STUDIES IN THE HISTORY
OF CHRISTIAN MISSIONS

R. E. Frykenberg
Brian Stanley
General Editors

STUDIES IN THE HISTORY OF CHRISTIAN MISSIONS

Alvyn Austin
China's Millions: The China Inland Mission and Late Qing Society, 1832-1905

Judith M. Brown and Robert Eric Frykenberg, *Editors*
Christians, Cultural Interactions, and India's Religious Traditions

Robert Eric Frykenberg
Christians and Missionaries in India: Cross-Cultural Communication since 1500

Susan Billington Harper
In the Shadow of the Mahatma: Bishop V. S. Azariah and the Travails of Christianity in British India

D. Dennis Hudson
Protestant Origins in India: Tamil Evangelical Christians, 1706-1835

Donald M. Lewis, *Editor*
Christianity Reborn: The Global Expansion of Evangelicalism in the Twentieth Century

Jon Miller
Missionary Zeal and Institutional Control: Organizational Contradictions in the Basel Mission on the Gold Coast, 1828-1917

Andrew Porter, *Editor*
The Imperial Horizons of British Protestant Missions, 1880-1914

Wilbert R. Shenk, *Editor*
North American Foreign Missions, 1810-1914: Theology, Theory, and Policy

Brian Stanley, *Editor*
Christian Missions and the Enlightenment

Brian Stanley, *Editor*
Missions, Nationalism, and the End of Empire

Kevin Ward and Brian Stanley, *Editors*
The Church Mission Society and World Christianity, 1799-1999

China's Millions

*The China Inland Mission and
Late Qing Society, 1832-1905*

Alvyn Austin

WILLIAM B. EERDMANS PUBLISHING COMPANY
GRAND RAPIDS, MICHIGAN / CAMBRIDGE, U.K.

© 2007 Alvyn Austin
All rights reserved

Published 2007 by
Wm. B. Eerdmans Publishing Co.
2140 Oak Industrial Drive N.E., Grand Rapids, Michigan 49505 /
P.O. Box 163, Cambridge CB3 9PU U.K.
www.eerdmans.com

Printed in the United States of America

15 14 13 12 11 10   7 6 5 4 3 2

Library of Congress Cataloging-in-Publication Data

Austin, Alvyn, 1945-
China's millions: the China Inland Mission and late Qing Society, 1832-1905 /
Alvyn Austin.
p.   cm. — (Studies in the history of Christian missions)
Includes bibliographical references and index.
ISBN 978-0-8028-2975-7 (pbk.: alk. paper)
1. Missions — China — History — 19th century. 2. China — Church history —
19th century. 3. China Inland Mission — China.   I. Title.

BV3415.2.A97   2007
266.00951'09034 — dc22

2006039059

Scripture quotations are from the King James or Authorized Version of the Bible.

Grateful acknowledgment is made to OMF International for permission to quote from CIM and OMF books, including those still in copyright, and from material in their archives.

Grateful acknowledgment is also made to the following for permission to use the photographs in this book: CIM/OMF, for pictures published in *China's Millions,* and in their books; Patricia Kennedy; Secker & Warburg, London; Royal Ontario Museum.

This book is dedicated to the two
who were my mentors as I was writing it.

GEORGE ALEXANDER RAWLYK
1935-1995

He had in his pocket a map of all the ways to or from the Celestial City. Wherefore he struck a light (for he never goes without his tinder-box).
　　　　　　　　　　　　　John Bunyan, *The Pilgrim's Progress*

DIANA LARY

There are no shortcuts to the Earthly Paradise, especially when one has no idea where it is. The towns, hills, streams and valleys of China spread out before one, in all directions. . . . The Earthly Paradise is not just one place. It is the whole of China.

　　　　　　　　　　　　Jonathan Spence, *God's Chinese Son*

"Open-air Preaching in China," by Thomas Eyres, a CIM missionary in Shanxi, published in *China's Millions* (GB), January 1892. Before Christianity could become a Chinese religion it had to be born again. This preacher is using a banner of the wordless book, which reduced the Christian doctrines to the pure symbolism of colors. The banner was colored, from the top, black to represent sin, red for the blood of Jesus that washes away sin, white for holiness, and gold (or yellow) for heaven. This produced a simple catechism for converts: I have sinned; Jesus loves me; Jesus saves me; and Jesus will take me to heaven. Since this woodcut depicts Shanxi province, where it was reported that "eleven out of every ten" people smoked opium, we can assume that most of the audience were drug addicts. The preacher may be a Chinese evangelist or a missionary in Chinese dress, which would lead to quite different interpretations.

Contents

FOREWORD	xiii
LIST OF ILLUSTRATIONS	xv
ACKNOWLEDGMENTS	xvii
PREFACE	xxi
ABBREVIATIONS	xxx

Introduction	1
Putting on Chinese Dress	1
The Wordless Book	2
Sectarian Conversion	11
Jesus Opium	14
The Conspiracy of Silence	15
Then and Now	28
One Pilgrim's Progress	29

PART I: THE FIRST GENERATION, 1832-1880

1. Black Barnsley, 1832-1851	33
London, 20 November 1860, "About Breakfast Time"	33

A Market Town in the County of Coveting	36
John Wesley Comes to Barnsley	38
Cheapside	41
Troubled Waters	46
Thunder and Lightning	48
The Blessed Hope	53
2. The Wicket-Gate, 1851-1865	**59**
The First Pilgrimage	59
The Odd Sparrow	65
The Heavenly Kingdom	70
The Heavenly Questions	72
The Earthly Family	75
3. Calling the Pilgrim Band, 1865-1866	**78**
The First Vision	78
The Great Revival	82
Spurgeon's Wordless Book	86
The Team	90
The Brethren	94
The Establishment	98
The Helpers	100
The General Director	103
The Last of England	107
Appendix 1: Passengers on the Lammermuir	109
4. The Land of Strangers, 1866-1875	**111**
The First Generation	111
The Wicket-Gate, Again	114
The Pigtailed Tribe	120
The Outrage	123
The Riot Season	128
The Native Missionary Association	132
"The Bombshell Scattering Us"	136

Contents

5. The Valley of the Shadow, 1875-1880	139
The Pilgrims' Map	139
The Great Famine	144
The Land of the Yellow Emperor	150
The Temple-Land	154
The Man Who Stood by the Gate	160
The Religion of the Golden Pill	163
The Chinese Wordless Book	167
The Essay Contest	169
The Opium Sot	171
The Overcomer of Demons	175

PART II: THE SECOND GENERATION, 1875-1888

6. National Righteousness, 1875-1888	181
The Second Vision	181
The Exchanged Life	186
The Council of Management	188
The Ladies' Council	195
The Anglo-Oriental Anti-Opium Society	199
The Candidates	203
The Cambridge Seven	206
Appendix 2: London Council Members and Referees, 1872-1876	210
7. The Octopus, 1875-1888	217
The Second Generation	217
The China Council	225
The Scattering	227
Tea-Shop Evangelism	233
Gossiping the Gospel	237
Jesus Opium	241
Appendix 3: Course of Study for Probationers, 1886	250

8. The Heavenly Invitation Offices, 1880-1888 — 255
   Teacher Hsi — 255
   The Demoniac among the Tombs — 260
   The Red Pills — 264
   The Shanxi Spirits — 268
   The Baptists — 270
   The Oberlin Band — 274
   The Great Origin: Taiyuan — 278
   The Cambridge Seven — 280
   The Feeder of the Sheep — 283

PART III: THE THIRD GENERATION, 1888-1900

9. The New World, 1888-1900 — 291
   The Third Vision — 291
   The Transatlantic Cables — 298
   Toronto the Good — 301
   The North American Council — 305
   The Divine Healers — 309
   A New Beginning — 312
   The Great Design — 315
   The Associates — 317
   The Candidates — 320
   Chart 1, Applicants: Residence, 1888-1901 — 322
   Chart 2, Denominational Affiliation, 1887-1915 — 326

10. God's Ambassadors, 1888-1899 — 332
    The Third Generation — 332
    The High Tides — 339
    Chart 3, Growth of the CIM by Provinces, 1885-1899 — 345
    Chart 4, Growth of the Chinese Church by Provinces, 1885-1899 — 347
    The Book of Arrangements — 349
    The Breakdown — 351

Contents

11.	**The Middle Eden, 1888-1899**	**354**
	The Venerable Chief Pastor	354
	North Shanxi	362
	The Opium Dream	365
	A Wealthy Place	371
	The Rules for the Middle Eden	379
	The Converts	381
	The Cambridge Seven	383
	The Pastor's Wife's Dream	387
	The Pastor's Death	391
12.	**The End of the Middle Eden, 1900**	**395**
	The Spirit Boxers	395
	Making Sense	400
	The Killing Time	409
	The Exodus	415
	The Last Pilgrim	417
	The Last Exodus	419
13.	**The Aftermath**	**421**
	The Blood of the Martyrs	421
	Returning to the Ruins	426
	Beyond the Jade Gate	431
	The Model Province	435
	Postscript	438
	Conclusion: Something Happened	**440**
	The Shanxi Spirits	440
	The City of Brotherly Love	443
	Testing the Spirits	448
	The Delectable Mountains	454
	BIBLIOGRAPHY	459
	INDEX	480

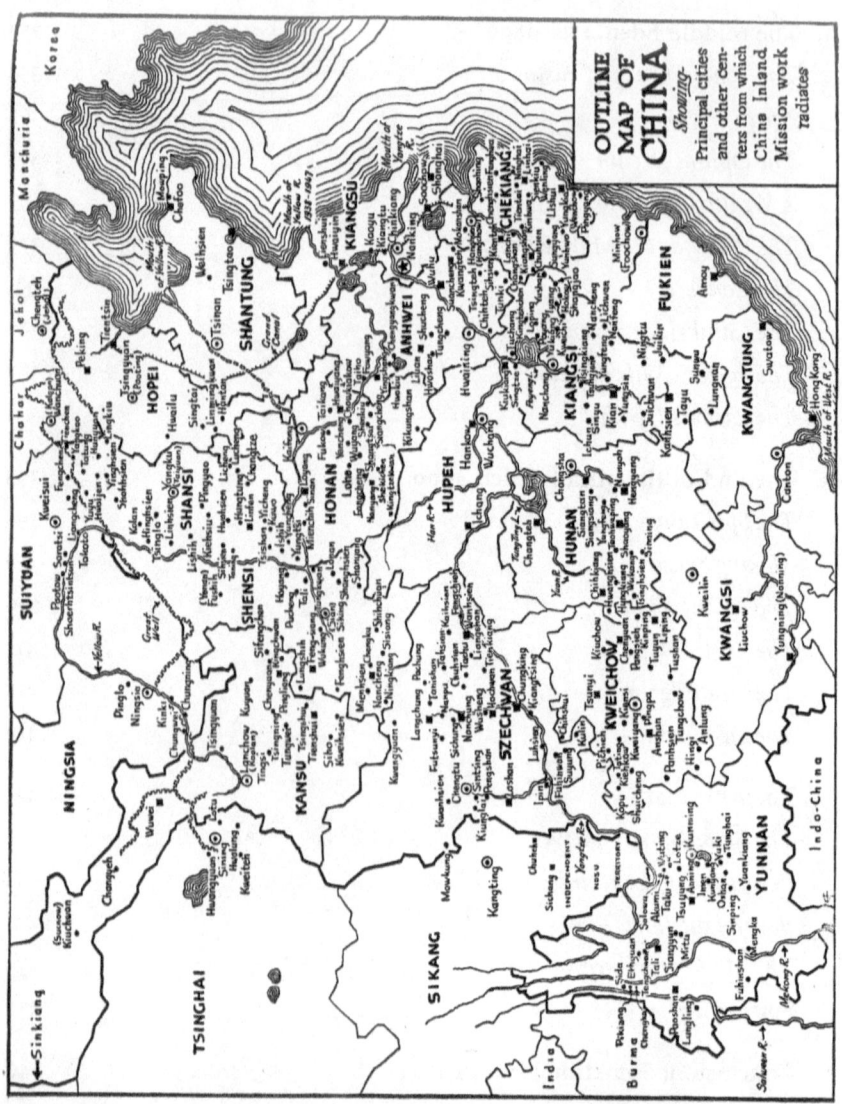

CIM map of China in the 1940s. Starting with the coastal provinces in the 1860s, the CIM expanded "like a bombshell scattering us" in the 1870s. By 1900 it had 800 missionaries in fifteen (of eighteen) provinces; by the 1930s, there were over 1,200 missionaries as far as Tibet and Sinkiang (now Xinjiang).

Source: *China's Millions* (NA), August 1949.

Foreword

The conservative evangelical tradition is not generally renowned for its veneration of saints. However, James Hudson Taylor's place in evangelical hagiography has been secure ever since the publication in 1911 and 1918 of the two volumes of his biography written by his son, Dr. Howard Taylor, and daughter-in-law, Geraldine Guinness. The graphic nature of Hudson Taylor's vision of the perishing millions of Chinese, dying without the saving knowledge of Christ, was intrinsic to his magnetic appeal to the Christian imagination in his own day, and has remained so subsequently. No less compelling was the extraordinary spiritual ambition displayed by Taylor's formation of a mission which set out to evangelize the largest nation on earth with a sublime indifference to the elaborate paraphernalia of committees and fund-raising that other missions deemed so indispensable. Perhaps most attractive of all to a sector of the Christian constituency that tends to value activism more than holiness, Hudson Taylor appeared to symbolize the perfect union of the two — mystic as well as missionary, man of prayer no less than man of action.

This book is not another biography of James Hudson Taylor, yet his enigmatic personality and pervasive influence are indelibly imprinted on the pages of this history of the China Inland Mission during his lifetime. Alvyn Austin seeks to sidestep the aura of sanctity which has enveloped Taylor himself and focus our attention instead on the ordinary women and men, whether foreign missionaries or Chinese evangelists, who staffed his mission and gave their lives (some of them literally, especially during the Boxer Rising) for the implementation of Taylor's vision. In so doing, Austin breaks new ground. Using the CIM archival collections in London, Toronto, and Wheaton College, Austin tells the story of the internationalization of what was originally a British mission, the first Protestant missionary agency to undergo such a process of radical dissociation from the constraints of national identity, one which was immensely significant for the future of evangelical missions, especially those based in North America. Indeed, the China Inland Mission, perhaps more than any other single organization, was responsible for fashioning the international network of conservative evangelicalism in the twentieth century.

Austin's account of the work of the CIM is the first to draw out the connections between the mission's converts and the myriad sects and secret societies that were such an important component of Chinese folk religion at the time. Of particular interest is the intriguing portrayal of Pastor Hsi Shengmo, hymn writer, controversial organizer of refuges for opium addicts in Shanxi province, and architect of a style of Chinese Christianity that challenged the preconceptions of European rationality in its preparedness to employ the gifts of healing and exorcism in the contest for spiritual territory. Pastor Hsi took the simple gospel symbolism of the "wordless book," introduced to China by CIM missionaries in about 1880, and incorporated it into the traditional *wuxing* color cosmology of Chinese culture. The result was the creation of an indigenous Chinese evangelical tradition that was to prove more enduring in China than the work of the China Inland Mission itself. The expanding popular Christianity of rural China today may owe more to Hsi's proto-pentecostal tradition in Shanxi than most previous scholarship on Christianity in China has recognized.

China's Millions is an engagingly written book that will fascinate, entertain, illuminate, and no doubt provoke lively reactions. It invites the reader to step into one of the most important yet least understood narratives of modern Christian history, a narrative that is still unfolding to this day as the long course of Christian history in China continues to defy western patterns and predictions.

BRIAN STANLEY

List of Illustrations

CIM map of China in the 1940s	xii
Pastor Hsi and his disciples, 1890s	xxii
CIM headquarters in Shanghai, about 1905	xxv
CIM missionaries in Chinese dress	3
Dr. Howard Taylor and Geraldine Guinness Taylor	17
Cheapside in Barnsley, Yorkshire, in the 20th century	38
The young Hudson Taylor	60
William Burns in Chinese winter clothes	69
The *Lammermuir* party, May 1866	106
A typical city street in China	113
Mule litter in Shanxi	137
Map of China with English names	141
Modern map of Shanxi in pinyin	143
Scenes of the Great Famine of 1877-78	147
Gatekeeper Sung and elders of the Hongdong church, 1890s	162
Opium addicts	175
Occasional Paper cover	183
Benjamin Broomhall in his study at Pyrland Road, 1880s	191
The Cambridge Seven in England	219
The Cambridge Seven in China	220

LIST OF ILLUSTRATIONS

Stanley Peregrine Smith	224
The Hundred	230
Keepers of Pastor Hsi's opium refuges, 1890s	257
Timothy and Mary Richard in 1884	271
Dixon E. Hoste, bachelor, in Shanxi	282
The first North American party of CIM missionaries	292
The China council	333
Map of South Shanxi with pinyin names	356
"The Two Roads" evangelistic banner	366
Mrs. Hsi, the second, younger wife of Pastor Hsi	374
The women's Bible school at Huozhou, about 1904	388
Boxers setting fire to a church	399
Archibald E. Glover and his family, March 1900	417
Elder Hsü (Hsü-pu-üin) in South Shanxi, in 1900	429
The Trio and Topsy in England	432
Three veterans: Shanghai, April 1905	457

Acknowledgments

I first came across Mrs. Howard Taylor's story of Pastor Hsi almost thirty years ago when I was doing research for *Saving China: Canadian Missionaries in the Middle Kingdom, 1888-1959*. A book with that long a gestation incurs many "without whoms," people without whom this book would not have been written. Unfortunately, I can only acknowledge those who read the manuscript. Even that is a daunting list.

Above all I would like to thank Brian Stanley of the Currents in World Christianity (CWC) project, whose grace and scholarship brought together a vast international community of mission scholars. He and Robert Frykenberg read the entire manuscript through three or four successive revisions, each longer than the previous. Brian is an author's best friend, a punctilious editor. Without him, this book would not have been published.

Brian Stanley was director of the Currents in World Christianity (CWC) project of the 1990s, successor to the North Atlantic Missiology Project, which was based at University of Cambridge and funded by The Pew Charitable Trusts of Philadelphia. CWC became the most intensive and extensive modern scholarly assessment of the history and impact of British- and North American-sponsored Christian missions between 1740 and 1968. It focused, in its own words, "on the complex inter-relationship between mission theology, theory and policy," giving "full weight to both the social, economic and political contexts within which mission theory was forged, and to the deeply held theological convictions which motivated the movement." The CWC conferences in England, Scotland, Canada, the United States, and South Africa may prove as pivotal in (re)writing the history of missions as the great missionary conventions of a century ago were in shaping the modern missions enterprise. I am proud to be included in the CWC publications series, Studies in the History of Christian Missions.

Among the scholars associated with the Institute for the Study of American Evangelicals at Wheaton who encouraged my interest in the CIM were Joel Carpenter, Wilbert Shenk, Grant Wacker, Dana Robert, and the ever-inventive editor of the ISAE Bulletin, Larry Eskridge. A special thank you to Mark Noll, who stepped in as outside reader of my thesis after the tragic death of George Rawlyk, a day none of us will forget. George Rawlyk was a great bear of a man who provided an entree for Canadian historians, such as Marguerite Van Die and John Stackhouse, to enter this international dialogue.

I would like to offer a special thanks to Dan Bays, the resident China hand in all these networks. As the leading historian of indigenous fundamentalist/pentecostal movements in China, he has shaped our understanding of Chinese Christianity. He also took time out from his busy schedule to read three or four versions of this book.

I would also like to thank China scholars Linda Benson and Gary Tiedemann, who shares my interest in eccentric missionaries. In Barnsley, I corresponded with Harold Taylor, from far-off Australia, with Ian Welch, and in Cambridge with Sue Anderson, who told me of her great-great-grandfather, Stanley Smith.

Going back, this book was once my thesis, and I would like to thank my committee and the community of scholars at York University. Diana Lary, to whom this book is dedicated, has always been my strongest supporter and good friend. (She tells me I have inspired her to write a novel about a CIM woman in the 1920s living in Pingyao, one of the cities in my story.) Ramsay Cook and Margo Gewurtz were on my thesis committee, and other readers included Bernie Frolic, Peter Mitchell, Bernard Luk, Jamie Scott, Molly Ungar, and Bill Westfall.

I came along at the end of the old China Inland Mission, a child during the reluctant exodus of 1950-51. My mother Lilian Reeks went to China from England in 1929, and my father John Austin from Canada in 1931. They met and married in China — in the British consulate — and had four sons, Stephen, Norman, Paul, and myself. At the tail end of the Second World War, they were forced to evacuate to India, where I was born. We returned to China, to the far northwest, Lanzhou, the last Chinese city before the Gobi Desert. So my earliest memories are of looking out from the city walls over the Yellow River and the yellow sand stretching to infinity. My family returned to Toronto, where, after my mother died, my father married Emma Sullivan, one of God's gifts to the old CIM.

Acknowledgments

As my scholarly work came to focus on the CIM, some people connected to the mission read various versions of my thesis, although I must admit they did not always agree with my conclusions. I would like to thank particularly the late David Michell, the late Margaret Bunting, the late Karin McLean, Norman Cliff and his sister Estelle Cowley, Dr. Timothy Fung, the current general director of OMF International, who shared his research on CIM medical missions, and Chris Wigram, who gave permission to quote from CIM sources.

Finally, when I had completed the final draft of the manuscript, along came two scholars who more than anyone else contributed to my understanding of the Boxer movement at the grassroots level. Andrew Kaiser lives in Taiyuan and works for Shanxi Evergreen Service, a Christian development and aid organization founded by the children of Peter Torjeson (whose Chinese name was "Green Leaf"), a CIM Norwegian associate. The Torjesons were invited to northern Shanxi to continue the work their parents had started fifty years earlier. Andrew Kaiser generously shared his manuscript history and commented on the Chinese chapters of this book. Henrietta Harrison also shared her work on Catholics in Shanxi.

A book cannot be written without archives, and I would like to thank the librarians and custodians of the various CIM/OMF archives who fetched papers and copied pictures. First is Rose Carleton, the indefatigable administrator of the Overseas Missionary Fellowship office in Toronto (Mississauga), who allowed me free access to the library — for decade-long loans — and the photographic archives. I look back fondly on my days in the School of Oriental and African Studies (SOAS) at the University of London, and in the Archives of the Billy Graham Library at Wheaton College. In Toronto, I consulted the Tyndale College and Seminary (formerly Toronto Bible College) Archives, the United Church of Canada Archives, and Wycliffe College.

I also gratefully acknowledge the generosity of the Overseas Missionary Fellowship in permitting me to call this book *China's Millions,* which was the title of the mission's magazine (now called *East Asia's Millions*). Furthermore the OMF has granted permission to use quotations and illustrations from the CIM/OMF archives in SOAS, the OMF in Toronto, and the Archives of the Billy Graham Center, and to quote from published sources, some of which are still under copyright.

As always, I would like to thank my friend James Bracken, who has been at my side throughout the long gestation of this book.

These people helped shape this manuscript, but William B. Eerdmans turned it into a book. In conclusion I would like to thank my editor, Mary

ACKNOWLEDGMENTS

Ruth Howes, who turned out to be a CIM "M.K.," or mish-kid, with fifty years' experience in editing religious books. She went out of her way to verify facts and look up sources. My thanks go to all these people, but the mistakes — and the tone — of this book are mine alone.

Preface

"The story of Hong Xiuquan and his Taiping Heavenly Kingdom is as strange as any to be found in Chinese history," wrote Jonathan Spence in *God's Chinese Son: The Taiping Heavenly Kingdom of Hong Xiuquan*.[1] The story of Pastor Hsi Shengmo, the "Overcomer of Demons," and the missionaries — one generation later, in the wretched "opium villages" of Shanxi — is equally strange. It is positively narcotic.

Shanxi (old spelling Shansi) in the late Qing (old spelling Ch'ing) dynasty was one of the saddest places on earth. In 1877-79 it was the epicenter of the Great North China Famine, one of the worst in modern history, when five million perished in the one province alone, one-third of its population. Afterwards, in desperation the survivors turned to opium to ease a myriad of physical ills brought on by malnutrition, and to religious sects to exorcise the hungry ghosts and fox demons. As one missionary remarked, "If there is a place in the whole world where it is harder to do missionary work than right here in Opium drugged Shansi province, which is probably one of the worst in the whole Empire, I do not want to know of it." Preaching in Shanxi, another said, was "like trying to save a race of drunkards."[2] Yet it was precisely among these "opium fiends" that Pastor Hsi created the most successful indigenous sect of "god-worshippers" in China between the Taiping Rebellion and the Boxer Uprising. "Many people say that opium-smokers cannot be brought under the power of the Gospel," a third missionary commented. "They have been. Some of our best

---

1. Jonathan D. Spence, *God's Chinese Son: The Taiping Heavenly Kingdom of Hong Xiuquan* (New York: W. W. Norton, 1996), p. xxi.
2. Nat Brandt, *Massacre in Shansi* (Syracuse: Syracuse University Press, 1994), pp. 48-49.

Pastor Hsi and his disciples, 1890s. Before his conversion, Pastor Hsi had been an opium addict and member of a Daoist sect, the Religion of the Golden Pill. Afterwards, cured of opium and appointed as "watcher over the sheep" in Shanxi, he would bring his converts down from the hills, hundreds of them begging to be baptized. The missionary baptized up to 200 a day because he could not refuse.
Source: Mrs. Howard Taylor, *Pastor Hsi*, vol. 2, *One of China's Christians* (London: CIM, 1903).

men in the church have been opium-smokers."[3] As many as nine out of ten — male and female — in some congregations were reformed addicts, which imparted a drugged aura to the sect, extravagant, visionary, hallucinatory — and extremely anti-foreign. One could call it narcotic Christianity.

This book presents a vast panorama of nineteenth-century evangelical missions, as it traces three generations of pilgrims from Great Britain and North America who made their way to China, where they happened to end up in Shanxi province. There is a large cast of characters: we do not meet Pastor Hsi until Chapter 5. Chapter 1 starts in Barnsley, a coal-mining town in Yorkshire, and traces the life of a chemist's son named James Hudson Taylor. He went to China as a spiritual waif in 1853, at the age of twenty-one, and dropped into the middle of the worst civil war in Chinese history. Invalided home, on 25 June 1865 he had a "Heavenly Vision" while walking on the stony beach at Brighton, and the next morning, with ten pounds and a prayer, he

---

3. *China's Millions* (NA), August 1893, pp. 110-11.

opened a bank account in the name of the China Inland Mission, which became universally known as the CIM.

Taylor was one of the great storytellers of the Victorian age, who could take a simple poignant anecdote that showed how God was working in his own life, and amplify and refine it until it gained mythic proportions. His "Brighton vision" became the most enduring stereotype of the heathen Chinese until well into the twentieth century. He invented the term "China's Millions," which was the title of the CIM's monthly magazine, published from 1875 to 1950. (The CIM changed its name to the Overseas Missionary Fellowship after expulsion from the People's Republic of China in 1950; the journal is still published under the title *East Asia's Millions*.)

"A million a month in China are dying without God," he saw in his mind's eye, as the waves at Brighton dissolved into millions of souls "lying in Christless graves." "If every Chinese," he wrote, were "marshalled in single rank and file, allowing one yard between man and man, they would encircle the globe more than ten times at the equator. Were they to march past the spectator at the rate of thirty miles a day, they would move on and on, day after day, week after week, month after month; and more than twenty-three years and a half would elapse before the last individual had passed by."[4] And so on forever, falling over the abyss, they would march in single file to eternal blackness. "Father, father, where am I going? What lies before me in the darkness? Oh father, I am frightened. Help me! Help me! . . . What do your books say? Tell me! Help me!"[5]

This book is not another biography of Hudson Taylor, although it presents a perspective quite different from either the hagiographic biographies or the attacks by his critics. One hundred years after his death, he is one of the most famous missionaries of all time, in the pantheon with William Carey and David Livingstone. The adoring biographies written by his son and daughter-in-law, Dr. and Mrs. Howard Taylor (Mrs. Taylor, Geraldine Guinness, was the real author) are required reading in many Bible colleges today.[6] *Hudson Taylor's Spiritual Secret* (1932), an abridged version of the two-volume *Hudson Taylor and the China Inland Mission* (1911 and 1918), has sold 380,717 copies in the Moody Press edition alone, which does not include any

---

4. JHT, *China: Its Spiritual Need and Claims* (London: CIM, 1865), p. 8.
5. *Pastor Hsi*, vol. 1, p. 141 [not in single vol.]. These are supposedly the dying words of Gatekeeper Sung's daughter before his conversion: see Chapter 5 note 63.
6. Daniel W. Bacon, *From Faith to Faith: The Influence of Hudson Taylor on the Faith Missions Movement* (Philadelphia: OMF, 1984), p. 133. *Hudson Taylor's Spiritual Secret* (Chicago: Moody Press & CIM, 1932) is an abridged version of Mrs. Taylor's two-volume *Hudson Taylor and the China Inland Mission* (1911 and 1918).

of the CIM/OMF editions, or those printed and distributed by other publishers. It has been described as "a spiritual classic to be placed on the same shelf as *Pilgrim's Progress*. . . . [It] has a timeless, intrinsic quality."[7] The late Anthony James (Jim) Broomhall, Taylor's great-nephew, wrote the definitive biography, a seven-volume, 4,000-page compendium entitled *Hudson Taylor and China's Open Century* (1981-89), to which I am greatly indebted. In 2005, to celebrate the 140th anniversary of the founding of the CIM (1865) and the 100th anniversary of Hudson Taylor's death, OMF Hong Kong published a lavish photo album entitled, *Christ Alone: A Pictorial Presentation of Hudson Taylor's Life and Legacy*.[8]

Rather, my purpose in this book is to shift the spotlight away from the founder to the "pigtailed tribe" of Hudson Taylor's "helpers" (as he called them), the footsoldiers of the CIM. By the time of his death in 1905, the CIM was an international "octopus,"[9] with eight hundred men and women at sixty stations in fifteen of the eighteen provinces of China. It was the largest and most influential Protestant mission, and constituted one-quarter of the entire Protestant mission force in China. Unlike denominational missions, which had head offices in London, New York, or Toronto, the CIM was based in Shanghai, where it had a huge "plant" set amidst manicured lawns. It had national branches in England, Canada, Scotland, Australia, New Zealand, and the United States, and "associate missions" (such as the Scandinavian Alliance), which had headquarters in Sweden, Norway, Denmark, Finland, Germany, and the United States. By the 1930s, when the CIM reached thirteen hundred missionaries, it comprised one-third of the total Protestant force in China. Altogether, the "Register of CIM Missionaries and Associates (1854-1949)" gives a total of 2,679 missionaries who served in China.[10] The Overseas Missionary Fellowship is still the largest Protestant mission in East and Southeast Asia, with eleven hundred missionaries from twenty-five nationalities, located in thirteen countries from Japan to Indonesia, including unofficial missionaries in China itself.

The CIM called themselves a tribe, "a peculiar people," in the biblical if not the modern sense. If evangelical Christianity is "a luxuriant undergrowth

---

7. John C. Pollock, *Hudson Taylor and Maria: Pioneers in China* (New York: McGraw-Hill and CIM, 1962), pp. 10-11. The British edition, entitled *Faith's Venture*, has sold over 50,000 copies.

8. Irene Chang, James Hudson Taylor III, James Hudson Taylor IV, Joyce Wu, Janey Yiu, and Lisa Yu, editors, *Christ Alone: A Pictorial Presentation of Hudson Taylor's Life and Legacy* (Hong Kong: OMF Hong Kong, 2005).

9. *HTCOC* 6, p. 23.

10. Ibid, p. 209. The manuscript "Register" is in CIM/SOAS.

Preface

CIM headquarters in Shanghai, about 1905. Built in the 1890s on a spacious site on Woosung Road, the compound consisted of three-story buildings with accommodation for 200 missionaries. This photograph, taken by Dr. William T. Clarke, a Canadian working in Sichuan, shows his wife, Ethelwyn Naylor.
Source: Patricia Kennedy family collection.

of weeds that requires only opportunity to flourish,"[11] the China Inland Mission was a thicket unto itself. It was a "mixed multitude" from almost every evangelical church in Christendom: Plymouth Brethren who refused to share communion with apostates; Methodists, Presbyterians, and Baptists, each with their own creed; prayer-book Anglicans who established dioceses of episcopal rectitude; Quakers who sat like statues in marble listening to the silent spirit;[12] Salvation Army types who marched through Chinese villages with tambourines and blood-and-fire banners; Swedish holy women who specialized in praying for the sick and dying; jump-up revivalists from the American Midwest trying to recreate "burned-over districts" in China; pentecostals who hoped to acquire the Chinese language supernaturally by speaking in tongues; conventional missionaries who were "repelled" by the "extreme piety" of their colleagues; and Canadians, one generation removed from the farm, who tried to explain the vagaries of British "mission home eti-

---

11. George Marsden, in *Christian Week*, 28 April 1992.
12. *HTCOC* 6, p. 324, noted the first missionaries of the English Society of Friends went under the wing of the CIM in 1883.

quette" to over-enthusiastic Swedish Americans. What were those mendicants doing in inland China? Who did they think they were, barely literate, some of them, in either English or Chinese, dressed in native clothes like peasants, setting up shop and starting to cast out devils? Where did they learn the secret language of demonology, a phenomenon rarely seen in Britain in three hundred years?

To discuss the China Inland Mission in the abstract would be contradictory and confusing. Work among the tribespeople of Yunnan and Guizhou could not compare with the head office at Shanghai or the stuffy Englishness of the Chefoo School for missionaries' children. Shanxi has been chosen as a microcosm, the reality to show the illusion, because it was both typical and larger-than-life, where the best and worst aspects of the CIM were played out. Shanxi was the success story of the CIM: the safest province; the largest number of missionaries; the most hospitals, schools, and opium refuges; second in the number of converts; and the most experimental methods. Yet it was such a fractious place that some referred to a "Shanxi spirit," which A. J. Broomhall described as "a whirlpool of complaints, misunderstandings, derelict spiritual morale and finally resignations from the CIM and BMS [Baptist Missionary Society]."[13] At least fifty Shanxi missionaries resigned from the CIM and left the province; three committed suicide.

At the end of the road sits Pastor Hsi in his utopian community called "The Middle [i.e., Chinese] Eden." He is not Kurtz in Joseph Conrad's *The Heart of Darkness*, but rather he appears as an angel of light, wearing an immaculate white gown with a scarlet sash that proclaims in gold letters, "Jesus came into the world to save sinners." The people called him "Living Jesus," as if he were an avatar or bodhisattva, as he went about casting out demons and curing opium addicts. He would lead his followers down from the hills in their hundreds, begging to be baptized; the missionary baptized up to two hundred a day because, he said, "it was not his place to reject them."[14]

Like Hong Xiuquan, leader of the Taiping Rebellion, Pastor Hsi was a failed scholar who considered his Chinese Christianity to be superior to the missionaries' version. Like Hong, he was converted through a vision in which he ascended into heaven and the Holy Spirit descended into his soul three times in the night. After the defeat of the Taiping Rebellion, Pastor Hsi, naturally, renounced any revolutionary ambitions, although he came to the attention of the Chinese government authorities as a bully and leader of a hetero-

---

13. Ibid., pp. 288-91.
14. Francis Price, "Description of Mission Work in Shansi, 1877-1889," in Brandt, *Massacre in Shansi*, p. 116.

dox religious sect. Rather, he was a businessman — Shanxi money-changers were the shrewdest bankers in the Empire — who built a network of opium refuges in four provinces of northwest China. These "Heavenly Invitation Offices" employed some two hundred workers and reportedly treated "probably not less" than 303,000 men and women, and made "probably more than 1000 converts."[15] (That ratio, of three hundred inquirers to one convert, was pretty good compared with most mission schools or hospitals.) He set up his converts in a sort of franchise philanthropic business, in which he provided his own special "medicine" — "attractive-looking" red pills he called "Life Restoring Pills," which the Holy Spirit had revealed in a second vision — and they would share the profits.

The problem was, both Pastor Hsi's pills and the missionaries' "medicines" turned out to be morphine (or morphia, the terms are interchangeable). We do not know whether his 303,000 addicts became "morphinomaniacs," as many soldiers in the United States Civil War and the Crimea became addicted to hypodermic morphine. The historian Sterling Seagrave suggests that at least in mass terms, "Chinese first became opium addicts, then graduated to morphine, then to heroin. By 1924, China was importing enough heroin from Japan each year to provide four strong doses of the drug to every one of the nation's 400 million inhabitants."[16] We do know that Pastor Hsi's opium refuges dispensed "anti-opium medicines" so freely that a black market sprang up in various kinds of imported and home-grown morphine. And along the way, the red pills became so common that morphine was popularly known as "Jesus opium," a cheap fix when the craving came on.[17]

Pastor Hsi died on an omen-filled day in 1896, and four years later his little sect was wiped out during the Boxer uprising. Most historical studies of the Boxer movement have concentrated on Shandong, where it all began, or the siege of the Beijing legations, the thrilling second act. But they forget the dénouement — like the last act of *Hamlet*, with bodies strewn over the stage — Shanxi, where it all ended. In Shandong most Christian victims died at the hands of Boxer mobs; in Shanxi, they died as a result of a policy of terror encouraged, if not initiated, at the highest state level. The larger significance of Pastor Hsi is now revealed. All global events are ultimately regional, as Joseph

---

15. Marshall Broomhall, *The Chinese Empire: A General and Missionary Survey* (London: Morgan & Scott and CIM, 1907), p. 213.

16. Sterling Seagrave, *The Soong Dynasty* (New York: Harper & Row, 1985), p. 334. Presumably, Seagrave is speaking of broad historical trends rather than individuals.

17. The term is used by both Seagrave, p. 334, and Jonathan D. Spence in the chapter, "Opium," in *Chinese Roundabout: Essays in History and Culture* (New York: W. W. Norton, 1992), p. 250.

Esherick says in *The Origins of the Boxer Uprising*.[18] Through the lens of Pastor Hsi's little Christian sect one can get a village-level view of what the Boxers were up against.

This book is about more than just the strange opium dream of Pastor Hsi and his addled Christians in a remote province of a crumbling Empire, a ghost dance at the end of civilization — compelling though that story may be. It is more, even, than a corporate history of the China Inland Mission, important though that study would be. Rather, I use the CIM as a prism through which to examine two large questions: How did nineteenth-century British evangelicalism feed into twentieth-century American fundamentalism, and eventually into worldwide Protestant patterns of the twenty-first century? And to pose the question in a deceptively simple fashion, how did evangelical Christianity become Chinese?

The CIM's motto could have been "Only Connect."[19] Born on the sectarian fringe, the CIM was one of the small "unnoticed religious movements" that grew out of the 1859 "Great Revival" in England.[20] Allying itself with Church, Chapel, and Dissent, it built a dense network of Bible schools, training institutions, orphanages, city missions, and foreign societies. It achieved respectability on the coattails of the YMCA and the Keswick conference, a prophetic, holiness summer camp in England's Lake District. The CIM's motto could have been "Only Connect." Born on the sectarian fringe, the CIM was one of the small "unnoticed religious movements that grew out of the 1859 "Great Revival." Hudson Taylor was deeply influenced by the German pietist tradition, and his first allies were the faith missions in England and continental Europe established by Karl Gutzlaff and George Muller.

If the Bible schools were the "regional co-ordinating centers" for twentieth-century American evangelicals,[21] in mid-nineteenth-century England the CIM helped build their prototypes. Hudson Taylor was present at the creation of, among others, Mildmay Park, Spurgeon's Baptist Pastors'

---

18. Joseph W. Esherick, *The Origins of the Boxer Uprising* (Berkeley: University of California Press, 1987), p. 1.

19. Alvyn Austin, "Only Connect: The China Inland Mission and Transatlantic Evangelicalism," in *North American Foreign Missions, 1810-1914: Theology, Theory, and Policy*, ed. Wilbert R. Shenk (London: Curzon and Grand Rapids: Eerdmans, 2003).

20. Eugene V. Stock, *The History of the Church Missionary Society: Its Environment, Its Men and Its Work*, vol. 3 (London: CMS, 1899), p. 20.

21. Joel A. Carpenter, "Fundamentalist Institutions and the Rise of Evangelical Protestantism, 1929-1942," *Church History* (March 1980), p. 67. See also his major study, *Revive Us Again: The Reawakening of Amerian Fundamentalism* (New York: Oxford University Press, 1997), and Virginia Lieson Brereton, *Training God's Army: The American Bible School, 1880-1940* (Bloomington: University of Indiana Press, 1990).

Preface

College, Grattan Guinness's East London Missionary Training Institute, Dr. Barnardo's orphanages, the anti-opium movement, D. L. Moody's tours of Britain which made him famous, and the founding of Keswick.

In Toronto, that most British of cities, the CIM became "Americanized" — or at least Canadianized. It was one of a number of evangelical movements that established colonial branches in Canada, which became beachheads for expansion into the United States: the YMCA, and by a separate path, the YWCA, the Salvation Army, John Nelson Darby's Plymouth Brethren, Keswick Holiness, prophetic conferences, and faith missions, all of which became hallmarks of the militant anti-modernism that called itself Fundamentalism.

This book also traces how this same "simple faith" was transplanted to China, where it was simplified to its basics: "Jesus loves me, this I know." It melded with Chinese folk religion, which was concerned with magic, secret writings, transformations, healing, exorcisms, and wrestling with the spirit world. The story of Pastor Hsi holds a key to understanding Chinese Christianity today. In the outburst of "Christianity fever" that has been sweeping China since 1978, when the antireligious legislation was repealed, some Christian leaders make Pastor Hsi seem quite ordinary. Most converts still join Christian churches for healing or exorcism, for good luck and fat babies.

Some readers may feel I have presented an overly benign picture of Christianity in Shanxi. I have a simple explanation. Christianity came to that sad, sad land as a gleam of hope for suffering humanity. It promised to heal the sick, to exorcise the demon-possessed, to cure opium addicts and help them become good, and in the next life it promised a savior to take them to paradise. One can believe that this strange sect was everything its critics said: its statistics were inflated, its converts opium addicts, its message simplistic and superstitious. Yet the manifestations the critics proscribed were exactly what gave it deep roots among the people: simple devotions, miracles, exorcism, healing, drug rehabilitation, and the "Larger Hope" (as Stanley Smith called it) that everyone would be saved, some in this life and some in the life to come. Of such simple believers was the kingdom of heaven at the end of the Qing dynasty in a remote corner of the Chinese Empire.

Abbreviations

ABGC	Archives of the Billy Graham Center, Wheaton College, Wheaton, Illinois
BMS	Baptist Missionary Society
C&MA	Christian and Missionary Alliance
CES	Chinese Evangelisation Society
CIM/ABGC	CIM/OMF Archives in the Archives of the Billy Graham Center, Wheaton College, collection 215.
CIM/SOAS	CIM/OMF Archives at the School of Oriental and African Studies, University of London
CIM/Toronto	CIM/OMF Archives at OMF, Toronto.
CMS	Church Missionary Society
GB	Great Britain
HTCOC	A. J. Broomhall, *Hudson Taylor and China's Open Century*, 7 vols. (Sevenoaks, UK: Hodder & Stoughton, and OMF, 1981-1989). Note: AJB uses parentheses (to indicate pinyin spelling and other minor changes) and square brackets [for editorial insertions]. Quotes follow his format.
HTCOC 1	Book 1, *Barbarians at the Gates* (1981).
HTCOC 2	Book 2, *Over the Treaty Wall* (1982).
HTCOC 3	Book 3, *If I Had a Thousand Lives* (1982).
HTCOC 4	Book 4, *Survivors' Pact* (1984).
HTCOC 5	Book 5, *Refiner's Fire* (1985).
HTCOC 6	Book 6, *Assault on the Nine* (1988).
HTCOC 7	Book 7, *It Is Not Death to Die!* (1989).
IMA	International Missionary Alliance

Abbreviations

JHT	James Hudson Taylor
MBI	Moody Bible Institute, Chicago, Illinois
LMS	London Missionary Society
NA	North America
OMF	Overseas Missionary Fellowship, the name adoped by the CIM after the exodus from China. (The name is now OMF International.)
PMS	Pentecostal Missionary Union
ROM	Royal Ontario Museum
SIM	Sudan Interior Mission
SPG	Society for the Propagation of the Gospel
SVM	Student Volunteer Movement
TBC	Toronto Bible College (successor to TBTS)
TBTS	Toronto Bible Training School
TSA	Tyndale University College and Seminary Archives (successor to TBC)
UCA	United Church of Canada/Victoria University Archives, at Victoria University in the University of Toronto
Frost, "Memoirs"	Henry W. Frost, "The Days that are Past," typescript memoirs (932 pages), at CIM/Toronto, copy at CIM/ABGC.
Growth of a Soul	Hudson Taylor in Early Years: The Growth of a Soul, vol. 1 of Dr. and Mrs. Howard Taylor, Hudson Taylor and the China Inland Mission (London: CIM, 1911).
Growth of a Work of God	Vol. 2 of Taylor and Taylor, Hudson Taylor and the China Inland Mission (London: CIM, 1918).
McKay, "Faith and Facts"	Moira Jane McKay, "Faith and Facts in the History of the China Inland Mission 1832-1905" (Master's Thesis, University of Aberdeen, 1981).
Pastor Hsi	Mrs. Howard Taylor, Pastor Hsi, vol. 1, One of China's Scholars: The Culture and Conversion of a Confucianist (CIM, 1901), and vol. 2, One of China's Christians (1903). An abridged single volume was published in 1903, which went through 28 printings by 1991 under various titles, most commonly, Pastor Hsi: Confucian Scholar and Christian. The most recent publication is Geraldine Taylor, Pastor Hsi: A Struggle for Chinese Christianity (Inverness, Scotland: Christian Focus Publications, 1997). Note: Unless specified, quotes are from the 1903 single volume, which is readily accessible. The copy I have is the 23rd printing of 1962, with a Foreword by D. Martyn Lloyd-Jones.

Introduction

In laying out gardens, pavilions, wandering paths, small mountains of stone, and flower plantings, try to give the feeling of the small in the large and the large in the small, of the real in the illusion, and of the illusion in the reality. Some things should be hidden, and some should be obvious, some prominent and some vague. . . . Here is a way to show the real amidst an illusion: arrange the garden so that when a guest feels he has seen everything he can suddenly take a turn in the path and have a broad new vista open up before him, or open a simple door in a pavilion only to find it leads to an entirely new garden.

Shen Fu, *Six Records of a Floating Life* (1809)[1]

Putting on Chinese Dress

One of the curiosities of China missions is that we, a century later, can look at a group photograph of turn-of-the-century missionaries — say, the delegates to the Shanghai Missionary Conference of 1890, a long scroll with hundreds of men and women in serried ranks — and guess each person's theology just from the clothes they are wearing. Most are in Western clothing, the men in suits and leather boots, and the women in corsets and bustle dresses that would have been fashionable a decade earlier in London. These were the liberals, the modernizers, who claimed their social gospel was universal to all

---

1. Shen Fu, *Six Records of a Floating Life*, written in 1809, translated by Leonard Pratt and Chiang Su-hui (Markham, Ont.: Penguin, 1983), pp. 60-61.

human societies — as long as it wore Western clothes. In the front row sits Hudson Taylor, a tiny, elf-like figure with a long white beard, who is wearing a Chinese gown and a black cap with a red button, the insignia of a scholar, and hidden behind his back, he has his hair braided into a long queue or pigtail. Scattered throughout the group are other men similarly dressed, and women wearing gowns like peasant women. These were Hudson Taylor's footsoldiers, the members of the China Inland Mission (CIM) and other faith missions. They were the conservatives who later would be called fundamentalists, those who were not willing to compromise their evangelical theology, who put on "native dress" as soon as they stepped off the boat. They looked like mendicant monks out of the floating world.

The CIM was derisively nicknamed the "pigtail mission" because of its strict policy concerning Chinese clothing. On arrival in China the recruits were outfitted with cotton gowns and high felt boots with thick paper soles, and sent inland with no luggage, no language, no words. The men had the added indignity of the queue, shaving the front of their heads and braiding the crown into a pigtail; until their hair grew in, a year or more, they would wear a cap with a false queue hanging down the back.

The question of native dress was not trifling, judging from the controversies and compromises it engendered. Conventional missionaries, who seldom ventured beyond the foreign concessions, said wearing Chinese clothes was "demeaning," that the Chinese would "lose respect" if foreigners "descended" to their level. It was not only foolhardy but also seditious; it upset the balance of imperialism. The CIM defended Chinese dress as neither disguise nor eccentricity, but as an attempt to build a three-self Chinese church — self-supporting, self-propagating, and self-financing — shorn of its foreign trappings. Western clothes aroused fear and suspicion; native dress was like a spiritual passport — "God's Ambassadors" — that allowed them to pass unnoticed.

One could be cynical and suggest that Hudson Taylor created the China Inland Mission as an emigrant society for adventurous, pious English clerks to start afresh, to reinvent themselves in a Chinese village, far away.

The Wordless Book

Hudson Taylor had the amazing ability to reduce incomprehensibly complex ideas into simple object lessons: the Chinese Empire, he liked to state, was 44 times the size of Great Britain and Ireland, or 104 times the size of England; every day, 33,000 Chinese died, equivalent to the population of Leeds, or Lon-

Introduction

CIM missionaries in Chinese dress; Hudson Taylor and Jennie Faulding Taylor (front row, right). This undated, unidentified photograph was probably taken in 1899-1900, while the Taylors were in Shanghai for a missionary conference; he suffered a heart attack there and retired to Switzerland, where Mrs Taylor died in 1903.   Source: OMF/Toronto.

don's deaths in three months; and so on. His "heavenly vision" at Brighton Beach, on 25 June 1865, with its grim message that "a million a month in China are dying without God," became *the* most powerful Western image of China for the nineteenth century and beyond. Stripped of its connotations of hellfire, it became a trope for the unlimited number of consumers for Standard Oil's advertising campaign, "Oil for the Lamps of China," or for Ford cars.[2]

When Hudson Taylor was young and believed in the "blitz-conversion" of China, he would "scatter a thousand gospels," literally tossing them over the

---

2. Perhaps the most graphic depiction of China's marching millions appears in Frank Capra's famous wartime propaganda film, "Why We Fight." While the narrator (Walter Huston) intones about four hundred million marching four abreast in a never-ending line, the screen is filled with a myriad of faces and crowds of people. Frank Capra, "Why We Fight," film 6, "The Battle of China" (1943), rereleased on DVD by Goodtime DVD.

heads of the crowds, hoping that some seed would fall on fertile ground. After the bloody suppression of the Taiping rebellion, he realized that the printed word needed to be accompanied by the preached word, either by a foreign missionary, or a native preacher or biblewoman. Indeed, he wrote in 1877, "putting a whole Bible or Testament into the hands of an unconverted and uninstructed *heathen,* in an unconverted *language* (you will understand me, my brethren), *without* printed note, or comment, or preface — *without* preached note and comment — *without* explanatory tract, and *without* the comment of Christian life, is the most unsuccessful, and is, so far as my experience goes, *sometimes* even *hurtful.*"[3]

Do not perplex the people with dogma, Taylor cautioned. "Talk theory to the heathen, and they are generally unmoved." Rather, missionaries should preach that they had "an infallible help for every opium smoker among them, for every drunkard, for every fornicator, for every gambler . . . and you will see that that Gospel *is* good news to your hearers, can command attention, and will accomplish the mightiest changes of which the mind of man can conceive, or the heart of man can desire."[4] The problem was, the only people who listened were opium smokers, drunkards, fornicators, and gamblers.

Converting 400 million Chinese one person at a time was a lonely, unrewarding profession — and every missionary dreamed of the day when he or she would baptize by the hundreds. From trial and error, Taylor and the CIM perfected two forms of personal evangelism. Starting from a central city, such as the capital of a province, a male missionary — in gown and pigtail — would make evangelistic tours of the neighborhood, covering the same ground over and over until he was recognized, then ignored. He would conduct what was called "teashop evangelism," stopping wherever people gathered, at religious shrines — setting up a table next to the Buddhists and Daoists — and marketplaces, at village wells and teashops, preaching and handing out tracts. Once he had established a beachhead, an outstation staffed with a native preacher, he would move there by himself. As circumstances permitted, he brought his wife to share his mud-brick house. Since Chinese women did not appear in public, only missionary women could enter the secluded inner chambers where they lived. This intensive house-to-house visiting was called "gossiping the gospel,"[5] as the women used simple devices such as "the wordless book" and a five-finger mantra to interest the

3. JHT, "Itineration Far and Near as an Evangelizing Agency" (speech to the Shanghai Missionary Conference, 12 May 1877), in *China's Millions* (GB), October 1877, pp. 122-25; quote at p. 124.
4. Ibid., p. 122.
5. *HTCOC* 6, p. 103.

Introduction

women at their own level and thereby teach the rudiments of Christianity, along with sewing and hygiene.

The wordless book, which is depicted on the cover of this book, appears at crucial points in the narrative. It is a simple mnemonic device that consists of four pages of colors to explain God's plan of redemption: black for sin; red for Jesus' sacrifice; white for sanctification; and gold for heaven. It has been widely used for a century and a half in Britain and North America for the instruction of boys and girls, and around the world to teach non-Christian adults in the mission fields.[6] The equation that the minds of converts in China were as simple as the children of England, and that what was suitable for the latter was adaptable to the former, was such a common trope of nineteenth-century missions that it passes almost without notice.

When the four-color wordless book was taken to China about 1880, the strangest thing happened. There it encountered another wordless book, that is, the ancient Chinese color cosmology known as *wuxing*, the Five Elements, that assigned meanings to five colors — yellow, red, white, and black, plus green — correlated with the directions, elements, seasons, *feng shui*, and human destiny. Each color has significance in daily life, from the color of an actor's face in Peking Opera to the red envelopes presented to children at the new year. As Sunzi wrote in *The Art of War* (500 B.C.E.), "There are not more than five primary colors (green, yellow, red, white, and black), yet in combination they produce more hues than can ever be seen."[7] Throughout history, each dynasty has chosen its auspicious color, with yellow/gold reserved for the emperor. Nowadays, of course, since the communist revolution, as the national anthem of China says, "The East is Red."[8]

Wittingly or unwittingly, the missionaries were presenting the Christian message in colors that the peasants already understood — new wine in old

---

6. Ruth Overholtzer wrote a short history of the wordless book called "That Little Book," which is at the Child Evangelism Fellowship website: http://www.gospelcom.net/cef/wordless. From anecdotal evidence, I can trace its continuous use since the 1920s. For example, when I was cleaning out the effects of my stepmother, Emma Sullivan Austin, a former CIM missionary, I discovered three copies of the wordless book, small, medium, and large, dating back to the 1930s, which she used in China and in Canada.

7. Sunzi, *The Art of War*, trans. John Minford (New York: Viking, 2002), vol. 5, p. 8.

8. Diana Lary has written a provocative paper on the meaning of the various shades of red in the Chinese revolution: "Chinese Reds," in Ian Germani and Robin Swales, eds., *Symbols, Myths and Images of the French Revolution: Essays in Honour of James Leith* (Regina: Canadian Plains Research Centre, 1998). "From its birth, China's Communist revolution was a red revolution, since it followed the Russian revolution. The dominance of red in the communist symbolic system was incredibly fortunate for the Chinese Communists, given the importance of the various reds within Chinese colour [cosmology]" (publicity text).

wineskins, as it were. (That was why they emphasized the correct sequence, otherwise the people might confuse the meaning.) And, as Jacques Gernet noted of the seventeenth-century Jesuits, who utilized similar techniques of mass evangelism, such as holy pictures, talismans, rosaries, and other visual symbols, the "assimilation was instantaneous." If the reaction of the Confucian elite was hostile to the Christian message, the common people "behaved towards the Christian missionaries in exactly the same manner as they were accustomed to behave towards the Buddhist monks."[9]

In deconstructionist terms, the missionaries were appropriating the colors of Chinese folk religion and giving them a new, secret meaning. Here is how the wordless book worked. In 1893, Mrs. Howard Taylor, the CIM historian, used it to teach a congregation of Buddhist nuns, "religious women . . . [who] belonged to an organized order of religious worshippers." She also had a five-finger mantra, an early version of "the gospel glove":

Thumb: "There is only one true God."
Forefinger: "The true God loves us."
Middle finger: "The true God can forgive sin."
Ring finger: "The true God keeps us in peace."
Little finger: "The true God leads us at last to heaven."[10]

When one slow sister finally got it, the others stood around clapping, "Her heart is opening! Her heart is opening!" like a lotus opening its petals, like a bodhisattva reaching enlightenment.

The wordless book was also used by the Church Missionary Society, which was closely allied with the CIM, as shown in reports from its far-flung missions in China and Africa. In China, Rev. Robert Stewart wrote a report on the efficacy of Christian schools as evangelistic agencies in Fujian province in 1893. (Stewart and other missionaries were killed in a grisly massacre in 1895; see Chapter 10.) He recounted an amusing story which is worth quoting because it illustrates the confusion when a missionary named Collins encountered a group of coolies, and how the wordless book acted as a cultural bridge.

"There is a great interest awakened in A-cai," said the native clergyman to me [Collins]. "I went there and stayed two nights and all the village

---

9. Jacques Gernet, *China and the Christian Impact: A Conflict of Cultures*, trans. Janet Lloyd (Cambridge: Cambridge University Press, 1985), p. 74.
10. Joy Guinness, *Mrs. Howard Taylor: Her Web of Time* (London: CIM, 1949), p. 132.

came to listen." "Where is A-cai?" I asked, as the name was unfamiliar. "Down by the sea — it is the village to which the school was moved this year," he answered. Directly he said that, I remembered that the schoolmaster was a very earnest man, a true Christian, and a keen student of his Bible, and I had been expecting to hear further news of him. I had heard that he had twelve scholars coming to his school every day, and sixteen at night — boys whose work prevented them coming at any other time — so I was heartily glad when I found myself seated in a large boat that sails daily down to the sea-coast villages. . . . The people crowded round me, and I . . . gave myself up at once to silent prayer, for it is a very real trial for me to be overhauled and mauled by a crowd on a hot June morning, and to answer with perfect equanimity a thousand questions, each more extraordinary than the one before; to have every garment pierced and felt by every hand that can reach it, and to be catechised on the state of the tea-market, and the value of a dollar in England. Presently an old man came and sat down near me, and in answer to a question as to where he was going, said, "To A-cai." So at once he struck up a friendly talk. He had heard the Gospel from the schoolmaster, Mr. Ding, and at once, to my complete surprise, asked me to read some of it to him, "As Mr. D. does every evening." Out came my Testament, and the fire of questions ceased as I read St. John iii. 1-18. I thought this old man promised well for A-cai.

A crowd of coolies with their loads joined us from another boat, and the noise and confusion preventing conversation, I opened my ink-bottle and letter-case to write. "What's he got there — is he eating opium?" shouted a man who was too far off to see, and took the pen for a pipe-stem. That gave me an opening, and they carried away a very distinct idea of what English Christians out here think of the opium question. I overheard one man say reflectively to his friend, some time after, "He says what they hate most is opium."

Shortly after, another man took the ink for morphia; for some reason it was connected with opium in his mind. They then conversed about foreigners in general, and some of their ideas were new to me. I gathered that there was a race of foreigners who were all women, no men! that there was one kingdom which no ship built with iron nails could ever get to, and so on. At length I made a last effort, and quoting St. John iii. 12, caught their attention, and with the help of the little "wordless book," had a capital time with them.[11]

11. Mary E. Watson, *Robert and Louisa Stewart: In Life and in Death* (London: Marshall

INTRODUCTION

If one follows the internal logic of this strange dialogue, there in a nutshell is the plot of my book: the missionary hears of an indigenous church which has grown up beyond his ken, led by a charismatic teacher; he sets out on a perilous journey to see for himself. Along the way he is bombarded with political questions — tea and dollars — and he responds by reading the Bible. He starts to write — if a missionary could not preach, it seems, he had a compulsion to write — and the coolies automatically assume he is smoking opium. He gives them an earful about evil England — "perfidious Albion" — and the evils of the opium trade. The subject of opium naturally leads to morphine, which for some reason they connected with opium, and then everyone has a capital time with the wordless book.

This could have startling results. One striking example comes from another place and culture, among the Yoruba of Nigeria, as reported by J. D. Y. Peel in *Religious Encounter and the Making of the Yoruba*. In 1877 a missionary of the Church Missionary Society started using the wordless book in outdoor preaching. He thus "abandoned verbal discourse altogether for pure symbolism. . . . [He] described its message as 'the heart washed by the blood of Christ' and confirmed the great impact it had on audiences; on one occasion a man responded by simply exclaiming, 'the truth is come.' While the overt message was powerful enough in its simplicity, especially to the young runaway slaves who constituted most of the population of Leki, its impact must have been enhanced by its coincidence with Yoruba modes of signification," such as the "'country' letters used in the solemn communication of chiefs." Peel notes how the missionaries picked up on this color symbolism, particularly using white things, such as jars of salt and sugar. "But the 'wordless book' made use of the whole range of the black/red/white color triad."[12]

The wordless book is more complex than it appears, Peel continues, with a brilliant analysis.

> As Victor Turner pointed out, basic symbols such as the three colors derive a strong emotional charge from their multi-referential character, which any user will find himself evoking without intending it. And not only was each symbol enhanced by having more than one reference, but the entire sequence of them was enhanced as well. The story line of [James] Read's "wordless book," which he devised to convey the plan of

---

Brothers, 1895), chapter 5. Available at: http://anglicanhistory.org/asia/china/stewart/05.html. Thanks to Ian Welch for this reference.

12. John David Yeardon Peel, *Religious Encounter and the Making of the Yoruba* (Bloomington: Indiana University Press, 2000), pp. 168-69.

redemption, can also be read in another way, as a symbolization of the history that the mission was attempting to make at a concrete level. Without doubt, the master metaphor used by the missionaries for their project was of bringing light into darkness; so the black/white opposition could also stand as a color-coding of heathenism/Christianity, African/*oyinbo*, tradition/modernity, past/future, a typological contrast projected onto the course of real cultural change. Red would then signify the struggles and suffering, the self-sacrifice of missionaries and the persecution of converts, which would lead from black to white; and gold the enhanced wealth and power which would result from enlightenment (*olaju*). Black-white-red-gold thus vividly encapsulates the course of cultural history which the mission was inviting the Yoruba to adopt.

I employ the wordless book in several ways, literally and metaphorically, in this book. First, it is an historical document, a text that can be deconstructed like any other text: it was invented at a particular moment in time, and has a historical and social context that can be mapped and understood. It was invented in 1866 by Charles Haddon Spurgeon, the most famous preacher in England, to teach illiterate "orphans" in his orphanages. His first version had only three colors, black, red, and white, and the emphasis was on the blackness of sin: "Do not be afraid to look on your sins," he warned his listeners, "and meditate upon them until they even drive you to despair."[13] Nine years later, in 1875, Taylor was present when the wordless book was revised by Dwight Lyman Moody, the American preacher, who added the gold for heaven. This seemingly innocuous addition had serious theological implications, for it represented the shift in evangelical teachings towards an emphasis on Keswick Holiness and glory theology, rather than hellfire and damnation.

Once Moody endorsed the wordless book, it spread throughout the transatlantic evangelical world. Fanny Crosby, the hymnodist ("Blessed Assurance"), kept a copy in her purse — now that would be a sight, the blind singer teaching the sighted to "read" colors. In 1895 Amy Carmichael, the devotional missionary author, took it to India, where she made a satin flag of four colors which, she reported, was a "most useful text for an impromptu sermon." Dr.

---

13. Charles Haddon Spurgeon, sermon # 3278, "The Wordless Book," delivered 11 January 1866, published in vol. 57 (30 November 1911) of his *Sermons* by Passmore & Alabaster. Spurgeon's entire 63 volumes of *Sermons* have recently been republished by Pilgrim Publications of Pasadena, Texas, under the title *Metropolitan Tabernacle Pulpit*. See Chapter 3 note 35.

INTRODUCTION

Baedecker smuggled it into Russian prisons, where he converted political prisoners of the Czar.[14]

In 1924 Ruth Overholtzer discovered a copy in Harry Ironside's bookstore attached to the Moody Church in Chicago. Inspired by Spurgeon's sermon, she and her husband J. Irvin Overholtzer founded Child Evangelism Fellowship (CEF) in 1937. The CEF "owns" the wordless book and added a fifth color, "green to grow in the knowledge of God." It has published many versions, often with explanatory scripture references, such as John 3:16. According to its mission statement, CEF is "a Bible-centered, worldwide organization composed of born-again believers whose purpose is to evangelize boys and girls with the Gospel of the Lord Jesus Christ and to establish (disciple) them in the local church for Christian living." It has 1,200 missionaries overseas and an estimated 40,000 volunteers in the United States and Canada.[15]

Finally, I employ the wordless book as a prism through which the "simple faith" of Victorian working-class evangelical piety took on Chinese dress and entered late Qing China. Pastor Hsi's use of the wordless book in Shanxi illustrates in vivid detail how Chinese folk religion, visions, healing, exorcism, and opium refuges formed a matrix of evangelism.[16] In other words it can be seen as part of a long continuum of "contextualization," or "inculturation," or "indigenization," of Christianity in China.

---

14. Overholtzer, "That Little Book."

15. Nowadays, the wordless book is ubiquitous in the evangelical subculture. There are wordless book pencils, coffee mugs, videos, comic books, bumper stickers, Rubic's Cubes, and bracelets for little girls, each emblazoned with four or five colors. There is even something called Wally the Gospel Walnut, "a Creative Object Lesson made from a Jumbo Sized Real Walnut with wordless book Ribbons Inside that scroll in and out of the mouth." See website www.kedhelper.com/CCM/walnut.htm. Betty Smartt Carter's *I Read It in the Wordless Book: A Novel* (Grand Rapids: Baker Book House, 1996) is a "snappy" coming-of-age novel about Southern fundamentalists, "deeply religious, deeply flawed people," who find "grace is as violent and unpredictable as it is tender and constant." One reviewer commented that it "is definitely not for young readers." See bettycart@juno.com and review by Anne Callahan at www.acloserlook.com/9607acl/fiction/ireaditinthewordlessbook.html.

16. In her study of the Canadian Presbyterian mission in North Henan, the neighboring province to Shanxi, Margo S. Gewurtz identified 1,500 named converts and, working with Chinese scholars, has reconstructed village-level networks of family and religion. She identified six pathways to Christian conversion and the growth of rural parishes, namely: markets and fairs, medicine, opium, family and kinship patterns, female converts and sectarianism. See "Do Numbers Count? A Report on a Preliminary Study of the Christian Converts of the North Henan Mission, 1890-1925," *Republican China* 10, no. 3 (June 1985): 18-26. To this list I would add exorcism and what Gary Tiedemann calls "water rights Christians" (see footnote 21), those who thought the missionary would use political pressure to intervene in their lawsuits.

Introduction

Sectarian Conversion

In the growing literature on religious conversion, Daniel Bays and Murray Rubinstein, respected historians of evangelical Protestants in China and Taiwan respectively, use the terms "commonalties" and "congruences" between pietistic evangelicals and traditional Chinese beliefs.[17] According to Rubinstein, a cultural transmitter (missionary) can only adapt the cultural patterns of one society to another if he finds common ground in "the existence of key parallel cultural patterns and structures" (the wordless book). Once he has found the congruences, he can move toward accommodation.[18] "Christianity may be rather strange and new, but not totally so," Alan Hunter and Kim-Kwong Chan write in the authoritative *Protestantism in Contemporary China*. Like Christianity, traditional Chinese sects offer "prayers, healing, fellowship, a system of morality, rationale for suffering and promise of salvation."[19] At a more mundane level, other congruencies include: the style of literary declamation or "scripture quoting"; congregational worship and scripture study; initiation and funeral rituals; an afterlife with a paradise and hell; a pantheon of supernatural beings, heavenly angels to save suffering humanity and demons to torment them; and a millenarian eschatology that promises salvation from coming catastrophe.[20]

In their travels, the missionaries found that the brightest and most attentive listeners were male and female members of native religious sects, existing organizations whose members were already on a spiritual pilgrimage. They made an concerted effort to target these sects. One missionary, Francis Huberty James, listed fifty in Shandong province alone that he had investigated and had tried to convert their members to Christianity.[21] "The simple

---

17. Daniel H. Bays, "Christianity and the Chinese Sectarian Tradition," *Ch'ing Shih Wen-t'i*, 4, no. 7 (June 1982): 33-50. Murray A. Rubinstein, *The Protestant Community on Modern Taiwan: Mission, Seminary, and Church* (Armonk, N.Y.: M. E. Sharpe, 1991), p. 9.

18. Rubinstein, *Protestant Community*, p. 129.

19. Alan Hunter and Kim-Kwong Chan, *Protestantism in Contemporary China* (Cambridge: Cambridge University Press, 1993), p. 71.

20. Rubinstein, *Protestant Community*, p. 136. Bays, "Christianity and the Chinese Sectarian Tradition," pp. 37-45.

21. Francis Huberty James, "The Secret Sects of Shantung, with Appendix," *Records of the General Conference of the Protestant Missionaries of China, Held at Shanghai, May 7-20, 1890* (Shanghai: American Presbyterian Press, 1890), pp. 196-202. I discuss James as a pioneer in Shanxi in Chapter 5. See also Daniel H. Bays, "Christianity and Chinese Sects: Religious Tracts in the Late Nineteenth Century," in Suzanne Wilson Barnett and John King Fairbank, eds., *Christianity in China: Early Protestant Missionary Writings* (Cambridge: Harvard University Press, 1985), pp. 122, 125-26; Bays, "Christianity and the Chinese Sectar-

sincerity of the followers of this religion has attracted the attention of European missionaries," Joseph Edkins wrote of one group. "They exhibit more depth and reality in their convictions than is common in other sects in China. This, added to their firm protest against idolatry, has led to . . . efforts to instruct them in Christianity."[22] Another sect the missionaries targeted was the "orphan colony" of Chinese Jews in Kaifeng, whom they tried to convince that Christianity was the successor to Judaism.[23]

Susan Naquin and Daniel Overmyer, leading historians of Chinese religious sects, distinguish two kinds in the late Qing: the religious teachings [*jiao*] which promoted salvation of believers and society in general, and "heterodox sects" or "secret societies" [*hui*], which had "a veneer of religious coloration to attract supporters" but whose purpose was political revolution. The "sutra-recitation *jiao*" were organized congregations characterized by quasi-monastic living, a vegetarian regimen, and congregational activities in a sutra hall. They attracted a literate, well-to-do urban audience and thus were visible to the authorities. "They live a life half clerical, half lay, characterized by sincere beliefs and the study of scriptures." They stressed vegetarian vows, and called each other "vegetarian friends," and cooperated in building chapels called "vegetarian halls for the purpose of worship."[24]

"Meditational sects," on the other hand, seem like Plymouth Brethren in Chinese dress, with "no halls, sutras, or vows," and only simple exercises and incantations. They survived for centuries as "small scattered groups of believers" bound by "long and loose chains of teachers and disciples. Followers of this religion, normally concerned with private devotions, also anticipated a period of great cataclysms when they would cast aside their ordinary lives and, following the deity sent to lead them, join together and rise up to usher in a new and perfect world in which all people found salvation through their

---

ian Tradition," pp. 45-49; and R. G. Tiedemann, "Christianity and Chinese 'Heterodox Sects': Mass Conversion and Syncretism in Shandong Province in the Early Eighteenth Century," *Monumenta Serica* 44 (1996): 339-82.

22. Joseph Edkins, *Religion in China: Containing a Brief Account of the Three Religions of the Chinese, with Observations on the Prospects of Christian Conversion amongst that People*, 3rd ed. (London: Trubner & Co., 1884), p. 187.

23. William C. White, *Chinese Jews: A Compilation of Matters Relating to the Jews of K'aifeng Fu* (Toronto: University of Toronto Press, 1942), pp. vi-vii. See also Alvyn Austin, "Scholars, Archaeologists and Diplomats: China Missions and Canadian Public Life," in *Religion and Public Life in Canada: Historical and Comparative Perspectives*, ed. Marguerite Van Die (Toronto: University of Toronto Press, 2001), p. 138.

24. David K. Jordan and Daniel L. Overmyer, *The Flying Phoenix: Aspects of Chinese Sectarianism in Taiwan* (Princeton: Princeton University Press, 1986), p. 27.

Introduction

faith and their faith alone."²⁵ Such sects offered people a way to be good and gain merit, and thus be saved from the coming cataclysm and be assured of paradise. Their purpose was, in the words of C. K. Yang, "to bring universal deliverance to tortured humanity."²⁶

Using the word "vegetarian" as a signifier, the reports of the China Inland Mission sound as though every other convert was a "vegetarian friend." The first convert in Wuhu, who "had been a vegetarian for some years, and ... was about to become a priest," converted many members of his sect, Former Heaven, Sien-t'ian (*Xiantian*).²⁷ Similarly in Shaanxi, the first convert had been "a vegetarian for many years, and a very zealous idolater."²⁸ "I had felt led to speak specially of the conscious need of many, of something better than idolatry to satisfy the heart," one missionary wrote, "and of the inability of those who eat herbs [a popular method of meritorious fasting], by that means to get rid of their sins" [square brackets in original]. He was pursued by two vegetarian women who "wished to hear more about the gospel. ... One of the women repeated after me, sentence by sentence, a few words of prayer; and then nothing would satisfy her but that we should go back to her house and write down a prayer for her to use."²⁹ Once they became Christians, however, the old women could not remain vegetarians: they had to participate in a public ceremony during which they ate meat, for, as one missionary explained in what seems a macabre notion, "without shedding of blood is no remission" of sins.³⁰

Although many converts may have come to Christianity through sectarian conversion, some had suspect motives. By putting themselves under the missionaries' protection and disguising themselves as Christians, they hoped to avoid prosecution when they were brought before a magistrate. As Christians, they claimed they did not have to pay the "idol tax" to support "heathen theatricals" and the ceremonies for the state pantheon. In Taizhou, Zhejiang province, an illiterate carpenter named Ling was converted by "the simplicity

---

25. Susan Naquin, *Millenarian Rebellion in China: The Eight Trigrams Uprising of 1813* (New Haven: Yale University Press, 1976), pp. 2-3.

26. Quoted in Daniel Overmyer, *Folk Buddhist Religion: Dissenting Sects in Late Traditional China* (Cambridge: Harvard University Press, 1976), p. 6.

27. *China's Millions* (GB), May 1876, p. 137. This is one of the only occasions in the CIM records when a sect was identified by name.

28. Ibid., December 1880, p. 148.

29. Ibid., July 1875, p. 11.

30. Ibid., May 1877, p. 52. For the conversion of vegetarians, see Nishan J. Najarian, "Religious Conversion in Nineteenth-Century China: Face-to-face Interaction Between Western Missionaries and the Chinese," in *Social Interaction in Chinese Society*, ed. Sidney L. Greenblatt, Richard W. Wilson, and Amy Auerbacher Wilson (New York: Praeger, 1982).

of the Gospel, and with its suitability with his case." He offered the missionaries a Buddhist temple and "Buddhist nunnery, and Mr. Ling's wife was formerly a novice in it. The abbess being dead, the building has been sold." The missionary had quite a bonfire that day: the idols were removed from their pedestals and the largest, the Goddess of Mercy, "dismantled and dethroned, was broken up, and used as fuel to cook our evening meal" — except for her head, which was sent to a museum in England. The situation turned out to be more complicated than it appeared. Ling and his fellow Buddhists were embroiled in a row with Roman Catholics in the next village who were aggressively pursuing land cases in the magistrates' courts. "The people somehow seemed to have got the idea that we were possessed of considerable political power which could be exerted on their behalf if they were to join us." When the CIM refused to intervene in lawsuits, they ceased attending. "Such persons," warned the Chinese pastor, "really are of the generation of vipers; they wish to escape the wrath of the mandarins, but do not fear God."[31]

Jesus Opium

One of the historical debates about late Qing China concerns opium. What was the connection between opium and the missionary enterprise, which nineteenth-century Chinese considered the twin scourges of Western imperialism, and "in some secret way connected together, as part of the general commercial enterprise of the British nation"?[32] Through the CIM one can trace the continuum of the anti-opium campaign from the Houses of Parliament in England to the wretched opium refuges of Shanxi. The Anglo-Chinese Society for the Suppression of the Opium Traffic (later, when opium was legalized, of the Opium Trade) was not just a sideline for the CIM, but its "other society." It was run in England by CIM secretary Benjamin Broomhall, who was editor of two anti-opium journals, *China's Millions*, its foreign policy, and *National Righteousness*, its domestic cause. In Shanghai the CIM gathered information from the remote regions of China and forwarded it to England where it formed the factual backbone of the crusade. At the tail end were those like Pastor Hsi who claimed to have treated over 300,000 addicts. As Hsi spiraled out of control, the CIM decided to support him at all costs,

---

31. *China's Millions* (GB), October 1876, p. 198; March 1877, p. 27; and July 1876, p. 170.
32. James Bromley Eames, *The English in China: Being an Account of the Intercourse and Relations between England and China from the Year 1600 to the Year 1843 and a Summary of Later Developments* (London: Curzon Press, 1909; reprint, New York: Barnes and Noble, 1974), p. 169.

Introduction

hush up his tantrums, because everything depended on the stories he concocted out of smoke and mirrors. Opium was the cause that made the CIM famous.

There has been considerable study of the anti-opium lobby as a political movement, but little on opium rehabilitation at the grassroots level. One important question in particular has never been examined: how did morphine (or morphia) come to be called "Jesus opium"?[33] Quitting cold turkey could kill a confirmed addict, so the opium refuges needed some sort of palliative, a regimen of physical and spiritual therapies to get over the side effects of withdrawal. Nothing was more effective than morphine, a new drug refined in the 1850s, administered either in pill or hypodermic form. The hospital in Taiyuan, Shanxi, made the first experiments with hypodermic morphine, which involved gradually diluting the dosage over a three- or four-week period until finally the doctor was injecting pure water. The treatment was so successful that the gentry presented the hospital with a plaque that proclaimed, "The wonderful needle is like that of old," as if the hypodermic was a miraculous new kind of acupuncture.[34]

Although British officials condoned the opium trade, which was after all legal, they immediately condemned the trade in morphine. In 1885 the British Legation, fearing a "panic should it become generally known that a foreign poison was being extensively sold," warned the Zongli Yamen, the Chinese Foreign Office, "so that they might take steps to prevent the circulation of so dangerous a substance, and promised British cooperation in necessary restrictions." Such restrictions were not implemented and the trade increased through the 1890s.[35]

The Conspiracy of Silence

"Even yet it would puzzle a stranger to know the real state of things," one CIM missionary wrote, "could he see our periodical statistical forms as sent to Shanghai, which show literally *nothing*, and at the same time hear the workers on the Si-gan [Xian] Plain singing with all their hearts, 'To God be the glory, Great things He hath done.'"[36] A historian, too, is puzzled when he tries to pen-

33. Seagrave, *The Soong Dynasty*, p. 334; and Spence, "Opium," in *Chinese Roundabout*, p. 250. See also above, Preface, note 15.
34. *China's Millions* (GB), February 1887, p. 28.
35. P. D. Coates, *The China Consuls: British Consular Officers, 1843-1943* (Hong Kong: Oxford University Press, 1988), p. 177.
36. *China's Millions* (GB), February 1895, p. 19.

etrate the labyrinthine workings of the China Inland Mission, and comes up with blank statistics and pious rhetoric. An aura of secrecy permeated the CIM, inside and outside, at every level and to such an extent that A. J. Broomhall, the official historian, used terms like a "conspiracy of silence"[37] and "cocoon of silence."[38] By the 1890s the rank and file in China were in open rebellion; the London office was not on speaking terms with Shanghai; Toronto would not reveal its finances; Australia was in debt; and Hudson Taylor was threatening to resign and take the work with him. The silence extended to the mission's archives, where Taylor decreed that "nothing detrimental to the mission be written and any documents which might prove an embarrassment in later years were to be destroyed." After Mrs. Howard Taylor (Geraldine Guinness), his daughter-in-law and the official historian of the CIM, finished writing her books, the records were purged so that little material remains, in the CIM archives or elsewhere, "which does not merely substantiate what they wrote."[39]

Mrs. Howard Taylor fashioned Hudson Taylor's oft-repeated stories into a two-volume history, *The Story of the CIM* (1893), which was superseded by another two-volume work, *Hudson Taylor and the China Inland Mission* (1911 and 1918), which sold 50,000 copies by 1929 and is still in print. Mrs. Taylor's biographer, her niece, admitted that she took poetic license, snipping and splicing with "the touch of an artist.... There are beautiful things, things very nearly ideal, and she instinctively found that side of life, and gloried in it.... Undoubtedly, Aunt Geraldine made some things sound unbelievably good, and we don't see them like that, but perhaps the fact that she did may make a few of us not only wish that we could, but believe that we may. There are other facts than the things present, other and far greater ones, and it is her prayer and mine that some who read the record of God's ways in her life may experience the uplift that comes of being more sure of God than of anything else in the universe."[40] In Shakespearean drama, this is called the willing suspension of disbelief.

Mrs. Taylor applied the touch of an artist to the mission archives. Some letters, too sacred to destroy but too delicate to leave intact, have been censored in a unique way. Hudson Taylor was often quite affectionate with his wife, and sometimes his letters overstepped the bounds of Victorian propriety. One letter reads:

37. *HTCOC* 6, p. 60.
38. *HTCOC* 7, p. 134.
39. Moira Jane McKay, "Faith and Facts in the History of the China Inland Mission 1832-1905" (master's thesis, University of Aberdeen, 1981), p. 63. Hereafter cited as McKay, "Faith and Facts."
40. Joy Guinness, *Mrs. Howard Taylor*, p. 5. Mrs. Taylor also wrote a biography of her brother, Dr. Whitfield Guinness, *Guinness of Honan* (London: CIM, 1930).

Introduction

Dr. Howard Taylor and Geraldine Guinness Taylor. He was Hudson Taylor's son and she was the daughter of Grattan Guinness, the silver-tongued Irish orator who established the East London Missionary Training School. After writing their histories of the CIM, the records were purged so that little material remains "which does not merely substantiate what they wrote." Source: Joy Guinness, *Mrs. Howard Taylor: Her Web of Time* (London: CIM, 1949).

My own precious treasure, how I do long to throw my arms around you, to feel . . .

At this point, Mrs. Howard Taylor, censoring her father-in-law, carefully pasted a thin strip of paper across the next line, both front and back, so it is impossible to read. The next line continues

. . . with kisses. Tomorrow it will be a month since I left you . . .

(The offending word is probably "bosom." This is not an isolated example.)[41]
Another level of secrecy started in China, where after a disastrous brush with British officials in 1866-68, Taylor resolved never to tell the British authorities

41. JHT to Jennie Faulding Taylor, his second wife, 21 March 1881, CIM/SOAS, file 267.

where his people happened to be, lest the consul prohibit the journey and revoke their passports. He also kept his friends in London in the dark in case they accidentally revealed vital information, which might have repercussions in China. Since the right of foreigners to travel in interior China was barely recognized by treaty rights, the CIM, pushing ahead of the flag, was "always in scrapes" with both British and Chinese officials, because of their "utter want of discretion."[42]

The antipathy was echoed by some consuls — though far from all, for the CIM had friends in high places — such as Consul F. S. Bourne (1893), who claimed the CIM was subject to no law, neither Chinese nor foreign. He deplored "the apparent mania in Europe for sending out uneducated and impulsive young men and letting them rush up-country; the religious fervor which was their only recommendation soon evaporated in the dry, matter-of-fact, apathetic Chinese environment; some lost their mental balance and many more their nerve."[43] (Losing one's nerve in the CIM sense meant reverting to Western clothes and all that entailed.)

The secrecy extended to England where nothing was said that might upset supporters. At the top of the list was money, where it came from and how it was spent. The CIM statement of its "faith principles," which was printed in every issue of *China's Millions,* had five clauses:

1. no solicitation of funds or missionaries
2. no guaranteed salary
3. no debt
4. faith in God alone to supply one's needs
5. nondenominational in its membership.

Significantly, four of the five statements have to do with money: no solicitation, no salary, no debt, perpetual poverty. In other words, money was the external signifier of inner grace. In the history of Christianity, there have been many movements that equated poverty with saintliness, and faith principles implied "a better brand of Christian or at least one which connotes greater faith and trust in God."[44] The fifth rule, nondenominational membership,

42. Consul R. J. Forrest at Ningbo (1875), quoted in Coates, *China Consuls,* p. 216.
43. Ibid., pp. 183, 185. Two popular images of CIM-type missionaries are the fictional Edwina Crane, the "plain, somewhat horse-faced" spinster in Paul H. Scott, *The Jewel in the Crown,* and Gladys Aylward, as portrayed by Ingrid Bergman in the film *Inn of the Sixth Happiness.* Miss Aylward was a London chambermaid who applied to the CIM in the 1930s; when she was rejected for lack of education, she went to China on her own: see her biography by Alan Burgess, *The Small Woman* (London: Evans Brothers, 1957).
44. Harold Lindsell, "Faith Missions since 1938," in *Frontiers of the Christian World*

Introduction

was equally contentious, for the Anglicans mistrusted the Baptists, and the Plymouth Brethren refused to share communion. So virtually nothing appears in the records about money or denominational affiliation, both of which happen to be the preoccupation of historians.

The CIM archives are scattered and fragmentary to say the least. The records of the head office in Shanghai perished in the expulsion of 1950 — there are references to files being burned in the courtyard — and whatever survived was destroyed during the Cultural Revolution. The OMF head office is now located in Singapore, whose archives started in 1950. There are three historical research archives for the CIM:

- LONDON: After Mrs. Howard Taylor wrote her books, the purged records were put into storage for a hundred years, until A. J. Broomhall wrote his books. Broomhall organized and catalogued the material, and deposited it at the School of Oriental and African Studies (SOAS), University of London. Broomhall further censored the material, such as inking out offending words in letters that had escaped his great aunt; in *Hudson Taylor and China's Open Century*, he often used ellipses [. . .] to excise offending words such as "heathen" or "degraded Chinese." (For examples, see Chapters 5 note 2, and 6 note 1.) The SOAS archives consist of financial records, minutes of the London and China Councils, and the "Hudson Taylor material," i.e., letters to and from Taylor and his immediate family. Some letter-books list each letter received from China, 800 to 900 a year, from all parts of the Empire, of which only a dozen or two survive, those personally connected with Hudson Taylor. Even the correspondence of the London Council is gone — probably because it was too hot to handle.
- TORONTO: The Toronto branch (founded 1888) moved frequently, and most of its records were destroyed in 1958 when it moved from 150 St. George Street to 1058 Avenue Road. The archives of the Overseas Missionary Fellowship, now located in Mississauga, Ontario, contain printed material, including a complete run of the British, North American, and Australian editions of *China's Millions;* it also has the unpublished 932-page typescript memoirs of Henry W. Frost, North American director, and a bound volume of 948 applications to the Toronto office between 1888 and 1915. The photographic collection is large, and three albums compiled in China are outstanding.
- PHILADELPHIA: The American branch (founded 1901) remained in

---

Mission since 1938: Essays in Honor of Kenneth Scott Latourette, ed. W. C. Harr (New York: Harper & Row, 1962), pp. 193-94.

Germantown in Philadelphia until the 1980s, when it relocated to Robesonia, a tiny place in central Pennsylvania, and then to the Denver area. (The retirement home, Lammermuir House, was and still is in Lancaster, Pennsylvania.) Its archives have been donated to the Archives of the Billy Graham Center (ABGC) at Wheaton College, collection 215. This collection includes the correspondence and minutes of the Toronto, London, and Shanghai Councils from 1901. The ABGC has also assembled a very large number of personal papers and oral history interviews from American and Canadian CIM/OMF missionaries.

External sources for the CIM are meager. In England the CIM's public face was genial, ecumenical, bewhiskered with Victorian rectitude. Its annual meetings were chaired by great philanthropists and church leaders: Lord Shaftsbury called it "one of the nicest and snuggest little societies I know . . . small in magnitude and yet it is very vast in operation."[45] Nevertheless periodic attempts by the Foreign Office to pierce the hagiographic aura were unsuccessful when they discovered that the London Council knew little about what was happening in China. So we catch glimpses of the CIM in parliamentary debates and anti-opium delegations, and in the histories of allied institutions like the Plymouth Brethren, the Church Missionary Society, Dr. Barnardo's Homes, and the Keswick movement.

The first attempt to "say what has never been said" was John C. Pollock's biography, *Hudson Taylor and Maria* (1962). Mrs. Howard Taylor, he wrote, not only hid Hudson Taylor's unpleasant side but also ignored his humanity, "expunging, or at least severely censoring her father-in-law's sense of humour [and] she suppressed one complete love affair and half of another, and incidents which to her generation may have seemed derogatory or too private." As a representative of the *amor vincit omnia* school of biography, Pollock presents Taylor's story as "one of the great love stories of all time."[46]

Ten years later Pat Barr wrote *To China with Love: The Lives and Times of Protestant Missionaries in China 1860-1900*, the first modern history of the British missionary enterprise. It is a rollicking book — a great read that belongs on the same shelf as *The Hermit of Peking*[47] — in which Taylor plays a comic opera role as one eccentric among many in the stifling white enclaves of nineteenth-century China. Barr's introduction sets her tone: "This is a true

---

45. *HTCOC* 6, p. 303.
46. Pollock, *Hudson Taylor and Maria*, pp. 11, 9. This book sold 40,000 copies in several editions by the 1980s and is still in print.
47. Hugh R. Trevor-Roper, *The Hermit of Peking: The Hidden Life of Sir Edmund Backhouse* (London: Macmillan, 1976).

Introduction

story about the sort of people whom I find interesting.... Today, for many of us, their ideas are so artless as to seem almost quaint, their language so unfamiliar as to need the interpretation of modern psychology, their ambitions so over-blown as to seem practically incredible."[48]

The first scholarly examination of the CIM by an outsider was Moira Jane McKay's dissertation (1981, under Professor Andrew Walls at the University of Aberdeen), "Faith and Facts in the History of the China Inland Mission 1832-1905." McKay applied the historical discipline to what had previously been treated devotionally, thus providing a new way of looking at the history of the CIM. Without her thesis, A. J. Broomhall could not have written his books, and I could not have written this one. McKay examined the inner working of the London Council and acknowledged both the faith of "faith missions" and the facts about money and influence. She outlined the debate over faith missions, and placed the CIM on the moderate side — compared with the Plymouth Brethren or the Swedish Americans, who tried to live off the land — for it occasionally abrogated its policy of no solicitation. McKay's important contribution is the compilation of biographies of the forty members and referees of the London Council, who included such luminaries as Thomas Barnardo and John Morley of the YMCA, but few clergymen. (See Appendix 2.)

Anthony James (Jim) Broomhall, a retired CIM/OMF doctor, published the definitive *Hudson Taylor and China's Open Century* between 1981 and 1989. Broomhall, who died in 1994, was an aristocrat within the CIM, the great-nephew of Hudson Taylor, i.e., the grandson of Hudson Taylor's sister Amelia and her husband Benjamin Broomhall. (It is amazing to think that three generations could span 165 years, from Benjamin's birth in 1829 to A. J. B.'s death in 1994.) A. J. Broomhall was born in Shanxi, the son of Dr. Benjamin Broomhall Junior, the tenth of the Broomhall children and the fifth to serve in the CIM, who worked as a medical doctor at the Shouyang hospital from 1903 to 1930. Jim Broomhall himself served under the CIM in China and Thailand, from 1938 until he retired to write his histories.[49] His cousin of the next generation is the other historian of the CIM, Dr. Norman Cliff.[50]

---

48. Pat Barr, *To China with Love: The Lives and Times of Protestant Missionaries in China 1860-1900* (London: Secker & Warburg, 1972), p. xi.

49. "Broomhall, Anthony James (1911-1994)," biographical entry in *Biographical Dictionary of Christian Missions*, ed. Gerald H. Anderson (New York: Macmillan Reference USA, 1998), pp. 92-93.

50. Dr. Norman Cliff, a grandson of A. Hudson Broomhall, earned his doctorate from the University of Buckingham with a dissertation entitled *A History of the Protestant Movement in Shandong Province, China, 1859-1951*. He is the author of *Courtyard of the Happy Way* (Evesham, Worcs: Arthur James, and London: OMF, 1977), a history of the

INTRODUCTION

Hudson Taylor's own family continues to influence the OMF, even to the fifth and sixth generation. James Hudson Taylor III (known as Jim), the grandson of Herbert Hudson Taylor (the eldest son of Hudson Taylor and his first wife, Maria Dyer, born in London in 1861), was the seventh general director of the OMF from 1980 to 1991. He is the father of James Hudson Taylor IV, known as Jamie, who married a Chinese woman named Yeh-Min Ke (Mimi) and is the father of James Hudson Taylor V. As the mission history put it, "Chinese blood is now immersed in the Taylors' next generation as they are growing up among us."[51]

A. J. Broomhall had to steer a delicate balance, not just in the larger world of China mission history, but with the conflicts between his grandfather and his great-uncle, who sometimes stopped speaking to each other for years. *Hudson Taylor and China's Open Century* is invaluable to the historian, since Broomhall "deliberately avoided" the classic biographies and went back to the original sources to present an "unexpurgated, unembellished collection of facts."[52] He was nothing if not thorough: his account of the Yangzhou riot of 1867 takes up one hundred pages. His exhaustive, often daily scope is indicated by the fact that the first book (400 pages) deals with China missions from the Nestorians to 1851, two years before Taylor's arrival; the founding of the CIM in 1865 (when Taylor was thirty-three) does not occur until book four, which traces but two and a half years, July 1865 to December 1867.

As for outside histories, unfortunately Mark Noll's *History of Christianity in the United States and Canada* is typical: he has two photographs of CIM missionaries, and mentions it in a list of societies.[53] Because of its British roots and its "fundamentalist" theology, histories of American missions tend to skim over "the known facts" about the CIM. Paul Varg's *Missionaries, Chinese and Diplomats*, for example, a cold war critique (1958), dismisses the CIM as largely English; its missionaries "lived in extremely modest circumstances when compared with those who enjoyed a regular salary from a denominational mission board, and consequently they were able to get closer to

---

Chefoo School's internment in the Japanese prisoner-of-war camp at Weixian, and *A Flame of Sacred Love: The Life of Benjamin Broomhall, Friend of China, The Man Behind Hudson Taylor, 1829-1911* (1998).

51. A complete family tree for the Hudson Taylor/Benjamin Broomhall/Grattan Guinness clan can be found in Irene Chang, James Hudson Taylor III, James Hudson Taylor IV, Joyce Wu, Janey Yiu, and Lisa Yu, editors, *Christ Alone: A Pictorial Presentation of Hudson Taylor's Life and Legacy* (Hong Kong: OMF Hong Kong, 2005), pp. 192-95. Quote at p. 121.

52. HTCOC 1, pp. 12-13.

53. Mark A. Noll, *A History of Christianity in the United States and Canada* (Grand Rapids: Wm. B. Eerdmans, 1992), pp. 533-34.

Introduction

the people."⁵⁴ (One would have thought that getting closer to the people would make the CIM intriguing, not dismissable.) Thirty years later Jane Hunter referred to it in a single footnote.⁵⁵

Except for a few travelers' accounts, that is about it. Turn-of-the-century explorers like Sven Hedin were always stumbling into CIM outposts in remote places, where invariably they "received every possible kindness" before pushing on.⁵⁶ One such encounter was described by the young Australian journalist George Morrison, tramping off the beaten track in Chinese dress. "You will be delighted to hear what a blessed time I am having with the Missionaries," he wrote his mother in 1893, tongue firmly in cheek:

> To-day, for instance. Called 7. Breakfast 7.30. prodigiously long grace then prayers, including psalms, bible-reading and prayer for 20 minutes. Then to hospital. Address by Doctor to outpatients kneeling down in outpatients' room among a lot of dirty Chinamen. Then lunch with grace and then a special prayer for one of the seven missionary divisions of China. Then afternoon tea with grace and special prayer for the conversion of all Unitarians. Then to dinner with Doctor — grace, and in the evening, music, hymns, etc., and a most blessed conversation concerning the conversion of a sea-captain by the Doctor's sister and then family prayers. Then home or would have had more. Total 10 hours, having sung 26 hymns, 25 being out of tune, have had prayers 17 times and have put in a gracious word for Heathen of all lands and of every colour.⁵⁷

Forty years later, John King Fairbank, then a young Sinologist hunting for Tang dynasty relics in Shanxi, commented that the CIM had stations "in almost as many places as the China Travel Service of today and would tell you at least as much about local conditions." He stayed at the home of a Mr. Trickey, who wore "Chinese garb, abhors foreign-style houses, sees the student-officials as communistic enemies, and works and prays for and to a

---

54. Paul A. Varg, *Missionaries, Chinese and Diplomats: The American Protestant Movement in China, 1890-1952* (Princeton: Princeton University Press, 1958), pp. 214-15.

55. Jane Hunter, *The Gospel of Gentility: American Women Missionaries in Turn-of-the-Century China* (New Haven: Yale University Press, 1984), p. 288, note 19.

56. Sven Hedin, *The Silk Road*, trans. F. H. Lyon (London: Routledge, 1938), p. 268. See also Alexander Hosie, *Three Years in Western China: A Narrative of Three Journeys in Ssu-ch'uan, Kwei-chow, and Yun-nan* (London: George Philip & Son, 1890), p. 55; Edwin J. Dingle, *Across China on Foot; Life in the Interior and the Reform Movement* (Bristol: J. W. Arrowsmith, 1911), p. 75.

57. Pearl, *Morrison of Peking*, p. 67.

close personal god — a whole-souled way of life to express a literal and all-embracing, all-satisfying faith — strong in morale, adequate but not modernly-scientific in intellectual life." Despite his Chinese appearance, Trickey was "conservative politically, fitted to live and work in any clime but never cease to be an Englishman." He maintained "the forms and standards of Wesleyan England" of a generation earlier, eating pudding, reading *The Times* (two months out of date), and preparing his children for an English boarding school. His medical colleague asked, "Our economic troubles . . . are essentially moral questions, don't you think?"[58]

The harshest critic was almost a lone voice, Alexander Michie, a British opium businessman in Tianjin, author of *Missionaries in China* (1895). He contrasted the Chinese toleration of foreign merchants, whose purpose was intelligible (supposedly), with the hatred directed against "irresponsible evangelists who go about the country retailing the figments of their own excited brains as the pure gospel." And he added, the "most eccentric missionaries are naturally those, many of them single women, belonging to Mr. Hudson Taylor's China Inland Mission." Chinese dress was not a way of getting closer to the Chinese, Michie charged, but merely "to wear the clothes of the poor and eat their food may be nearer to formal condescension than to true sympathy."[59]

Of interest to the historian, Michie described the practice of faith healing as a "species of thaumaturgy."

> They here meet the Chinese on their own ground of spiritualism, and in cases of sickness or trouble, the missionaries are ready to back the foreign against the native Deity, after the example of Elijah with the prophets of Baal. In other words, they live by prayer, not privately merely, but often openly, and by way of challenging their opponents. When a patient dies for whose recovery special prayer has been made, and the petitioners are self-pledged to a successful issue, they do not look at the material cause of death, but examine the mechanism of their prayer as if it were an experiment in physics that had miscarried.

Unfortunately the Chinese saw that the "poor Inland missionaries" were subject to the same illnesses, and consequently their influence was limited to those "within the incandescent sphere of their direct personal attraction."[60]

58. John King Fairbank, *Chinabound: A Fifty Year Memoir* (New York: Harper & Row, 1982), p. 112.
59. Alexander Michie, *Missionaries in China* (London: Edward Stanford, 1891), pp. 52-53, 38.
60. Ibid., pp. 54-56.

Introduction

If the CIM archival sources are limited, its propaganda is overwhelming. For a group of yeomen with limited education, they certainly were prolific writers: between 1865 and 1952, "almost 300 titles were published by CIM authors," with an additional 259 by 1984.[61] At their best, the CIM were reliable, scholarly witnesses. The *Atlas of the Chinese Empire*, "specially prepared . . . for the China Inland Mission" (1907), was an important reference work which the explorer and diplomat Sir Alexander Hosie described as "my constant companion [which], while it contains much excellent work, has many blemishes."[62] F. W. Baller, head of the CIM men's language school, produced the standard textbook and *Kuoyü Dictionary* [*Guoyu*, the national dialect] for language instruction, until it was superseded forty years later by another CIM text by R. H. Mathews. *Mathews' Chinese-English Dictionary*, considered the most comprehensive until the introduction of *pinyin* spelling, is still in print. Others wrote scholarly studies on their corner of the vineyard, like Samuel Clarke in Yunnan or "the Trio," Eva and Francesca French and Mildred Cable, whose books on Central Asia provided almost the only information about "events in these hermetically sealed regions."[63]

More has been written about Hudson Taylor than almost any other nineteenth-century missionary except David Livingstone: biographies in many editions, a film ("The Man Who Loved China"), radio dramas and stage plays, children's stories, even a coloring book: "Whew! It was hard work being a missionary in China. . . ."[64] He was a skilled publicist, whose "manifesto," *China: Its Spiritual Need and Claims* (1865), sold 3,000 copies within three weeks and went through eight editions before 1900. During the CIM's first decade, 1865-75, he published thirty-nine pamphlets called *Occasional Papers*, that were superseded by the larger *China's Millions*, attractively bound, with woodcuts. "*The Millions*," as it was called, was an "effective tool" with wide circulation among Christian leaders, politicians, and affiliated societies. With Taylor as editor, every issue had "a cutting edge, more than one, carrying its messages of many kinds deep into the awareness of readers. It must report to donors, inform and incite to action. . . . It was also the conductor's baton. . . . So he crystallized his messages in his own mind and re-echoed them in a hundred and one different ways, never tiring of them."[65]

---

61. Bacon, *From Faith to Faith*, p. 139.
62. Sir Alexander Hosie, *On the Trail of the Opium Poppy: A Narrative of Travel in the Chief Opium-Producing Provinces of China*, vol. 1 (Boston: Small Maynard & Company, 1914), p. 191.
63. Hedin, *Silk Road*, p. 295.
64. Sheila Miller, *My Book about Hudson* (Singapore: OMF, 1975), unpaginated.
65. *HTCOC* 6, p. 162.

"Another basic principle which he followed," writes Norman Cliff, "was 'Only sell success' — a phrase which has a modern ring about it. In the context of *China's Millions* it meant omitting any references to setbacks and dismissals. It was important to show to the mission supporters in Britain that the mission was making progress in its programme of evangelizing China."⁶⁶ As a result, *The Millions* employed an elaborate code: the word "excitement," for example, was code for a riot, and "danger" for murder, as in "God had been blessing us with an excitement." "Attention is drawn to our Mission," Hudson Taylor wrote in an oblique reference to the consul's threat to revoke all CIM passports. "Satan will surely use all his arts to hinder and to stumble, to raise up jealousies or murmurings, to divide those who should be united, to lead one or another to grieve the Holy Spirit of GOD, and hinder spiritual blessing."⁶⁷ Those are strong words, but only one skilled in exegesis would recognize that those who were grieving the Holy Spirit and hindering blessing were those who should be united, the members of Taylor's own family, his brother-in-law Benjamin Broomhall and the London Council.

Despite Taylor's heavy hand — he often rewrote reports simply to make them legible — *The Millions* was the CIM's internal dialogue, the voice of the rank and file through which they spoke to each other and their sister societies. It contains a multiplicity of voices, unheard in the biographies of worthies, arranged in chronological order. Yet, the historian echoes Alexander Michie's frustration at

> [the] extreme subjectiveness . . . and the corresponding absence of objectiveness. Their thoughts are full of themselves, their doctrines, their organisation, their methods, their efforts, their disappointments, their piety, their charity, their humility and self-effacement; while the condition of the Chinese mind and conscience is passed over with some threadbare commonplaces, as if no account need be taken of that great factor in the problem!⁶⁸

It is easier to describe what *China's Millions* does not say, rather than what it does. There is no landscape, no reference to natural resources or business prospects, nothing about other foreign residents, almost nothing about Chinese or international politics. There is no personal information on the missionaries' class, education, and background, their church affiliation, nationality, or any "family secret" that might cause friction. Finally, to hide the location

---

66. Cliff, *Flame of Sacred Love*, p. 53.
67. *China's Millions* (GB), January 1888, p. 15.
68. Michie, *Missionaries in China*, p. 40.

of their people, the reports deliberately avoided mentioning place names: one missionary in Henan wrote:

> We returned to-day from our visit to all the surrounding county cities. We were well received in each, as well as in the towns and villages through which we passed. . . . I should have gone on to another prefecture, and to the capital, but I have neither enough money nor books to go as far as the latter place; at least I will try and visit the former, and go from thence to a third prefecture when homeward bound.

He concluded, "The Lord has given us encouragement from individuals who came to ask the way to Zion."[69]

That said, *China's Millions* tells more about Chinese peasant Christians than other mission publications. Their testimonies, sanitized though they may be, jump out at the reader with internal clues to authenticate them: "vegetarian" would be meaningless to an English supporter, but as a signifier of Buddhist sectarianism it opens a cosmology for the historian. One missionary woman reported that the magistrate's wife invited her into the *yamen*, the official residence, while the magistrate sat in the next room and questioned her through his wife: "Why had we come? Were we going to do trade? Had we brought anything to sell? Who had sent us? Were we going to rent a house? How long were we going to stay? Had our queen sent us to China?"[70] These certainly indicate the magistrate's confusion when confronted by a foreign woman traveling alone.

How does a historian deal with such opaque sources, where words are meant to hide more than they reveal, where the "real world" drops away and pilgrims wander a timeless landscape that could be Palestine, could be the Middle Ages, could be *Pilgrim's Progress?* One can throw up one's hands and declare all is allegory — or one can ask why and how did the CIM write its history as allegory? If one assumes that everyone, missionaries and Chinese, were independent actors in a cosmic drama, *China's Millions* tells a far stranger story than they could have imagined.

I have three assumptions as I tell this story. First, the congruency between the real world and the inner world is often inverse: the inner spirit burns white-hot when the outside forces are at their blackest. Second, everyone has his or her own agenda. And third, Chinese dress was not an exotic fashion, but an agonized decision to "go native."

69. *China's Millions* (GB), August 1875, p. 24.
70. Ibid., June 1891, p. 76.

INTRODUCTION

Then and Now

Alexander Michie's critique was echoed a century later by Bob Whyte, director of the China Study Project of the British Council of Churches, in his survey of Christianity in China, *Unfinished Encounter* (1988). "Of Hudson Taylor's greatness there need be no doubt," he states, but the institutional CIM functioned as "a separate denomination with its own congregations," and in this sense was more of an obstacle to the development of a Chinese church than denominational societies. Chinese dress was "a superficial means of adaptation, masking a rigid and narrow theological understanding. . . . Our criticism of the CIM may seem to be very hard, but it has been made necessary by greatly exaggerated claims as to its achievements that are still being made in some quarters."[71]

Nevertheless, historians can trace a direct line from the CIM to the resurgence of Christianity in the People's Republic of China since 1978, when the proscription against Christianity was lifted. Alan Hunter and Kim-Kwong Chan in their authoritative study *Protestantism in Contemporary China* (1993), call it "Christianity fever." From one million Protestants in 1949, the government figure for 2001-02 is 15 million Protestants, although some "reputable Christian research groups [including the Overseas Missionary Fellowship] conclude that *there are now 40-50 million Christians in China.*"[72] Wildly exaggerated estimates range as high as one hundred million, or more, of whom 95 percent are underground or "secret" Christians. The most spectacular growth has been among radical Protestant congregations that refuse to associate with the state-recognized (and state-controlled) Three-Self Church Movement. They are called "house churches" or "unregistered" churches, many of which are lineal descendants of churches planted by the China Inland Mission. They are politically controversial because they pose a challenge to the bureaucratic control of the government Bureau of Religious Affairs, and many of their activities verge on "superstition" and "magic."

Now as then, the manifestations of peasant Christianity include a gospel of suffering and salvation; petitionary prayer, that is prayer for specific blessings (health and wealth); "magic formulae . . . couched in a mysterious and incomprehensible language";[73] visions; spirit possession; miraculous healing; Christian exorcism;[74] personal charisma; and the role of women as "religious

---

71. Bob Whyte, *Unfinished Encounter: China and Christianity* (London: Fount Paperbacks, 1988), pp. 119-23.
72. Hunter and Chan, *Protestantism in Contemporary China*, pp. 4, 67-70.
73. Gernet, *China and the Christian Impact*, p. 89.
74. Gernet (pp. 89-90) describes exorcism in the seventeenth century; Hunter and Chan (pp. 146-49) discuss it in the twentieth.

specialists" inside the family. Many Christians today "interpret their lives as a series of minor epiphanies or miracles. Belief in ghosts and devils is still widespread, and prayer in the name of Jesus is thought to be an effective remedy against possession and evil spirits. . . . We were frequently told that a main reason for conversion is hearing of or experiencing healing by Jesus, which appears to be a common phenomenon in China today." Hunter and Chan report that spiritual healing, or the belief in spiritual healing, attracts as many as 70 percent of believers in some locations.[75]

If one needs proof that sectarian religion is alive in the People's Republic, consider the *Falun Gong* (or *Falun Dafa*). In 1999 *Falun Gong*, the Religion of the Law, a brand-new sect, came out of nowhere to embarrass the Chinese government by holding a silent vigil of ten thousand people outside the headquarters of the communist party. Started by an overseas Chinese in New York, it combines Buddhist meditation, Daoist vegetarian and alchemical practices, and *taiqi* exercises, with an emphasis on health and healing. If you live right, *Falun Gong* promises, you can live for two hundred or three hundred years. The movement claims 80 million members — more than Protestants — including many party members. The government, always suspicious of movements that threaten the state, has reacted with a massive, continuing crackdown, burning its books and imprisoning its leaders.

One Pilgrim's Progress

Consul Bourne, quoted above, described the outer pilgrimage of the China Inland Mission: the religious mania in Europe that sent uneducated and impulsive young men and women into the interior of China, where their religious fervor evaporated in the apathetic Chinese environment. Some lost their minds, some lost their nerve.

F. W. Baller, head of the men's language school, saw the inner pilgrimage, "a sad procession passes before me of bright promising men who have sacrificed the prospect of great usefulness, yea life itself, and all for the lack of a little common sense." Some acted "like simpletons. I knew one young fellow who smiled serenely with an air of ineffable wisdom when urged to use an umbrella . . . to shield him from the sun. He said the promise was that the sun should not smite him by day. Need I say that he is now at home with an enfeebled brain?" Baller concluded that "many of the strongest die the soonest after coming to this country, while others who could not get

75. Hunter and Chan, *Protestantism in Contemporary China*, pp. 7, 174.

their lives insured if they tried, go on year after year and do splendid service for God."⁷⁶

If one pilgrim could typify the journey, she might be Maggie Mackee, a lively Scottish woman who arrived in China in March 1887. She was "very happy," she reported in April, with her first experience of Chinese life after being cooped up in the language school. It was a walk to a country village where she witnessed the baptism of three men and one woman. By June she noticed "a great many opium cases," including one particularly sad case, a young woman suicide who died in her arms. The opium trade was England's sin, she wept: "Oh, may GOD have mercy on our land that sent and forced this soul-damning opium on these poor people!" By the end of the summer, there had been no rain for weeks and "a special procession of devil-worshippers" passed by the mission station: "Just think — 'devil-worshippers!' I did not know until the other day that they really worshipped the devil, and it was a revelation to be told calmly by my teacher that he did. I do wonder what their ideas of the devil are. . . ." A few days later she witnessed "a fine fire" to burn the idols of an old "vegetarian" convert.

Miss Mackee died in January 1889 of smallpox, after less than two years in China, and three weeks after she reached her permanent station. "I scatter the seed and expect GOD to use it, in what way I cannot say," she wrote in her last letter.⁷⁷

One wonders what Miss Mackee's ideas of the devil were.

---

76. Frederick W. Baller, *Letters from an Old Missionary to his Nephew* (Shanghai: American Presbyterian Press, 1907), pp. 19-20.
77. *China's Millions* (GB), January 1888, pp. 10-11, and April 1889, pp. 43-44.

PART I

The First Generation
1832-1880

I think it is a wonderfully significant thing that in all these pictures of the missionary field and of the state of the world, we see heathenism painted black. That is the colour that it should be painted.

A Victorian Quaker,
in Elizabeth Allo Isichei,
Victorian Quakers

CHAPTER 1

Black Barnsley

1832-1851

Yorkshire, circa 1760

I dreamed I was in Yorkshire, going from Gomersal-Hill-Top to Cleckheaton; and about the middle of the lane, I thought I saw Satan coming out to meet me in the shape of a tall, black man, and the hair of his head was like snakes. . . . But I went on, ript open my clothes, and shewed him my naked breast, saying, "See, here is the blood of Christ." Then I thought he fled from me as fast as a hare could run.

John Nelson, a Methodist stonemason[1]

London, 20 November 1860, "About Breakfast Time"

A curious procession materializes out of the cold grey fog in New Bond Street, the haute fashion district of London's West End. It is led by a Chinese "boy," a "'fine man physically,'" dressed *à la chinois* in black silk gown and thick-soled, high-stepping boots, with a pigtail hanging down his back. Back in China he had been a "house painter and interior decorator"[2] — sounds respectable, like a Yorkshire tradesman — but in Victorian England, he looks like music hall Chinaman. He is holding aloft a sixteen-month girl, "'in En-

---

1. E. P. Thompson, *The Making of the English Working Class* (London: Victor Gollancz, 1963), p. 43.
2. *HTCOC 3*, p. 177.

glish dress, her white drawers down almost to her ancles' [sic] in the fashion of a decade back." Three paces behind is a young English woman in an old-fashioned poke bonnet and hoop-skirt. "That must be his wife," the onlookers whisper; she married a Chinaman! But that child, with her golden curls, she is *definitely not his*. Bringing up the rear is a white man, "'short and unimportant in appearance,'" also wearing a Chinese gown and pigtail. His gown is not silk, though, but cotton, and shabby, because "his own old English clothes [were] unfit for wear." He is only twenty-eight, but he shuffles like a chronic invalid who is not expected to live long.[3]

Every family — especially an Anglo-Chinese family — needs an ancestor, the one individual who breaks away from the main trunk to found a new branch, a new ancestral shrine. Here, at the moment they stepped onto the English stage, was Hudson Taylor with his family, fresh off the boat. It was more than just the gendered exoticism that shocked the onlookers, the males in pigtails and the females smelling of mothballs, or the way they upset class and racial boundaries: the well-dressed servant and the shabby master. Behind the studied casualness lurked an element of theatricality, a performance, a self-conscious calling attention to oneself. And like theatrical folk everywhere, there was a frisson of sexual ambiguity.

Appearances are deceptive.

Hudson Taylor was bringing home his bride, Maria Dyer, the most eligible woman on the China coast. Born in Malacca and raised in Singapore, orphaned twice over by parents and stepparents, she had lived in England for a few years with her grandparents and then returned to China to teach school. Although her costume was old-fashioned, it was definitely English. Even in China, she refused her husband's request to wear Chinese clothes, which were "a special trial" for her. She died within ten years, in China in 1870, aged thirty-three, six months after the death of her eighth child. Little Gracie, the golden-haired child carried by their Chinese servant, also went "home" to China, where she died in 1867, not yet eight years old.

Although the servant, named Wang Lae-djün ("Chinese characters not found"),[4] told everyone he had left his wife and child to follow the foreigner and learn the foreign religion, that was a convenient fiction, for he was running away from his wife's "irascible temper."[5] He remained in London for four years, more collaborator than servant, helping Hudson Taylor translate the Bible into "romanized Ningbo vernacular." He returned to China as the

---

3. Ibid., pp. 233-34; internal quotes from the Archives.
4. *HTCOC* 4, "Personalia," p. 456.
5. Ibid., p. 312.

first ordained Chinese pastor in the China Inland Mission and became "bishop" of Zhejiang for forty years.

Hudson Taylor, the invalid, did not die; he lived for another forty-five years. He was a tiny, doll-like man, a bit over five feet tall. "I have often thought that God made me little in order that He might show what a great God He is," he would say.[6] He was a true original, yet typically "Yorkshire." He might be compared with other Yorkshire originals, such as Samuel Smiles — the perfect name — a Leeds bookseller who wrote books like *Character* and *Self-Help*. Everyone, Smiles declared, even a chemist's son from Barnsley, could pull himself out of the muck of the coal-mines by his bootstraps as long as he had "Character." One was not born with Character, like a silver spoon, but one created it through persevering effort. "The battle of life," Smiles wrote, "must necessarily be fought uphill; and to win it without a struggle were perhaps to win it without honour."[7]

Or perhaps Taylor could be compared to Sir Titus Salt, the "Great Yorkshire Llama" himself. A self-made millionaire, Salt spun a worldwide empire from the gossamer called alpaca, the finest "lustre cloth" for ladies' shawls. He built a company town called Saltaire, centered around a "cyclopean" mill, one of the largest buildings in England, which produced "30,000 yards of alpaca cloth daily, or some 5,688 miles of it a year, which, as the crow flies, would reach from Saltaire over the land and sea to Peru." Salt was one of the great philanthropists of the Victorian age, who spent £100,000 to build stone cottages for his workers, "designed to nurture self-improvement, politeness, orderly behaviour, and good health." To combat the moral anarchy of a mill town, he also built public baths, a library, high school, and two chapels, Methodist and Congregational, and prohibited pubs from setting up shop.[8]

That was the heroic stuff from which Hudson Taylor was made. He too discovered a worthless commodity — heathen Chinese souls — and built a metaphorical "factory in the East" which employed hundreds of English men and women as foremen and supervisors, and thousands of Chinese workers. In a way, Taylor was a more astute businessman: he raised hundreds of thou-

---

6. Henry W. Frost, "The Days that are Past," (CIM/Toronto), p. 215. Hereafter cited as Frost, "Memoirs." Frost was the CIM's North American director from 1888 to 1932.

7. In David Bebbington, *Evangelicalism in Modern Britain: A History from the 1730s to the 1980s* (London: Unwin Hyman/Routledge, 1989. Reprint, Grand Rapids: Baker Book House, 1992), p. 166.

8. Jim Greenhalf, *Salt and Silver: A Story of Hope* (Bradford, Yorkshire: Bradford Libraries, 1998), pp. 39, 54. Saltaire is now a tourist attraction which features a gallery of David Hockney's paintings. See also John Styles, *Titus Salt and Saltaire: Industry and Virtue* (Shipley, Yorkshire: Salts Estates, 1994).

sands of pounds and never had to show a profit — or even a product, none he could bring home to mother, except Maria Dyer and Wang Lae-djün. Like Ezekiel's wheel rolling in the middle of the air, Taylor's business was run on faith that the Lord would provide and, as Pat Barr put it with some exaggeration, he "sought money where it existed and the pocketbooks of the rich simply fell open at his confident coming."[9]

A Market Town in the County of Coveting

At the beginning of *Pilgrim's Progress*, the Pilgrim named Christian flees from the City of Destruction with his fingers in his ears, leaving his wife and children behind. He is clothed in rags and has a great burden of sin on his back, and in his hand he carries a book. Beware the wrath to come, he shouts to all who have ears to hear, when the city shall be burned with fire from Heaven. He meets Evangelist, who points the way across the plain to yon Wicket-gate, almost invisible in the wall around Beelzebub's Castle. Christian falls into the Slough of Despond, is dragged down by his burden of sin, and his companions, Obstinate and Pliable, desert him at the first sign of danger. He is rescued, but again is diverted from the narrow path by Mr. Worldly Wiseman, who dwells in the town of Carnal Policy. Again Evangelist points the way to the Wicket-gate, and this time Christian makes haste like one treading on forbidden ground.

The City of Destruction: in Hudson Taylor's allegory, that would be Barnsley: "Black Barnsley" as it was called. John Bunyan, writing *Pilgrim's Progress* in the aftermath of the English Civil War (1677), would have recognized the human sins of Barnsley, a hotheaded town in the West Riding (since 1974, the South Riding) of Yorkshire. But living before the Industrial Revolution, Bunyan could not have imagined the physical blackness of Barnsley 150 years later, and the soul-destroying ferocity of the dark satanic mills. Everything was black: the buildings, constructed from that glorious golden Yorkshire sandstone, were as black as if they had been burned by fire; the people's clothes, their hands and faces — and their lungs — were indelibly stained.

During the years of Hudson Taylor's childhood, from 1832 to 1853, Barnsley was where the Industrial Revolution happened. To give some idea of the sudden transformation, in 1832 Barnsley was relatively isolated, a regional center of the linen industry as it had been for a century. Throughout the valley, white squares were scattered among the fields like a vast checker-board, the bleach-

---

9. Barr, *To China with Love*, p. 6.

ing yards where flax was laid out (a process known as crofting) to bleach.[10] Linen was notoriously difficult to mechanize — the strands are too brittle — and power-looms were not introduced until 1837. There were 4,000 handlooms in Barnsley, one for every adult: some cottages had as many as six. With the coming of the railway in 1840, King Coal put an end to the linen industry. By 1853, when the population reached 50,000, Barnsley was the fastest growing conurbation in England. The linen industry had been mechanized. But by 1900 it was gone, both hand-weaving and machine-weaving, as Barnsley became a center of heavy industry, glass-making, iron, steel, and coal.

Hudson Taylor was born during the "days of May" of 1832, a revolutionary moment in British history. For months Britain had teetered on the brink of civil war over the passage of the Reform Bill, which was signed into law a couple of days after Taylor was born. The bill, one of the cornerstones of British democracy, restructured Parliament by abolishing the old "rotten boroughs" and giving their political representation to the new industrial towns, like Barnsley. Above all, it helped define the middle class in monetary terms with one stroke of an indelible pencil, by granting universal suffrage to all male £10 householders.[11] (It also specifically disenfranchised women householders.) The whole country was in a state of "unparalleled excitement" with riots and mass meetings, and Yorkshire was under martial law. "In some places the bells of the churches and dissenting chapels were tolled all night, in others they were muffled."[12]

On 21 May, at the height of the agitation, Hudson Taylor was the firstborn of one of the newly enfranchised ratepayers. With a population of 10,000, Barnsley was the largest town in the West Riding, halfway between Sheffield and Leeds. (To a North American, the distances are Lilliputian: Sheffield is fourteen miles south and Leeds nineteen miles north — a day's journey apart, before the coming of the railway, which does it in an hour. Barnsley is 178 miles north of London.) Once it was known as "Bleak Barnsley," a medieval market town on a windy ridge overlooking the Dearne River valley. The valley contains the largest exposed coalfield in England (which continues southward to become the Doncaster concealed coalfield) and substantial deposits of iron.

There is not much left of Hudson Taylor's Barnsley, though he is recog-

---

10. Harold Taylor, "Bleachworks of Barnsley & their Industrial Archaeology," in Brian Elliott, ed., *Aspects of Barnsley: Discovering Local History* (Barnsley, Yorkshire: Wharncliffe Publishing, 1993). I am indebted to Harold Taylor — a local historian whose common ancestor with Hudson Taylor died in 1744 — for generously sharing his research on Staincross and Barnsley.

11. Thompson, *Making of the English Working Class*, pp. 888-89.

12. James Taylor, *The Age We Live In: A History of the Nineteenth Century, from the Peace of 1815 to the Present Time* (London: William Mackenzie, 1900), pp. 18, 14.

THE FIRST GENERATION

Cheapside in Barnsley, Yorkshire, in the 20th century. The "Taylor's Chemists" was founded by James Taylor as the best chemist shop (pharmacy) in town. Hudson Taylor grew up upstairs behind the baise curtain.   Source: Author's collection.

nized as a local historical figure, and Taylor relatives are well known in the district. Barnsley is one of those English cities that, in an ill-fated attempt at urban renewal, demolished its downtown core in the 1960s, so Cheapside has been replaced by a pedestrian mall and May Day Green is a flea market. The linen mills are gone, as are the weavers' tenements, the glass factories, the iron smelters, and the vast railway yards. The coal mines have been closed, and the pitheads landscaped into parks. The air is clean, and the buildings, scrubbed of a century's soot, glow golden in the sunshine. Barnsley still has a reputation for working-class laddishness: whenever a television sitcom needs a seedy character, they invariably choose Barnsley as the locale.

John Wesley Comes to Barnsley

Hudson Taylor was a fourth-generation Methodist, since his great-grandfather had been converted on his wedding day in 1776. The role of Methodism has been an historiographical puzzle since E. P. Thompson wrote *The Making of the English Working Class* (1962), in which he set out to "rescue the poor stockinger, the Luddite cropper, the 'obsolete' hand-loom weaver, the 'utopian' artisan, and even the deluded follower of Joanna Southcott, from the enormous condescension of posterity."[13] Early Methodism attracted many artisans and yeomen, Thompson argues, who became political radicals in the tragic years between the American Revolution and the defeat of Napoleon when Britain became a police state. They were black-coated, street-corner "ranters," like the stonemason John Nelson, quoted above, who "familiarized the lower classes to the work of combining in associations, making rules for their own governance, raising funds, and communicating from one part of the kingdom to another."[14] In short, Methodism nurtured a rudimentary class consciousness — organizing people horizontally into "classes" rather than vertically into guilds of watchmakers, weavers, tailors, cordwainers, ribbon-dressers, hosiers, breeches-makers, china burners, jappanners, engravers, mercers, etc.[15]

The classic CIM biographies recount Hudson Taylor's genealogy — the ancestor's ancestors — as a providential flow of Methodist piety from generation unto generation. Put in their historical context, the generations of Taylors show the other side of Thompson's equation: the social progress of Methodists from an indigent, crippled factory worker to his middle-class, nonconformist grandchildren. As Wesley noted, "religion must necessarily produce both industry and frugality, and these cannot but produce riches.... For the Methodists in every place grow diligent and frugal; consequently they increase in goods. Hence they proportionately increase in pride, in anger, in the desire of the flesh, the desire of the eyes, and the pride of life. So, although the form of religion remains, the spirit is swiftly vanishing away."[16]

John Wesley was born in Epworth, just over the border in Lincolnshire, and visited Yorkshire many times. "A wilder people I never saw in England," he wrote of Huddersfield; "the men, women, and children filled the street as we rode along, and appeared just ready to devour us." John Nelson warned, "No other preaching will do for Yorkshire, but the old sort that comes like a thunderclap upon the conscience. Fine preaching does more harm than good here."[17] (The original phrase "thunder-clap conversion" was from Count Zinzendorf, the eighteenth-century Moravian pietist: "donner hinein schlagen," to hit people like a clap of thunder. We shall hear echoes of thunder-and-lightning conversion in China, where the term was translated from German to English by Karl Gutzlaff as "blitz-conversion.")[18]

13. Thompson, *Making of the English Working Class*, p. 12.
14. R. Southey, *Life of Wesley and the Rise of Methodism* (1820), quoted in ibid., p. 46.
15. Thompson, *Making of the English Working Class*, pp. 170-71.
16. Ibid., p. 391.
17. Ibid., p. 31.
18. I am indebted to Gary Tiedemann for this quotation.

THE FIRST GENERATION

Hudson Taylor's great-grandfather, James the first, was a stonemason in Staincross, across the valley, who became so absorbed in reading the Bible he was late for his wedding ceremony. Oh dear, his wife said to herself, don't tell me I have married a Methodist! After an accident damaged his leg, the family moved to a small house at the top of Old Mill Lane, on the outskirts of Barnsley. Reduced to penury, James obtained work in a linen warehouse owned by a Quaker industrialist named Beckett. James and his wife Betty were the first Methodists in Barnsley, and became objects of ridicule — "baiting the Methodists," it was called. One writer noted that "scarcely any people raged against the Methodists or persecuted them with that ferocity as the people of Barnsley. For some years a preacher never went there without several persons in company."[19] James Taylor preached on May Day Green until some drunks rubbed broken glass in his face, temporarily blinding him. Mr. Beckett, who also happened to be the magistrate, urged him to press charges, but he refused, saying the Lord would deal with them. Indeed the Lord did, for one was struck blind and "had to be led by a dog through the familiar streets, and ultimately sunk into extreme poverty."[20]

When Wesley made his second visit to Barnsley in 1786, he stayed in the Taylors' home. He wrote in his diary:

> Friday, June 30, 1786: I turned aside to Barnsley, formerly famous for all manner of wickedness. They were then ready to tear any Methodist preacher in pieces. Now not a dog wagged its tongue. I preached near the Market Place to a very large congregation, and I believe the truth sank into many hearts. They seemed to drink in every word. Surely God will have a people in this place.[21]

(The "Wesley Steps," where he preached, have been preserved — with a plaque unveiled by Queen Mary — attached to the Pitt Street church.)

By 1794, when the Methodists erected their first chapel, James Taylor was on the building committee, but he died the following year, aged forty-six. His eldest son John, age seventeen, assumed the responsibilities for the household, and became class leader in his father's stead. He married Mary Shepherd, daughter of a gaoler and local preacher from Bradford (who, the Taylor family claimed, was the son of William Shepherd, one of Wesley's first seven traveling preachers).[22]

---

19. *Barnsley Chronicle* of 1905 quoting an 1813 source, in HTCOC 1, p. 98.
20. *Growth of a Soul*, pp. 13-14.
21. Ibid., p. 19.
22. HTCOC 1, pp. 377-78 note 13, goes into detail on this genealogy.

John became a skilled artisan, a maker of the slender reeds used in linen handlooms, a specialized trade much in demand. He lived near the chapel and his workshop employed several hands. Through frugality and diligence, his trade prospered, and he became a man "of great consequence to the staple trade of the town."[23]

John and Mary Taylor had seven children who survived, and all joined the upwardly mobile middle classes. Of the four sons, the eldest took up his father's trade; James (the second, Hudson Taylor's father), with educational advantages unknown to his parents, became a chemist (a druggist) with one of the best shops in town; the next "went his own way and became a wealthy stockbroker"; and the youngest became a Wesleyan minister. Apprenticed to a chemist in a neighboring town, James the second married the girl next door, Amelia Hudson, the eldest daughter of the Methodist minister. She was a sweet submissive woman who had been sent to a Quaker school and then worked as governess in a castle. In a painted portrait, she looks like one of Charlotte Brontë's heroines, with her hair pulled back under a lace cap. ("Mother would hardly have seemed Mother without that modest head-gear.")[24] They were married in 1831, and with an advance from his father, purchased a chemist shop at 21 Cheapside, a prime location on Market Hill.

Cheapside

Cheapside was opposite May Day Green, the market and "pleasure ground" that on Feast Day was transformed into a medieval fair, with minstrels, jugglers, and circus acts. Among more innocent pleasures, they still baited bears in the green and held noisy political demonstrations.[25] Although Barnsley escaped the Luddite machine-smashing in 1812 — it had no machines yet — it was a hotbed of working-class agitation. After one particularly violent strike in 1829, labor unions were outlawed, and not until the Chartist agitation of 1848 did the working class of Barnsley rise again. Later, Barnsley became the headquarters of the militant National Union of Mineworkers.

Lest one mythologize the pre-industrial handloom weavers, we should

---

23. *Growth of a Soul*, pp. 21, 25.
24. Ibid., p. 45.
25. Brian Elliott, "Bulls & Bears on May Day Green," *Making of Barnsley* (Barnsley, Yorkshire: Wharncliffe Publishing, 1988), pp. 335-417. Barnsley was "one of the last towns to witness the gruesome spectacle" of bear-baiting, which was not abolished until 1835, to be replaced by dancing bears.

note that they were looked down upon as "degraded beings." Barely a hundred yards from the Taylors' back door, squalid tenements stretched row upon row down the hill. A report of the Barnsley Board of Health (1852) gave a graphic description of the basements where the looms were kept going fifteen hours a day:

> In the window is generally a small aperture for the admission of air. Immediately under this window an aperture runs an open channel to carry off the liquid refuse of the neighbouring houses, so that every breath of air that comes into the weaving shop is poisoned in its passage over the filthy and stagnant gutter. Add to this the fact that the permeable nature of the drains allows much of the liquid sewerage to saturate the ground.

No wonder one linen manufacturer commented that the linen had "the most offensive and unhealthy odour."[26]

No wonder, too, that when the coal mines opened, offering steady work and higher wages, a father would prefer to send his children down the mine rather than take up weaving. "Take 100 collier-boys and 100 weaver-boys," one weaver told another investigation, "and the collier boys will be the strongest and healthiest." Deep-shaft mining may have been less debilitating, but it was infinitely more dangerous. In 1838, when Hudson Taylor was six, a terrific storm flooded a shallow pit mine in Silkstone, and twenty-six children drowned, between the ages of seven and fifteen. In 1866 an explosion killed 358 men and boys. "The Silkstone catastrophe was just one of many such disasters which Barnsley people gradually learned to live with."[27]

An interview with one weaver child contained in a report on Employment of Children (1842) sounds surreal, since the questions were excised:

> "I have been to Sunday school; I can read; I don't go to the evening school; I don't know who St. Paul was, nor St. John, but I know about St. Matthew. Jesus Christ was born in heaven, but I don't know what happened to him; he came on earth to commit sin, yes to commit sin." Can spell tolerably and can write a little. "Scotland is a country, but I don't know where it is; I never heard of France."[28]

---

26. Harold Taylor, "Taylor Row and the Handloom Weavers of Barnsley," in Elliott, ed. *Aspects of Barnsley*, vol. 5, p. 52.

27. David H. Pill, "Barnsley," in *Yorkshire: The West Riding* (London: Batsford, 1977), p. 167.

28. Harold Taylor, "Taylor Row," p. 58.

With May Day Green in front and the sewers behind, James Taylor could cross class lines as the poor man's doctor, much like a modern druggist. He would have dispensed a lot of opium, particularly in the form of laudanum, since Black Barnsley had a high incidence of black lung and digestive diseases. His career started at an opportune moment, just as the old-time trade of apothecary was regulated into the new profession of pharmacy. One of the Pharmacy Acts classified opium as a dangerous drug that could only be sold by registered chemists.

Educated and prosperous, James Taylor was a more complex personality than his forebears. He was "his own worst enemy," A. J. Broomhall (his great-grandson) concluded. "He was painfully shy even among equals, and only at ease among familiar friends. His rich and influential clients, who came to him because of his reputation for sound diagnosis and treatment, as well as honesty, found him uncommunicative. He would even go upstairs rather than face some of them. But his home was wide open to his Methodist friends when they came into town."[29]

Studious and methodical, he was a scientist who spent his life concocting elixirs and tinctures, a bookkeeper who calculated interest tables to "four or five places of decimals," and a preacher who gave a literate, effective sermon. He was a great reader of theology, sermons, biographies, medicine, French literature, and, surprisingly, considering the time and place, everything he could get his hands on concerning China, starting with Karl Gutzlaff's *Journal of Three Voyages along the Coast of China* taken in 1831-33. According to pious legend, Hudson Taylor was consecrated at birth for the evangelization of China. China remained in the news during his childhood — the build-up to the Opium War and China's opening to missionary activity — and as James instructed his children in the progress of Methodist missions around the world, he grumbled, "Why don't they send them to China?"[30]

James doted on Amelia and the children, who lived above the shop: James Hudson (James the third, known as Hudson, born 1832), William Shepherd, who died young, Amelia Hudson (1835), Theodore, who also died, and Louisa Shepherd. Drawn together by the death of their brothers, Hudson and Amelia became inseparable companions. Pale and tiny, he was "delicate" and had to be kept indoors, under the constant attention of his mother, who more than made up for his father's nondemonstrative nature. Hudson took after the musical, affectionate, submissive Hudson side of the family. "There is some-

---

29. *HTCOC 1*, p. 289.
30. John C. Pollock, *Hudson Taylor and Maria: Pioneers in China* (New York: McGraw-Hill and OMF, 1962), p. 16.

thing in my nature that seems as if it must have love and sympathy," he once told his mother.[31] He was a happy, curious child, with his grandfather's irrepressible sense of the absurd.

Behind the curtain that separated the shop from the family, James Taylor was, in Mrs. Howard Taylor's measured words, "decidedly a disciplinarian." He "dread[ed] the consequences of over-indulgence, that he went, perhaps, too far in the opposite extreme." Like many fathers of his time, he saw himself as "the direct representative of Him 'from whom every fatherhood in heaven and on earth is named.' To permit disobedience would be not only unfaithfulness to God, but cruel injustice to the children."[32] He ran his family like a laboratory: his wife Amelia lived in "painful subjection," and the children were trained to such "prompt and loyal obedience to their earthly parents that they would be prepared to render like submission to the will of God."[33] He demanded punctuality: if a meal was delayed five minutes, five minutes times five people equals twenty-five minutes "lost which can never be found again." At meals, everyone would sit in silence while he expounded the news of the day and construed the scriptures.

Nothing shows James Taylor's contradictions more than his attitude towards money. Throughout Europe in the 1830s, and Yorkshire in particular, where there was so much new money, "an almost morbid cupidity was elevated into a cult of money for its own sake, a philosophy that frequently went side by side with harebrained schemes of rash investment."[34] James was bringing in "more than enough" to support his family, but he took frugality to an extreme. He would pay his debts on the day they were due: "If I let it stand over a week," he would say, "I defraud my creditor of interest . . . if only a fractional sum."[35] Generous with the poor, he was "tight-fisted" with his family, keeping them in "needlessly low water" (sister Amelia remembered in her old age). "See if you can do without," was one of his maxims, and at dinner he would ask "cheerfully": "So, let us try to practise it now, for the sooner you begin, the stronger will be the habit. . . . Who will see if they can do without to-day?"[36] Here, exactly reversed in how money was "earned," are Hudson Taylor's faith principles, which he instituted into the China Inland Mission.

---

31. *Growth of a Soul*, p. 64.

32. Ibid., pp. 46, 54. Hudson Taylor's son Howard (Dr. Howard Taylor) often stayed with his grandparents as a child.

33. *HTCOC 1*, pp. 287-88.

34. Alan Palmer, ed., *The Age of Optimism*, "Milestones of History," vol. 8 (London: Weidenfeld and Nicholson, 1974), quoted in Greenhalf, *Salt & Silver*, p. 26.

35. *Growth of a Soul*, p. 32; *HTCOC 1*, pp. 288-89.

36. *Growth of a Soul*, pp. 47-48.

Curiously, James Taylor did not believe in sending his children to school, perhaps from frugality, perhaps from fear of contamination. Consequently, Hudson Taylor did not attend school until he was eleven, an unhappy experience that lasted two years. At home, Father taught the children French, Latin, and arithmetic, while Mother taught English, music, and natural history. Likewise, James "heartily approved" of Sunday schools — for the poor — but did not allow his own children to attend, so that he could personally supervise their spiritual life.

One last word on Father James: in 1866, when Hudson Taylor took the CIM pioneers to China, Mother came to London to see him off but Father was too shy to face the hubbub of a dockside parting. "I can't mix with strangers," he wrote, but "I shall ever pray for you." Perhaps, A. J. Broomhall suggests, he "sensed his inferior social position or lack of social graces, for . . . he was, he wrote, naturally bashful."[37]

When Hudson Taylor grew up, he had two "voices" in speaking and writing. Father's was the angry voice, harsh, uncompromising, demanding. Hudson Taylor tried to keep Father's voice under control, and few heard its fury. Mother's voice was the flowery, scripture-quoting, moral tales recounted in *China's Millions*, ineffably sad and ofttimes cloying. Mother was the first in a long line of CIM saints.

In 1848, at the age of sixteen, Hudson Taylor was apprenticed to a bank, where he damaged his eyesight by close work. This was another "days of May" — the year Karl Marx published his *Communist Manifesto*, the Chartist agitation reached fever pitch, and Barnsley became a center of the "Radical conspiracy." It was also a pivotal moment in Hudson Taylor's life. He could have followed his father into the middle class and become a chemist. Instead, he "fell from grace" and flirted with Chartism, convinced that socialism could change the world.[38] It was easy to believe in utopia when a "Chartist secondhand bookseller" in Barnsley explained the Chartist Land Plan: "They would divide the land into small farms, and give every man an opportunity of getting his living by the sweat of his brow."[39] Taylor's "spiritual life shrivelled up," and was not resolved until a year later, when he was "soundly converted." Then, he asked God to give him some task, "some self-denying service, no matter what it might be, however trying or however trivial. . . . For what service I was accepted I knew not. But a deep consciousness that I was not my

---

37. *HTCOC 4*, p. 159.
38. *HTCOC 1*, p. 293.
39. A Barnsley linen-weaver speaking to the Chartist National Convention, 1848, in Thompson, *Making of the English Working Class*, p. 326.

own took possession of me." As distinctly as if a voice had spoken, the command came: "Then go for Me to China."[40]

Troubled Waters

In 1832 — the year of Taylor's birth, the year of the Reform Bill, a year of both revival and cholera — a Scottish Presbyterian minister in London named Edward Irving was encouraging his fashionable congregation to speak in tongues, one of the first modern instances of the phenomenon. Eight years earlier, in 1824, he had proposed a new strategy of missions in a speech to the London Missionary Society — sending out "roving figures" who called themselves "revivalists" or "evangelists." These men — and a few women, for this was a period when "female ranting" was still common along the sectarian fringe — took their enthusiasm out of the churches and into the marketplaces, factories, and theatres. They should be sent forth, Irving urged, "destitute of all visible sustenance, and of all human support" and should be "compelled to rely on God alone."[41]

Some British revivalists adopted the frontier techniques of the American Charles Grandison Finney — who came like a "great wave from America."[42] Finney argued that spiritual movements could be "got up" — as opposed to "prayed down," which might happen once in a lifetime — by the application of scientific methods, "the right use of constituted means. It is not a miracle, nor dependent upon a miracle."[43] The means included singing, protracted meetings, and the "mourner's bench in front of the congregation where penitents would kneel in agony while the congregation prayed a volley over their heads.

"Religious ideas have the fate of melodies, which once set afloat in the world, are taken up by all sorts of instruments," wrote George Eliot in her first novel *Scenes of Clerical Life*. Set in 1832-33, the year of Hudson Taylor's birth, the novel describes the advent of evangelicalism into Milby, a linen-and-coal town much like Barnsley. "Evangelicalism was . . . gradually diffusing its subtle odour into chambers that were bolted and barred against it. . . . Nevertheless, evangelicalism brought the idea of duty, that recognition of something to be lived for beyond the mere satisfaction of self."[44]

---

40. J. Hudson Taylor, *A Retrospect* (CIM, 1875), in *HTCOC 1*, pp. 354-55.
41. Bebbington, *Evangelicalism in Modern Britain*, pp. 75-77.
42. I. E. Page, ed., *John Brash: Memorials and Correspondence* (London: C. H. Kelly, 1912), quoted in ibid., p. 164.
43. Rosalind Goforth, *Goforth of China* (Grand Rapids: Zondervan, 1937), pp. 178-79.
44. George Eliot, *Scenes of Clerical Life* (1857; republished London: Penguin, 1973), pp. 319-20.

The experimental spirituality of the 1830s led to schisms in the 1840s, as church leaders tried to rein in the free spirits. The most spectacular was the Great Disruption of 1844, which split the Presbyterians into the established Church of Scotland and the Free Church, over the question of state patronage for ministers. On a smaller scale the "Beaconite" controversy among the Quakers separated Friends from Friends, traditional Quakers with their distinctive dress and speech from "preaching Quakers" who had more in common with evangelicals in other churches. The Wesleyan Methodists, too, were split by the Reform Movement Secession of 1849. Like the Primitive Methodists and Bible Christians a generation earlier, the split was led by lay class leaders ("the older 'sectarian' tendency") who wanted to "re-form" Wesleyan revivalism, to rescue it from the educated clergy and bring back Wesley's emotional revivals. The lay leaders called the seminary-educated preachers "Rationalistic," "artificial" or "man-made" ministers, and accused them of trying to modernize the church into a liberal, and Liberal party, organization. Preachers should only be in the churches, one lay leader advocated, "as silent spectators, obedient serfs, or as the servants of Christ in priestly bondage."[45]

Hudson Taylor, aged seventeen and newly converted, walked out of the Wesleyan Methodist Connexion with his father and the other class leaders to form what would become the United Methodist Free Churches. His application to the Chinese Evangelisation Society the next year, 1850, is vague concerning his denominational affiliation: "at first I joined the Wesleyan Methodists, as my parents and friends were members of that body. But not being able to reconcile the late proceedings with the doctrines and precepts of Holy Scripture, I withdrew, and am at present united to the branch Society."[46] Neither the biographies by Mrs. Howard Taylor nor Pollock's *Hudson Taylor and Maria* mention this episode, but its consequences were momentous for the China Inland Mission. Having left the church of his fathers, Hudson Taylor could pick and choose, unfettered by dogma, from the storehouse of religious ideas. He never became a *member* of another church, that is, he never "joined" one church, though he felt free to share communion with all. He was (re)baptized by the Plymouth Brethren and in a burst of enthusiasm, baptized his sister Amelia in a local stream. Later, he was ordained by the Baptists,

---

45. John Kent, "The Wesleyan Methodists to 1849," in *A History of the Methodist Church in Great Britain*, 4 vols., ed. Rupert Eric Davies and E. Gordon Rupp (London: Epworth Press, 1965-88), vol. 2, p. 247. For the decline in Wesleyan membership after 1849, see Alan D. Gilbert, *Religion and Society in Industrial England: Church, Chapel and Social Change, 1740-1914* (London: Longmans, 1976), pp. 190-92.

46. HTCOC 2, p. 30. *Growth of a Soul* does not mention the schism, even though JHT's application to Pearse, dated 25 April 1851, is quoted extensively at pp. 101-4.

though this too was not publicized lest the CIM be identified with one church, which would reduce its interdenominational appeal.⁴⁷

Taylor's secession from the Wesleyan Methodists left a mistrust of "priestcraft," which made his relations with denominational missions difficult. The CIM remained a lay organization: even when it reached eight hundred members, no more than a handful were ordained. Many would have agreed with the American A. T. Pierson "that the distinction of clerical and lay is Anti-Scriptural, Romish and from the Devil." Yet, in a very British contradiction, Taylor himself sought ordination to increase his social status in China, and as he wrote, "most of us believe in ordination, and not a few are ordained."⁴⁸

Thunder and Lightning

In 1839, when Hudson Taylor was seven, tensions between China and Britain escalated into the First Opium War. The Opium Wars, the First in 1839-42 and the Second in 1857-59, *were* about opium, whatever apologists may argue — that opium was merely the spark or that the wars were the inevitable clash of civilizations — isolationist China versus capitalist free trade.⁴⁹ As early as the 1790s, Britain's insatiable desire for Chinese tea was draining the British economy of silver, which was the only payment the Chinese merchants would accept. The British East India Company, which had a monopoly on British trade "east of the Levant," had to come up with a new commodity the Chinese wanted — and were willing to pay for with hard cash. This turned out to be

---

47. Similarly, neither *Growth of a Soul* nor Pollock, *Hudson Taylor and Maria*, mentions his (re)baptism or the spontaneous baptism of Amelia, which were revealed by HTCOC 2, p. 42. Amelia "always regretted it, acknowledging that they were immature and over-zealous." JHT's lack of formal church affiliation was not unique within the CIM. According to the "Personnel Records" of North American missionaries in the 1940s, several missionaries were listed as having no "home church": CIM/ABGC, file 4-82.

48. In McKay, "Faith and Facts," p. 121. The China council discussed the "Ordination of Missionaries on Furlough" on 10 March 1924, and the London council took up the issue on 24 October 1924, in CIM/SOAS.

49. An example of this view would be Harry Gelber, *Opium, Soldiers and Evangelicals: Britain's 1840-42 War with China and Its Aftermath* (New York: Palgrave Macmillan, 2004), whose promotional material states: "This book questions the universal belief that England's 1840-42 war with China was an 'Opium War.' What really worried London was 'insults to the crown,' the claim of a dilapidated and corrupt China to be superior to everyone, threats to British men and women and seizure of British property, plus the wish to expand and free trade everywhere. It was only much later that general Chinese resentment and Evangelical opinion at home — and in America — persuaded everyone that Britain had indeed been wicked and fought for opium."

opium, grown in the British colonies in India, in Patna, near Calcutta. By the 1830s, opium had become the engine of the world's economy, the most traded and profitable international commodity, equivalent, say, to cars or oil today. The EIC inaugurated a three-way trade that lasted into the twentieth century: Indian opium to China; Chinese silver to India to pay for governing the Raj and for tea and silk to Britain; and Indian cotton to Britain, where it was manufactured in the mills of Lancashire and exported back to India and China.

By 1839, opium was a serious problem in China, impoverishing the addicts and draining the imperial treasury. The Daoguang Emperor tried to outlaw opium smoking and appointed a "drug czar," an incorruptible official named Lin Zexu, to stop the smuggling in the Canton area. Commissioner Lin went after the rich merchants who controlled the trade, then the addicts; he even wrote a letter to Queen Victoria. "So long as you do not take it yourselves, but continue to make it and tempt the people of China to buy it, such conduct is repugnant to human feeling and at variance with the Way of Heaven." When all else failed, Commissioner Lin imprisoned the foreign traders inside their warehouses in Canton, and seized 20,000 chests — an astounding 2,000,000 pounds — of opium, which he flushed out to sea. The British merchants tricked Commissioner Lin, though, because they signed a paper that transferred ownership of the confiscated opium to the custodianship of the British consul. The opium, thus, was British crown property, and its expropriation must be revenged by war. The Chinese never forgot that Hong Kong was "stolen" by a trick.

When news reached Britain months later, the Tory Foreign Secretary Lord Palmerston gave in to the mercantile lobby, and sent twenty gunboats to force the mighty Chinese Empire to pay full indemnity for the confiscated opium. There were few who did not succumb to the nationalist jingoism, because the anti-opium movement had barely begun. One who did speak courageously for the Chinese side was the leading evangelical parliamentarian, the future Lord Shaftesbury (Palmerston's son-in-law), who gave a three-hour speech denouncing the opium trade. The future Liberal Prime Minister, William Gladstone, thundered in Parliament against this "iniquitous traffic": "The great principles of justice are involved in this matter. . . . They gave us notice to abandon the contraband trade. When they found that we would not, they had the right to drive us from their coasts on account of our obstinacy in persisting in this infamous and atrocious traffic. . . . [T]his I can say, that a war more unjust in its origin, a war more calculated in its progress to cover this country with permanent disgrace, I do not know, and I have not read of."[50]

---

50. Quoted in Maurice Collis, "Morality and the Opium Trade," in *China Yesterday and Today*, ed. Molly Joel Coye and Jon Livingston (Toronto: Bantam Books, 1975), pp. 150-52.

The war dragged on for two years, until the British Navy sailed up the Yangtze River, the lifeline of China's east-west trade, to Yangzhou, at the junction of the Grand Canal, which controlled the north-south trade. Thus, with a handful of gunboats, they brought the Celestial Empire to its knees and forced the emperor to sign the Treaty of Nanjing, the first in a long line of "unequal treaties." The Treaty of Nanjing paved the way for the missionary movement because it removed the strictures against Christianity. It ceded the island of Hong Kong as a British colony and opened five "treaty ports," foreign enclaves or "concessions" along the coast where the foreigners could own property and run their own government: Canton (now Guangzhou), Amoy (Xiamen), Swatow, Ningpo (Ningbo), and Shanghai. The most valuable privilege was "extraterritoriality," or "extrality" as it was popularly known, which meant that a foreigner had diplomatic immunity from prosecution in Chinese courts, and could travel freely throughout the Chinese Empire protected by the Union Jack.

The most colorful personality of the First Opium War was a swashbuckling Pomeranian (or Prussian) named Karl Friedrich August Gützlaff (1803-51), or as he called himself in English, Charles Gutzlaff. (Since he called himself Gutzlaff, I shall do so too.) Gutzlaff, who had been sailing the China Seas when Hudson Taylor was born, is remembered today for his hypocrisy, a missionary who disguised himself as a Fujianese fisherman, while he worked as a translator for opium smuggling ships, selling opium off the front of the boat while distributing tracts off the stern. This was "a classic case of the inattentive right hand," in Pat Barr's memorable phrase.[51] It is easy to laugh at Gutzlaff's fevered rhetoric, his posturing, but it is hard to overstate his influence. Eugene Stock, the Editorial Secretary of the Church Missionary Society, painted Gutzlaff like a Boy's Own Adventure story:

> Ascending the rivers, landing here and there at the risk of his life, pursued by pirates, harassed by the police, stoned by the mob, haled before magistrates, but giving medicine to crowds of sick folk, and distributing literally hundreds of thousands of tracts and portions of Scripture. His method was much criticised but his adventures excited unbounded interest in England and America, and certainly gave the Christian public a new idea as to the possibilities of missionary work in China.[52]

Many claimed Gutzlaff's mantle as blitz-converter of the nations, among them David Livingstone in Africa and Hong Xiuquan, the Taiping King, in

---

51. Barr, *To China with Love*, p. 16.
52. Stock, *A History of the Church Missionary Society*, vol. 1, p. 466, quoted in ibid., pp. 227-28.

China. Although Hudson Taylor never met Gutzlaff, he institutionalized the latter's ideas of mass evangelism and native agency into the CIM. As A. J. Broomhall noted, "Gutzlaff's courage, originality, adventurousness, adaptability to Chinese customs, his principles and methods, left a deep impression on the young man who was to follow him. When Hudson Taylor reached China, his own actions and attitudes suggest that he was emulating Gutzlaff, albeit subconsciously."[53]

Gutzlaff was an uncanny linguist who "could pick up the nuances of each local dialect after only a short period of fierce concentration." He would disguise himself as a Fujianese sailor, and even got himself adopted by a Fujianese family so he could become a citizen of the Chinese Empire.[54] In order to convert the Chinese, he wrote, the missionary should "learn from their own mouth their prejudices, witness their vices, and hear their defence, in order to meet them effectually. . . . In *style* we ought to conform entirely to the Chinese taste." Yet, even though he was a "free" or independent missionary, responsible only to God, he worked as "the interpreter and Chinese-language secretary to the newly appointed British superintendent of trade, and so [was] in an excellent position to know the state of anti-pirate campaigns and social conditions of the Chinese countryside."[55]

After the Opium War and the subsequent treaties that tolerated Christianity, Gutzlaff founded the Chinese Union, a band of native evangelists who would spread the gospel beyond the treaty ports. He based the Union "on the principle that China's millions could never be converted to Christianity by foreign missionaries: Chinese Christians themselves must carry out the evangelization of the empire while Western missionaries would serve as instructors and supervisors."[56]

Like Edward Irving's revivalists who were "compelled" to rely on God, Gutzlaff said that his evangelists "simply [went] preaching the Word of the Cross . . . from house to house, from city to city. . . . How this is to be done they do not know, but leave the whole with entire childlike confidence in their father in heaven. If he withdraws his support we must naturally sink, if he upholds, he will do it with his miraculous power."[57] Their reports were fantastic:

---

53. *HTCOC 1*, p. 180.
54. Jonathan D. Spence, *God's Chinese Son: The Taiping Heavenly Kingdom of Hong Xiuquan* (New York: W. W. Norton, 1996), pp. 20-21.
55. Ibid., p. 88.
56. Jessie G. Lutz and R. Ray Lutz, "Karl Gützlaff's Approach to Indigenization: The Chinese Union," in *Christianity in China: From the Eighteenth Century to the Present*, ed. Daniel H. Bays (Stanford: Stanford University Press, 1996), p. 269.
57. Gutzlaff, quoted in *HTCOC 1*, p. 324.

262 converts in their first year (1844) — doubling the number of Protestants in all China. By 1849, the Union counted 1,000 evangelists travelling inland, who claimed a total of 2,871 baptisms, carefully itemized, from Mongolia to Tibet.[58]

As Jessie G. Lutz points out in her history of the Chinese Union, Gutzlaff's approach demanded a great deal of trust: trust in the power of the Holy Spirit working through the printed Word to bring about the "thunder-and-lightning conversion" of China, and more important, trust in the native evangelists. James Legge, the learned sinologue who translated the Chinese classics into English, was one of Gutzlaff's fiercest critics. Since he was a full-time government employee, Legge asked, "Was it reasonable to believe that Gützlaff was able to organize and carry on a great spiritual movement among the people so sunk in apathy, sensuality, covetousness, and deceit as the Chinese? Where was the necessary organization of infant communities, the oversight of them, and the discipline?"[59]

In September 1849, riding the crest of publicity, Gutzlaff returned to Europe, his first furlough in twenty-three years, to drum up support among his societies. "Preceded by an aura of romance and fame, Gützlaff was equal to expectations. He had a genius for inspiring confidence and enthusiasm upon initial contact and he made the most of it. He was, wrote one writer, like electricity. Setting himself a killing schedule that called for travel by night after twelve-hour days of public lectures, meetings with executives of mission societies, sermons, and so forth, he conducted a blitz tour of England and Scotland. Crossing to the continent, he had an interview with the queen of Holland, received a commendation from the Literary Society of Leyden, met with the Moravians about founding a mission in Inner Asia, and established an English women's support society."[60] With an "intolerable assumption of omniscience," he carved up China and assigned each province to a different society: Berlin University got the western provinces of Shaanxi, Gansu, Sichuan, and Tibet; Danzig (now Gdansk, Poland), the free port, "took charge" of Guizhou, a sea of mountains near Burma; and to the English Chinese Evangelisation Society, Gützlaff recommended "the provinces of Shantung, Chekiang, and Fukien . . . accessible by sea."[61]

Meanwhile, predictably, the Chinese Union unraveled. A missionary committee launched an investigation and summoned each preacher for question-

---

58. These are itemized in Lutz and Lutz, "Gützlaff's Approach," p. 273.
59. Ibid., pp. 282, 285.
60. Ibid., p. 274.
61. *HTCOC 1*, p. 336.

ing. They were critical of the preachers' understanding of Christian doctrine, and of Gutzlaff's failure to monitor their activities. "Testimony indicated that a significant minority of the Chinese Union members were opium smokers, that some of the preachers had never left the Hong Kong area, and that some of the colporteurs had resold their tracts to book suppliers to be repurchased by Gützlaff." The committee's report reached Europe while Gutzlaff was in the middle of his triumphal tour, and the controversy became acrimonious. Some societies withdrew their support, while others, including the Chinese Evangelisation Society, suspended judgment. The collapse of the Union, they believed, was a failure of *means* — the untrained, untrustworthy individuals — but the *goal* of extensive evangelism by "native agency" remained unchanged.[62]

In November 1850, Gutzlaff returned to Hong Kong, where he threw himself into reorganizing the Chinese Union. But he was already sick with rheumatic fever, and died eight months later, in August 1851, of overwork at the age of 48. The Union was dissolved.

Lest one dismiss the Chinese Union, it had earth-shaking repercussions. Even if some preachers were opium addicts and opportunists, the majority were sincere, if simple, believers who actually did make preaching tours of Guangdong and Fujian. In the tragic aftermath of the Opium War, the Word fell on fertile soil in the Canton delta, which was suffering from endemic opium addiction, piracy, robbery, warfare between ethnic groups and clashes between villages. The Hakka, a persecuted ethnic minority, were particularly receptive to heterodox teachings, including Christianity. The majority of the Chinese Union's preachers were Hakka, as were most of their converts. Years later, missionaries would go into Hakka villages and discover groups of secret "god-worshippers" who had been converted by one of Gutzlaff's preachers. One was Hong Xiuquan, who by 1850 had raised the standard of the Taiping Rebellion to drive the Manchu demons from China.

The Blessed Hope

In 1849, while Gutzlaff was touring Europe, in Yorkshire Hudson Taylor heard his call to China. "For every man, woman and child in Barnsley, four thousand are dying in China," he wrote his sister Amelia, a number concocted out of thin air. "I have not the slightest idea *how* I shall go, but this I know, I *shall* go."[63] He

---

62. Lutz and Lutz, "Gützlaff's Approach," p. 275.
63. *HTCOC* 2, pp. 24-25.

subscribed to a magazine called *The Gleaner in the Missionary Field*, published by the Chinese Evangelisation Society, Gutzlaff's English support society. In August 1850, Hudson Taylor wrote to George Pearse, the foreign secretary of the Chinese Evangelisation Society, an epistle from a soul on fire. "We cannot be too much in earnest in the prosecution of this great work," he started. "The missionaries should be men of apostolic zeal, patience, endurance, willing to be all things to all men. May the Lord raise up suitable instruments, and fit me for this work." He had studied Gutzlaff's reports published in *The Gleaner* and, startlingly direct, asked Pearse: "On Dr. Gutzlaff's return will the Institution be remodled [sic] or can further frauds be prevented in any way?" He closed by saying he would try to "gather a few pounds if possible" and forward them to the committee.[64]

Pearse, jumping to the conclusion this was an application, asked Taylor for a statement outlining his spiritual experiences, his religious views, education, and general health. He also suggested that Taylor take medical training to prepare himself for China. So, on his nineteenth birthday, Taylor started an apprenticeship with a surgeon in Hull, a Dr. Hardey. Hull was a fishing town on the Yorkshire coast, linked by train to Barnsley, where the fictional Robinson Crusoe and the humanitarian William Wilberforce had been born — quite the legendary pair. Like all ports, it was a hotbed of religious enthusiasms, including a gathering of Southcottians, followers of the Messiah Joanna Southcott, "the Woman Clothed with the Sun."[65] Taylor boarded with his aunt but, determined to live on faith, he moved to a rooming house in a part of town aptly named Drainside, where he learned how to be poor. He subsisted on oatmeal and rice so he could give away six-tenths of his income in the form of tithes and tracts. Meanwhile he was teaching himself Chinese from a dictionary.

In Hull, Taylor came under the influence of Andrew Jukes, a mystical independent preacher who wrote books on millenarian prophecy, "the blessed hope" that Jesus would return imminently, but also built a high-gothic cruciform chapel. He was, Taylor thought, a "man with a message, a prophet or seer of rare spiritual illumination."[66] Jukes was a member of the Christian

---

64. JHT, letter to G. Pearse, 7 August 1850, in *HTCOC* 2, p. 23.

65. Had I world enough and time, I would recount the story of the prophetess Joanna Southcott and her "spiritually incarnated son," John "Zion" Ward, who founded the British-Israel movement. She made a few converts in Barnsley, and Ward was more successful there in the 1830s. See J. F. C. Harrison, *The Second Coming: Popular Millenarianism 1780-1850* (New Brunswick, N.J.: Rutgers University Press, 1979), p. 158.

66. *HTCOC* 2, pp. 42-43. For more on Jukes, see F. Roy Coad, *A History of the Brethren Movement: Its Origins, its Worldwide Development and its Significance for the Present Day* (London: Paternoster Press, 1968), pp. 78-79.

Brethren, a radical evangelical movement that grew out of the religious ferment of the 1820s and '30s. Though not related to the German Brethren, the Christian Brethren chose the name to indicate their search for the primitive, apostolic church where all members shared everything in common. The movement started in 1828 as a Bible study group of young Church of Ireland students at Queen's College, Dublin. They gathered on the simple premise that true believers should be free to "break bread," to share communion, with all who follow Christ. In other words, they did not need an Anglican minister to administer the sacraments, but could bless and serve the bread and wine to each other.

Two leaders of those Dublin meetings show the opposite temperaments of the Brethren. Anthony Norton Groves (1795-1853) was a sweet, sympathetic soul, an Exeter dentist who gave up his profession to study for the Church of England priesthood. Studying the Bible with single-minded purpose, he came to the conclusion that he could no longer believe in Anglican exclusivity and gave away all his income, £1,000 a year, everything "beyond [his] modest immediate needs," to the neighborhood poor. "The Christian motto should be — labour hard, consume little, give much, and all to Christ." Since his wife shared his calling to foreign missions, they went to Baghdad as independents, where they worked for four years (1829-33) under extremely adverse circumstances, followed by twenty years in India, where his "attempts to work with existing missionaries were largely negated by his idealistic approach."[67]

Another Irish Brethren was John Nelson Darby (1800-82), one of the strangest mystics of the nineteenth century. Darby's attempts to reconcile the prophetic scriptures of Daniel and Revelation took him into the realm of prophetic dreams; his inner light was the jagged lightning of apocalyptic end-times. "His energy was prodigious, and his gifts scarcely less so," writes F. Roy Coad, an historian of the Brethren movement.

> When he died, he left behind him some fifteen hundred churches — in Britain and on the Continent, in North America and the West Indies, in New Zealand and Australia — who looked to him as their founder or their guide. His writings fill over forty ample volumes, and include comments and controversy over most of the great ecclesiastical events occurring during his long lifetime. . . . Darby's English style was often slovenly, tortuous and obscure, and his thought was rarely systematized

---

67. For more on Groves, see ibid., pp. 15-24 and throughout. Quote is from biographical entry in *Biographical Dictionary of Christian Missions*, ed. Gerald H. Anderson (New York: Macmillan Reference USA, 1998), pp. 264-65.

— "to analyse his position is often to refute it." Yet few who have remarked on this trait have noticed the semi-hypnotic effect of his involuted prose: an effect that has permeated the customary language and imagery of his most extreme followers until they have become almost incomprehensible to the uninitiated.[68]

Darby's distinctive contribution was a theology called *dispensational premillennialism*. Since this eschatology, marginal in nineteenth-century England, became *the* cornerstone of twentieth-century American fundamentalism, some explication is needed here, as the term will occur again.

Postmillennialism, the doctrine Taylor grew up with, is the theology of Progress, that humankind can achieve perfection through the progressive improvement of human nature and morality. The millennium — the thousand years of peace, also known as the Kingdom of God on Earth — could be achieved by human effort. Only *after* the millennium — the post of postmillennial — will Christ return. Consequently, the Second Coming will always be at least one thousand years in the future.

Premillennialism is its opposite. It teaches that Christ will return *before* the millennium, and that the Second Coming will precipitate the apocalyptic battle of Armageddon. Darby created a further refinement called *dispensationalism*, which divided History into Ages or "Dispensations," including the Dispensation of the Garden of Eden, the Dispensation of the Mosaic Law, the Dispensation of Jesus Christ, and the present Dispensation of the Church, which was nearing its latter days.

The vexatious question on which dispensationalism turns, is the seven-year period known as the *Tribulation*. The placing of the Tribulation — before or after the Second Coming, before or after Armageddon, before or after the Millennium — was so contentious it fractured the Brethren not once, but many times, into "pre-trib pre-mill" and "post-trib pre-mill" camps. *Pre-tribulationists*, like Darby, taught (and teach) that Christ will come *before* the Tribulation: when he appears in glory, the "living true saints" will be taken out of the world to meet him in the air in the "secret rapture." Thus they will avoid the Tribulation, which will be inflicted only upon the unsaved. *Post-tribulationists* were more pessimistic: they taught that the Antichrist will purify the saints for seven years, which will end with the Second Coming. Both agreed, though, that the end was vertiginously near: the common view was that Christ could return at "any moment — before the morning dawned, be-

---

68. For Darby, see Coad, *History of the Brethren Movement*, pp. 26-35, and throughout; quote at p. 106.

fore the meeting closed, and even before the speaker had completed his address."[69]

In 1848, about the time Hudson Taylor came into the Brethren orbit, Darby split the movement. He believed that the Church of England was a "church in ruins," an "ice-palace" of formalized ritual and "the secret working of heresy," and demanded that his followers must "come out" from the "apostate" churches. As a "nonsectarian fellowship," the Brethren attracted Anglicans, Baptists, Quakers, Methodists, and others who did not feel the need to sever their connection with their churches. The Exclusive (or Closed) Brethren practiced "second-degree separation," that is, they refused to associate with anyone who associated with anyone who was apostate. The Open Brethren, like Groves, held the same tenets, but without second-degree separation. The Plymouth Brethren were somewhere in the middle. In other words, the Open Brethren would shun Anglicans but be willing, in theory, to share communion with Plymouth Brethren, but the "PBs" would not sit down to the Lord's table with them. Thus, the Brethren movement started "with universal communion, but ended with universal excommunication."[70]

Some mid-nineteenth-century evangelicals considered premillennialism to be a heresy whose "mystical vagueness" was "a fruitful source of confusion and misunderstandings in the face of the immediate practicalities of life."[71] Moreover, with its passive assumption that "human effort could not in fact bring in God's Kingdom," premillennialism "cut the nerve of missions": why send missionaries to evangelize the heathen if only the return of Christ would be sufficient to establish the kingdom of God?[72] Nevertheless, by the 1850s premillennialist teachings were spreading far beyond the Brethren, among Baptists and Presbyterians, even among moderate Calvinists in the Church of England. By the 1880s premillennialism turned itself inside out to became the theology of missions: if the end was imminent, human "means" could kick-start the prophetic clock. As it is written, in the last days — "this generation" — even "these from the Land of Sinim" would be among the Elect.

---

69. Ernest R. Sandeen, *The Roots of Fundamentalism: British and American Millenarianism 1800-1930* (Chicago: University of Chicago Press, 1970), p. 140.

70. A. A. Rees, quoted in P. L. Embley, "The Early Development of the Plymouth Brethren," in *Patterns of Sectarianism: Organization and Ideology in Social and Religious Movements,* ed. Bryan R. Wilson (London: Heinemann, 1967), p. 225.

71. Coad, *History of the Brethren Movement,* p. 114.

72. Dana L. Robert, "The Crisis of Missions: Premillennial Mission Theory and the Origins of Independent Evangelical Missions," in *Earthen Vessels: American Evangelicals and Foreign Missions, 1880-1980,* ed. Joel A. Carpenter and Wilbert Shenk (Grand Rapids: Wm. B. Eerdmans, 1990), p. 32.

Hudson Taylor became caught up in prophetic speculation and developed his own theory which he called "First Fruits." As the name suggests, it was a version of pre-tribulationist premillennial dispensationalism, that some believers would be raptured up while the majority would remain on earth to suffer the Tribulation.[73] He started expounding his views so fervently that his parents thought he was "unbalanced" by these "new notions from Scripture." "I wish, dear mother," he wrote, "you saw clearly the truth of the second coming of our Lord.... One, if genuinely believed in, which would alter the indolent and apathetic state of the Church."[74]

The immediate effect on Hudson Taylor was more practical: he sorted his possessions and gave away everything he would not need when Christ appeared. Then he started packing his bags for China.

---

73. Frost, "Memoirs," p. 472.
74. HTCOC 2, pp. 52, 43.

CHAPTER 2

The Wicket-Gate
1851-1865

> *In these pages I propose to record the result of a journey into a region which lies at our own doors — into a dark continent that is within easy walking distance of the General Post Office.*
>
> George Sims, known as "Dante of the London Slums,"
> *How the Poor Live,* and *Horrible London* (1889)[1]

The First Pilgrimage

The Pilgrim has extricated himself from the Slough of Despond, bedaubed with mud, and has escaped from the socialist sophistry of Mr. Worldly Wiseman. He finds himself at the wicket-gate, in the shadow of Beelzebub's Castle, where far above, the demons rain flaming arrows on the pilgrims who pass below. He knocks at the gate, which opens a crack. "Here is a poor burdened sinner," he says. "I come from the City of Destruction, but am going to Mount Sion." A hand reaches out, and Good-will pulls him inside to safety. Good-will takes him to the House of the Interpreter, where the Interpreter shows him a series of tableaux and explains the significance of each. In one room (the unsanctified human heart), a man (the Mosaic Law) tries to sweep the black dust (original sin) but only raises choking clouds; when a damsel sprinkles the dust with water (the gospel), it is cleansed "with pleasure." In other rooms, a professor weeps in an iron cage, and two children, Passion and Patience, sit on little chairs. Interpreter gives Christian new clothes to wear, a

---

1. Julian Pettifer and Richard Bradley, *Missionaries* (London: BBC Books, 1990), pp. 219, 267.

The young Hudson Taylor, painted by his aunt in Hull in 1852. In Hull, Taylor came under the influence of the Plymouth Brethren and started to live on faith. He went to China the next year under the Chinese Evangelisation Society.

Source: Dr. and Mrs. Howard Taylor, *Hudson Taylor In Early Years: The Growth of a Soul* (London: CIM, 1911).

pure white robe, and points to the Cross, just visible in the distance, where he will lose his burden of sin.

Two hundred years later, Hudson Taylor needed to pass through two wicket-gates as he went from from his own land, Yorkshire, to the far country, Inland China, first through London — "darkest London," in General Booth's memorable phrase — then Shanghai, where he was literally showered with flame-tipped arrows from the city walls as he camped in the no-man's-land between warring armies.

Hudson Taylor made his first visit to London in September 1851 with his sister Amelia to see the Great Exhibition. He was nineteen and she was celebrating her sixteenth birthday, two fresh-faced, blue-eyed young people from the North Country. Amelia was suitably awed with Prince Albert's extravaganza, the Crystal Palace, which displayed treasures from all over the world. It was like a glass fairyland, she said, as she gazed up into the domes soaring overhead, with the sunshine lighting up the ferns and tropical plants. Hudson bought her a pineapple, her first taste of such an exotic fruit, as a birthday treat. More interesting was a "Chinese village" with imported Chinamen and a temple filled with idols.

Hudson Taylor was never intrinsically interested in the outside world. After leaving Barnsley, he wandered physically and spiritually: one place was the same as another, one church as good as another, depending only whether the Holy Spirit was present. He had come to London to meet the directors of the Chinese Evangelisation Society, the organization that was going to send him to China. He had eagerly read their journal, *The Gleaner in the Missionary Field*, which was filled with reports from Karl Gutzlaff and Issachar Roberts, the independent missionary from Tennessee. Roberts had taught Hong Xiuquan, the Taiping King, after his conversion by the evangelist Liang A-fa. The year before, 1850, when Taylor had sent his unexpected application, the secretary George Pearse had advised caution, that he should take medical training to prepare himself for China.

Pearse met Hudson and Amelia at the Bank of England, where he was a wealthy stockbroker, and whisked them off to Tottenham, a railway suburb in north London. There, after chapel one Sunday afternoon, Hudson Taylor was introduced to the men and women who would be his friends and supporters for the rest of his life, his adopted family. Unfortunately, Taylor had missed Gutzlaff during his English visit the year before, but he did meet one of his German colleagues, Dr. Wilhelm Lobscheid, renowned as a daring pioneer. Looking him up and down, Lobscheid remarked, "They call me a red-bristled barbarian devil, and you see how dark I am. *You* would never do for China."

To which Hudson Taylor replied, "But God has called me, and He knows the colour of my hair and eyes."[2]

The CES was a tiny organization with no missionaries that was run by two congregations of Brethren. They were not the Exclusive (or Closed) Brethren of Andrew Jukes and John Nelson Darby, for Taylor had already found the "PBs" (Plymouth Brethren) narrow and exclusionary. One assembly was at Hackney, where Pearse and W. T. Berger worshiped, along with Philip Henry Gosse, a naturalist and geologist who wrote the *Manual of Marine Zoology*. One catches a brief grimpse of Hudson Taylor in the memoirs of his son Edmund Gosse, the classic *Father and Son*, which paints a bleak picture of a Brethren childhood.[3]

The other assembly was the Brook Street chapel, Tottenham (which survives today), built and financed by Luke Howard (1772-1864). Like many Brethren congregations, they were Quakers who had seceded during the Beaconite controversy and started an independent "unsectarian" meeting. Howard was a member of the prominent family which included John Howard and Elizabeth Fry, the hospital and prison reformers. Although Luke Howard and his family had left the Society of Friends, they retained their social and family connections with Quaker philanthropists and politicians, which became a significant link in the anti-opium crusade.

Since Quakers were barred from the universities, Luke Howard went into business and founded a family firm, Howard & Sons, manufacturers of pharmaceutical chemicals, while he pursued his scientific hobby: watching clouds. Luke Howard is known to history as "the man who named the clouds" because he classified them into four categories and ascribed the names they bear today: cirrus, cumulus, stratus, and nimbus. His sons, Robert and John Eliot, became professional quininologists, experts in the distillation of the antimalarial drug quinine. In 1851 both were fathers of young families, not much older than Taylor himself. Like the Taylor-Broomhalls, the Howards formed a dynasty within the CIM, when Robert's son Theodore became the third generation to join the London council in 1873, then became home director in 1879.

Also present that Sunday was William Thomas Berger, "dear Mr. Berger," the manufacturer of Berger's Rice Starch, which was famous throughout England. He built two chapels, one for his factory workers in East London and another at his estate, named "The House Beautiful, Saint Hill" in East

---

2. *HTCOC* 2, p. 38.
3. Edmund Gosse, *Father and Son: A Study of Two Temperaments* (London: Heinemann, 1907; reprint, 1958), pp. 61-62. *HTCOC* 2, pp. 448-49.

The Wicket-Gate

Grinstead. A generation older than Taylor, Berger and his wife became Taylor's mentors, and he is credited as the "co-founder" of the China Inland Mission. During its first years, 1865-72, Berger and George Müller kept the mission afloat financially. Almost as crucial in Taylor's life, hovering in the background was Miss Mary Stacey, a Quaker lady who organized bands of women who sewed and raised money.

Hudson Taylor, obsessed with the Chinese souls who were perishing without hearing the gospel, was restless to sail as quickly as possible, but the Chinese Evangelisation Society seemed to stall. He quickly realized that the CES was run by businessmen who were "intensely sincere and impractical." He returned to Hull to finish his apprenticeship with Dr. Hardey, during which he formulated the financial and faith principles of the CIM, living on faith that the Lord would provide. One year later, in September 1852, Pearse offered to support him to study medicine at the London Hospital.

> The C.E.S. early showed the culpable lack of business sense which in the end destroyed it, and Hudson shrewdly declined to commit himself too deeply. It paid his fees, but for board and lodging he let the secretary think his father paid, and allowed his father to suppose the Society paid, while he . . . existed on a loaf of bread and a pound of apples a day.[4]

London Hospital was one of those cavernous institutions built in the eighteenth century where scientific medicine coexisted with old-fashioned heroic treatments like bleeding and cupping. Amputations were performed without anaesthetic, and the stench of gangrene and carbolic was overwhelming. It was the charity hospital for the East End, which made Barnsley seem like a Sunday school picnic. Respectable people who never ventured further than St. Paul's could not imagine the degradation and criminality that lurked behind the monuments of Empire. As Taylor walked from Soho, where he boarded with his uncle, to the hospital in Whitechapel, he entered the world of Dickens, Mayhew, and General Booth. Dickens needed an armed escort when he ventured at night into the warrens "of sickening smells, these heaps of filth, these tumbling houses, with all their vile contents. . . . Wherever Mr. Rogers turns the flaming eye [of the flashlight], there is a spectral figure rising, unshrouded, from a grave of rags."[5]

---

4. Pollock, *Hudson Taylor and Maria*, p. 22.
5. Kellow Chesney, *The Anti-Society: An Account of the Victorian Underworld* (Boston: Gambit Incorporated, 1970), pp. 114, 117.

THE FIRST GENERATION

While Taylor survived on bread and apples, he was performing surgery and dissecting cadavers. The city preyed on his mind, darkening his thoughts, and his letters drift into apocalyptic tones: "Oh! dear Mother, I do wish you were out of that Babylon of Confusion, Sectarianism," he wrote. "The moment a man is called Reverend he takes on a higher standing in the eyes of the world and worldly Christians than his poor local brother who may be far more holy." Mother, startled, joked about his "instability." When someone offered him a ticket to see the state funeral of the Duke of Wellington, he "declined, thinking it was the world worshipping its Idol and classed in the lust of the flesh, the lust of the eye and the pride of life."[6] His regimen lasted a couple of months, until he cut his finger while dissecting, contracted septicemia, and returned home to Barnsley. After a long, painful convalescence, he recovered with a deeper sense of urgency.

Events were unfolding in China, a once-in-a-lifetime open door. *The Gleaner* had been following the story of the Taiping Rebellion since the conversion of Hong Xiuquan. In 1852 it announced that a "Christian" army forty thousand strong had broken out of south China and was marching north toward the Yangtze River. In November, the rebels besieged Changsha, capital of Hunan province, which was the only major city to repel their advance. Hankou went up in flames a month later, and in March 1853, the Heavenly King was carried in his palanquin into the old Southern Capital, Nanjing, which lay in ruins after a bloody siege. By then, the Taiping armies, swollen with conscripts, prisoners, and deserters, reached one hundred thousand, and they launched a northern expedition to capture Beijing, which they called "the Demon's Den."

Hong declared Nanjing would be his capital, which he renamed the Heavenly City, or New Jerusalem, and there he put on the yellow robe and the yellow shoes and ascended the Dragon throne as the first Emperor of the Heavenly Kingdom of Great Peace, *Taiping Tianguo*. He ordered mass printings of Gutzlaff's Bible and instituted public readings of the Ten Commandments. *The Gleaner*'s enthusiasm exceeded all bounds. "Can anyone conceive of the number of preachers and teachers, the amount of Scriptures and tracts that will be needed for T'ien-the's [*Tiandi*, Emperor of Heaven] army just as soon as access can be had to them?" As soon as access could be had, *The Gleaner* predicted hopefully, the Emperor of China would be a Christian!

In September 1853, two years to the day after he visited the Crystal Palace, Taylor terminated his medical studies without finishing his degree, and sailed for China as an "agent" of the Chinese Evangelisation Society with instruc-

---

6. *HTCOC* 2, pp. 62, 68.

The Wicket-Gate

tions to proceed forthwith to Nanjing.[7] Before the ship reached Land's End, he had a spiritual crisis. The square-rigged sailing ship — "the doomed *Dumfries*" — ran into a storm off the coast and was almost shipwrecked. Taylor was wracked with guilt: should he wear a "swimming-belt" during a storm? Did a life jacket constitute "means," which would indicate a want of faith and "remove me from the direct and immediate leadings of God"? He gave it away, preferring to rely on faith to protect him. Fortunately, since the ship passed through no more storms, he did not have to test his resolve. As the ship languished in the tropics, he read *The Law of Storms* and *Pilgrim's Progress*.[8]

The Odd Sparrow

After five and a half months at sea, Hudson Taylor arrived bedraggled and unannounced in Shanghai on 1 March 1854. The biographies linger long and lovingly on his first term in China from 1854 to 1860: 300 pages in Dr. and Mrs. Howard Taylor's *Growth of a Soul* (1911); 75 pages in John Pollock's *Hudson Taylor and Maria* (1962); and 400 pages spread over two volumes of A. J. Broomhall's *Hudson Taylor and China's Open Century* (1982).[9] All agree, at varying levels of candidness, that in the topsy-turvy world of Shanghai under siege, Hudson Taylor was "an odd sparrow," as W. A. P. Martin, dean of the American missionaries, called him, "a mystic absorbed in religious dreams, waiting to have his work revealed. Not idle but aimless." He "forever looked poor,"[10] and would come round at meal times, always waiting for his remittance which never came. Sometimes he was forced to borrow a string of cash from his servant or pawn a bar of soap — his last bar! — until in unexpected ways, by prayer alone, God reminded some friend at home and Taylor's ship came in.

Broomhall described how Taylor appeared to his contemporaries:

> Brazenly dressed as a Chinese when he attended community functions, when he called at Gibb, Livingstone & Co. to cash credit notes, and even at the consulate, young Hudson Taylor was affronting the very people to whom he owed his security. Even Issacher [sic] J. Roberts, unkempt but

---

7. *Growth of a Soul*, p. 175.
8. The voyage of the *Dumfries* is in ibid., pp. 184-98, the swimming-belt at p. 191. See also *HTCOC* 2, pp. 88-116 and 103-4 respectively.
9. *Growth of a Soul*, pp. 198-503; Pollock, *Hudson Taylor and Maria*, pp. 25-104; *HTCOC* 2, pp. 112-411, and *HTCOC* 3, pp. 22-226.
10. Ralph Covell, *W. A. P. Martin: Pioneer of Progress in China* (Washington: Christian University Press, 1978), p. 21; Pollock, *Hudson Taylor and Maria*, p. 79; *HTCOC* 2, p. 110.

Western in appearance, was less despicable. This nobody, this pauper without degree or title, neither flotsam of the mercantile and seafaring world nor accredited representative of any church, hatless and "pigtailed," was disgracing the respectable community he had entered.[11]

Yet, W. A. P. Martin remembered fifty years later, "when the vocation found him, it made him a new man, with iron will and untiring energy."

For years, Taylor had been dreaming of living in the interior of China, "far away from all human aid, there to depend on God alone for protection, supplies and help of every kind. . . . I thought to myself, when I get out to China I shall have no claim on anyone for anything; my only claim will be on God."[12] In Shanghai, he dropped into one of the worst civil wars in human history.

Shanghai was China's wicket-gate. The foreign concession was barely a decade old, since it had only been opened as a treaty port after the Opium War. It was a malarial outpost on the muddy flats twenty miles up the Huangpu River, consisting of half a dozen streets between the creek and the walled Chinese city. The *Shanghai Almanac* of 1854 listed 270 foreign male residents, not counting the thousands of sailors, mercenaries, deserters, vagabonds, and ne'er-do-wells, the flotsam of every Oriental port. The two dozen missionaries made up one-third of the married couples.[13] Most of the residents were single young men, newly arrived apprentices called "griffins," who had been recruited in London as silk appraisers. These spirited young men with nothing to do gave their nickname to the wild Mongolian ponies they imported, and they amused themselves playing polo — the griffins on their griffins — and organizing paper hunts "to shake up the liver."[14]

Dr. James Henderson, the author of *Shanghai Hygiene or Hints for the Preservation of Health in China* (1863), acknowledged "the general relaxation and debility which unavoidably supervene during a *protracted residence in sultry climates*" [his italics] as a result of the Englishman's diet. Dinner in Shanghai, he wrote, began

> with a rich soup, and a glass of sherry; then they partake of one or two side dishes with champagne, then some beef, mutton or fowls and bacon, with more champagne, or beer; then rice and curry and ham; afterwards game, then pudding, pastry, jelly, custard, or blancmange, and more

11. *HTCOC* 2, p. 294.
12. Pollock, *Hudson Taylor and Maria*, p. 20.
13. *HTCOC* 2, p. 122.
14. Frances Wood, *No Dogs and Not Many Chinese: Treaty Port Life in China 1843-1943* (London: John Murray, 1998), p. 22.

champagne; then cheese and salad, and bread and butter, and a glass of port wine; then in many cases, oranges, figs, raisins and walnuts are eaten with two or three glasses of claret or some other wine; and this A W F U L repast is finished at last with a cup of strong coffee and cigars.[15]

The Shanghai foreign cemetery was filled to overflowing, he concluded ominously, and had to be enlarged several times in the 1850s.

While Taylor was at sea worrying about swimming belts, a secret society known as the Triads (or Red Turbans, or Short Swords) had captured the Chinese walled city of Shanghai, where they were in turn besieged by 40,000 Imperialist (i.e. Chinese government) troops, the so-called "Imps." ("Imp" is a slippery word. The Taipings used it racially to define the Manchu "demons" that the One True God had commanded them to exterminate; the foreigners used it politically as an abbreviation for the Qing "Imperial" forces, which were, of course, ethnically partly Manchu and partly Chinese.) Taylor spent his first night in Dr. William Lockhart's hospital in the no-man's-land between the city wall and the Qing army, where he collected "balls" (cannon and musket) as souvenirs. A month later, after the Battle of Muddy Flats, he moved into the walled city as the only resident missionary. The carnage was horrible, he wrote, heads hung by their queues and the unburied dead eaten by dogs: "the very thought of it makes your blood run cold."[16]

Hudson Taylor met his first interpreter as soon as he stepped off the boat, a white man in a Chinese gown and queue. This was the Reverend Joseph Edkins (1832-1905, exactly Taylor's lifetime) of the London Missionary Society, late of London University, "a scholar of fluid dynamics and Milton's *Paradise Lost* as well as of biblical theology."[17] Like Gutzlaff, Edkins was an uncanny linguist, who had already been in China for six years, and was, according to his colleague Griffith John, "diving into the depths of Buddhism, unfolding the mysteries of the Chinese language and literature," and becoming an expert on the Chinese occult.[18]

Edkins took Hudson Taylor on tours of the devastated countryside, and taught him how to wear "the native costume . . . not to deceive them, but merely to avoid the astonishment that foreign clothes always produce."[19] He also taught Taylor how to run away when a crowd started throwing mud and bricks. Like Bunyan's Interpreter, Edkins pointed out the grisly tableaux and

15. Ibid., p. 29.
16. Ibid., p. 28; *HTCOC* 2, p. 142.
17. Spence, *God's Chinese Son*, p. 288.
18. *HTCOC* 2, p. 292.
19. JHT to CES in ibid., p. 148.

explained their meaning: "rows upon rows of houses . . . some burned down, some blown in," black skeletons telling of "the misery of hundreds if not thousands of poor Chinese" driven from their homes in the dead of winter. With the shifting battle lines, some villages changed hands five or ten times in the course of the thirteen-year Taiping rebellion, and were sacked each time.

A few years later, Hudson Taylor's second interpreter was William Chalmers Burns, a Scottish firebrand who had ignited revivals among factory women in Aberdeen, Catholics in Ireland, and Scottish emigrants in Upper Canada during the 1830s and 1840s, before he sought "a sterner and more self-denying service" in China. His revivals were described "in the strictest sense [as] cardiphonia — the voice of an instrument that could sound only as the breath of the eternal Spirit of God swept over it. . . . His function and vocation was rather that of the old prophets uttering from time to time the message and the 'burden' given to them under the immediate impulse of the Spirit."[20] Burns took Taylor along the rivers that fan out from Shanghai, introducing him to every village and planting "the seed-thoughts" that were to grow into the China Inland Mission. In the matter of Chinese dress, though, the younger Taylor was the mentor. After ten years in country, Burns was still wearing a Western suit — and wondered why, in those perilous times, he was always arrested and brought back in chains.

Man cannot live on air, and Hudson Taylor had mundane concerns — such as staying alive. His relations with the armchair industrialists of the Chinese Evangelisation Society deteriorated quickly. What did they know about Chinese politics or how to send money through native banks? They continued to order Taylor to move to Nanjing, as if one could sail through the Heavenly Navy, but did not send his stipend, which was supposed to be £70 [$350 U.S.] a quarter. Instead, Taylor was sustained by personal gifts from his family and from friends, the Howards, Pearse, and Berger. In 1857 Taylor and his colleague, Dr. William Parker, resigned from the CES to form an independent Ningbo [old spelling Ningpo] Mission, in a quiet treaty port 150 miles down the coast, where Taylor had already established a shop-front chapel.

In Ningbo Taylor met his final interpreter, Wang Lae-djün. In Shanghai Taylor had made a few converts, including a "repentant *amah* who had to be disciplined,"[21] but the first male to be baptized in Ningbo showed more promise. He was Ni Yong-fa, a cotton spinner and "the leader of a reformed Buddhist sect which shunned idolatry and was searching for the truth." One

---

20. Islay Burns, *Memoir of the Reverend William C. Burns, M.A.: Missionary to China from the English Presbyterian Church* (London: James Nisbet & Co., 1870), pp. 213-14.

21. *HTCOC* 3, p. 159.

William Burns in Chinese winter clothes. This was an advertisement for Hudson Taylor's speaking tour of England, New Year's 1866. Burns, one of Taylor's mentors during his first term in China (1853-60), escorted him around Shanghai. Taylor introduced Burns to the advantages of traveling in Chinese dress.

Source: A. J. Broomhall, *Hudson Taylor and China's Open Century*, book 4, *Survivors' Pact* (Sevenoaks, UK: Hodder & Stoughton, and OMF, 1984).

evening when Taylor was preaching "the glad tidings of salvation through the finished work of Christ," Ni stood up and declared, "I have long sought for the truth — as my father did before me. . . . I have found no rest in Confucianism, Buddhism, Taoism, but I do find rest in what I have heard tonight. Henceforth I believe in Jesus." (This is what Gutzlaff would have called thunderbolt conversion.) Ni took Taylor to a meeting of his unnamed sect, and as a result Taylor's first converts and preachers were all former members.

Wang Lae-djün, a house painter and interior decorator, overheard a conversation in the next yard between the lady of the house and one of these converts, a basketmaker who refused to make incense containers after he became a Christian. Why Wang was so interested in incense baskets and idol taxes is never explained, but Taylor baptized him in 1859, near the end of Taylor's first term. When Hudson and Maria were invalided home to England the next year, Wang accompanied them.

The Heavenly Kingdom

The Taiping Rebellion hung like a pall over Taylor's first term. It had started in 1848, five years before he arrived, and ended in 1864, four years after he left. Hong Xiuquan, the Heavenly King, had been a Hakka peasant in a remote part of Guangdong province, who failed the civil service examinations several times. In 1837 he had a dream in which he ascended to heaven in a sedan chair, where his soiled heart was sliced out and he was given a new, clean heart. He was cleansed by a female deity who called herself "Mother" and him "Son." She took him to God the Father, a tall, erect deity seated on a throne dressed in a black dragon robe, with a luxuriant golden beard that reached down to his belly. Years later, Hong read a Christian tract entitled "Good Words to Admonish the Age," which seemed to provide an explanation of his dream in Christian terms: Hong was literally the second-born, Chinese Son of God the Father, and thus the Younger Brother of Heavenly Elder Brother Jesus.

On the basis of his vision, the historian Rudolf Wagner argues, Hong created "a complete world view based on the materials authenticated through the vision" and confirmed through the foreign books, namely the Bible and later *Pilgrim's Progress*. Visions were important in Chinese folk religion, with "a set of conventions" regarding their authentication "within the context of canons of rationality." They were not dreams, but rather were imposed from above while the visionary was in a passive state ("dozing"), or as psychologists call it, a fugue state. Visions can be "differentiated from spirit possession and madness through external confirmation: an event within the vision is confirmed by another event outside the vision that is visible to all." Once the vision was written down, it would "move into a radically different category. It would become a mandate from God or Heaven to be obediently followed even if it involved the most fundamental changes and dangers." Indeed, Wagner shows that the older Jesuit emphasis on healing and magic gave way to psychological and spiritual exorcism in the nineteenth century, the power to interpret dreams and wrestle with the spirit world.[22]

22. Rudolf G. Wagner, *Re-enacting the Heavenly Vision: The Role of Religion in the Taiping Rebellion* (Berkeley: Institute of East Asian Studies, University of California Press, 1982), pp. 4, 22–24.

The Wicket-Gate

In 1848, after years of preaching to his Hakka neighbors, Hong launched a full-scale rebellion to exterminate the demons — the non-Chinese Manchus — who had deceived the people from the One True God's way. He established the *Taiping Tianguo*, the Heavenly Kingdom of Great Peace, and declared himself the Heavenly Emperor. As his armies marched northwards from Guangdong, Hong established his capital city at Nanjing in 1853, which he renamed the Heavenly City, the New Jerusalem. The Heavenly King had a keen eye for imperial spectacle. He was an intensely visual person, and like all emperors or emperors-in-waiting he paid attention to the color symbolism of the *wuxing*, the five-color cosmology. As he entered triumphally into Nanjing, he wore the imperial yellow dragon robe and yellow slippers, and was escorted by hundreds of soldiers and officials in their distinctive uniforms, "red and yellow robes, their hair hanging long around their faces below their scarlet hoods or turbans, or sometimes stuffed into a cloth bag or pouch around their neck."[23]

Even W. C. Burns, Taylor's mentor, with his knowledge of the Yangtze delta, was unable to venture further than thirty miles before he was stopped by the Heavenly Navy. Inadvertently, though, Burns reinforced the Taiping cosmology, but this happened after Taylor had left China. In 1860 the Heavenly King received a copy of Burns's translation of *Pilgrim's Progress*, which was illustrated with Chinese-style woodcuts. This became Hong's favorite reading, for he found here in illustrated form another clue to authenticating his vision. "The man called Christian," Spence writes, is presented

> as being the product of a dream, but a dream so vivid we can understand with all our souls how Christian staggers under the weight of his guilt and sin. . . . The illustrations heighten the emotion of various episodes: Christian's baby in his mother's arms, stretching out his hand toward his disappearing father; the burden falling off Christian's back as he prays before the cross of Jesus; and Christian, flanked by the guardian knight and shepherds, gazing through a telescope toward the New Jerusalem.[24]

E. P. Thompson, in *The Making of the English Working Class*, called *Pilgrim's Progress*

---

23. Ibid., p. 201.
24. Spence, *God's Chinese Son*, pp. 280-81. Wagner, *Re-enacting the Heavenly Vision*, also discusses the impact of the illustrated *Pilgrim's Progress* on Hong Xiuquan, particularly the "pope and paganism" woodcut.

the inner spiritual landscape of the poor man's Dissent — of the "tailors, leather-sellers, soap-boilers, brewers, weavers and tinkers" who were among Baptist preachers — a landscape seeming all the more lurid, suffused with passionate energy and conflict, from the frustration of these passions in the outer world: Beelzebub's Castle, the giants Bloody-man, Maul, and Slay-Good, the Hill Difficulty, Doubting Castle, Vanity Fair, the Enchanted Ground; a way "full of snares, pits, traps, and gins."[25]

Stripped of its seventeenth-century English specificity, put into Chinese clothes, *Pilgrim's Progress* provided a timeless dreamland, a different spiritual landscape.[26]

The Heavenly Questions

Only four foreign emissaries managed to penetrate as far as the Heavenly Capital, but all were rebuffed. In April 1853, the British plenipotentiary took a scouting expedition; he reached the walls of Nanjing but refused to get off the boat when he was given an audience with only low-ranking official. He did receive an edict from the East King, however, a former charcoal burner named Yang Xiuqing, who claimed to be a channel for the voice of God the Father and had recently been elevated to the rank of "the Comforter" and "the wind of the Holy Spirit" (or Holy Ghost).[27] The East King wrote in his own hand,

> A decree to the distant English, who have long recognized the duty of worshipping Heaven (God).... The Heavenly King, the Supreme Lord, the Great God, in the beginning created heaven and earth, land and sea, men and things, in six days; from that time to this the whole world has been one family, and all within the four seas brethren: how can there exist, then, any difference between man and man?

---

25. E. P. Thompson, *The Making of the English Working Class*, pp. 34-35.
26. *Pilgrim's Progress* was translated into many languages and widely published from the 1860s on. African Christians, for example, asked why the story ends when Pilgrim crosses Jordan and arrives at the Celestial City; that should be the beginning, not the end: the joy in heaven, communing with the ancestors, and walking the streets of gold, the rewards for a holy life on earth.
27. Spence, *God's Chinese Son*, pp. 222-23.

The Wicket-Gate

The British plenipotentiary rejected the document, which he was "unable to understand, and especially that portion which implies that the English are subordinate to your Sovereign." The Taiping religion, he reported to Whitehall, appears to be a "spurious revelation," with a true Old Testament base perhaps, but "superadded thereto a tissue of superstition and nonsense."[28]

Six months later, the French minister — and his wife who came along for the ride — refused to sit at a lower level while the Taiping official sat on a dais. Nevertheless, in Gallic fashion, he was impressed by "the strength of this revolutionary movement, which promises nothing less than to accomplish a complete transformation, at once religious, social and political in this immense Empire, by tradition a land of custom and immobility."[29]

Since the American gunboats were occupied elsewhere in 1853, sailing into Edo [now Tokyo] harbor with Commodore Perry's expedition to open Japan, it was not until May 1854 — two months after Taylor arrived — that the American minister took two Protestant missionaries to the Heavenly Capital. They were fired upon from the shore because the Taiping garrisons were "unfamiliar with the markings or flags of foreign vessels" and suspicious of the American flag. The minister also received an edict from the East King, which was "couched in language so peculiar and unintelligible as to cause [him] much astonishment." In reply, he sent "a historical memoir of the U.S. of America, together with a drawing of their National Flag, which his excellency, the Commissioner, desires to be submitted to your Chief authorities, to prevent any misapprehension on their part."[30]

Finally, a month later the British could "no longer contain their curiosity" and sent a low-level expedition to Nanjing. Frustrated at not being allowed to land, the British submitted to Yang Xiuqing, the East King, "thirty questions on a wide range of topics — trade prospects, troop numbers, laws, tariffs, initiation rites, examinations, the common treasury, separation of males from females, opium prohibitions, ranks of nobility — and two intrusive ones on a matter of different import: what does it mean when Hong Xiuquan says he is Jesus' younger brother; and why, among his many titles, does the East King include those of 'Comforter' and 'Holy Ghost'?" In reply, they received one of the strangest diplomatic missives ever sent from the head of one state to another.

The Taiping emperor did not answer their questions, but rather posed a series of fifty questions of his own, which "show with great clarity the questions that are troubling the Taiping Celestial Court about their heavenly

---

28. Ibid., p. 198.
29. Ibid., p. 203.
30. Ibid., pp. 206-7.

claims." The epistle asked: "Your nations having worshipped God for so long a time, does any one among you know," followed by such conundrums as:

1. How tall God is, or how broad?
3. What his appearance or color is?
4. How large his abdomen is?
5. What kind of beard he grows?
6. What colour his beard is? . . .
9. Whether his first wife was the Celestial Mother, the same that brought forth the Celestial Elder Brother Jesus? . . .
12. Whether he is able to compose verse?
25. How rapidly can he compose verse?

And concerning Heavenly Elder Brother Jesus:

16. How tall Jesus is, or how broad?
33. What his appearance or colour is?
34. What kind of beard he grows?
35. Of what color his beard is?
36. What kind of cap and clothes he wears?
37. Whether his first wife was our elder sister?
38. How many children he has had?

It concluded with: "Whether all the Heavens are of Equal height? What the highest Heaven is like?"[31]

These questions seemed utterly absurd to the British, who were unable to grasp their import; to the Taipings, however, they were perfectly sensible.[32] The British — none of whom had theological training — replied in Sunday-school terms that God the Father was a spirit and therefore invisible; he did not have a body, so he had no beard nor hands nor children, and his robes and throne were metaphorical, not "real."

Hudson Taylor, crisscrossing the Shanghai hinterland in Chinese dress, tried to penetrate into the Taiping territory, but failed each time. He seems to have swallowed the general opprobrium of the Taiping "heresy." He warned the CES not to publish Issachar Roberts's fabrications, which were "too credulous" and "deficient in judgement."[33] He told his mother not to believe what

---

31. Ibid., pp. 230-31.
32. Wagner, *Re-enacting the Heavenly Vision*, pp. 44-45.
33. *HTCOC* 2, pp. 156-57.

she read in *The Gleaner:* "I am afraid their [the Taiping] success would do more harm than their destruction. Their errors are great and their impostures so numerous."[34] Nevertheless, like the conundrum of the swimming-belt, Taylor claimed the problem was "means": the means were weak — Hong Xiuquan and his corrupt doctrines — not Gutzlaff's goal of blitz-conversion of China's millions.

The Earthly Family

Hudson Taylor's first term in China was divided into two parts. The first four years, when he was constantly in motion, he spent as a bachelor in a predominantly married missionary world. His success at winning the hearts and minds of the Chinese was overshadowed, at least in the biographies, by his great adventure, the love story of Hudson Taylor and Maria Dyer. Mrs. Howard Taylor drew a veil across the details because they were "too delicate," but once Pollock revealed all, they have been incorporated into the legend. *The Man Who Loved God*, a play that toured the world in the 1990s, dramatized their courtship and marriage to the point of caricature, like "a tragi-comedy of Victorian mores enacted in a Manchu world of missionary romance."[35]

Maria Dyer was born in Malacca in 1835, three years younger than Taylor, and was brought up to be a missionary's wife. He told his mother that she was, "despite the slightest cast of the eye, a good looking girl." Although only nineteen, she had seen a lot of sadness: her father died when she was six, followed by her baby brother, who had been dropped on his head. Widow Dyer married a Mr. Bausum and then died. Bausum remarried, and died, and his widow married a widower, Mr. Lord, who also died. Maria's sister Burella died in 1857, shortly after her own marriage, and so on. Yet, in England and along the China coast, her extended family was a who's who of missions: her grandfather and uncle were directors of the LMS in London, and her brother-in-law became Anglican bishop of Victoria (Hong Kong).

In 1852, at fifteen, she had returned to Ningbo to teach at a school for blind girls run by the redoubtable Mary Ann Aldersey. Miss Aldersey was an eccentric if there ever was one. Twenty years earlier, she had been the first unmarried woman missionary in China; now at sixty, she had a reputation among the Chinese as a "witch" because of her nocturnal wanderings. Every evening, rain or shine, she would walk along the top of the city wall and open

---

34. JHT to his mother, November 1854, ibid., p. 223.
35. *HTCOC* 3, p. 57.

a bottle of smelling salts, which, the people claimed, released demonic powers. W. A. P. Martin said the Chinese attributed several earthquakes to her powers: "The wonder is that they did not burn or stone her as a witch."[36] Miss Aldersey had the audacity to refuse Hudson Taylor permission to visit Maria, her ward. He was a pigtailed "ranter," she shouted, "a canting Plymouth Brethren. He does not keep the Sabbath.... He is short, you are tall. And — and, he wears Chinese clothes!!"[37]

Love won out, and Hudson and Maria were married in January 1858, in English dress at her request, with his pigtail cut off. Although they both caught typhoid during their honeymoon, their marriage was "the happiest year of my life," Hudson Taylor remembered. They were "blissful, discovering they were perfectly matched and of one mind on everything." Soon, Maria was in the family way. "So home-letters began to include requests for tablecloths, cutlery, tumblers and wine glasses, to be charged against the account he kept with his parents."[38]

After his marriage, Taylor settled down in Ningbo, where he experimented with evangelistic techniques that centered around the mission compound. In addition to preaching in the street chapel, he and Maria adopted a boy who became the nucleus of a small orphanage, which led to a boys' school, while Maria started a school for girls. One of his innovations would have far-reaching ramifications. After a wave of opium suicides in 1859, he opened the first "opium asylum" run by missionaries for the treatment of opium addicts. Immediately he was overwhelmed by people begging him "to take pity on their condition" and to do an act of merit by helping them to reform. In three months he admitted 133 addicts. This asylum had a short tragic history. Not one in ten addicts was serious, and Taylor had "exceeding difficulty" keeping order since he could not prevent them from smuggling in opium. Of the few who were cured most went back to smoking and many perished "by famine and the sword" when the Taipings ravaged that district a few months later. It had a sequel when a conscience-stricken opium inspector in India sent £3,000 to the CMS for the relief of addicts in China, which was used to build the CMS hospital in Hangzhou.[39]

---

36. W. A. P. Martin, *A Cycle of Cathay: Or China South and China North with Personal Reminiscences* (New York: Fleming H. Revell, 1896), p. 210. See biographical entry in Anderson, ed., *Biographical Dictionary of Christian Missions*, p. 9.

37. Pollock, *Hudson Taylor and Maria*, p. 84.

38. *HTCOC 3*, pp. 127, 132.

39. This account is based on ibid., pp. 195-96, and a report by Rev. G. E. Moule (JHT's antagonist in Hangzhou, see Chapter 4), "The Opium Refuge and General Hospital at Hangchow," *Chinese Recorder*, September-October 1874, pp. 256-62.

The Wicket-Gate

As the story of his first baptized convert, Ni Yong-fa, indicates, Hudson Taylor was acutely aware of the possibility of converting members of native religious sects. "I was preaching in the temple of the guardian god of the city one afternoon," goes one typical account, and "had been dwelling on the love of God, and the blessing of sonship given to believers," when a "Buddhist vegetarian" asked, "When a man believes and wishes to join the church are there any ceremonies to be observed?" Taylor "told him of baptism . . . and explained it as typical of death to the world and regeneration, resurrection — a new creature." The man said, "I greatly believe in Jesus, I *do* believe in him and will come to be baptised. . . . When I heard you preach I found what I wanted. I was so overjoyed if you had said I must be immersed in fire instead of water I should have desired it with all my heart."[40]

Hudson and Maria's domestic happiness was happening against the backdrop of the Second Opium War, which broke out in 1857. Like the First Opium War (1839-41), the British found a pretext for war when the Chinese seized the *Arrow*, a Chinese ship flying a British flag. This time, however, the Taiping Heavenly Navy controlled the Yangtze beyond Nanjing. In Ningbo, a quiet backwater, a convoy of pirates massacred the crew of several Portuguese ships which had sought safety in the harbor. A few months later, the Taiping armies came within a hair's breadth of capturing the city, with horrifying consequences. "We are living only from night to day and from day to night," Taylor's colleague wrote. "The people here are thirsting for our blood. Satan has filled the multitude with lies." By that time, however, both Hudson and Maria were in precarious health. Maria's pregnancy had gone badly. On the hottest day of the year, at the height of the riots, she gave birth to Grace. As Maria lay dying, Hudson prayed "the prayer of faith" for healing, his first experiment with faith healing. Both mother and baby recovered, and she went on to give birth to five sons and three daughters before she died in 1870. Hudson's health, never robust at the best of times, gave out and in 1860 they returned to England with Wang Lae-djün.

---

40. JHT, letter of May 1857, in *HTCOC 3*, p. 62.

CHAPTER 3

Calling the Pilgrim Band
1865-1866

Over the dark blue sea, over the trackless flood
A little band has gone in the service of their God.
The lonely waste of waters they traverse to proclaim
In the distant land of Sinim Immanuel's Saving Name.
They have heard from the far-off East the voice of their brother's blood:
"A million a month in China are dying without God."

Grattan Guinness, "The Voice of Thy Brother's Blood,"
on the sailing of the *Lammermuir*, 26 May 1866
(and so on for 14 stanzas)[1]

The First Vision

The Pilgrim has been brought to a stony beach. It is the 25th of June 1865, a date commemorated as Hudson Taylor's "Heavenly Vision" and the founding of the China Inland Mission. Four and a half years earlier, Taylor had returned as an invalid from China with Maria and little Gracie, and Wang Lae-djün, his "young Chinese brother." The doctors warned he could never return, that the ocean voyage was too dangerous; he had no committee to send his remittance so how could he live in the far country without money? Perplexed and confused by God's guiding, he settled into a crowded house at 30 Coburn Street, in the depths of East London. These were what the biographies call "the hidden years" (1860-65), a life in the shadows, out of the public

1. *HTCOC* 4, pp. 160-61.

glare.[2] He took a year to recuperate, during which he finished his medical degree and was ordained. He and Wang finished their translation of the Bible into a romanized Ningbo dialect. Then he began to create a family and a network of supporters who were, like him, on fire for the salvation of China. He and Maria had four children in quick succession, of whom one died, but earthly attachments did not slow him down.

Always his mind was on the far country, and how to get back there. He kept a large map of China on his wall, with pins indicating the Protestant missions along the coast; the rest of the country was blank, without a single gospel pin. He liked to tell the story of a Chinese man called "Peter," who had been recruited in London by another missionary and taken back to China, where he became Taylor's evangelist. While traveling by boat, Peter fell overboard, but when Taylor called for help, the fishermen yelled, "It is not convenient!" "This to Hudson Taylor was a picture of the godless mind, indifferent to the value of life, of a human soul, concerned only for personal profit; and of the apathy of Christians, enjoying their own security and faith in Christ while others died in sin and ignorance, unwilling to raise a hand."[3] (There was a certain slippage here, a transference between the sins of the godless mind in the far country and the negligence of Christians here, in his own land.)

More and more Hudson Taylor was convinced God was calling him to start his own mission society, not run by armchair directors in England like the Chinese Evangelisation Society or the Church Missionary Society, but directed from the field, where it could be adaptable and mobile, ready to be deployed as circumstances changed and doors opened. He studied his Bible and came to the conclusion that the biblical way to recruit suitable men and women was "to pray, first that God would send them out and second, that the Church's spiritual life would be so deepened that men would be unable to stay at home."[4]

Now, after four years in England, while he was attending a church service at Brighton, suddenly he was possessed by an "incubus of heathendom on one's soul. Could not bear it. Distress of mind tremendous." He left the church and went for a walk on the beach. Perhaps he glanced up at the domes of the Brighton Pavilion, the pleasure palace built by the late, reprobate King George IV as a chinoiserie fairyland; now, at the instructions of the good

---

2. For the hidden years, see *HTCOC 3*, pp. 227-441.
3. *Growth of a Work of God*, pp. 4-6. *HTCOC 2*, pp. 371-73, stated, "He told the story again and again in after years, and published it in his books."
4. McKay, "Faith and Facts," pp. 80-81.

young Queen Victoria, it had been stripped of its contents and abandoned, a reminder of the transience of this world. As he looked out to sea, the lapping waves turned black, like one of Luke Howard's cumulus thunderclouds. He saw the face of Peter, drowning, and millions of others, all the death and destruction he had witnessed in China. He took up his Bible, at Job 17:9 (KJV), "The righteous shall also hold on his way," and wrote: "Prayed for 24 willing skilful workers at Brighton, June 25/65." The next morning, with £10 and a prayer, he opened a bank account in the name of the "China Inland Mission."[5]

Emerging from obscurity Hudson Taylor wrote his "manifesto," a hundred-page compendium entitled *China: Its Spiritual Need and Claims; with Brief Notices of Missionary Effort, Past and Present*, that made him a celebrity overnight. (The title echoes W. H. Medhurst's *China: Its State and Prospects* of 1838, one of the books Taylor had read in Barnsley.) *China's Spiritual Need and Claims* (its later title) sold three thousand copies in three weeks, was reprinted twice within the year, and went through eight editions before 1900. This book, it was said, stirred the evangelical churches of Britain to their missionary duty as no document had done since William Carey's pamphlet seventy-three years earlier (1792).

Hudson Taylor had the amazing ability to reduce incomprehensibly complex ideas into simple, indelible images of "missionary arithmetic." *China's Spiritual Need* is filled with facts and word-images of "the wonderful nation of China, 'its great antiquity, its vast extent, its teeming population, its spiritual destitution, and overwhelming need.'" He saw in his mind's eye the 400 million Chinese falling into eternal darkness: "A million a month in China are dying without God" became his slogan. (See Introduction.) To personalize 400 million individuals, Taylor recounted the story of drowning Peter, and of the first convert, Mr. Ni of Ningbo. Then he itemized the statistics of the eighteen provinces, one by one. In the sixty years since Robert Morrison arrived at Macao, there were still only one hundred Protestant missionaries in the whole Chinese Empire, and all were clustered near the coast. In the far northwest, Gansu — larger than France and Spain put together — had "No missionary."

---

5. Taylor's Brighton Beach vision has been retold many, many times from *China: Its Spiritual Need and Claims* onward. *Growth of a Work of God*, pp. 31-32. A. J. Broomhall in *HTCOC* 3, pp. 454-55, "Appendix 4, Brighton 25 June 1865," reconstructed the vision by piecing together various accounts and JHT's "reminiscences scribbled down by Geraldine Howard Taylor." McKay, "Faith and Facts," p. 83, noted that JHT used the name "China Inland Mission" six months before the Brighton vision: an entry on 20 December 1864 states "J. H. Taylor in account with China Inland Mission"; by June 1865 he had received 26 donations in the name of the CIM.

Shanxi, Sichuan, on and on, one after another, adding after each, "No Protestant missionary." "Should not these provinces immediately be occupied?" Taylor asked rhetorically.⁶

Having decided to assemble a "team" for China, Taylor came out of the shadows and threw himself into a year of activity, making looping tours of the Midlands, Scotland, Ireland, and the West Country, speaking three or four times a day and writing hundreds of letters. One indication of the changing times was that he traveled by train and got to know the schedules intimately. He was an exotic man, "small, quiet and unassuming," as mannered as a Chinese scholar in black silk gown, as he moved effortlessly from drawing-room to chapel, from London to Dublin, from Spurgeon's Metropolitan Tabernacle to the Twig Folly Mission in the East End. He was not an orator, but he exemplified a new style that was gaining favor, the Bible teacher. Often he was so moved by his own testimony that he wept like a child. James Meadows, one of the first to join, recalled that he was "never charmed with Mr. Taylor's eloquence; he was a man of fluent speech, well chosen words always, but he never stirred one's soul by eloquence of speech, but the eloquence of his life of Faith in God is a continuous power for good."⁷

Taylor's lectures were advertised like scientific lectures cum curiosity shows:

> A Lecture on China and the Chinese, by Rev. H. Taylor MRCS
> The Lecture will embrace the geography, antiquity and population
> of the Empire and the manners, customs, languages and religion
> of the people and will be largely
> ILLUSTRATED BY
> MAPS, DRAWINGS, IDOLS, ARTICLES OF DRESS
> and other objects of interest brought from China.
> ADMISSION FREE.
> NO COLLECTION.⁸

"No collection" was Hudson Taylor's faith principle, that the Lord would provide — a novel idea, that a religious organization did not beg for money — and true to his word, he never brought up the subject of money and had no offering box. He did, however, accept personal donations, which he claimed came from God and discreetly put in his purse. One pious legend

---

6. *HTCOC 4*, pp. 49-58.
7. Ibid., p. 141.
8. Barr, *To China with Love*, p. 7.

concerns the greenhouses of Langley Park, where Sir Thomas Beauchamp (brother-in-law of Lord Radstock, the evangelist, and father of Montague Beauchamp of the Cambridge Seven) took the insurance off and donated the premium to the CIM. When a violent storm shattered greenhouses for miles around, Langley Park escaped without a broken pane.[9]

There was a whiff of Oriental magic in Taylor's meetings, something more than the prosaic miracles of popular preachers. He described a contest that he had held with the heathen priests, like the battle between Jehovah and Baal, when the

> writer has seen God, in answer to prayer, quell the raging of the storm, alter the direction of the wind and give rain in the midst of prolonged drought. He has seen Him, in answer to prayer, stay the angry passions and murderous intentions of violent men, and bring the machinations of His people's foes to nought. He has seen Him, in answer to prayer, raise the dying from the bed of death, when human aid was vain; has seen Him preserve from the pestilence that walketh in darkness, and from the destruction that wasteth at noon-day.[10]

He spoke "about idols and idol worship so vividly" that the impression was "never forgotten," and when he lowered his voice, and whispered about exorcism and devil worship, his audience shivered. "Go home to your family and tell them!" he said.[11]

God was raising the dying in China! Go home and tell them that!

The Great Revival

In 1859, while Hudson Taylor was still in China, a revival broke out in Northern Ireland that led to a religious movement so pivotal in British religious history that it came to be called the Revival or "Awakening of '59." (In the secular realm, 1859 was equally momentous, with the publication of Darwin's *On the Origin of Species* and John Stuart Mill's essay *On Liberty*.)[12] Although Taylor

---

9. *Growth of a Work of God*, p. 36.
10. Ibid., p. 40.
11. Mildred Cable and Francesca French, *A Woman Who Laughed: Henrietta Soltau Who Laughed at Impossibilities and Cried: "It Shall be Done"* (London: CIM, 1934), pp. 50-52.
12. For J. S. Mill's anti-evangelicalism, see Bebbington, *Evangelicalism in Modern Britain*, p. 106.

missed the first phase of the revival, he arrived in Britain in time to reap its benefits. As J. Edwin Orr noted, "there is reason to believe that the whole [of the China Inland Mission's first] party [of 1866] was made up of converts and workers of the 1859 Awakening."[13]

If one reads the pages of *The Revival* — another innovation, a magazine founded solely to spread information about the revival — one gets the impression of a sustained, nationwide movement, "that a single phenomenon, revival, was already aflame throughout Britain."[14] Evangelical tradition, such as J. Edwin Orr's *The Second Evangelical Awakening in Britain* (1949), claims the revival was the national manifestation of a movement of the Holy Spirit that had swept America in 1857-59.[15] It had started in Hamilton, Canada West (Ontario), a grimy industrial town known as "the Birmingham of Canada," when an American Methodist evangelist with Quaker roots, Mrs. Phoebe Palmer, introduced a new teaching concerning Holiness. (Hamilton remained a source of working-class religious movements, and thirty years later Hudson Taylor called his first Canadian recruits there.) After her initial success, Mrs. Palmer returned to New York City, from where revivals spread throughout the United States and Canada. As the fires were waning in America, they sparked across the Atlantic to Ulster, then from Ireland to Scotland and Wales, and finally to England. "The tendency of British evangelicals to turn to the United States for inspiration and example meant that once the American revival had burst into flame a British conflagration was assured."[16]

Recent historians have tended to be more circumspect. John Kent, while not denying the impact in Ireland, Scotland, and Wales, provocatively entitled his chapter: "1859: The Failure of English Revivalism." The "much desired major English revival of 1859-60 did not take place,"[17] he argues. *The Revival* (the journal) failed to "discriminate between spontaneous popular revival, deeply rooted in the community, and meetings carefully designed to promote the work of the gospel."[18] At first, in Ireland, there had been mass conversions

---

13. Quoted in McKay, "Faith and Facts," p. 88.

14. Bebbington, *Evangelicalism in Modern Britain*, pp. 116-17.

15. J. Edwin Orr, *The Second Evangelical Awakening in Britain* (London: Marshall, Morgan & Scott, 1949).

16. Richard Carwardine, *Trans-atlantic Revivalism: Popular Evangelicalism in Britain and America, 1790-1865* (Westport, Conn.: Greenwood Press, 1978), pp. 159-97; quote at p. 159. See also Kathryn Teresa Long, *The Revival of 1857-58: Interpreting an American Religious Awakening* (New York: Oxford University Press, 1998).

17. John Kent, *Holding the Fort: Studies in Victorian Revivalism* (London: Epworth Press, 1978), p. 32.

18. Bebbington, *Evangelicalism in Modern Britain*, pp. 116-17.

and emotional prostrations, "sleeps" and "trances" reminiscent of the convulsive 1820s and 1830s. In Scotland, particularly Banffshire, it was said that scarcely a town or village had not been visited by the Spirit; five of the Lammermuir party came from Banffshire.

Yet in England there was "no evidence of prostration or hysteria"[19] — one researcher has discovered only three such instances.[20] England did not have a tradition of revivalism, as the United States did, and besides, "no religious movement could hope to be 'national' if it hardly moved the Church of England at all."[21] The London revival was primarily one of preaching, for as one contemporary wrote, the English were "accustomed greatly to repress . . . the indications of powerful feelings, and especially of religious emotions," and everything proceeded with "greater tranquillity and less sympathetic excitement."[22] Even the efforts of the American professional revivalists who toured England in 1859 — Charles Grandison Finney, the grand old man, and James Caughey, who had both toured Britain in the 1840s, and Phoebe Palmer, fresh from New York — were "marginal."[23] The real revival, Kent argues, came years later, in 1873-75, when the orotund shoe salesman from Chicago, Dwight Moody, and his singing evangelist Ira Sankey brought their harmoniums and anecdotes to England.

Alan D. Gilbert comes to the same conclusion using different evidence. Focusing on the statistical growth rates for the Methodist and Baptist denominations, Gilbert charts a "succession of short-term cycles, and that the peaks and troughs of these cycles occurred at intervals of between five and ten years." There were five peaks between 1845 and 1885, each of which coincided with a time of "revival," but these did not last. Consequently, the growth in church membership was due to "sporadic periods of extremely heavy recruitment which compensated for longer intervening phases of virtual stagnation or actual decline." Gilbert has a novel explanation for "the 1859-60 Revival," that it coincided with a political struggle over church rates, the taxes imposed to support the state church. "During the second half of 1859 the Liberation Society launched a concerted nationwide drive to harness popular support for a Church Rates Abolition Bill." This "confrontation produced precisely the kinds of organisational strategies successful in a revival. House-to-house visitation by lay volunteers, pamphlet distribution, public meetings, and

---

19. Orr, *Second Evangelical Awakening*, p. 101.
20. B. Hardman, doctoral dissertation, University of Cambridge, 1964, quoted in Bebbington, *Evangelicalism in Modern Britain*, p. 117.
21. Kent, *Holding the Fort*, p. 71.
22. Orr, *Second Evangelical Awakening*, p. 65.
23. Kent, *Holding the Fort*, p. 71.

large-scale advertising campaigns advocating (or denying) the social and spiritual benefits of voluntarism in religion, were carried on in most areas."[24]

In any event, it is generally agreed that "something happened" in 1859-60, and that its ripples continued to reverberate for the rest of the century. It may not have swept new converts into the churches in dramatic numbers, but it did lead to a quickening of the spiritual life of those within the fold, and the redoubling of organized, transatlantic efforts for spreading the gospel. *The Revival* (later renamed *The Christian*, once the fires had cooled) itself was one example: it was founded by Richard Cope Morgan in 1859 as an eight-page weekly pamphlet, and soon had a circulation of 80,000.[25] It is also evident that the primary beneficiary was the Brethren movement, just coming to maturity as a denomination, which "created much of the network responsible for the new temper and drew in many of the converts."[26]

Once this revivalist temper was taken to China, in an entirely different context, each of these facets emerged as templates for Hudson Taylor's strategy of missions that he called "concentration and diffusion": lay leadership; the influence of the Brethren; the attempt to deepen the spiritual life among the missionaries and the blitz-conversion of the heathen; the intensive distribution of tracts door to door; and even the spiritual benefits of "volunteerism" in religion.

In Britain, Hudson Taylor joined a select company of urban evangelists, each with his own hobby-horse, who had come of age in 1859 in Ireland and Scotland. Their interconnections spread beyond Britain to continental Europe, Canada, the United States, Australia, and South Africa. One life-long supporter was Lord Radstock, Granville Augustus Waldegrave (1833-1913), the "gentleman evangelist" who once preached to the Czar of Russia. (This led to the coining of the word "radstockism.") The Waldegraves were "the first family of British Evangelicalism," headed by Samuel Waldegrave, Bishop of Carlisle. Lord Radstock, a year younger than Taylor, had been a soldier during

---

24. Alan D. Gilbert, *Religion and Society in Industrial England: Church, Chapel and Social Change, 1740-1914* (London: Longmans, 1976), pp. 190-92, 194. Gilbert's thesis, that the 1875-76 expansion coincided with "a massive popular disestablishment campaign," has been contradicted: see Bebbington, *Evangelicalism in Modern Britain*, p. 115.

25. Bebbington, *Evangelicalism in Modern Britain*, pp. 104-6ff. For Morgan and JHT, see *HTCOC 3*, pp. 394-95. For Morgan and Barnardo, see Gillian Wagner, *Barnardo* (London: Eyre & Spottiswoode, 1979), p. 42. Morgan (1827-1908) was the founder of Morgan & Scott, the CIM's publishers, and a CIM referee (see Appendix 2). Scott's daughter, Mary, went out under the CIM in 1887 and married Archibald Orr Ewing, the CIM's wealthiest benefactor.

26. Bebbington, *Evangelicalism in Modern Britain*, p. 117. Kent, *Holding the Fort*, pp. 126-27.

the Crimean War, where he was converted, and became a revivalist "in the Evangelical seaside and watering-place tradition." A "wealthy, eccentric Anglican" who pleased himself ecclesiastically, he was an adherent of the Welbeck Street Plymouth Brethren chapel. About 1873 he came to unorthodox views, and started to practice faith healing.[27] Radstock's mother, Dowager Lady Waldegrave, who owned banks and coal mines (including the Silkstone mine in Barnsley), was also a generous supporter.

At the lower end of the social (and oratorical) scale was Richard Weaver, "the converted prize-fighter, from the mines of Lancashire," who preached "about Hell and the torments of the damned in an imagery derived from the dense darkness of the coal-pit, the flames of the firedamp, and the suffocating vapour of the choke-damp."[28]

Spurgeon's Wordless Book

The exemplar of the post-revival evangelical style was Rev. Charles Haddon Spurgeon (1834-92), the most famous British preacher of his day. Two years younger than Hudson Taylor, he had started preaching at sixteen, and by nineteen was called to a moribund, though historic, Baptist church in South London near Tower Bridge. He quickly became famous as a public speaker and "personality," since he was adept in using modern media. His Sunday sermons, given extemporaneously, were transcribed by stenographers and published in the "Penny Pulpit" by Friday. His lectures, entitled "John Ploughman's Talks," were influential throughout the world; translated into many languages, such as French, German, Arabic, and Urdu, some issues sold up to one hundred thousand copies. (Spurgeon's sermons, recently reprinted, occupy sixty-three volumes, plus another fifty of commentaries, sayings, anecdotes, illustrations, and devotions.)

In 1859, as news of the Irish revival was reaching England, Spurgeon started construction of the Metropolitan Tabernacle, completed in 1861, supposedly the largest church edifice in the world. It was (and is) at a strategic location at the Elephant & Castle transportation hub, and was built upon the site where the Southwark Martyrs were burned at the stake. It seated five thousand people — "people of all classes and no classes" — with room for

---

27. Kent, *Holding the Fort*, pp. 126, 148.
28. Ibid., chapter "Weaver, Radcliffe and the English Revivalist Network," pp. 99-122, quotes at pp. 114, 118. (Radcliffe was a CIM referee and accompanied JHT to North America in 1888; see Chapter 9.)

another thousand standing. There was nothing "churchy" about the Tabernacle; "Baptist church" was dropped from its name; outside it looked like a Roman temple (or the British Museum), a monument of Empire, while the inside was a plush opera house, a vast oval coliseum with two levels of cast-iron balconies rising to the gods.[29] There was no pulpit; rather the stage sat in the middle surrounded by the audience, furnished only with a table and the organ console.

Spurgeon's voice was his instrument, which could sway an audience of twenty thousand — without a microphone. His preaching style was florid and flamboyant — it had to be, to fill that space — yet simple, in the "market language" of the people,[30] which some considered "clumsy," "theatrical," and even blasphemous.[31] Others, however, admired his "high order of pulpit oratory," his "daring homeliness," and his "fresh and striking" illustrations.[32] He believed (like the fictional Alice in Wonderland, like Dwight Moody and Hudson Taylor) that a sermon without illustrations was like a house without windows.[33]

Hudson Taylor came into Spurgeon's network by 1864, when he took Maria and Wang Lae-djün to the Metropolitan Tabernacle. Spurgeon invited him to address a weekday meeting and to give a lecture on China, and a "mutual admiration which never faded grew from that beginning."[34] When Taylor had his Brighton Beach vision in June 1865 and announced the formation of the China Inland Mission, Spurgeon promoted the cause and publicized the CIM in his sermons and writings.

Spurgeon must have been preoccupied with the blackness of Taylor's vision, for on 11 January 1866, a Thursday evening, he gave a talk entitled "The Wordless Book," on the text from Psalm 51:7: "Wash me, and I shall be whiter than snow." This was the first mention of the wordless book as a teaching device, which in this first incarnation had only three colors: black, red, and

29. The original Metropolitan Tabernacle burned in 1898; the subsequent building was bombed during the Blitz. It remains an active evangelistic congregation, which conducts mass advertising campaigns in the London Underground.

30. G. N. Hervey, "Spurgeon as a Preacher," *Christian Review* 22 (1857): 296-316.

31. Lewis A. Drummond, *Spurgeon: Prince of Preachers* (Grand Rapids: Kregel Publications, 1992), p. 281. Charles Haddon Spurgeon, *C. H. Spurgeon's Autobiography*, compiled from his diary, letters, and records, by his wife [Susannah T. Spurgeon] and his private secretary [Rev. W. J. Harrald], 4 vols. (London: Passmore and Alabaster, 1897-1900), vol. 1 (1834-54), p. 311. "Sermons and Sermonizers," *Fraser's Magazine* 55 (1857): 84-94.

32. Spurgeon, *Autobiography*, p. 348.

33. Quoted in "The Christian Hall Of Fame" website, of Canton Baptist Temple, Canton, Ohio: http://www.cantonbaptist.org/halloffame/spurgeon.htm.

34. *HTCOC* 3, p. 390; *HTCOC* 4, p. 60.

white. "I daresay you have most of you heard of a little book which an old divine used to constantly study," Spurgeon started, as though it were already known. "The old minister used to gaze upon the black leaf to remind himself of his sinful state by nature, upon the red leaf to call to his remembrance the precious blood of Christ, and upon the white leaf to picture to him the perfect righteousness which God has given to believers through the atoning sacrifice of Jesus Christ his Son. I want you, dear friends, to read this book this evening." Spurgeon emphasized the blackness of sin: "Do not be afraid to look on your sins, and meditate upon them until they even drive you to despair."[35]

The wordless book was not invented in a vacuum, for Spurgeon had several motives. Increasingly his mind was turning to the evangelization of children, especially the poor on his doorstep. He had recently established his Pastors' College, which trained hundreds of Baptist ministers for churches throughout Britain and the Empire as well as overseas missions, and part of their practical work was combing through the neighborhood to attract children to the ragged school. "A child of age five," he declared in the same sermon, "if properly instructed, can as readily believe and be regenerated as anyone." The orphanages presented a marvelous opportunity but they also presented a conundrum: how to evangelize children in the mass? Simple devices like the wordless book were the answer, along with choruses like "Jesus Loves Me," animated marching and clapping, and magic lantern talks, thus combining religious education and entertainment in one children's service.

A few months later, Spurgeon purchased land at Stockwell, where he laid the cornerstone of an orphanage that would accommodate seven hundred boys, soon to be followed by one for girls. It is astonishing that every nineteenth-century evangelical organization seemed to establish an orphanage, including the CIM. These grew into huge institutions: one thousand boys and girls at George Müller's in Bristol; the same at Dr. Barnardo's Homes on Harley Street in the East End; and hundreds more at the Mildmay orphanage, at Annie Macpherson's Home of Industry, and the Quarrier Homes in Glasgow. These British orphanages despatched eighty thousand "home children" to Canada alone, and more to Australia and New Zealand, where they were sent onto farms to start a new life.[36] It would be a mistake to dismiss the orphanage movement merely as social control over a recalcitrant, industrial

---

35. Spurgeon, sermon # 3278, "The Wordless Book," 11 January 1866, in vol. 57 of *Sermons* (30 November 1911). See Introduction note 13.

36. Kenneth Bagnell, *The Little Immigrants: The Orphans Who Came to Canada* (Toronto: Macmillan of Canada, 1980), flyleaf.

proletariat, part of the civilization-and-uplift of Victorian Britain. Their size alone signifies the enormity of the problem: a cholera epidemic in the summer of 1866 swept the East End, killing 1,407 in a single week.[37]

The orphanage movement, which was run by the same philanthropists who ran the anti-slavery and anti-opium campaigns and acted as referees for the China Inland Mission, presented certain theological conundrums. One was the debate over the existence and nature of hell, whether a just and loving Father would condemn those who had never heard the gospel — whether children at home or heathen overseas — to eternal punishment. Working in the poor parts of London, where one in eight children died before their first birthday, Spurgeon could not help being aware of the inordinately high death rates caused by overcrowding, disease, and the Industrial Revolution. "[I]t would probably be fair to say that, by the time a child reached the age of ten, it was likely that he would have experienced at least one death in the family and possibly more," wrote Geoffrey Rowell in *Hell and the Victorians*. "Evangelical addresses to children on the subject of death become more comprehensible against this background."[38]

The same message was reinforced by Hudson Taylor's vision. "Because the doctrine of hell was used to encourage missionary effort, and indeed in some circles was treated as the sole *raison d'être* of evangelism, it is not surprising that to attack hell was seen by many as an attack on missionary work and evangelism."[39] As we shall see, going soft on the doctrine of hell was the most pernicious heresy within the CIM, which had to be rooted out, root and branch.

Many of the orphanage leaders were Brethren and others who were motivated by premillennial prophecy. As Gillian Wagner noted in her biography of Thomas Barnardo, "Millennial influence had a dual effect on those who believed its eschatological doctrines. In the first place they tended to believe that social change would only produce greater corruption in the world; therefore they did not look with favour on any sort of radical approach to social problems. But secondly, because they believed themselves to be living in an important age in history with only a limited time in which to achieve their objectives, their work had an urgency and a positive quality about it."[40]

There was one more inspiration for the wordless book. British society in

---

37. Ibid., p. 20.
38. Geoffrey Rowell, *Hell and the Victorians: A Study of the Nineteenth-Century Theological Controversies Concerning Eternal Punishment and the Future Life* (Oxford: Clarendon Press, 1974), p. 12.
39. Ibid., p. 191.
40. Wagner, *Barnardo*, pp. 38-40.

the 1860s witnessed an explosion of color, as the manufacture of the bright, metallic aniline dyes created colors never seen in nature. Mauve was patented in 1856, which led to a "mauve mania"; mauve was succeeded by magenta and Britannia violets, and the myriad colors of the artificial rainbow. As new colors were invented, they had to be defined according to a new science of color theory, which assigned a meaning according to random criteria to such displays of color as "the secret language of flowers," flags and bunting, ladies' dresses and interior decoration. They were christened with exotic names that disguised their origin as black coal tar: Turkey red, Tyrian purple, bleu de Lyons, Zanzibar brown, Chinese vermilion.[41] Magazines spilled forth with colored lithographs and even something as mundane as railway signals had to be color-coded. What would have happened if the Victorians had chosen green for stop and red for go (as happened during the Cultural Revolution in China)?

The Team

The year 1865-66 — six years after the revival, once the converts had matured in the faith and were looking for a career — was memorable for the beginnings of three organizations which employed the streams of young, dedicated Christian workers: the CIM, Dr. Barnardo's Homes, and the Salvation Army. All three established their headquarters within a few blocks of each other in the matrix of East End, a stone's throw from the London Hospital. Each was the vision of one charismatic leader who controlled the minutest details until his death, and afterwards through his extended family. Like Hudson Taylor, General William Booth and Dr. Thomas Barnardo mistrusted committees, preferring an autocratic leadership based on personal and family ties of loyalty. Curiously, each imposed a uniform on its members: the blood and fire of the Salvationists, the suits and middies of Barnardo's orphans, and the Chinese dress of Taylor's pigtailed tribe.

During the 1860s the established foreign missions, such as the Church Missionary Society and the London Missionary Society, expanded rapidly in all parts of the world. They were becoming multinational corporations dispatching professional "agents," virtually independent of their respective denominations. The LMS, which developed a two-tiered staff of ordained ministers and lay assistants, was worried that artisans would use mission work as

---

41. Simon Garfield, *Mauve: How One Man Invented a Colour that Changed the World* (London: Faber and Faber, 2001); for color naming, see pp. 176-77.

a step up the social ladder. The application specifically asked: "Does the desire of improving your worldly circumstances enter into the motives of this application?"[42] Another, the Melanesian Mission, was equally frank: it wanted High-Church Anglican "gentlemen missionaries," who were by birth and breeding "free from preconceived notions," having "no taint of the common and fatal heresy concerning the natural inferiority of the black races." They should wear "well-cut well-brushed clothes; who are men of the world, of tact and discrimination; who will say and do the right thing, at the right time and place; whose experience is varied and conversation interesting."[43]

As early as 1864 *The Revival* was pleading: "Where is the channel through which simple hearted labourers who, brought to Christ through those remarkable Revivals, wished to devote themselves to missionary work in far lands, could reach their purpose? But I could find no such channel."[44] The CIM created the channel, and opened the floodgates for shop-clerks, bookkeepers, and governesses to go to China.

Like the Salvation Army, the CIM stressed, at least in theory, the equality of women. Just as the revival opened doors for consecrated but uneducated lay men, it offered careers for women as Sunday school teachers, deaconesses, social workers, home missionaries, and foreign missionaries. (In modern jargon they are described as "professional altruists.") Since the churches prohibited women from being preachers — that is, preaching to men and women from a pulpit — the idea of women as "teachers" — speaking to women and children in a classroom — emerged out of "the laicism, search for novelty, sensationalism, and emphasis on holiness typical of the revival generally."[45] The Salvation Army went one better: even if they did not ordain women, women officers held the same rank as their husbands.

Taylor founded the CIM as a "special agency" for less qualified, Spirit-filled workers. "There is ample scope for the highest talents that could be laid upon the altar of God," he pleaded, as well as for "persons of moderate ability and limited attainments."[46] Just as he never asked for money, he never asked

---

42. David A. Nock, *A Victorian Missionary and Canadian Indian Policy: Cultural Synthesis vs Cultural Replacement* (Waterloo: Wilfrid Laurier University, 1988), p. 12, discusses the class-based recruitment strategies of the LMS. McKay, "Faith and Facts," pp. 96-103, considered various missions, including the LMS (pp. 97-99).

43. David Lockhard Hilliard, *God's Gentlemen: A History of the Melanesian Mission, 1849-1942* (St. Lucia, Queensland, Australia: University of Queensland Press, 1978), p. 31, in McKay, "Faith and Facts," pp. 99-101.

44. *The Revival*, 10 March 1864, in ibid., p. 92.

45. Carwardine, *Trans-atlantic Revivalism*, pp. 187-88.

46. Marshall Broomhall, *The Jubilee Story of the China Inland Mission* (London: CIM,

for recruits, although his message was plain: his audience's own sense of "blood-guiltiness" would make it impossible for them to *stay* home. Wisely, he directed the university men, ordained ministers, and medical doctors to other societies, such as the CMS, LMS, or the Baptist Missionary Society, where their gifts and graces would be appreciated. Above all, they must be men and women "full of faith and the Holy Ghost," experienced in the art of saving souls, the one-on-one confrontation which led another to Jesus Christ. If they didn't know how to save souls by now, they would never learn in China, in another language, among hostile people. Finally, they needed a strong constitution, for they would be forced to live among cesspools and riots in inland China, far from Western doctors.

In creating an institution as complex as the China Inland Mission, Taylor had to draw upon several overlapping but distinct constituencies. The first was the core of family and old friends who could be trusted to take care of personal matters, such as forwarding funds, training recruits, and stoking the publicity machine. These were mostly the Brethren whom Taylor had met in 1851, the businessmen who had sponsored the Chinese Evangelisation Society. Beyond this were his allies in the broader world of missions — Maria Taylor was related to leaders of both the LMS and CMS — schools, churches, and denominational complexes like the Metropolitan Tabernacle and Mildmay. These tended to be newer friends, younger men and women he met between 1860 and 1866. Finally, there were the individual applicants, the team of hand-picked men and women who would accompany him to China.

The first person Hudson Taylor called upon was his sister Amelia, who had married the boy next door from Barnsley, Benjamin Broomhall (1829-1911), and had founded a parallel branch of the Taylor clan. Benjamin was a YMCA success story, a draper's assistant who worked his way up to his own "bespoke" — i.e., made to order — tailor shop in New Bond Street, London, with a large home in Bayswater. Dapper, even worldly, in frock coat and top hat, Broomhall "loved to bring men together in large social conferences." He was active in two "societies," the YMCA and the Anti-Slavery Society, and his "breakfast gatherings" at Hotel Cecil "might be expensive, but Mr. Broomhall was so trusted by wealthy Christian men . . . that whenever he judged that the right time had come for such a social conference, the funds were always ready."[47]

1915, reprinted 1929), p. 30. McKay, "Faith and Facts," p. 92, stated that Taylor's term "simple hearted labourers" led some to speculate that the CIM missionaries were drawn from the forges and mines of England. This class did predominate among the *Lammermuir* party, but by the 1870s, most recruits were what A. J. Broomhall called the artisan or "yeoman" class — shopkeepers, secretaries, and YMCA workers.

47. *HTCOC* 7, p. 75.

Amelia Hudson Taylor Broomhall, known as "Mother Broomhall" to generations of missionaries, was second in the mission's affection only to Hudson Taylor. Like her own mother, also named Amelia, Mrs. Broomhall lived in the shadows: "She never went to China, performed no acts of outstanding courage, had no spectacular achievements to her credit, swayed no audiences with her eloquence. Hers was an unusually sheltered life, from beginning to end surrounded by deep family love. . . . But the sum total of a mission's quality is not contained in its outward activity. . . . Without the Amelias, there would be no Mission."[48] There were many, many Amelias in the China Inland Mission.

When Hudson Taylor asked the Broomhalls to join the CIM in a formal capacity, Benjamin was too busy with his business and societies, but he and Amelia did move to 30 Coburn Street, Taylor's home off Bow Road, to look after Maria and the children while Hudson was touring the country. Their own children, who eventually numbered ten, and the Taylor children who were eventually seven grew up lock-step like brothers and sisters.

When the Pilgrim fled the City of Destruction, he did not leave a committee to forward remittances, answer letters, or act as referees. If he had, it might have looked like the China Inland Mission when Hudson Taylor departed: the London committee, A. J. Broomhall commented, was like "a rope of sand."[49] Taylor left the "entire administration" in the "sole charge" of the wealthy starch manufacturer, William Thomas Berger (1812-99, see Chapter 2). The mission histories call him "co-founder" of the CIM — or, in a bizarre anatomical image, "the nursing father and Mrs. [Mary] Berger the nursing mother of the Mission from its infancy."[50]

A member of the Hackney Brethren assembly whom Taylor had met that memorable Sunday afternoon in 1851, Berger had been a director of the CES, and often sent Taylor money outside regular channels when the CES "forgot" to send his remittance. During the critical year 1865-66, when Taylor was assembling his CIM team, the Bergers were the calm in the eye of the storm as preparations reached a feverish pitch. He personally paid for the printing of 3,000 copies of *China: Its Spiritual Need and Claims*, contributed hundreds of pounds for passages and outfits, and a further £2,000 for a printing press. More, he and his wife opened their home — "The House Beautiful, Saint Hill" — to fifty or sixty candidates, where its spacious lawns gave them a res-

---

48. Phyllis Thompson, *Each to Her Post: Six Women of the China Inland Mission* (Sevenoaks: Hodder & Stoughton and OMF, 1982), pp. 40-41.
49. *HTCOC* 7, pp. 126-27.
50. Broomhall, *Jubilee Story*, p. 79.

pite from the grimy East End. Quietly, the Bergers practiced the ministry of hospitality, and supervised the candidates' "reading, village evangelism and personal part in activities at Saint Hill . . . to judge their character and potential as missionaries."[51]

Berger was a different personality from Taylor, complementary in some respects, dogmatic in others. Charles Judd, who went out in 1867, recalled him as "one of the finest men I have ever met in my life — unquestionably." Tall and thin, he was "decisive and sharp in manner. Quick, a little bit inclined to be severe, but very loving; at the bottom of his heart there was intense love." Mary was "a bright energetic little body . . . so efficient and yet so much out of sight."[52] Unfortunately, A. J. Broomhall concludes, Berger's "gifts did not include public relations." "In communicating with the public he was pedestrian, too formal to inspire, too stilted for easy reading."[53]

The Brethren

The influence of the Brethren on the China Inland Mission is still controversial. Historians of the Brethren movement claim Hudson Taylor as one of their own. As secretary Richard Hill whispered to Geraldine Guinness Taylor, herself a second-generation Brethren: "You know of course that the great majority of the earliest supporters were either or practically P.B.s [Plymouth Brethren]."[54] Yet in her thirty books the word "Brethren" never passed Mrs. Taylor's pen, hidden behind a cloud of euphemisms like "chapel" and "meeting." A. J. Broomhall went to great lengths to deny the "false label" that Taylor was connected with the Plymouth Brethren, that is, John Nelson Darby's Exclusives who practiced second-degree separation, which Taylor "repudiated," as well as the equally "false label" that Taylor was a "Baptist." Broomhall did acknowledge that "the non-sectarian, trans-denominational practices and principles of the China Inland Mission . . . owed much" to the non-Plymouth or Open Brethren, like Berger, Grattan Guinness, and the Howard family.[55]

Foremost among the Brethren was Taylor's most generous benefactor, George Müller (1805-98), the abstemious Prussian (like his contemporary Karl Gutzlaff) who is called "the grandfather of the faith missions movement." Born near Halberstat, Germany, and educated at the University of

51. *HTCOC 4*, pp. 348, 351.
52. Ibid., p. 168.
53. Ibid., p. 166. *HTCOC 5*, p. 338.
54. McKay, "Faith and Facts," p. 290.
55. *HTCOC 3*, "Appendix 2, Hudson Taylor and the Brethren," pp. 446-50.

Halle, Müller was appointed as a missionary to London by the Society for Promoting Christianity among the Jews of England in 1829. He resigned to become pastor of a small congregation at Teignmouth, where he married Mary Groves, sister of Anthony Norris Groves, the self-sacrificing missionary in Persia and India. Together they instituted Norris's faith principles in a larger and permanent form. Müller turned the principle of not asking for money into a high art. In 1834-35 he founded two institutions in Bristol: a Bible school cum mission society, the Scriptural Knowledge Institution for Home and Abroad, which funneled tens of thousands of pounds to missions throughout the British Empire; and an orphanage that grew into the largest social service agency in the west of England.

All this was run by faith: no public appeals, not even a mite box (like the Society for Waifs and Strays) at the back of the room. "There was a supernatural ease with which Müller discovered the secret that God's people will give sacrificially to God's work," wrote Roger Steer, his biographer.[56] Such faith might have produced a carefree attitude toward money, an inner conviction that the Lord would provide. But Müller's diary, *A Narrative of Some of the Lord's Dealings with George Muller. Written by Himself* (1850, with annual updates), shows a man deeply, intensely, prayerfully obsessed with money. It is surely one of the strangest textbooks ever written on fiduciary economics:

> January 4, 1836 . . . one dish, three plates, two basons, two cups and saucers, and two knives and forks. . . . All this money, and all these articles have been given . . . *without my asking any individual for any thing;* moreover, almost all has been sent from individuals concerning whom I had *naturally* no reason to expect any thing, and some of whom I never saw.[57]

Day after agonizing day, year in and year out, from 1834 to 1898: one million printed words.

Although Müller had given financial contributions to Taylor since 1857, they do not seem to have met until 1863, when Taylor took Wang Lae-djün to Bristol to sit at Müller's feet. "Through the kindness of dear friends, many of whom never heard of our names before," Taylor wrote, "all expenses have been covered and we have returned richer than when we went."[58] The grand old man — he

---

56. Roger Steer, *George Muller: Delighted in God* (London: Hodder & Stoughton, 1975), p. 56.

57. George Muller, *A Narrative of Some of the Lord's Dealings with George Muller. Written by Himself* (n.p., 1850), pp. 164-65.

58. *HTCOC 3*, pp. 329, 444-46, "Appendix 1, George Müller (1805-98)."

was nearing sixty, almost gaunt-looking, with a white beard and unruly hair — bequeathed two gifts to the young man. The first were his mottoes, which became the watchwords of the CIM: "Ebenezer" ("Hitherto hath the Lord helped us") and "Jehovah-Jireh" ("the Lord will provide"). Taylor transcribed them into Chinese, and printed them on the cover of every issue of *China's Millions: Yi-ben-yi-shi-er* and *Ye-he-hua-yi-la*.[59] Müller's second gift was his system of divine bookkeeping: each donor was given a numbered receipt, which Müller published in consecutive order, anonymously, on regular occasions. This system satisfied the auditors, while maintaining the fiction that all gifts came from God, that humans were merely "means," God's visible hand.

By 1866 Müller had become the CIM's largest donor, ahead of Berger, and during its early years he kept the mission afloat. From the fragmentary financial records, Moira McKay has ascertained that Müller contributed one-third of the CIM's income between 1866 and 1871, a total of £780 to the general fund and £560 to individual missionaries; this does not include money he gave Hudson Taylor personally for his own use, nor money he remitted directly to China. (By contrast, Berger gave £741 to the general fund and £125 to individuals.)[60]

Another of the Brethren who "wore the stigma of sectarianism, though it was quite foreign to his thoughts,"[61] was Henry Grattan Guinness (1835-1910), the "silver-tongued herald" of the 1859-60 revival. Born into the wealthy Guinness brewing family of Dublin, he broke away from the Church of Ireland to become a professional revivalist who specialized in outdoor preaching, once addressing fifteen thousand people from the top of a cab. Guinness happened to be in Canada when the Irish revival broke out in 1859; one boy who was converted under his ministry, in Chatham, Ontario, was Albert Benjamin Simpson, later founder of the Christian & Missionary Alliance[62] (see Chapter 9 for more). Returning to Dublin, Guinness gathered a group of young men for Bible study. When he invited Hudson Taylor to address the group, they all applied to join the CIM and over a dozen went to China.

When Guinness himself applied to the CIM, Hudson Taylor reluctantly had to turn him down, since with a wife and three children, there was "little likelihood of his being able to learn the language sufficiently well to be as useful in

---

59. In the 1830s Müller received a diamond ring and before selling it he scratched these mottoes on a pane of glass. JHT adopted them in 1857.
60. McKay, "Faith and Facts," pp. 217-19.
61. Joy Guinness, *Mrs. Howard Taylor: Her Web of Time* (London: CIM, 1949), p. 15.
62. Lindsay Reynolds, *Footprints: The Beginnings of the Christian and Missionary Alliance in Canada* (Willowdale, Ont.: Christian and Missionary Alliance in Canada, 1982). Darrel Robert Reid, "'Jesus Only': The Early Life and Presbyterian Ministry of Albert Benjamin Simpson, 1843-1881" (Ph.D. diss., Queen's University at Kingston, 1994).

China as he was at home."⁶³ Rather, Taylor asked him to "train me the men" — and presumably, the women — which Guinness more than fulfilled. He established the East London Missionary Training Institute in 1873, around the corner from the CIM's original home at Coburn Street, and opposite Dr. Barnardo's Homes on Harley Street, the first interdenominational Bible school in England. (The first Bible school was Johannes Janick's Berliner Missiongesellschaft, founded in 1800; there were also denominational Bible schools in England, such as the CMS trainng school in Islington and Spurgeon's Baptist Pastor's College.) By 1900 he had trained fifteen hundred men and women for foreign missions, and had created several faith missions such as the Regions Beyond Missionary Union.⁶⁴ Like Hudson Taylor, Guinness was the patriarch of a dynasty still prominent in evangelical circles a century and a half later: one daughter, Geraldine, married Hudson Taylor's son Howard and became the historian of the CIM; the other, Lucy, founded the Sudan United Mission with her husband Karl Kumm. Grattan's grandson Desmond Guinness helped found the Inter-Varsity Christian Fellowship in the 1920s, and a generation later Oswald (Os) Guinness was a prominent evangelical theologian.⁶⁵

The Guinness family shows the other preoccupation of the Brethren, their concern for premillennial eschatology, and how "the blessed hope" of the imminent Second Coming deepened as it went down through the generations. Grattan Guinness wrote *The Approaching End of the Age* in 1870, and instructed eight-year-old Geraldine on the Second Coming: "He may not come in my lifetime, but I believe He may come in yours."⁶⁶ Fifty years later she still hoped for the Second Coming "within the next few years. It was the most living hope of her life."⁶⁷ Her sister Lucy, on her deathbed, hoped that her four-year-old son "when he was old enough would learn by heart the prophetic passages in Daniel 2, 7 and 9; 1 Thessalonians 4; and 2 Thessalonians 2. I want him to study Revelation, and the Lord's closing prophecies of the three Gospels. If he will do that for Mother's sake when he is fifteen or sixteen, he will understand afterwards why I wanted him to do so. In the later days when he lives he may perhaps see the restored Jewish state, in those unutterable days he may understand and tell."⁶⁸

63. Joy Guinness, *Mrs. Howard Taylor*, pp. 17-18.
64. Christof Sauer, "Reaching the Unreached Sudan Belt: Guinness, Kumm, and the Sudan-Pioneer-Mission" (D.Th. diss., UNISA [South Africa], 2002); see esp. pp. 37-72.
65. The family history by Michelle Guinness, *The Guinness Legend* (London: Hodder & Stoughton and OMF, 1989), examines both branches of the family, the brewing/banking branch and the missionary evangelicals.
66. Ibid., p. 21.
67. Ibid., p. 214.
68. Ibid., p. 201.

The Establishment

Back in the 1830s, when David Nasmith founded the London City Mission, one clergyman had advised him: "I very much fear, that in the present circumstances of the church, you will find yourself repelled at every step in *any* plan which contemplates the co-operation of different denominations. In the first place, you must secure the consent of the bishop, or you will not get the clergy to act, and without the clergy you will find it hard to move the lay members of the Establishment."[69] Twenty years on, the religious landscape of Britain had changed from the schismatic 1840s to the undenominational Keswick Holiness movement of the 1860s and 1870s. The Church of England was more willing to accommodate radical evangelical movements within and without the church. Meanwhile, the sectarian fringe had toned down its anti-state-church rhetoric, marked by "a shift of emphasis among revivalists away from theology towards ethics."[70] In fact, the most enduring evangelical association of the 1860s proved to be the unlikely alliance of the evangelical wing of the Church of England and the Brethren.

The YMCA provided one undenominational (or nonsectarian) model for the CIM, since it remained an "association," not a "denomination" that stressed "come-out" separation. Thus it was able to attract *men* from all walks of life according to age, gender, and special interest, not necessarily by denominational or social homogeneity. As an organizational model, though, the YMCA had little relevance: it was too democratic, had too many committees, too many secretaries. It was, after all, a men's club — with leather chairs, billiard rooms, lecture halls, and gymnasia — whose purpose was the self-help of its members. It was not, as the CIM would become, a tribe composed of married and single men, married and single women, and children growing up within the fold, whose representatives in Britain were only the "agents" of the real family far away, over the dark blue sea.

According to Eugene Stock, secretary of the Church Missionary Society, the Church of England had barely been touched by the revival of 1859-60. As he wrote, the revival "lies outside the range of vision of the modern Church historian, and so do the movements that have sprung from it." Nevertheless, there were a few pockets of enthusiasm within the church, and it was these small "unnoticed religious movements," Stock concluded forty years later,

---

69. Clyde Binfield, *George Williams and the Y.M.C.A.: A Study in Victorian Social Attitudes* (London: Heinemann, 1973), p. 53.
70. Bebbington, *Evangelicalism in Modern Britain*, p. 162.

Calling the Pilgrim Band

that contributed "whatever of life and power the Evangelical wing of the Church possesses today."[71]

One of these unnoticed movements was the annual Mildmay Conferences for Christian Workers convened by Canon William Pennefather (1816-73), whom Stock called "the George Müller of the Church of England."[72] In 1856, he had convened a conference for the spiritual life that brought Brethren and Churchmen together. Clergymen and dissenting ministers, lay leaders, nobility and bankers, men and women together with "large numbers of the middle-class and peasantry" gathered to "glorify God and pray for an outpouring of the Holy Spirit on England such as had been witnessed in America."[73] Pennefather taught them to "expect things." In 1864 he became curate of the parish of St. Jude's in Mildmay Park, Newington, a pleasant railway suburb of Islington, North London, where like Müller, he built an empire on faith.[74]

A simple man, Canon Pennefather "simply asked his Heavenly Father for whatever was needed for this or that project according to his Father's will, and who found these childlike requests granted."[75] The Mildmay Conference grew into a regional organizing complex with a worldwide reach, a 1500-seat church, an orphanage, a deaconess home, hospital, missionary training school, and a 2500-seat conference hall that had an air of "severe respectability, reminding one of a Friends' or Moravian Meeting House."[76] Mildmay, the historian David Bebbington concludes, "introduced a section of the Evangelical party in the Church of England to higher spiritual aspirations than were normally entertained in the middle years of the century."[77]

While he was in England, Hudson Taylor attended every Mildmay Conference, where he was often the featured speaker. In 1864, he experienced the second blessing there, and four months after his vision at Brighton Beach, he announced from the pulpit the formation of the "China Inland Mission," the first time the name appeared in print. That very morning he had received the first copies of *China: Its Spiritual Need and Claims*, his manifesto, and Pennefather "gave permission for the pamphlet to be sold at the doors and for me to plead for China in the evening." As a result, he sold two hundred copies

---

71. Stock, *The History of the Church Missionary Society*, vol. 3, pp. 20-21.
72. Ibid., quoted in *HTCOC 3*, p. 390.
73. Carwardine, *Trans-atlantic Revivalism*, p. 172.
74. Bebbington, *Evangelicalism in Modern Britain*, chapter "The Mildmay Circle," pp. 159-64.
75. *HTCOC 3*, p. 390.
76. *China's Millions* (GB), July 1888, p. 77.
77. Bebbington, *Evangelicalism in Modern Britain*, p. 159.

that day.[78] After Pennefather's death in 1873, Taylor's close relations continued with his widow, who carried on the work for twenty-five years. ("My dear," Geraldine Guinness whispered, "Mrs. Pennefather *was* Mildmay.")

The Helpers

The road to Zion was dangerous, Taylor warned those who applied to become one of his team. "Their funds may become exhausted . . . and communication with the free ports may be difficult or impossible. Or they may be robbed of all they possess, and may find themselves destitute in the midst of strangers. But they cannot be robbed of His presence and aid, whose are the gold and the silver, and the cattle on a thousand hills."[79]

On 26 May 1866, the "*Lammermuir* party" sailed for China, commemorated ever after as "Lammermuir Day." In addition to Hudson Taylor and Maria (two months pregnant, her seventh) and their children (Gracie, age seven, Herbert five, Howard four, and Samuel two), the team consisted of sixteen adults: one married couple, Lewis and Eliza Nicol, five single men, and nine single women (see Appendix 1). What was exceptional was their ordinariness. Five came from London and one from Barnsley, making a total of ten from England; five came from Banffshire, Scotland, a center of spontaneous revivals, and one woman from Limerick, Ireland. Including those he had sent before and after the *Lammermuir*, by the end of 1867, Taylor had thirty-five missionaries under his aegis, making the CIM — from the beginning — the largest mission in China.

There was something experimental, almost casual, about Taylor's recruitment of single women. "The younger they were the sooner they would be fluent in Chinese," he remarked rather bloodlessly. Mary Bausum was family, Maria's stepsister, the daughter of her stepfather's second wife. She was only fifteen, returning to teach in her mother's school, yet she was "considered one of the party and not as a child."[80] Mary Bell and Mary Bowyer were Anglican deaconesses, graduates of the Mildmay college. In addition, there were two other teachers and two governesses. Louise Desgraz, the Taylor family's Swiss governess, had been employed by William Collingwood, a well-known watercolor painter in Liverpool who had once aspired to join Gutzlaff as a missionary-artist. On the whole, reflecting the British class system, the

---

78. *HTCOC 4*, pp. 83-86.
79. Ibid., pp. 57-58.
80. Ibid., p. 106.

women tended to be better educated than the men, some of whom could barely sign their name.

Two women stood out, Jane Faulding known as Jennie (she was to become the second Mrs. Hudson Taylor) and Emily Blatchley, members of Regent's Park chapel, a prominent Baptist church where Taylor had many friends. Jennie had known Taylor since she was nine, before he went to China, and at nineteen she was mature enough to know God was calling her, and that she could trust Hudson Taylor with her life. Her father, a wealthy piano manufacturer who supported Taylor's work in the abstract, was not so sure when his daughter started attending prayer meetings in the mission home. He took some persuading, through the intervention of the minister Dr. William Landels, who took Jennie's side. Emily Blatchley was the opposite. She was from a working class, non-Christian family who gave her permission to go to China. Desperately shy, she was another Amelia, who glowed with love for Hudson Taylor, and in her eyes he could do no wrong. As preparation, both women attended the Home and Colonial Training College, near Gray's Inn.

At a meeting for "the deepening of the spiritual life" in Perth, Scotland, Taylor received three applications, including that of George Duncan, a gentle giant, a stonemason "not specially gifted or cultured" but a "stalwart Highlander possessed of great grit and perseverance — a man in the frontier tradition." Years later, Taylor reminisced that the pioneers were "humble people. If they were to offer to our Mission now they might not be accepted — George Duncan, for example," who was "willing to live anywhere and endure anything if only souls might be saved."[81] Lewis Nicol, a blacksmith from Arbroath, and his fiancée Eliza Calder, wrote unctuously that their evangelistic experience had been limited to teaching Sunday school and visiting "the low dens of iniquity."[82] At Liverpool, eight or nine persons gathered in a snowstorm: "Half of those present either became missionaries themselves or gave one or more of their children to be missionaries and the rest became permanent supporters at home."[83]

In Eversden, near Cambridge, Annie Macpherson, the headmistress of a boarding school for girls, gathered an evening class of young men, including Will Rudland, an "agricultural engineer" (a blacksmith who fixed farm machinery). He put a sign "Quench not the Spirit" above his forge, and "got hold of a book on Chinese and tried to study it in the evenings by forge firelight."

---

81. Barr, *To China with Love*, p. 33.
82. *HTCOC 4*, pp. 81-82.
83. Ibid., p. 124.

Watching the "ravens ... over the autumnal fields [he] longed to commit himself recklessly to their care."[84] (Miss Macpherson moved to London, where she opened an orphanage, and in 1869 escorted her first five hundred children to Canada.)[85]

As significant as the applicants that Hudson Taylor accepted were those he rejected. The "patently unsuitable" were easy to weed out. Others were too "denominational" on matters like paedo-baptism and come-out separation. Still others had strong personalities who would have challenged his authority, such as Tom Barnardo, one of Guinness's Dublin group. Barnardo became so besotted that he followed Taylor to London to pursue his application, and stayed with the Taylors at the Coburn Street House. (During World War II, Number 30 Coburn Street miraculously escaped the German Blitz while everything around was destroyed. It is now commemorated with a blue historic marker as Dr. Barnardo's first home in London, with no mention of Hudson Taylor or the CIM.) Taylor tried to put him off, suggesting Barnardo take a medical degree to equip himself. He was "so overbearing that it tries some of us a little," Taylor wrote. Finally he was turned down because of his "strong Plymouth Brethren beliefs — 'peculiarities' was the word used — and his unwillingness to accept the necessity of [Taylor's] 'headship and government' in the China Mission as well as his inexperience."[86]

Barnardo found his calling when he chanced upon a destitute boy — "Jim Jarvis, My First Street Arab" — who guided him through the warrens of Whitechapel, under bridges and over rooftops, pointing out bundles of children, "heaps on 'em! More'n I could count."[87] Although Barnardo moved away from his Brethren background, he remained a CIM referee, and every party of departing missionaries held a farewell meeting at Dr. Barnardo's Homes and Miss Macpherson's Home of Industry — presumably to teach the orphans that children in China were worse off than they were, and that they should be grateful for what had been given to them. And, over the years, some of Barnardo's orphans found a home in inland China.

Another applicant whom Taylor rejected was Timothy Richard, an eloquent Welshman who became "one of the most greatest missionaries to China." A convert of 1859, Richard was a student at Haverfordwest Baptist College in Wales. "But as I was a Baptist, they recommended me to apply to

---

84. Barr, *To China with Love*, p. 9.
85. Bagnell, *Little Immigrants*, pp. 19-27 and throughout, discusses Annie Macpherson from a Canadian perspective.
86. For Barnardo and JHT, see Wagner, *Barnardo*, pp. 14-23. *HTCOC 4*, pp. 118-19 and throughout.
87. Wagner, *Barnardo*, p. 33.

the Baptist Missionary Society," was his terse comment — but then, his relations with the CIM always were terse. Richard finished his education, was ordained, and went to China with the English Baptists, where he became a pioneer in Shandong.[88] We shall meet him again in Chinese dress.

The General Director

Determined not to repeat the disaster of the Chinese Evangelisation Society, Taylor named himself general director of the CIM in order to give himself "flexibility and finality in decision-making."[89] The general director, he stated in *The Book of Arrangements of the C.I.M.* (1886), was "the highest authority and responsibility in the Mission . . . and ultimate appeal is to him. He himself should be a Missionary, and intimately acquainted with all the circumstances of the work in China; he must be a man of a loving and sympathetic disposition, a man of faith and prayer and one who has commended himself to his fellow workers in the field and at home. With the right man in this post, all other needful arrangements can be rendered valid." Moira McKay comments, "Taylor did not become a dictator to satisfy his own megalomania but because he was convinced that it was far better to have authority vested in one man than in a committee."[90]

Hudson Taylor did not see himself as the remote head of a multinational corporation dispatching agents hither and yon, but as a benign father figure with an extended family of "helpers," who would give him prompt and loyal obedience (as his father put it) as they would obey God. They must be spirited enough to survive in China, but not so independent to challenge his leadership. W. T. Berger suggested a formal written contract with each missionary, but Taylor felt that would be unnecessary, that a "verbal pact involving loyalty based on mutual confidence and love could be stronger by far than any written bond."[91]

As the only *man* with field experience — both Maria and Mary Bausum had lived most of their lives in China — Taylor spoke forcefully to the recruits. "In the first place," runs his pencilled memorandum,

---

88. Timothy Richard, *Forty-Five Years in China: Reminiscences by Timothy Richard* (New York: Frederick A. Stokes Company, 1916), p. 29; William E. Soothill, *Timothy Richard of China: Seer, Statesman, Missionary & the Most Disinterested Adviser the Chinese Ever Had* (London: Seeley, Service & Co., 1924), p. 27; *HTCOC 3*, p. 193.
89. *HTCOC 4*, p. 69.
90. McKay, "Faith and Facts," p. 148.
91. *HTCOC 4*, pp. 107-8.

it was stated that I was feeling called by God to do a work in China, in which I desired helpers. That such helpers must be satisfied that God has called them individually to labour in China for the good of the Chinese; must go to China on *their own responsibility;* and must look to *God* for their support, and trust *Him* to provide it, and not lean on me....

As to guidance and direction, it was stated that in every respect what I deemed requisite must be complied with. That *where* we should go to, where and when different individuals should be located, the positions they should occupy, etc., must be left to me to determine....

That it was not for the brethren themselves to decide what they were fit for, or when they were to go, but that in all points save those of conscience on which Christians of various denominations differed, it was to be understood fully that I should direct.

... that the relation between us was this: — that as far as possible they should feel responsible for affording me all the help in their power in the work of the Mission, and that I should feel myself responsible for guiding, directing, and helping — pecuniarily and otherwise — as I might be able, and deem advisable, those assisting me.[92]

In his letters, Taylor did not mince words:

it is as *helpers* in the work among the *Chinese* that we desire and pray for your co-operation and fellowship. We do not request you to assist us in the general direction of affairs of the mission, either at home or in China; nor do we ask you to share in our responsibilities as trustees for the funds committed to our care. Nothing is further from our thought than the formation of a committee or committees for the management of our affairs.... None of you will suppose that immediately on your arrival in China you will be in a position of such knowledge of the language, people, habits, etc, or of the local peculiarities of the work, as would enable you to give any real help in the direction of affairs.[93]

In 1903, when Hudson Taylor retired and appointed D. E. Hoste as acting general director, he defined his "system of government." The CIM was not a church, he wrote,

---

92. A. J. Broomhall dates this document to 2 February 1866, while McKay, "Faith and Facts," p. 15, dates it to the first *Principles & Practice of the CIM* (1867).

93. JHT to Berger, July 1867, in *HTCOC* 4, p. 353.

but a voluntary union of members of various denominations agreeing to band themselves together to obey the Saviour's last command in respect to China; holding in common the same fundamental truths, accepting the Directorship rule of the Mission, and receiving where needful, such ministrations as God may make possible from its funds.

The first Directors (J. Hudson Taylor and W. T. Berger), were not selected by a body of Donors on the one hand, nor, on the other, by a body of workers in China, — no such bodies then existing in connection with us; but they believed themselves called of God. God justified them in this conclusion, by providing the co-operation of donors and of Christian men and women of various capacities, who gave themselves to the work. As it grew, and as circumstances called for them, Councils, Secretaries, Treasurers, Directors, etc., have been given for the home work; and in like manner, among the workers in China, men and women for various posts have been raised up and appointed. None of these have been *elected*, but all have been *selected*, according to their God-given or acquired capacities. It is to those whom we may call the rank and file among us, however, that God has given the special privilege of devoting themselves *entirely* to giving the Gospel to the heathen and building up the native churches, — the work for which the Mission exists, and to which they felt themselves called of God. Others have had to give more or less of thought and time to the help of their brethren. . . .

If the Directors and Members of our Councils are godly and wise men, walking in the spirit of unity and love, they will not lack Divine guidance in important matters, and at critical times; but should another spirit ever prevail, no rules could save the Mission nor would it be worth saving.[94]

These last sentences are harsh, uncompromising words written by an old man who had weathered many battles over directorship and "democracy." More than once "another spirit" had prevailed and Hudson Taylor had despaired that the directors and councils were neither godly nor wise.

---

94. "Letters written by The Rev. J. Hudson Taylor on the occasion of his retirement from the office of General Director, in January, 1903, relating to the appointment and other matters appertaining to the position of General Director and other officers of the China Inland Mission," CIM/ABGC, file 5/12.

The Lammermuir party, May 1866. After his "Brighton vision" in June 1865, Hudson Taylor recruited about thirty missionaries for the CIM, and sailed with "the first party" on the *Lammermuir*. This photograph, taken in the garden of Pyrland Road a few days before their departure, was widely distributed for publicity. Hudson Taylor (front center) sits surrounded by his family, between his first wife, Maria Dyer (right), and Jennie Faulding, who became his second wife after Maria's death, with four children in front. Emily Blatchley stands behind him. Will Rudland, the blacksmith, is second from left front, next to the troublemakers, Lewis and Eliza Nicol.   Source: Marshall Broomhall, *The Jubilee Story of the China Inland Mission* (London: CIM, 1915)

The Last of England

"China, China, China is now ringing in our ears," wrote Spurgeon, "in that special, peculiar, musical, forcible, unique way in which Mr. Taylor utters it."

The year of frenzied activity came to an end. Taylor had given his team their marching orders. The tickets for eighteen adults and four children (who counted as one adult) cost a total of over £800 ($4,000 U.S.). Farewell meetings were held at dozens of churches throughout London. Three hundred pieces of luggage, wooden crates, and lead-lined trunks, each carefully labeled, were piled at the East India docks. The "printing and lithography presses, with type and other accessories," and "a large supply of medicines, with the requisite apparatus for commencing a hospital and dispensary," were stowed in the hold.[95]

A historic photograph was taken of "the *Lammermuir* party" and sold at one shilling for the whole party, or sixpence for individual portraits. George Duncan, the Scottish mason, stands head and shoulders above the rest. James Williamson and John Sell appear mature and strong, while Will Rudland, the Cambridge blacksmith, poses awkwardly but unselfconsciously among the girls. Lewis and Eliza Nicol, the married couple, are seated and relaxed. Mary Bausum, the fifteen-year-old, is holding Mary Bowyer's hand. Jennie Faulding is seated with little Grace Taylor leaning against her knee. Hudson Taylor and Maria hold the two older boys, while Emily Blatchley directly behind them is half hidden, with a shy smile.[96]

Five days after Taylor's thirty-fourth birthday, a large and emotional group of well-wishers gathered at the East India docks. The Howards and Miss Stacey came from Tottenham, Mr. Berger from East Grinstead with two of his factory managers, and representatives of church and mission societies. Hudson's mother came from Barnsley, and stood beside her daughter — the two Amelias. John McCarthy recited the epic poem by Grattan Guinness entitled "The Voice of Thy Brother's Blood." Taylor left everything in Mr. Berger's hand, but gave him no instructions, except to look "prayerfully to God for guidance, [and] to act without unnecessary delay in every matter as it arose."[97]

After the well-wishers had dispersed, each caught up in his or her own thoughts, one person remained on the dock, and for her the parting was a bit-

---

95. *HTCOC* 4, p. 211.
96. For the *Lammermuir* voyage, see ibid., pp. 145-208; description of photograph at p. 157.
97. Ibid., p. 70.

ter disappointment. She had literally given up everything to sail on the *Lammermuir*, but at the last moment the doctors forbade her; now she was homeless and penniless. Her name was Grace Ciggie, aged twenty, a tough street evangelist from Glasgow who had been raised by her grandmother after her parents died, then by a friend, who also died. At one meeting, she approached Hudson Taylor. "I had no home ties, it was true; but was I fit? Then, too, I had never heard of a young girl going to a heathen land — was it practicable? This latter question I decided to ask Mr. Taylor. He saw no reason why I should not go, even though but twenty years of age, if called of God, and if called, surely the fitness would be given by Him."

After the *Lammermuir* sailed down the Thames, Grace took a boat to Glasgow because it was cheaper than the train, and returned to the Salt Market, "one of the vilest and most wicked places in Glasgow, inhabited almost exclusively by thieves and women of ill-repute. It was hardly fit for a man to go into such a place — could it be God was sending a young girl there, uncalled by man, unprotected, and without means of support — could that be God's will for me?"[98] The Salt Market proved a good preparation for China.

Grace Ciggie finally sailed for China in 1869. By then she was engaged to George Stott, whom she had met once, four years before on the East India docks. Stott, an irascible character, had been a farmer near Aberdeen who lost a leg to tuberculosis and became a schoolteacher. When he heard Taylor's call, he thought to himself, "surely no Society would have sent a lame man to such a country to pioneer work," but he applied anyway, saying, "I do not see those with two legs going, so I must go." Taylor fitted him up with an artificial leg — "Stott's leg or outfit" appears regularly in the correspondence[99] — and sent him a few months ahead of the *Lammermuir*. After their hastily arranged marriage in Shanghai, George and Grace returned to his station in Wenzhou, where they remained for twenty-six years, until his death.

Who would have suspected that within five years, four of the *Lammermuir* party — all young people in good health — would have died, and four more by 1874? Little Gracie Taylor died in 1868, a cathartic moment, followed by Maria and five-year-old Samuel in 1870; George Duncan died in London in 1873, where he had been sent to recuperate from tuberculosis. By contrast, Will Rudland labored for forty years in Taizhou, where he died in 1913, after the Chinese Revolution — the last surviving member.

---

98. Ibid., p. 105; Grace Stott, *Twenty-six Years of Missionary Work in China* (London: Hodder & Stoughton, 1897), pp. 2-4.

99. *HTCOC* 4, p. 65.

APPENDIX 1

Passengers on the Lammermuir 26 May 1866

Hudson Taylor — age 34.
Maria Dyer Taylor — age 29, d. Zhenjiang 1870.
Grace Dyer Taylor — b. Ningbo 1859 — d. Hangzhou 1867.
Herbert Hudson Taylor — b. London 1861 — CIM missionary 1881.
Frederick Howard Taylor — b. London 1862 — CIM missionary, member of London, China, and Philadelphia Councils, CIM historian — d. 1946.
Samuel Dyer Taylor — b. Barnsley 1864 — d. Zhenjiang 1870.
Lewis Nicol — blacksmith from Arbroath, Aberdeen — leader of anti-JHT faction, cause of "Xiaoshan outrage" — fired 1867.
Eliza Calder, his wife — from Arbroath — fired 1867.
George Duncan — stonemason from Banffshire — m. Catherine Brown 1872 — d. 1873 in London of TB.
Josiah Jackson — carpenter/draper from Mildmay — "let go" by JHT 1884, returned to Shanghai in secular business — d. 1906 Shanghai.
William Rudland — blacksmith from Eversden, Cambridgeshire — m. Mary Bell, and two other wives — d. 1913, still member of CIM.
John R. Sell — from Romford, Essex — engaged to Jane McLean — d. 1867 Ningbo of smallpox.
James Williamson — carpenter from Arbroath — CIM explorer — m. 1878, still in CIM in 1891.
Susan Barnes — from Limerick — resigned 1867.
Mary Bausum — age 15, Maria Taylor's stepsister, joining her stepmother in Ningbo — m. Stephan Barchet (pre-*Lammermuir* pioneer) 1868, they resigned same year over believer's baptism and church governance.
Jane (Jennie) Faulding — Baptist from Regent Park Chapel — graduate of

Home and Colonial Training College — m. JHT in London 1871 — d. 1903 at Davos, Switzerland.

Emily Blatchley — Regent Park Chapel — graduate of Home and Colonial Training College, "rt. hand secretary" of CIM — d. 1874 of TB.

Mary Bell — from Malvern — m. Rudland — d. 1874.

Mary Bowyer — Anglican, Mildmay deaconess school — m. F. W. Baller (sinologue, head of CIM language school, compiler of dictionaries) 1874 — d. 1909.

Louise Desgraz — from Switzerland, governess to Collingwood family — m. Edward Tomalin 1878 — d. 1909.

Jane McLean — Anglican biblewoman from Inverness — graduate of Mildmay deaconess school — joined by her twin sister Margaret in 1867 — both resigned 1868 after Sell's death to join LMS in Shanghai.

Elizabeth Rose — Methodist, from Barnsley — m. James Meadows (pre-*Lammermuir*) 1866 — d. 1890.

CHAPTER 4

The Land of Strangers
1866-1875

SPEED thy servants, Saviour, speed them,
Thou art Lord of winds and waves;
They were bound, but thou hast freed them,
Now they go to free the slaves;
Be thou with them:
'Tis thine arm alone that saves. . . .
    When they reach the land of strangers,
    And the prospect dark appears,
    Nothing seen but toils and dangers,
    Nothing felt but doubts and fears,
    Be thou with them:
    Hear their sighs, and count their tears. . . .
        John Wesley, *Collection of Hymns for the People called Methodists*

The First Generation

Once again the Pilgrim is at sea. Hudson Taylor has assembled his little band and (as his Irish friend put it) set out to traverse the dark blue sea to "the distant land of Sinim," that mythical realm of idolatry. He tried to warn them in his oracular way that it "was necessary between the comforts of home and the privations of China to have a sea voyage to break us in."[1] How different was this voyage from the first — but the world had changed since 1853. Then, he

1. *HTCOC* 4, p. 158.

had been alone and friendless, an odd sparrow seeking his vocation, traveling on a leaky sailing ship. Then, he had agonized about swimming-belts and "human means." Now he was responsible for twenty-one souls, his wife and four children, and sixteen adults. They were traveling in comparative luxury, the only passengers on the *Lammermuir,* a new clipper ship (a smaller version of the famous *Cutty Sark*), powered by steam and sail. After paying for their outfits and passages, the China Inland Mission still had £2,000 [$10,000 U.S.] in the Bank of England and 900 taels (ounces of silver) in credit at the "Oriental Banking Corporation" in Shanghai.

But something went fearfully wrong. A mutiny broke out over a pair of stockings! His daughter-in-law put it elliptically in her official history: "Never surely were travelers more prayed for, as the long months of the voyage wore on, and none could have more needed such aid . . . ; and, very determined were the onslaughts of the enemy, first to wreck the unity and spiritual power of the missionary party, and then to wreck the ship on which they traveled, sending them all to the bottom."[2] There had been personality conflicts before they left England, but everyone had been on their best behavior and deferred to Taylor's leadership. Now, on board ship, "personalities were being changed before [their] eyes." The "devil possessed" first mate was saved and became a lamb, while the missionaries dissolved into factions.

By the time they reached the equator, Taylor reported there were "germs of ill-feeling and division among our party." Lewis Nicol — the Scottish blacksmith, whom Pat Barr characterized as "an obstinate, whining, social climber"[3] — discovered that someone had forgotten to pack an extra pair of stockings in his outfit. He had seen "a list of articles supplied to the Presbyterian missionaries," and they received better outfits. Taylor apologized and offered to give Lewis a pair of his own stockings, as well as "light clothes" for the tropics, adding that everyone had "a good useful outfit, for which we ought to be thankful." As for the Presbyterians, he reminded him in a conflation of English and Chinese class consciousness, they "were persons of different position in society; and that moreover they were to wear these [Western] things when in China, which we should not do."[4] Then Nicol refused to join the communion service in the saloon since the converted sailors were neither baptized nor church members.

2. *Growth of a Work of God,* pp. 70-71.
3. Barr, *To China with Love,* p. 10; *HTCOC* 4, more circumspect, called Nicol "a brawny blacksmith of twenty-three."
4. *HTCOC* 4, p. 181; for examples of outfits, Miss Jean Notman (1864) and George Crombie (1865), see pp. 470-71. Hers included "1 winter dress, 2 skirts, 1 crinoline. . . ." His included "frock coat, doe trousers, waistcoat, tweed trousers, coat, vest, 3 linen coats and vests," and so on.

A typical city street in China. A bean-curd (tofu) seller's shop near the women's language school in Yangzhou. The scene would be familiar to many CIM missionary pioneers, who were the first Westerners, wearing Chinese clothes, to visit many inland cities. Their reception could range from idle curiosity to hostile riots, even death.   Source: OMF/Toronto.

As they steamed through the Straits of Malacca, the dividing line between West and East, the Anglican deaconesses, Mary Bowyer and Jane McLean, asked Taylor to baptize them. They had been baptized as infants and had graduated from Mildmay, but studying the Bible with Taylor convinced them "that they had never before received true baptism." (It was not uncommon during the long months of travel for missionaries to study the Bible and change their theological views: the exemplar was Adoniram Judson, who left Massachusetts a Congregationalist and arrived in India a Baptist, then challenged the Calvinist theology of Baptist foreign missions.) Taylor, remembering how he had impulsively baptized his sister Amelia, hesitated, weighing the consequences. At their insistence, he baptized them and Elizabeth Rose, a Barnsley Methodist "girl with little education," in a secluded stream at Anjer, at the tip of Java. If it were done, it were better to do it before they arrived in Shanghai, he reasoned, where the women would be under the nominal charge of the Church of England clergyman. (The baptisms were never reported publicly, lest Taylor be accused of "sheep stealing.")[5]

In the China Sea, a few days out of Shanghai, all hell broke loose. Looking at the red sunset, Taylor pronounced with a prescience worthy of Luke Howard that it was "like those preceding a typhoon . . . a strange, unearthly tone." The first typhoon spiraled them like a cork into the path of the second. For three weeks they could do nothing except "commend ourselves, and more especially the crew, to God's keeping." On 30 September 1866, after four months at sea, the *Lammermuir* limped into Shanghai, its sails shredded, and the masts splintered until they "hung by the wire shrouds; swinging about most fearfully." Miraculously, beyond bruises and dysentery — and Maria's pregnancy — not one life had been lost, nor one bone broken: the next ship arrived with only six survivors of twenty-two on board. "May we live as those who are alive from the dead," said Sister Rose.[6]

The Wicket-Gate, Again

The Taiping Rebellion had ended in a fiery reckoning in 1864 when the Heavenly King, Hong Xiuquan, committed suicide, or in the dynastic euphemism, "ascended to Heaven." A month later, in May, the Qing general Zeng Guofan

---

5. Ibid., pp. 92-93, "Baptisms at Anjer." The baptisms were not mentioned in *Growth of a Work of God*, except for an elliptical reference (p. 79), that "a spirit of discord again crept in. It was on different grounds this time and with other members of the party, but the outcome was the same — criticism, discontent, loss of power and blessing."

6. For typhoons, see *HTCOC 4*, pp. 196-208.

blew up the walls of Nanjing and massacred its inhabitants. He told the emperor, "Not one of the 100,000 rebels in Nanjing surrendered themselves when the city was taken but in many cases gathered together and burned themselves and passed away without repentance. Such a formidable band of rebels has been rarely known from ancient times to the present."[7]

During the Taiping Rebellion, Shanghai had been "a city of refuge" for up to a million Chinese, who had "rushed pell-mell along the roads and through the streets like a herd of stricken deer." (Hong Kong, Taiwan, and other treaty ports also grew rapidly with the explosion of refugees.) Now, two years later, Shanghai was a ghost town. "Across a fifty-mile swath of land one might see almost every house destroyed, wantonly burned by one side or the other, or stripped of its doors and roof beams . . . [and] villages where every man and boy has been pressed into service by one army or another, and the women carried off, where 'human bones lie bleaching among cannon balls' and only the elderly are left to pick among the debris. . . . On many riverbanks, sometimes for tens of miles, every hut or house is gutted and the people sleep as best they may under rough shelters of mats or reeds."[8]

The Second Opium (or Arrow) War ended with the harsh Treaty of Tientsin (1859) and the Peking Convention of 1860. One clause inserted in the French language version of the treaty — but not the Chinese version — by the French translator, a Roman Catholic priest, and copied by the British, American, and other "unequal treaties," granted foreign missionaries and traders the right to travel anywhere in the Chinese Empire, and to rent or buy property outside the treaty ports. Nevertheless, travel beyond the ports was dangerous and barely controlled by either the British or Chinese governments. As late as 1874, a British consul named Augustus Margary was murdered when he led an expedition from Burma into Yunnan. But then, he was wearing a tropical white suit and waving a Union Jack, which made him a target.

The day the *Lammermuir* docked in Shanghai, the *North China Herald* announced: "The doom of foreign residents in China is evidently sealed. A *jehad* has been proclaimed against them in Hunan and they are to be swept from the face of the Flowery Land."[9] This, despite its sarcasm, was the first warning of an anti-Christian crusade that was to continue more or less intermittently for thirty years. Changsha, the capital of Hunan, had resisted the Taiping siege for several years, in large part because Zeng Guofan, the provincial viceroy, orga-

---

7. Jonathan D. Spence, *The Search for Modern China* (New York: W. W. Norton, 1990), p. 178.

8. Spence, *God's Chinese Son*, pp. 305, 303.

9. *North China Herald*, 29 September 1866.

nized regional armies of "braves" (so called because they wore chest badges with the character "brave"). The military campaign against the Taipings was accompanied by a propaganda campaign against the "god-worshippers" in general, i.e. the Protestants who worshiped Shangdi, the One True God.

After the rebellion, a "torrent of violently anti-Christian pamphlets and tracts" emanated from Hunan. The most notorious was called "A True Record to Ward Off Heterodoxy," or "Death Blow to Corrupt Doctrines," which was regularly published into the 1890s. By a homonym in Chinese, the name for "the Lord of Heaven" (*Tianzhu*), the name the Roman Catholics selected to translate God, sounds with a different tone like "the Pig of Heaven." Like a perverse *Pilgrim's Progress*, the "True Record" is illustrated with woodcuts depicting the secret rituals of pigtailed Christians worshiping a crucified pig, which is stuck with arrows like St. Sebastian. It accused missionaries of bewitching the Chinese through the vapors of their printed books, of perverted sexual practices, and using human eyes to make medicine. This was the most common charge against missionaries from 1600 to 1950 — that the "Brigands of the religion of Jesus" "scooped out the eyes of the dying, opened foundling hospitals to eat the children, cut open pregnant women (for the purpose of making medicine of the infants), &c." A poster plastered on the CIM gate read: "What a beast is this Jesus whose venom has reached to China."[10] The "True Record" was such "a farrago of obscene calumnies" that the prim Victorian missionaries could not bring themselves to translate it in its entirety for an English audience.[11]

The Chinese government had no mechanism for dealing with "missionary cases" at the local level. Particularly serious "incidents," where gunboats were involved, would be taken up to the highest diplomatic level. After the Second Opium War, which ended in 1858, the Chinese government created the Zongli Yamen, the equivalent of a Ministry of Foreign Affairs, which dealt with the foreign ambassadors in Beijing. The Qing state launched a half-hearted "Self-Strengthening Movement" to rebuild the economic and agricultural base us-

---

10. Paul A. Cohen, *China and Christianity: The Missionary Movement and the Growth of Chinese Antiforeignism 1860-1870* (Cambridge: Harvard University Press, 1963), details the history of the *Bi-xie zhi-shi* ("A record of facts to ward off heterodoxy," 1861) and its abridged version *Bi-xie shi-lu* ("A true record to ward off heterodoxy"). The quote is from "Statement with Affidavit, made by Missionaries from Yangchow," signed by JHT, George Duncan, William Rudland, and Henry Reid, to Consul W. H. Medhurst, 31 August 1868, in British Foreign Office, *British Parliamentary Papers*, vol. 29, *China: Correspondence, Dispatches, Circulars and other Papers Respecting Missionaries in China 1868-72* (Shannon: Irish University Press, 1971), pp. 15-16.

11. Cohen, *China and Christianity*, p. 47.

ing Western technology (guns, arsenals, railways, telegraphs) and Chinese ideas. This was a failure in the long run, only delaying the inevitable revolution until 1911. The Taiping Rebellion might have been that revolution — one of those great "what ifs" that historians ponder — it *could* have changed China, and indeed, came within a hair's breadth of succeeding. After its defeat, its revolutionary Christian ideology also had to be crushed. The local magistrates, guided by the traditional rules for the management of barbarians and the regulation of heterodox religions, did not know how to deal with these new missionaries wandering through their districts, preaching seditious doctrines, yet who must be protected according to foreign treaties.

The British consuls, too, had to adjust to the new rules, though their adjustment was complicated by the changed relations with the Foreign Office in London. The opening of telegraph lines across Russia meant that diplomatic communications, which used to take six months for a letter from Shanghai to London, and a year for a reply, now took a fortnight or less. Whitehall took more effective control in dealing with the Chinese government, state to state, issuing instructions to its agents, who were expected to implement the policies in the field. P. D. Coates, the official historian of the China consular service, noted, "Henceforward consuls were tamer officials who were expected to deal with local issues in accordance with general Legation guidance, to negotiate as many local settlements as they could, and to refer unresolved disputes to the Legation. Direct influence from the consulates on the shaping of British policy towards China had virtually ceased."[12]

Meanwhile, there was a distinct hardening of attitude among the consuls that Coates called "more and more minatory." In 1864 Sir F. W. A. Bruce, retiring as ambassador, warned Lord John Russell at Whitehall concerning "the tradition among British consular officers of imposing settlements on the Chinese without seeking to persuade them, a method which might carry particular matters through but could not achieve friendly relations." The following year, Russell reminded the incoming ambassador, Sir John Rutherford Alcock — a veteran China diplomat who was then ambassador to Japan — that he should "strongly inculcate the importance of consular officers cultivating friendly relations, adding that the Chinese were not barbarians but according to oriental notions highly civilized and that in recent years they had been perfectly disposed to listen to reason." Nevertheless, right up to 1900, the British Legation stressed that representations to the Qing government would be disregarded unless they were accompanied by threats and force.[13]

12. Coates, *The China Consuls*, pp. 151-52.
13. Ibid., p. 156.

THE FIRST GENERATION

In the treaty ports, Coates concluded, the consular officers "tended to act much like referees in a football match, trying impartially to ensure that Chinese authorities and British merchants observed the treaty rules for the commercial game and not themselves participating in the game." The expansion of the missionary force in response to the opening of China, determined to push their treaty rights to the limit, upset the rules. The Foreign Office tended to be cool to missionaries: one consul summed up the general attitude when he asked what would happen "if Buddhist or Taoist priests built temples in England and went round the country to denounce Christianity as a farce." He concluded, "I don't see what you have to complain about." In 1864 the Foreign Office stipulated "that the claim to acquire land in the interior should not at present be asserted, in 1869 [it] spoke of injudicious missionary proceedings, and in 1871 correctly forecast that unchecked Christian propaganda would either end in the expulsion or massacre of missionaries or end in more hostilities, ruinously expensive and disastrous both for the Chinese state and for trade."[14]

By 1866 the Protestant missionary contingent had grown to two hundred men and women, mostly British, though Americans were increasing in numbers. Although missionaries could travel into "the interior," few ventured beyond the treaty ports, the original five of 1842 and the nine added in 1860. Some did manage to "occupy" a neighboring city, but opening a station was fraught with difficulty. The British consul could refuse the permit, or as a last resort withdraw the missionary's passport. Renting a house — buying one was impossible for another ten years at least — had to be done with subterfuge, by middlemen, and if the negotiations were discovered by the Chinese authorities, the offending landlord would be punished severely. Once the missionary managed to rent a property, he would literally sit down and "possess" it. George Stott stalked Wenzhou as his "prey," and once he had rented a house he refused to leave the city for two and a half years, seeing no other foreigner. He left only to pick up his bride Grace Ciggie. Whenever a crowd threatened, he would take off his wooden leg and wave it in their faces to shame them for persecuting a one-legged man.[15]

Into this blasted landscape, Hudson Taylor was proposing to take his naïve "helpers," far beyond the consuls' reach, disguised in Chinese gowns and queues. However pious his rhetoric, he was determined to enter "Inland China"

---

14. Ibid., pp. 171, 179-80.
15. Because he went to China before the *Lammermuir*, George and Grace Stott wore Western clothes. In her autobiography, *Twenty-Six Years of Missionary Work in China*, Grace never mentioned the subject of Chinese dress — most unusual for a CIM biography; furthermore the photographs show her and her husband in Western clothes.

by enforcing his treaty rights if necessary. He was to change his mind later, after bitter experience with the heavy hand of British diplomacy. Even such a dispassionate observer as Hosea Ballou Morse, in *The International Relations of the Chinese Empire* (1918), claimed Taylor started the CIM "for the purpose of forcing the previously unsettled question of the right of residence inland, and of 'planting the shining cross on every hill and in every valley of China.'"[16]

One of the casualties of the Taiping defeat was Karl Gutzlaff's dream of the Chinese Union, the blitz-conversion of China by "native agency," that is, by paid or unpaid preachers who would itinerate ahead of the foreign missionary, like John the Baptist preparing the way for the Messiah. It was not just a difference of style. Conventional missionaries, frightened by the violence, retreated inside their compounds, where they invited the natives to enter their foreign churches and schools. Hudson Taylor's strategy of extensive itinerations, rather than intensive church-building, upset the diplomatic balance. So did Chinese dress, the use of native evangelists and biblewomen, and the deployment of unmarried women in inland China. (In 1866 there were only thirteen unmarried Protestant women missionaries in China, such as the teachers and nurses of the Society for Promoting Female Education in the East, who were confined to Hong Kong. Hudson Taylor's women were the first to travel inland.)

But Gutzlaff's concept of "native agency" did not die. He had taught William Chalmers Burns, the English Presbyterian who had introduced "the seed-thoughts" that were to become institutionalized in the China Inland Mission. Theologically, as Jessie and Ray Lutz have noted, Gutzlaff's strategy went to the heart of missions: the very definition of a Christian and the qualifications of an evangelist. This was the difference between Gutzlaff's (and Müller's) German pietism and confessional missionaries such as the CMS and LMS, who sought to reproduce "daughter" denominations in foreign countries. "Gützlaff was interested in promoting an awareness of sin and a conversionary experience of rebirth. . . . Christian communities would come into existence and continuing instruction occur after baptism, but Gützlaff defined a Christian as one who had seen the light and accepted Jesus' offer of grace."[17]

Moreover, he did not expect a changed life initially among his converts.

Gützlaff argued throughout that if one treated Chinese Christians as children, they would respond as children, taking no responsibility; if

---

16. Hosea Ballou Morse, *The International Relations of the Chinese Empire*, 2 vols. (London: Longmans, Green, & Co., 1918), vol. 2, p. 226.
17. Lutz and Lutz, "Gützlaff's Approach," p. 271.

one treated them as adults and gave them responsibility, they would respond accordingly and accept the duty of evangelism as their own. Like many of pietist persuasion, he looked for a conversionary experience as the mark of a Christian. A sense of sin, repentance, and rebirth was fundamental; outward practices, no matter how desirable, did not define a Christian. Future growth in Christian knowledge and moral reform would follow conversion as the Holy Spirit and the missionary did their work. He took sinners where they were; lapses were disturbing, though not necessarily cause for excommunication. Rather one should love and trust the sinner and bring him to renewed repentance. True to his pen name, Gaihan [*aihan*, Lover of the Chinese], Gützlaff never abandoned his love for the Chinese people nor his goal of the conversion of China in his lifetime. To do so would have been to acknowledge that his life had been a failure.[18]

The same could be said of Hudson Taylor.

The Pigtailed Tribe

When the *Lammermuir* party finally reached Shanghai they were given space in an empty *go-down* (warehouse) to unpack their outfits and spread out their sea-wet clothes to dry. They succumbed to a turmoil of emotions, "ready to sing" one moment and depressed the next. "I cried bitterly and could not help it," said John Sell, who had been seasick for four months. Jennie Faulding, the brightest and most observant, was cheered by the colonial architecture of the Bund, the boulevard along the riverfront. "There is so much English mixed with what is foreign," she wrote approvingly. "I heard the gong of evening idol-worship, but we got back in time for Christian Chinese worship in a nice chapel under Mr. Gamble's house. . . . I could understand a good deal." She saw many idols and idol-worship, which were "a lurid demonstration of the enslavement by Satan of those who were 'without God and without hope.'"[19]

Hudson Taylor remained in Shanghai for only one day before he set sail again to take two young women to Ningbo, Mary Bausum to join her stepmother, and Elizabeth Rose to marry her fiancé James Meadows after four years apart. Taylor had lived in Ningbo, had married Maria Dyer there, and

18. Ibid., pp. 279-80.
19. *HTCOC* 4, pp. 222-23.

spoke the dialect. He had dispatched twelve pioneers there in advance of the *Lammermuir* between 1860 and 1866, and hoped to make it his base of operations. Taylor was pleased that the men and women had begun to move outside the city: the Crombies and George Stott at Fenghua, thirty miles south, and John Stevenson at Shaoxing, ninety miles west. However, Taylor was distressed that they had all gone back to wearing Western clothing, eating Western food with knives and forks, and all that entailed. Moreover, they refused to accept "the Lammermuir pact," the written statement everyone had signed on board ship, which reinforced Taylor's leadership, designated the missionaries as his "helpers," and stipulated Chinese dress.

Putting on Chinese clothes was not a case of button, button, where's the button? In a hierarchical society like China where every button, every peacock feather, every ripple of silk — the symbolism of every color — denoted one's status, how did one choose the correct costume? Back in the seventeenth century the Jesuit Matteo Ricci put on the saffron robes of a Buddhist priest, but once he found out how despised priests were by the Chinese gentry, he exchanged it for the silk robes of a court scholar to convert China from the top down. Ever since, missionaries who adopted Chinese clothes chose a secular costume like Confucian gentlemen. They did not want the Chinese to confuse them with Buddhist priests. That would give quite the wrong message: the credulous people might expect a miracle.

Nineteenth-century Protestants who "went native" were quite experimental: silk gown or cotton; Chinese gown and Western pith helmet and shoes ("top and bottom," as it was called); gown, felt boots and umbrella, but no pigtail; pigtails, real or false, black or blond. Chauncey Goodrich took to wearing "formal Chinese dress" when he arrived in Peking in the 1860s,[20] as did Timothy Richard, who would wear his Imperial Order of the Double Dragon emblazoned on his chest. Even Hudson Taylor could dress up when he had to, like "a Chinese gentleman in official costume" straight out of the eighteenth-century novel *The Scholars*, wearing a "long blue silk robe, confined by a girdle round the waist, and over this, a short jacket of dark brown satin; black satin boots, and a cap with a very broad brim, red tassel, and a gilt button (the 'mark of literary distinction')."[21] The everyday costume of the CIM was more humble, as befitted their social station in England. Their cotton gowns, thin in summer and wadded in winter, and thick paper-soled boots made them look like poor teachers.

It was easier for a male English shop assistant to pass through the needle's

---

20. Ibid., p. 321.
21. Ibid., p. 302.

eye and emerge as a Chinese teacher than for an Irish governess to become a Chinese lady. One Western stereotype was that in China, the men wore skirts and pigtails, while the women wore trousers. The CIM women wore wide "blue trousers, a silk pair for best occasions and cotton for everyday wear, with a black apron wrapped over itself at the back." It felt "clumsy," and since they had to adopt Chinese hair styles, they felt it was not "natural to go without either hat or bonnet, and many other things we have been accustomed to wear."[22]

Maria Taylor had never worn Chinese dress in all her years in China, even after their marriage. She put it on only after her husband suggested she set an example for the *Lammermuir* women. "I had a misgiving before leaving England," she wrote to Mrs. Berger, "about the *ladies* wearing Chinese dress on this ground: — the Chinese despise their own families, while they respect foreign ladies; will they treat us with as much respect, and shall we have as much weight with them, if we change our dress? . . . I know that those who prefer the foreign dress think that it commands respect," she concluded. "It commands *fear*, not respect; and far be it from us to wish to inspire such fear."[23] The *North China Herald* inveighed against the "injustice" and "cruelty" of forcing foreign women to wear Chinese gowns. Hudson Taylor, it thundered, was "either a fool or a knave, and we have reason to believe that Mr. Taylor is not a fool."[24]

When "we first come out from England," one CIM woman remarked, "we have all our English ideas. We go scampering about through the streets, and that does not do at all."[25] Maria Taylor warned, "Things which are tolerated in us as *foreigners* in *foreign* dress could not be allowed for one moment in native ladies. . . . But the nearer we come to the Chinese in outward appearance, the more severely will any breach of their notions of propriety be criticized. Henceforth I must never be guilty, for instance, of taking my husband's arm in the street! And in fifty or a hundred other ways we may most inadvertently shock the Chinese by what would seem to them grossly immodest and unfeminine conduct."[26]

An unmarried woman traveling alone or with another woman is a stock character in Chinese tales, and invariably she is in disguise, running away, a mendicant nun or healer, an immoral woman, a fairy or demon, or all of the

22. Ibid., pp. 233, 239.
23. Maria Taylor, 14 June 1867, in ibid., pp. 332-33.
24. Ibid., pp. 226-27.
25. *China's Millions* (NA), July 1896, p. 90.
26. HTCOC 4, p. 230. A slightly different version appears in *Growth of a Work of God*, p. 92.

above. "Female missionaries were of particular consular concern" to the consuls, explains P. D. Coates. "[Consul R. W.] Hurst said that when travelling alone in the interior they were protected by the supercilious Chinese contempt for womankind, and the general though not unanimous consular opinion was in doing so they did not expose themselves to much risk, although they were bound to be considered immoral women. On the other hand C. F. R. Allen pointed out that being bigger than Chinese women they risked being taken for men masquerading as women."[27]

The Outrage

Taylor's first term in Ningbo formed the centerpiece of *Hudson Taylor and Maria;* the "Hangzhou outrage" became the rollicking satire of Pat Barr's *To China with Love.* What a "deplorable spectacle," she wrote, "the only two groups of English missionaries resident outside the treaty ports quarrelling over the use of knife or chopstick, 'taking testimonies' about one man's sexual propriety and sneering about another man's grammar. But major issues were involved which rankled long, and it was only the first of many occasions when emotive phrases about the 'proper conduct for young unmarried ladies,' the 'presumptions of priests,' and the dangers of 'going native' were to be bandied around in missionary circles."[28]

Returning from Ningbo, Hudson Taylor had to ponder the future of the China Inland Mission. The recruits could not stay in Shanghai, nor could he trust them in Ningbo, where the missionary community comprised six denominations, none of whom (including the CIM) wore Chinese clothes. With no fixed destination, how could he know where the Spirit led? His goal from the beginning was to occupy a strategic inland city — not a treaty port — and use it for a foothold, while he expanded itinerations outwards. He decided upon Hangzhou, the capital of Zhejiang, located near Hangzhou Bay at the terminus of the Grand Canal. If Hangzhou was closed, the Lord would lead elsewhere, open another door.

Hangzhou is halfway between Shanghai and Ningbo, about one hundred miles as the crow flies, but considerably further overland. Taylor could have taken them by boat in three or four days, but he decided they needed a leisurely, thorough introduction to the people. "Most of the places on the way to Hangzhou will be familiar to me," he assured them, "as I have often visited

---

27. Coates, *China Consuls,* pp. 184-85.
28. Barr, *To China with Love,* p. 35.

them and preached in them."²⁹ Taylor chartered four canal junks, or houseboats, to take them up the Huangpu River to the Grand Canal at Jiaxing: "one [boat] for the women, one for the men, a third for the Chinese employees as a kitchen and laundry — and a small boat for John Sell whose 'bronchitis' and coughing were so troublesome as to prevent others sleeping."³⁰ In addition to the missionaries, there were five Chinese servants and the preacher Mr. Tsiu from Ningbo, as well as twenty boatmen — a contingent of fifty. They would travel ten or twenty miles, then pull up in the shadow of the next walled city and stay a few days, walking around and distributing tracts. At Jiaxing, they hoped to drop off Lewis and Eliza Nicol, the thorns in Taylor's flesh, along with Mr. Tsiu, where after two months in country they were expected to sink or swim. But they could not rent a house, and so they passed on, another city without a Christian witness.

The whole route was nothing but "ruin, ruin, ruin."³¹ Of Songjiang Hudson Taylor wrote, "Once populous suburbs are now heaps of ruins, covered with weeds and brushwood. I was told that three-fourths of the people had perished from the sword, famine, or pestilence."³² Jiaxing used to be a "city of palaces . . . [and] is now the greater part of it in ruins; of all its former glory we could see only the debris of lordly mansions. . . . And its condition fairly represents that of many of the cities and towns which we have seen."³³ The crowds were friendly, though, belying the stereotype of the "violent Chinamen," and the women — still wearing Western dress because their Chinese outfits were not yet ready — were a special attraction. When they went for a walk, Jennie Faulding reported, "we are as much run after as the Queen would be; but at the same time the people are not rude."³⁴

By stages they reached Hangzhou two months after they left Shanghai. The city has been famous since antiquity as one of China's beauty spots: "Heaven above, Hangzhou below" is a common saying. Located on the tidal-flats near the mouth of the Qiantang River, Hangzhou is surrounded by tiers of mist-enshrouded mountains; the West Lake, Dongting, looks like a brush painting come to life, with willow trees in the foreground and pagodas crowning the distant hills. Hangzhou commands a strategic harbor, the terminus of the Grand Canal, the artery that carries much of China's internal commerce from the south to Beijing. It was the capital of the Southern Song

29. *HTCOC 4*, p. 231.
30. Ibid., p. 228.
31. JHT, 19 June 1867, in ibid., p. 299.
32. JHT, 29 October 1866, in ibid., p. 232.
33. Ibid., p. 236.
34. Ibid., p. 234.

The Land of Strangers

dynasty (1127-1279 C.E.), which imparted an urbane cosmopolitanism of a seaport. When Marco Polo visited in the 1200s, under the Mongols, it was the largest and most efficient city in the world, with a population of over a million.[35]

Now Hangzhou was a city ravaged. It had been besieged and sacked three times during the Taiping Rebellion and huge areas inside the walls had been leveled. After a week of "exceedingly prolix" negotiations, "involving much tea, much talk and much manoeuvering," Taylor managed to rent a dilapidated mansion with thirty rooms, "quietly isolated among acres of ruins." Moving twenty-five adults and children from the houseboats into One New Lane required great secrecy. "Before daylight on Wednesday morning, we passed quickly and noiselessly through the city, and established ourselves in it." The city officials thought they were planting mines under the city walls and "believed we were spies of some rebellious army, not yet heard of."[36]

Hangzhou already had six Protestant missionaries, three married couples representing three societies: Rev. D. D. Green of the American Presbyterians; Rev. Carl Kreyer of the American Baptists; and Rev. George E. Moule of the Church Missionary Society. A. J. Broomhall commented pointedly, "When the Greens, Kreyers or Moules left their premises they did so as gentlemen and ladies in their own or hired sedan chairs, receiving the deference foreigners in foreign dress had come to expect. Foreigners mixing with the Chinese, on foot and in Chinese clothes, were introducing a completely new relationship. When the two types met, the subject could not but be discussed."[37]

Arriving at the end of November, the CIM recruits set to work with hammers and nails to transform the haunted mansion into a home fit for the living. They constructed windows with glass from Shanghai and hung bedsheets to hide the holes in the walls. Their furniture consisted of packing crates covered with tablecloths made from no-longer-needed English dresses. Their plan, Taylor explained, was to live "as quietly, and as little seen as possible; the study of the language affording sufficient occupation. By the time that any of this party are ready for mission work among the people, it will have become a well known fact that a party of foreigners are dwelling in the city, and that no disturbance or mischief has resulted therefrom, and we shall thus get among them with less difficulty, and excite less suspicion than might

---

35. Jacques Gernet, *Daily Life in China on the Eve of the Mongol Invasion, 1250-1276*, trans. H. M. Wright (Stanford: Stanford University Press; London: Allen & Unwin, 1962), is a history of Hangzhou during the Southern Song dynasty.

36. For renting a house, see *HTCOC* 4, pp. 241-50; quotes at pp. 245-46, 249, 267.

37. Ibid., p. 265.

otherwise be."³⁸ By Christmas, they had started a school, medical work, sewing classes and a chapel that attracted fifty or sixty people.

If the Chinese were curious about these secretive foreigners, so too was George Moule. Moule was the eldest of three brothers who all entered the Anglican ministry: he himself was to become bishop of Mid-China; Arthur was archdeacon in Ningbo; while Handley stayed home and became bishop of Durham and a prominent Keswick Holiness teacher (and a close friend of the CIM). George Moule was proper Church of England. At Ningbo (where Taylor had known him in 1858) and then in Hangzhou, Moule had built gothic chapels where he would preside in a surplice and preach from the Book of Common Prayer — it was as familiar as Devonshire. He prided himself on building a congregation of Christians, and never traveling more than twenty miles into the countryside.

The first trouble came when Moule learned that Taylor had baptized the Mildmay deaconesses, and that they had brought no introduction from their home clergyman. He was so outraged he could never bring himself to raise the subject with Taylor — though he expressed himself forcefully to Eugene Stock at the CMS in London. He quickly found the weakest links in the CIM, Lewis and Eliza Nicol, and started to ask questions. The first issue, naturally, was Chinese dress. "Are you aware that we had only old dirty Chinese cast-offs in which we were such figures that it tempted more than Mr. Taylor to call us Coolies?" Nicol wrote to Mr. Berger. "You at home can have no idea of what Chinese cast-off clothes are. . . . It is . . . common to see the Chinese day by day take off their clothes and pick the vermin (lice) off them." Maria Taylor was shocked by Nicol's "downright *falsehood*" about the CIM outfits: "Neither Mr. Nicol nor any other of the brethren had a single article in his Chinese outfit but what was quite new and *clean*. . . . They were dressed as *gentlemen*" [italics in original].³⁹

It escalated from there. "Within three months George Moule came to the conclusion that neither Hudson Taylor's policy nor his personal integrity could bear scrutiny. If damage to the missionary cause was to be averted, the responsibility for taking action rested upon him, George Moule. . . . He must as far as possible put things right in Hangzhou, and bring the state of affairs to the notice of influential people in Britain. At first his aim was reform of the CIM. Later, only its dissolution would satisfy him."⁴⁰

It was a sad, sordid imbroglio. Nicol, eager for an audience, would ferry

---

38. Letter from Emily Blatchley in ibid., p. 249.
39. Ibid., p. 284.
40. Ibid., pp. 263-65.

The Land of Strangers

scurrilous, wildly imaginary tales to Moule about the secret life inside the haunted house. The men lived in one building, while Taylor and his family shared the other with the single women. Taylor would kiss the women goodnight, Nicol declared, and would make "nocturnal visits" to their rooms. Exasperated beyond belief, Moule warned him "that by domiciling in (your) own house so many unmarried females" Taylor was "doing that which if I am not mistaken would be viewed with mistrust and disapproval even in England. . . . Living as you all do in very confined premises, having some of the restraints of social etiquette relaxed (as you may conceive) by your relation to these ladies as their physician, and some by the position you have assumed as their spiritual pastor . . . [and] as their easily accessible friend and adviser of experience in China . . . *you would be more than human if you were not capable of being tempted to lay aside* in some measure the reserve with which for their sakes and your own they ought to be treated." Taylor, he thundered, should "put a speedy end" to the CIM so "further perils may be averted."[41]

This would seem to be a tempest in a teapot, except that Nicol's unbalanced attitude endangered the party and led to a riot. He and Eliza wanted to live alone in a Chinese city, so Taylor rented a house in Xiaoshan, ten miles away. The agreement with the landlord stipulated "that, though foreigners, those who were to reside there had adopted the Chinese dress." The Nicols moved there in January 1867 — and defiantly took off their Chinese clothes and put on foreign suits. "I felt God's blessing could not rest upon a work commenced in the spirit in which *it seems to me* Mr. Nicol was commencing his," said Taylor. A riot ensued — known as the "Xiaoshan outrage" — in which the evangelist was flogged and the missionaries escaped by boat. "Had he been fluent in Chinese, he [Nicol] said, he would have stayed in Chinese clothes. He would wear them again when he could speak freely. But he felt insecure. Foreign clothes gave him 'protection and respect.'"[42]

By May 1867, in its usual sarcastic tone, the *North China Herald* announced, "This happy family has, we learn, exploded. The ladies were required to dress in Chinese costume and to eat Chinese chow-chow, and rebelled against both edicts. The former proceedings drew down on them

---

41. Ibid., pp. 288-92. William Berger defended Taylor's "intimacy with . . . the sisters," whom he had known since childhood, such as Jennie Faulding, and that Taylor kissed the other women "only under peculiar circumstances": *HTCOC 5*, p. 145. McKay, "Faith and Facts," p. 102, quotes a correspondent to the *Chinese Recorder* (1900): "Kissing is regarded as a vicious and unspeakable act [by the Chinese], yet our missionary women kiss their husbands and brothers in the streets when they meet after being parted for a time."

42. For the Xiaoshan outrage, see *HTCOC 4*, pp. 354-56, 277-84, 299-301; quotes at pp. 255, 278.

unfavorable notice from the Chinese, and the latter seems to have disagreed with their constitutions. They have accordingly returned to Ningpo."[43] In Ningbo the CIM reunited briefly after the cathartic deaths of John Sell, whose bronchitis had kept them awake, and little Gracie Taylor, the first CIM martyrs. Nicol and the others agreed to sign a "survivors' pact," a written document (quoted in Chapter 3) which replaced the verbal agreement before they departed.

The mutiny continued for another year, until early 1868 when five members resigned or were fired. The survivors' compromise, though, established a two-tier family, the pre-*Lammermuir* pioneers not bound by CIM regulations (like James Meadows and George Stott), "half in and half out of the CIM circle,"[44] and the *Lammermuir* party and those who came after.

The Riot Season

The CIM gained its nickname in this period, "Constantly In Motion." With barely any language, the men were "deployed" with Chinese preachers to cover the province of Zhejiang, both north and south of Hangzhou Bay. The strategy was "both systematic and methodical. There was no aimless wandering."[45] Once they were assured of tolerance by the provincial governor in Hangzhou, they could move outside the capital to the district cities, and from the prefectural cities down to the county towns and villages. In particular they would target markets and religious fairs, where they would set up their tables beside the other religious healers and sectarians. They would stay "a few days here and a few days there (as Americans would call it, 'prospecting') and feeling their way, as God led them on, step by step, as to where they should establish their mission."[46]

By November 1867, the end of its first year, the CIM had twenty-five missionaries at eleven stations in Zhejiang and Jiangsu, a twenty-four-day journey from the northernmost at Jiaxing to the south at Wenzhou.[47] They had baptized twenty-five converts ("one for each member of the mission," the *North China Herald* noted)[48] and had one hundred enquirers. By the follow-

43. *North China Herald*, 18 May 1867, p. 60.
44. *HTCOC 5*, p. 53.
45. *HTCOC 4*, p. 260.
46. David Hill, speech to CIM annual meeting, *China's Millions* (GB), July-August 1881, p. 89.
47. *Growth of a Work of God*, p. 131.
48. *North China Herald*, 30 May 1869, p. 243.

The Land of Strangers

ing summer Taylor decided the Chinese church in Zhejiang was strong enough to be turned over to "native agency," and ordained Wang Lae-djün, his collaborator in London, as the "pastor and in effect bishop of an expanding network of churches."[49]

It was time to move inland, into the nine unoccupied provinces that had been Taylor's goal since his vision at Brighton. Moving up the Grand Canal, Taylor established several stations near the junction with the Yangtze River, at Zhenjiang, Yangzhou, Anqing, and eventually Nanjing and Hankou. This "Yangtze advance" was an interesting strategy that by-passed Shanghai, the normal port of entry. Living on a houseboat outside the city walls of Yangzhou, famous for its wealth and the beauty of its women, near the junction with the Yangtze River (which the British had bombed during the First Opium War), Taylor spent several weeks "gently feeling our way among the people." Armed with a dispatch from the *daotai* (the prefect or head official of the county) and instructions from the British Minister in Beijing, he managed to rent a house inside the city in July 1868, and established his headquarters there, since the head office was wherever he happened to be. As others moved there over the next few days, they numbered thirteen foreigners, plus nineteen Chinese servants, preachers, and printers. Maria Taylor was eight months pregnant, and Mrs. Rudland was also pregnant. But they were not to stay there long.[50]

On 22 August a crowd estimated at eight to ten thousand forced its way into the CIM compound in an orgy of looting and burning. The missionaries literally had to jump over the wall in "our blood-stained clothes," with the result that Mrs. Taylor and Mrs. Rudland were badly bruised and Mr. Reid almost lost an eye. The "Yangzhou riot" followed a predictable pattern. It was fomented by the gentry who whipped up anti-foreign passions through big-character posters and rumors of dead babies. When a crowd gathered outside the house and started throwing stones, Taylor, demanding his treaty rights, called on the prefectural official to punish the agitators. The prefect was in a double bind since the ringleaders were the "head-men" of the city, wealthy scholars and friends of Zeng Guofan, now governor-general of three provinces (Jiangsu, Jiangxi, and Anhui). "For it was evident," Taylor wrote in his affidavit, "that though the Prefect would write a polite note, he feared the unpopularity of taking any decided steps in our favour."[51]

49. *HTCOC 4*, pp. 153-54.
50. *HTCOC 5*, pp. 70-73, and a map of the Yangzhou property on p. 83.
51. The Yangzhou riot and its aftermath are the most documented events in CIM history. Cohen, *China and Christianity,* pp. 180-84, regards it as *the* pivotal event in relations between Britain and China. He listed five "incidents" (more serious than "cases") involv-

Fleeing down-river to Shanghai, Taylor reported the incident to the British consul in Shanghai, W. H. Medhurst. Immediately, everything was taken out of his hands. The *North China Herald*, which only a few weeks before had described a CIM tract as "sickening twaddle" and "a farrago of nauseous cant," called for "prompt and decisive punishment" to ensure the safety of all foreigners.[52] The diplomatic process went through two phases. In September Medhurst steamed up to Yangzhou in a man-o'-war with seventy marines. Medhurst, a man of the old school, felt foreigners were not always right and the Chinese not always wrong, but nevertheless he had a "sovereign contempt for Chinese officials, and in dealing with them preferred a bludgeon to a rapier."[53] He inflated the CIM losses from 1,100 taels to 2,000 taels "so as to include reparation for the loss to Mr. Reid of the sight of one eye, and for the various injuries."[54] He also demanded an apology, which became the sticking point for the Chinese, who were willing to pay a "gratuity" of 1,000 taels, which would have demonstrated their "benevolence" not their guilt.[55]

The ambassador Sir Rutherford Alcock, in tune with the Foreign Office's conciliatory policy, admitted that while technically Taylor had the right to purchase land, "whether it may be consistent with wisdom or prudence to seek to enforce the right, or practicable to do so in effect, having in view the safety of the missionaries themselves, and the maintenance of peace, order, and good government wherever they may elect to settle themselves, is another question."[56] By November the diplomatic maneuvers ended with an official Chinese apology, the degradation of the city officials, and the return of the premises to the CIM.

The second phase exploded three months later in Britain, when the reports started to arrive from China. "What right have we to send missionar-

---

ing the Zongli Yamen and Protestant missionaries during the 1860s: all were British, and three involved the CIM (the others were in Fujian and Taiwan). Coates, *China Consuls*, p. 223. *HTCOC 5* described the "riot season" (also riots at Zhenjiang and Anqing), pp. 76-187, 215-20, etc. Quotes from "Affidavit of 31 August 1868" (see note 10 above), *British Parliamentary Papers*, p. 17.

52. *North China Herald*, 30 May 1868 and 28 August 1868, p. 415.
53. Coates, *China Consuls*, pp. 222-23.
54. W. H. Medhurst, Nanjing, to Sir R. A. Alcock, Beijing, 15 September 1868, in *British Parliamentary Papers*, p. 26.
55. Medhurst to Alcock, 17 September 1868, in ibid., p. 33; and Zeng Guofan to Medhurst, 14 September 1868, p. 35. In his letter of 8 October to Medhurst (p. 39), Zeng minimized the injuries: Mr. Reid's wound was slight, "and as to the wives of Messrs Taylor and Rudland, I must deny their being wounded at all. This is a very important point. . . . The sum of 770 taels for medical expenses will, therefore, have to be largely reduced."
56. Alcock to Lord Stanley, London, 11 September 1868, in ibid., p. 38.

to the interior of China?" asked the Duke of Somerset in the House of Lords, as he demanded the recall of all missionaries: "A missionary, indeed, must be an enthusiast; if he is not an enthusiast, he is probably a rogue. (A laugh.) No man would go and live up one of those rivers and preach Christianity unless he were an enthusiast, and if an enthusiast, he readily incurs dangers."

In the meantime there had been a switch of foreign secretaries, and though the Earl of Clarendon admired the spirit of missionaries, he felt they should follow, not precede, the flag. They must be restrained from causing "a state of riot and bloodshed such as men of peace and goodwill should be the last to bring about." The British navy was in China "to protect the floating commerce of British subjects against piratical attacks," to be used only under "very peculiar" circumstances "when it is clearly shown that without such interference the lives and properties of British subjects would, in all probability, have been sacrificed.... Her Majesty's Government cannot delegate to Her Majesty's Servants in foreign countries the power of involving their own country in war."[57]

William Berger, home secretary of the CIM, knew less than the Foreign Office, because Hudson Taylor kept him in the dark too, lest he inadvertently reveal incriminating details in the *Occasional Papers*. Finally, in desperation, he plaintively wrote to Taylor, "Will you kindly send me word whether you sent for the gunboat?"[58] He realized, of course, he might not receive a reply for six months or more. In public, Berger put on a brave face and spoke with such authority everyone assumed he knew whereof he spoke. The riot was started by the gentry, he said without a shred of evidence; the common people were not violent except when "acted upon by others they become excited, and proceed to vent their feelings."[59] As the CIM's support in England dwindled, it was rescued financially by George Müller, who contributed £6,200 to Hudson Taylor and the CIM between 1868-73, including £1,940 in 1870-71, one-half the income. "He was now largely assisting twenty-one missionaries, who with twelve wives constituted the entire staff of the Mission."[60]

Yangzhou became another CIM allegory: "Put not your faith in princes." Avoid publicity and "the limelight."[61] Do not trust consuls, never tell them anything. Work in secret. Seven years later when the CIM was making covert

---

57. *Times* (London), 10 May 1869, 6.
58. HTCOC 5, p. 168.
59. *Times* (London), 14 April 1869, p. 4.
60. McKay, "Faith and Facts," pp. 247-52, itemizes Müller's contributions as well as those of Berger and other individuals. According to the receipts, which do not list all Müller's contributions, he gave almost £35,000 to JHT and the CIM between 1860 and 1874. See also Steer, *George Muller*.
61. HTCOC 5, p. 143.

explorations in all directions, Taylor's instructions were explicit: "First, the absolute necessity of desisting from making any representation, private, semi-official, or official, of any difficulties in the work to H. M. Consul or consular offices. Second, if possible to avoid personal (dealings) with Mandarins. . . . Anything which may, fairly or unfairly, be termed indiscretion, may be taken as a reason for steps seriously embarrassing to the operations of the Mission, and which might place some, if they continue their work, in a position of antagonism to law and order."[62]

In the apocalyptic struggle for China's soul, the British consuls might be doing the devil's work. By threatening to revoke passports, by sending gunboats, by high-handedly degrading provincial governors, by demanding minatory concessions, the flag obstructed the gospel. Out there in the countryside, the CIM knew that ultimately its protection came from the blind eye of the Chinese officials: one could travel better as a lamb than as a wolf.[63]

The Native Missionary Association

Before the church could put down roots, the missionaries had to itinerate for years, making themselves visible so they would be recognized next time they passed through. Once they gathered a few believers, they would press forward, leaving behind Chinese pastors, either local or imported, to shepherd the flock. In May 1877 Taylor gave a paper to the Shanghai Missionary Conference, entitled "Itineration Far and Near as an Evangelizing Agency." It may be the nineteenth century in England, he said, but in China, where Satan still held sway, it was the first century A.D., and first-century, apostolic methods must be employed. His speech was cloaked with vagueness, saying only that the CIM had "recently traversed considerable districts" of nine provinces. "Suppose two men, A and B, thus to spend two years in itineration and colportage all over a province, and then to separate, each taking a new companion with him, and confining himself to half a province. These companions we will call C and D. After the third year A and C divide their half prov-

---

62. JHT, memorandum to every member of CIM, 1874, in *HTCOC* 6, p. 28.

63. Coates, *China Consuls*, p. 183, gives an odd, back-handed compliment to the CIM's prowess. C. T. Gardner, consul at Amoy, suggested that "as many British missionaries, especially those connected with the China Inland Mission, were acquainted with trade, some of them might with advantage to British trade and without detriment to their spiritual work act as commercial travelers; 'being ostentatiously engaged in trade, they would be less liable to suspicion and dislike than if only engaged in proselytisation, the motive for which the Chinese find it difficult to understand.'"

ince, and each, again taking another companion, itinerates more and more thoroughly over a quarter of a province. . . ."[64]

Since native Christians could carry the gospel far in advance of the missionaries, one convert, Lo Ah-ts'ih of Hangzhou, tried to revive Gutzlaff's Chinese Union by founding a "native missionary society." He spent two years "engaged in evangelistic work in the interior," and on his return, he called the native believers together and "explained his plan for the formation of a native missionary society; namely that each (church) member should give something each month. . . . This money, he said, should not be used for any purpose but the spread of the Gospel; *not* for the poor (or) a fund from which they could borrow money."[65]

The temptation was always there, though, to regard the church as a benevolent society. "And when the doors are opened, in rushes everyone," wrote George Stott in Wenzhou, "street strollers and loungers, rowdies, travelling tradesmen of all kinds, hawkers crying out their wares, conjurers, fortune-tellers, musicians, thieves and beggars: the shaven pate of a Buddhist priest, the cowl of a Taoist priest may also be seen, and the noise is almost beyond description."[66] The only people missing from Stott's portrait are opium addicts, for Wenzhou in 1870 was not yet consumed by opium.

Ironically, the Taiping Rebellion, far from suppressing the growth of popular religious movements, spurred the proliferation of sects, of which the Christian god-worshipers constituted one, each promising to save suffering humanity. Many survivors responded to the social and political instability by joining an association that could offer protection, mutual support, and a sense of purpose. Some were based upon clan membership, others were organized as revolutionary societies dedicated to the overthrow of the "foreign" [i.e. Manchu] Qing government. Regardless of their organization, each functioned as an alternative family operating outside traditional gentry-dominated social institutions. They were thus regarded as "heterodox" by Qing authorities who undertook to control their influence and at times to suppress them violently.

Susan Naquin, a leading scholar of Qing sectarian religious communities, noted these new sects appealed to individuals "for whom the normal paths to salvation were unappealing or unattainable or for whom normal community structures were unavailable."[67] They included elderly men and women with-

---

64. JHT, "Itineration Far and Near."
65. John McCarthy in *HTCOC* 5, p. 335.
66. Stott, *Twenty-Six Years*, p. 27.
67. Susan Naquin, "The Transmission of White Lotus Sectarianism in Late Imperial

out intact families, monks without temples, migrant labor and itinerant workers, urban immigrants, and peasants whose village and temple organizations were dominated by others.[68] These were exactly the sort of people who flocked to the missionary, begging to be healed, begging for influence with the magistrate, begging for opium, begging.

Looking out at the crowd of dead, sullen faces, how could a missionary hope to do more than throw a handful of tracts like buckshot over their heads? To say the Christian message fell on stony ground is an understatement. The crowds would "flit about, go and come, and never sit down,"[69] unless one of the "lewd fellows of the baser sort" came in and whipped them up.[70] "Coldness, indifference, carelessness are often shown by the people."[71] They were "proud, rude, callous, and annoying to the last degree."[72]

Coming out of their haunted houses into this disreputable netherworld, missionaries learned to recognize a glimmer of hope in the blankest faces, the slightest awakening of spiritual interest. While traveling from village to village, writes Daniel Bays, they would ask who were "doctrine-lovers," that is members of religious sects who were already on a religious pilgrimage; they were "better listeners, and some had become converts and the core of new churches."[73] Taylor's first male convert in Ningbo, Ni Yong-fa, had been a sect leader who took Taylor to meetings and preached to his fellow sectarians. A decade later George Stott's first convert in Wenzhou was the "interesting case" of an aged Buddhist priest. The priest could not be baptized and be "a follower of Christ while wearing the priestly garb, and living on the gains of idolatry." So one day, "putting on clean garments, he went to a mountain stream near by, prayed on the bank, then plunged in and baptized himself." He went home and converted his village and told Stott that he was "known for miles around as the turncoat priest." He continued to live in the temple and would take inquirers to his secret room, saying, "Elder brother, I have been a priest for sixty years, and worshipped these things until two years ago; but they never did me any good." He pointed them to Jesus, telling them "that

---

China," in *Popular Culture in Late Imperial China*, ed. David Johnson, Andrew Nathan, and Evelyn Rawski (Berkeley: University of California Press, 1985), p. 257.

68. Daniel Overmyer, "Alternatives: Popular Religious Sects in Chinese Society," *Modern China* 7, no. 2 (April 1981): 156-57.

69. Stott, *Twenty-Six Years*, p. 7.

70. *China's Millions* (GB), December 1875, p. 80.

71. Ibid., February 1877, p. 15.

72. Ibid., August 1876, p. 182.

73. Daniel H. Bays, "Christianity and Chinese Sects: Religious Tracts in the Late Nineteenth Century," in Barnett and Fairbank, eds., *Christianity in China*, pp. 124-25.

some tens of good men had entered the religion, and were going to eternal happiness in heaven.... He died in the temple, but, we believe, a true disciple."[74]

The dominant sectarian tradition in North China was White Lotus, which traced its origins back to the dissolution of the Buddhist and Nestorian monasteries after 800 C.E. The typical sect survived for centuries as small scattered groups, bound by "long and loose chains of teachers and disciples." The primary deity was the Eternal Venerable Mother, *Wu-sheng Lao-mu* (Our Eternal Mother in the World of True Emptiness), the creator goddess who had sent her sons and daughters to populate the Eastern Land. In the beginning they were crowned with rainbows of light and flew on wheels, but gradually they got lost in "the red-dust world," this *samsara* world of illusion. The goddess weeps for them in their suffering and sends spiritual messages through "inspired leaders and revealed books," calling on them to recover their true natures and return home. At the end of this corrupt age, this *kalpa* ("eon"), the story continued, the believers will be saved from famine, drought, and floods.[75]

Chinese popular religion is "deliberately syncretistic," states Daniel Overmyer, that is, it weds diverse elements from Buddhism and Daoism into a new religion, "the self-conscious creation of a new religious system.... Something distinctive, new, and greater than the sum of its parts. At the same time that sectarians claim to be creating something new, they also claim that it is primordial, a restoration of the 'true' unity underlying the component traditions."[76] As one missionary added, "I fancy there are a great many Chinese today who would be willing to mix in a little Christianity along with the other elements."[77]

---

74. Stott, *Twenty-Six Years*, pp. 32-34.

75. David K. Jordan and Daniel L. Overmyer, *The Flying Phoenix: Aspects of Chinese Sectarianism in Taiwan* (Princeton: Princeton University Press, 1986), pp. 21-23; Daniel L. Overmyer, *Folk Buddhist Religion: Dissenting Sects in Late Traditional China* (Cambridge: Harvard University Asia Center, 1999), pp. 135-38. Like Quakers, Chinese sects showed that millenarian expectations, which could inspire revolution at the creation of a new sect, could become quietist in more peaceful times.

76. Jordan and Overmyer, *Flying Phoenix*, p. 10.

77. J. G. Bompas, a Canadian Presbyterian in North Henan, to R. P. MacKay, Toronto, 13 December 1919, UCA, North Henan Mission correspondence. There are many such deliberately syncretic sects in China and Taiwan today, such as *Yiguandao* or Unity Sect, which incorporates Buddhist and Christian elements.

"The Bombshell Scattering Us"

The scandals and riots of the first years were followed by years of "tunnelling through rock."[78] By 1875 the CIM had reached its nadir, with Hudson Taylor at death's door in England, while Jennie Faulding Taylor, his second wife whom he married after Maria's death in 1870, was giving birth to their third child. Five of the eighteen *Lammermuir* adults had died, including George Duncan, the gentle giant, dead at twenty-nine. "I often feel the grave to be very near indeed," wrote Mrs. Annie Crombie, whose three babies died; "yet many of the young and strong have gone to rest, and I am here to suffer, or to stand still and wait, *not to do*."[79] Of the fifty-three missionaries sent out in one way or another by the CIM, only twenty-two adults (and eighteen children) remained in the mission, and of those only four or five men and three or four women were much good: "some lack ability, others reliability," said Taylor.[80] The middle-class recruits (tradesmen and printers) tended to drift off into secular work, while the enthusiasts joined other missions, in which they did not have to wear Chinese dress.

After opening three provinces in its first decade (Zhejiang, Jiangsu, and Anhui), the CIM issued an appeal in 1875 for "the Eighteen" — two new missionaries to "occupy" each of the nine provinces that still had no resident missionary. The arrival of twenty-two recruits in 1875-76 was "like a bombshell scattering us."[81] Taylor dispatched them to explore every corner of the empire, in total secrecy, from Guizhou to Xinjiang, from the borders of Tibet to Manchuria. This was a golden age of the CIM, the heroic explorations that, once revealed, made it famous. One step at a time, they walked clear across China, making some of the most prodigious journeys of the nineteenth century. What Taylor had once written of the Jesuits could well apply to his own missionaries: "Entering by stealth, living in concealment, ever and anon meeting with imprisonment, sufferings, torture, and death itself, they have presented a remarkable instance of fidelity to their calling."[82]

"As a rule," Taylor concluded, "single young men must commence such work, and they should commence it as soon after their arrival in the field as possible, before their health and strength are too much worn down. The physical strain of months and years spent in such labours is very great." And do not forget the single and married women, the "female agency." "Like Pe-

---

78. *HTCOC* 5, p. 289.
79. *China's Millions* (GB), December 1875, p. 73.
80. *HTCOC* 5, p. 391.
81. *HTCOC* 6, p. 86.
82. JHT, *China: Its Spiritual Need and Claims* (1865).

The Land of Strangers

Mule litter in Shanxi. This was the most common form of traveling long distances in China. The litter would carry the missionary's bedding as well as boxes of Bibles and tracts. This photograph shows the Guguan Pass, known as the "Gates of Heaven," on the Big Road from Beijing to Xian. T. W. Piggott, who resigned from the CIM, established a station of the independent Shouyang Mission near here, where he watched the troop movements of the Boxers.
Source: Mrs. Howard Taylor, *Pastor Hsi*, vol. 1, *One of China's Scholars* (London: CIM, 1901).

ter," he wrote, "I have traveled much with 'a sister, a wife,' and have been helped, and not hindered. . . . A lady missionary, in travelling, can also do much for the sick of her own sex."

James Cameron, another Scottish giant, made several spectacular journeys in eight years, "one man and a mule" traveling through every province of China (including a foray into Hunan). He was a shipbuilder from Arrow-on-the-Tyne, aged twenty-nine, who reached Burma in 1875. From there he walked through Yunnan, "south of the clouds," in the wake of the Margary murder, to Tibet, then back to Hong Kong. His next trip took him from Shanghai as far as Korea, then along the Great Wall into Gansu. "I liked to come in contact with them," he wrote, "and to speak the gospel to them in their own homes." A. J. Broomhall concluded, "Many remarkable things were being done in China by many remarkable men and women, but perhaps none comparable with the 'itinerations' of this calm, courteous Scotsman, preparing the way always self-effacingly for others to reap where he sowed."[83]

As they moved inland, these men and women took the system developed at the coast of extended itinerations and intensive preaching. They had acquired strategies for moving invisibly among the people, even in hostile territory (such as Yunnan after the Margary murder), barely attracting attention. They knew how to attract a crowd — like Stott waving his wooden leg — and when to retreat and shake the dust from their shoes. Moreover they had learned to distinguish doctrine-lovers from the merely curious and to offer them "something better."

In the next chapter, we shall see how these themes worked out in microcosm in one inland province, Shanxi, after the Great Famine.

---

83. For more on Cameron, see *HTCOC 6*, pp. 146-53, 215-31; quotes at pp. 146, 231.

CHAPTER 5

The Valley of the Shadow
1875-1880

When Thou wouldst light the darkness, Lord,
Then I would be the silver lamp.
Whose oil supply can never fail,
Placed high to shed the beams afar,
That darkness may be turned to light,
And men and women see Thy face.

Pastor Hsi, "A Song of Sacrifice"[1]

The Pilgrims' Map

Now there are three Pilgrims tramping the dusty yellow plains, two young Englishmen of "the Eighteen" scattered like a bombshell through the interior of China, and their Chinese preacher. Francis James (1851-1900) was twenty-five, the son of a Berkshire storekeeper and had some education, for he would become a university professor and an authority on Chinese religious sects. His friend Joshua J. Turner was getting along "nicely with the language and is the nicest-spirited man that has come out here recently," their superintendent John McCarthy told Hudson Taylor. "He is thoroughly at one with your views as to works and *loves* the Chinese — not merely piteous — does not speak of them as 'poor creatures' — He will be a great help to James and James will get on well with him." Since Turner had been in China for only ten months, and James for seven, neither was fluent in the language. They were accompanied

---

1. Francesca French, translator, *The Songs of Pastor Hsi* (London: Morgan & Scott and CIM, 1920), p. 11. Also published in *Pastor Hsi* (single vol.), p. 295.

by "Yao Sien-seng" (i.e. Mr. Yao), "a first-rate Nankin man who has lived most of his time in Honan and travelled all over the North. . . . He is an enquirer and quite *fung-siu* [?] about going."²

Be warned.

The road is harrowing. "The suffering was so terrible that it was said that in all history, even in that of China, the distress had never been equaled. It struck terror into the hearts of all."³ The missionaries met many like one old woman of sorrows who asked them to tell her if she will have any more grief in her lifetime?" They pointed her to Zion, "a place where there is no more sorrow, nor crying, neither shall there be any pain, and of Him who is the Way to that happy place . . . without any merit of her own."⁴

China used to be measured in "stages," the distance one man could walk in one day: "We travel along very leisurely — Chinese carts scarcely ever hurry, or exceed the regulation pace of three to four miles per hour. . . . When the carts are heavily laden the pace is slow indeed."⁵ Each stage was one day's journey away from the white man's world, one day's journey inland. The men and women of the China Inland Mission were renowned walkers. They would get up while it was still dark, 3:00 or 4:00 a.m., set out with their bedding and literature and walk until nightfall. They might cover sixty *li* (twenty English miles) a day; if the journey was by water, they would cover more distance to less advantage. In the mountains, five miles as the crow flies might take a full day.

In 1875, just as he was scattering the Eighteen, Hudson Taylor started a new magazine, *China's Millions,* and in its first issue he printed a map of China he had invented so that supporters in Britain could follow their itinerations. The map used different shadings to designate the provinces, which even he admitted gives "our Map a somewhat peculiar appearance." The "novel feature," though, was that it substituted nice, cozy English translations for the awkward, hard-to-pronounce, easy-to-forget Chinese names. Ominously, a "dark line that winds through the center of the Map from north to south, separates the totally unevangelized provinces from those that are partially occupied by the soldiers of the Cross."⁶

---

2. John McCarthy, Chinkiang, to JHT, 11 October 1876, in CIM/SOAS, file 232. A censored text appears in *HTCOC 6,* pp. 72-73: the phrase, "He is thoroughly at one with your views," is quoted but the rest — "piteous poor creatures" — is clipped.

3. Timothy Richard, *Forty-Five Years in China,* p. 97.

4. *China's Millions* (GB), July-August 1880, p. 83.

5. Ibid., October 1884, p. 130.

6. JHT, "Special Notice," ibid., October 1875, p. 44. Unlike most of JHT's fabulations, this map was not a success. It was printed twice in *China's Millions,* and then disappeared.

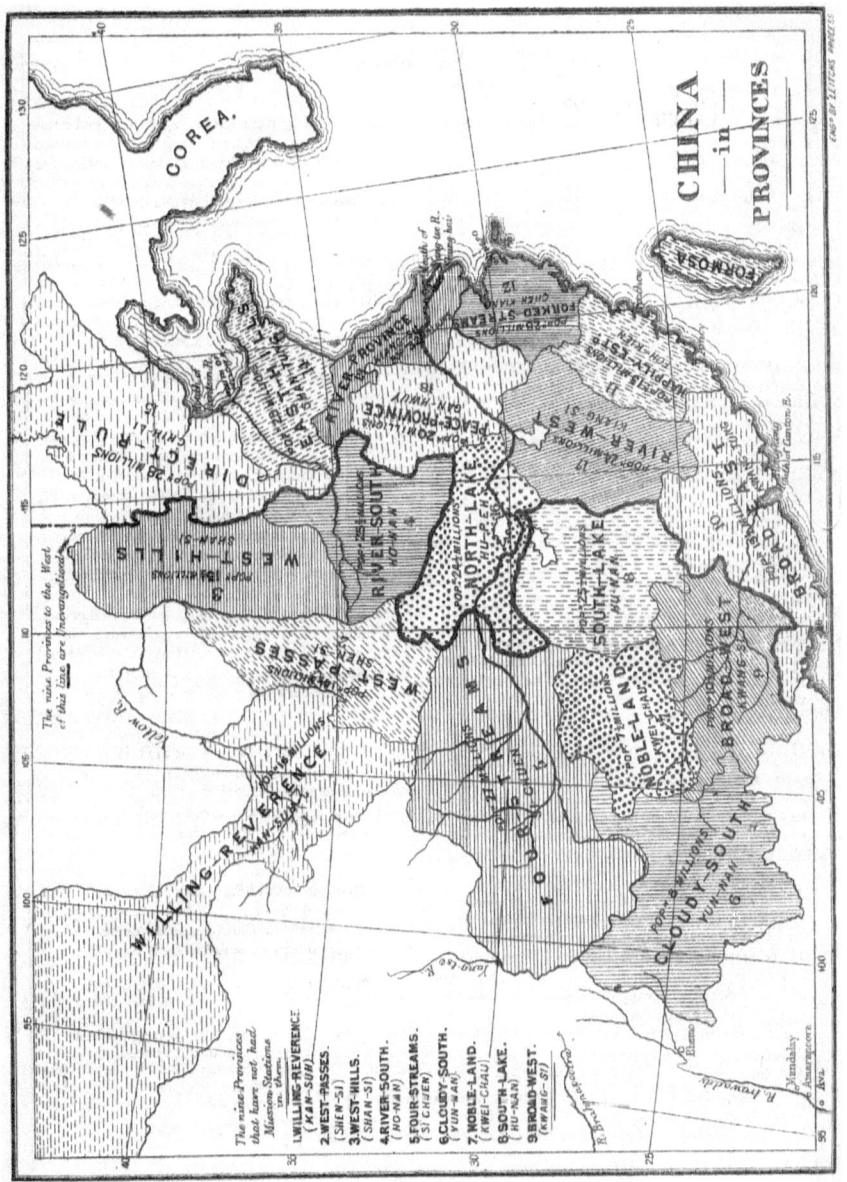

Map of China with English names. One of the first issues of *China's Millions* had this unusual map which substituted cozy English names for the hard-to-remember Chinese names. Shanxi ("West-Hills") is at the north center.
Source: *China's Millions* (GB), October 1875.

THE FIRST GENERATION

Since James and Turner selected *West-Hills* (Shanxi) as their destination, one can trace their journey according to this map. (I have put the names of the provinces in *italics,* along with my interpolations.) First, they had to leave the City of Destruction, so far away it is off the map; by 1875, ocean liners had reduced the ocean voyage from Britain to six weeks, barring typhoons, shipwrecks, or pirates. Crossing the equator twice, their first glimpse of the "Celestial Kingdom" (the conventional name for China, home of "the Celestials," or the "Flowery Kingdom") was of the broad rice-paddies of *Broad-East* (Guangdong). After a brief stop to salute the flag in Fragrant Harbor (Hong Kong), they sailed up the coast past *Happily-Established* (Fujian), where the people drank fragrant tea, to *Forked-Stream* (Zhejiang), where the people spoke with forked tongues. Far out to sea, where the dark ocean turned yellow, they passed Gutzlaff Island, at the entrance to Broad River (the Yangtze). They disembarked at Upper Sea (Shanghai), the port city of *River-Province* (Jiangsu).

From Upper Sea, the wicket-gate, they had the choice of three routes to *West-Hills.* They could continue their sea voyage up the coast around the peninsula of *East-Hills* (Shandong) to *Direct-Rule* (Zhili), where the Emperor ruled in more than oriental splendor. There they could hook up with the "Big Road," the imperial highway from Northern Capital (Beijing) to West Peace (Xian). After crossing the North China plain and climbing the mountains, the road entered *West-Hills* from the northwest through the pass known as the "Heavenly Gates."[7] (This was the route taken by the Empress Dowager in 1900 when she fled the post-Boxer turmoil; it is paralleled by the railway today.)

Instead, they took a river steamer up Broad River through *Peace Province* (Anhui), a desolate ruin, past the Southern Capital (Nanjing), once the New Jerusalem of the Taiping Heavenly Kingdom, now utterly destroyed. They could have continued upriver through *North-Lake* (Hubei), the economic heartland, and the Three Gorges to *Four-Streams* (Sichuan). Striking overland they would have gone through *West-Passes* (Shaanxi) and entered *West-Hills* from the back-door, from the southwest. Our pilgrims are attempting the impossible, entering Shanxi from the southeast: from *North-Lake* they traversed *River-South* (Henan), crossed the Yellow River in an inflated pigskin raft, and then climbed the black granite cliffs of the Great Fog (Taihang) mountains. Eventually they reached the high plateau that forms the watershed of the Dividing Waters (Fen River), and hence to Great Origin (Taiyuan), the capital.

7. Nat Brandt, *Massacre in Shansi* (Syracuse: Syracuse University Press, 1994), p. 15.

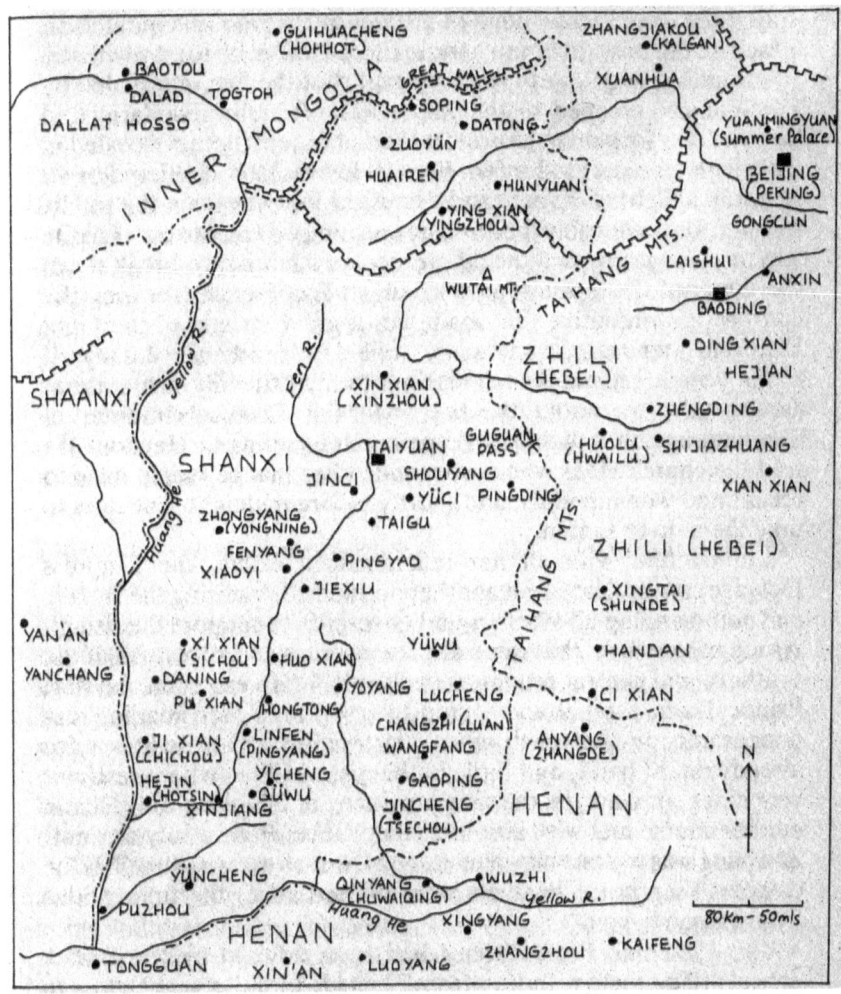

Modern map of Shanxi in pinyin. In 1878, during the famine, the CIM and the English Baptists (BMS) established stations at Taiyuan, the provincial capital. After the controversy with Timothy Richard, the CIM withdrew to Pingyao and concentrated on south Shanxi, under Pastor Hsi, whose work radiated from Linfen (then called Pingyang). The Oberlin Band was at Taigu, south of Taiyuan, while the various Scandinavian Alliances claimed the north between the branches of the Great Wall. T. W. Piggott broke with the CIM and BMS to establish an independent mission at Shouyang. Source: A. J. Broomhall, *Hudson Taylor and China's Open Century,* book 6, *Assault on the Nine* (London: Hodder & Stoughton and OMF, 1988).

The Great Famine

Turner, James, and Yao left the Yangtze at Hankou on 15 October 1876 with a mule cart containing "3000 Gospels, about 1300 small books, and a large number of tracts."[8] They probably had copies of W. C. Burns's illustrated translation of *Pilgrim's Progress*, as well as *The Two Friends*, a popular tract, and several large colored posters. But with their emphasis on the printed word, they probably did not carry any devices — such as scientific instruments or magic lanterns — that could appeal to the illiterate peasants.[9]

They had to travel surreptitiously through Henan, which had a reputation of being "bitterly anti-foreign." Another CIM missionary, Henry Taylor (no relation of Hudson Taylor), reported he had to catch an audience "with guile," preaching that "'The Great Emperor has issued a proclamation of very great importance — holding in my hand a copy of the New Testament — come and hear it read.' This not only brought them together but made them curious — as I declared the rights of 'another King, one Jesus.' Some who listened responded heartily."[10] This could be considered as close to sedition. After he left, the Chinese burned his "stinking" books because the smell of the ink caused people to fall "down in the street in a swoon, upon whom it was supposed that we had exerted our satanic influence."[11]

"Shanxi" means "West of the Mountains," not the gentle "West Hills" of Taylor's imagination but the Taihang range which separates Shanxi from the North China Plain. Stone steps climb one valley and down the next, like stairways to heaven. Far overhead, thousand-year-old pagodas crowned the peaks and temples clung to the cliffs like spider webs, guiding and guarding travelers. "Cuttings are made through these hills," pointed out James, "in some cases 70 feet deep, and so very narrow as sometimes to barely admit the passage of the cart. . . . At other places a second road runs parallel to the first from 10 to 30 feet above the level."[12]

"The scenery was grand," commented Turner, and on 15 November they crossed the border into Shanxi. The harvest had been good, and everything looked "well cultivated." The only sad note was the number of opium fields,

---

8. J. J. Turner, "Province of Shan-si," *China's Millions* (GB), June 1877, p. 70.
9. *Growth of a Work of God*, p. 320, stated that JHT used images in evangelism as early as 1872: "Every night we collect large numbers by means of pictures and magic-lantern slides."
10. M. Henry Taylor, Henan, letter to JHT, 4 June 1875, in CIM/SOAS, file 225. *China's Millions* (GB), November 1875, p. 60.
11. M. Henry Taylor, "Second Visit to Honan *(River-South Province),*" *China's Millions* (GB), August 1876, p. 181.
12. *China's Millions* (GB), May 1877, p. 57.

The Valley of the Shadow

now barren after the harvest. "The people seemed rather suspicious of us; I should judge that the greater part of them were opium-smokers."[13] They visited three southern prefectures, Zezhou, Pingyuan, and Puzhou, and greatly encouraged, they returned to Hankou, having traveled seventeen hundred miles in three months. They remained there only long enough to re-equip themselves before setting out again.

Their second trip turned them into white ghosts.

Rain had failed in the spring of 1877, and by summer North China was in the grip of drought, which deepened when the locusts came, and through the next year. By 1879, when the rains finally fell, the Great North China Famine had claimed nine million victims, five million in Shanxi alone, one-third of the population.[14] (The population of Shanxi did not regain its prefamine level until the 1920s.) "People resorted to eating dried leaves, tree roots, bark, sawdust, dried mud, and even baked pellets of finely ground stone mixed with soil or millet husks—which caused terrible stomach cramps and eventual death."[15] Pingyang [now called Linfen], halfway to Taiyuan, was the epicenter, and after a brief survey of conditions there, Turner and James pushed north to Taiyuan, the capital, where in April 1877 they almost succumbed to "famine fever" (typhoid).

Their diaries are heartrending. Francis James:

> Outside one village we passed to-day there was a group of women who begged us to relieve them, and one called out several times, "Buy my two girls," "Buy my two girls"... Never met this before. Cartloads of women and girls have passed us on the way to the capital and other cities to be sold. Saw a dead woman lying close by.... *Dogs eat the dead, and the starving eat the dogs.*[16]

Joshua Turner:

> We saw men who were once strong and well-clothed, staggering along the frozen ground with only a few rags to shield them from the piercing

---

13. Ibid., June 1877, p. 71.
14. The standard monograph on the famine is Paul Richard Bohr, *Famine in China and the Missionary: Timothy Richard as Relief Administrator and Advocate of National Reform, 1876-1884*. See also Henrietta Harrison, *The Man Awakened from Dreams: One Man's Life in a North China Village 1857-1942* (Stanford: Stanford University Press, 2005), pp. 28-32. Comparable famines occurred in North China in 1920-21 and 1959-62.
15. Brandt, *Massacre in Shanxi*, p. 21.
16. Francis James, "Scenes in the Famine Districts," *China's Millions* (GB), May 1878, pp. 69-70.

wind. Their feeble steps, emaciated bodies, and wild looks told, only too plainly, that they were about *to spend their last night on earth*. . . . No one pitied them; no one cared for them, for . . . there were hundreds of corpses lying along the road. We saw them. . . . Outside some of the cities we observed a heap of skulls, bones, rags, and pieces of human flesh.[17]

Timothy Richard, who reached Taiyuan later:

January 29th [1878]. 140 li south [of Taiyuan]. Passed four dead men on the road. . . . Passed two men apparently just dead. One had good clothes on but had died of hunger. . . . January 30th. 290 li south. Saw fourteen dead by the roadside. . . . Saw men grinding soft stones . . . into powder . . . to be mixed with any grain or grass seed, or roots and made into cakes. . . . We passed many houses without doors and window frames. . . . The owners had gone away and died. . . . Saw only seven [dead] persons today, but no woman among them. This was explained by meeting carts daily full of women being taken away for sale.[18]

David Hill, who joined James and Turner:

The husband eats his wife, the children eat their sons and daughters, and in their turn children eat their parents.[19]

In psychological terms, famine is the cruelest death. As Joseph Esherick noted in *The Origins of the Boxer Uprising*, "It has no perceptible cause, nor any human remedy. Floods come from breaks in dikes: one can affix blame for the breaks, and take measures to repair them. But peasants can do nothing to fight a drought but wait, and pray for rain. Waiting makes men restless — especially young men."[20] What could a starving peasant do? He could not walk somewhere else, for there was as bad as here — and the roads were clogged with refugees, so by the time they reached safety his wife and children would have starved beside the road. Women, demure bound-feet wives and daughters who seldom ventured beyond the family gate, threw themselves in front of strangers and begged for food. One Catholic priest calculated that the

17. "Letter from Mr. J. J. Turner *(Terrible Suffering in Shan-si),*" *China's Millions* (GB), May 1878, p. 70.
18. Richard, *Forty-five Years in China*, pp. 130-33.
19. *China's Millions* (GB), September 1878, p. 115.
20. Esherick, *Origins of the Boxer Uprising*, p. 281.

Scenes of the Great Famine of 1877-78. Left: the horrors of living skeletons and unburied dead. *Left: Below.* The caption reads: "The living eat the dead. . . . What will not famine compel men to do?" *Right:* a dead mother lies inside while the grieving father buries the baby. The Great Famine was one of the worst in modern Chinese history — an estimated five million victims died in Shanxi alone, one-third of the population. The CIM raised £8,000 (about $40,000 U.S.) in Britain for famine relief.

Source: Woodcuts by a Chinese artist, published in *China's Million* (GB), September 1878.

evil carts hauled away a hundred thousand women and children from one county alone and sold them into slavery.[21]

The spirit world was aghast, weeping at the sufferings of humanity. The city god was paraded through the streets accompanied by firecrackers to awaken the water dragon, who was holding back the rain clouds. When this did not work, they held penitential processions, led by spirit mediums in trances who pierced their bodies with knives to draw the gods' pity. "When the Eternal Mother heard this, tears rolled down her cheeks like pearls because of the scattered and lost ones about to be destroyed, with no way of escape." In desperation, she summoned "all the many gods and Buddhas" — the Jade Emperor and his court, all the Buddhas that ever were and ever will be, all the compassionate bodhisattvas, sages and immortals, all the denizens of the other world — and emptying Heaven, sent them to earth to rescue suffering humanity.[22]

She sent her people messages written on the planchette, the divination stick wielded by a spirit medium who transcribes her words in a trance. These spirit-writing books [*fuqi*] were new scriptures in which Our Eternal Mother could make spiritual statements that were published the next morning as her divine revelations. Her warnings of the calamities at the end of this *kalpa* ("age" or "eon") had a prophetic echo with the missionaries' message. Disasters will arrive, she predicted, "famine, drought, and floods. The people of Shantung [Shandong] will starve to death while they eat each other; husbands and wives will not look after each other, and fathers and sons will be divided." Though the disasters seem to end, "again calamities will occur, mountains will shake, the earth will move, the Yellow River will overflow, and people will drown. There will be a plague of grasshoppers, a dark rain will fall continually, houses will collapse, and there will be no place to dwell."[23]

By the time the Protestant missionaries arrived in Shanxi, there were already 22,780 Roman Catholic converts, led by thirty Western missionaries and eighteen native priests. The Protestants, however, were much more effective at distributing famine relief, even though they were newcomers. "One scholar reports that 127,110 taels (ounces of silver) of relief were distributed by

21. *HTCOC* 6, p. 170.
22. Jordan and Overmyer, *The Flying Phoenix*, pp. 60, 22.
23. Ibid, pp. 21-23. This is quoted from a *baoquan*, or "Precious Volume," called the "Dragon Flower Scripture," published in 1654. The authors examine four *fuqi*, or planchette scriptures. Two were published in Shanxi, one in the Song dynasty and the other, "The Illustrated Book on Returning to the True Nature," in Yangzheng county, dated 1878, the height of the famine (pp. 51-53). See also Overmyer, *Folk Buddhist Religion*, pp. 135-38.

Protestants to 100,641 individuals in Taiyuan, Pingyang, and Zezhou prefectures. The Catholic effort, for which we have less information, was reportedly limited to 14,416 taels of relief to 2,800 families."[24]

This is more astounding considering there were only four Protestant missionaries in Shanxi in 1877: Joshua Turner and Francis James of the CIM, Timothy Richard (the Welshman whom Hudson Taylor had rejected — see Chapter 3) of the Baptist Missionary Society, and David Hill, a veteran of the Wesleyan Methodist Missionary Society. They were joined by three or four others in 1878, of whom one died of famine fever. Their eyewitness accounts, along with reports from Shandong, Zhili, Henan, and Shaanxi, stirred the conscience of Europe and North America. The Lord Mayor's China Famine Relief fund, sponsored by the Archbishop of Canterbury, raised over £50,000, of which £8,000 came through the CIM, and another £5,000 through other missions. Although this was "a drop of water in the ocean" of need, nevertheless the fund-raising campaign was one of the largest in England.[25]

The CIM, with stations in seven provinces and itinerants in eight more, was in a position to provide much of the famine information. Hudson Taylor, who left China in late 1877, happened to be in England as the first reports came from his far-flung correspondents, which he collated in *China's Millions*, sometimes devoting a whole issue to the famine with little regular (i.e., evangelistic) news.[26] Since famine relief was a departure from the CIM's emphasis on evangelism, it required some theological adjustment. By divine providence, Taylor argued, the famine "synchronizes with the wider opening up of China to missionary effort, thus giving us the call to help, and affording us the opportunity of showing practically that Christianity teaches men to 'love this [sic] neighbor as himself.'"[27]

The drought was compounded by the logistics of moving grain through

---

24. Roger R. Thompson, "Twilight of the Gods in the Chinese Countryside: Christians, Confucians, and the Modernizing State, 1861-1911," in *Christianity in China: From the Eighteenth Century to the Present*, ed. Daniel H. Bays (Stanford: Stanford University Press, 1996), pp. 60, 56.

25. *HTCOC* 6, p. 183. *China's Millions* (GB), September 1878, p. 123.

26. These issues of *China's Millions*, with a larger distribution than normal, are among the primary documents of the famine. In addition to its own reports, they reprinted eye-witness accounts from diplomats, Catholic priests, newspapers like the *Shanghai Courier* and *China Telegraph*, and statements of eminent Chinese like Zeng Guofan and the Chinese ambassador to France. Articles included: "What has been done for the relief of sufferers"; "Rotting grain at Tien-tsin"; and "Has the relief distributed by missionaries done any appreciable good?"

27. JHT, in Brandt, *Massacre in Shansi*, p. 21. *China's Millions* (GB), September 1878, p. 120.

the mountains. The passes presented scenes of "frightful disorder" where "fugitives, beggars and thieves absolutely swarmed."[28] At first the missionaries tried to distribute cash, a tactic that raised suspicion among the authorities, especially in areas where the government had limited control. "Any distribution made in the districts where the Chinese had started no relief would inevitably lead to an insurrection among the desperate inhabitants," wrote a consul, and would lead to "the pillage of one or two *yamens*, and the murder of a few mandarins [and] would have been the signal for a general conflagration."[29] Rather, working with the officials, Richard learned the most important lesson in orderly famine relief. When Jesus had fed the five thousand, *"He made them sit down,"* for, Richard realized, a "sitting crowd cannot crush."[30]

One successful venture was an orphanage in Taiyuan opened by Timothy Richard and his wife Mary, the only Protestant woman in the province. Its inmates numbered "Orphans, 822; Aged and Widows, 334 — Total, 1156," and it provided outdoor relief for others.[31] Richard wrote to Hudson Taylor in London offering to turn the orphanage over to the CIM if Taylor could provide suitable women to run it. In 1878 Taylor sent his wife, Jennie Faulding, to Shanxi while he stayed in England with the children. Her companions, Anna Crickmay (later Mrs. Joshua Turner) and Celia Horne, were the first unmarried Protestant women in the interior of China, a precedent that opened doors for women, married and single, to journey into the farthest reaches of inland China.

The Land of the Yellow Emperor

Shanxi appears on a map of China as a rectangle near the top left corner, cut off from the rest of China by the mountains on the east, the Yellow River on the south and west, and by the two arms of the Great Wall in the north. With an area "one and two-thirds the size of Scotland,"[32] it was a mountain fastness as old as time itself. *The Christian Occupation of China* (1922) described Shanxi as

> a great loess plateau, ascending gradually from an altitude of 2,500 feet in the south to over 5,000 feet in the north. This plateau is intersected by

28. *China's Millions* (GB), October 1879, pp. 135-36.
29. R. J. Forrest, formerly Consul in Ningbo, in *HTCOC 6*, p. 176. See also Introduction, note 42.
30. *HTCOC 6*, pp. 166-67.
31. Ibid., p. 179.
32. *China's Millions* (GB), June 1877, p. 70.

The Valley of the Shadow

short and irregular mountain ranges. A series of depressions or sunken alluvial plains gives evidence of former lakes. These regions form the most fertile and populous sections of the province. Tatungfu [Datong], Taiyüanfu, Pingyangfu, and Chiehchow [Jiezhou] are situated in these former lake basins. . . . Communication by both rivers and roads in Shansi is extremely difficult, owing to the nature of the soil and to the shallow swift currents of the rivers. . . . Cart roads radiate in all directions in the plains. Many of them are, however, below the surface of the fields, and during the rainy season either become running streams or are so deep with mud that they are almost impassable for two or three months of the year.[33]

This central valley varies from ten to sixty miles wide, and is so fertile it can produce two crops in one summer — if it rains; otherwise, the sandy soil dries up and blows away. (The Shanxi landscape can be visualized from photographs of Mao Zedong's wartime capital at Yanan, which happens to be across the Yellow River in Shaanxi, where the communist soldiers lived in caves in the loess cliffs.)

According to Andrew Kaiser, a Christian aid worker in Shanxi, there was a joke circulating in the province when the national "Go West" initiative was being pushed in the 1990s. For purposes of government grants and subsidies, Shanxi was not officially considered part of the western provinces (Shaanxi, Gansu), nor was it one of the eastern coastal provinces (Hebei, Shandong). *Shanxi bu shu dong, ye bu shu xi. Shanxi bu shi dongxi:* "Shanxi doesn't belong to the eastern part of China or the western part of China — Shanxi isn't anything!" The word play relies on the Chinese word for an unspecified thing or object [*dongxi*] being composed of two simple characters: one meaning east [*dong*] and the other west [*xi*]. This peculiar exemption meant Shanxi got nothing — not even respect. Kaiser said that "Shanxi residents — even officials — were often quite proud of this!"[34]

Taiyuan, the capital, is one of the oldest cities in China, and its massive walls, now demolished, were thirteen miles in circumference and built about 1000 B.C.E. It sits at the northern end of a broad plain, the watershed of the Fen River, which flows from the north, gathering what little rainwater it can

---

33. Milton T. Stauffer, ed., *The Christian Occupation of China: A General Survey of the Numerical Strength and Geographical Distribution of the Christian Forces in China Made by the Special Committee on Survey and Occupation, China Continuation Committee 1918-1921* (Shanghai: China Continuation Committee, 1922), p. 185.

34. Andrew T. Kaiser, Shanxi Evergreen Service, Taiyuan, Shanxi, communication to author, 13 September 2003.

across the parched ground, until it exits three hundred fifty miles to the southwest, at the bend in the Yellow River. Back in the 1200s Marco Polo described Taiyuan as a terminus of the Silk Road and a "great center of trade and industry, which supplies great quantities of the equipment needed for the Great Khan's armies." Ever since, Taiyuan and Pingyao, thirty miles south, have been the headquarters of China's "native banking" system, which was based on pawnshops and "long-distance remittances, specializing in particular in drafts and credit accounts for traders and merchants all through the empire," as far as Canton, Mongolia, and Japan. The bankers had buried so much gold and silver in their backyards, it was said, that Shanxi was a "solid mountain of precious metal."[35] (The home of one of these Shanxi bankers, the Qiao family mansion, with its myriad subsidiary courtyards and eerie lack of privacy, was the setting for the film *Raise the Red Lantern*, which depicted the extended household of a traditional patriarch with four wives.)

Shanxi people describe themselves as *laoshi*, which means either honest and straightforward or stick-in-the-mud and close-minded. One recent guidebook described their character as

> conservative, simple, and thrifty. The man from Shanxi, the *Shanxiren*, is often the butt of Chinese jokes, taking a role somewhat like that of the Scotsman in the humor of English-speaking peoples. Although the people of Shanxi do have a reputation for being hard-working and good at business (including banking), they are also expected to be honest and straightforward in their dealings. Even when the *Shanxiren* becomes rich, so goes the stereotype, he does not spend money in ostentatious living . . . rather he puts it away for hard times.[36]

In its present incarnation, Taiyuan sits at the bottom of most lists. Zhu Rongji, the foremost architect of China's recent economic reforms, supposedly described Taiyuan as the most *luan* of all *shengcheng* [provincial capitals]. *Luan* is one of those fearsome words in Chinese, which means "chaotic," such as the chaos that accompanied the Cultural Revolution. There have been recent attempts to clean up the city, but it still has the worst pollution on earth, only slightly below Lanzhou and New Delhi. The new mayor ordered a face-lift in response to Zhu's comment, which meant the uncompensated demolition of two million square meters of "temporary or illegal buildings."

---

35. Brandt, *Massacre in Shansi*, pp. 16-17.
36. Leo J. Moser, *The Chinese Mosaic: The Peoples and Provinces of China* (Boulder, Colo: Westview Press, 1985), pp. 76-77.

The Valley of the Shadow

This was a cruel blow to Taiyuan's fledgling entrepreneurial class. Street peddlers and vegetable carts were also outlawed and forced into giant markets — where they pay rent and are out of sight of official motorcades. "This can be a very sad place to live," says Andrew Kaiser, who works at Shanxi Evergreen Service, "especially when one's job brings one into regular contact with officials who are coming up with these ideas."[37]

There are now perhaps fifteen thousand Protestants in Taiyuan. As many as ten thousand would consider themselves in some ways associated with the registered Three-Self church, which is very evangelical. Catholics are far more numerous, especially in the rural areas surrounding Taiyuan. There are still many villages where everyone is Catholic. Many are fifth-, sixth-, or more generation Catholics, who trace their roots back to the early 1700s. They are to Catholicism what a typical Chinese is to Buddhism.[38]

Halfway down the Fen River, about one hundred fifty miles south of Taiyuan, is Pingyang, now called by its ancient name Linfen, the main prefectural or *fu* city of South Shanxi. It was supposedly the oldest walled city in China, built by the Yellow Emperor at the dawn of time (he acceded to the throne in 2696 B.C.E., since 1911 was counted as the 4,607th anniversary). All *lao-bai* (the "old hundred surnames" of the Chinese people) trace their ancestry to the Yellow Emperor and his twenty-five sons. Here at Pingyang, he taught humans how to be human: how to sow and reap millet, how to raise silkworms, how to wear clothes. He invented the wheel, copper coins, the Chinese writing system, and the five-color *wuxing* — the cosmological interrelationship of yellow earth, green wood, red fire, white metal, and black water.

This may seem like ancient history, but even today the Yellow Emperor is spoken of in Shanxi as though he lived the day before yesterday.[39] Moreover, archaeology confirms successive Stone Age cultures in the Fen-Wei valley, dating back to the "oldest homo sapiens," 100,000 years ago.[40] There are 200 paleolithic and 500 neolithic sites in the province, and three-quarters of all

---

37. Kaiser communication.
38. Ibid.
39. Justin Hill, *A Bend in the Yellow River* (London: Phoenix House, 1997), pp. 5-7. Hill, an ESL teacher, was "bombarded with facts and figures" concerning the Yellow Emperor and Guandi when he arrived in Yuncheng in 1993. Speeches and tourist information about Shanxi invariably begin with a recitation of the Yellow Emperor, Yao and Shun, and so on, with lists of famous *Shanxiren*.
40. Dennis A. Etler, "The Fossil Evidence for Human Evolution in China," at website http://www.cruzio.com/~cscp/index.htm. The fossils discovered in Shanxi are 150,000 years younger than Peking Man, and are described as the first "fully modern Homo sapiens."

ancient (i.e., pre-thirteenth century, Yuan and earlier) "cultural relics" in China are found there.[41]

The Temple-Land

The missionaries called Shanxi a "temple-land." They did not mean that as a compliment: to them Shanxi was a god-saturated, idolatrous place, the seat of Satan. More dispassionately, Shanxi has always been a crossroads of religious movements, imported religions that migrated along the Silk Road — Jews, Christians, Nestorians, and Muslims from the Middle East, Buddhists and magicians from India, lamas from Tibet and shamans from Mongolia — mixing with the native religions that percolated up from the yellow earth. Hongdong, north of Pingyang, was a center of the White Lotus sect. Taiyuan was the home of Pure Land Buddhism, which worshiped Amida Buddha, the Buddha of Compassion who promised to take the faithful to his Western Paradise in the Pure Land. The Yellow Emperor's cult temple is nearby, as well as the birthplace of Guandi, the God of War, at Yuncheng, which has a shrine slightly smaller than the imperial palace. In the far north, Datong was the capital of the Northern Wei dynasty (386-532 C.E.), which produced some of the most ethereal Buddhist sculpture ever created. The Yungang Grotto is considered one of the major repositories of Buddhist art in China, with fifty-three caves housing as many as 51,000 sandstone carvings.[42] Out in the desert, Datong is dominated by a colossal Buddha more than sixty feet tall, portrayed in a pose of reconciliation.

The most important pilgrimage shrine in Shanxi was (and is) Wutaishan, the Mountain of Five Peaks, 120 miles northeast of Taiyuan, which is considered one of the four holy mountains sacred to Chinese Buddhism. It is dedicated to Manjusri, the Buddha of Wisdom, whose name is translated from the Sanskrit *Pancasika,* which literally means "mountain with five peaks." Temples have been built at Wutaishan since the Han dynasty and now number in the hundreds, with tens of thousands of images. One particular attraction is a mechanical Buddha that emerges from a lotus flower as the monk grinds away behind the scenes.[43] Since Manjusri is the Buddha of Grammatical Science, Wutaishan is laid out with geometric precision as a living *wuxing.* Each

---

41. See website for "Armchair Traveller: Shanxi Province," at http://ess1.ps.uci.edu/~oliver/shanxi.html.
42. Ibid.
43. Ibid.

The Valley of the Shadow

of the five peaks is dedicated to one of the five celestial colors, and everything on that peak — the temples, the images, even the flowers on the hillsides — is either red, black, white, green, or yellow.

The best place to imagine Shanxi before the famine is, unexpectedly, in Toronto, in the Bishop White Gallery of the Royal Ontario Museum. According to the guidebook, the gallery is the re-creation of a major North Chinese monastery hall from the golden age of Chinese Buddhism, from the Tang (617-907 C.E.) to the Yuan (or Mongol 1234-1368 C.E.). Everything came from a fifty-mile radius of Pingyang. A huge fresco (40 feet wide by 30 feet) which dominates the north wall, came from the "Monastery of Joyful Conversion" [*Xinghua Si*] at "Little Peace Village." Dated to about 1325, it depicts Maitreya, the Buddha of the Future, enthroned in paradise, flanked by Transcendent Wisdom and Universal Goodness. On the east and west walls are Daoist processions from the Dragon Gate Monastery, depicting the stars and planets marching in stately homage to the First Principle. An image platform contains twelve monumental statues of Guanyin, the Goddess of Mercy, reaching out to save suffering humanity.[44]

This is Mahayana Buddhism at its most exuberant, bedecked with pearls and jewels, gazing sloe-eyed down from paradise. Shanxi idols are distinctive, easy to identify in museums around the world, including the British Museum, the Victoria & Albert, the Metropolitan, Berlin, and Kansas City. They have noble features and powerful bodies that show "a tendency toward a mature and relaxed corpulence." According to the British Museum, "Wooden sculptures, often life-size or over, were common in North China from about the 10th to the 14th centuries, and are particularly associated with Shanxi."[45]

The "Monastery of Joyful Conversion" is a suggestive name, and the re-created hall contains both Buddhist and Daoist images. This, in museological terms, suggests the syncretic nature of Shanxi religious movements, and the "joyful conversion" as old deities died and new ones were born. There was a curious parallel between the entry of Protestant Christianity in the late nineteenth century and an event that took place in Shanxi three thousand years ago, at the end of the Shang dynasty (1122 B.C.E.), known as "the enfiefment of the gods." The main deity of the Shang kings was named *Shangdi*, usually translated as "Lord on High," who lived in the Heavenly City Shang with the ancestors of the royal family. Humans could speak to Shangdi through oracle

---

44. William Charles White, *Chinese Temple Frescos: A Study of Three Wall Paintings of the Thirteenth Century* (1940), detailed the Shanxi art that was available on the international markets during the 1930s. Quote from Royal Ontario Museum pamphlet, "The Bishop White Gallery: Wall Paintings and Wood Sculptures from Shanxi Province, China."

45. Exhibit text in British Museum.

bones, bones of animals and turtles which were inscribed with the earliest form of Chinese writing.

When the Shang dynasty was conquered by the Zhou dynasty, the new rulers introduced a pantheon under *Tian* or "Heaven." "Heaven was in turmoil, with no one in charge. The deities were being 'killed' and returning to Earth as humans, where they were readily employed as soldiers on both sides."[46] Heaven, arching above human affairs, was distant, impersonal, the capricious forces of fate that sweep over humans like wind over grass. As his final defiant gesture, the last Shang emperor shot an arrow into Heaven and committed suicide. Heaven won, and gradually the worship of Shangdi faded away. Nevertheless, the Chinese never forget an old god, and temples dedicated to Shangdi survived; they are unusual because Shangdi, being a spirit, is invisible and therefore the temples have no images.

Twelve hundred years later, another god was born near Pingyang, Guandi the God of War, one of the most popular deities throughout East Asia. He was a loyal general at the end of the Han dynasty (221 C.E.) whose adventures were immortalized in *The Romance of the Three Kingdoms*. He appears on temple doors as the Red-Faced General in a ferocious attitude, one foot raised and brandishing his jeweled sword. Seated and benign, he is a scholar, the patron of those who believe in discipline and order, such as bookkeepers, soldiers, and police. "He is interdenominational, being worshipped by Buddhists as a temple protector, by Confucianists as a patron of literature, and by Daoists as a powerful exorcist." It is worth noting that Guandi is also the patron deity of spirit mediums, and acts "as a spirit control for mediums and an exorciser of demons."[47]

The Jesuits, who arrived in China in the 1600s, fixated on Shangdi *because he was invisible.* They came up with a theory that Shangdi — about the time Moses encountered the Burning Bush — was an immortal, invisible, omnipotent creator-god, a monotheistic Jehovah, who had revealed himself to the ancient Chinese people. The worship of Shangdi, performed with burned sacrifices in Hebraic fashion, the Jesuits claimed, was corrupted by the "idolatry" of Confucian ancestor worship, Daoist magic, and, later, the images of Buddhism. The Jesuits' rivals, the Franciscans, aware of the danger of associating Christianity with Chinese folk religion, claimed the Jesuits were condoning "ancestor worship" by employing the name Shangdi. As a result of the "Confucian rites" controversy, the pope prohibited the use of Shangdi, and Roman

---

46. Keith Stevens, *Chinese Gods: Fo Hsiang Shen Hsiang* (London: Collins & Brown, 1997), pp. 59-60.

47. Ibid., p. 150.

Catholics had to invent a new name with no connotations, *Tianzhu*, "the Lord of Heaven."[48]

When Protestant missionaries arrived in the nineteenth century, they too agonized over the "term question," how to translate God Almighty. Gutzlaff had selected "Shangdi" for his elegant translation of the Bible in the 1840s, which was copied in the Taiping Bible. Among the vocal opponents of Shangdi was W. C. Burns, Hudson Taylor's mentor and translator of *Pilgrim's Progress*, who proposed a variety of alternatives. Nevertheless, despite — or because of — the Taiping "god-worshippers," Shangdi became the common Protestant name for God, which was translated as "the True God" or "the One True God."

The CIM records provide a tantalizing glimpse of a series of religious revivals in Shanxi that predated their arrival by fifty years, in which Christianity was part of a continuum of new sects. About fifty years before the missionaries arrived, that is, about 1830, a Buddhist "reformer" started a sect in northeast Shanxi. He called it simply "the Secret Religion, because the members do not openly declare themselves such, as the Government has more than once terribly persecuted them, thinking them guilty of disloyalty to the present dynasty. As far as we can ascertain, the charge seems wholly without foundation."[49] This reformer preached of a coming calamity, and promised salvation through self-denial, charitable works, and devotion to images. Even Mrs. Howard Taylor waxed sympathetic when she described him as "living in poverty and loneliness. . . . With burning enthusiasm he called on men and women to repent, and turn from their selfishness and evil ways, exhorting them to cultivate virtue, care for the needs of others, practise benevolence, spend time and money in the relief of suffering, [and] accumulate merit." He attracted a large following of Confucianists, Buddhists, and Daoists, "men and women alike" who banded into "well-organized societies."[50]

The Secret Religion reached as far south as Pingyang, where in 1853 it encountered the Taiping god-worshipers. After the Taipings captured Nanjing, they sent a Northern Expeditionary Force into Shanxi to take Taiyuan, then move along the Big Road east to Beijing. At Pingyang the Taiping army was welcomed with "spontaneous public support," and they moved on to Hongdong, the next city north on the Big Road, which also welcomed them. But then they changed their minds and instead of continuing to march north

---

48. David E. Mungello, *Curious Land: Jesuit Accommodation and the Origins of Sinology* (Honolulu: University of Hawaii Press, 1989), discussed this at length.

49. Rev. Samuel B. Drake, "The Story of Mr. Fan, of P'ing Yang Fu, Shan-si," *China's Millions* (GB), September 1883, pp. 127-29. Elder Fan (see Chapter 8) was a member of the Secret Religion.

50. *Pastor Hsi*, pp. 90-91.

to Taiyuan, they turned eastwards. This proved to be disastrous, since they got lost in the mountains and never reached Beijing. After the devastation they had caused in central China, why would they have been welcomed at Pingyang and Hongdong? The historian Jen Yu-wen attributes this to the desire of the common people for the restoration of Chinese rule from the "barbarian" Manchu dynasty and the moral discipline of the Taiping army.[51] In any event the Taipings went away and never returned, so Shanxi did not endure the devastation of the Yangtze cities.

Enter the Roman Catholics in 1861, on the coattails of Western imperialism. The Franciscans had a long history in Shanxi going back to 1700, when they claimed two thousand converts in Taiyuan. In 1724, the Qianlong Emperor proscribed Christianity as a heterodox sect, over the so-called Rites controversy, but Christian families and communities persisted. Henrietta Harrison, the historian of Catholicism and Boxers in Shanxi, notes, "For many years after the expulsion of the Jesuits there was only a single Cantonese priest in the province, but the number of Catholics continued to grow and the faith was assimilated into local social structures and ideologies in ways which shocked later missionaries."[52] The Sino-French Convention of 1860 not only allowed Catholic missionaries under French protection to travel and purchase land in the interior; it also confirmed the edict that called for the return of religious property which had been seized after 1724. The Franciscans who traveled to Shanxi quickly reclaimed the mission their confrères had left almost a century and a half earlier.

The Catholic church offered something no other sect could: protection from lawsuits and a 40 percent cut in taxes. Although the imperial government had issued a declaration of toleration for Christians, this did not always filter down to the local magistrate. There was no mechanism for dealing with "missionary cases," except for the cumbersome, high-level Zongli Yamen. In fact, Roger Thompson argues that the compromise worked out by the Franciscans in Shanxi in 1861 had far-reaching ramifications, because it became the model for diplomatic relations between China and the Western Powers until the Boxer Uprising. (Thompson also noted that the Franciscans had a Pastor Hsi kind of indigenous leader, the native catechist Paul Wu, who actively took up cases of Christian village persecution with provincial authorities.)[53]

51. Jen Yu-wen, *The Taiping Revolutionary Movement* (New Haven: Yale University Press, 1973), pp. 179-80.
52. Henrietta Harrison, "Village Politics and National Politics: The Boxer Movement in Central Shanxi" (unpublished paper courtesy of the author).
53. Roger Thompson, "Twilight of the Gods in the Chinese Countryside," pp. 60, 56; for Paul Wu see pp. 62-64.

The Valley of the Shadow

When the Franciscans demanded that the provincial governor issue a proclamation outlining the rights and freedoms of Chinese Christians, their proposed regulations all concerned money and taxes. Catholics should be exempt from paying "idol taxes" or having "to contribute money for opera, sacrifices, or temple repairs because Christians, who believe in God *(tianzhu)*, need to use this money to pay for their own chapels *(tianzhu tang)* and ceremonies *(libai)* so that they can show proper respect to their religion." Article five stated that "magistrates must punish any non-Christian who extorts from, harasses, harms the crops of, or acts violently toward or beats Christians who refuse to pay monies for activities injurious to their beliefs."[54]

Since the problem had been expressed in monetary terms, so too was the compromise. Christians were to be exempt from paying that portion of their taxes used to support local temple festivals, which often included performances of opera, but they still had to pay for public projects, such as bridge and road repairs, irrigation, local security, crop-watching, and the corvée labor. The former, the French minister declared, were "wasteful" or "useless" expenditures, while the latter he deemed "useful" or "public." Once that principle was established, the government had to determine the exact percentage: 60 percent of taxes were deemed "useful," and 40 percent "useless."[55]

Thompson argues that the payment of opera taxes was *the* main cause of conflict between Christians and their neighbors. Not only was it economic, he goes further, but the refusal to pay temple taxes upset the moral order of the villages. The Western dichotomy between the sacred and the secular was inconceivable, and by dividing taxes in those terms, "the Chinese government had called into question an implicit communal understanding of proper behavior with respect to ritual observances. By defining the ritual observances of local communities as voluntary and non-inclusive, the stage was set for desacralizing temple resources."[56]

Nevertheless, as Henrietta Harrison notes, the Catholic church grew into a sizable minority in central Shanxi, including several powerful Christian villages. "The diocesan compound in Taiyuan with its huge cathedral built in the early 1870s reflected the size and history of the Catholic community." When Dr. Schofield of the CIM arrived in 1881, he could hardly believe he was in China as he looked at the gorgeous high altar, shrines, confessionals, holy pictures, the stations of the cross and holy water stoops. The Catholics were not always popular with the local population, but there was little history of

---

54. Ibid., p. 57.
55. Ibid., pp. 57-60.
56. Ibid., p. 71.

open antagonism. By 1898, the Catholic church counted 26,961 adherents and thirty-six foreign missionaries.[57]

Finally, with the famine, the Protestant missionaries came to Shanxi. They seemed to have lots of silver and grain, which they distributed freely, without demanding that the recipient join the church. But from the beginning, they refused to get involved with lawsuits. Rather they preached a gospel of sin and suffering, and possible persecution. Nevertheless, the Protestants did accept the 60/40 percent compromise worked out by the Catholics. Dr. Schofield wrote in his diary on 22 September 1881 that "a proclamation has just been issued by the Chinese Government in Pekin [Beijing] extending to Protestant native Christians the same privileges which have long been accorded to the native adherents of the Romish priests, viz. complete exemption from all taxes levied for the support of idolatrous rites and ceremonies."[58]

By the end of the nineteenth century, Shanxi was tired and worn-out, like a thousand-year-old idol that had been painted so many times the features were obscured by layers of gilt. The iconoclastic Protestant missionaries contributed to the decimation of the idol population of Shanxi by lighting bonfires to burn the "paraphernalia of idolatry" given up by their converts. But their activities were minuscule compared to the tomb robbers, temple vandalizers, archaeologists, and revolutionaries of the twentieth century. By the 1920s Shanxi had gained a reputation in the international art market as "the most fruitful source" for monumental temple paintings and sculpture from the highest periods of Chinese art, ripe for the picking.[59] The Swedish Orientalist Osvald Siren and John King Fairbank, the American historian, poked around Tang temples and left with crates of loot.[60]

The Man Who Stood by the Gate

As the famine abated in 1879, the Protestant missionaries, who now numbered nine, turned their minds from famine relief to evangelism. The first convert was a "doctor" named Sung, who had been hired by David Hill as the gatekeeper at Pingyang: Gatekeeper Sung, later Elder Sung. (The only time his full name was given, in a list of pastors who survived the Boxer uprising, it is

---

57. Harrison, "Village Politics."
58. Thompson, "Twilight of the Gods," p. 56.
59. White, *Chinese Temple Frescos*, p. 15.
60. John King Fairbank, *Chinabound: A Fifty Year Memoir* (New York: Harper & Row, 1982), p. 112.

The Valley of the Shadow

spelled Song-Ch'ang-Keng.)[61] The gatekeeper was a pivotal person in a walled society, part coolie and watchman, part language teacher and evangelist. He sat inside the gate, keeping an eye out for robbers and hostile intruders while welcoming the good people to come inside and eat the Jesus religion. For us, a century later, Gatekeeper Sung swings the gate the other way to reveal an unexpected vista of Chinese religious sectarians waiting outside.

The first record of Gatekeeper Sung is J. J. Turner's report on the baptism of five "native brethren" in November 1880. He was aged fifty, a native of Pingyang, "by profession, a doctor, well known throughout the neighbourhood." He had sought in vain for soul satisfaction in the native religions, he testified, and had converted to Christianity and destroyed his idols a year before. He was now, Turner wrote, a "consistent humble believer . . . a gradual conversion."[62]

Let us hear Gatekeeper Sung's testimony in his own words, filtered through the missionary's words: "I formerly feared death," he started, abruptly, not unexpectedly from one surrounded by death and dying. In his youth, he had worked in a "tobacconist's shop" — a thinly disguised opium shop? — until his health failed, and he fell into debt. He studied medicine in Huaiqing, North Henan, then returned to open a medical shop in Pingyang. During the famine, when his only daughter was dying, she asked what would happen to her soul, but he "did not know the truth himself, and there was no one else to teach her."[63]

His testimony continues, with a startling ring of truth:

> On hearing the Taoist doctrines, I determined to enter that sect. I studied their books, and for twenty-five years abstained from all meat. I, moreover, followed the Buddhists in reciting the incantations. Instead of obtaining peace, my heart became increasingly wretched and unsatisfied. Then came the great famine. In the first year of the famine, I saw a boy with the gospel of Matthew; he lent it to me, and I read it. I was immensely taken with the life of Jesus, but what struck me so was that such a good man should come to such an end. I remember weeping over the story of the crucifixion, but at that time, though I loved Jesus, I did not know he could save me. . . . Some time after, Mr. Hill came to P'ing-yang; the famine was at its height, my daughter-in-law and daughter both died in the space of three days. At that time Mr. Hill came to my house to ask me to look after a young connection of mine who had been cast out by

---

61. *China's Millions* (NA), October 1901, p. 104.
62. J. J. Turner, Pingyang, to JHT, London, 29 November 1880, in CIM/SOAS, file 257.
63. *China's Millions* (GB), April 1881, p. 42. Compared to this chaste testimony, *Pastor Hsi*, vol. 1, pp. 139-44, devoted a chapter, "First-Fruits," to Sung; for an overwrought version of his daughter's death, pp. 141-42 (see also Preface, note 5).

Gatekeeper Sung (#9) and elders of the Hongdong church, 1890s. A former member of a Daoist sect, Sung was the first convert in South Shanxi; as gatekeeper for the Christian mission, he invited his former sectarians inside. He died in 1902, aged 75. Elder Sï, Pastor Hsi's brother-in-law and successor, is #7; he was stabbed by the Boxers and died of his injuries. The Hongdong church was Pastor Hsi's mud-brick "cathedral" where he presided as "bishop." Source: Mrs. Howard Taylor, *Pastor Hsi*, vol. 2, *One of China's Christians.*

his parents, and was nearly starved. I told him my circumstances. . . . He promised to help me, adding, he would pay for the keep of the child.[64]

What is one to make of Gatekeeper Sung's testimony, other than the obvious, that many of his family starved during the famine but he was saved by rice and money from the missionary? By his own reckoning, he had joined a Daoist sect twenty-five years earlier, i.e., about 1852, about the time of the Taiping Northern Expedition, and had learned an eclectic range of religious exercises, hoping for immortality and salvation from the coming cataclysm. He grew "wretched and unsatisfied" when his breathing exercises did not save him from the famine.

Even in translation, there is something formulaic in Sung's repudiation of his old religion and conversion to the new: indeed, it was a common trope in Chinese sectarian autobiographies. Gatekeeper Sung's abrupt beginning could have been copied from the spiritual autobiography of Lo Qing (1443-

---

64. "The Hung-t'ung Conference, Aug. 1st and 2nd. Deeply Interesting Native Testimony," *China's Millions* (GB), January 1887, p. 7. (Hereafter cited as "Hung-T'ung Conference. Mr. Sung.") See also *Pastor Hsi*, vol. 1, pp. 140-41.

The Valley of the Shadow

1527). Patriarch Lo was the legendary founder of Gatekeeper Sung's sect, the Wu-wei (Nonactivism) branch of Daoism:

> Fearing impermanence and the sufferings of birth-and-death, I took the first step, observing that all things in the world course on impermanence, all that has form is empty and lost.... When my parents died, I was abandoned and left alone.... Fortunately, the celestial buddhas protected me and I grew up to adulthood. I constantly maintained a vegetarian diet, feared birth-and-death, and desired to have some control over the path ahead [i.e., my future].[65]

Gatekeeper Sung's testimony continued with another startling admission: "I happened to see a copy of the treaty of the Western powers with China. I noticed particularly that each western kingdom took its year's date from the birth of Jesus (Anno Domini) 1800 odd years ago. On thinking the matter over it came to me, Well, if the doctrine of Jesus is 'the heavenly doctrine,' is it not right that time should be so reckoned? and will not China, too, soon own His sway?" How did Sung get a copy of the Beijing Convention? How many hands had it passed through? Of course, the treaty gives more than the date of Jesus' birth: Sung would have learned that Christian converts were exempt from paying idol taxes, and that missionaries possessed enormous diplomatic power backed up by gunboats.

Finally, Gatekeeper Sung closed with a moral. His mind filled with questions, he visited Mr. Hill, who gave him a book called "Questions and Answers on the Heavenly Doctrine." After studying the book for five months, Sung started praying to the One True God, even though he continued "incantations." His wife, a zealous idol-worshiper who recited incantations a hundred times a day, also converted, and now, "since we have believed in Jesus we have had the deepest fellowship."[66]

The Religion of the Golden Pill

Gatekeeper Sung had been an adept of the *Jindan Jiao*, the Religion (or School, or Doctrine) of the Golden Pill, or Golden Elixir, a Daoist sect that

---

65. Daniel L. Overmyer, *Precious Volumes: An Introduction to Chinese Sectarian Scriptures from the Sixteenth and Seventeenth Centuries* (Cambridge: Harvard University Asia Center, 1999), p. 96. This is from a *baoquan* called "On Awakening to the Way through bitter toil."
66. "Hung-T'ung Conference. Mr. Sung," p. 7; see also *Pastor Hsi*, vol. 1, pp. 142-43.

taught a variety of breathing and alchemical techniques for healing and long life. Sung welcomed his fellow sectarians into the mission and, one can say with some assurance, most of the early converts in Shanxi were former members of *Jindan Jiao*. The famine had shattered the old sectarian networks, since the first victims would have been the elderly lay leaders, the spirit mediums who were always in precarious health, and pregnant and old women. Joining the Christian church — in name if not in deed — was a providential escape: the missionaries gave food, money, and political protection, a refuge where he could stitch together his sectarian network. Gatekeeper Sung had the perfect vantage point to spot his old friends, sitting at the gate.

The Golden Pill, according to Timothy Richard, was the most widespread and powerful of all secret societies in North China, counting forty thousand members and centered at Pingyang. It had the distinction, in historical terms, of being one of the oldest religious sects, since it was founded during the Song dynasty (c. 1050 C.E.) and spread rapidly during the Mongol invasions. By the 1400s the Golden Pill merged with other Daoist sects under a common name, the Complete Perfection *(Quanchen)* sect.

Richard had a controversial theory that the Golden Pill was unique in that it contained elements of Nestorian Christianity, which had flourished in the Taiyuan — Xian corridor during the Tang dynasty (618-907 C.E.). Their most famous relic is the Nestorian monument in Xian, dated 781. Nestorianism was supposedly persecuted out of existence during the Ming dynasty, but some Golden Pill patriarchs told Richard that the Nestorians had dispersed among the Muslims, one explanation for the large population of Muslims in northwest China, while others joined the Religion of the Golden Pill. They used the old Chinese dichotomy of *yin-yang* to express Christian philosophical ideas (good/evil, word/flesh, spirit/soul), thus "putting the search for immortality on a moral and spiritual basis . . . but with a new and higher meaning." Richard concluded, "Add to this the circumstantial evidence that several of the leaders of the Kin Tan Kiao [*Jindan Jiao*], whether they have joined the modern Christians or not, have decided that the essential doctrines of the Kin Tan Kiao and Christianity are the same." One evidence was the daily worship of the sun at sunrise and sunset. Another was its name, "the Learning-to-do-good Sect" *(Xuehao jiao)*, for its teetotalism and prohibition against tobacco and opium.[67]

---

67. The Nestorian lineage was supported by P. Yokio Saeki, a professor at Waseda University in *The Nestorian Monument in China* (London: Society for Promoting Christian Knowledge, 1916; reprint, 1928), pp. 48-61; quotes at p. 55. It has been discussed recently by Ralph Covell, *Confucius, the Buddha, and Christ: A History of the Gospel in Chinese* (Maryknoll, N.Y.: Orbis Books, 1986).

The Valley of the Shadow

The Nestorian lineage is interesting, whether true or not, for Pastor Hsi and his Chinese Christians believed it: the *indigenous Christianity that arose in southern Shanxi was seen as a restoration of ancient Chinese Christianity.* Therefore they possessed an older, "truer," and "purer" tradition of Christianity than the "corrupt" missionary variety.

Daoist sects were different from the Buddhist and White Lotus congregations that characterized CIM conversions near the coast (see Chapter 4). They were elemental and experiential, concerned with inner and outer alchemy through transformations and breathing exercises *(taiqi)*, as well as invulnerability rituals, spirit mediums, and planchette writings. One opponent described the Golden Pill in words that sound suspiciously similar to official denunciations of the *Falun Gong* today: "There is a class of heretics who practice breathing exercises.... They speak of the field of cinnabar ... the three apertures, ... fate, and yin and yang.... All that they teach is useless in times of danger."[68] Perhaps that was what Gatekeeper Sung meant when he said he feared death, that the teachings did not protect him from the famine.

Like many religious sects, the Golden Pill could become a political rebellion. In 1891 the *Jindan Jiao* and a brother society, a vegetarian sect known as *Zaili*, were involved in an uprising in Manchuria that started as a conflict between Mongols and Chinese immigrants from Shanxi, who had been sent there to colonize the grasslands. It escalated into a full-scale anti-Christian, antiforeign, antidynastic rebellion, and engulfed an area of several thousand square miles. It was suppressed when well-armed government troops massacred twenty thousand sectarians, which led to a widespread suppression of religious sects throughout North China.[69]

Until recently, references to the Golden Pill were "fragmentary and superficial," at least in English. This has been remedied by Daniel L. Overmyer's magisterial *Precious Volumes: An Introduction to Chinese Sectarian Scriptures from the Sixteenth and Seventeenth Centuries*, which traces its lineage and influence in detail.

The Golden Elixir school was best known for its inner or physiological alchemy, in which bodily organs, processes, and fluids were identified with those of the alchemical furnace. This quest for nurturing the "in-

---

68. Overmyer, *Folk Buddhist Religion*, p. 124.
69. Richard Shek, "The Revolt of the Zaili, Jindan Sects in Rehe (Jehol), 1891," *Modern China*, April 1980, p. 163. Saeki, *Nestorian Monument*, p. 6, commented: "We may feel pretty sure that it was the descendents of the Chinese Nestorians who were so piteously massacred by the Chinese soldiery in 1891."

ner elixir" *(nei-dan)* was expressed in symbolic terminology based on ancient systems of classification, such as the sixty-term cycle of the "celestial stems and earthly branches," the sixty-four hexagrams of the *Book of Changes*, and the interaction of the Five Phases (wood, fire, earth, metal, and water). This symbolism also involved that of metals, such as mercury and lead, which were associated with psycho-physiological processes.[70]

By the time of the Qing Dynasty, the Golden Elixir had gained accretions of "the dark furnace" and the "Dark Furnace Pass," a "point between the eyebrows where the soul can escape." Its hymns became obscure incantations, such as the prayer toward the north: "At the *zu*-hour [11:00 p.m.–1:00 a.m.] (offering of) incense, the Dark Warrior divine general [*Xuan-wu shen-jiang*] receives the incense smoke and the Black Lotus Bodhisattva rejoices. They receive and guide the lost to return to their old home. In the Purple Yang Palace, buddhas and patriarchs rejoice. The Divine Lord of the Northern Bushel [i.e. the Big Dipper] sends down blessings. With devotion and sincerity, advance. Do not shorten the incense; the Divine General of the North will not obstruct you." These prayers are "repeated for the east, south, and west, with the deities involved being the Blue-Green Dragon, Vermilion Bird, and White Tiger divine generals, respectively. Each is paired with a bodhisattva of the appropriately colored lotus." In fact, Overmyer concludes, most of Golden Elixir scriptures was "a conflation of the five peaks, directions, and phases [and colors] with the rulers of different courts of purgatory."[71]

No wonder, when asked to give his testimony, Pastor Hsi — one of Gatekeeper Sung's converts from the Golden Pill — would get angry and speak in generalities. "As to the whole system of Buddhist idolatry and Taoist magic, what rubbish it really is!" he would say.[72] When pressed further, he would denounce his old religion as a "delusion." He had been attracted by "the promise of immortality" — what he called "refining and eating 'the pill'" and "living continually without aging" — but "came to realize what he ever afterwards maintained, that the whole system is a dark mystery of spiritualism and devil-worship."[73] How could he explain the field of cinnabar and the Dark General who guards the eyebrows?

---

70. Overmyer, *Precious Volumes*, p. 48. I have transliterated his Chinese into pinyin.
71. Ibid., pp. 86-88.
72. *Pastor Hsi*, vol. 1, p. 86; also single vol., pp. 13-16.
73. "Hung-t'ung Conference," pp. 5-6, "The Testimony of Mr. Hsi."

The Valley of the Shadow

The Chinese Wordless Book

By 1879, the China Inland Mission and the Baptist Missionary Society had both established stations in Taiyuan. The CIM pioneers, Joshua Turner and Francis James, had been joined by two seasoned veterans, Samuel Drake and Thomas Wellesley Piggott, and the women, Anna Crickmay and Celia Horne. The BMS consisted for the moment of Timothy Richard and his wife, since his Shandong colleagues had returned to their stations. The BMS claimed responsibility for the area north of Taiyuan — as far as Mongolia — while the CIM took the south, to the Yellow River. Since "the time had not yet come for street preaching, nor yet the opening of a Public Preaching Hall," the missionaries "held united consultation and prayer" how to attract different segments of Chinese society.[74] Using the house-to-house distribution tactics of the 1859 revival, they distributed twenty thousand tracts called "the Duty of Thanksgiving for the Cessation of the Famine." Their campaign operated at several levels: the refuge for widows and orphans, sectarian conversion through Gatekeeper Sung, preaching and tract distribution, and a literary campaign aimed at the scholar gentry class.

The CIM women found a ready audience among the famine victims under their care. Winter was coming on, so they employed the women in sewing wadded clothing for themselves and for distribution to the poor. "There was a large pile of them made, and we very soon got through them; and then another pile was made, and thus, week after week, distribution was made to these poor people in their distress." In the orphanage, "a new phase of missionary work was entered upon" when they realized the children needed "some kind of industry that might be useful to them in after life." The girls were taught to braid straw, spin cotton, and embroider articles for sale, such as a "little embroidered comb-case (it is a common thing amongst the Chinese to carry a little comb, with which they comb out their moustache)."[75]

While sewing scraps of cloth one of them — probably Jennie Taylor, the most adaptable of missionaries — had the brilliant idea of using the "wordless book" within the sewing circle, so they could "gossip the gospel" while they sewed. The four-color wordless book had been invented in 1875, as a refinement of Spurgeon's three-color version, by the American evangelist Dwight L. Moody, who added the gold page for "the glories of Heaven." By

---

74. David Hill, "The Triennial Examinations for the Kü Jan Degree," *Chinese Recorder*, November-December 1879, pp. 463-64; and "The Kü Jan Examination," March-April 1880, pp. 143-46.

75. David Hill, speech to CIM annual meeting, in *China's Millions* (GB), July-August 1881, pp. 89-93; quotes at pp. 90-91.

1877 it was being used by the CMS in Africa (see Introduction), where the missionaries noticed its congruence with native color symbolism. Now, a few years later, it was used for the first time in China.

The first mention came from David Hill, the saintly Wesleyan Methodist, in his keynote address to the CIM's annual meeting in May 1881. He had just returned from Shanxi, where he had spent four years through the whole famine period, and thus was one of the first eyewitnesses to reach England. He had high praise for the CIM men, his colleagues in distributing relief, but he particularly admired the "adaptiveness" of the women. They had sent him a small wordless book, which he pulled out of his pocket, in the form of "a coloured silk folio, for a lady to use and put her coloured silk thread into." It was sewn from scraps of four colors of silk: black, red, white, and yellow.

"And what is the lesson that is taught?" Hill asked.

> First of all, the black indicates the blackness of sin — that whoever lives in the habitual commission of sin has his heart blackened by it. The next is the red, pointing them to the blood of our Lord Jesus Christ, which cleanses from all sin. The next is the white, which shows the purity of those who believe in the Lord Jesus Christ for salvation, that their sins are all cleansed away, and that they are washed and made white in His most precious blood. And then the last part is golden, which refers to the golden streets of the heavenly Jerusalem; thus are lessons taught to these poor women.[76]

Was it merely coincidence that the first use of the wordless book in China occurred in Shanxi, where the five-color *wuxing* had been invented five thousand years before? Did the missionaries recognize the congruence? After all, the Religion of the Golden Pill was drenched with symbolic colors, as Gatekeeper Sung could have explained, and they would have seen Wutaishan, the holy mountain painted as a living *wuxing*. But it was not just the Chinese who were obsessed with color cosmology symbolism. One missionary, who signed himself "F," wrote several articles in the *Chinese Recorder* on "Colour-Names in Mencius." He gave the classical references for white (such as birds, snow, gems, horses, man's skin and hair), yellow, azure [or green], red, and the "5 terms denoting *dark* or *black*," which he said were "indicative of the conditions of their [Chinese] minds." He quoted Mencius, "To enjoy food and delight in colours is nature."[77] Closer to home, Timothy Richard was also exper-

76. Ibid.
77. "F," "Colour-Names in Mencius," *Chinese Recorder*, January-February 1880, pp. 59-64.

imenting with traditional Chinese colors in a Christian setting. His Baptist colleagues noted with horror that he hung "a large white satin cross, flanked by yellow streamers 'exactly like those used in Buddhist temples' in the Taiyuan chapel."[78]

At the end of his talk, almost in passing, David Hill mentioned another innovation of the CIM women, which was to have far-reaching implications: the first opium refuge in Shanxi. As Miss Crickmay went visiting from house to house, she discovered that many women were opium addicts; in fact, after the famine, it was estimated that 70 percent of the adult population of Taiyuan smoked opium, mostly domestic. "At once letters were sent to Pekin, and medicine was purchased; the opium pills were brought down from Pekin, and sold to the people," Hill reported.[79]

The Essay Contest

While the women missionaries were targeting the low end of the social scale, the males were trying to attract the social elite. Timothy Richard "came out of the horror [of the famine] with the one word 'Education' branded into his soul, a word which became the key-note of his life."[80] Sacks of grain and carts of cash could save individuals, but when millions were dying they were a drop in the eternal ocean. The people must be educated, Richard said, so that famines would not occur again; they needed better crops and better technology to produce more grain. They needed primary schools, middle schools, high schools, and, he dared dream, a university (a dream which he realized after the Boxer Uprising). Like Matteo Ricci three centuries earlier, Richard believed "in the principle that as water flows downhill more easily than it is pumped up, so truth will progress more rapidly when it is advocated by educated men."[81]

Richard argued that the apostolic method of missionary work was laid down in Matthew 10:11: "And into whatsoever city or town ye shall enter, inquire who in it is worthy; and there abide till ye go thence." Among the "worthies" in Qing China he "included both those who gave evidence of

---

78. Brian Stanley, *The History of the Baptist Missionary Society 1792-1992* (Edinburgh: T&T Clark, 1992), p. 191.

79. Hill, speech to CIM Annual Meeting 1881, p. 91.

80. William E. Soothill, *Timothy Richard of China: Seer, Statesman, Missionary & the Most Disinterested Adviser the Chinese Ever Had* (London: Seeley, Service & Co., 1924), p. 106.

81. Ibid., p. 122.

seeking after religious truth, and those who had the power to mould public opinion. . . . Richard targeted his message at two groups — the devout teachers of the different religions (especially the leaders of the reforming sects), and the highly educated scholar-officials who formed the imperial civil service."[82]

Richard, Hill, and Francis James initiated a campaign aimed at the scholars. Every three years the Qing government held civil service exams, when tens of thousands of candidates would gather in each provincial capital to sit for the *Xiucai*, the lowest level degree (sometimes called "B.A."). The exam of 1879 — the first after the famine — was particularly important both to demonstrate the government's stability and to fill the many state jobs that had come vacant through death and retirements. As the scholars emerged from the examination halls, the missionaries set up a table outside, among the fortune-tellers and idol makers. In one day they distributed "between 10 and 20,000 Tracts and handbills"; each package contained the prayer of thanksgiving, a tract called "The Mirror of Conscience" and a commentary on the Ten Commandments.[83]

Gatekeeper Sung came up with a new idea. He suggested that Hill hold a literary contest offering cash prizes — thirty taels of silver (£7 10s or $36 U.S.), a substantial sum — for "first-class literary essays upon Christian themes." Although the topics were ostensibly Christian, they were framed in open-ended terms that Confucianists, Buddhists, Daoists, and sectarians would each have interpreted in their own way: "The Regulation of the Heart"; "The Source of True Doctrine, or the Right Way"; "Rewards and Punishments"; "Images of the Gods"; and "On Opium."[84] They received 110 essays — written by men ignorant of Christianity — and not surprisingly, most "altogether ignored the Christian teaching . . . others, and I am happy to say the best, introduced more or less of Christian truth." All were "thoroughly Confucianistic" in their condemnation of idolatry and opium smoking, and "the need of moral power, of Divine assistance, is expressed again and again."[85]

Hill was so pleased with the success of this contest that he wrote two articles for the *Chinese Recorder*, advocating its use elsewhere.

---

82. Ibid.
83. Hill, "Triennial Examinations."
84. *Pastor Hsi* (single vol.), pp. 38-39.
85. Hill, "Kü Jan Examination."

The Valley of the Shadow

The Opium Sot

After David Hill read the essays, he announced the four prize-winning essays. The author — actually the author of three of the four, under different pseudonyms — was reluctant to claim his prize and sent a relative to get it for him. No wonder. The man who finally presented himself was a broken-down scholar, a fixer at the yamen, an opium sot given to hallucinations, far from the "first-class" scholar Hill had hoped for. Gatekeeper Sung, though, recognized him as a fellow member of the Golden Pill. Hill, too, recognized that under the opiated shell was a spiritual pilgrim, a sinner God had come to save. His name was Hsi Liao-chih (pinyin Xi Liaozhi), the second or third convert in Shanxi. (Like Gatekeeper Sung, the CIM sources are reticent about his personal name. Inexplicably, *Pastor Hsi*, the biography, never reveals it, using circumlocutions like "Fourth Son" before his conversion, and his self-appointed title, Shengmo, Overcomer of Demons, afterwards.)[86]

Hsi had read Hill's tracts but could not make heads or tails of the teachings and was afraid of being bewitched by the foreign religion. He was overtly antiforeign, because he blamed England for imposing the "black mud" of opium on China. However, he was surprised and reassured that Gatekeeper Sung and other members of the Golden Pill were enquirers, whereupon the following conversation occurred:

Hsi: "May I ask what you do here?"
Sung: "Oh, we are helping the foreigner."
Hsi: "And don't you fear being bewitched?"
Sung: "No, indeed, no more would you if you knew him."[87]

"One glance, one word, it was enough!" Hsi wrote in his autobiographical account. "As stars fade before the rising sun, so did his [Hill's] presence dissipate the idle rumours I had heard. . . . I beheld his kindly eye and remembered the words of Mencius, 'If a man's heart is not right his eyes bespeak it.' I realized I was in the presence of a true man."

Impressed by Hill's personal sanctity, Hsi accepted his offer of employment to live in Pingyang and help him write literary tracts. The two months

---

86. Hsi's baptism is in a letter from J. J. Turner to JHT, 29 November 1880, in CIM/SOAS, file 257. This is the only place in the entire CIM records when the Chinese characters for Hsi's original name appear. The romanization was given twice: *Growth of a Work of God*, p. 349, in a footnote, called him "Hsi Liao-chuh" (a misprint), and in *HTCOC* 6, p. 483.

87. "Hung-t'ung Conference," pp. 5-6, "The Testimony of Mr. Hsi."

he spent there were the only sustained contact he had with foreigners in his first six years as a Christian.[88] "Thanks be to God, He afterwards saved my soul," Hsi wrote. "Mr. . . . Hill led me to the gate, God caused me to enter." While helping Hill to translate the New Testament, Hsi wept like Gatekeeper Sung over the sufferings of Jesus and, he testified, suddenly "the Holy Spirit influenced his soul and 'with tears that flowed and would not cease' he bowed and yielded himself, unreservedly" to God. The experience was so real that his testimony henceforth was a solemn evocation of "the reality to him of the Heavenly Vision."[89]

We know more about Pastor Hsi than any other nineteenth-century Chinese Protestant, except Hong Xiuquan, thanks to Mrs. Howard Taylor's two-volume biography, *One of China's Scholars (Pastor Hsi): The Culture and Conversion of a Confucianist* (1901) and *Pastor Hsi: One of China's Christians* (1903), and an abridged single volume, *Pastor Hsi: Confucian Scholar and Christian* (1903). "Pastor Hsi" was entirely a CIM creation: he was not mentioned in any source outside the CIM, except for a couple of comments in the *Chinese Recorder*. Mrs. Taylor's book made "the name of Pastor Hsi . . . almost as well known as that of Hudson Taylor himself."[90] In addition to her own visit to Pastor Hsi's home in 1894, Mrs. Taylor drew upon Hsi's autobiographical notes (which seem from the quotations to amount to a few pages in Chinese, a spiritual autobiography). She also relied on Dixon E. Hoste, Pastor Hsi's "fellow-worker and most valued friend" for ten years, who became Hudson Taylor's successor as general director of the CIM. One could not get a more official imprimatur.

Pastor Hsi is a compelling story told with the verve of firsthand experience, but more, it was the first popular mission book to explore issues like demon possession, opium addiction, and exorcism in a candid and "scientific" way. The first volume, which deals with Hsi's "heathen" life up to the time of his conversion, lays out in precise detail every book he studied. In the absence of personal information, Mrs. Taylor faked it: concerning Hsi's wedding, she wrote in a footnote, "The wedding is one that the writer witnessed in northern China, and is introduced in default of information as to the actual marriage of young Hsi himself."[91] She outlined the Four Books and Five Classics of the Confucian canon which he had studied, cribbed from authors like Samuel Wells Williams, and gave a garbled account of the Religion of the

---

88. There is a parallel here with Hong Xiuquan, who studied for only a few months with Issachar Roberts in Canton before returning to his village.
89. *Pastor Hsi*, pp. 46-48 [vol. 1, pp. 176-79].
90. Joy Guinness, *Mrs. Howard Taylor*, pp. 170-71.
91. *Pastor Hsi*, p. 6.

The Valley of the Shadow

Golden Pill. Her lack of understanding of his sectarian background is indicated by the subtitle to the first volume, *The Culture and Conversion of a Confucianist*, making him seem more respectable than he was. When the abridged volume was issued, this material that grounded Hsi in his Chinese setting was considered too arcane for English readers and was edited out.

D. E. Hoste wrote the introduction to volume 2, in which he hesitantly admitted that Pastor Hsi possessed "comprehensiveness of mind and foresight which enable men to frame measures on a large scale, with the strengths of will, practical resourcefulness, and capacity for the management of others, essential in carrying such projects to completion." Yet "there were points in his character which rendered his co-operation with foreign missionaries a matter of difficulty. By nature and by training, his temper was autocratic and independent. . . . His confidence was not easily won; indeed, a tendency to overmistrust and suspicion concerning those whom he did not know well, was a distinct weakness in his character."[92]

Hsi Liao-chih was born in the fifteenth year of the Daoguang Emperor, who reigned 1821-50, which would make it 1836, "just before the accession of Queen Victoria." He was thus four years younger than Hudson Taylor, and about forty-one at the time of the famine. He was the fourth son of a well-to-do peasant family in a village identified only as "Western Chang Village" [Xizhang Cun? or old spelling Hsi-Chang Ts'un?], half a day's journey (thirty to fifty *li* or ten to twenty miles) east of Pingyang in the foothills. The Hsi family owned some terraced fields and lived in a courtyard built into the hillside. He had married at the usual age of sixteen, but his wife died, then his parents, and the land was divided among the four sons. At thirty, he married a second, younger wife, aged sixteen, from a nearby village, who was related to Gatekeeper Sung and other converts. "A warm attachment grew up between them [Pastor Hsi and his wife], which deepened through all the years of their united life." Mrs. Hsi became the mother figure of Pastor Hsi's Christian sect and continued the work after his death.

As a child, Hsi felt different, because he, like Gatekeeper Sung, had a morbid "fear of death."[93] But he excelled at his studies and passed the *Xiucai* degree at sixteen, a remarkable achievement: that would have been about 1852, a year before the Taiping Expeditionary Force passed through Pingyang. Shrewd and ambitious, Hsi was "wholly absorbed in the pursuit of power" with a temper and fearlessness that gained him respect among local bullies. When his village became embroiled in a conflict over control of the local fair, they elected him

92. Ibid., p. xiii.
93. Ibid., p. 2.

headman; he resolved the dispute by bringing in several hundred armed men from friendly villages. Hsi mixed "among the gentry" and "had a following in the lowest class of hangers-on at the mandarin's office."[94]

The Hsi family were doctors and healers, well known for their skill as diagnosticians, and members of the *Jindan Jiao* for generations. In particular, they kept a drugstore of secret recipes handed down from father to son.[95] He joined the Golden Pill society at thirty (1866), about the time he remarried. He was suffering from some chronic illness, but the breathing exercises made his condition worse, not better. About 1870 he started to use opium to alleviate the coughing. Before this time, opium *smoking* had been nonexistent in Shanxi, but now smoking local opium was becoming "fashionable."[96]

Mr. Wellman, a colporteur of the British and Foreign Bible Society, who toured southern Shanxi in 1870, described what he called the "opium villages": "Si-ho-ch'en was formerly very rich" but the "present town is half in ruins and the people have almost wholly given themselves up to the opium pipe. . . . Opium smokers are said to be 70 per cent" of the 4,000 families in Wan-hsi-hsien, and so on. One man accosted him, demanding to be cured of opium: "You bring Bibles, why not bring anti-opium pills? You brought us opium, and now you bring us holy books and refuse to cure us — why not bring us anti-opium books or pills and not these 'glad tidings books' that contain nothing about opium."[97] Ten years later, the problem had grown so large it was reported that in some parts of Shanxi, "eleven out of every ten smoked opium!"[98]

Opium was for Hsi "a swift descent." He spent a year and a half without leaving his bed. In delirium he was haunted by ghosts, "faces he had known in youth, changed, sunken, degraded like himself. . . . From the opium suicide's dishonoured grave they beckoned in the darkness, 'You are one of us.'" One night as he prepared to die, wearing his burial clothes, Hsi's spirit ascended to heaven where a voice spoke, "Go back! Go back!"[99] Then, when the famine came, the dream faces took on earthly reality, as family and friends died. The fact that he and his family survived the famine indicates they were wealthy enough to have considerable grain stored in the back of the cave.

94. Ibid., p. 10.
95. Ibid., p. 2.
96. Ibid., p. 16.
97. Quoted in Dr. John Dudgeon, "Notes of a Bible Tour in South Eastern Shansi," *Chinese Recorder*, January 1871, pp. 213-14. Wellman seems to have been preoccupied with two subjects, opium and coal deposits, sometimes in the same sentence.
98. *Pastor Hsi*, p. 101.
99. Ibid., pp. 5, 15, 17. Compare Hsi's dream with Hong Xiuquan's Heavenly Vision in Chapter 2.

The Valley of the Shadow

Opium addicts. From the 1890s to the 1930s, it was impossible to avoid the sight of opium addicts in China. The CIM was one of the leaders in the crusade to stop the opium trade between England and China.   Source: Pat Barr, *To China with Love: The Lives and Times of Protestant Missionaries in China, 1860-1900* (London: Secker & Warburg, 1972).

The Overcomer of Demons

By the time Hsi arrived at Mr. Hill's house, he was an addict of ten years standing. Once converted, he tried to break off opium with "the usual medicines" (unnamed) that Hill supplied. "It was as though the enemy of souls, seeing his prisoner escaping, fell back on his opium-habit as an invincible chain to bind him.... Medicines were given in larger doses, and native as well as foreign drugs were tried, but all without avail." Conscious of the power of Satan, Hsi cried out, "Devil what can you do against me? My life is in the hand of God. And truly am I willing to break off the opium and die, but not willing to continue in sin and live! . . . Though I die, I will never touch it again!" Again the Holy Spirit descended, "flooding his heart with peace."[100] A third time, Hsi wrote, "the Holy Spirit descended, filling and overflowing my heart."

As a sign of his new birth — "a new man in a new world" — Hsi took on a new name in religion, Hsi Shengmo, "the Overcomer of Demons." The "Christian life must be one of conquest," he declared, battling in spirit against

100. Ibid., pp. 51-52.

the Chinese underworld. (It is interesting to note that "Conqueror of Demons," using different characters, is one of the titles of Guandi, the tutelary god of Pingyang.)[101]

Despite their belief in thunder-and-lightning conversion — in the abstract — the missionaries did not know how to respond to this extraordinary individual, who pushed himself forward and demanded precedence because of his spiritual visions. He had a slight cast in one eye, which gave his face an odd, unbalanced appearance, and a sharp glancing look like an eagle. His energy and ideas overwhelmed the missionaries. He had a student-teacher relationship with David Hill, but after Hill left, Hsi did not have such cordial relations with Joshua Turner who replaced him. When he asked Turner to baptize him immediately, relayed through Gatekeeper Sung, Turner told him to wait. "I fear it is yet too early; I fear lest, coming on too quickly, he will go back too soon." Hsi replied urgently that his desire "to worship God is not because of Mr. Hill, but because of God's own teaching; I know for myself; I have read his word; I know my sins are great; I ought to go to hell. I know, too, that Jesus is able to forgive my sins, able to save me from sin, able to save me from hell, and to give me to live in heaven forever."[102]

In November 1880 Joshua Turner baptized the "first fruits" of Shanxi, five men including Gatekeeper Sung, Hsi Shengmo, and two brothers, all former adepts of the Golden Pill. Considering his hagiographic fame, the first references are ambiguous. Turner's baptismal record, which gave the Chinese characters for his name — a conventional name that meant "Intelligent and Upright" — stated he was aged forty-five, a native of a village in Hsiang-ling Hsien (Xiangling County). "He is a Shiu-ts'ai [*Xiucai*] and a man of great ability and influence. He came to us at the beginning of the year. He had read Christian books and he soon broke off his opium, demolished his idols, and accepted Christ as his savior. He is a man of quick temperament, and his conversion was rapid and full of joy. He is serving the Lord in his own neighbourhood."[103]

The account in *China's Millions* is more fulsome:

Mr. Hi [sic] is naturally impulsive, with a strong tendency to asceticism. He embraced eagerly the teachings of Scripture, and exerted himself in bringing before his friends the truth he had so recently learnt. He spent

---

101. Ibid., pp. 55, 58. For "Conqueror of Demons," see Clarence Burton Day, *Chinese Peasant Cults: Being a Study of Chinese Paper Gods* (Shanghai: Kelly & Walsh, 1940), p. 52.
102. "Hung-t'ung Conference," p. 6, "Testimony of Mr. Hsi."
103. Turner to JHT, 29 November 1880, in CIM/SOAS, file 257.

The Valley of the Shadow

much time in prayer, and frequently fasted. On one occasion, his wife being ill, and doctors being unable to cure her, he ordered a week's fasting and prayer; at the end of which time the malady was completely cured. He also tells us of others who have been restored to health in answer to prayer.

He no longer holds any situation with us, nor does he receive a cash [a small copper coin with a square hole in the center, worth about a penny] from us; on the other hand, he has been most generous in helping another of our natives who was in difficulties. He is working now amongst those living in or around his own village, fifty *li* from P'ing-yang, has daily worship, and regular Sunday service. He speaks of erecting a small chapel on his own land, and at his own expense.[104]

In other words, Hsi had nothing to do with the foreigners, except to report his exploits. Moreover, he was acting like a traditional healer, casting out demons (his wife's euphemistic illness) and fasting to purge his body. His independent streak — "he no longer holds any situation with us," implying he once did — was a foretaste of things to come. Hsi returned to his village, where (according to Mrs. Howard Taylor) he learned "all he could from occasional intercourse with the missionaries, and [was] taught of God, often in quaint surprising ways, through the enlightenment of His Word applied to the daily experiences of life."[105]

We shall return to Shanxi, but first we must journey back to London to introduce the second generation of pilgrims.

---

104. W. L. Elliston, "The Work of God in P'ing-yang, Shan-si Province," *China's Millions* (GB), April 1881, p. 42.
105. *Pastor Hsi*, p. 75.

PART II

The Second Generation
1875-1888

Ho, my comrades! See the signal Waving in the sky!
Reinforcements now appearing, Victory is nigh!
Hold the fort, for I am coming! Jesus signals still;
Wave the answer back to heaven, "By Thy grace we will!"

See the mighty host advancing, Satan leading on:
Mighty men around us falling, Courage almost gone!
Hold the fort, for I am coming! Jesus signals still;
Wave the answer back to heaven, "By Thy grace we will!"

P. P. Bliss

CHAPTER 6

National Righteousness

1875-1888

If you want hard work, and little appreciation; if you value God's approval more than you fear man's disapprobation; if you are prepared to take joyfully the spoiling of your goods, and seal your testimony, if need be, with your blood; if you can pity and love the Chinese in all their mental and moral degradation, as well as literal filth and impurity, you may count on a harvest of souls now and a crown of glory hereafter "that fadeth not away," and on the Master's "Well done." You would find that, in connection with the China Inland Mission, it is no question of "making the best of both worlds." The men, the only men who will be happy with us, are those who have this world under their feet: and I do venture to say that such men will find a happiness they never dreamed of or thought possible down here.

Hudson Taylor, general letter to candidates, January 1875[1]

The Second Vision

We have turned the page. The Pilgrim has been brought back to the stony beach for a second blessing. Ten years before, in June 1865, Hudson Taylor had a vision of a million Chinese souls a month sweeping over into eternal darkness, and prayed for "24 willing skilful workers." Now, in June 1875 he had another vision at Brighton, and the China Inland Mission was reborn. More

---

1. *Growth of a Work of God*, p. 269. A censored version appeared in *HTCOC* 5, p. 435: the phrase "if you can pity and love the Chinese in all their mental and moral degradation, as well as literal filth and impurity," has been excised.

than merely revitalizing an insignificant foreign mission, Taylor also helped to create an evangelical movement, "an epoch of spiritual revival in the home churches"[2] that was to dominate British and North American evangelicalism well into the twentieth century. The Brighton Convention for the Promotion of Scriptural Holiness (31 May to 4 June) was followed by the Mildmay Conference (23 to 25 June) and the Keswick Convention (28 June to 2 July) in the Lake District. And thus, the movement received its name: Keswick Holiness.

Only six months before, at Christmas of 1874, the CIM had reached its nadir — "pathetic in the extreme," Eugene Stock of the Church Missionary Society called it[3] — with a dispirited force in China and disarray in England, while Taylor himself was bedridden, paralyzed from the waist down. "It seems very unlikely that either we or you will ever see China again," his wife told him. This was the second time Taylor had returned from China since he escorted the *Lammermuir* party in 1866, trying desperately to administer both ends, Britain and China, simultaneously. The first was in 1871-72 after Maria Dyer Taylor died of childbirth and William Berger, the London director, retired for personal and theological reasons. When Berger sold "Saint Hill," his estate that had served as the mission home, Taylor acquired a small house at 6 Pyrland Road, near Mildmay in Islington, which was to be the London headquarters for twenty years, and appointed a temporary council of management.

Since the council members were volunteers with busy careers, none had the time or expertise to devote themselves to running the British operations of the CIM, so these duties fell on the shoulders of Emily Blatchley, Taylor's sweet, faithful amanuensis from the *Lammermuir* party. She cared for Hudson and Maria's children — the four who survived — and when he married Jennie Faulding in 1871 and returned to China, she became "Hudson Taylor's mouthpiece" in Britain.[4] Miss Blatchley, according to Grattan Guinness, "though unknown to the world, was a true heroine, and an instance of this noble, Christ-like self-sacrifice for the good of others.... Not content with caring for Mr. Taylor's children, she became a Secretary of the Mission. She wrote in its interest thousands of letters; she kept its accounts; she edited its *Occasional Papers;* she helped to bear its burdens; she worked long hours, and often far into the night.... She daily remembered its missionaries by name at the Throne of grace, and pleaded continually its cause with God."[5]

---

2. *Growth of a Work of God*, p. 264.
3. Stock, *The History of the Church Missionary Society*, vol. 3, p. 244.
4. *HTCOC 5*, p. 365.
5. *Growth of a Work of God*, p. 262.

Occasional Paper cover, with Hudson Taylor's two mottoes on either side. This was the CIM's first periodical, published between 1865 and 1875, when it was superseded by China's Millions.
Source: OMF/Toronto.

But Emily contracted consumption and faded rapidly, forcing Hudson and Jennie to return to England in 1874 to reorganize the home front. In the midst of these personal tragedies, the CIM's finances collapsed. "Pray for funds," he wrote his mother. "We have over 100 agents native and foreign [but only eighteen missionaries], 170 mouths to feed daily and that number to clothe, not to count the wives and children of the native helpers." He added, "We have more than 50 buildings — houses, chapels, and schools to keep in repair, and four-fifths of them to pay rent for. . . . The travelling expenses involved in the work in China, now extended to five provinces, are not small."[6] The bare-bones expenses of the mission amounted to £100 a week or £500 a month, yet the council was so negligent in forwarding money that on one occasion there was 67 cents in the Shanghai bank. "It seems to me that our good

---

6. JHT to mother, 1 May and 11 July 1874, in *HTCOC* 5, pp. 407-8.

friends have forgotten that the main object of *all* the home operations is the reception and transmission of funds *to China*," Taylor wrote angrily. "I've been in China nearly four months, and not a penny has been sent."[7] "The Lord will provide" was the CIM's motto, and somehow he always did: when they prayed for £235, in came a cheque, the proceeds "From the sale of plate," for £235, 7 shillings and 9 pence.[8]

The worst was yet to come. Before he left China, Hudson Taylor slipped while climbing onto a boat and sprained his ankle, forcing him to walk with crutches. The sea voyage accentuated the injury, and "the vibration of railways, cabs and omnibuses, etc., since reaching land," caused a "delayed concussion of the spine."[9] Paralyzed in his back and legs, he had to remain in bed for three months, using a rope to turn from side to side. Jennie was confined to the next room, where she gave birth prematurely and almost died. Two other women died at the Pyrland Road home within ten days, and others arrived from China blind and lame, broken in body and spirit.

Hudson Taylor was always at his best running the mission from his sickbed. He pinned a map of China to the bedposts and turned his bed into the CIM's boardroom. In the mornings he would meet with the council and read the correspondence. In the afternoons, he held Chinese lessons for the recruits. Between, he dictated hundreds of letters and audited the accounts. When things seemed at their darkest, Taylor made one of his most audacious moves. In January 1875 he issued an

AN APPEAL FOR PRAYER
ON BEHALF OF MORE THAN 150 MILLIONS OF CHINESE

> There are nine provinces of China, each as large as a European kingdom, averaging a population of seventeen or eighteen millions, but all destitute of the pure Gospel. About a hundred Roman Catholic priests from Europe live in them, but not one Protestant missionary....

For years he had been praying for "the Eighteen," two male missionaries to open each of the nine provinces without a resident missionary. "Warm-hearted young men," he continued, "who have a good knowledge of business, clerks, or assistants in shops who have come in contact with the public and learned to cover the wants and suit the wishes of purchasers, are well fitted for this work." With the murder of the British diplomat Margary in the news, this was "a brave

---

7. JHT to Emily Blatchley, ibid., p. 369.
8. *Growth of a Work of God*, p. 270.
9. *HTCOC* 5, p. 420.

and defiant act, made from a paraplegic's bed," A. J. Broomhall commented. This appeal, published in *The Christian* and Spurgeon's *Sword and Trowel*, had an immediate and dramatic result — sixty applications within the year.[10]

By June, Taylor was hobbling on canes, and the Brighton convention was his first public appearance. He had the amazing ability of being in the right place at the right time. In 1860 he arrived in England in the heightened spiritual atmosphere of the 1859 revival and gathered the enthusiasts to establish the China Inland Mission. In 1864 he was one of the first speakers at Mildmay, and in 1865 he announced the formation of the CIM from its platform. During the 1870s he was present at some of Britain's most important religious events. In 1872 he introduced Dwight L. Moody, then an unknown American on his second tour of Ireland and Britain, and two years later welcomed him back with his singing accompanist, Ira Sankey, on the tour that made them international celebrities. In the historic conferences of 1875, he shared platforms with Moody and with Hannah and Robert Pearsall Smith, and gathered the Keswick devotees for the Eighteen.

In July, the first issue of *China's Millions* was published just in time to be distributed at the Keswick conference, and it immediately became an effective, attractive publicity agent. Not all the publicity was favorable, though. There was considerable criticism that the CIM had an excessively high death rate because its missionaries lived in the native style. Taylor was at pains to refute this, comparing the CIM with the respected Church Missionary Society: out of thirty-four clergymen the CMS had sent to China in thirty years, only fifteen lasted more than four years. "In the ten years of the China Inland Mission," he stated somewhat disingenuously, "(excluding those who have gone out within the last four years) of 39 persons of both sexes, 32 were able to stay more than four years, and 25 are still in connection with the Mission." He also broke his traditional reticence about finances, and announced that an "immediate outlay of about £1000 is required . . . and we trust God will incline the hearts of His people to send special contributions for this, as a large saving to the Mission in rent will thus be effected."[11] (This lapse from the strict policy of "no solicitation" was rare.)

"We all had visions at that time," wrote John W. Stevenson, who was later appointed deputy China director.[12] The rebirth of the CIM was so spectacular that in just over a decade it had become an "octopus"[13] with tentacles that

---

10. Ibid., pp. 428-29. *Growth of a Work of God*, pp. 265-66.
11. *HTCOC 6*, pp. 58-60.
12. *HTCOC 5*, p. 428.
13. China missionary Chauncey Goodrich, quoted in *HTCOC 6*, p. 8.

stretched from London to Chicago to the farthest reaches of the Chinese Empire. Each level of the mission experienced the collective vision in a different way. The directors in London saw an unending stream of applicants, young men and women who came in their hundreds begging to be sent to China: they had the pick of the crop. The CIM doubled with the Eighteen in 1875-76, redoubled with "the Thirty" in 1878-79, again with "the Seventy" ("And the Lord sent forth seventy also ...") in 1882-84, and again with "the Hundred" in 1886-88. By the end of 1888 the CIM had 332 missionaries in China.[14] One friend got so carried away she asked, "Why stop at the Seventy? Ask for seven hundred, a thousand. That was the spirit."[15] There "seemed no limit to the number who could be sent to China, and provided for."[16]

In Shanghai, every week would bring another party, who stayed long enough to be fitted in Chinese clothes and sent inland before the next group arrived. In this period the CIM achieved its distinctive tiered organization with settled work near the coast and widespread itinerations inland, with stations in nine provinces. It had large institutional nodes — the men's language school at Anqing, the women's school at Yangzhou, business offices at Shanghai and Hankou, and the school for missionaries' children at Chefoo — and strings of stations descending from the provincial capitals to outstations in the deep countryside. The rapid expansion had its dark side, as poorly trained enthusiasts were thrown into situations far beyond their understanding.

The Exchanged Life

Between 1870 and 1876, writes David Bebbington, there was a "change of religious climate" in Britain as holiness teachings "ushered in a new phase in Evangelical history." Advocates of holiness "spoke a new spiritual language" and urged Christians to seek "a second decisive experience beyond conversion." This was called a "second conversion," or "the Second Blessing," which would "endue them with power." "Afterwards they would live on a more elevated plane. No longer would they feel themselves ensnared by wrongdoing, for they would have victory over sin. They would possess holiness, enjoying the 'higher life.' ... They shared the belief that holiness comes by faith. Effort, conflict, endeavour were rejected as the path of sanctification."[17] This spiri-

---

14. *China's Millions* (GB), annual report, July 1889, pp. 88-89.
15. HTCOC 6, p. 354.
16. HTCOC 7, p. 43.
17. Bebbington, *Evangelicalism in Modern Britain*, pp. 179, 151.

tual plane was variously called "the higher life," "the deeper life," or Hudson Taylor's preferred term, "the exchanged life."[18]

"The strength of Keswick," wrote Clyde Binfield in his history of the YMCA, which became a major avenue for Keswick teachings, "was that it sought to turn the ceaselessly striving, seeking faith which had been the peculiar glory of Victorian Christianity, into a resting faith.... Resting, buoyant trust, rather than burdensome, conscience-stricken struggle was to be the springboard for an active, manly Christian life."[19] "Resting" was the operative word, as one of Taylor's favorite hymns, by Sophia Piggott, put it: "Jesus, I am resting, resting, in the joy of what Thou art."

Taylor claimed to be an exponent of the holiness teachings before they were called Keswick; he had experienced the second blessing as early as 1864 when Canon William Pennefather opened the Mildmay Institute to spread scriptural holiness. The way to convert 400 million Chinese, Taylor proposed, was not through struggle — what he would call "means," through gunboat diplomacy, argumentation, and personality conflicts — but by a resting faith in God, like a feather on the ocean, trusting where the Spirit led, closing one door and opening another. Taylor was often criticized for his dreamy spirituality and detachment from the mundane world. No one, though, could accuse him of lacking sinew or "manliness." Indeed his passivity was his power; prayer and devotions were the answer to life's troubling questions, the big ones (Modernism), as well as the small (whether to wear a pith helmet in the noonday sun).

Taylor sought to institutionalize Keswick piety in the CIM — and one can track the spread of Keswick ideas by the use of the familial "dear," which became a hallmark of Keswick: dear Mr. Berger, dear Mrs. Broomhall. One common phrase was "saved to serve," and as Stuart Piggin wrote on missionary motivation, "There were many whom Keswick's message led straight to the mission field. From the early 1880s onwards, the argument was ever more frequently advanced that amongst the clearest indications of the true willingness to conform with God's will, and the surest route to present sanctification, was the offer of oneself for foreign missionary service.... All alike sought ... to recreate abroad the intense fellowship of Keswick circles."[20]

---

18. For Taylor and Keswick, see ibid., p. 152.

19. Clyde Binfield, *George Williams and the Y.M.C.A.: A Study in Victorian Social Attitudes* (London: Heinemann, 1973), pp. 220-21.

20. Stuart Piggin, "Assessing Missionary Motivation," in D. Baker, ed., *Religious Motivation: Biographical and Sociological Problems for the Church Historian*. According to McKay, "Faith and Facts," p. 159, by the 1880s Taylor estimated that "two thirds of those in the China Inland Mission were 'among the brethren' as a result of Keswick."

Holiness teachings sprang from diverse roots: Wesleyan Holiness, Quaker spirituality (which spoke of "resting" in the Inner Light), the Brethren search for "the heavenly calling" of the church, and Moody's revivals, all of which had influenced Hudson Taylor's pilgrimage.[21] Several institutions that spread Keswick teachings, such as the YMCA and Mildmay, became his allies. The Mildmay conferences combined devotional intensity with remarkable energy, and by the 1870s the complex contained a Bible school, a deaconess training center, a settlement house, an orphanage, schools, and a hospital. When Moody returned to America after his 1873-75 tour, he was constantly talking about England and sent Emma Dreyer, his colleague and the founder of Moody Bible Institute, to study the Mildmay methods, which he tried to replicate at his schools at Northfield, Massachusetts, and Chicago.[22]

The Council of Management

Hudson Taylor had returned to England in 1871 ostensibly because of his own health, but more serious was the resignation of William T. Berger, the cofounder of the CIM. A strict member of the Brethren, though not the Exclusive Brethren, Berger had not always seen eye to eye with Taylor's enthusiasms, such as his "overstressing of the passive, receptive aspect of 'holiness.' They [Berger and the council] replied emphasising the need for active resistance to evil and of effort to obey God."[23]

Berger had come to a theology called the "non-eternity of punishment" or the "conditional immortality" of sinners not justified by faith in Christ. This was one of a number of eschatological reactions against the idea of eternal hell for the perishing millions even though they never had a chance to hear the gospel. It went by a number of names depending on varying concepts of the afterlife, such as annihilationism, restitutionism, universal restoration, the eternal hope or the larger hope. Influenced by Darwinism, conditionalists denied the existence of the immortal soul, although God did offer "conditional immortality" to those who believed in Christ. The souls of the unregenerate would be "annihilated" since they were "unfitted to receive the gift

---

21. Bebbington, *Evangelicalism in Modern Britain*, pp. 153-55 (Wesleyan Holiness), pp. 155-57 (Quakers), and pp. 157-59 (Brethren).

22. This is contained in a letter from Emma Dreyer to Charles Blanchard, president of Wheaton College, January 1916, concerning the founding of Moody Bible Insitute, in MBI library, Chicago.

23. *HTCOC* 5, p. 214.

National Righteousness

of immortality," either immediately upon death or at a "second death" after a period of suspended animation.[24] Some, citing scripture, argued that the biblical *"aeion"* did not mean "eternity" but merely a conditional period of time, an "eon" or an age, and that after an "age," the souls of the unregenerate would be saved.

This debate may seem academic, but it had a deeply disturbing effect on the CIM, forcing not only Berger's resignation, but also other leaders like Stanley Smith of the Cambridge Seven, and Hudson Taylor II, Hudson Taylor's grandson, as late as 1921. The CIM had been founded on Hudson Taylor's vision at Brighton, and its grim message — a million a month were dying without God — was reiterated again and again in *China's Millions* and other propaganda. In particular, pathetic deathbed scenes were featured as didactic moral lessons. If sin and hell were removed as a motivation for conversion, heaven vanished too, since both depended on the idea of an eternal soul. One can hear echoes of this debate in the testimony of Pastor Hsi (see Chapter 5): "I know my sins are great; I ought to go to hell. I know, too, that Jesus is able to forgive my sins, able to save me from sin, able to save me from hell, and to give me to live in heaven forever."[25]

Taylor was fighting a two-pronged attack, for liberal missionaries were discovering that "threats of hell were not necessarily the most effective way of proclaiming the gospel." Some were turning toward conditionalism as a way of dealing with the moral dilemma of the righteous heathen.[26] Others, like Timothy Richard and Joseph Edkins, were studying the religions of China, not to condemn them but to find the good in other religions and incorporate that spirituality into a syncretistic Christianized Confucianism.

The debate over conditionalism, John Morley of the YMCA stated, was "a living issue in the seventies, but had ceased to be so by the eighties and nineties: men were then more interested in the rights of nations and imperial policy."[27] As Hudson Taylor wrote at Berger's resignation, "Many Churches of England, Baptist, Brethren, etc., are expelling all who hold non-eternity. Some work is quite broken up on account of it."[28] Berger had been expelled by the Hackney Brethren assembly, and he wrote, "Need I say that I desire to be incognito as to the subject . . . for were it to get abroad that I even favoured

---

24. Geoffrey Rowell, *Hell and the Victorians: A Study of the Nineteenth-Century Theological Controversies Concerning Eternal Punishment and the Future Life* (Oxford: Clarendon Press 1974), pp. 180-211.
25. "Hung-t'ung Conference," p. 6, "Testimony of Mr. Hsi."
26. Rowell, *Hell and the Victorians*, "Missionary Theology," pp. 190-92.
27. Ibid., p. 4.
28. *HTCOC 5*, p. 339.

it, my usefulness, some say would be at an end."²⁹ In fact, George Müller withheld his contributions from the CIM until Berger formally resigned.

Even after Berger retired to Cannes, he continued to offer advice to Hudson Taylor and contribute substantial sums (£1,000 at a time) to Taylor and the CIM. Occasionally, he could speak sharply, such as his warning in 1889 that Taylor was "almost claiming for yourself shall I say Divine and infallible guidance. . . . This seems to me to partake of the spirit of infatuation, and may involve you in separating from your co-director, the Council, Secretaries, and many friends if they should differ from your view of God's leadings."³⁰

When Berger resigned, Taylor created a temporary council of management under an honorary president, Theodore Howard, the grandson of Luke the meteorologist and son of Robert the quininologist — the third generation of his family to serve with the CIM. There were two honorary secretaries, Henry Soltau and Richard Hill, an architect, who both had busy careers and could give no more than nominal oversight. Emily Blatchley did most of the work. After her death, Taylor organized a formal London council, with an inner council of management and nineteen "Referees" throughout Great Britain who could provide information to friends and enquirers. Although this arrangement was meant to be "for the time being," since the council was merely advisory and none had any field experience, it remained the administrative structure, copied in the China council, until Taylor's death in 1905.³¹

For years Hudson Taylor had been pressuring his sister Amelia to join him in China, even after she married Benjamin Broomhall in 1858 and moved to London. Benjamin considered going to China, but a friend advised against such a step: "You have qualifications of a different kind. You must do work involving public relations."³² After Benjamin and Amelia moved to London he opened a custom tailor shop at 20 New Bond Street, the heart of the fashion district, while the family lived in a large house at Bayswater, then at Godalming, Surrey. He remained a member of the Wesleyan Methodist church, a strict sabbatarian and temperance advocate, and was active in the YMCA — George Williams was his friend for fifty years — and the Anti-Slavery Association. Benjamin had a great gift for dealing with the public — "enthusiasm itself," was one description³³ — but he was not good at finances, and consequently his business went bankrupt.

Providentially, Hudson Taylor proposed in 1875 that Benjamin and

29. Ibid., p. 317.
30. McKay, "Faith and Facts," p. 149.
31. Ibid., p. 192.
32. Norman Cliff, *Flame of Sacred Love*, p. 39.
33. *HTCOC* 6, p. 353.

Benjamin Broomhall in his study at Pyrland Road, 1880s. Broomhall married Hudson Taylor's sister, Amelia, and became the British Home Director in 1875. "B.B." and Amelia were much loved by the young missionaries, and sometimes intervened in conflicts with Hudson Taylor. As editor of *China's Millions* and *National Righteousness,* Broomhall was a leader of the anti-opium crusade in Britain. Five Broomhall children served as CIM missionaries in China, including Marshall, later British Home Director, and Gertrude, who married D. E. Hoste, Hudson Taylor's successor. Source: Norman Cliff, *A Flame of Sacred Fire: The Life of Benjamin Broomhall, 1829-1911* (Carlisle, UK: OM Publishing, 1998).

Amelia join the CIM in a full-time capacity as the mission's home secretary in England. "I have found my destiny," Broomhall declared. "Administration, journalism, dealing with the Christian public, selecting candidates — were these not just the kinds of work for which he had a genuine aptitude?"[34] They moved their ten children to the cramped house at Pyrland Road, which was so overflowing with candidates that the children had to eat standing up in the kitchen. In 1878 Taylor brought his own seven children to live there while he sent Jennie to Shanxi to organize the famine work, so in one day Amelia's children went from ten to seventeen.

34. Cliff, *Flame of Sacred Love,* p. 40.

The Broomhalls were full members "attached to the Mission in the same way as the missionaries,"[35] in other words, he was the only member of the London council who had voting authority in the mission's policy, rather than being merely advisory. He was also the only one who was paid. But an unusual financial arrangement had to be made, since Broomhall could not sustain his family on a missionary's stipend in middle-class London. Taylor hesitated "to show favouritism to his close relatives," but he guaranteed them a separate house in Pyrland Road and a regular income, an arrangement that placed them outside the normal conditions of service.[36]

Benjamin was a dapper sociable man who "counted among his friends bishops, moderators and presidents of these churches, as well as many local church pastors."[37] When he joined the CIM in 1876, it had 38 missionaries; when he retired twenty years later at the age of sixty-six, it had 630, of whom all the British had passed through his hands — several times, coming and going. More irenic and more ecumenical than Taylor, "half Methodist, half Anglican," he helped steer the CIM away from the sectarian Brethren toward the denominational and undenominational associations like the YMCA, the CMS, Mildmay, and Spurgeon's Tabernacle.[38]

B.B.'s great-grandson Norman Cliff, author of an affectionate biography, described his plan of action. "Using the many contacts in the churches which he had made in his earlier 20 years in London, he began making whistle-stop tours of the country. He would take a missionary on furlough with him to a church with which he had already made arrangements for a meeting. After introducing the missionary, he would go to a nearby town and make further appointments before returning to join in the meetings at the first centre. When the missionary had been escorted to the second town, Benjamin would proceed to make contacts in yet another town. With this strategy a group of towns would be covered in one round trip, and news of the work of the CIM shared with an ever-widening circle of Christians of various denominations."[39]

Moira Jane McKay, whose thesis was the first scholarly examination of the CIM, has made a major contribution to understanding the inner workings of the London council by compiling biographies of the seven members of the council of management and nineteen referees of 1872, plus the thirteen referees added in 1876 (see Appendix 2). It is a distinctive slice of British evangelicalism.

35. Minutes of London council, 18 February 1876, in *HTCOC* 6, p. 60.
36. Cliff, *Flame of Sacred Love*, p. 40.
37. Ibid., p. 45.
38. McKay, "Faith and Facts," traced this interdenominational shift.
39. Cliff, *Flame of Sacred Love*, p. 48.

In time the London council, like the China council, would become an extension of Hudson Taylor's own family, but at the beginning, he relied on his old friends.[40] Six of the seven members of the council of management can be traced. Two were deacons at Bryanston Hall, an Independent chapel in Portman Square that had sponsored Stephan Barchet, a pre-*Lammermuir* pioneer: the honorary treasurer John Challice, a businessman in Picadilly and director of six companies, and William Hall, a manufacturer of footwear. Challice was such a dedicated friend that his "In Memoriam" in *China's Millions* (1887) praised his "unremitting services as treasurer . . . ; to him the office was no sinecure; most scrupulously and conscientiously he examined the accounts from week to week making a private audit of every page."[41]

The other four were members of the Tottenham Brethren assembly, Theodore Howard and three members of the Soltau family, brothers Henry and George, and their brother-in-law Richard Hill, who had married Agnes Soltau. Henry W. Soltau, their father, was a Plymouth Brethren leader from Exeter, a barrister of "'sparkling wit, keen intellect, and extensive literary acquirements,'" who had met Taylor in 1865. He was in "his full vigour" then, and eventually six of his nine children served under the CIM in England, China, and Australia. Henry was honorary secretary from 1872 until he went to China in 1875, to pioneer the route from Burma, when he was replaced by George, who trained the candidates at his Lamb and Flag Ragged School and City Mission.[42]

Beyond the inner council, Taylor appointed referees "in various parts of the country, whose known sympathy will be helpful to strangers to the mission, and from whom such may learn its character and *bona fide* nature."[43] The first nineteen included ten Brethren, four Anglicans, three Baptists, and T. B. Smithies, a Primitive Methodist and editor of *The British Workman*. Since Brethren, both Open and Exclusive, made up half the membership, including the four on the council, this confirms Richard Hill's comment, "You know of course that the great majority of the earliest supporters were either or practically P.B.s [Plymouth Brethren]."[44] Geographically, most of the referees were based in London (13), with individuals in Barnstable, Liverpool, Bristol, and Brighton in England, and two in Dublin. They included such well-known "names" as Canon Pennefather, George Müller, Dr. Thomas Bar-

---

40. *HTCOC 5*, pp. 346-49, "A Council of Management."
41. McKay, "Faith and Facts."
42. *HTCOC 4*, pp. 140-41; *HTCOC 5*, p. 349.
43. *HTCOC 5*, p. 350.
44. McKay, "Faith and Facts," p. 290.

nardo, John Eliot Howard, Samuel Morley, and Grattan Guinness, as well as two titled aristocrats, Lord Radstock and the Marquis of Cholmondeley.

It is worth noting who is missing: there were only four clergymen — most unusual for a religious organization — including two Anglicans, Canon Pennefather (who died in 1873) and another parish priest, and two Baptists. Rev. William Landels was pastor of Regent's Park chapel, which sponsored Emily Blatchley and Jennie Faulding, a prominent Baptist church with "a large proportion of young men and many persons of social distinction." The absence of ministers emphasizes that the CIM was a lay organization, led by lay men and women, many of whom shared Taylor's residual mistrust of "educated ministers" and "priest-craft." Also absent were Wesleyan Methodists, Presbyterians, Salvation Army, or Quakers, though Taylor had friends among those denominations. More significant, not one of the council of management or the referees had any overseas experience: there were no CIM missionaries on furlough, for example, or directors of other mission societies.

When Broomhall took over as full-time secretary in 1876, there was a sea-change as twelve new referees were added. Nine were clergymen, three Anglicans (including Pennefather's successor at St Jude's), three Baptists, two Wesleyan Methodists, and one unknown. Only one Brethren was added, Richard Cope Morgan, editor of *The Christian* and chairman of Morgan & Scott, the CIM's official publishers, though he was hard to pin down ecclesiastically. The two Wesleyans included Rev. William Arthur, Broomhall's minister at Bayswater, who was a retired missionary from India, and Rev. Alexander McAuley, a Scotsman who was president of the Wesleyan Conference and secretary of home missions. There was also a noticeable shift upwards in class, with the addition of luminaries such as George Williams, founder of the YMCA, and Charles Haddon Spurgeon. Finally, Taylor appointed a field secretary who had experience in China: Charles Fishe, who with his brother Edward had been among Guinness's students in Dublin and joined the CIM in 1866.

Taylor's parting words gave Broomhall few instructions: "The all-important thing is to improve the character of the work; deepen the piety, devotion and success of the workers; remove stones of stumbling if possible; oil the wheels when they stick; amend whatever is defective and supplement as far as may be what is lacking. This is no easy matter when suitable men are wanting or only in the course of formation." As A. J. Broomhall commented, "Conspicuous, perhaps, in his evaluation is the absence of any reference to intelligence, initiative, energy or authority."[45] How was Broomhall to respond when Taylor, half a world away in 1881, telegraphed cryptically, "RECEIVE

---

45. JHT to Broomhall, 1879, in *HTCOC* 6, pp. 382-83.

AND SEND OUT 42 MEN AND 28 WOMEN"; or a few years later, "BANDED PRAYER. NEXT YEAR ONE HUNDRED NEW WORKERS TO BE SENT. PLEASE ACT AS SOON AS POSSIBLE"?[46] Taylor added, "We are not anxious as to the means for sending them forth or sustaining them...."[47]

From the beginning, there were rumblings from the London council and referees about their subordinate status. As Moira McKay notes, "Throughout Taylor's lifetime, there were difficulties as to the precise nature of the Council's powers." Mrs. Howard Taylor's official histories never allude to the controversies and consequently seldom mention London, for as D. E. Hoste warned her: "Be careful of anything that implies criticism of the home end. Everything depends on how you introduce it."[48]

The most controversial disagreement concerned *The Principles & Practice of the CIM*, introduced in 1876 and virtually unchanged into the 1930s, and *The Book of Arrangements* of 1886. These were meant to be windows for the London council "on the obscure administrative domain of the directors in China."[49] London was dismayed, believing it was "witnessing an authoritarian departure from the comfortable family relationship between Hudson Taylor and the missionaries that had satisfied all for twenty-five years." "Law had replaced the grace and love demonstrated by Hudson Taylor," they contended. "Now the Mission is growing so large we don't want it to be a big machine, but what it has been in the past — a family, only a larger one."[50]

"No thought occurred to them," A. J. Broomhall concluded, "that this logical step in the Mission's development would provoke years of disharmony and be the reef on which the CIM could have come to grief."[51]

The Ladies' Council

After the disaster of the *Lammermuir* party, the CIM did not send out any single women until 1878, when Jennie Taylor took the two women to Shanxi. Since no missionary couple was either willing or suitable to train a newly arrived unmarried woman, there seemed no place for them in China. The attitude of the London council seems to have been bewilderment: "There are two

---

46. Cliff, *Flame of Sacred Love*, pp. 50, 52.
47. JHT, appeal to the Churches in Great Britain and Ireland, 7 January 1882, in *HTCOC* 6, p. 303.
48. McKay, "Faith and Facts," p. 150.
49. *HTCOC* 6, p. 421.
50. *HTCOC* 7, p. 37.
51. *HTCOC* 6, p. 423.

or three apparently suitable ones who have offered themselves; but none of us seems quite to know your mind about it," Richard Hill wrote tentatively. In response, Taylor replied, "If there are one or two *suitable* female candidates, who could harmonize with Mrs. Duncan [widow of George Duncan], live with her, and work under her, by all means send them if you can. The great difficulty . . . is to find them suitable homes."[52] As late as 1885 — when the CIM had more women than men — the mission was still publicly silent on the subject of single women. Privately Taylor could write, "Our brethren in nearly every province are urgent in their cries for reinforcements; our sisters, were they to come out in ten times the number," would all find more than enough to do. Yet publicly he could not announce that women were being sent inland. "Keep it quiet," he wrote, "until success or otherwise appears."[53]

Once Benjamin Broomhall took over as home secretary, Amelia became the "Home Mother" to the ever-expanding household, a ladies' council unto herself. Norman Cliff writes that "an effective teamwork emerged." In addition to looking after the children and a stream of candidates, she would

> comfort young ladies who were leaving home to go to a strange and unknown distant land. She had to help Benjamin as he rushed off to take meetings all over the country. . . . Amelia was also to supervise the household staff and entertain the many visitors who came for information about the mission. . . . Amelia supervised the young people upon their arrival, and then, when they had been accepted by the London Council, Henrietta Soltau took them over for training at her nearby institute.[54]

While Amelia looked after the home, Jennie Taylor handled the correspondence when Hudson Taylor was in China — which was much of the time between 1876 and 1884 — acted as the mission treasurer and editor of *China's Millions*, and handled relations with the councils and committees. This personal approach was no longer sufficient when the CIM became an international corporation with three hundred agents in China. In 1886 Hudson Taylor created a ladies' council, under the "chairman" Henrietta Soltau, the youngest sister of Henry, George, and Agnes. She had looked after their aged father until his death, when she opened a small boarding school for CIM children, her own private enterprise run on faith principles, which grew into the Women's Training Home.

52. *HTCOC 5*, pp. 392-93.
53. *HTCOC 6*, p. 387.
54. Cliff, *Flame of Sacred Love*, pp. 42-43.

National Righteousness

Between 1886 and the Great War Miss Soltau personally prepared 547 women who were accepted as CIM missionaries and many times that number who were rejected.[55] Her duty was to "receive all and sundry" women who applied, "keep them for a limited time in her house and seek to form an estimate of their suitability for the work." The training home differed from the Broomhalls' home, where "each inmate should be given full opportunity for freedom of expression so as to reveal her natural characteristics, whereas in the Training School necessary discipline should exercise a salutary restraint on idiosyncrasies, its very rules and regulations inducing a conformity which, for the time being, must mask individuality."[56]

One woman who passed through Miss Soltau's hands was Evangeline French, who became a pioneer in Shanxi, and later, with her sister Francesca French and Mildred Cable, became famous as "the Trio" of Central Asia. Eva was a high-spirited woman, raised in France and Switzerland, fluent in French and German, highly intelligent and educated at the University of Geneva. She was also "painfully undomesticated . . . a tornado of a girl," who became subdued in the holy atmosphere. The accommodation was spartan, she wrote late in life, four women in one room divided by curtains, and the regimen strict. The matron told Miss French she was too well dressed and should learn to sew her own clothes, by hand. The garment she produced was "sufficiently dowdy, even for a missionary." For Miss French, "It was as though she had slipped a sheath over her personality. . . . Not until ten years later was that old mask finally discarded."[57]

Mildred Cable and Francesca French's biography of Miss Soltau has a classic title, *A Woman Who Laughed: Henrietta Soltau Who Laughed at Impossibilities and Cried: "It Shall Be Done."* For a CIM biography, it is surprisingly frank concerning theological controversies within the CIM, and shows Miss Soltau's pilgrimage away from the exclusive Plymouth Brethren of her family, through the second blessing of Keswick Holiness, to what some called "the third blessing" of divine healing.[58] After her father's death Miss Soltau felt under "the searchlight of the Holy God," until she was consumed by mi-

---

55. Cable and French, *A Woman Who Laughed*, p. 153.
56. Ibid., pp. 146-47.
57. Mildred Cable and Francesca French, *Something Happened* (London: Hodder & Stoughton, 1934), pp. 31-37.
58. Faith healing in Britain was typically part of a small sectarian community, such as "The Peculiar People" (that was their name), a tiny group in a few villages east of London: see Mark Sorrell, *The Peculiar People* (Exeter: Paternoster Press, 1979). Bethshan was one of the first healing institutions, which multiplied rapidly with the advent of Pentecostalism in the twentieth century.

graines and failing health.⁵⁹ A visitor told her about Bethshan, "the Home of Healing" in North London "where the restoring power of the all-conquering Christ was claimed in the treatment of human illness." The friend said, "You are unwilling to see where you have been trained in error. Beware lest you regard the tradition of man as more important than the commandments of God." Miss Soltau took this to mean she was not to be bound by old ideas and prejudices, such as the injunction against women preachers, but could receive direct commandments from God. This was a liberating moment, and in the silence Miss Soltau heard a voice say, "Loose her and let her go."⁶⁰

Miss Soltau's biography also illuminates the growth of women's work as a separate department of the CIM as a result of the London council's decision in 1883 that "the sisters be recognized as equals."⁶¹ This was due to the CIM's unique policy concerning marriage. The CIM regulations stated explicitly — up to 1950 — that candidates, male and female (with few exceptions), were to be sent out unmarried and to remain unmarried during their two-year probationary period in China. As the *Principles & Practice* stated:

> Owing to the great mortality rate which has been found to prevail among ladies who arrive in China newly married, or who marry on arrival, unmarried candidates of either sex, whether engaged or otherwise, will be expected to defer marriage until the completion of the second year from the date of the arrival of the one who last reached China. . . . [Since] the Directors of the Mission only send to China such persons as in their judgement possess the requisite qualifications, they may feel compelled in the event of a decidedly unsuitable engagement or marriage, to advise retirement from the Mission, and in case of noncompliance, to exercise their power of dismissal.⁶²

In England as in China, the CIM followed the rule of avoidance to keep the sexes apart except under "spiritual" circumstances: the men's home was strategically located an hour's walk from the women's; engaged couples could not meet unchaperoned or travel on the same vehicle. They had to obtain the permission of the council before they became engaged, even before they notified their own parents.

---

59. Cable and French, *A Woman Who Laughed*, p. 96.
60. Ibid., pp. 98-99.
61. *HTCOC* 6, p. 382.
62. *Principles & Practice of the China Inland Mission*, attached to minutes of North American council, Niagara-on-the-Lake, 20 July 1889, p. 3, in CIM/ABGC.

National Righteousness

The Anglo-Oriental Anti-Opium Society

Before he joined the China Inland Mission Benjamin Broomhall had been active in the YMCA and the Anti-Slavery Association, one of many small societies. When the anti-slavery movement was disbanded after the American civil war, many leaders turned to another international cause, the anti-opium crusade. After Broomhall joined the CIM, he became a key player at the highest level, as a director of the Anglo-Oriental Society for the Suppression of the Opium Trade (SSOT, the "Anglo-Oriental" was dropped), and editor of two anti-opium journals, *China's Millions* and *National Righteousness*.

Opium is the most effective pain remedy known to humankind. Because of its almost magical properties, it has been used to treat a wide range of illnesses since ancient times. It suppresses pain (arthritis, cancer, headaches, infant teething), "useless coughing" (tuberculosis, lung and throat diseases), diarrhoea (dysentery, cholera), and nervous and mental problems (depression, neurasthenia, boredom, sleeplessness). It also suppresses the pain of hunger and can produce a worker with superhuman endurance — reason for its spread both among the industrial poor in England and coolies in China. Opium has had a long history in England, and by the mid-nineteenth century opium and laudanum were in "open sale and popular use," available from chemists (such as Hudson Taylor's father), green-grocers, and grog-shops. It was particularly popular in the fen country of Cambridgeshire where the damp climate caused chronic ague, and in the industrial cities, such as Barnsley, where it soothed a myriad of ills.[63]

There was a brief flurry of anti-opium sentiment during the First Opium War with China (1839-41) when Gladstone denounced this "pernicious article" as a cause for war, but the debate was carried on at the level of parliament and big business.[64] The British little knew or cared that opium formed *the* economic base for the emerging British Empire. To them it was a commodity like any other, an economic question, not a moral one.[65]

---

63. For the anti-opium crusade in England, see Virginia Berridge and Griffith Edwards, *Opium and the People: Opiate Use in Nineteenth-Century England* (London: St. Martin's Press, 1981). For China, see Kathleen L. Lodwick, *Crusaders against Opium: Protestant Missionaries in China 1874-1917* (Lexington: University Press of Kentucky, 1996).

64. Berridge and Edwards, *Opium and the People*, p. 174.

65. Hartmann Henry Sultzberger, *All About Opium* (London: Wertheimer, Lea and Company, 1884), was a rationalization by a German businessman who condemned "the ever-increasing attacks" on opium, "this most unjustly abused article" (pp. iii, vii). P. D. Coates, *The China Consuls*, p. 176, stated that "[Consular] Officer after Officer forcefully expressed the opinion that opium in China was far less evil than alcohol at home." One re-

One of the tragic consequences of both the Crimean War and the American Civil War was the indiscriminate use of opium and its derivative, morphine. Morphine (or morphia) is an alkaloid of opium, ten times stronger — heroin is ten times stronger still — but once it was refined in medical form (in Germany in the 1840s), it could be controlled and diluted indefinitely. The development of morphine went hand-in-hand with the invention of the hypodermic needle, invented in 1843 and publicly demonstrated in 1855, just in time for the Crimean War.[66] Hypodermic morphine was a medical miracle: it could bring back a man literally from the edge of the grave, restoring rosy cheeks within minutes. But it created a generation of "morphinomaniacs," wounded soldiers who had become addicted in the battlefield hospitals.

Social historians tend to dismiss the domestic anti-opium crusade as a form of "social control," a moral crusade that went hand-in-hand with temperance and sexual purity. As such, it contributed to the medicalization of society and the disease theory of addiction, mental illness and racial degeneration. The "opium dens" in East London were a racist myth, they argue, fabricated by the "antidrug hysteria."[67] Now that "substance abuse" and drug cartels are international problems, scholars have a more sober reassessment of nineteenth-century opium. It was opium, and opium alone, that opened China to Western imperialism, William O. Walker claims in his recent study: British foreign policy based on free trade "could not succeed without recourse to drug addiction and war."[68] The CIM had an indirect involvement in the medicalization of opium through the Howard family, whose pharmaceutical company manufactured quinine, one of the palliatives used to treat withdrawal.

The main anti-opium organization, the SSOT, was founded in 1874 by Edward Pease, a banker, and his relative Sir Joseph Pease, an evangelical liberal MP, who brought the issue before the House of Commons. The SSOT was not

---

marked: "the excessive opium-smoker is a perfectly harmless creature, whose kindly instincts, if he has any, are not even dulled by indulgence in his vice, whereas the drunkard is too often a terror to his wife and children, a pest to his neighbours and a disgrace to his country." R. K. Newman, "Opium Smoking in Late Imperial China: A Reconsideration," *Modern Asian Studies* (Winter 1995), attempted to quantify "addiction" by differentiating recreational smokers from the "opium sots," and claimed that the opium problem was exaggerated by the missionaries.

66. H. H. Kane, *The Hypodermic Injection of Morphia: Its History, Advantages and Dangers. Based on the Experience of 360 Physicians* (New York: Chas. Bermingham, 1880).

67. Dean Latimer and Jess Goldberg, *Flowers in the Blood: The Story of Opium* (New York: Franklin Watts, 1981), p. 3.

68. William O. Walker, *Opium and Foreign Policy: The Anglo-American Search for Order in Asia, 1912-1954* (Chapel Hill: University of North Carolina Press, 1991), p. 7.

National Righteousness

a mass movement like the temperance or anti-slavery crusades; it was a political lobby whose goal was to create "an educated public opinion" that would apply "parliamentary pressure to obtain definite political action."[69] It was a single-issue coalition of politicians, medical men, and "nonconformist and evangelical denominations, with the missionaries as a distinct and active grouping, increasingly so towards the end of the century."[70]

The SSOT raised debates in the House of Lords on the opium question every year except one between 1878 and 1885. In 1881 the Archbishop of Canterbury, Cardinal Manning, and Lord Shaftesbury, "a triumvirate which might well overawe evil itself," chaired "an influential meeting" that demanded the British government treat China as a diplomatic equal and support its efforts to suppress the traffic and prohibit poppy growing in India.[71] In 1882-83 they held 180 public meetings on the opium trade, culminating in a petition of 75,000 signatures which Broomhall helped present to the House of Commons. "We must be as pungent as we can," he said. "We have no need to go cap in hand humbly to Ministers ... or any other official. We must demand, and press our demand."[72]

The year 1885 marked the apogee of the anti-opium movement, when the British government signed the Chefoo Convention that legalized opium in China, as long as a duty was paid when it was imported. The Chefoo Convention effectively fragmented the anti-opium lobby since one could no longer claim that Britain was "forcing" opium on China. After 1885 some anti-opium advocates turned to lobbying the Indian government, others supported a reform movement in China. Broomhall, who by now had a halo of snow-white hair and beard, founded a new organization called the Christian Union for the Severance of the Connection of the British Empire with the Opium Traffic, which "was closely identified with the missionary view of things."[73] Broomhall also founded its journal, *National Righteousness*, whose primary goal was to awaken the "conscience of England" and to "mobilize Christians

---

69. Berridge and Edwards, *Opium and the People*, p. 179, noted that the SSOT remained "obstinately elitist. It never attracted any significant body of working-class support."

70. Ibid. Mildmay also sponsored anti-opium conferences and petitions; its director, Rev. F. S. Turner, was editor of *The Friend of China*, the official organ of the SSOT: see *Chinese Recorder*, January-February 1879, p. 80.

71. David Edward Owen, *British Opium Policy in China and India* (New Haven: Yale University Press, 1934), pp. 262-63. Benjamin Broomhall, *The Truth About Opium Smoking* (London: Hodder & Stoughton, 1882), p. 5.

72. HTCOC 7, pp. 75-76.

73. Berridge and Edwards, *Opium and the People*, pp. 183-84. HTCOC 7, p. 628 note 20, noted that the "names" of the Christian Union included such CIM stalwarts as Dr. Barnardo, Eugene Stock, Grattan Guinness, Major-General Hoste, and C. H. Spurgeon.

to ceaseless involvement 'until this great evil is entirely removed.' "[74] (The title came from Proverbs 14:34: "Righteousness exalteth a nation, but sin is a reproach to any people.")

Broomhall retired from the CIM in 1895 to devote himself full time to the Christian Union; on his deathbed in 1911, when he was told that the British government promised the "extinction" of the opium trade with China within two years, he proclaimed, "A great victory. Thank God I have lived to see the day."[75]

The opium trade was for the CIM, as for most missionaries, a moral question, a blot on the national righteousness of England. *China's Millions* played all the themes of the anti-opium crusade. Hardly a month passed without some tragic vignette of opium suicides, emaciated bodies, or scholars reduced to penury. Some reports were so detailed a historian could use them to reconstruct the opium trails of a century ago. For example, Arthur Eason reported on smuggling in the Golden Triangle from Burma to Yunnan: "I asked my teacher to ascertain the number of opium dens" in Dali, Yunnan, he reported; they numbered 245. "Frequently on the road here I met as many as from sixty to 100 coolies in a company carrying opium to Hu-nan, Kwang-si [Guangxi], Canton, Kiang-si [Jiangxi], and Fu-kien [Fujian]. Each coolie carries from ninety-three to 100 English pounds."[76] Other reports tracked the growth of domestic opium in Sichuan, Shaanxi, Shanxi, and other provinces.

China's Millions also emphasized the Chinese point of view, reprinting interviews and letters from statesmen like Li Hongzhang, the foreign minister, and the Chinese ambassador to England. It also reported comments of ordinary Chinese who hated Christianity, the "foreign religion," because of its connection with "foreign mud." Arthur Eason quoted one Chinese who accused England of "plotting the nation's destruction" by sowing this dreadful seed. "A day of retribution is drawing nearer upon those who introduced it to satiate their own covetousness," Eason warned.[77]

Opium "is eating out the very vitals of the nation" went another typical account: "It is the source of poverty, wretchedness, disease and misery, unparalleled in . . . any other country. It debases the debased to the very lowest depths of degradation. It closes the eye to all pity, and the heart to all shame

---

74. *HTCOC 7*, p. 72. Dr. J. L. Maxwell of Taiwan stated (p. 75), "It was Mr Broomhall's keen perception of the secret of the weakness of the anti-opium movement *in the ignorance and apathy of the Churches.* There could be no hope of victory until the Churches had been thoroughly aroused."
75. Ibid., p. 519.
76. *China's Millions* (GB), July-August 1885, p. 102.
77. Ibid.

and sympathy. See that poor wretch with the emaciated frame; he has parted with his land, his house, his furniture, his children's and his own clothing and bedding, and either sold his wife or hired her out for prostitution, and *all for opium*, to satisfy an insatiable appetite."[78]

The Candidates

China's Millions was not primarily an anti-opium journal or a fund-raiser: it was a devotional text whose goal was to deepen the piety of its readers. Its message was reiterated in a hundred and one different ways: surrender your old life, "exchange" it for a new life of faith — and "step out on the promises" of God. That message determined the type of applicants the CIM attracted. They were young people without "attachments" (engaged to be married) or "obligations" (in debt or looking after parents). Some were "so full of joy, it was the natural outcome of a heart full of the love of Christ that they should want to rush to the darkest unhappiest places in the world to tell it out. To others, and these perhaps deeper natures, the sense of sacrifice was so intense that the offer meant keenest pain . . . to break away from the tender ties of home."[79]

Since the CIM stressed spiritual qualifications over educational or social, it demanded a genuine experience of Christ's power in the individual life of the applicant and zeal in winning souls. "Have you definite reason to believe that you have been blessed to the conversion of others?" the Candidates' Schedule (application form) asked.[80] At least one candidate was rejected because he could not pray spontaneously in public. When God gave a call, Hudson Taylor believed, he generally gave *"qualifications"* such as health and language ability. On occasion when the CIM accepted a candidate "full of faith and the Holy Ghost" contrary to doctor's orders, "we have either seen God in answer to prayer Himself interpose, or there has been afterwards a thorough breakdown, involving much sorrow and expense. On the other hand I should be sorry to be guided *only* by a Physician's judgement, and we very seldom are."[81]

Rather than class or education the CIM developed a "capacity standard," defined as the "ability to take advantage of opportunities." The majority continued to be what A. J. Broomhall called the "yeoman class," artisans, shop clerks, ste-

---

78. Ibid., July-August 1876, p. 82.
79. Obituary of May Rose Nathan in Marshall Broomhall, *Martyred Missionaries of the China Inland Mission, With a Record of the Perils and Sufferings of Some who Escaped* (London: CIM, 1901), p. 44.
80. McKay, "Faith and Facts," p. 108.
81. Ibid., p. 109.

nographers, and governesses. Nevertheless, after the disaster of the *Lammermuir* party, the CIM's social qualifications edged upwards, particularly during the boom years of the 1880s.[82] In one month of 1886 the candidates included a wine merchant from Calcutta, a druggist's assistant, the son of a Welsh publican, a former Africa missionary, a Cambridge graduate and an artist.[83] By this time Hudson Taylor could reminisce about the "humble people" of the early years. "If they were to offer to the Mission now they might not be accepted."[84]

The CIM Archives in London (SOAS) contains a "List of Missionaries" who went to China between 1853 (Hudson Taylor) and 1895. The information is scanty, giving only the name, the date of arrival and marriage, and occasionally death or resignation. Starting in 1880, the records begin to include home address, age, and occupation. Of the 248 who joined by 1885, the year of the Cambridge Seven, they can be tabulated thus:

	Male	Female	Total
1862-74	26	24	50
1875 (the Eighteen)	10	5	15
1876	6	6	12
1877	—	1	1
1878 (the Thirty)	14	14	28
1879	6 (1 MD)	—	6
1880	4 (1 MD, 1 Rev)	5	9
1881	4	4	8
1882 (the Seventy)	3 (2 MD)	5	8
1883	7	12	19
1884	19 (1 MD)	27	46
1885 (the Seven)	29 (1 Rev)	17	46
Total	128	120	248

Of the 50 who went out during the first decade, only 18 remained in active membership by 1875, due to deaths, resignations, firing, marriage outside, or joining another mission. Since only five married couples were accepted before 1885, this meant that 238 individuals went out unmarried, 115 women and 123 men. Nevertheless within two or three years most had married. Contrary to

---

82. If the Canadian statistics (Chapter 9) are any indication, showing a ratio of seven applicants for every accepted candidate, the CIM must have received thousands of applications.
83. McKay, "Faith and Facts," p. 106.
84. Barr, *To China with Love*, p. 33.

the public perception of the CIM as a repository of "redundant women," the gender breakdown shows that the numbers of men and women were almost equal. The geographical breakdown of the 83 individuals who listed their residence shows that almost half (39) came from London, mostly middle-class suburbs from South Kensington to Islington. One-quarter (21) came from Manchester, Liverpool, and other cities in England. There were 6 from Ireland and 18 from Scotland. (Fourteen of the Scottish candidates joined in 1884, 12 from Glasgow alone, which led to the opening of a Scottish office.)

Among the occupations listed for the men were lawyer, ornamental carver, jeweler, teacher, photographer, commodities traveler, bank clerk, and civil servant. Other than Hudson Taylor, who had been ordained by the Baptists, there were only three clergymen, all Anglicans, including W. W. Cassels of the Cambridge Seven. For the women, occupations include dressmaker, "smallware makeup" [piecework], teachers, and stationer's clerks, but many merely state: "home duties," "at home," "keeping brother's house," and far too often, "nil."

For fifteen years Hudson Taylor was the only medical doctor, until two joined in 1880 and two more in 1882. Over the next few years, several experienced British missionaries spent their furloughs in the United States, where medical education was more readily available, and obtained their "M.D. (U.S.A.)" degree. One was Arthur Douthwaite, a pioneer of the Eighteen, who crammed three years' work into one year at Vanderbilt University in Nashville, Tennessee.

If one person was both representative and catalyst for the respectability of the CIM it was Dr. Harold A. Schofield (1851-83), who was described by Timothy Richard as "one of the most brilliant medical missionaries who ever came to China."[85] He graduated from London University at eighteen, received an M.A. and bachelor of medicine from Oxford and further training in Vienna and Prague. He directed a Red Cross hospital in Turkey during the war with Serbia, and again in the war against Russia, where he helped administer hypodermic morphine. He was married, though his wife had to pass the physical and theological qualifications to join the CIM. They arrived in Taiyuan, Shanxi, in 1880, where he started medical work, then died tragically three years later, aged thirty-two, of cholera.

Dr. Schofield took his cousins, Florence and Jessie Kemp, daughters of a well-known Baptist family from Rochdale, England, to be his assistants in the hospital. Since they were not members of the CIM, but went out at their own expense, they did not need to pass the physical or spiritual qualifications. Nor

---

85. Richard, *Forty-Five Years in China*, p. 151.

were such friends and relations, governesses and tutors, bound by CIM rules regarding Chinese dress. The *Book of Arrangements* stated in black and white: "none of our missionaries resident in the interior are at liberty to invite their friends for residence or prolonged stay in the premises of the Mission without the written permission of the Superintendent.... These remarks do not apply to hospitality to travellers passing through."[86] Florence married Dr. Ebenezer Henry Edwards, Schofield's successor, but she had conditionalist views and a special dispensation had to be given. Jessie married Thomas Wellesley Piggott, an Anglo-Irish aristocrat who endowed the Schofield Memorial Hospital. They formed quite a CIM dynasty in Taiyuan.

The Cambridge Seven

In 1884-85, the CIM was catapulted "from comparative obscurity to an almost embarrassing prominence" by the recruitment of the Cambridge Seven.[87] They were seven young aristocrats who joined the CIM in 1885 in one of the grand heroic gestures of nineteenth-century missions. Charlie Studd was one of the most famous men in England, as a member of the All-England cricket team. Their recruitment sparked an "irresistible" movement. "No such event had occurred before; and no event of the century has done so much to arouse the minds of Christian men to the . . . nobility of the missionary vocation." Eugene Stock of the CMS (which received dozens of applications as a result of the Seven) claimed they were "a gift from God," a reward for Hudson Taylor's unselfishness in pleading "the cause of China and the World" and not his own organization.[88]

The Seven started with Stanley Peregrine Smith ("S.P.S."), "a percussion cap! — the gun already loaded in many cases." Smith was an orator, "scintillating," erratic, introspective, bookish, a man of peculiar habits and "infectious devotion."[89] Son of a successful London surgeon, he went up to Cambridge in 1879 where he made a name for himself "on the river" as captain of the University Eight rowing team. A nominal Christian in that male world of theater, racing, and cards, he saw "the transience, the emptiness of all this world could offer"[90] and helped found the Cambridge Inter-Collegiate Christian Union, forerunner of many student organizations including the Student

86. *HTCOC* 6, p. 423.
87. John C. Pollock, *A Cambridge Movement* (London: Marshall, Morgan & Scott, 1953), p. 87.
88. Stock, *History of the CMS*, vol. 3, pp. 284-85.
89. *HTCOC* 6, p. 339, quoting Dixon Hoste; p. 353, quoting John Stevenson.
90. Ibid., p. 340.

National Righteousness

Volunteer Movement and the Varsity Christian Fellowship. Smith had a soapbox in Hyde Park where he preached "not the milk and water of religion but the cream of the Gospel."[91] He provided the defining moment of the party at a meeting at Edinburgh University. Some students came to heckle, expecting "professedly religious people of their own age as wanting in manliness, unfit for the river or cricket-field, and only good for psalm-singing and pulling a long face. But the big, muscular hands and long arms of the ex-captain of the Cambridge Eight, stretched out in entreaty, while he eloquently told the old story of Redeeming Love, capsized their theory."[92]

The second was Charlie Studd ("C.T."), a "Roman candle, impulsive, unpredictable, even unbalanced."[93] Charlie was the third brother to captain the Cambridge cricket team, following John Edward Kynaston (later Sir John, the Lord Mayor of London) and George, who became a pentecostal minister in Los Angeles. Charlie grew up on a palatial estate that had its own "first-quality cricket ground in the days when country-house cricket was at its height." After his conversion, when he spoke with "quiet but intense and burning utterances of personal testimony to the love and power of a personal Saviour, opposition and criticism were alike disarmed, and professors and students together were seen in tears."[94] Shortly after he arrived in China, Studd came into an inheritance of £50,000 ($250,000 U.S. at that time, and perhaps $5 million today), which he invested in "the Bank of Heaven" and donated £5,000 each to D. L. Moody, George Müller, Dr. Barnardo, Annie Macpherson, and the Salvation Army. Moody used his money to establish Moody Bible Institute in Chicago; General Booth sent fifty missionaries to open work in India. On his marriage, Studd gave away the rest so that he and his bride could "start clear with the Lord at our wedding."[95]

Rev. William Wharton Cassels, "Will the Silent," was at twenty-seven the oldest of the group. Born in Oporto, Portugal, the ninth of thirteen children of a British merchant (port wine), Cassels was inordinately reserved with "something more than introspection." He was "a fervent lover of order.... To him obedience to marching orders was fundamental. And so were unity, order, and authority."[96] After graduating from Cambridge, he was ordained cu-

---

91. Ibid., p. 362.
92. *Growth of a Work of God*, pp. 386-87.
93. *HTCOC 6*, pp. 341, 330-32.
94. *Growth of a Work of God*, p. 387.
95. Norman P. Grubb, *C. T. Studd: Athlete and Pioneer* (London: Religious Tract Society, 1933; reprint, Grand Rapids: Zondervan, 1937), pp. 59-60.
96. Marshall Broomhall, *W. W. Cassels: First Bishop in Western China* (London: CIM, 1926), pp. 136-37.

rate of a working-class parish in Lambeth where his boundless energy went into running a Sunday school for three thousand children and "vigorous open-air work."[97] As the first Anglican clergyman in the CIM, Cassels raised ecclesiastical problems, since he was bound to sticky Episcopal regulations concerning Eucharist, baptism, catechism, confirmation, major and minor orders, and nominal control by a bishop. His biographer Marshall Broomhall noted that "it is one thing to profess principles and another to embody them."[98] For forty years he worked to create a Church of England enclave within the CIM, which was elevated to the Diocese of East Sichuan in 1895, an unusual cooperative venture, a CMS diocese under CIM control, and he was consecrated bishop by the Archbishop of Canterbury.[99]

The Polhill Turners came next. Cecil was a soldier, a lieutenant in the Royal Dragoons in Ireland. In China, he became a restless wanderer, edging towards Tibet and pentecostalism, settling for a time in Xinjiang then moving to Darjeeling, India, then back to Sichuan on the Tibetan border. Brother Arthur, at twenty-two the youngest of the group, was studying for Anglican holy orders. Ecclesiastically, he was ordained by Cassels as the curate at the cathedral in Baoning (now Langzhong), East Sichuan, where he remained for thirty years.

The sixth was Montague Beauchamp, a nephew of the evangelist Lord Radstock and son of Sir Thomas Beauchamp, who had taken the insurance policy off his greenhouses which were miraculously preserved during a hailstorm (see Chapter 3). Montague joined the Cambridge Seven as an independent, self-supporting missionary, not officially attached to the CIM. When he did join officially, he renounced an inheritance of a quarter of a million pounds — over $1.25 million U.S. ($25 million today) — because it was conditional on his returning to England. Instead he chose to live on a CIM stipend.[100] He was a providential philanthropist who anonymously contributed the construction cost of many CIM buildings, including the Shanghai headquarters.

The final member was Dixon E. Hoste, another soldier who loved order. The grandson of the Gentleman Usher to Queen Victoria and son of a major-

---

97. Ibid., p. 24.
98. Ibid., p. 136.
99. Cassels was nominally under Bishop George Moule, Taylor's CMS antagonist from Hangzhou, who had reconciled himself to the CIM but kept Cassels under "closer supervision than was normally demanded" (ibid., p. 139). Moule's brother, Rev. Handley Moule, the Principal of Ridley Hall, Cambridge, and later Bishop of Durham, was a Keswick teacher and friend of JHT.
100. *HTCOC* 6, pp. 425-26.

National Righteousness

general, he grew up in a family of "uncompromising Christians" characterized by "military precision." Dixon Hoste did not attend Cambridge, but joined the Royal Artillery, where "he shrugged off all but garrison religion in any form." Converted under Moody's revival, he decided he must give himself to Christ "as completely as he had given himself to soldiering." He applied to the CIM, he wrote in his diary, because it was "thoughtful, sober-minded, feet on the ground: this gained *my* confidence. So much cackling *before* they have their egg! (CIM) show the *real* thing."[101] (In other words the CIM thanked God in advance of receiving the answer to their prayers.)

Taylor considered sending the Seven as part of the Seventy but recognizing their publicity value, he sent them on tours of England, Scotland, and Ireland. Their story in *China's Millions* sold 50,000 copies and, republished as *The Evangelisation of the World* by Benjamin Broomhall, it sold 20,000 copies and was distributed free to every YMCA and YWCA in the British Empire and the United States. Robert Speer, a founder of the (American) Student Volunteer Movement, stated that three books had influenced his life: the Bible, *The Personal Life of Livingstone*, and *The Evangelisation of the World*.[102]

The Cambridge Seven, the official history by John C. Pollock, ends at Victoria Station: "Carriage doors were shut, a whistle blew, and at 10 a.m. the Boat Train drew slowly out. The Cambridge Seven were on their way to Dover and Calais, Brindisi, Suez, Colombo and China."[103] I find it inexplicable that the official history ends with their departure and does not follow them to China, as though their recruitment in England were the whole story. Victoria Station was not the end, but only the beginning, for until they arrived in China the Cambridge Seven were ordinary young men — ordinary, rich, athletic, educated, pious young men caught in a grand romantic gesture. It was in China that the percussion caps and Roman candles went off.

---

101. Ibid., pp. 335-37.
102. *Growth of a Work of God*, p. 378. Although CIM historians stated the title contributed to the watchword of the SVM, "the evangelization of the world in this generation," Dana Robert, "'The Crisis of Missions': Premillennial Mission Theory and the Origins of Independent Evangelical Missions," in Carpenter and Shenk, eds., *Earthen Vessels: American Evangelicals and Foreign Missions, 1880-1980*, noted that A. T. Pierson had used the watchword earlier. She also noted that it appealed to both postmillennialists and premillennialists.
103. John C. Pollock, *The Cambridge Seven* (London: Marshall, Morgan & Scott, 1955), p. 117.

APPENDIX 2

London Council Members and Referees 1872-1876

The first council of management met on 4 October 1872 at 51 Gordon Square, home of Joseph Weatherley. They met again the next day and on the 8th, the day before Hudson Taylor left for China. By 1873 nineteen referees had been named, and thirteen more were added in 1876. The information is from Moira McKay, "Faith and Facts in the History of the China Inland Mission, 1832-1905," pp. 259-91, as well as "Personalia" in *HTCOC* and other sources.

Council of Management:

John Challice — Honorary Treasurer (d. 1887) — Dover Street, Picadilly. Challice was a London businessman, director of six companies, and deacon at Bryanston Hall, a Congregational (or Independent) chapel in Portman Square that had supported the CIM since 1861.

Richard Harris Hill — Honorary Secretary — Westminster. An architect and civil engineer, Hill married Agnes, sister of Henry and George Soltau. He assisted in building Barnardo's Homes, Mildmay, the Bethnal Green Cottage Hospitals, and the CIM headquarters at Newington Green. Hill's father, an Anglican clergyman, had joined the Plymouth Brethren under H. W. Soltau, and Richard Hill remained in "happy fellowship" with the Brethren.

Henry Soltau — Honorary Secretary — 6 Pyrland Road (CIM home). Son of Henry W. Soltau, a barrister and Plymouth Brethren teacher from Exeter who met JHT in 1865, Henry was one of six children connected with the CIM. He went to China in 1875, where he pioneered the route from Burma and was one of the first Westerners to cross China from west to east.

Theodore Howard — Chairman — (d. 1915) Bickley, Kent. Son of Robert Howard, Theodore Howard was the third generation of the Brook Street (Tottenham) Brethren family to be associated with the CIM. In addition to being chairman and home director (1879) of the CIM, he was honorary treasurer of the Regions Beyond Missionary Union and other faith missions.

William Hall — Edgeware Road. Like Challice, Hall was a businessman, a manufacturer of footwear, and deacon at Bryanston Hall. He was a supporter of the CIM from 1865.

George Soltau — Myddelton Square (East London). Son of Henry W. and brother of Henry, George Soltau was in charge of the Lamb and Flag Schools and associated with Barnardo's Homes. He was appointed assistant secretary of the London council in 1875, when Henry went to China.

Joseph Weatherley — Gordon Square. The first council of management met in his home, but he left the council by 1876.

Referees in 1872:

Dr. Thomas John Barnardo, FRCS, FRGS — Stepney Causeway. Founder and director of Barnardo's Homes.

Henry Bewley (1814-76) — Dublin. An evangelist and printer, Bewley was the printer of the CIM's *Occasional Papers*, and printed four to five million tracts at his own expense. He was responsible, with J. Denham Smith, for the erection of Merrion Hall, a Brethren assembly in Dublin.

William Henry Hugh, 3rd Marquis of Cholmondeley (1800-84) — Norfolk and London. Tory MP for Norfolk and South Hants, hereditary Grand Chamberlain of England. Cholmondeley was "a typical Evangelical churchman," according to his obituary in *The Times*, a generous supporter of "good and charitable works, especially such as were endorsed by the Evangelical Party." His estates in Cheshire had an income of £40,000 per annum, and after his death were sold for £300,000.

Robert Cleaver Chapman (1803-1902) — Barnstable. A solicitor and son of a rich Yorkshire merchant, Chapman was converted to the Church of England in 1823, then changed his views on believers' baptism and became pastor of a "Strict" or "Close" Baptist chapel in Barnstable. He came to Brethren views and established an Open Brethren hall in Grosvenor Square, London. "Chapman's long life and the simple holiness of his character made him the outstanding patriarch and counsellor of the nineteenth century Open Brethren. . . . Barnstable became a 'Mecca' of Brethren" (Coad, *History of the Brethren Movement*).

William Collingwood (1819-1903) — Liverpool. Collingwood left the Church of England and joined the Brethren. A landscape painter and member of the Royal Water-Colour Society, he was responsible for building Crown Street Hall, the permanent base for Liverpool Brethren. In 1850 he applied to Gutzlaff to go as a missionary artist to China, but he withdrew in order to get married. He met JHT in 1853 and was a regular donor to CES and CIM. Louise Desgraz, one of the *Lammermuir* stalwarts, was a governess in his home.

Rev. C. Graham — Shepherd's Bush. He is not mentioned in Crockford's (Anglican clergy), and nothing is known of him.

Henry Grattan Guinness — Harley House, Bow Road. The "silver-tongued" Irish evangelist and founder of East London Institute.

John Eliot Howard, FRS (1803-83) — Tottenham. He was a manufacturer of quinine, the son of Luke Howard.

Rev. William Landels (1823-99) — A Scotsman, Landels was the first pastor of Regent's Park Baptist chapel. He differed from traditional Baptist policy by admitting to the Lord's Supper persons not baptized by total immersion. He was a popular preacher who could attract eighteen hundred people to a Sunday evening service.

Rev. William Garrett Lewis — Bayswater. An "active Baptist" minister, he was a schoolteacher in Brixton, then minister of Westbourne Grove Chapel (where JHT attended regularly), "one of the largest religious edifices in the metropolis." He urged JHT to publish *China: Its Spiritual Need and Claims* (1865), and was a founder of the London Baptist Association.

John Morley (1807-96) — Upper Clapton. Morley was the older brother of the Congregational leader and political reformer, Samuel Morley, and both were involved in the early YMCA. After retiring as senior partner in a textile firm in 1855, he joined the Brethren and financed the construction of Clapton Hall.

George Müller — Bristol. A founder of the Brethren movement in Britain.

Rev. William Pennefather (1816-73) — Mildmay Hall, Islington. Pennefather was the Church of England vicar of St. Jude's, Mildmay Park, where he established a complex of schools, orphanages, a hospital and a chapel, which continues today.

Granville Augustus William Waldegrave, Lord Radstock (1833-1913) — East Sheen. Son of Dowager Lady Radstock (herself an important supporter of the CIM) and brother-in-law of Sir Thomas Beauchamp, Radstock was a member of the "first family" of English evangelicalism. He was a wealthy, eccentric Anglican layman who pleased himself ecclesiastically, and was a member of the Welbeck Street Plymouth Brethren chapel. About 1873 he started to practice faith healing. He was also president of the Heart of Africa Mission.

Rev. William Lewis Rosenthall — Forest Hill, London. He was vicar of St. Saviour's Anglican church.

Joseph Denham Smith — Dublin. A Congregational pastor, Smith was a leading evangelist of the 1859 revival. He threw his lot in with the Irish Brethren, and with Bewley, was responsible for the construction of Merrion Hall. He held a successful tour of England and the Continent, and later settled in London.

T. B. Smithies (1815-83) — Highgate, London. A Primitive Methodist and energetic temperance worker, Smithies was editor of *The Band of Hope Review*, *The British Workman*, and similar works. He was "a warm friend" of the CIM, and a holiness speaker at Mildmay (Bebbington).

Henry Varley — Clarendon Road. Well known as an evangelist, Varley was associated with the Brethren assemblies at Highgate and Swindon, before taking charge of the West London Tabernacle, Notting Hill. He was a financial supporter of the CIM from 1866; in 1883 he contributed £500, the proceeds from his Bible readings and evening meetings.

Colonel Woodfall — Brighton. A member of the Plymouth Brethren before joining the Open Brethren, Woodfall was often JHT's host.

Referees Added in 1876:

Charles Thomas Fishe — Field Secretary. Dublin. The younger son of Colonel Fishe, of the Madras Horse Artillery, Charles was one of Guinness's students. In 1867 he was assistant secretary of the CIM under W. T. Berger, and went to China in 1869. He married Nellie Faulding, sister of Jennie (the second Mrs. JHT). He returned to England because of health.

Rev. William Arthur (1819-1901) — Belfast. Wesleyan Methodist minister and missionary to India from 1839-61, he retired because of health. He was secretary of the WMMS and director of the Wesleyan Mission House. He was Broomhall's pastor in Bayswater, and a well-known writer of prophetic literature, such as *The Tongue of Fire* (1856). (See Cliff, *Flame of Sacred Love*, pp. 32-33.)

Rev. Dr. James Culross (1824-99) — Perthshire. Awarded a D.D. from St. Andrew's University, Culross was minister of Stirling Baptist church for twenty years, training men for the Baptist ministry. He moved to Highbury Hill, London, then returned to Glasgow. He published twenty-five books on devotional and mission topics.

Rev. Daniel Bell Hankin — Milday Hall. Hankin became vicar of St. Jude's, Mildmay Park in 1875, after Canon Pennefather's death.

Rev. William Haslam (d. 1893) — Mayfair. Born in Dublin, Haslam was a Church of Ireland priest who held charges in Cornwall and Bath before becoming perpetual curate of the Curzon Chapel in Mayfair. He was also a missionary with the Church Parochial Missionary Society, and author of *A Personal Christ* and *The Lord is Coming*.

Rev. Alexander McAulay (1818-90) — Glasgow and London. Born in Glasgow, he was a Wesleyan Methodist minister and missionary, and secretary of the Metropolitan Chapel Building Fund. He was a supporter (with William Arthur) of the CIM since 1866. In 1876 he was president of the Wesleyan Conference and secretary of the Home Mission Department. After retiring, he went as a missionary to the West Indies and Africa at his own expense.

Rev. Alexander McLaren (1826-1910) — Manchester. Son of a Glasgow business man, McLaren was a Baptist minister in Southampton and Union Chapel, Manchester, where his preaching attracted such crowds that a larger church was built. He was "a brilliant expository preacher although he lacked other qualities of a successful pastor." He was president of the Baptist Union and the first Baptist World Conference (1905).

Richard Cope Morgan (1827-1908) — London. Morgan was founder and editor of *The Revival* in 1859 (later *The Christian*), and chairman of Morgan & Scott, the CIM's official publishers (including *China's Millions*). According to his obituary in *The Times*, he "was ready to assist many efforts of practical philanthropy," including becoming a trustee of Barnardo's Edinburgh Castle. Morgan appears to have become "eccentric," for he published an article in *The Christian* attacking the basis of faith missions. (See Bebbington.)

National Righteousness

Captain Reynold Ducie Moreton (1835-1919) — Mildmay Hall. The third son of Lord Moreton, Earl of Ducie, Leicester, Moreton was a retired naval captain who was in charge of Mildmay Hall.

Rev. Josiah Pearson — Nothing is known.

Rev. Marcus Rainsford — Pimlico. A graduate of Trinity College, Dublin, Rainsford was minister of Belgrave Chapel, Pimlico. He was a well-known Anglican millenarian and spoke at the 1878 Mildmay Second Advent conference.

Rev. Charles Haddon Spurgeon (1834-92) — London. The most famous nineteenth-century English preacher, he founded the Metropolitan Tabernacle, and was a supporter of JHT and the CIM from 1865.

Sir George Williams (1821-1905) — London. A draper's assistant, Williams was "the most probable founder of the YMCA" in 1844-45. He first appeared in *China's Millions* in 1880, when he chaired a farewell meeting in the Aldersgate YMCA. He was president of the YMCA and the Band of Hope Union, the Bible Society and London City Mission, and according to *The Times*, of any society for the suppression of smoking, drinking, and gambling. Despite his nonconformist background, he joined the Church of England, and attended Portman Chapel (see Challice above). He was knighted in 1894.

Brethren: 19

T. J. Barnardo	Colonel Woodhull	H. Bewley
Theodore Howard	R. C. Chapman	H. G. Guinness
W. Collingwood	Henry Soltau	George Soltau
R. H. Hill	John Eliot Howard	R. C. Morgan
J. Morley	R. Morrison	Lord Radstock
J. Weatherley	J. Denham Smith	C. T. Fishe
H. Varley		

Church of England: 8

Marquis of Cholmondeley	Rev. William Pennefather	G. Williams
Rev. D. B. Hankin	Rev. W. L. Rosenthall	Rev. William Haslam
Rev. H. Rainsford	W. Hall	

Baptist: 5

Rev. Wm. Landels
Rev. A. McLaren
Rev. W. G. Lewis
Rev. C. H. Spurgeon
Rev. Culross

Congregational:

J. Challice

Wesleyan Methodist: 2

Rev. W. Arthur
Rev. Alexander McAulay

Primitive Methodist:

T. B. Smithies

Unknown:

Rev. C. Graham
Rev. J. Pearson

CHAPTER 7

The Octopus
1875-1888

When you go to China, what will you have to face? . . . I dare say the thoughts of many as they read this question will turn at once to the outward and visible things we have to face — the dirt and discomfort, the strange, dreadful-looking dishes we have to eat, the contempt and ridicule we often meet with, the consciousness that we are living over a sleeping volcano, which, if God were to withdraw His restraining hand, might at any moment burst forth and destroy us all. . . . You will have to face the devil himself; you have actually dared to attack the very citadel of his kingdom, where he has reigned without a rival for thousands of years, and he will soon let you know and realize his presence and power as you have never felt it in Christian England. . . . You will have to watch the awful struggle between light and darkness; yea, and if you are to prove a true sister you must enter into conflict with them. . . . Lastly, just because you are face to face with the devil, you must face God. . . . Have I drawn the shadows too darkly?

Miss Hessie Newcombe, Church of England Zenana Mission,
martyred 1895 in Fujian.[1]

The Second Generation

Now there are eighteen, thirty, seventy, one hundred pilgrims at sea. Gone are the days of sails and windjammers; they travel by ocean liners, albeit in third

---

1. *China's Millions* (NA), April 1896, p. 48.

class, as an identifiable group among the international travelers. Like the Cambridge Seven, they sailed through the Straits of Gibraltar, past Brindisi and through the Suez Canal. At every port of call east of Suez — Aden, India, Malaya, Singapore, Hong Kong, Shanghai — they see the Union Jack, the sign of the expanding British Empire. Somehow "the distant land of Sinim" seems less distant when it is only one month's journey away, compared to Hudson Taylor's five months at sea.

Before they left Britain, the candidates attended a round of farewell meetings, large and small. They came from diverse backgrounds, from all walks of life and all parts of England, Scotland, Ireland, and Wales, plus one or two from Europe. Just as they had been streamlined into a family through the mission home and training institutes, the farewells had become standardized. The five or six young men or women would proceed to the platform during the singing of a missionary hymn like "From Greenland's icy mountains," where they were introduced by dignitaries such as Lord Shaftesbury or George Williams. Each was asked to give a brief testimony; one Welsh woman gave hers in Gaelic.[2] The service ended with a dedication of these young people to a life of missionary service — "God's ambassadors" — and closed with an emotional "God be with you till we meet again." In addition to their home churches, the farewells culminated in grand gatherings at the Aldersgate YMCA, Spurgeon's Metropolitan Tabernacle, Mildmay Hall, Guinness's East London Missionary Training Institute, Dr. Barnardo's Homes, and Annie Macpherson's Home of Industry.[3]

Then came the final farewell. Mildred Cable and Francesca French described one group of young women standing on the London docks, "whose dress was of a plain and severe order, several of them wearing small black bonnets which had certainly not been selected from any notion of coquetry. . . . Senior among them was a woman of heroic type" — Miss Henrietta Soltau, head of the women's training institute — "who looked as one does who has counted and accepted the cost of whatever life might require of her. Her broad forehead, strong features and general independence of deportment, spoke of reliability, enthusiasm and tenacity of purpose. By her side stood a young woman whose manner showed timidity, but whose eyes shone with a fire of zeal, revealing a spirit which one felt would not quail before martyrdom. . . . I caught the sound of a well known chorus led in a magnifi-

---

2. A Miss Jones at the Welsh Chapel, Shirland Road: *China's Millions* (GB), March 1881, p. 40.

3. Ibid., December 1884, pp. 150-51, listed farewell meetings in London, Glasgow, and Edinburgh for thirty departing missionaries in two months: four women sailed on 27 August, seven women and two men on 24 September, eight men on 8 October, and nine women on 22 October.

The Cambridge Seven in England. 1. Charlie Studd; 2. Dixon E. Hoste; 3. Rev. William Wharton Cassels; 4. Stanley Peregrine Smith; 5. Charles Polhill Turner; 6. Rev. Arthur Polhill Turner; 7. Montague Beauchamp. The recruitment of the Cambridge Seven in 1884-85 catapulted the CIM "from comparative obscurity to an almost embarrassing prominence," and was a catalyst for student missionary movements on both sides of the Atlantic. Source: Phyllis Thompson, *D. E. Hoste: "A Prince with God": Hudson Taylor's Successor as General Director of the China Inland Mission 1900-1935* (London: CIM, 1947)

THE SECOND GENERATION

The Cambridge Seven in China. As soon as they arrived in China, the Seven changed into Chinese clothes. Standing, l. to r.: Studd, Beauchamp, and Smith; seated, A. Polhill Turner, Hoste, C. Polhill Turner, and Cassels. Source: Thompson, *D. E. Hoste.*

cent soprano by the heroic woman: 'Stayed upon Jehovah, hearts are fully blessed, Finding, as He promised, perfect peace and rest.'"[4]

We have met some pilgrims on the road to Shanxi: who were the others, Hudson Taylor's forgotten footsoldiers? There was Robert J. Landale, "a gentleman of means and education," the son of a lawyer at the Supreme Court in Edinburgh and a graduate of Oxford University. Since he paid his own expenses, he went to China independently in 1876 as a "traveler," with no obligation on either side, and joined the CIM in 1878; he became a pioneer explorer of Shanxi, Hunan, Guizhou, and Guangxi.[5] Alexander Hoddle was the son of a banker at the Bank of England who had lived in Canada for ten years. Converted by Quakers, he was a YMCA secretary in Newcastle-on-Tyne.[6] George

---

4. Cable and French, *A Woman Who Laughed,* pp. 12-14.
5. *HTCOC* 6, p. 71.
6. Hoddle and the following were Boxer martyrs in Shanxi: see his obituary in Robert Coventry Forsyth, *The China Martyrs of 1900: A Complete Roll of the Christian Heroes Martyred in China in 1900* (London: Religious Tract Society, 1904), p. 435.

The Octopus

Stokes was a printer and a diligent Christian worker who conducted a ragged school in one of the roughest neighborhoods of Dover.[7] Maria Aspden, a native of Preston, was headmistress for twenty years of Emmanuel Infants' School. She had long desired to become a missionary, but duty to her parents kept her at home. Finally the way opened up.[8]

When the "sporting hearties" of the Cambridge Seven arrived at Shanghai in April 1885, everything seemed under construction. The city wall, where Hudson Taylor had collected cannon balls in 1853, had been demolished to make way for the racetrack. The Bund, the stately boulevard along the river, was a forest of bamboo scaffolding hiding half-finished hotels and bank buildings. But some things never changed: again Shanghai was a beleaguered Western enclave at war with China, filled with refugees from the Sino-French war in south China and Vietnam. Since the British consul would not issue documents for inland travel, the Seven, dressed in Chinese outfits with artificial pigtails, held long-remembered meetings for "the baptism of the Holy Ghost on our own hearts" and "the outpouring of the Spirit on China."[9]

They arrived on the cusp of the transformation of the China Inland Mission, between the bombshell of the Seventy and the explosion of the Hundred. They were among the last to see the CIM in its old incarnation and in fact, precipitated the creation of the new. The CIM had always shunned the Westernized cities of the coast, maintaining only a run-down "transit home" in Shanghai and business offices in Yangzhou and Hankou. "A missionary charged with conducting the Mission's business in Shanghai had rented premises in his own name and after defecting, to run them as a private boarding house, was claiming them for himself." Taylor rented two Chinese houses "a stone's throw from the British consulate," and a year later purchased a swampy patch of land on Woosung Road. Drained and leveled, Woosung Road became the site of the international Head Office, with ivy-covered, three-storey brick buildings around a manicured lawn. Except for the curving tile roofs and the gazebo, one would hardly have thought one was in China.[10] But that was in the future, thanks to Montague Beauchamp's generous gift.

Since the CIM did not yet have a language school, the intention was to send the Seven inland where senior missionaries would induct them into "the mysteries of Chinese, with its strange tones and wonderful characters."[11] This

---

7. Ibid., p. 433.
8. Ibid., p. 460.
9. Ibid., pp. 374-75.
10. Ibid., p. 372-73.
11. W. W. Cassels, letter from P'ing-yang, 9 July 1885, *China's Millions* (GB), November 1885, p. 145.

had been the path for scores of men and women since the inception: the current membership stood at 163, and reached almost 200 by the end of 1885. Since Sichuan, the original destination, was closed, Taylor assigned them to Shanxi, which was considered the safest inland province. Taiyuan had nine missionaries, the CIM's largest inland station, and further south at Pingyang was Pastor Hsi's "remarkable work of God" under "native agency," with hundreds of converts ready for baptism, if only they had missionaries to instruct them.

In Shanghai the Seven divided. Cecil and Arthur Polhill Turner, Charlie Studd, and Montague Beauchamp, who were not technically members of the China Inland Mission, went on a round-about inspection through Sichuan and Shaanxi, and entered Shanxi from the southwest corner. On the river they were "Etonians 'on a continuous picnic,'" refusing to study and praying to receive the language supernaturally. "If anyone should have received it, surely men who have forsaken all and followed Christ could expect it as a mark of God's approval," A. J. Broomhall commented. "How many and subtle are the devices of Satan," Taylor warned them, "to keep the Chinese ignorant of the gospel." Language study was a "necessary means": "If I could put the Chinese language into your brains by one wave of the hand I would not do it," he would say to new missionaries. Studd and Cecil Polhill Turner did manage to convince a few missionaries to follow their example, but eventually they saw the error of their enthusiasm and "knuckled down to study and in time became fluent."[12]

The other three, Stanley Smith, the "percussion cap," Rev. William Cassels, "Will the Silent," and Dixon E. Hoste, the soldier who believed in military precision, went up the coast to Chefoo, Tianjin, and Beijing, where they held meetings for the deepening of the spiritual life. One American missionary wrote admiringly, "They visited no remarkable places in Peking, saw no sights, wondered at nothing, but made it their one object while here to seek for themselves and for Christians the power of God's Spirit according to His Promise." The historian Pat Barr exclaimed incredulously, "that such educated, energetic young men who had never before set foot beyond Suez should stay for two months in the capital of one of the world's most colourful, sophisticated cultures and wonder at *nothing*. How insular they were, arrogantly hidebound by the moral imperatives and exclusive judgements of their narrow faith."[13] In-

---

12. *HTCOC* 6, pp. 374-75. This was the first (recorded) experiment with pentecostal tongues in the CIM and, except for Edward Irving in the 1830s, one of the first among orthodox evangelicals. It mirrored the expectations of some Pentecostal missionaries in 1906-08 described in the Conclusion.

13. Barr, *To China with Love*, p. 111.

The Octopus

deed, they were more than naive: they were blinded by the Spirit. Stanley Smith rhapsodized about the road ahead, "Oh, when He steps on the scene, how the hills melt before Him!"[14]

Escorted by Benjamin Bagnall, the "genial, kindly, hospitable" agent of the American Bible Society,[15] the three left Beijing by ox-cart across the North China Plain and through the mountain pass known as the Heavenly Gates, and arrived at Taiyuan, thirty-three stages from Beijing. Since there was no place there to hide such large, big-nosed athletes, they continued nine days south to Pingyang, where they joined the others. Their teacher was Frederick W. Baller, the mission's best linguist, who used the language lessons as the model for the course that he created the following year. By July Cassels was able to write, "We are a very happy party, enjoying our work, enjoying our walks on the city walls."[16]

The first disconcerting note occurred a few days after they arrived. C. H. Rendall, only two years out but suffering "incessantly from intense weariness," died at a remote village. They brought his body to the city "in mortal terror, they said, of the wolves they could hear prowling around" during the night.[17] "The country round here bears sad traces of the famine," Hoste wrote from the epicenter of the Great North China Famine six years earlier: "the villages are more than half depopulated; and broken down houses, ruined walls, and neglected roadways and bridges, speak on all hands of a departed prosperity." The ominous landscape echoed in his heart: "It seems to me that now we are out here Satan will do all he can to keep our lives from being really mixed up with the Chinese; of course I am speaking conscious of my own inexperience."[18]

Stanley Smith, picking up the language faster than the others, felt like "a soul out of communion" amidst the "dreadful disclosures of the power of darkness."[19] "Foreign things," he thundered in an oblique reference to the

14. Stanley Smith, letter from Peking, 4 May 1885, *China's Millions* (GB), September 1885, p. 115.

15. Forsyth, *China Martyrs of 1900*, p. 423. Bagnall joined the CIM as superintendent of Shanxi but he was one of those who clashed with Pastor Hsi. He was killed during the Boxer Uprising at Baoding, Zhili.

16. W. W. Cassels, letter from P'ing-yang, 9 July 1885, *China's Millions* (GB), November 1885, p. 145.

17. Mrs. Florence Edwards, "Further Tidings from T'ai-yüen," ibid., December 1885, p. 155.

18. D. E. Hoste, "Tidings from Kuh-wu Hien" [Quwu Xian], ibid., January 1886, p. 8. HTCOC 6, p. 376.

19. Stanley Smith, letter from P'ing-yang, 8 October 1885, in *China's Millions* (GB), February 1886, p. 26.

Stanley Peregrine Smith. "S.P.S." was a "percussion cap" with a "sunny" personality. In China, he was influenced by Timothy Richard and became a scholar of Chinese religions, moving towards a "Larger Hope" theology that all humans will be saved, some in this life and some in the next. After many years of controversy, he was forced to resign from the CIM in 1904, although he remained at his station, Lu'an, for another twenty years. Source: Thompson, *D. E. Hoste.*

comfortable residences in Taiyuan, with their tablecloths and rosewood pianos (brought at great expense through the mountains), are the missionaries' idols. "There is a very subtle snare here to speak of western things, and to have them as proofs of the superiority of western intelligence." Wishing he could be a "beggar with his one pot," Smith stated: "*Possessions* — there is the snare."[20]

It was easy to get lost in time out there, tramping the dusty plains day after day, year in and year out. Stanley Smith must have had a pocket-watch, when it worked, but he had to juggle three calendars: the Western one which tells the days of the week and the months; the Chinese calendar which tells the phases of the moon; and the Church of England Book of Common Prayer, which delineates the Christian year. It may have been the nineteenth century in England, but as he walked, he imagined he was living in the Holy Land at the time of Jesus. The centuries collapsed, as though they never were, and he felt he could perform miracles, cast out devils, and speak in tongues like the apostles. Eventually he went too far, adopting quasi-Buddhist notions of universal salvation, and had to resign from the CIM. Like W. T. Berger, Smith came to conditionalist views concerning eternal punishment which he called "the Larger Hope" — that all human souls would be saved, some in this life and some, after sufficient punishment, in the next. Smith, the North American director Henry Frost wrote, because of his long contact with "the mystery of the Christless multitudes of heathenism" had made "the unintentional mistake of interpreting the Scriptures by heathenism rather than heathenism by the Scriptures."[21]

Stanley Smith's pilgrimage was exceptional only because it was larger than life. His swings from enthusiasm to despair, from visions and supernatural gifts to "delusions and snares," was typical of the second generation. As Benjamin Broomhall commented, "The hour of success is often the time of danger . . . a snare and not a blessing."[22]

The China Council

Hudson Taylor remained the China director long after he delegated the British side to Benjamin Broomhall and the London council. "He himself held the reins, firmly, very firmly at times when discipline was needed, but very loosely in the case of men and women whom he could trust to plan and work

---

20. Ibid., March 1888, p. 33.
21. Frost, "Memoirs," p. 653.
22. *HTCOC* 6, pp. 376-77.

and use scarce funds responsibly."²³ As early as 1882, when he began to plan for the Seventy, Taylor realized the mission was too far-flung for him to govern from his back pocket. He circularized his ideas for the "development and perpetuation of the Mission's work in China" under an appointed council of provincial superintendents and a deputy China director.²⁴

This caused a "constitutional crisis" among the rank and file, since they regarded Taylor as a father and each wanted direct, personal access to him. "There was a good deal said that was unpleasant, and bad feelings aroused," recalled James Meadows, one of the stalwarts.²⁵ Taylor stressed that the superintendents were not higher or better, but lived on the same faith principles. "The Mission was a fellowship of equals, some voluntarily serving the others, from himself as their leader to the local secretaries and housekeepers. 'For love of the brethren,' of the Chinese and the Lord himself, they were gladly sacrificing the pleasure of field work in a place of their own, to be servants of the rest."²⁶

Taylor appointed John W. Stevenson as deputy China director "to act as my deputy in districts which I cannot personally visit, and generally in matters requiring attention during my absence from China."²⁷ Stevenson was a tall genial Scotsman, son of a laird in Renfrewshire, a man of simple, self-denying, methodical habits. His "hearty greeting, cordial hand-grip, and sympathetic enquiry . . . went far to strengthen the family bond which binds the Mission."²⁸ One of Taylor's first recruits, Stevenson had sailed to China in advance of the *Lammermuir* party. In his first term he established a small church in Shaoxing, an aristocratic city in Zhejiang famous for the many scholars it provided for China's civil service. In his second term, he walked from Burma through Yunnan to Hankou, a distance of nineteen hundred miles, and was the first explorer to cross China from west to east. Meanwhile, his wife and children remained in England to free him from family worries; in fact, except for brief furloughs they did not live as a family from 1875 to Stevenson's death in China in 1918. With his personality, Stevenson remained the deputy director and corporate memory for thirty years.

The London council was the model for the China council, which Taylor established in 1886. Its function was also advisory, "to assist the Director and

---

23. Ibid., p. 211.
24. Marshall Broomhall, *John W. Stevenson: One of Christ's Stalwarts* (London: CIM, 1919), p. 61. *HTCOC* 6, pp. 383-86.
25. *HTCOC* 6, p. 385.
26. Ibid., p. 381.
27. Marshall Broomhall, *John W. Stevenson*, p. 61.
28. Ibid., p. 84.

his Deputy with its counsel and co-operation in all such matters of gravity as the Director or his Deputy may feel it useful to lay before them." Their first duty was to "achieve harmonious co-operation, by defining the practices which had been evolved by common consent over the years," and the practical application of the *Principles & Practice* and the *Book of Arrangements*.[29]

Like the London council, the China council was dominated by members of Taylor's extended family: three of the six or eight who attended regularly were relatives by blood or marriage.[30] This intertwined family was to cause difficulty when some felt that "Shanghai" was harsh and uncompromising and they appealed to "London" as the court of last resort. Benjamin Broomhall, who had a personal relationship with each missionary as strong as Taylor's own, often sided with the dissidents, even though he did not necessarily have access to the facts. According to A. J. Broomhall, the conflict between London and Shanghai was continual from 1886 to 1893, when the mission was reorganized along more "democratic" lines.

From the outside, the China council seemed a small secretive body that decided the fate of one-third of the missionaries in China. From the inside though, its workings were more mundane: keeping track of three hundred missionaries at seventy-seven stations in fourteen provinces. The council met four times a year for several days of meetings, prayer, and fasting, to oil the wheels of the CIM system. They processed arrivals, arranged language training, awarded junior and senior missionary certificates, sanctioned marriages, dealt with personal problems and illnesses, and allowed some to go home on furlough. There was little substantive discussion of policy, international politics, or denominational controversies, for that was beyond their advisory capacity.

The Scattering

The first duty of the China council was to bring order to the far-flung octopus. During the mission's first decades, the experience of each probationer was unique. The ideal was a six-month apprenticeship to a senior missionary

---

29. *HTCOC* 6, pp. 421-22.
30. At one important meeting in 1922, which decided that the CIM would join the National Christian Council, five of the twelve were members of JHT's extended family: General Director D. E. Hoste (married to JHT's niece, Gertrude Broomhall); London Secretary Marshall Broomhall (JHT's nephew and Hoste's brother-in-law); Dr. Hudson Broomhall, Marshall's brother; Dr. Howard Taylor, JHT's son; and J. J. Coulthard, JHT's son-in-law: China council minutes, 17-22 April and 17-22 May 1922, in CIM/ABGC, file 2/39.

— who might have only a year of language himself — and an old-fashioned Chinese teacher, usually a poor scholar down on his luck, a dismal process. Others were sent out after a few weeks, sink or swim. The women had yet a different experience, since they had to be cloistered with a married couple or "live around" at different stations during their two-year probation.

After the Seven's misguided expectations of pentecostal tongues, it was obvious that the CIM had to upgrade its language requirements. At the first China council meeting, F. W. Baller, the linguist, was set apart for "preparation of aids to student probationers." His first recommendation was the translation of "Miss," a delicate matter considering the number of single women in the field: "Nü Kiao-sï" should be used for "all unmarried Lady Missionaries as both Siao-hsieh [*xiaojie*, 'little sister'] and Ku-niang [*guniang*, 'older sister'] are objectionable."[31] Taylor was so pleased with Baller's "Course of Study for Probationers," he sat the examination himself.[32]

The curriculum (see Appendix 3) was "a very thorough course of a remarkably high standard" spread over six years.[33] It was the best language training in China at the time in any mission, and became the standard course of study: *Baller's Mandarin Primer* — known simply as *Baller's* — was used in most language schools until the outbreak of World War II in the Pacific. The *Primer* was "of greatest value to beginners" since it contained a "scientific arrangement" of words, "elucidating the elements of the language, and providing some practical means of communication between [Chinese] teacher and [foreign] scholar." It included a "dialogue with an enquirer; terms used in surgery, medicine, banking, trade, building, family relationships, religions, travelling; agreements with boatmen; passport; deeds of sale and rental; etc., etc."[34]

The first four sections took two years, with written and oral exams every six months. After passing these, the "Probationer" became a "Junior Missionary," the prerequisite for marriage and a voice in station policies. If the probationer could not pass three sections after two years, he or she might be dismissed or sent to a station where the language was not necessary, such as the Chefoo School or the Shanghai office. The course was an ideal that most fulfilled, and indeed the CIM was known for its linguistic proficiency. Nevertheless, some — especially the treaty port directors and their wives — never did complete the course and were granted honorary certificates after fifteen years "in consideration of long and faithful service."

---

31. China council minutes, 13-24 November 1886, in CIM/SOAS, file 73.
32. McKay, "Faith and Facts," p. 120.
33. Ibid., p. 116.
34. "A Mandarin Primer," advertisement in *China's Millions* (NA), March 1895, p. 41.

The Octopus

Surprising is the emphasis on Chinese culture and religion, on how to explain Christianity in Chinese terms. The probationers should be conversant with "Chinese Ancient and Modern History," geography and government; they should be able to name the emperors of the Qing dynasty and the officials in their district. They translated the Confucian books, starting with the *Sacred Edict*, the Qianlong Emperor's document that promoted loyalty and proscribed Christianity and other heterodox sects. They then proceeded through collections of proverbs, the *Thousand Character Classic*, Mencius, and Confucius, read in both colloquial and literary ("easy *wen-li*") styles. At the end, the missionary should be familiar with the Chinese "School and University course with the steps leading to Chwang-yuen" (Chuang-yuan), the lowest scholars' degree. Nor was folk religion neglected: the missionary was advised to keep an annotated calendar of local religious festivals, "beliefs and ceremonies."

One further point should be noted, the emphasis on the history of the China Inland Mission. Since the mission had not yet produced a "history," this meant devotional study of *China's Spiritual Need and Claims* (1865), the *Principles & Practice*, and the *Book of Arrangements*. The final examination included writing a history of the CIM in romanized Chinese: thus was loyalty inculcated along with language.

The language schools opened in 1886 just in time for the Hundred. The women's school was at Yangzhou, an important city at the junction of the Yangtze River and the Grand Canal, where they could be dispatched in any direction. This was a sacred place in CIM history, where Hudson Taylor and the *Lammermuir* party had faced the "riot season" of 1867-68. It was an emotional moment when the young women were shown the monument where the rioters had broken down the wall. Since then, the CIM had obtained a compound large enough to house thirty or forty women.

The lady superintendent, the counterpart of Henrietta Soltau in London, was another of the austere spirits of the CIM, Mariamne Murray. She and her sister Celia had arrived in 1884 with four other women from Glasgow — "One of the best parties that ever went to China." Both were "widely experienced and in their thirties, going at their own expense," since the mission could not assume responsibility because they were older than the normal age. Nevertheless Mariamne remained in China for thirty-seven years, until she retired of old age in 1921. As confidante of generations of women, she was a one-woman ladies' council, a position that was later formalized, consulted by the superintendents as an equal though she did not sit on the council. Her work was to deepen the piety of her charges and prepare them as fast as possible for the rigors of inland China.

The Hundred: composite photograph. "Portraits of a Hundred Missionaries, Who left for China during the year 1887, in connection with the China Inland Mission." The CIM launched several recruitment campaigns, starting with the Eighteen in 1875-76, the Thirty in 1882-84, the Seventy ("And the Lord sent forth seventy also . . .") in 1884-85, and the Hundred in 1886-88. By the end of 1888 the CIM had 332 missionaries in China.   Source: *China's Millions,* bound with 1888 volume.

The Octopus

Despite the success of many (most?) women at adapting to China, there was always an undercurrent among the mission leaders that women were not suitable for mission work on the grounds of health and intelligence. Dr. Arthur W. Douthwaite, a twenty-five-year veteran, made his personal views clear in 1898 in an address he gave on the "Relation of the Marriage Question to Missionary Work":

> Women are liable to certain functional disorders, which are readily provoked by the disturbance of their emotions, in consequence of the break-up of home associations, the long voyage, the entire change of surroundings on reaching their destination, the effect of a strange climate, the study of a difficult language and the enforced sedentary life while engaged in study. Of course I don't say that *all* lady missionaries are thus affected, but many are, and unfortunately, functional disturbance sometimes leads to structural change, and a long list of evils follows.

Furthermore, Dr. Douthwaite was not convinced that the women could master a difficult language like Chinese.

> It may also be well to bear in mind the fact that, while young men of somewhat defective education, may, if otherwise fit, be accepted as missionaries, because, under the stimulus of compulsory study of a foreign language, their minds will develop, and a desire for general improvement stirred up; the same cannot, as a rule, be said of young women, who seldom make any effort to improve their general education after leaving school, or at any rate, after marriage.[35]

The men's school at Anqing (old spelling Anking), further up the Yangtze, was under Baller himself. Son of a Chelsea carpenter, Frederick William Baller (1852-1922) sailed for China in steerage at the age of twenty. In 1878, at the height of the Great Famine, he escorted Jennie Taylor and the single women into Shanxi, another party of men to Shandong, and a third to Guizhou. By 1885 he was a veteran of the "roving" life, an "experienced, capable missionary, but dry at heart." As Headmaster Baller of Anking, he had a reputation of being "by far too authoritarian for mature men to tolerate."[36]

---

35. Dr. A. W. Douthwaite, "Relation of the Marriage Question to Missionary Work," address delivered in London, 1898, in CIM/SOAS, item 8516, pp. 4-5.

36. *HTCOC* 6, p. 376.

He was a scholarly autodidact who insisted that study, not supernatural gifts, was the royal road to learning.

Baller's sardonic, avuncular style is evident in *Letters from an Old Missionary to his Nephew* (1907), his published "talks" to the men. "You say that . . . your audience listened with open-mouthed attention. This I can quite believe. I have often listened to preachers in the same attitude myself. You will, however, do well to bear in mind that the open mouth, like the open door, means different things to different people. It may express surprise, admiration, bewilderment, or speechlessness."[37] "Words are your tools," Baller told his students, advice he exemplified in his life. He wrote the *Mandarin Primer* (1887, with twelve editions by 1911) and *An Analytical Anglo-Chinese Dictionary* (1900). After 1900 Baller was set apart for translation work and over the next twenty years produced a Mandarin Bible, Chinese versions of the lives of Hudson Taylor, George Müller, and Pastor Hsi, and the authoritative translation of the *Sacred Edict* into English. His "illustrated Scripture portionettes" had a circulation of thirty million copies.[38]

The language schools extended the CIM policy of avoidance between the sexes. Distance aroused curiosity on both sides that could range from lighthearted teasing to censorious gossip. Charlie Studd recalled when "four or five of us young bachelors were talking about marriage, and most of us (and I among them) were rather against it, and for using utmost caution — please don't laugh, don't roar."[39] Strategies for meeting a woman who might make a suitable wife often led to extreme measures: on one occasion, two men each wrote to an unsuspecting woman proposing marriage, and in case she turned him down, asking her to act as a go-between with two or three others.[40] Two generations later (1919), Arthur E. Beard remembered the "flutter" of male hearts when three "young lady workers" passed through Anqing. "Roy and I had been spending some time each afternoon in prayer and one of our topics was 'a future partner in life' for we did not want to remain bachelors but serve the Lord in 'double harness.'"[41] Meanwhile, Hudson Taylor shook his head sadly, "In matters of the heart few accept advice." When one couple married without consulting him, he said, "I see the importance of being firm, more than ever."[42]

---

37. Baller, *Letters from an Old Missionary*, pp. 3, 30. These were originally published in several issues of *Chinese Recorder*, 1907.
38. Marshall Broomhall, *F. W. Baller: A Master of the Pencil* (London: CIM, 1923), p. 42.
39. Grubb, *C. T. Studd: Athlete and Pioneer*, p. 77.
40. *HTCOC 7*, pp. 35-36.
41. A. E. Beard, *South of the Great Wall* (Whangarei, Australia: private, 1976), pp. 11-12.
42. *HTCOC 6*, p. 297.

The Octopus

The deepest, darkest family secret of the China Inland Mission (and, sadly, every other China mission) was the number of unhappy marriages: not even A. J. Broomhall — the last keeper of the secrets — could broach that issue. With this sort of desperation, many couples scarcely knew each other before their wedding. As soon as the engagement was announced, they were deliberately sent to separate stations and might have met only once or twice under strained circumstances. Some, like James Meadows, resolved the situation by sending their wives home to Britain once the children reached school age.

The time available for language study varied from a few weeks to eight months depending on circumstances and exigencies of "the work." Once or twice a year Hudson Taylor or John Stevenson would go to Yangzhou and Anqing for the "scattering" of workers; no one, not even Taylor, knew their assignments until this ritual, the most solemn commission of their young lives.[43] Taylor gave each his or her final instructions: "God will direct your path" and "Keep yourself from idols." Then they were gone, "in the dark with God."[44]

Tea-Shop Evangelism

The "Inland Mission" was described as a "veritable octopus" whose tentacles reached to the farthest extremes of the Chinese Empire. This caused disequilibrium between the "concentration" of mission stations at the coast and the "diffusion" of the far-flung itinerants. At one level this was a clash of temperaments, as the freedom of living like a Chinese, "one man and a mule," gave way to the strictures of station life. At a deeper level it was a clash of theologies: what was more important, that each Chinese hear the gospel once, or that established congregations be nurtured in the faith?

In Zhejiang, the older stations were still run by the "remaining unstable missionaries of the *Lammermuir* era and their wives,"[45] as fractious as ever. "Some lack ability, others reliability," Taylor wrote.[46] All had gone back to wearing Western clothes "for self-protection." The northern part of Zhejiang, based at Hangzhou, had long since been devolved to Pastor Wang Lae-djün, Taylor's colleague in London, who ran it as a "bishop" with two ordained Chi-

---

43. Emma Forsberg described "the scattering" at Yangzhou in *China's Millions* (NA), January 1895, p. 12.
44. *Pastor Hsi*, vol. 2, p. 57.
45. HTCOC 6, p. 155.
46. HTCOC 5, p. 391.

nese pastors, two evangelists, and two preachers — and no missionaries. He submitted annual reports which were included in *China's Millions,* the only Chinese to be considered a "full member," even though he received no salary. Zhejiang was a mature church with a network of chapels, and it became the "nursery" that supplied Chinese "evangelists, colporteurs, Scripture readers and schoolteachers" to staff Taylor's expanding mission.[47] In 1883 Wang reported that the churches were trying to be self-supporting and had "contributed this year 85 [Chinese] dollars and 65 cents — quite a sum for these poor people to raise. Of this sum 8 dollars and 85 cents was spent for the relief of poor members."[48]

By 1884, eighteen years after the *Lammermuir,* the veterans had sadly diminished in number: three pioneers from 1862-66, seven from the *Lammermuir* (including Hudson and Jennie Taylor), and a few from the early 1870s. Surprisingly, seven of the pioneers in Zhejiang were listed as "Rev.," though when and where they were ordained (and into what denomination) was not specified.[49] These included James Meadows (Shaoxing), George Stott (Wenzhou), Will Rudland (Taizhou), and James Williamson (Fenghua). Williamson was a Presbyterian, though the others seem to have been Baptists. (Wang is merely identified as "Pastor.")

Presumably, like Western clothes, ordination was seen as a credential for working in the treaty ports, but sometimes it gave them ideas above their station. Even Will Rudland, the Cambridgeshire blacksmith who had written "Quench not the Spirit" above his forge (see Chapter 3), normally the humblest of missionaries, succumbed to "spiritual pride." He was "getting very up-ish and conceited" — Taylor's words. "Printing his papers and letters (in the *Occasional Paper*) is not doing him any good." A surge of anti-foreign riots in Taizhou "so scared Rudland that in panic he changed into foreign dress to awe them. That garb meant the power of consuls and gunboats behind him, and the threat of reprisals if they should go too far — as if trust in God was a fair-weather safeguard." Meanwhile, his wife Mary was gossiping that she saw "one of the younger Chinese missionaries kissing the evangelist's wife. . . . Both men left, insulted, as two others had done previously, and in shame William Rudland wrote offering to resign from the Mission."[50]

Yet, as Rudland showed, once these individualists found their niche, with a certain independence, they had long and useful careers. Rudland moved to

47. Ibid., p. 376.
48. Wang Lae-djün, annual report for "Cheh-kiang, North," *China's Millions* (GB), August 1883, pp. 105-6. *HTCOC* 6, pp. 155-56, 371.
49. *China's Millions* (GB), August 1883, pp. 102-11.
50. *HTCOC* 5, pp. 383-84.

The Octopus

Taizhou after the Yangzhou riot (1868), and remained there until his death in 1913, the last survivor of the *Lammermuir* party. He nurtured a flourishing church, though Taylor confided that he "questioned whether one-third or a half of the people he had baptised were true believers." Only by bringing such men back to humility before God, Taylor continued, would their work become more than "wood, hay and stubble."[51]

The pre-*Lammermuir* pioneers like James Meadows, the first man Taylor had sent out in 1862, did not feel bound by the "Lammermuir pact" — which they had not signed — the agreement which stipulated that Hudson Taylor's "helpers" must wear Chinese dress at the inland stations. Meadows and his wife Elizabeth Rose, the Methodist from Barnsley on the *Lammermuir*, settled down in Shaoxing for forty years, wearing Western clothes. Despite difficult relations with Taylor, he was appointed superintendent of Zhejiang and a member of the China council in 1886, on the assumption that he would have to accept the *Principles & Practice* if he had to enforce it. He died in 1914, after fifty-two years of service in the CIM.[52]

George Stott, the one-legged schoolteacher from Aberdeen, and his wife, Grace Ciggie, the Glasgow street evangelist, typified this generation. A. J. Broomhall concluded, amply confirmed by Grace Stott's autobiography, that Stott, "the Scottish dominie, ruled his little kingdom with a rod of iron." Grace, as tough-minded as he, knew how to get on with him. "Remarkably, the Chinese Christians in gratitude for the gospel accepted his powerful paternalistic regimen and thrived. At a time of tension the Church paradoxically grew and spread." The enduring indigenous Protestant church in Wenzhou dates from those beginnings and today reveres George's memory.

Stott resented Hudson Taylor's "interference" and complained to London, threatening to resign. He was "impossible," Taylor said. "There was nothing for it but to let him go and, at last, Josiah Jackson [a London carpenter from the *Lammermuir*] too — in some ways also a successful missionary but a thorn in the side for twenty years."[53] Stott died five years later at W. T. Berger's home in Cannes, and Grace remained at Wenzhou for another twenty years, until she retired to Toronto.

After 1886, the probationers settled down to a more routine preparation in the language schools. Once they had gained the rudiments, the young, healthy males were taken on itineration trips in expanding circles as they

---

51. *HTCOC* 7, p. 273.
52. *HTCOC* 6, pp. 385-86.
53. *HTCOC* 7, p. 34. According to China council minutes, 25 November 1886, in CIM/SOAS, file 73, new missionaries could be assigned to the outstations of Wenzhou, but "Stott himself and his pastoral work in Wenchau remain disconnected."

gained experience. They would distribute sheet tracts and Baller's illustrated Scripture portionettes as a "preparatory agency," but as Taylor stressed, the printed word, "in an unconverted *language . . . without* printed note, or comment, or preface," had to be accompanied by the preached word. By this time, they also had simple popular evangelistic devices to attract a crowd, illustrations, photographs, posters, banners, the wordless book, and above all, magic lanterns. As they negotiated the tracks between rice paddies that served as roads, in inns and teashops, they would try to strike up a conversation with each individual or gather larger crowds at markets or religious festivals.

Once they gained experience they would travel to a distant province, going upriver as far as they could and then overland. That one or two foreigners in Chinese dress could travel among the common people with gentleness and sincerity was in large part due to the friendliness of the Chinese people. Besides, the British consuls would never rescue a wayward missionary with the casual violence of the Yangzhou riot. By the same token the people had come to suspect that the CIM were "harmless eccentrics," an occasional nuisance but courageous and self-sacrificing.[54]

Each province, each village was different. Guiyang, the capital of remote Guizhou, was occupied quietly when the Chinese officials turned a blind eye; once the men were established, they brought the first foreign women into southwest China and established a beachhead in Yunnan. In Shaanxi, in the northwest, the stations in the Hanzhong plain, a fertile district accessible from Sichuan, were "expanding, with six self-supporting voluntary preachers and lively congregations." But the provincial capital of Xian — "imperial Changan" of the Tang dynasty, which had been the capital of China for fifteen hundred years — was a "haughty" city, so hostile that the officials would not let a westerner inside the city gates; "the only possible way to work was still to keep moving from one place to another, but covering the same territory again and again."[55] Hunan, "the most bitterly hostile province," home of Zeng Guofan's anti-Taiping, anti-Christian armies, remained out of bounds until one tiny station was opened in 1897 a few miles inside the border.

Jiangxi, inland from Zhejiang, shows how the CIM's message was carried ahead of the missionaries by native Christians. The first convert was a Captain Yü, a former soldier in the anti-Taiping army, who had heard "the rudiments of a distorted gospel from Taiping rebels" and attracted by their anti-

---

54. Coates, *The China Consuls,* pp. 179-85, quoted one "superciliously disdainful" consul (p. 180) who described a clergyman in Chinese Turkestan: "I believe he occasionally distributes bibles and tracts but in other respects he is a respectable and harmless traveller."

55. *HTCOC* 6, p. 390.

idolatrous message joined a "devout Buddhist" sect. In 1876 he was baptized by a Chinese pastor in Zhejiang and returned to his home in Yushan, "over the wall" in southern Jiangxi, to convert his fellow sectarians. This was near the cult center of the Celestial Masters, the so-called "Daoist Popes," and among the first converts were Buddhist women vegetarians, who were baptized in groups of ten or twenty. Captain Yü became a "sort of high priest in his district," so that when the missionaries arrived, they found "a maturing church sending evangelists farther afield into Jiangxi, and planting daughter churches."[56]

Gossiping the Gospel

In 1883, at Hudson Taylor's insistence, the London council made the momentous decision that "the sisters be recognized as equals" in seniority and the management of station affairs.[57] This policy was unusual among nineteenth-century evangelical associations, although such attitudes were not uncommon in the holiness tradition which gave birth to both the CIM and the Salvation Army. Its appearance in the CIM is an indication that Hudson Taylor and Benjamin Broomhall were shifting the mission away from its strict Brethren beginnings toward the broader, nondenominational Holiness teachings of Keswick, the YMCA, and the Salvation Army.

By the 1880s the Salvation Army was to the CIM what the Brethren had been in the 1860s, the unobtrusive ally in the background, even though there were no identifiable Salvationists on the London council or among the referees. General Booth himself, despite his connections with East London and Barnardo's Homes, is strangely absent from CIM publicity: he does not seem to have been a platform speaker at the great farewell services, nor a sponsor for practical slum evangelism. Nevertheless, among the testimonies given in *China's Millions*, several mention the candidate's Salvation Army background. This would explain the enthusiasm of someone like Stanley Smith marching through the Chinese villages with "blood and fire" banners; it would also explain the CIM's policy concerning the equality of women.

56. Ibid., pp. 395-96. Dr. and Mrs. Howard Taylor, *"By Faith": Henry W. Frost and the China Inland Mission* (Philadelphia: CIM, 1938), p. 160, discussed North American women at the Guangxin women's river. The Celestial Master in 1940 was the 63rd-generation descendent of Laozi's disciple: Clarence Day, *Chinese Peasant Cults: Being a Study of Chinese Paper Gods* (Shanghai: Kelly & Walsh, 1940), p. 51; Hans Kuhn and Julia Ching, *Christianity and Chinese Religions* (New York: Doubleday, 1989), pp. 139-40.

57. HTCOC 6, p. 382.

Hudson Taylor was determined not to repeat the tragedy of many missions, in which the husband fulfilled the language requirements while his wife was forced to limp along in pidgin, talking to the servants and looking after her husband and children. Since the CIM demanded that the women, like the men, be full missionaries, they were compelled to go out unmarried and pass the probation and language exams. There were a few "lone wolves" like Annie Royale Taylor, one of the "intrepid lady explorers" of Tibet, who was constantly moving beyond her nearest colleagues, deep into Xinjiang, joining up with Cecil Polhill Turner in Darjeeling, India, until she reached closer to Lhasa than any other foreigner.[58] Most women were more timid. They "lived around"[59] for the first two years until they married and moved to their husbands' stations, or remained single and settled at permanent stations. This led to some unusual ménages, such as at Hanzhong, Shaanxi, where George King lived in one house with his wife, Dr. Harriette Black, a registered physician, and her three sisters from Belfast;[60] next door George Parker and his Chinese wife Minnie shared a house with a changing arrangement of single men.

Minnie Parker was unique, the only Chinese woman married to a white missionary in mainland China. Although there was a long history of merchants and clerks having Chinese mistresses, even "wives" of varying degrees of respectability, of the hundreds of missionaries in nineteenth-century China, there were only three recorded interracial marriages, and two were in the CIM: George Parker and Shao Mianzi, and Anna Jakobsen and Ch'eng Hsiu-chi, whom we shall meet later in Shanxi. The third was the Canadian Presbyterian George Leslie Mackay in Taiwan.[61]

George Parker was one of the Eighteen, who arrived in 1876 and six months later set out to explore the far reaches of Gansu. (This was the same time as Francis James and Joshua Turner were reconnoitering Shanxi.) Shao

---

58. Annie Royale Taylor appears in histories of the exploration of Tibet, such as Peter Hopkirk, *Trespassers on the Roof of the World: The Race for Lhasa* (London: J. Murray, 1982).

59. Eva Jane Price, *China Journal 1889-1900: An American Missionary Family During the Boxer Rebellion* (New York: Scribner's, 1989), p. 109.

60. King resigned because the CIM would not grant a furlough to his sick wife. His son, Dr. George King Jr., joined the mission in 1910: Frank Houghton, *George King: Medical Evangelist* (London: CIM, 1930).

61. George Leslie Mackay, the "black-bearded barbarian" of Taiwan, explained his marriage to the Foreign Mission Committee simply, "I am thinking how I can do most for Jesus." In large part *because* of his interracial marriage, Mackay has become a national hero of Taiwan since the 1990s. See Alvyn Austin, entry in *Dictionary of Canadian Biography*, vol. 13, pp. 653-55. For a discussion of Western and Chinese attitudes toward intermarriage at the time, see Frank Dikotter, *The Discourse of Race in Modern China* (Stanford: Stanford University Press, 1992), pp. 58, 87.

The Octopus

Mianzi was a schoolgirl in Yangzhou, "a fine girl, intelligent and active as a Christian, well suited to be a [Chinese] pastor's wife in a year or two." Against all odds, the couple fell in love and determined to marry. The problem was not *just* racialism, though "[n]o objection was raised to an inter-racial marriage *per se*." Taylor's main objection was legal, that Parker would become the "son-in-law" of a Chinese family, subject to Chinese law — and his in-laws. Besides, the CIM had signed a contract with her father that in return for her upbringing and education, the mission would arrange a Christian marriage to a Chinese, since her parents were afraid she would be forced to marry a missionary and be taken abroad. "I entreat you to abandon the thought," Taylor wrote to Parker, and trust God to provide "a true helpmeet suited to you."[62]

Nevertheless, Taylor relented after several of Parker's colleagues threatened "to resign if in their opinion he was disciplined or forced to yield." Theodore Howard, chairman of the London council, also supported Parker's cause at home. Minnie's father, an "opium smoker out to make trouble," was mollified when Parker paid him "compensation for his expenditure on her since her birth" — in other words, a dowry. The problem of their visibility if they remained in Yangzhou was solved by sending them first to Hanzhong, then to Lanzhou, Gansu, the most remote station in the CIM, seventy-two stages from Hankou. Mrs. Parker proved to be strong and courageous: once she and her husband walked from Lanzhou across Xinjiang to the Trans-Siberian railway, and then she charmed the folks in England with her grace and manners. When George died in 1931, Minnie Parker became the senior missionary in the CIM. Their daughter, Mrs. Mason, another CIM "character," was among the last CIM missionaries to leave Shanghai in 1950.

Other missionary wives were outstanding pioneers in their own right. Thomas Botham, who coined the phrase, "one man and a mule," spent years itinerating the Xian plain before he managed to rent a room at an inn. He warned his fiancée, Ellen Barclay, living in Lanzhou, "The place won't do for you." She joined his traveling life and Botham was never so happy as when he was itinerating with his wife on one side of the mule and his bundles of books on the other. "Models of faithful perseverance," A. J. Broomhall concluded, Thomas and Ellen Botham "demonstrated the soundness of Hudson Taylor's contention that China's families could be given the gospel systematically by persistence in going to them."[63]

The first experiment with stationing unmarried women without a foreign

---

62. For the Parker marriage, see *HTCOC 6*, pp. 247-48, and *HTCOC 7*, pp. 129-30.
63. *HTCOC 7*, p. 130.

male's protection was in 1886 in southern Shanxi, when Pastor Hsi's wife offered to look after two women from Taiyuan. This was so successful that Taylor instituted districts of "women's stations" where the women worked under the supervision of Chinese pastors. The most notable was the Guangxin River, "the women's river" in southern Jiangxi (including Yushan, the center of Captain Yü's Christian sect), where the women missionaries and Chinese pastors operated a string of stations, and male missionaries were not permitted to visit.[64] Suffice it to say, during the 1880s the position of single women was shifting as the CIM worked out the implications of equality.

Most of the time the presence of single women caused no difficulties, but occasionally a group of women would be stranded while traveling or be mistreated by Chinese authorities. In 1891 one such incident at Yichang, the entry to the Yangtze gorges, brought down outrage against the "misguided and dangerous" policy of sending defenseless women into heathen China dressed like natives. The scholar and philologist Max Müller commented that unmarried women missionaries "seem to have given greater offense than in their ignorance they imagined," since "the Chinese recognize in public life two classes of women only — married women and single women of bad character. What good results could the missions expect from the missionary labours of persons so despised by the Chinese?"[65]

Women's work was by definition settled work: the rationale was that only women could reach Chinese women in their homes. Women's work was sometimes called "gossiping the gospel."[66] Using simple devices such as the wordless book and the five-finger mantra ("Thumb: There is one True God . . . ," see Introduction), they conducted itineration on an intimate, more intensive scale, starting in their own courtyard, their neighborhood, the city and nearby villages. Miss L. M. Forth described one village trip in Shanxi, where she was taken into a cave that the Christians had transformed into "a little miniature meeting-house. . . . Though small, it was beautifully clean; new mats on the tiny kang [mud-brick bed], and a number of small booklets hanging from the wall." After a short prayer meeting, she witnessed a bonfire of idols " — only pieces of paper — the god of riches, the god of the kitchen,

---

64. *HTCOC* 6, pp. 394-99.

65. Stanley P. Smith, *China from Within: Or the Story of the Chinese Crisis* (London: Marshall Brothers, 1901), p. 219. Worse than being equated with sing-song girls, stated Miss L. M. Forth in a letter from Hoh-chau, Shansi, published in *China's Millions* (GB), January 1893, p. 12, was that the Chinese thought the women missionaries had a power "similar to their sorcerers, and that the safest way is to say nothing to us." (See reference in note 67 for further quotes.)

66. *HTCOC* 6, p. 103.

The Octopus

and the god of skill. . . . From there we went into the open air, where we had a very informal meeting for about two hours; the Christians talking to the men, while I sat some distance off, surrounded by a number of women and children, who were charmed by my singing, 'Jesus can help little children to be obedient to their mother's words,' varied by, 'to not swear, or get angry,' etc. They made me sing it over and over again, some of the boldest joining in."[67]

From such small beginnings — "singing the gospel" — grew the church, for without Christian women and families, it would remain a sect of males. As was said of Edith Whitchurch, "many souls were saved, demons cast out, the sick were healed, and opium-smokers reclaimed."[68] The order was intentional: more souls were saved than demons exorcised, more exorcisms than faith healing, more healing than cured opium addicts.

Jesus Opium

Of all the transformations that occurred in a missionary's life, surely the strangest was the notion that people with "no special medical knowledge" could go to China and start healing the sick. One can understand why a trained physician would feel called to establish a Western hospital, like Peter Parker in the 1840s or Harold Schofield in the 1880s, and why generations of doctors and nurses would follow in their footsteps. It is harder to comprehend how a lay missionary, male or female (for the CIM was not alone in this regard), could take a bottle of pills to China and start dispensing them like water. English evangelicalism had a submerged current of "non-conformist thaumaturgy,"[69] but supernatural healing was for most missionaries a "gift" acquired in China. It started experimentally when a missionary fell sick far from medical aid. Praying "the prayer of faith," anointing with oil and laying on of hands (described in James 5:13-15) were common in the CIM and probably every missionary participated in one of these "waiting meetings," on either side of the sickbed. Hudson Taylor had been healed miraculously several times, and gained a reputation as a healer and a "man of prayer."

The missionaries' urge to heal was intensified by the sickness of China. Everywhere they went, they were besieged by the halt and the lame, as in Jesus' day. Those who tugged at the missionaries' sleeves were, by definition, be-

---

67. Forth, *China's Millions* (GB), January 1893. The congruence with Confucian morality is obvious.

68. Forsyth, *China Martyrs of 1900*, p. 452.

69. Jon Butler, *Awash in a Sea of Faith: Christianizing the American People* (Cambridge: Harvard University Press, 1990).

yond the help of Chinese medicine, otherwise why come to the foreigner? "A very slight knowledge of some homeopathic medicines has won us many a friend amongst rich and poor," confided Anna Crickmay from Taiyuan.[70] In the early years, the missionaries would carry a little black bag filled with various "tinctures" (alcoholic plant extracts) and mixtures that could be prepared on the spot.[71] They had two manufactured drugs in their repertoire: spirits of camphor (alias camphorated tincture of opium, alias paregoric), which was useful for "summer cholera," and liquid quinine (possibly manufactured by Howard Brothers), which "acted like a charm for ague," colds, and malaria.[72] "I had a good supply of quinine and gave it out freely," wrote Timothy Richard of Shandong in the 1870s. "To the people around it seemed nothing short of miraculous."[73]

The missionary's introduction to opium was likely an opium suicide, and the stories were legion. A midnight call wakes the household; the missionary follows a man with a lamp through the dark streets and enters a room filled with the "hideous wailing" of Daoist priests calling back the soul of the suicide. "When we arrived, we found the man already dead, quite cold. They asked us if we had no plan to bring him to life again."[74] Lethal doses of opium slow the heart until it gradually stops beating. Dr. Schofield's instructions for opium suicides were "(1) A speedy and thorough evacuation of the stomach, and (2) the use of various stimuli to counteract the drowsiness which ensues as soon as the drug has been absorbed into the system." In other words, get everyone out of the room, keep the patient awake by walking, by "artificial respiration, steadily persevered in for three or four hours," and administering

---

70. Anna Crickmay, "Women's Work in Shan-si," *China's Millions* (GB), March 1881, p. 35.

71. Homeopathy was well-known and respected in the eastern U.S. in the nineteenth century, and was still being used in China, recalls the daughter of CIM missionaries. "My great grandfather on my father's side was a homeopathic doctor in upstate New York. His daughter took medicines with her when she and her husband and five children migrated from Massachusetts to Alberta to homestead in 1900. My father took medicines with him to China in 1925, and as long as I can remember we had homeopathy's *Materia Medica,* and a large Chinese-made wooden box with lots of small squares for small bottles which came from Boericke and Tafel in Philadelphia where there was a famous homeopathic hospital. And because of homeopathic remedies, I was brought through typhoid fever in Jiendeh, Zhejiang, when we were running ahead of the Japanese in 1937 and no hospital was near."

72. Soothill, *Timothy Richard of China,* p. 71. The Jesuits introduced quinine, which was a New World discovery, to China in the seventeenth century.

73. Timothy Richard, *Forty-Five Years in China,* pp. 78-79.

74. Thomas H. King, "Tidings from Shan-si," in *China's Millions* (GB), November 1884, p. 139.

The Octopus

stimulants such as coffee, sulphate of zinc, or native drugs. The patient's stomach was flushed with a dilute solution of potassium permanganate, which counteracted the drug by making it nonabsorbable. Opium suicides were "terribly common" in Taiyuan, Schofield wrote, with forty cases brought to the missionaries in one year. Normally, Schofield sent the stimulants with directions for their use, although he personally attended six patients, of whom two died.[75]

Opium suicides were simple compared to withdrawal from a long-standing addiction: if undertaken without guidance, quitting "cold turkey" could kill a weak addict. Physically, withdrawal produces the opposite effect that the drug has on the body. If, for example, opium was originally taken to alleviate diarrhoea, it paralyses the intestinal muscles; the body learns to function doubly hard to counteract the paralysis so that when the drug is withdrawn, the bowels collapse. Within the bounds of Victorian propriety, Mrs. Howard Taylor described these symptoms in the biography of *Pastor Hsi*: "Water streamed from his eyes and nostrils. Extreme depression overwhelmed him. Giddiness came on, with shivering, and aching pains, or burning thirst. For seven days he scarcely tasted food, and was quite unable to sleep. . . . The agony became almost unbearable; and all the while he knew that a few whiffs of the opium-pipe would waft him at once into delicious dreams."[76]

The physical symptoms peak on the third day and last for a week, when the physical dependence is broken. Then the psychological need kicks in, what the Chinese called "the craving" or "the yen," much worse than the physical symptoms. "This craving must indeed be terrible, in imagination and in reality, for whenever one speaks to Chinese about abstaining from opium, they invariably speak of 'the craving' as the insurmountable difficulty."[77]

As opium smoking exploded "on a massive scale" in the 1870s, the Chinese government reacted with laws of "increasing complexity and severity" against opium addicts, opium growers and sellers, and makers of pipes. The penalties were punitive: parents of opium-sellers were beaten according to the laws against "parents who cannot stop their children from stealing," not because their children were "evil but just because they were weak, like drinkers or lechers. But smoking could be done in secret: the severer the penalties the

---

75. R. H. A. Schofield, "Medical Mission, T'ai-yüen Fu, 1882," ibid., October 1883, pp. 135-36.

76. *Pastor Hsi* (single volume), p. 51.

77. Rev. Samuel B. Drake, "The Story of Mr. Fan, of P'ing-yang Fu, Shan-si," in *China's Millions* (GB), September 1883, p. 128.

more secret the smoking, so it got harder to catch the smokers."[78] At the local level the prohibitions against opium depended on the provincial authorities and the local magistrate, who more than likely grew opium himself.[79]

Chinese religious societies tried in various ways to combat the opium problem. There was a flood of popular Confucian literature across the North China plain in the 1880s, some copied from missionary tracts, "manuals of personal cultivation and morality" that exhorted the people to virtue.[80] Addicts brought shame on their families, the Confucians stressed, and the family must restore the wayward children to filial piety, frugality, and honor. Daoist and Buddhist sects opened shelters for addicted members that used various techniques of herbal medication, massage, hot baths, bleeding, religious devotions, and just keeping the patients contented and occupied.[81]

At the grassroots level, all Protestant congregations had a rule that no opium smoker could be baptized until he broke off the habit. Some of them organized anti-opium societies, like temperance societies in Britain, to "wage war with the opium trade" by distributing books, by "making opium medicine procurable by the people," and giving "assistance to those who really desire to cease opium smoking. We hope not only to reform, but also to save many."[82]

---

78. Jonathan Spence, "Opium," in *Chinese Roundabout* (New York: W. W. Norton & Company, 1992), pp. 237, 243. An unnamed author (probably Dr. John Dudgeon) in "Report of the Opium Refuge at Peking for 1878-79," *Chinese Recorder*, XI, no. 3 (May-June 1880), pp. 196-207, quoted a Christian "native Anti-opium Society" in Beijing that blamed the "many stupid people who cannot get rid of the vice and who treat it as some precious thing" (p. 197).

79. Spence, *Chinese Roundabout*, pp. 253-54, cited the ambiguous case of Zhang Zhidong, who as governor of Shanxi in 1884 eloquently pleaded to banish all opium; by the 1890s he was getting rich from opium taxes and proposed using opium revenue to purchase foreign weapons. Zeng Guoquan, his successor, was a powerful suppresser of opium in Shanxi but later used opium revenue in Shanghai affairs. Li Hongzhang used opium taxes to make up for deficits in the police and armies.

80. Daniel H. Bays, "Christianity and Chinese Sects: Religious Tracts in the Late Nineteenth Century," in Barnett and Fairbank, eds., *Christianity in China*, pp. 129-30.

81. Joseph Westermeyer, *Poppies, Pipes, and People: Opium and Its Use in Laos* (Berkeley: University of California Press, 1982), pp. 189-218, described a Buddhist temple in Laos in the 1970s that treated thousands of drug addicts through a regimen that started with a "pungent herbal medication" to induce vomiting, followed by alternating sweat baths, cold showers and massage. The abbot was self-disciplined, "highly intelligent, poorly educated, empathetic and a master of applied psychology. He is humble, unassuming but has complete confidence in his power to influence the people for good" (pp. 201-2). He might be compared with Pastor Hsi.

82. Samuel Drake started a society in Pingyang in September 1882 with thirty-three men: *China's Millions* (GB), July 1883, p. 87.

The Octopus

The first missionary "opium asylum" in China was opened by Hudson Taylor in 1859 after a wave of suicides in Ningbo (see Chapter 2). There was considerable debate in the missionary community whether to put opium treatment in the hands of nonmedical personnel — i.e., clergymen — or make it a department of the medical work. In China, as in England, the doctors won. The first *medical* opium asylum was "twenty-four native beds in three large wards" of the Hangzhou hospital where the treatment lasted from fifteen days to three weeks and cost $2. It consisted "mainly in an immediate prohibition of the opium-pipe" and the administration of "stimulants and tonics" to alleviate the withdrawal symptoms. The doctor admitted patients once a month to give himself "a little breathing time" between groups, for when too many were passing through the critical stages at the same time the refuge could be a dangerous place, with the inmates on the verge of a "mutinous spirit," hurling "furniture and other heavy missiles."[83]

The most memorable of the anti-opium activists was Dr. John Dudgeon of the London Missionary Society, whose stream of articles in the *Chinese Recorder* and elsewhere had a wide readership. Dudgeon was "an emotional and touchy man of very strong opinions,"[84] who opened an experimental refuge in an abandoned temple in Beijing. He recommended such anti-opium "tonics" as "Doctor Osgood's or Dr. Peck's quinine and belladonna pills," and stimulants like "a high dilution of sulphate of strychnine . . . [or] a hypodermic dose of ergot."[85]

In the late 1870s Dudgeon discovered the most effective "tonic" of all: morphine (morphia). Morphine was a miracle, it could raise people from the edge of the grave. Just three weeks' use, however, was enough to make an addict for life. But morphine was not just a palliative, something to ease the pain, it was a stronger form of opium, a "substitute" that had to be administered in decreasing doses (gradual reduction versus cold turkey). The problem was that once morphine slipped out of the missionaries' hands, rather

---

83. Rev. G. E. Moule, "The Opium Refuge and General Hospital at Hangchow," *Chinese Recorder*, September-October 1874, pp. 256-62, especially pp. 259-60. A Canadian doctor in North Henan described the addicts crowding around him "more like hungry wolves than men": Margaret H. Brown, "History of the Honan (North China) Mission of the United Church of Canada, Originally a Mission of the Presbyterian Church in Canada, 1887-1951," 4 vols. (United Church Archives, Toronto: typescript, 1970), chapter XXI, p. 10.

84. Barr, *To China with Love*, pp. 62, 88-89. Dudgeon was one of those rambunctious missionaries Barr loved to skewer: he split the LMS when he was evicted from his drug storeroom.

85. Letter from "Another Missionary" to "A Symposium on the Cure of the Opium Habit," *Chinese Recorder*, October 1887, pp. 396-99; quote at p. 397.

than using the pills to stop smoking, many addicts ingested them as cheap substitutes for opium whenever the cost was prohibitive or while they were traveling.[86] As one critic charged, morphine addiction was like "changing one's tipple from colonial beer to methylated spirits."[87]

Dr. Dudgeon by his own account admitted how things could go wrong when the "native keepers" created a black market in anti-opium medicines. His refuge had two kinds of pills, foreign white pills (morphine) that were "used exclusively inside" where dosage could be monitored, and black pills that Dudgeon prepared, "a very effective home-made pill, after a recipe of his own," which he "exclusively sold outside. It might have been expected, although at the time it was not foreseen, that the white pills would also come to be in demand outside among the friends of those who had been cured inside, and of others who had been cured outside through their report. And so it was." A lucrative black market grew up in both kinds of pills until the smuggled white pills (morphine) "realized a sum sufficient to pay for the original cost of the ingredients and at the same time for the entire inside gratuitous consumption." This split the church — "a great boon became ere long a serious stumbling block" when "the native committee did nothing to guard against its possible evil consequences."[88]

The first experiment in the hypodermic injection of morphine seems to have been conducted by Dr. Harold Schofield in Taiyuan in 1882. The hypodermic needle was another miracle, putting the dosage under the control of the physician. Dr. Schofield had learned the technique in the battlefield hospitals he ran during the Turkish wars, and he started a dispensary as soon as he had a "slender acquaintance with the language." Only five in-patients were opium addicts. "One patient was helped successfully to give up the vice by the administration of morphia hypodermically, thrice daily, as a substitute for opium, and gradually diminishing the dose, ending at last with pure water, which was injected beneath the skin for several days until the cure was complete."[89] Schofield was "very much elated with the success of his first trial,"

---

86. Spence, *Chinese Roundabout*, p. 250. Dudgeon wrote several articles for the *Chinese Recorder* on morphine, such as "Is Morphia Volatilizable?" January-February 1883, pp. 56-63.

87. Barr, *To China with Love*, p. 89.

88. Dudgeon considered several options, such as disguising the pills by making them the same color, or making the white pills smaller and less potent. "Report of the Opium Refuge at Peking," pp. 199-203.

89. R. H. A. Schofield, "Medical Mission, T'ai-yüen Fu, 1882," *China's Millions* (GB), October 1883, p. 136. An article by Dr. A. P. Peck in the *China Medical Missionary Journal*, vol. 3, no. 1 (January 1889), published an alternative treatment for opium addicts by not us-

The Octopus

but he died before he could perform any more. In his last report, he pleaded, "To do this work well requires a man to give himself to this one thing; it needs no special medical knowledge. If one could be established, I would gladly give all the medical advice necessary."[90]

Schofield's death postponed further experiments with opium refuges. His successor Dr. Ebenezer Henry Edwards had no time for opium refuges. At his earlier station in Sichuan, he wrote pointedly: "The suffering they endure during the first few days after giving up the pipe must be something very severe, notwithstanding all the medicine given them (opium in any form being withheld)."[91] (This was a reference to morphine.) He established the Schofield Memorial Hospital in Taiyuan in 1885 with one ward for men and a smaller one for women. The majority of the opium patients (160 within a few months) were soldiers from a nearby cavalry camp, who were sent (and paid for) by their commanding officers.[92] This is an indication of the drugged condition of the Chinese army; the Chinese government continued to send addicted soldiers to mission hospitals to dry out through the 1930s.

By 1890 the CIM had a variety of refuges in eight or nine provinces. They ranged from professional medical wards, to refuges run by Chinese keepers nominally under missionary control, down to primitive shelters run by Chinese Christians. "I would not attempt to open a chapel at first," wrote George King of Xian,

> but would send a couple of men to open a shop, and call it Kiu-shï-t'ang [Salvation Hall — a title often taken by native medicine shops, and occasionally used for Protestant chapels]. The natives should sell suitable medicines, and especially remedies for curing opium-smokers. After a time, shorter or longer according to circumstances, the selling of tracts

---

ing pills that contain opium, including the use of Nux vomica, ipecae, belladonna, and Piperine. A typical anti-opium pill produced by Wyeth & Bro. contained *Pulv. Opii* (pulverized opium) 750 grains. Of these pills, from two to eight per day may be needed at first, according to the amount of opium previously consumed, to be gradually dropped one by one until both opium and medicine are stopped. I am grateful to Dr. Patrick Fung for this reference. Myra Scovel and Nelle Keys Bell, *The Chinese Ginger Jars* (New York: Harper & Row, 1962), pp. 38-39, suggested another unusual treatment using cantharides, the ground up beetle known as "Spanish fly." It was mixed with vaseline and bandaged to the patient's arm, where it would form a large blister, which was extracted with a hypodermic and injected into the patient as a form of auto-inoculation.

90. Schofield, annual report for 1882, *China's Millions* (GB), July 1883, p. 85.
91. Dr. Ebenezer Henry Edwards, "Tidings from Si-ch'uen Province," ibid., April 1884, p. 52.
92. William Key, letter from T'ai-yüen, ibid., June 1885, p. 66.

and useful books might be added. . . . By very slow degrees a resident missionary and a chapel might be introduced, if desired. . . . The books published by the Hankow Tract Society and the Shanghai American Press, on religion, science, history, etc., would sell well, and not stir up opposition, and open the way quietly for the Bibles and public preaching. [Square brackets in original; pinyin for Kiu-shï-t'ang is *Jiushi Tang*.][93]

In Yunnan, Arthur Eason compounded his own medicine "of native drugs; the formula is from a tract on the evils of opium smoking, published by Mr. Griffith John, of Hankow. It is so difficult to get medicine of foreign manufacture from the ports so far as here, and this seems very little inferior to the morphia or compositions containing the same."[94] Meanwhile, "Another Missionary" in Shanxi (possibly Stanley Smith) reported he injected morphine hypodermically, although the results were not "a startling success." He followed the treatment of "Dr. Bartholow in his work, recently issued entitled 'Hypodermatic Medication,' adapted, of course, to the special requirements of cases." The needle did have the advantage of breaking the connection of *smoking* opium, he said. "The use of hypodermic solutions of morphia and of other medicines is a profound mystery to the Chinese. . . . I do not know why it may not be kept a secret from them and used in this way. The danger of their acquiring the habit of using morphia by the needle is so small that it need not be taken into account."[95]

The use of morphine — a sophisticated medical treatment and a lucrative business — shows how far the CIM had come since the blacksmiths and governesses of the *Lammermuir*. The "system" that the CIM evolved in its second decade proved to be remarkably resilient. It was capable of absorbing endless numbers of men and women, providing them with a smattering of language and cultural training and sending them into the far reaches of China. At its best the CIM was a family; at its worst, when Shanghai refused to talk to London, when informal "arrangements" became carved in stone, it dissolved into factions. As it grew, it was necessary to bring order to the enthusiasts, to establish regulations concerning Chinese dress, finances, conduct with Chinese and fellow missionaries, and not least language lessons. Many felt that the *Principles & Practice* were too authoritarian, that commit-

---

93. George King, "Localized Work — Si-Gan [Xian] Fu," report for 1882, ibid., July 1883, pp. 80-81.
94. Arthur Eason, "Opium Smoking in China," ibid., July-August 1885, p. 102.
95. Letter from "Another Missionary" in *Chinese Recorder*, October 1887.

tee rule had replaced grace. Yet once the probationer passed the exams and became a fully accredited "member," he or she had remarkable freedom to get close to the people.

In the first decade the theological congruence between CIM pietism and Chinese popular religion was their millenarian eschatology in the face of human tragedy. In the second they added Keswick Holiness teaching. This passive faith that their lives were in God's hands gave them a spiritual passport into Chinese life. It made each incident they encountered, from the opium sots to the haughty mandarins, both unexpected and instantaneously literal. Unfortunately, as the use of morphine indicates, when the inexperienced enthusiasts were sent into the far reaches of China, they did not, could not, take into account that their small needles had ramifications far beyond their ken — as we shall see in the next chapter, when we examine Pastor Hsi's work of God in Shanxi.

APPENDIX 3

Course of Study for Probationers
1886

First Section [6 months]

- Joseph Edkins' *Progressive Lessons*, chapters 1-24.
- The whole of John's Gospel (Mandarin).
- The Sacred Edict (Mandarin), chapters 1, 2.
- Special attention is recommended to the tones and aspirates.
- One hymn to be written out neatly in Romanised.
- Chinese Characters should be written with a Chinese pencil. A short daily practice in writing will greatly aid the memory.
- In Examination analyse the first 50 different characters in the first Chapter of John and tell from memory the number of each radical found in the said 50 characters.
- Write from memory the characters of the 18 provinces and the capitals.
- Indicate the course of the three principal rivers, viz: — the Yang-tsze, Yellow and Pearl Rivers.
- Locate and describe two lakes, viz: — the Tung-ting and Po-yang.
- Give the boundaries of China proper and of each of the 18 Provinces.
- Pass a short examination on the *Principles and Practice*, and the *Instructions* of the C.I.M.

Second Section

- Edkins' *Progressive Lessons*, chapter 24 to end.
- Matthew, Mark, Luke and Acts (Mandarin).
- The Sacred Edict (Mandarin), chapters 3-9.
- Old Testament History (Mrs. McCartee), chapters 1-20.

The Octopus

- The English Book of Common Prayer, Peking Edition, first 22 pages.
- Mr. [Griffith] John's Sheet-tract "Rejecting the False and Reverting to the True."
- In Examination analyse the first 100 different Characters in first chap. of Mark, and tell from memory the number of each radical found in the said 100 Characters. Write from memory the characters of all the Fu's [fu cities, or prefectural capitals] of the Province in which Probationer is residing.
- Hold a conversation with a Chinese Teacher before Examiner of not less than 15 minutes.
- Give a short address to the Heathen before Examiner.
- Present 2 hymns written out neatly in Romanised.
- Pass an Examination on the *Principles and Practice,* and *Instructions* of the C.I.M.
- Pass an Examination on "China's Spiritual need and claims."

Third Section

- Romans to Revelation (Mandarin).
- Genesis to Joshua (Mandarin).
- The Sacred Edict (Mandarin), chapters 10-16.
- Old Testament History, chapters 21-50.
- The English Book of Common Prayer, Peking Edition, pages 24-44.
- Mr. John's Catechism of Christian Doctrine.
- Mr. John's Sheet-tract "Origin of all things."
- Mr. John's Sheet-tract "Leading the Prince in the Right Way."
- Mr. John's Sheet-tract "True way of seeking happiness."
- In Examination give details regarding all the C.I.M. Stations — date of opening and history; also write from memory the names in Chinese characters, if obtainable.
- Give a list of the Chief Civil and Military Authorities of the province in which Probationer is residing.
- Write in romanised from dictation The Apostles' Creed, The Lord's Prayer and the Ten Commandments.
- Pass an Examination on the *Principles and Practice,* and *Instructions* of the C.I.M.
- Pass a fuller Examination on "China's Spiritual need and claims."

Fourth Section

- Judges to Ezra (Mandarin).

- Old Testament History, chapter 51 to end.
- [W. C.] Burns' Mandarin Pilgrim's Progress, volume I.
- [W. A. P.] Martin's Evidences of Christianity (Mandarin), first section.
- The English Book of Common Prayer, Peking Edition, last half.
- Collection of famous sayings.
- The Book of Surnames.
- The Thousand Character Classic.
- The Great Learning with Commentary.
- Mr. John's Sheet-tract "True Saviour of the World."
- Mr. John's "Salient Doctrines of Christianity."
- Mr. John's Sheet-tract "Exhortation to Repentance."
- Mr. John's Sheet-tract "On the Atonement."
- Hold a conversation on a subject previously communicated to Probationer to be carried on with a Chinese Teacher for at least 20 minutes before Examiner.
- Write one hymn in romanised from dictation.
- Write a brief history in English of the CIM. Spelling, writing, and composition will be noted.

Fifth Section [beginning of 3rd year]

- Nehemiah to Jeremiah (Mandarin).
- Burns' Mandarin Pilgrim's Progress, volume II.
- Martin's Evidences of Christianity (Mandarin — second section).
- Mr. John's easy Wen-li Gospel of Matthew.
- Confucian Analects with Commentary.
- The Three Character Classic with Commentary, two volumes.
- The Book of Rewards with Commentary.
- Repeat and write from memory the Character called Ten Stems, and Twelve branches, and explain the uses and significance of these separately and in combination.
- Give in a previously prepared written paper containing a list of all Chinese Dynasties from the Hia [Xia] downwards — in character and romanised.
- Write from memory the style of reign of each Emperor of the Present Dynasty and be able to tell the date of accession of each Emperor to the Throne.
- Write one Hymn in romanised from dictation.
- Pass an Examination on the *Principles and Practice,* and *Instructions* of the C.I.M.

The Octopus

Sixth Section [4th year]

- Lamentations to Malachi (Mandarin).
- Martin's Evidences of Christianity (Mandarin), last section.
- Mr. John's Easy Wen-li Luke and Acts.
- Mencius with Commentary.
- The Doctrine of the Mean with Commentary.
- Mr. John's book "Gate of Virtue and Wisdom."
- Sheet-tract "Superstitious Customs Exposed."
- "Leading the people in the right way."
- "On Regeneration."
- "Truth concerning God."
- Write a sermon on a given text in romanised Mandarin, and preach to Chinese Christians another sermon before Examiner.
- Give in a previously prepared paper, written in Romanised Mandarin, giving a brief history of the C.I.M. up to date: and also explain and define in romanised Mandarin the chief points in the *Principles and Practice*, and *Instructions* of the C.I.M.

Addendum

In addition to the above course, though not required for the Examinations, it is recommended that the Missionary make himself familiar with the following subjects:

- Beliefs and ceremonies connected with Births, Marriages and Deaths.
- Superstitions and rites throughout the year. To this end a calendar should be kept and each festival and other event connected with the religious life of the Chinese should be carefully noted as it occurs, together with all local information, that the Teacher or other friend can supply.
- The School and University course with the steps leading to Chwang-yuen [chuang-yuan]
- The Chinese Government and all the Chief Civil and Military Officials — Metropolitan and provincial.
- Tauism [Daoism] and Buddhism.
- Confucianism — including Ancestral worship.
- Popular ideas and notions regarding man in this life and after death.
- The history and influence upon the nation of such famous men, as Yao, Shun, Yu, T'ang, Wen, Wu, Chou Kung [the Duke of Zhou], Confucius, Mencius, and Chu-hsi [Zhu Xi].
- Chinese Ancient and Modern History.

- The following English works most of which will be found in the library of the Training Homes may be mentioned as containing useful information, bearing upon some of the above subjects [ten books including S. W. Williams, *Middle Kingdom*, J. Doolittle, *Social Life of the Chinese*, and J. Edkins, *Religions in China*].

Source: Moira Jane McKay, "Faith and Facts in the History of the China Inland Mission 1832-1905," pp. 116-20: reference CIM/SOAS Archives J131.

CHAPTER 8

The Heavenly Invitation Offices

1880-1888

*When Thou wouldst slay the wolves, O Lord,
Then I would be the keen-edged sword,
Clean, free from rust, sharpened and sure,
The handle grasped, my God, by Thee —
To kill the cruel ravening foe
And save the sheep for whom Christ died.*

Pastor Hsi, "A Song of Sacrifice."[1]

Teacher Hsi

Opium has brought us back to Shanxi. At the end of Chapter 5, Hsi Liao-chih, a broken-down opium addict, became a Christian after he won the literary essay contest sponsored by David Hill. He was cured of his addiction — through "the usual medicines" — and experienced a Heavenly Vision of the Holy Spirit descending and filling his heart with light. As "a new man in a new world"[2] he took on a new name in religion, calling himself defiantly, Hsi Shengmo, "the Overcomer of Demons." Hsi had conquered his own inner demons and, convinced of his divine call, he was ready to subdue the demons of Shanxi. He stayed with Hill for two months, as much teacher as student; this was the only sustained contact he had with foreign missionaries for six years. He returned to Western Chang Village, in the foothills near Pingyang, where he learned "all he could from occasional intercourse with the missionaries,

1. French, trans., *The Songs of Pastor Hsi*, p. 11.
2. *Pastor Hsi* (single volume), p. 63.

and [was] taught of God, often in quaint surprising ways, through the enlightenment of His Word applied to the daily experiences of life."³

As an adept of the Religion of the Golden Pill, Hsi was used to studying obscure scriptures, and his Bible reading, unaided by explanations, was literal and imaginative. Every time he stumbled on a stone or had a confrontation with one of the "under-shepherds," he saw this as the direct intervention of Satan. Since he had no preconceived notions of "the Christian life," he continued to cultivate opium and tobacco, until he recognized this was "a stumbling block" to others. He destroyed his opium crop, and at the same time adopted Hebraic (kosher) eating habits, banishing pigs from his farm. "They are filthy," he insisted. "We must have nothing to do with that which is impure."⁴ (One could read this in two ways. In Christian terms, he adopted the Mosaic dietary laws, which were common in Shanxi among the Muslims. In Chinese terms, he was following a vegetarian diet to accumulate merit.) He also adopted Saturday as his Sabbath, though he did it inadvertently through a calendrical error, but reverted to Sunday under the missionaries' instructions.

As the leading Christian in southern Shanxi, Teacher Hsi created a sect whose difference from the other religions that sprang up after the famine was that it was Christian. Aged 44 in 1880, when he was baptized, Teacher Hsi was a theatrical, domineering personality, with a cast in one eye that gave him an eaglelike glance. He had formerly been a scholar and local bully. Now, released from the lethargy of opium and armed with a copy of the treaty rights, he took on the role of arbiter of village disputes. According to Mrs. Howard Taylor, the most sympathetic of biographers, Hsi thought "that his zeal and energy must be employed to clear the way of the Lord, sweeping aside all obstacles and hindrances, with the means whereby he had hitherto successfully dominated those around him. Thus when troubles arose, and believers were persecuted contrary to treaty rights, he even went up to the capital and interviewed the Governor of the province, setting on foot legal proceedings that covered their enemies with confusion. For as followers of the Western faith, he and other Christians could claim the protection assured to foreigners."⁵ Persecution was not resumed, since "everyone seemed to hold the foreign religion in wholesome fear."⁶

3. Ibid., p. 75.
4. Ibid., p. 77.
5. Ibid., pp. 276-77. Roger R. Thompson, "Twilight of the Gods in the Chinese Countryside," pp. 66-67, considered the persecutions and "missionary cases" in South Shanxi during the 1890s.
6. *Pastor Hsi*, pp. 73-74. Timothy Richard, "Christian Persecutions in China — Their

The Heavenly Invitation Offices

Keepers of Pastor Hsi's opium refuges, 1890s. Shanxi was infamous for its wretched "opium villages" where "eleven out of every ten people smoked opium." It was like "preaching to a nation of drunkards," one missionary said, and most converts were reformed addicts. Pastor Hsi established a successful philanthropic business, a string of forty opium refuges in four provinces of northwestern China. Supposedly they treated over 300,000 addicts, using various kinds of morphine.
Source: OMF/Toronto.

Hsi was elected headman of his own village — as Mrs. Taylor quaintly put it, "chairman of the Parish Council" — despite his protestations that as a Christian, "under no circumstances can I have anything to do with sacrifices in worship of the idols, or with the festivities of the temple and seasons. I will at all times pray to the living God for the prosperity of the village, and for abundant harvests." Since the elders had noticed that "Hsi's prayers in the name of Jesus were remarkably effective," they agreed to his stipulation that "the entire village take the same position." They closed the temple and conducted no public ceremonies for one year, and prayed to the One True God — Shangdi — for their crops. In treaty terms, he must have persuaded the whole village not to pay the idol taxes, 40 percent of the total taxes due to the state, which would have supported such opera performances. By the end of the

---

Nature, Causes, Remedies," *Chinese Recorder*, July-August 1884, p. 242, referred to this incident: "Some of the Christians were imprisoned and severely tortured."

year, the "harvests were good, money matters successfully dealt with, and peace and contentment reigned." After being elected headman for four years, Hsi announced triumphantly that "the idols must be quite starved to death."[7]

As Hsi matured, he "mellowed" into an austere, charismatic figure, immaculately dressed in a white gown with a scarlet ribbon across his chest that read "Jesus came into the world to save sinners." He could preach a sermon on St. Paul's shipwreck with such emotion that tears streamed down his cheeks like an old-fashioned marketplace storyteller, making it come alive to these peasants in a landlocked sea of mountains.

The only problem was that he disliked foreigners. He manipulated the missionaries adeptly, playing them off against each other and against other contenders to his leadership. Joshua Turner, who baptized Hsi, admitted he did not go to "the town where these brethren live, as I intended to do, because there is a great deal of ill-feeling and speaking against the 'foreign religion,' and I think my presence would only hinder the cause."[8] Dixon E. Hoste, who was to become Hsi's colleague for ten years, summarized the situation: "He was rather an extreme case, because all the circumstances were extreme. Here was a man of exceptional force of character and organizing power, and whose education and position gave him weight; then, a man of exceptionally deep spiritual life; and, further, circumstances had been such that he had never had missionary supervision, but really, he had been left practically alone. He found Turner inadequate, as, indeed, 99 out of 100 of us would have been, under the circumstances. Mr. Hsi was, indeed, a very difficult man to get on with, in those days."[9]

Turner's successor Samuel B. Drake, under Timothy Richard's influence, objected to "scriptural colportage" and never ventured near Hsi's home. The reports in *China's Millions* contain little more than Hsi's own accounts dictated during his visits to the "mother-church" in Pingyang.[10] In one typical account — filtered through layers of censorship — Robert J. Landale, the Edinburgh lawyer, wrote: "There is one gentleman down the southern part of my province, a man of wealth among the Chinese, a man of landed property,

---

7. *Pastor Hsi*, pp. 81-83.

8. J. J. Turner, "Shan-si Province: Progress at P'ing-yang Fu," in *China's Millions* (GB), December 1881, p. 148.

9. D. E. Hoste, CIM/SOAS, file 305. On its cover in Geraldine Taylor's handwriting (including ellipses), "Notes of Mr. Hoste on his relation w. Hsi . . . Chapter 12 (In 1886) . . . Wisdom of D. E. Hoste recognized by JHT while DEH was still in Shansi," p. 26. Hoste wrote this account about 1899 to provide her with information for the biography. (See also Conclusion.)

10. Marshall Broomhall, *W. W. Cassels*, p. 71.

but one who considers the whole of his time, and influence, and means must, as a matter of course, be at the feet of the Lord Jesus. We never told him that. He said, 'Why, the Lord has redeemed me; He shed His blood, He spared nothing in working out my redemption; therefore I consider that granary of mine, full of rice, is for the use of the brothers and sisters, if they need it.' I may say this was in the time of persecution."[11] There is a note of surprise here — "We never told him that" — that echoes in the missionaries' reaction to many "quaint surprising" things *they* never told him.

The CIM, like most Protestant missions, was unwilling to get involved in political disputes such as Hsi stirred up. By 1884 he was so notorious that the Pingyang magistrate put up a proclamation "warning the people from learning religion and getting involved in the evils of the religion professed by the T'ai-p'ing rebels." The provincial chancellor announced that the degrees obtained by a scholar would be confiscated if he converted to Christianity, and to set an example he rescinded Hsi's degree. This time Hsi enlisted Timothy Richard and Samuel Drake to "petition the governor of the province on his behalf, and after a few weeks' delay, the degree was restored to him." Although the *daotai*, the district official, said that "such talk grated on his ears," at some level he must have been convinced that Hsi's congregation in an isolated village posed no threat, that he was the teacher of a religious sect *(jiao)*, not a secret society *(hui)*.[12]

Hsi's work was "large and spreading" with meetings "to worship God (according to the reckoning of the natives) in twenty-seven villages, spread over five counties."[13] At one place one hundred "Christians and candidates for baptism" met weekly, thirty-five of them women.[14] ("I wish they would come out in T'ai-yüen in the same manner," Miss Emily Kingsbury whispered parenthetically, "but the people of P'ing-yang seem different to what they are in this city — they are much more simple-hearted.")[15]

---

11. R. J. Landale, annual report of P'ing-yang station, 15 April 1882, in *China's Millions* (GB), July 1883, p. 87 (italics in original). Sharing his grain would be a common act of benevolence for a sect leader.

12. Timothy Richard, "Christian Persecutions in China," pp. 241-44; and "The Political Status of Missionaries and Native Christians in China," *Chinese Recorder*, March 1885, p. 104. S. B. Drake, "Shan-si Province: Eighteen Persons Baptised," *China's Millions* (GB), August 1884, p. 106. *HTCOC* 6, p. 401.

13. Thomas Wellesley Piggott, "Shan-si Province: The Work in P'ing-yang Fu and the Surrounding Towns and Villages," *China's Millions* (GB), September 1884, p. 113.

14. Drake, "Shan-si Province," p. 106.

15. Emily E. Kingsbury, "Work in P'ing-yang Fu, Shan-si," ibid., October 1884, p. 126.

The Demoniac among the Tombs

After the Great Famine, many survivors, plagued with a host of physical illnesses, turned to the opium pipe, so they were sick and addicted. In addition, if the missionary records can be trusted, the famine caused an epidemic of mental illnesses, madness, and possession by malignant spirits. It is not to be wondered that people were plagued with hungry ghosts when missionaries would find skeletons at the back of the caves, unburied since the famine. The famine had shattered the old religious networks, leaving the people further bereft. Pingyang was a burned-over district, ripe for a "better" religion that promised spiritual healing in this world and a paradise in the next.

It is hard to document the practice of exorcism within the CIM, since the references are covert and elliptical. One explicit reference occurred in Ningbo about 1876 when the landlady, a "passionate, outrageous creature" who had caused the death of two daughters-in-law, had "the devil cast out of her, and she is now clothed, and in her right mind. . . . Her subdued manner in all things is truly marvelous."[16] In Wenzhou, where George and Grace Stott ruled the church with an iron hand, Mrs. Stott recorded the first exorcism she witnessed, in 1884, which came as a shocking and disturbing revelation.[17]

Most missionaries, being rational, educated Westerners, thought the demons of China were dirt and poverty, which should be exorcised with carbolic and whitewash. "Use the broom!" one Chinese pastor said in 1875. "Clean the dirt in your homes! Keep the cats and dogs and chickens and pigs outside, where they belong! Wash your whole bodies frequently in warm water! Poke some holes in your close houses; put in windows, and let in the fresh air of heaven! Do this and you will not only be rid of the fox demon, but you will be rid of the itch at the same time."[18]

A few missionaries, however, searched Chinese occult religions. One was John Livingston Nevius, pioneer of the influential "Nevius method" of building a self-supporting, indigenous church, who also wrote a book on *Demon Possession*. Nevius claimed that exorcisms were common among rural Chinese Christians, though seldom mentioned in missionary publicity. "No Protestant missionary, so far as I know, has ever given native converts instructions as to casting out spirits; and few, if any, have dreamed that their converts would have the disposition, the ability, or the opportunity to do so." The mis-

---

16. Ibid., January 1877, p. 3.
17. Grace Stott, *Twenty-Six Years of Missionary Work in China*.
18. Li Yu-ni of the Methodist Episcopal Mission in Fuzhou, in *The Christian Advocate*, 1875, p. 9.

sionaries would explain away demon manifestations because they were not in close contact with grass-roots village life and the Chinese were "ashamed" to tell them.[19]

Exorcism was something to be talked of in whispers, hinted at with the story of "the demoniac among the tombs." In the life of Jesus this story was considered so significant that it appears in both Mark 5:2-19 and Luke 8:26-39. When Jesus cast out an unclean spirit from a man who had broken his fetters and lived naked among the tombs, he asked the spirit its name. The spirit responded, "My name is Legion: for we are many." Jesus cast the devils into a herd of swine, which ran into the sea and were drowned. The demoniac was found with Jesus, "sitting, and clothed, and his right mind," and the people were afraid.

Very few missionaries, even in the CIM, ventured from watching a native Christian exorcism to participating in spiritual battles with "the Devil and his angels (or demons, whichever title be right)."[20] Yet, using the code phrases of the gospels — "my name is Legion," "seated and clothed" and "in his right mind" — as signifiers for exorcism, *China's Millions* seems to have been awash with exorcisms, performed by natives and missionaries alike. (Perhaps the most oblique reference was at the CIM's annual meeting in 1880, when the curate of Mildmay recounted the story of the disciples who forbade a man from casting out devils in Jesus' name "because he followed not with us." Jesus rebuked them; "Forbid him not, for there is no man that can do a miracle in My name, that can speak lightly of Me." This suggests that some CIM leaders in England knew more than they were willing to admit publicly.)[21]

Nineteenth-century evangelicals did not have a distinct theology to explain supernatural manifestations such as miracles and exorcisms. That did not come until the "latter rain" theology of twentieth-century pentecostalism, which taught that such apostolic gifts were withdrawn in apostolic times ("the cessation of charisms"), but were being reinstated in "these last days" as a witness. Groping in the dark, for exorcism and speaking in tongues were not isolated phenomena, the missionaries would give the rationalization, as one Chinese pastor put it: "In western lands, demons are no longer found, but in our Middle Kingdom they abound. Why? Because Christ in His day drove them out of Judea, and His Apostles and the succeeding genera-

---

19. John Livingston Nevius, *Demon Possession* (1898. 8th edition, Grand Rapids: Kregel Publications, 1968), p. 14.
20. John S. Rough, "Kiukiang," *China's Millions* (NA), April 1895, p. 51.
21. *China's Millions* (GB), July-August 1880, p. 100.

tions of Christians have for almost 2,000 years been casting them out in the west, and so they have had to come east to find a dwelling-place!"[22]

Pastor Hsi, the two-volume biography by Mrs. Howard Taylor, was the first popular book to discuss exorcism candidly for a Western audience. "It would never occur to a Chinese to question the existence of demons," she wrote. "We may regard such ideas as superstitious, and dismiss them without further thought, but facts remain; and some facts are startling as well as stubborn things."[23] Hsi Shengmo illuminates the progression of exorcism as a secretive practice among Chinese Christians before it came to the attention of the missionaries. When Hsi was first converted and tried to tell his fellow villagers the story of Jesus, the people would ask, "But is all this true, Teacher Hsi? Did Jesus really heal that demoniac among the tombs? Or is it only an honourable fable? Did He indeed open the eyes of the blind, make lame men walk, and cure even lepers? Why do you not respectfully invite Him to our neighbourhood? There are plenty of sick people here." Hsi "gladly laid his hands on their sick and prayed for immediate recovery.... And seeing these things with their own eyes, it was little wonder that men and women turned to the Lord."[24]

The historian Susan Naquin stresses the connection between healing and sectarian conversion. Sometimes the healer would make the people join the sect first "because the cure was difficult.... In most cases, however, it was the grateful patient, now cured, who (perhaps together with relatives who had been impressed by the cure) kowtowed to his 'doctor,' became his pupil and joined the sect. In many instances, the teacher then shared with his former patient the 'secrets' of the sects.... The healer's skill in curing illness was transformed into authority on religious matters as well, and the doctor-patient relationship only strengthened the sect teacher-pupil bond."[25]

This particular bond was emphasized by the practice of exorcism. Jan Jakob Maria de Groot, a nineteenth-century expert on Chinese sects who wrote a massive, six-volume compendium called *The Religious System of*

---

22. William J. Doherty, "'The Spirit That Now Worketh' in China," *China's Millions* (NA), April 1905, pp. 67-68. This illuminating article concerns demon possession and exorcism at Xinzhang (old spelling Hsin-chang), Zhejiang. The author wrote: "I refused to give credence to the statements of the natives until I visited the place personally. Undoubtedly there are things in connection with it that are not to be dismissed with a shake of the head and catalogued as superstition or tricks."

23. *Pastor Hsi*, pp. 64-65.

24. Ibid., pp. 71-72.

25. Susan Naquin, *Millenarian Rebellion in China: The Eight Trigrams Uprising of 1813* (New Haven: Yale University Press, 1976), pp. 29-30.

China: Its Ancient Forms, Evolution, History and Present Aspect, Manners, Customs and Social Institutions Connected Therewith, stated that every male had the potential to be a "demon expeller" since he "possesses a *shen* [spirit] or *Yang* [male] soul. But this *Yang* soul should be well developed: in other words, he should have vitality or health, bodily strength, boldness, intellect, and, above all things, moral rectitude, such as heaven possesses, which never deviates from the *Tao* [*Dao*] or right order of the universe." A Chinese exorcist was highly physical, cutting himself with spirit swords and leaping about like a madman. "Blowing on the sick, the swooned, or the mad, or spurting water on them from the mouth, or spitting upon them, preferably in the face, is a good means to drive out the indwelling spectres."[26]

Christian exorcism relied on a quiet, verbal (not necessarily physical) command "in the name of Jesus of Nazareth." In his early years Hsi would cast out any possessed who came if they promised to destroy their idols and worship the One True God. Later he "learned to distinguish between the greater and the lesser demons. With the latter he would deal summarily," but the greater demons could be conquered only "by prayer and fasting; and thus he would prepare himself for an encounter with the powers of evil." On at least one occasion the evil spirit was stronger than his own powers and temporarily took over his body. Hsi was constantly tormented by "the many onslaughts of Satan," he wrote in his autobiography, and "my wife and I for the space of three years seldom put off our clothing to go to sleep, in order that we might be the more ready to watch and pray."[27] This action, which seems extreme, puts Hsi fully in the Chinese spirit realm, for the Chinese word for "visions" means literally "dreaming with one's clothes on."[28]

Hsi did not have to look far for his first unclean spirit. Mrs. Hsi, his second, childless wife (his first had died young), thought her husband had been bewitched by the foreign drugs. She became deranged and possessed of "constant suggestions of evil" and "paroxysms of ungovernable rage" whenever he prayed. Hsi called for a three-day fast of the entire household and then in the presence of all he laid his hands on her head and commanded the spirit to depart. She was permanently cured and joined her husband as his partner, conducting the women's work and managing the women's refuges.[29] Another of

26. J. J. de Groot, *The Religion of the Chinese* (New York: Macmillan, 1910), pp. 45, 53-55. See also his *The Religious System of China: Its Ancient Forms, Evolution, History and Present Aspect, Manners, Customs and Social Institutions Connected Therewith* (Leyden: E. J. Brill, 1892).
27. *Pastor Hsi*, p. 80.
28. R. G. Wagner, *Re-enacting the Heavenly Vision*, pp. 22-24.
29. *Pastor Hsi*, pp. 68-70. An account by W. L. Elliston in *China's Millions* (GB), April

Hsi's cures was his wife's aunt who had burned her leg with oil; Hsi laid his hands on her and (she testified) on the third day, "I was healed, and descended from my couch. . . . Of course, I at once cast away my idols and worshipped the true God." She later went back to worshiping idols "for fear of persecution" and was "immediately smitten with a great illness and nearly died." Hsi cured her a second time.[30]

Pastor Hsi describes many exorcisms but one shall suffice, the first he performed for a missionary audience. In 1882 Hsi took his wife to Taiyuan to be baptized — presumably this was also the trip when he called upon the provincial governor demanding treaty protections for Christians — where he was asked to attend a possessed young woman. As he entered the room there was a lull in her seizure and Hsi, "laying his hands on her head, simply and earnestly prayed in the name of Jesus, and commanded the evil spirits at once to come out of her." When she fell into a swoon Hsi announced the spirits were gone. She remained well until he left the city, when she relapsed. "He is gone; he is gone!" she shrieked. "Now I fear no one. Let them bring their Jesus. I defy them all." She continued like this for a few days until she died of exhaustion.[31]

The Red Pills

As word got around that Teacher Hsi had the ability to cast out demons and cure the sick, he was besieged by enquirers begging to "eat the doctrine." He would encourage them to stay at his home for a month or more while he instructed them. Since the old people and children could not walk to the station at Pingyang, a twenty-mile round trip, they had no contact with the missionary, so Hsi built a chapel on his land, where he acted as the benevolent host. "Believers gathering from miles around for Sunday services were often weary, and too far from home to go back between the meetings for their mid-day meal. Some brought flour, bread, and other provisions; some had little or nothing to bring; and all needed the use of kitchen and guest-hall, not to speak of the women's apartments. Then benches for the meetings had to be provided; oil for the lamps; hot water for perpetual tea-drinking, . . . and many other hospitalities too numerous to mention."[32]

1881, p. 42, merely said that Hsi's wife was "ill, and doctors being unable to cure her," Hsi's fasting and prayer "completely cured" her "malady."

30. Ibid., January 1887, p. 10.
31. *Pastor Hsi*, pp. 116-18.
32. Ibid., pp. 84-85.

The Heavenly Invitation Offices

At this point, Hsi's influence spread only as far as his personal charisma — and he craved a larger audience. His wife had a dream in which the One True God commanded her to sell her jewelry to finance a "Christian drugstore" in a nearby market town. With his medical skills and the breathing exercises of the Golden Pill, Hsi opened a "neat and attractive" shop with a banner that read *Fuyintang*, literally "Hall of the Happy News" or "Gospel Hall." The missionaries, suspicious of a "medical mission station, on purely native lines, sustained and conducted apart altogether from foreign supervision," thought it "wiser not to render any direct assistance."[33] This meant that as Hsi was branching out he was thrown on his own resources.

All this was happening outside the foreigners' ken, but as they started encroaching on Hsi's turf, he polarized them into pro- and anti-Hsi factions. Some enthusiasts announced that "the Kingdom of God was about to be established in South Shanxi."[34] Others, such as Robert Landale, warned that Hsi "seems very independent of the opinions of the foreigner, and fortunately he seems to put the Bible where it should be. He would be a dangerous man if he got wrong in anything, for all the others look up to him."[35]

In 1881, two years after his conversion and one year after his baptism, things came to a crisis when a rival leader arose twenty miles from Hsi's home. His name was Mr. Fan (whose personal name was never given) of Fancun (old spelling Fan-ts'un), or "the Fan family village," near Hongdong, the county city twenty miles north of Pingyang. He had been a member of a reformed Buddhist sect that called itself "the Secret Religion," which practiced austerity, vegetarianism, idol worship, and devotions (see Chapter 5). It had been founded about "fifty years before" the missionaries arrived, i.e., about 1830, by a "reformer" who exhorted the people "to cultivate virtue, care for the needs of others, practice benevolence, spend time and money in the relief of suffering, [and] accumulate merit."[36] Samuel Drake said that the Qing government considered the society to be a political threat, and "more than once terribly persecuted them." The sect founder died during the famine time, and Fan made Christian converts among his fellow worshipers.

Fan Village was also the home of Gatekeeper Sung and other former members of the Golden Pill, and in the tumultuous relations between Hsi the Daoist and Fan the Buddhist, we can discern the larger confrontation between different strands within Chinese Christianity. Hsi's Christianity was

---

33. Ibid., p. 87. Compare this with George King's "Salvation Hall" in Hanzhong, Shaanxi (see Chapter 5).
34. *China's Millions* (GB), p. 120.
35. R. J. Landale, annual report, 15 April 1882, pp. 84, 87.
36. *Pastor Hsi*, pp. 90-91.

energetic and miraculous, dependent on yin and yang and controlling the spirit world; Fan established a meditative kind of Christianity that offered release from this transient world.[37] One should not overemphasize their differences, for Buddhism and Daoism — and Nestorian Christianity — had blended for fifteen hundred years in this corner of China. Hsi's sect became "non-sectarian," with local variants depending on whether the converts were from the Golden Pill or the Secret Religion.[38]

When Fan tried to convert his fellow sectarians, the "one great obstacle" was that most were opium addicts. Fan was not an addict himself, and he asked Samuel Drake to help him set up a "native opium refuge" in his village. It was a primitive affair conducted in a cave, "an indifferent middle-class cave ... with an indifferent chimney, a stove-bed, and a paper window, one square yard in size." It was furnished with "a good stock of winnowed grain of several kinds, a heap of coals, two stools, and one small stand." Fan gathered those who truly wanted to reform, and Drake supplied foreign "anti-opium pills" — i.e. morphine. When "the craving" came on, Drake would administer a pill and Fan would pray. The addict "had never prayed before, and a form of prayer was repeated to him; this prayer was repeated by him, and soon after he fell asleep." When news spread "there was quite a rush of visitors," who came to chat and smoke tobacco until the cave was more like "a smoking-saloon rather than a preaching-hall." The "circumstances were so peculiar," Drake concluded, "the experience so novel, and the work by night as well as by day was so trying and exhausting, that it has formed an epoch in my life." Of the nineteen patients, six were "cured of opium-smoking, and thirteen others nearly so."[39]

As long as Drake supplied the "anti-opium medicines," Fan's business prospered. Within a year he claimed to have "cured more than one hundred opium-smokers; twenty-five or six persons now meet in his house every

---

37. Naquin, *Millenarian Rebellion in China*, defines the difference between Buddhist and Daoist priests: the former will discuss theological concepts while the latter will struggle with the spirits.

38. I am suggesting that as Christianity mixed syncretically with Chinese folk religion, it produced different strands of indigenous Christianity. Given specific missionary temperaments and Chinese roots, different types of indigenous Christianity would emerge from, say, a Swedish holy woman working among women vegetarians, or a Church of England clergyman and a Daoist adept.

39. S. B. Drake, annual report for P'ing-yang, 14 May 1882, in *China's Millions*, July 1883, p. 87, stated that the event occurred the previous autumn (1881). His article, "The Story of Mr. Fan, of P'ing-yang Fu, Shan-si," in September 1883, pp. 127-29, is more detailed. The two years that elapsed between the event and its publication in *China's Millions* indicates how slowly the CIM released its "news."

The Heavenly Invitation Offices

Sunday for worship, and six of their number are applying for baptism."[40] With Drake's pills, Fan threatened Hsi's supremacy and Hsi was reduced to "coming at any time to the assistance of his friend." When Drake went on furlough (and later joined the BMS), the supply of pills stopped and Hsi saw his chance to act.

Pastor Hsi had a dream — his fourth heavenly vision — in which the Holy Spirit revealed a recipe for making anti-opium pills that could be concocted from drugs in his own drug store. Hsi's pills changed everything. They were red, "well made and attractive-looking," and the ingredients were "the best obtainable." Moreover, they were "inexpensive and easily made," and could be produced "in large quantities and at short notice."[41] He was no longer dependent on the foreigners' drugs, and the correct master-disciple relationship was restored with Fan. Hsi took over Fan's refuge in Fancun, which became "the laboratory" for his life's work. Now Fan had to come to *him* for medicines.[42] By 1885 Hsi had three or four refuges which dispensed the red pills with prayer and singing; by the time of his death eleven years later he had over forty refuges in four provinces, which he called "Heavenly Invitation Offices."

It is impossible to ascertain the ingredients of the pills for they had flowery Chinese names, though one is tempted to speculate they were some sort of refined opiate. There were three pills of varying strength, used successively: the Life-Imparting Pill, the Life-Establishing Pill, and the Health-Restoring Pill that the patients took home with them.[43] Framing the story of his pills as a divine revelation, Hsi claimed his treatment was primarily spiritual, "to save the souls of men." Manufacturing the pills was a sacred ritual preceded by days of prayer and fasting. It was a "difficult process, generally undertaken by Hsi himself," in which he used "a simple corrugated basket hanging from a rope." The powder was moistened and "kneaded to a particular consistency, so it would roll off into nice, firm, little balls when properly swung in the basket." The process required patience, but "when the basket was kept swinging they could turn out hundreds, if not thousands, of pills in the day."[44]

---

40. Drake, "Story of Mr. Fan," p. 129.
41. *Pastor Hsi*, pp. 99-100.
42. Ibid., p. 101.
43. Ibid., p. 165.
44. Ibid., p. 131. In the days before manufactured pills, each pharmacist (chemist) in England made his own pills using a manual machine that rolled the pill mass into a sausage shape which was cut into sections by a brass instrument with corrugated grooves and then rolled into spherical balls. Hsi's basket probably had grooves of split bamboo that worked on similar principles.

The Shanxi Spirits

While Teacher Hsi was creating his indigenous sect in south Shanxi, a different scenario was unfolding in Taiyuan, the provincial capital, where the CIM and the Baptist Missionary Society shared a Union Chapel. Since Timothy Richard and his wife Mary were the sole Baptist representatives, their relations were facilitated by the fact that Shanxi seems to have been set aside as a Baptist enclave within the nondenominational CIM. "Our relations with the Inland Mission had been the friendliest," Timothy Richard wrote, for "all were agreeable people, willing to differ amicably." Then "Mr. Hudson Taylor broke our harmony by ordering his members, in 1881, to have a separate place of worship, on the ground that I was not orthodox. . . . This came as a great surprise to Dr. Schofield and Mr. Landale, who called on me at once with Mr. Taylor's letter. They assured me that they had always found my addresses most helpful; but much against the wishes of most of them, the Inland Mission in T'ai-yuan fu had their separate place of worship and opened a separate school."[45]

A. J. Broomhall described the split between Hudson Taylor and Timothy Richard as a manifestation of what a few letters of the period referred to as "the Shanxi spirit." This was "a whirlpool of complaints, misunderstandings, derelict spiritual morale and finally resignations from the CIM and BMS."[46] It was more than just another outbreak of "missionary quarrels," the gossip and denominational controversies that were endemic among the China missions. Between 1881 and 1895 over fifty CIM missionaries in Shanxi resigned as a result: five couples and Miss Horne joined the BMS, so that when Richard left Shanxi in 1884, the entire BMS mission was former CIM; thirty-five "associates" of the Scandinavian Alliance Mission severed their connection and moved to Shaanxi and Gansu, the provinces to the west; while Thomas Piggott and Dr. Edwards started an independent work known as the Shouyang Mission.

A. J. Broomhall called Timothy Richard the "vortex" of the Shanxi spirit, because he departed from orthodox Christianity and started preaching "another gospel," a syncretic mix of Christianity, Confucianism, and Buddhism. More dispassionately, Brian Stanley, in *The History of the Baptist Missionary Society*, writes that the discord in Shanxi was "the first example in the BMS (and one of the first in Protestant missions as a whole) of the impact of the new theological liberalism on assumptions which had hitherto gone virtually

---

45. Richard, *Forty-Five Years in China*, pp. 152-53.
46. *HTCOC 6*, pp. 288-93, "Timothy Richard and 'the Shansi spirit'"; quote at p. 288.

unchallenged. Richard's liberalism did not consist in the overt denial or even reformulation of any major Christian doctrine — his opponents were unable to make the charge of unorthodoxy stick." Rather, Richard was arguing that "Christianity has the power of assimilating all that is good in other religions. We come here to counteract their false teaching and to fill up what is awanting just as Christ came not to destroy but to fulfil."[47]

Broomhall described the Shanxi spirit as a battle of the titans, Hudson Taylor versus Timothy Richard, with the others as pawns. It is possible to read the documents, fragmentary as they are, and reach a different conclusion. The main antagonist, as far as the missionaries were concerned, was not Richard but Hsi Shengmo, whose influence was more divisive. (Richard would have met Hsi between 1879 and 1884, both in Pingyang and Taiyuan. Richard wrote two articles about Hsi's troubles with the authorities for the *Chinese Recorder*. He also had a remarkable knowledge of the Religion of the Golden Pill, which he may have learned from the former sect leader.) Even after Richard left Shanxi in 1884, the Shanxi spirit continued to percolate through the 1890s and its rumblings could be felt as late as the 1930s. Although the Shanxi spirit may have been sparked by a theological debate, it was sustained by the discord and "derelict spiritual morale" that took many manifestations: Hsi's opium refuges in South Shanxi were one, the discord in Taiyuan another.

In CIM code language, "derelict spiritual morale" invariably meant returning to Western clothes, and Chinese dress did prove to be a stumblingblock. Similarly, "complaints" is shorthand for opposition to Taylor's autocratic rule and calls for "democracy" within the mission. Samuel Drake, for example, refused to obey Taylor's injunction against marrying Miss Sowerby, the sister of Rev. Arthur Sowerby, who had resigned from the CIM to join the BMS, and instead, escorted her to Chefoo, where they were married by the British Consul without Taylor's permission. They, too, had to resign from the CIM, and they joined the BMS.[48]

There must have been other explanations for the Shanxi spirit, since the English Baptists and the American Oberlin mission experienced the same derelict morale. One Oberlin missionary blamed the opiated condition of the people for the "deadness" of the work. After the famine, the devastated fields had been planted with opium poppies, a cash crop well suited to the sandy soil, and Shanxi became a major producer of domestic opium. Cultivation led to addiction, and in some villages the people said "eleven out of every ten

---

47. Brian Stanley, *The History of the Baptist Missionary Society 1792-1992* (Edinburgh: T&T Clark, 1992), p. 196.

48. *HTCOC* 6, p. 297.

people smoked opium."⁴⁹ One Oberlin missionary said, "If there is a place in the whole world where it is harder to do missionary work than right here in Opium drugged Shansi province, which is probably one of the worst in the whole Empire, I do not want to know of it." Preaching in Shanxi, another said, was "like trying to save a race of drunkards."⁵⁰ Yet it was precisely among these "opium fiends" that the CIM made its most successful converts.

The Baptists

Timothy Richard was one of the towering figures of China missions, the most brilliant mind of his generation: the subtitle of his biography by William Soothill called him "Seer, Statesman, Missionary & the Most Disinterested Adviser the Chinese Ever Had." Converted in Wales during the 1859 revival, he had applied to the CIM when Hudson Taylor was organizing the *Lammermuir* party (see Chapter 3). "But as I was a Baptist," he commented tersely in his autobiography, "they recommended me to apply to the Baptist Missionary Society."⁵¹ After studying at Haverfordwest Baptist College, Richard joined the BMS in Shandong in 1870. Shandong was a singularly tragic field, where he was the only survivor of twelve missionaries and for three years, 1874-77, the sole representative. Although he was not in the CIM, Richard was captivated by Taylor's vision of pressing beyond the treaty ports and accordingly, in 1875 he transferred the Chefoo station to the American Baptists and moved 250 miles inland to Chingzhou (now Weifang).

"It was at Chingzhou that Richard's missionary principles assumed their mature form," wrote Brian Stanley. "He observed that the reforming religious sects which were now so numerous in this part of China propagated their doctrines by means of self-supporting and self-managing societies, and concluded that 'the best way to make Christianity indigenous was to adopt Chinese methods of propagation.'" Richard's ideas of a self-supporting, indigenous church were refined by John L. Nevius into his *Methods of Mission Work* (1886), which formed the basis for the Three-Self Movement starting in the 1920s. The Three-Self Church is self-supporting (controlling its own money),

---

49. According to Jonathan D. Spence's chapter, "Opium," in *Chinese Roundabout: Essays in History and Culture*, p. 237, the reformer Zhang Zhitong "insisted" that smokers made up 80 percent of the population of Shanxi cities and 60 percent in the countryside; Governor Zeng Guoquan thought rural smoking higher than urban. By the early twentieth century, a million *mu* (300,000 acres) of land were planted with opium in Shanxi.

50. Nat Brandt, *Massacre in Shansi*, pp. 48-49.

51. Richard, *Forty-Five Years in China*, p. 29.

Timothy and Mary Richard in 1884. After Richard was rejected by the CIM, he graduated from a Welsh Baptist college and went to China to found the English Baptist Mission. He sought out "the worthies" among Chinese religious leaders and scholars to incorporate Chinese ideas into evangelical Christianity. When Hudson Taylor broke with him, several CIM missionaries in Shanxi resigned from the CIM to join the BMS. Source: Timothy Richard, *Forty-five Years in China: Reminiscences by Timothy Richard, D.D., Litt.D.* (New York: Frederick A. Stokes, 1916).

self-propagating (converts, education), and self-governing (political and denominational independence from missionaries). Later, Richard worked with the reformers at court and the Emperor himself to launch "the Hundred Days of Reform" in 1898. So his legacy is long and distinguished, and the Chinese churches of today owe him a debt.[52]

His ideas, as expansive as Hudson Taylor's vision of the blitz-conversion of China, were diametrically opposed to them, for the CIM supported a network of paid agents — gatekeepers, colporteurs, preachers, evangelists, and Biblewomen. Besides, Taylor had such a dark view of heathenism, he could never see anything good in non-Christian religions and was anxiously stamping out the pernicious heresy of conditionalism, which denied the eternal damnation of the heathen. Finally, there was the issue of class. Taylor was sending an army of evangelists to scatter the gospel far and wide among the common people. Richard believed that water trickled downhill, and that China — like Constantine's Rome — could be converted from the top down.

The influence of Richard's ideas on the CIM was apparent as early as 1878, when Hudson Taylor wrote that he "refuses to preach to the masses, is for circulation of moral and theistic tracts, not containing the name or work of Christ, to prepare the way, as he thinks, for the gospel. . . . The faith of one brother [Joshua Turner] has quite broken down, under the unhelpful influence largely of other missionaries, and we shall have to recall him."[53] Richard's "presence in Shansi causes me great anxiety for some of his views are so Romish [an allusion to Matteo Ricci], and his personal influence so strong that the CIM has no existence, scarcely, or place, or work or claims in the minds of [two CIM missionaries, presumably Turner and Samuel Drake]. This is not necessarily Mr. R's fault; it is rather the inevitable result of a strong and attractive character over weaker minds."[54]

In 1881, after Taylor ordered the CIM people to sever relations with Richard, Joshua Turner, Francis James, and Arthur Sowerby resigned along with their wives, followed by Samuel Drake and Celia Horne, the entire first generation of the CIM in Shanxi. Turner had remained in Pingyang throughout the famine, where he almost died from famine fever, and afterwards, since he had offended Hsi Shengmo, he turned Pingyang over to Drake and returned to Taiyuan. He resigned because of the inadequate stipend, Taylor reported, and "does not believe in looking directly to God."[55]

---

52. Stanley, *History of the BMS*, pp. 182-83.
53. JHT letter to Lord Radstock, 15 August 1878, in *HTCOC* 6, p. 192.
54. JHT letter to London, 6 March 1880, in ibid.
55. JHT to Mrs. Jennie Taylor, 10 November 1881, in CIM/SOAS, file 267.

Francis James married a "Belgian lady," a member of the CIM named Marie Huberty, and took on her surname, known henceforth as Francis Huberty James. She was thirty-two, highly educated and a graduate of the French Protestant School at Liège.[56] Similarly, Huberty James resigned over money. He had been insulted by Hudson Taylor, who practically accused him of appropriating famine funds when his CIM stipend did not arrive in time. He stated in his letter of resignation, "I must say I am not satisfied with the plan of support, and for myself I feel it would be a considerable help and convenience to me in my work to belong to a Society giving a stated salary. This was one of the chief reasons that influenced me in seeking to join the BMS." Taylor sniffed, "I myself more than once as a married man lived on a less sum: as a single man I have lived at times on one-fourth the amount." This was followed by four pages of close financial analysis.[57] We shall meet Francis Huberty James again.

As a result of the split, the CIM and the BMS divided Taiyuan, with the Baptists keeping the northern chapel, while the CIM built a new chapel in the south. Except for a BMS station north of Taiyuan, the CIM claimed the rest of the province, even though it had only two stations, in the far north at Datong and in the south at Pingyang. This was the CIM version of "comity." Comity usually referred to a cooperative division of a field claimed by two or more missions where one mission would build, say, a women's hospital and another would concentrate on education. The CIM (and the Alliance missions) seldom entered into comity agreements since they refused to be confined to one kind of work or one district. In the 1880s, with the burgeoning of missions in China, the CIM would claim a whole province on the basis of its extended itinerations, even if it did not have a resident missionary in that particular district. If the CIM deemed the other mission to be orthodox (such as the Canadian Presbyterians in North Henan or the Bible Christians in Yunnan), it would devolve its work and move elsewhere. With a liberal like Timothy Richard, the CIM could only establish a rival congregation, thus splitting the work, to present the orthodox gospel.

The Richard controversy had a sequel. In 1884 when Timothy and Mary Richard went on furlough, he took every opportunity to urge his views on the mission committee. He wrote "A Plea for China" in the *Missionary Herald*, which "appealed for volunteers for China, not merely from the Baptist colleges, but from parliament, the universities, business, and literature." He also

---

56. "List of Missionaries 1853-1895," record #74 (1876), Miss Marie Huberty, in CIM/SOAS, file 86.
57. Francis James to JHT, 20 June 1881, and JHT, "Remarks on Mr. James' Memo," with notation "[AJB: prior to 24 Mar/80]," in CIM/SOAS, file 261.

advocated "an inter-mission scheme to establish a high-class missionary college in every Chinese provincial capital, in order to bring about the "national conversion of China." The BMS committee rejected the scheme as impossibly expensive, and Richard, deeply wounded, resigned as secretary and treasurer of the Shanxi mission.[58]

Meanwhile, in Taiyuan, Richard's colleagues were writing to the BMS committee attacking his views. Turner and Sowerby — too liberal for the CIM, too conservative for Richard — "sent a long letter to the Committee, censuring me in regard to both my theological views and to my methods of work."[59] They stated that Richard was "devaluing evangelism, individual conversion, and work among the poor." Dr. Herbert Dixon, who had recently arrived in Taiyuan from the Congo — where he had "some missionary experience in an uncivilized country," Richard noted sarcastically — claimed Richard's message was "a conglomerate wherein Science, Heathenism, Roman Catholicism, and Christianity are bundled up into a new 'Gospel for Nations.'"[60]

When Richard returned from furlough in 1886, the Taiyuan people pointedly told him not to return — and he did not set foot in Shanxi again until 1902. He moved to Tianjin, where he resigned from the BMS to become secretary of the Christian Literature Society in Shanghai.

The Oberlin Band

Another event of 1881, the same year as the Richard controversy, was the arrival of the first representatives of the Oberlin Band, graduates of Oberlin College in Ohio, who arrived with a "ghost of an idea" of starting a daughter college, Oberlin-in-China. Twelve friends had applied to the American Board of Commissioners for Foreign Missions, asking to be considered as a group since they shared a common goal and could work in harmony: "We hope to establish a *center of influence* for the Chinese Empire and we plan in time to found an *educational institution* which shall command the respect of, and so influence the higher classes of China." The secretary recommended Shanxi as a "splendid field for new blood for the next generation" because it had a population of fourteen million but no missions except for "a small beginning by the Inland Mission who do a good work as scouts."[61]

---

58. The most complete description of this phase of the Richard controversy is Stanley, *History of the BMS*, pp. 189-95. See also *HTCOC 6*, pp. 292-93.
59. Soothill, *Timothy Richard*, pp. 156-57.
60. Stanley, *History of the BMS*, pp. 190-91.
61. Brandt, *Massacre in Shansi*, pp. 27-28.

The Heavenly Invitation Offices

Oberlin College had been founded in 1833 by Charles Grandison Finney, who invented "scientific revivalism," as a colony of Christian reverence. Its purpose, "for the training of teachers and other Christian toilers for the boundless and most desolute [sic] fields" in the American West, combined religious piety with social activism. The school promoted health food, coeducation, benevolence, voluntarism, and the holiness doctrine known as "perfectionism." It was open to women from the beginning, and admitted blacks the following year. "The college was soon a breeding ground of abolitionist preachers and the town a haven for runaway slaves. . . . A branch of the Young Men's Christian Association was founded in Oberlin in 1881, and within a year it was the largest YMCA in the world." By 1889, "one hundred and sixty Oberlin men and women were currently serving in missions as far afield as Africa, the Sandwich Islands, Jamaica, Turkey, Haiti, Bulgaria, Micronesia, Japan, and India," as well as among the Amerindians of the American West.[62]

When Martin Luther Stimson and his bride Emily Hall, the heralds of Oberlin, arrived in Tianjin in 1881, Richard escorted them to Taiyuan and helped them purchase a house. They were joined by two married couples and a single man the following year, including Iranaeus J. Atwood, who studied cataract surgery under Dr. Schofield and acted as the band's interim doctor. Stimson had been impressed by the smaller cities in the plain south of Taiyuan with populations from 15,000 to 20,000, and the Oberlin Band opened stations at Taigu, east of the Fen River, and Fenzhou, a prefectural *(fu)* city on the west.

Although the Oberlin Band were joined by two more couples in 1884 — a total of eleven, five married couples and a single man — it remained a "feeble Mission" that at one point was down to three members and had to abandon Fenzhou to concentrate on Taigu. "The roster of the Shansi Mission never went beyond a total of eighteen missionaries, including physicians [and single women], and then only in a four year period 1893-1896."[63] Although Nat Brandt does not use the phrase "the Shanxi spirit" in his history of the Oberlin mission, *Massacre in Shansi*, it is clear they were beset by the same whirlpool of derelict morale. Looking back on the first eight years, Charles Price gave several reasons why they had not yet opened a school or baptized one convert. He cited a "mysterious providence" evidenced by the high death rate and serious illness, which resulted in an "exceedingly short" term of service. Another was the "slowness of the work," the difficulty in learning the

62. Ibid., pp. 25-26.
63. Ibid., pp. 29, 33.

language, the opium addiction of the people, and "the deceitfulness and vileness of the heathen heart," which "closes the ear to the Gospel message."[64]

The Oberlin mission was also affected by the Richard controversy, when Charles Tenney converted to Unitarian views and refused to engage in street preaching. In particular, he argued that employing "natives" encouraged the unemployed — "empty cisterns which love no water" — to profess Christianity to get a salaried job. He even quoted Hudson Taylor, who had stated that reliable converts told him not to pay preachers with foreign money: "When you put a man into a street chapel on $5.00 per month, the fact is that everybody in the place soon finds out that he is the best paid and (according to their opinion) has the least to do of any man among them." Stimson, the patriarch, thought the ban against hiring natives to do mission work was "a relic of medieval times" and stubbornly continued to pay colporteurs and evangelists anyway. Despite objections, this "eventually became standard procedure simply because there were never enough missionaries to handle the Mission's workload." The episode left a sour taste in everyone's mouth, and Stimson, feeling "deeply wronged," resigned from the mission.[65]

It took eight years, until 1889, before the Oberlin Band baptized its first convert, Liu Feng Chih — "Deacon Liu" — a charismatic preacher whose story is uncannily similar to Pastor Hsi's. "He was an unusually tall, robust Chinese man in his late forties who sported a moustache that grew down from his upper lip in oriental fashion." He was known for his violent temper, and had at one time been very rich, the owner of camel trains that carried tea, cotton, and sugar to Manchuria and Mongolia. But Liu was addicted to opium and smoked three ounces a day. He heard that the American missionaries had opened an opium refuge at Taigu, and listened with rapt attention while the missionary preached on Luke 8:26-39, the story of the demoniac among the tombs. Liu stayed in the refuge for forty days, under constant surveillance, while the missionaries injected him with a weak solution of morphine. Despite the terrible suffering, he remained steadfast even when his nephew smuggled in opium pills and tempted him. "As daylight approached, Liu found he had lost his craving for opium, and he fell asleep for a long time. When he awoke, he felt transformed." He stayed at the station for several months and returned to his village with copies of the Old and New Testaments, where he spent his time reading and preaching. He was later employed as a teacher in the boys' school.[66]

---

64. Ibid., p. 37.
65. Ibid., pp. 37-38.
66. Ibid., pp. 9-12.

The Heavenly Invitation Offices

The Oberlin Band added a distinct American character to the homogenous British missions in Shanxi when Charles and Eva Price called their station "Little America" and hung an American flag over their house.[67] Separated by nationality, class, education, theology, and physical distance from the CIM — and by their stereotype that the CIM was not doing *real* mission work, only "scouting" — the Oberlin people did not have much direct contact until the CIM started opening stations near their district in the 1890s. Eva Price opened her house as a sanctuary for wandering CIM missionaries, and her diary provides a rare glimpse of the CIM from the outside. "No place but in Fen Cho fu do we get treated dis way," one Swedish man told her. "You shake hands wid us and your lady friends eat wid us at de same table. We tink we not lif long if we lif as de Chinese do." Eva commented, "It is a real treat for them to come to our American homes and to be treated as brothers indeed."[68]

On another occasion Mrs. Price befriended Sarah Seed who lived with another single woman at Xiaoyi. Miss Seed was a schoolmistress from Bradford, Yorkshire, who went out in 1883 at the age of twenty-nine; she married William Russell in 1891 and shortly after, had a nervous breakdown and took "an overdose of sleeping powder." (Mrs. Russell was one of three known suicides within the CIM; her death was not noted in *China's Millions* nor in the minutes of the China council.) "I only wish they could have thought it their duty to live in more comfort," Mrs. Price concluded of the whole CIM enterprise, "but they lived just about as the poorer Chinese do. I feel sure if she had taken better care of herself and lived in a more homelike way with good nourishing food, she could have stood it much longer here."[69]

Summing up the history of the Oberlin Band, Brandt notes that the goal of converting of fourteen million people in Shanxi was "so wildly improbable that it can only be labeled as misdirected fantasy. But the missionaries persisted, undaunted by any obstacle, real or imagined, undeterred by the comings and goings of missionary after missionary, unfaltering in the face of constant illness and death, and ever-eager and welcoming to a new crop of recruits."[70]

---

67. Ibid., p. 41.
68. Price, *China Journal 1889-1900*, p. 60.
69. Ibid., pp. 108, 110. Mrs. Russell's suicide is not mentioned in her record #152 (1883) in the "List of Missionaries 1853-1895," in CIM/SOAS, file 86.
70. Brandt, *Massacre in Shansi*, p. 38.

The Great Origin: Taiyuan

After the first generation of the CIM in Shanxi resigned, Hudson Taylor replaced them with people who were, A. J. Broomhall commented, "sufficiently at home with Christian theology and mission strategy to be unaffected by Richard's views."[71] They were also aristocrats in CIM terms, and since they were all self-supporting they displayed a certain *noblesse oblige* about obeying Hudson Taylor's rules concerning Chinese dress and simple living. Dr. Robert Harold Ainsworth Schofield was "a new phenomenon" in the CIM, a highly qualified physician and surgeon who had served with distinction in the Turkish wars. As soon as he arrived in Taiyuan he opened a dispensary, though he tried to restrict his medical practice until he got the language. "He had a large vocabulary which enabled him to speak without hesitation, and thus he made many (Chinese) friends." During his first year he treated fifty inpatients, including three operations under chloroform, and fifteen hundred outpatients. By his second year, he had 6,631 patients, including many wolf bites, and performed 292 operations, 47 under chloroform. In particular, he pioneered the *medical* treatment of opium addicts, establishing an "opium asylum" and administering the first experiment with hypodermic morphine (see Chapter 7).

He became infected with typhus from body lice and died tragically young, aged thirty-two. His last words were, "Tell Mr Taylor and the Council ... that these three years in China have been by far the happiest in my life." Then, his face "radiant with a brightness not of earth," he said, "Heaven at last," and was gone.[72] (In a postscript to Hudson Taylor, Mrs. Schofield added a special recognition, "Nothing could exceed Mr. Richard's attention and kindness to my dear husband." In turn, Richard called Dr. Schofield "one of the most brilliant medical missionaries who ever came to China.")[73]

Schofield and his wife had been praying that "God would open the hearts of the students at our Universities and Colleges to the needs of the Mission Fields of the world." His plea, amplified with the emotion of a Victorian funeral, became a clarion call to the next generation, and the CIM was besieged with college men, including the Cambridge Seven. "I have sometimes thought," Hudson Taylor wrote, "that in those prayers the greatest work of Harold Schofield was accomplished, and that, having finished

---

71. *HTCOC* 6, p. 291.
72. Ibid., pp. 314-17, "Harold Schofield: a seed in the ground." See letters from his wife and others, "Tidings from T'ai-yüen fu, Shan-si Province. Dr. Schofield's illness and death," *China's Millions* (GB), November 1883, pp. 155-57.
73. Richard, *Forty-Five Years in China*, p. 151.

the work that God had given him to do, he was then called to his eternal reward."[74]

Dr. Schofield's widow took the two children, one ten months old, to England, although they returned to Taiyuan, where she stayed for ten years.[75] His cousins, the Kemp sisters, barely six months in the country, with no mission skills except helping in the dispensary, were set adrift. "The Misses Kemp are not connected with us," *China's Millions* commented, "but we are very thankful for their presence and help."[76] Jessie married Thomas Wellesley Piggott and Florence married Dr. Ebenezer Henry Edwards, Schofield's successor, and they formed a cozy, close-knit dynasty. With Piggott's money and Dr. Edwards's expertise, they built the Schofield Memorial Hospital in Taiyuan, the first Western hospital in northwest China.

Tom Piggott was an Anglo-Irish aristocrat, as blunt and pugnacious as his name. Born in a country house near Dublin, he was the nephew of Lord Ashdowne and the brother of Sophia Piggott, the composer of "Jesus, I am resting, resting, in the joy of what Thou art," one of Hudson Taylor's (and Keswick's) favorite hymns. His obituary (written by Dr. Edwards) portrays him as a genial storyteller with a quick mind and a gift for language, of such forceful personality it was "impossible to remain unsympathetic in face of such zeal." As a boy, he had helped his father distribute tracts to the poor, had passed "uneventfully" through school and graduated with a BA from Trinity College, Dublin. He went to China in 1878 as an independent, half in and half out of the CIM, and put in five years of itineration as far as Manchuria and Kalgan. He settled in Taiyuan, where he and his wife established an Anglo-Irish household with a "rosewood piano and carved mahogany" furniture, and brought an English governess for their son, Wellesley Junior.[77]

Piggott was a leader of an "anti-CIM" faction within the CIM, and a thorn in Taylor's side for almost twenty years. He formed a "democracy" movement that challenged Taylor's autocratic rule and proposed that the rank-and-file should *vote* on the *Principles & Practice* — as if that were any way to run a mission. He was particularly critical of Chinese dress, for he changed in and

---

74. *HTCOC* 6, p. 317.
75. Mrs. Schofield was listed in *China's Millions* from 1884 onwards.
76. Schofield, annual report, 9 November 1882, in *China's Millions* (GB), July 1883, p. 85.
77. Ebenezer Henry Edwards, *Fire and Sword in Shansi: The Story of the Martyrdom of Foreigners and Chinese Christians* (Edinburgh: Oliphant, Anderson & Ferrier, 1900). For Piggott, see also Robert Coventry Forsyth, *The China Martyrs of 1900: A Complete Roll of the Christian Heroes Martyred in China in 1900 with Narratives of Survivors* (London: Religious Tract Society, 1904), pp. 34-38, 424-29.

out of Western clothes as he saw fit. When the China council was established in 1886 he demanded a place on it — as senior missionary in Shanxi, he felt he should be superintendent — and became increasingly outspoken when he was rejected. Hudson Taylor noted pointedly, "The one thing the work needs here is a head or captain, not too strong on the one hand [Piggott] nor a weakling [Dr. Edwards] on the other."[78]

As a compromise, Taylor appointed Piggott superintendent of South Shanxi, Pastor Hsi's territory. When Piggott reported that Hsi and his assistant Fan were "full of life and fire" but brought in "superstition and fanaticism,"[79] he "mortally offended Hsi and cannot return to Shanxi" (Taylor's words).[80] Taylor sent him out of the province, to Baoding, Zhili, on the imperial road to Shanxi, to open a business office for remittances and missionaries in transit, where he had no direct dealings with the Chinese. Hsi was getting to be a kingmaker.

The Cambridge Seven

The first foreigners to enter Hsi's hermetic world were the naive young men of the Cambridge Seven, who arrived at Pingyang in September 1885. Teacher Hsi had never met foreigners who could not speak Chinese and he was enchanted with their attempts to communicate by "pointing to verses of Scripture." He was charmed by Stanley Smith's "sunny nature," and Smith in turn was convinced Hsi was "really taught of God," although he found some of his practices "perplexing." Since the Seven had "no experience or settled theories of their own," they believed his genuineness and followed his guidance.[81] Moreover, they made the decision, virtually unprecedented in mission history, to work under him, rather than pull rank and impose their superiority over his work. D. E. Hoste explained, "It didn't require very much, whatever your theories on the subject might be, with regard to the relation of foreigner to Chinaman; and it wasn't any cleverness or ingenuity on our part to see that Pastor Hsi was head of it, and it was our place to recognize him in the position that he is. Not to become his helpers . . . [or] one of his lieutenants; that you cannot be, for one thing, and there is no occasion to be."[82]

78. JHT, Taiyuan, to Mrs. Jennie Taylor, 8 July 1886, *HTCOC 6*, p. 405.
79. Piggott, "Shan-si Province: The Work in P'ing-yang Fu and the Surrounding Towns and Villages," in *China's Millions* (GB), September 1884, p. 113.
80. *HTCOC 7*, p. 41.
81. *China's Millions* (GB), January 1886, p. 9, and F. W. Baller, "A Visit to Mr. Hsi," April 1886, pp. 45-46.
82. Hoste, "Notes of Mr. Hoste."

The Heavenly Invitation Offices

The seven young men stayed in Pingyang for three months studying the language under F. W. Baller, the master linguist, before they were dispersed to different cities where indigenous work had already started. Baller escorted William W. Cassels, the Anglican clergyman, and Montague Beauchamp, "the rich young ruler," to Xizhou (now Xi Xian, old spelling Hsi-chow), a county city west of the Fen River where another "remarkable work of grace" had been established by a former "Buddhist bishop" named Chang Chih-pen (pinyin Zhang Zhiben) and "a scholar and local school-master" named Ch'ü Wan-yih (pinyin Qu Wanyi).[83] A man had purchased a Gospel of Mark in Daning (old spelling Ta-ning), but had been confused by its obscure religious language and gave it to his friend, Teacher Ch'ü. Ch'ü and Chang began to worship it like a *baoquan*, a "precious volume" of scripture, burning incense to the book and to Jesus and the twelve apostles.[84] The two young Englishmen were "hopelessly at sea" in this strange environment. Since Cassels was better at understanding what the Chinese said and Beauchamp better at speaking, "they clung together as mutual ears and mouth."[85]

Cassels was impressed by the indigenous work, but "as a good Churchman he was exercised by the absence of much to which he was accustomed. Neither infant baptism nor confirmation were practiced in Shanxi, and the ordination of Pastors Hsi and Ch'ü was certainly not episcopal."[86] He panicked, and during an absence from the city the magistrate accused him of destroying an idol in a temple and locked his house; after he put pressure on the prefectural official the house was returned. Cassels remained at Xizhou for six months, until the end of 1886 when Hudson Taylor assigned him to start a Church of England diocese at Baoning, in East Sichuan.[87]

Stanley Smith, the firecracker, and Dixon E. Hoste, the soldier, remained at Pingyang. It was "an admirable combination," Mrs. Howard Taylor enthused, "Hsi, *plus* young, devoted, foreign workers."[88] Smith was making "wonderful progress in the language," and Hoste, despite his loss of face, sub-

---

83. The pinyin is from *HTCOC 7*, pp. 484-85.
84. Marshall Broomhall, *W. W. Cassels*, p. 65. *HTCOC 6*, p. 403. *China's Millions* (GB), February 1886, p. 18.
85. Broomhall, *W. W. Cassels*, p. 66.
86. Ibid., pp. 74-75. Since most CIM missionaries in Shanxi were Baptists, adult baptism was performed by immersion.
87. Bishop Cassels set up a family dynasty in the CIM. One daughter Jessie married P. A. Bruce, later headmaster of the famous Chefoo School for missionaries' children; Dorothy married Rev. Frank Houghton, Cassels' successor as Bishop of East Sichuan (1937-51) who later became general director of the CIM (1940-51). Frank's brother Stanley Houghton succeeded Bruce as headmaster of the Chefoo School.
88. *Pastor Hsi*, p. 161.

Dixon E. Hoste, bachelor, in Shanxi. Using a Cambridge boating metaphor, Hoste described himself as the "little man who sort of steered" Pastor Hsi, like the coxswain in a boat. He married Gertrude Broomhall, Hudson Taylor's niece, and became General Director in 1904. This delightfully informal snapshot is a contrast to his clipped, bearded appearance as an older man.

Source: Phyllis Thompson, *D. E. Hoste*.

The Heavenly Invitation Offices

ordinated himself doubly, first as "junior missionary" to Smith, then to Hsi, because he loved living among the Chinese and having his "utter rawness rubbed off." Smith, the dreamy intellectual, was also learning from Hsi: within a few months he was exorcising devils. "The more he was willing to let Pastor Hsi more and more keep his natural position, the more God seemed to bless him," wrote Hoste.[89]

At the beginning of 1886 Hsi asked Smith to "join him in opening a Refuge in Hung-t'ung city." Hongdong was the county (*xian*) city one stage north of Pingyang, and had always been a center of the Golden Pill and White Lotus sectarian religions. Even the Roman Catholics went back two hundred years, with a large cathedral. Hsi "had in his mind a very small place, and Stanley Smith went up there and saw that it would not do, and they looked about, and got the Hung-t'ung premises, which were in a dilapidated condition, and mortgaged them; then Mr. Taylor sanctioned Stanley Smith going there to be a missionary, practically." Smith was not "the man to run a big thing," Hoste recalled years later. He was a wonderful platform speaker, "but, so far as an oversight of God's church, he was as ignorant as a child . . . but he plunged along, and Pastor Hsi looked rather grim, but still he loved and appreciated him."[90]

It was a great temptation to interfere and correct Hsi when he pushed inexperienced converts into itinerant evangelism. In a schoolboy image Hoste wrote that Smith was acting like a "stroke," the pace-setter in rowing, "rather than a cox. It was a cox that was wanted, because Pastor Hsi was perfectly well able to stroke the boat; he had got plenty of men to pull behind him. What you want is a little man to sort of steer."[91] Hoste proved to be a wise and patient advisor, a little man who sort of steered Hsi for ten years until the latter's death. Smith on the other hand was so volatile that he lasted seven or eight months before he clashed with Hsi and had to be sent away. "God, in His providence, led S.P., away to the east of the Province, after that," said Hoste.

The Feeder of the Sheep

For years Hudson Taylor had been planning a pastoral visit to Shanxi, and by 1886 he could no longer delay. The mutinous Shanxi spirit had broken out

---

89. Hoste, "Notes of Mr. Hoste," p. 28. See also Phyllis Thompson, *D. E. Hoste: "A Prince with God"* (London: CIM, 1947), p. 55.

90. Hoste, "Notes of Mr. Hoste," pp. 25-28.

91. Ibid., p. 28. *HTCOC* 6, p. 411.

again, propelled by Piggott's criticisms of the China council. Moreover, Taylor had heard so much about Hsi Shengmo, the Overcomer of Demons, that he had to see for himself. Taylor's tour was a milestone both for the devotional spirit and the organizational decisions made behind the scenes. It was memorialized in a book by Montague Beauchamp, *Days of Blessing in Inland China*, often referred to in mission histories.[92]

In Taiyuan the CIM and BMS missionaries (Richard had resigned) gathered for a conference to hear Taylor's rambling, week-long talk on "the all-sufficiency of Christ for personal life and all the exigencies of service." He spoke a lot about persecution — that seemed to be on his mind. But, he asked rhetorically, were not the victories won by enduring persecution "ten thousand times better than writing to the Consul, and getting him to appeal to the Viceroy?" If the treaty rights were withdrawn, then the missionaries, having lost their privileged status, could "get shoulder to shoulder with our native converts, who are liable to be imprisoned, and robbed, and to have their tails and ears cut off."[93] This was explained to the converts. At a special examination for baptism in a village near Xiaoyi, "it was clearly pointed out that their profession would involve them in persecution, and even death might be the outcome." (Roger Thompson noted that those were prescient words, for during the Boxer time, the first CIM martyrs were the two women missionaries at Xiaoyi; the converts were tracked down from their names on a ceremonial banner.)[94]

Since Hsi could not come so far, the Venerable Chief Pastor Taylor went to him. At Hongdong, a "glorious conference" of three hundred Christians and enquirers was the largest Christian gathering ever held in Shanxi. J. W. Stevenson, the deputy China director, preached a sermon on "The Kingdom of God is not in words, but in power." Hudson Taylor "glowed with happiness" as men and women rose to give their testimonies. That afternoon he helped to baptize fifty-six men and women.[95]

Hsi invited Taylor to his home, the Middle Eden, a privilege he granted to few foreigners, for consultations concerning the church and "the financial basis and the extension of the Refuge work." Hsi certainly knew his way into an

---

92. Montague Beauchamp, *Days of Blessing in Inland China: Being an Account of Meetings held in the Province of Shansi* (London: Morgan & Scott, 1887). See also *Growth of a Work of God*, pp. 401-18. *Pastor Hsi*, pp. 167-79. *China's Millions* (GB), December 1886, pp. 160-65 (Taiyuan), and January 1887 (Pingyang).

93. Beauchamp, *Days of Blessing in Inland China*, pp. 52, 39.

94. Roger Thompson, "Twilight of the Gods," p. 61.

95. *HTCOC 6*, pp. 406-7. This number was exceeded by the 72 baptisms at the first "annual native conference" the previous spring: *Growth of a Work of God*, p. 403.

The Heavenly Invitation Offices

old man's heart: beside the washbasin was a new bar of Pear's soap. Taylor decided the time had come for a forward movement in Shanxi and he established a hierarchy of deacons, elders, and pastors. He ordained Gatekeeper Sung as pastor of the Pingyang congregation and the Scholar Ch'ü at Xizhou, and designated Elder Sï, Hsi's brother-in-law (his wife's sister's husband, and later his successor).[96] Another who was ordained, with disastrous consequences, was Elder Fan, who resented that his life's work had been taken over by Hsi. To ordain Hsi would have been a demotion, for he had been leader for six years, so Taylor merely confirmed his "divine appointment," making him "Superintending Pastor" of the three districts of South Shanxi, the "watcher over and feeder of the sheep of God."[97] In the twilight as the Christians sang the songs of Zion, Taylor felt as if he were living in the "days of heaven upon earth; nothing seemed difficult."[98]

The next morning they held a business meeting, which was to have farreaching ramifications. Many matters had to be discussed, such as the question of self-support for the church with its newly ordained pastors, and "the best way of spreading far and wide a knowledge of the Gospel." As his first request, Pastor Hsi asked for some single women missionaries to work under Mrs. Hsi. Then, pointing out the little opium refuge in a corner of the courtyard, he suggested opening refuges as beachheads for mission extension. Archibald Orr Ewing, the CIM's greatest benefactor, who accompanied Taylor's party, offered to pay the rent for Hsi's refuges and the salaries of the keepers if Hsi would "undertake all the responsibility, find and train workers, decide upon suitable localities, and establish Refuges as widely as possible." Presumably he would also supply the medicines, the famous red pills, while the missionaries would care "for the spiritual interests of the work." As a result of this meeting, Mrs. Howard Taylor added, "Mr. Orr Ewing was already winning for himself among Shansi Christians the beautifully suggestive name of 'Glory-face.'"[99]

"It all unfolded and developed in the most natural way," Mrs. Taylor concluded, in her omniscient style. "The key fitted the lock, opened the door, and gave access to a wide beyond of opportunity and promise."[100] Within six years, Hsi had opened forty refuges in four provinces, employing two hun-

---

96. *Pastor Hsi*, pp. 188-90. Elder Sï was such a "hopeless" addict that Fan refused him entry into the refuge. Sï appealed directly to Hsi, and after he was cured, lived in Hsi's home as a disciple and married Mrs. Hsi's younger sister.
97. *HTCOC* 6, pp. 405, 407.
98. *Pastor Hsi*, p. 184.
99. Ibid., pp. 214-15.
100. Ibid., p. 100.

dred men and women and treating two to three thousand addicts a year. But we are getting ahead of ourselves.

As soon as Taylor and his party left, Pastor Hsi moved into Smith's rooms and preached a sermon on "Now is the Son of Man glorified," in which he showed "how the principle works out in human experience and instancing his own." Elder Fan had been a troublemaker for years and now, in the absence of the missionaries, he "revealed his true colours." He organized a gang to break up the refuges, steal the medicine, and set up rival refuges. This culminated in a murderous attack when Fan screamed, "You used me as a ladder to rise upon. You keep us all away from the foreigners while working yourself into favour. Now they come along and make you a great man." The gang bound Hsi hand-and-foot and brought him to Benjamin Bagnall, the superintendent. The scene, Bagnall wrote, was like being in hell.[101]

For a while Elder Fan "flourished," opening twenty refuges that "employed men of disreputable character, anybody and everybody who would come to them, dragging the fair reputation of the Refuge work in the mire. These agents they sent out far and wide to sell Hsi's well-known medicines everywhere." Meanwhile Hsi remained calm, prophesying, "We do not need to fight in this battle. *Within three months* you will see the last of these spurious Refuges brought to an end." Plagued by mismanagement and a lack of pills, each of the false refuges closed or rejoined Hsi's organization within three months.

The story of Elder Fan had a sequel. Smith, too, had mortally wounded Pastor Hsi by sympathizing with Fan, "knowing that Hsi had not always been wise." As a result Smith could no longer stay at Hongdong. He moved to Luan, one hundred miles east on the road to North Henan, taking Fan with him. "Deluded by the devil," Fan "used every spite against us that he could possibly devise." Smith spent his first year "trying to pull down the spurious work. . . . It was rotten to the very core."[102] Fan remained at Luan during the 1890s, then disappeared from the records except for two cryptic footnotes in the first editions of *Pastor Hsi*, removed from later versions. Years after the troubles he confessed his wrongdoing and paid his respects to Hsi; despite the public reconciliation, he continued to live in "his old heathen surroundings, growing opium, and going to theatricals in the temples, though he has never worshipped idols."[103] After the Boxer uprising, Fan was "restored to church fellowship," although the missionaries did so "with a certain amount of fear

---

101. Ibid., pp. 196-200.
102. Stanley Smith, "Six Years in China," *China's Millions* (GB), July 1892, p. 91.
103. Footnote in *Pastor Hsi*, vol. 2 (1903), p. 238.

and trembling. He still gives us a good deal of anxiety, though he has his better moments." He told the missionary, "weeping, that he is not *free*."[104]

The white-hot fervor of South Shanxi climaxed in April 1887 when 214 people, including 52 "female enquirers," were baptized in a daylong ceremony. The male missionaries baptized most of the men, while Hsi baptized all the women and the rest of the men: saving face was important. This mass baptism, widely reported in Britain and China, raised many questions about the CIM and its methods. Even Hsi came to feel that they had acted without due caution and that "it was necessary to exercise greater care" in the future. Hoste wrote hesitantly years later, "I, myself, never regretted that baptism — never seriously, of course, I regretted it to some extent, but I mean, the wholesale denunciations of it. There had been baptisms before. We [the chapel at Hongdong] had taken over eighty, who had been baptized at P'ing-iang. As a matter of fact, of course, we were fearfully talked of for letting all sorts of ragtag and bobtail into the church, and there was no discipline, etc. As a matter of fact, those eighty whom we took from P'ing-iang were the lowest standard in the lot."[105]

Many missionaries were consumed by a "dread of Hsi," but as Pat Barr noted, "overt criticisms of Hsi were an embarrassment and tended to remain unvoiced."[106] Writing confidentially, Eva Jane Price of the Oberlin Band summed up the outside view: "Dr. Taylor is not liked very well by the members of our mission," and his "methods of work are not very satisfactory in many instances. . . . The Chinese profess to be Christians and are baptized and often make fine stories for *China's Millions* or the *Herald*, but only a very small proportion of them are genuine. As to Mr. Taylor himself, many feel that he is a hypocrite but I believe he is a good Christian man, striving honestly for the salvation of China and not self-glory. Those of his mission we have met we like very much and some of them are dear friends. Some are unwise and too easily deceived by these crafty Chinese, but we all get taken in too often."[107]

Stanley Smith, the person closest to the epicenter, summed up the inside view. Five years after the mass baptism, he reported that of the 214, only "fifty had definitely backslided, while another twenty were difficult to trace [i.e. a total of one-third had left]. Of the backsliders, most of whom had returned to opium smoking, less than twenty lapsed into idolatry, while some continued

---

104. Ibid., "Note to Fourth Edition" (added 1904), pp. 1-2.
105. Hoste, "Notes of Mr. Hoste," p. 51.
106. Barr, *To China with Love*, p. 139.
107. Price, *China Journal*, pp. 115-16.

to hold family worship." Nevertheless, as far as results, Smith confided, "I would not like to speak of much definite result. One gets more and more afraid of speaking of results."[108]

The Cambridge Seven marked the end of the second generation, which had started with the bombshell of 1875. Three events stand out in this chapter, each of which set off a chain of events. The first, which I emphasize, was the Cambridge Seven's decision to work under Pastor Hsi, to learn from him. Charlie Studd's experiments with speaking in tongues was the other side of the same coin. The third was Orr Ewing's offer to finance Pastor Hsi's opium refuges. After that, things spun out of control, as we shall when we return to Shanxi in Chapter 11. First we must follow the Pilgrim to Toronto to meet the next generation of pilgrims.

---

108. Phyllis Thompson, *D. E. Hoste*, p. 56.

PART III

The Third Generation
1888-1900

After this I beheld, and lo, a great multitude, which no man could number, of all nations, and kindreds, and people, and tongues, stood before the throne, and before the Lamb, clothed with white robes, and palms in their hands; And cried with a loud voice, saying, Salvation to our God, which sitteth upon the throne, and unto the Lamb. . . . And one of the elders answered, saying unto me, What are these which are arrayed in white robes? and whence came they? . . . And he said unto me, These are they which came out of great tribulation, and have washed their robes, and made them white in the blood of the Lamb.

Revelation 7:9-14 (KJV)

CHAPTER 9

The New World

1888-1900

[I]t became clear to us, as time went on, that we [the North American branch] could not look to the [China Inland] Mission in England for advice in the developing of our North American work. This was not because our English friends were lacking in wisdom, but because their experience had been insular while our need was continental.

Henry W. Frost, *Memoirs*[1]

The Third Vision

We have turned another page. Once again the Pilgrim is at sea. It is July 1888, three years after the Cambridge Seven, and Hudson Taylor is steaming across the Atlantic to the New World. In the thirty-five years since he sailed to China, he had been from Britain to China and back six times without crossing either the Atlantic or Pacific Oceans. Now that the Canadian Pacific Railway had opened a continent and shortened the distance to China by a week or two, Dwight L. Moody had invited Taylor to speak at a few meetings in "America." Yet when Moody suggested that Taylor establish an "American branch" of the

---

1. Frost, "Memoirs," p. 522. Henry Weston Frost's 932-page manuscript, which he entitled *The Days that are Past,* is *the* primary source for the CIM in North America and the basis for Dr. and Mrs. Howard Taylor's book *"By Faith": Henry W. Frost and the China Inland Mission.* (For JHT's visit see pp. 76-108.) It is interesting to contrast Frost's original, which is candid and fulsome, with the Taylors' official history. The OMF Archives in Toronto also has a bound volume of 950 applications to the Toronto office between 1888 and 1915 (copy in CIM/ABGC). Cited as CIM Application Records (Toronto).

The first North American party of CIM missionaries. In 1888 Hudson Taylor decided to take the Canadian Pacific Railway across Canada as an alternate route to China. After speaking at the Niagara prophetic conference, he established a North American branch based in Toronto. Three weeks later, he escorted twelve Canadians and two Americans to China. The North American branch became an important feeder of personnel and money to the mission, and tried to impose an American "fundamentalist" character on the more "tolerant" British CIM.
Source: OMF/Toronto.

China Inland Mission "that might work as a feeder of men and money," Taylor shook his head sadly, saying, "The Lord has given me no light about it."[2]

The fame of the Cambridge Seven had preceded him through the wide distribution of Benjamin Broomhall's volume, *The Evangelisation of the*

---

2. Marshall Broomhall, *The Jubilee Story of the China Inland Mission*, p. 184. The first North American party has been described several times: *Growth of a Work of God*, pp. 439-55. *HTCOC 7*, pp. 76-92; David Michell, *In God's Way: The Impressive Centennial Story of the China Inland Mission/Overseas Missionary Fellowship in North America* (Toronto: OMF, 1988). I have also written on the transplanting of the CIM to North America.

The New World

World. J. E. Kynaston Studd, a brother of the cricket player Charlie Studd, led an English delegation to Moody's school in Massachusetts in 1884, and brother George went in 1888, two events that helped transplant the British student missions movement to America. Moody, arguably the most famous man in America, had been instrumental in the Seven's conversion and recruitment, and used their example in his schools at Northfield, Massachusetts, and Chicago to inspire a new generation of North American students.

No, Hudson Taylor said, he was too old to start such an international venture that a North American branch would entail. It would be better if Moody and his friends started their own independent mission based on the CIM's faith principles. Nevertheless, he did accept Moody's invitation, and sailed to New York with his son Dr. Howard Taylor, the future historian, who had just completed his medical degree. They were accompanied by Silvester Whitehouse, Taylor's private secretary who was considering whether to join the CIM, and Reginald Radcliffe, the fiery evangelist of the 1859 revival, and his wife. At Northfield, where Moody had established a summer camp in the town of his birth, Taylor presided as an elder statesman over an "inspiring assembly" which formally inaugurated the Student Volunteer Movement for Foreign Missions.[3] The SVM, which chose as its watchword, "The Evangelization of the World in This Generation," was to become the foremost recruiting agency for overseas missionaries, sending out eight thousand college-educated men and women between 1886 and 1920.[4] Taylor was shocked by the casualness of American students — short-sleeved shirts and tennis racquets — and saw no reason to change his mind. Mrs. Radcliffe remarked, "There are big hearts and heavy purses in America, but like the old country, men are bound by preconceived notions."[5]

Taylor's next stop was the Believers' Conference at Niagara-on-the-Lake, Ontario, a quiet border town on the Niagara River, about ten miles north of Niagara Falls, on Lake Ontario. Standing at the edge of the cataract, Taylor had another vision. In 1865, staring into the lapping waves at Brighton Beach he had seen four hundred million Chinese marching around the equator.

---

3. *Growth of a Work of God*, p. 443.

4. There has been considerable study of the SVM. Valentin H. Rabe, *The Home Base of American China Missions, 1880-1920* (Cambridge: Harvard University Press, 1978). Michael Parker, *The Kingdom of Character: The Student Volunteer Movement for Foreign Missions (1886-1926)* (Lanham, Md.: American Society of Missiology, University Press of America, 1998). Nathan D. Showalter, *The End of a Crusade: The Student Volunteer Movement for Foreign Missions and the Great War* (Lanham, Md.: Scarecrow Press, 1998).

5. Mrs. Reginald Radcliffe to Mrs. Jennie Taylor, *HTCOC 7*, p. 83.

Now, at Niagara his emotions were as turbulent and unformed as the raging current. The Second Coming was near, time was running out, humanity was sweeping over the edge.

As soon as Taylor crossed into "British" Canada, the difference was palpable: "Collegians at Northfield and parsons at Niagara," he noted approvingly, and "the Premillennial Advent is prominent."[6] In his talk that evening Taylor did not mention the CIM; rather "he spoke, as a little child might speak, as a prophet might speak, as one who sees a vision of a needy land and a dying people might speak. And when, after a hour, he finished, there was a great sigh from the listening throng, followed by a silence which was profound."[7]

The next morning he left for Chicago to help Moody recruit students for what would become Moody Bible Institute. "My Father manages the trains," he waved a cheery bye, "and I'll be there."[8] After Taylor left, the conference broke into "organized pandemonium" as people became "intoxicated with the joy of giving," pledging $2,000, enough to support eight "North American workers" in China for a year. (This figure, $250 each per year, which Radcliffe translated from £50, was far too low, and had to be revised.) Led by God's guidance, Taylor abruptly canceled his tickets for China and announced the formation of a North American branch of the CIM. In his appeal, he said: "To have missionaries and no money would be no trouble to me, for the Lord is bound to take care of His own.... But to have money and no missionaries is very serious indeed. And I do not think it will be kind of you dear friends in America to put this burden upon us, and not to send from among yourselves to use the money. We have the dollars, but where are the people?"[9]

Just as Taylor had scooped up the converts of the 1859 Revival for the *Lammermuir*, he arrived in North America in time to catch the waves of mission enthusiasm that were sweeping through the college campuses and prophetic conferences. Within three months, from July to September 1888, Taylor received over sixty applications, of whom he accepted fourteen — two Americans and twelve Canadians — to join him immediately. The first was Susie Parker of Northfield, whose father gave her, saying, "I have nothing too precious for my Lord Jesus." A year later, when she died in China, he said simply, "I have given my best to Jesus."[10] The second was Edith Lucas, an educated

---

6. Ibid., pp. 82-83.
7. Taylor and Taylor, *"By Faith,"* p. 88.
8. *HTCOC 7*, p. 89.
9. *Growth of a Work of God*, p. 449.
10. Alvyn Austin, *Saving China: Canadian Missionaries in the Middle Kingdom 1888-1959* (Toronto: University of Toronto Press, 1986), pp. 6, 19.

The New World

Jewish convert, a "relative of the late Sir Moses Montefiore and the Rothschilds," who was working as a nurse in Moody's household.[11]

Taylor decided to establish a North American branch based in Toronto — not New York or Chicago — so he sat down with a railway timetable to chart "out an itinerary, date by date and city by city, until Toronto might be reached at an appropriate time."[12] He made huge looping tours from New York to Chicago, and beyond to Nebraska and Kansas, where he connected with the remarkable revivals conducted by Frederik Franson among Swedish Americans. He passed through southern Ontario twice from Windsor to Montreal, following the well-worn "sawdust trail" laid down by British, American, and Canadian evangelists. At each place Taylor connected with a colonial branch of British evangelicalism, and the recruits were predominantly first-generation British immigrants. In Guelph, it was the Plymouth Brethren, where John Nelson Darby had established several chapels and a summer conference.[13] In Hamilton — where Phoebe Palmer had ignited the great revival of 1857 — Taylor found a YMCA Bible study group "united in earnest prayer that seven of their number might be privileged to go as missionaries to China."[14] He called six immediately, and came back for seven more the following year.

At Belleville and Stratford, Annie Macpherson operated the Marchmount Homes, the distribution homes for the hundreds of orphans she brought from the slums of Britain to Canada. She had been Taylor's friend since 1865, and every departing party of CIM candidates spoke at her Home of Industry. She happened to be in Canada and encouraged Taylor, saying, "I believe there are more brave and well-educated men waiting for your beloved China in the Canadian colleges than in any other part of the globe."[15] One of her charges,

---

11. *HTCOC* 7, pp. 85-86. She married Archibald Ewing (not to be confused with Archibald Orr Ewing, the benefactor).

12. Taylor and Taylor, *"By Faith,"* p. 90.

13. Sandeen, *The Roots of Fundamentalism*, pp. 71-80, stated that Darby spent almost seven years in southwestern Ontario between 1862 and 1877, and established an annual conference near Guelph. For Methodist suspicion of Plymouth Brethren "supposed evangelists" in Ontario, see Phyllis D. Airhart, *Serving the Present Age: Revivalism, Progressivism, and the Methodist Tradition in Canada* (Kingston and Montreal: McGill-Queen's University Press, 1992), pp. 39-48.

14. *Growth of a Work of God*, p. 451.

15. *HTCOC* 7, p. 78. For the Marchmount Homes, see Bagnell, *The Little Immigrants: The Orphans Who Came to Canada*, pp. 24-27. In 1869 Annie Macpherson and Ellen Bilbrough escorted five hundred orphans to Canada. In 1870, accompanied by a group of one hundred, Miss Bilbrough was given the Belleville home. For Horne and Munro, see their applications in CIM Application Records (Toronto).

George W. Clarke, had been the first CIM missionary who had lived in Canada. Miss Macpherson had sent him there as a teenager, where "he worked on the transcontinental railways and as a lumberjack, earning enough to attend college." Returning to England, he applied to the CIM in 1875 and took the usual training at the East London Missionary Training College. He became a pioneer in Yunnan and Shanxi, where he opened the station at Datong; he outlived three wives and died in 1919 after forty-five years service.[16]

At Belleville, Taylor called two orphans who had grown up and joined the staff as child-care workers, William Horne and Jeannie Munro. In addition, he called the chaplain of the Marchmount Home, Rev. Robert Wallace, and his wife, Ellen Agnes Bilbrough, a woman of "limitless devotion" and "rare gifts," to act as surrogate parents, as William and Mary Berger had done during the infancy of the CIM.[17] They took the applicants into their home, where they judged their aptitude for service and trained them in practical work. Wallace was the senior member of the Toronto council and contributed "frequent and generous gifts" to the CIM; they even took an extended tour of China. After Ellen's death in 1901, Wallace married Hudson Taylor's favorite niece, Edith Broomhall, daughter of Benjamin Broomhall, thus cementing Taylor's transatlantic family. In 1915, when he retired from the Marchmount Homes, he joined the CIM staff as treasurer in Toronto and Philadelphia.[18]

Taylor's secretary wrote a confidential assessment of each candidate. Jeannie Munro was a "delicate intellectual lady," while her friend Rebecca Mackenzie was a "master-mind" who moved one with her eloquence. Susie Parker was a "quiet home-bird." Among the men, George Duff was "more of the butcher type and was engaged in that business." Hamilton Racey — who was to succumb to typhoid fever within six months — was a "great child-like" man, "so tender that you nearly weep when he speaks in simple style of his 'mother' and 'sister' in public."[19]

After a series of never-to-be-forgotten meetings on 25 September 1888, Taylor and the "North American *Lammermuir* party" were escorted to the Toronto train station in a hymn-singing, torch-lit parade down Yonge Street,

---

16. *HTCOC* 7, pp. 9-40.

17. For Agnes Bilbrough Wallace, see Bagnell, *Little Immigrants*, pp. 25, 193-94. Her papers are in the National Archives of Canada, including an account of their trip to China in 1896.

18. Frost, "Memoirs," pp. 515, 797-98.

19. S. F. Whitehouse, on board S.S. *Batavia*, to Mrs. Jennie Taylor, 5 October 1888, in CIM/SOAS, file 337. Whitehouse, aged 21, joined the CIM for four years, returned to China under the Bible Society of Scotland, then joined the BMS. He died during the Boxer Uprising in Taiyuan.

the main street. Taylor had appointed Henry Weston Frost as the Secretary for the United States and Alfred Sandham for Canada, with a grandly named "International Council." When Frost protested that he knew nothing about interviewing candidates or forwarding funds, Taylor replied, "Quite true, but the Lord will help you." This, Frost wrote, was "a distressingly simple word, characteristic of the man, but not exactly practical in its application."[20]

As the train steamed across the flat prairies, Taylor's vision at Niagara Falls continued to haunt his imagination. China *could be redeemed,* he declared, despite the chaos and the onslaughts of Satan. A year later he wrote a pamphlet called *To Every Creature* (1889), which dramatically showed his state of mind. In his most astounding piece of missionary arithmetic — he who had difficulty in converting English pounds to American dollars — Taylor calculated that the whole of China from Shanghai to Tibet could be evangelized by "one thousand whole-hearted [foreign] evangelists, male and female" in one thousand days. China was a nation of families, he calculated. Estimating the population at 250 million, and assuming each family unit had five members, "there will be about 50 millions of families; if fifty families were reached daily for 1,000 days by each of the 1,000 evangelists, every creature in China could be reached in three years' time, leaving the evangelists two or three Sundays for rest each month." Since these imaginary families lived in imaginary "courts or quadrangles containing from four to ten families each," the evangelist would need to spend only "four days in a village of 1,000 inhabitants, or two such workers would need to spend ten days in a market-town of 5,000."[21]

"Shall a work which 1,000 workers might accomplish in three years of steady work, after two years of preparation, be thought of as chimerical, and beyond the resources of the Christian Church?" he asked rhetorically. Evidently, the Shanghai Missionary Conference of 1890 did not think so. Taylor gave the opening meditation at the conference, in which he appealed for one thousand "men" over the next five years, not for the CIM alone but all Protestant bodies combined. Exactly 1,153 *men and women* did go to China between 1890 and 1895, in all Protestant missions, and thus Taylor's vision at Niagara sparked the explosion of the missionary movement at the high tides of imperialism.[22]

20. Frost, "Memoirs," p. 217.
21. JHT, "To Every Creature," *China's Millions* (GB), December 1889, pp. 171-73, and February 1890, pp. 14-17; it was published as a booklet. See *Growth of a Work of God,* pp. 479-82. *HTCOC 7,* pp. 116-17.
22. *Growth of a Work of God,* pp. 483-88, 537. *HTCOC 7,* pp. 138-43, "Third General Missionary Conference, Shanghai."

The Transatlantic Cables

The China Inland Mission was one of several British associations that established a branch in Canada as a beachhead to the United States — among them the Plymouth Brethren and the YMCA in the 1850s, and the Salvation Army in the 1880s.[23] Its transplanting illuminates the complex transatlantic cables that linked evangelicals in Britain, Canada, and the United States. In Britain the CIM had been present at the creation of many evangelical movements: Dr. Barnardo's Homes, Keswick, Moody's British revivals, the anti-opium crusade, and the faith mission movement, and it drew upon a wide range of schools and Bible institutes, including Mildmay, the East London Training Institute, and Spurgeon's Pastors' College.[24] In Toronto it repeated the process.

Using the transatlantic cables to transplant itself, it formed local networks of congregations, which publicized the CIM through the national denominations and associations across Canada. Simultaneously, Frost through his American connections used Moody's and A. B. Simpson's continental networks to expand into the United States. The CIM helped establish, among others, Toronto Bible College,[25] Vancouver Bible Training School,[26] Moody Bible Institute, the Philadelphia School of the Bible, and the Bible Institute of Los Angeles. In the United States it became "the favorite mission of American Fundamentalists" after it moved its North American headquarters to Philadelphia in 1901.[27] Nevertheless, well into the 1930s Toronto remained the

---

23. For the transplanting of the Salvation Army, see R. G. Moyles, *The Blood and Fire in Canada: A History of the Salvation Army in the Dominion, 1882-1976* (Toronto: Peter Martin, 1977).

24. In the 1920s with the collapse of the SVM, the British CIM helped create the Varsity Christian Fellowship and sent delegates (such as Desmond Guinness) to Canada and the United States to organize the first North American branches of Inter-Varsity Christian Fellowship.

25. Alvyn Austin, "Hotbed of Missions: The China Inland Mission, Toronto Bible College, and the Bible School Movement," in Grant Wacker and Daniel H. Bays, eds., *The Foreign Missionary Enterprise at Home: Explorations in North American Cultural History* (Mobile: University of Alabama Press, 2003).

26. Robert K. Burkinshaw, *Pilgrims in Lotus Land: Conservative Protestants in British Columbia 1917-1981* (Montreal and Kingston: McGill-Queen's University Press, 1995), pp. 60-75, stated that between 1917, when the CIM established a transit home in Vancouver, and 1947, when it was closed, the CIM and its daughter Vancouver Bible Training School were "the most important" institutions of the Vancouver evangelical network (p. 57).

27. Joel A. Carpenter, "Propagating the Faith Once Delivered: The Fundamentalist Missionary Enterprise 1920-1945," in Joel A. Carpenter and Wilbert R. Shenk, eds., *Earthen Vessels: American Evangelicals and Foreign Missions, 1880-1980* (Grand Rapids: William B.

more important center, as the publishing base and receiving home for Canadian and many American applicants.

Toronto used to be one of the great evangelical cities of the world, and the CIM struck deep roots into its fertile British soil. The CIM became Canadian in Canada as it was English in England because it was an association, not a denomination. If one looks at Canadian evangelicalism through a denominational focus, there were turf wars and denominational controversies as the denominations grew to national institutions, each an empire unto itself. But Canadian churches could not expand across the border: the United States did not need, say, a transplanted Church of England in Canada.

The interdenominational associations demonstrated the broad "irenic" consensus of Canadian evangelicalism, its inclusiveness and flexibility. Perhaps the greatest achievement of this cooperative spirit was the "common Christianity" of the Ontario public school system, broadly evangelical but not evangelistic. Canadian religion, the novelist Sara Jeannette Duncan wrote, was "not beautiful, or dramatic, or self-immolating; it was reasonable."[28] It was in this soil that the CIM flourished, and like other Anglo-Canadian organizations, crossed the border to bring an "attraction and freshness" to American religion.[29]

The strongest of Taylor's transatlantic cables was the Believers' Conference, held at Niagara-on-the-Lake every year from 1883 to 1898. "Niagara" was the "mother" of the prophetic meetings that proliferated between the 1880s and the First World War — "the Monte Cassino and Port Royal" of fundamentalism, the historian Ernest Sandeen called it — which attracted "virtually everyone of any significance in the history of the American millenarian movement." There, Keswick Holiness and premillennial dispensationalism coalesced into a "protodenominational fellowship" that came to be called "fundamentalism." Niagara was unique: a Canadian border town where American preachers came to study British teachings under Canadian and British teachers.[30]

Eerdmans, 1990), pp. 92-132, discussed the CIM and its Chicago connection with Moody Bible Institute and Wheaton College.

28. Sara Jeannette Duncan, *The Imperialist* (1904; reprint, Toronto: McClelland & Stewart, 1984), pp. 60-61.

29. This was one American's description of the Niagara Conference, in Sandeen, *Roots of Fundamentalism*, p. 132. John G. Stackhouse, Jr., *Canadian Evangelicalism in the Twentieth Century: An Introduction to Its Character* (Toronto: University of Toronto Press, 1993), contrasted the two *mentalités* of Canadian evangelicalism, which he calls "churchish" and "sectish." It is significant that "churchish" organizations tended to have British roots, while the "sectish" ones (such as the C&MA) showed a distinct American influence.

30. Sandeen, *Roots of Fundamentalism*, pp. 132-34. There has been considerable debate concerning the role of the Niagara Conference, and of premillennialism in particular, in

Since Shanghai was the head office, Taylor decided that Toronto should be an autonomous "branch," not an "auxiliary," equal to London and responsible for raising its own funds and supporting its own missionaries. London was appalled. Benjamin Broomhall, already embroiled with Taylor concerning the *Principles & Practice* and the *Book of Arrangements*, threatened to resign and take the council with him if Taylor made "the North American work an integral part of the Mission."[31] He warned that "when the authority is divided and the responsibility divided, there is weakness, and there is danger."[32] America would be a drain on the finances and, he said flatly, English people could never work in harmony with Americans. The North American "auxiliary" would succeed, Broomhall concluded, only if candidates came to London for approval, as one or two Canadians had already done.

Writing from China, Taylor's response was bleak: "If God has finished with the old China Inland Mission and wishes to start a new one, He will do it, and He will make no mistake. . . . But if it be God's will, I shall not move a finger to avert it." To Henry Frost, Taylor took the opposite tone: "if you have any godly men fit for the work, *don't keep them back*; and if you have any suitable women and a suitable escort . . . *don't keep them back*."[33] Staying in Shanghai long enough to send the North Americans inland, Taylor made a special trip to England to calm the council. They had not been at Niagara, he explained; they had not seen the leading of the Spirit. The CIM was too prominent to be torn apart by a family squabble. The council acquiesced to

---

American fundamentalism. Sandeen, who emphasized premillennialism, stressed Niagara's centrality, while more inclusive historians give it less prominence. George M. Marsden, *Fundamentalism and American Culture: The Shaping of Twentieth-Century Evangelicalism 1870-1925* (Oxford: Oxford University Press, 1980), pp. 3-4, argued that "Militant opposition to modernism was what most clearly set off fundamentalism from a number of closely related traditions, such as evangelicalism, revivalism, pietism, the holiness movements, millenarianism, Reformed confessionalism, Baptist traditionalism, and other denominational orthodoxies." Joel A. Carpenter, *Revive Us Again: The Reawakening of American Fundamentalism* (New York: Oxford University Press, 1997), is the most significant recent study. As to Niagara's prominence in transplanting the CIM, JHT said succinctly, "The work really originated at the Niagara Believers' Meetings" (*HTCOC 7*, p. 96). In 1989 the OMF unveiled a monument at the site of the Queen's Hotel to commemorate the Niagara Conference and JHT's visit.

31. Frost, "Memoirs," p. 256: the correspondence is quoted verbatim at pp. 237-48, and 256-64. The original letters are in CIM/ABGC, file 5/11. See also *HTCOC 7*, pp. 99-105, "No Crisis at All."

32. Robert Caldwell, London council, to Frost, 20 February 1899, in CIM/ABGC. Frost, "Memoirs," p. 244.

33. Both quotes from JHT to Frost, 5 March 1889, in CIM/ABGC. Frost, "Memoirs," pp. 253-54.

Taylor's vision. Although they sent fraternal greetings to Toronto, it took five years before harmony was achieved between London and Toronto.

In 1890 Taylor made a trip to Australia, where an interdenominational nucleus of Anglicans, Baptists, and Brethren had already established a temporary council. Because Australia was a British Dominion like Canada, Taylor was able to utilize the transatlantic/transpacific cables to connect with evangelicals throughout the British Empire. A few Australians had gone to China independently, where they had been accepted directly by the China council, and several British CIMers had migrated to Melbourne and Sydney. Harry Guinness, the son of Grattan, married a woman from Tasmania, Anne Nicoll, daughter of a CIM pioneer, George Nicoll, who was to become "the mother-to-be of future members of the CIM and other notables." Henry Soltau, the first honorary secretary, also moved to Australia after a term in China. The chairman of the Australia–New Zealand branch was Rev. H. B. Macartney, an Anglican curate, and the secretary was Philip Kitchen, a Plymouth Brethren.[34]

Toronto the Good

Three years before Taylor arrived, in 1885, Toronto city had acquired the nickname of "Toronto the Good" when D. L. Moody and Ira Sankey held a revival that drew an audience estimated at 25,000, half the adult population of the city. That year a Sunday school teacher named William Howland was elected mayor, promising to clean up the city, and under his tutelage it became a city run by and for evangelicals. It was the sort of place where the daily newspaper ran a contest to vote for the most popular pulpit preacher of the day.[35]

Hudson Taylor did indeed arrive in Toronto at an appropriate time. There was tremendous missionary excitement in the colleges and churches, but there was no outlet, no movement. By establishing the CIM, Taylor did not so much ignite "fires of missionary enthusiasm" as fan the glowing embers into flame. The University of Toronto, Queen's in Kingston, and McGill in Montreal all had branches of the Student Volunteer Movement ready to ignite with zeal to evangelize the world. The first Canadian Protestant missionaries had been sent overseas two generations earlier, in 1846, when the Maritime

---

34. For CIM in Australia, see *Growth of a Work of God*, pp. 488-98; *HTCOC* 7, pp. 146-52.

35. John Webster Grant, *A Profusion of Spires: Religion in Nineteenth-Century Ontario* (Burlington, Ont.: Welch Publishing, 1988), p. 175; for foreign missions, pp. 186-88.

Presbyterians sent John and Charlotte Geddie to the New Hebrides, and the Maritime Baptists sent Richard Burpee to the American field in Burma. Yet, by 1888, the national denominations supported only three small missions overseas, the Methodists in Japan (1873), the Presbyterians in Taiwan (1871) under the redoubtable George Leslie Mackay, and in India (1873).[36]

Just a few weeks before Taylor arrived in Toronto, Jonathan Goforth and his wife, the author and painter Rosalind Bell-Smith, had left the city "in Abrahamic ignorance" to establish the first independent Canadian mission on mainland China. Goforth had applied to the CIM, and had gone to London to be interviewed in 1886, along with his friend Alexander Saunders, a Scottish-born Canadian. But Broomhall had turned him down because of his Presbyterian "peculiarities."[37] Besides, like Timothy Richard and Thomas Barnardo in 1865, Goforth would have been too independent to remain under Taylor's authoritarian regimen. As a result Goforth pressured his own church to establish its own mission to China. Alex Saunders, more irenic, was accepted by the London council and underwent the usual training there, thus becoming the first official Canadian in the CIM. Goforth remained the best friend of the CIM, and by the 1910s he became the leading spokesman for fundamentalism in China.[38]

Taylor's visit was the catalyst for the creation of denominational missions that drew from a national constituency. By 1900 the Methodists had established the West China mission in Sichuan, which was to become a highly professional organization, reputedly the largest single mission run by a single church. The Anglicans had established the Diocese of Mid-Japan and another in India, and had a few representatives in China not yet organized into the diocese of Henan. The Baptists had missions in Bolivia and India, the Congregationalists in Angola, and the Presbyterians had a string of missions from Trinidad to Taiwan to the New Hebrides. But, like England in 1865, Canada had no "faith mission" that would send working-class, less educated workers overseas, until the CIM came along.[39]

---

36. Ruth Compton Brouwer, *New Women for God: Canadian Presbyterian Women and India Missions, 1876-1914* is the history of this mission.

37. Rosalind Goforth, *Goforth of China* (Grand Rapids: Zondervan, 1937), pp. 52-53.

38. Goforth's obituary in *China's Millions* (NA), pp. 43-44, noted: "No missionary not actually a member of the mission was ever more akin to it in spirit or more closely associated with it in actual service."

39. For JHT's impact on denominational missions, see Austin, *Saving China*. Rosemary R. Gagan, *A Sensitive Independence: Canadian Methodist Women Missionaries in Canada and the Orient, 1881-1925* (Montreal and Kingston: McGill-Queen's University Press, 1992), discussed mission enthusiasm prior to 1888.

The New World

The CIM entered Toronto under the auspices of the Christian Institute, a slum mission that deserves to be rescued from historical obscurity, for in its short life it was responsible for the establishment of the CIM, the Dominion branch of the Christian and Missionary Alliance (C&MA), Canada's first Bible school, and the Sudan Interior Mission — the largest Canadian-based, multinational faith mission, modeled on the CIM.[40] Located on Richmond Street West, the Christian Institute was run by Alfred Sandham, the eccentric editor of *Faithful Witness*. He was a YMCA secretary and numismatist, who had started out a Methodist and ended up, Henry Frost wrote, "I know not what."[41] During 1888-89, while Frost was still living in Attica, New York, Sandham housed the CIM's male candidates on the upper floor of the Christian Institute, where they would study Chinese characters by day — how? one asks, without a teacher? — and do practical soul-winning in the evenings.

In February 1889 Sandham helped found a new denomination, the Dominion Alliance, in Hamilton, forty miles west of Toronto. Hamilton was a grimy industrial city — "the Birmingham of Canada" — that spawned several working-class religious movements, from Phoebe Palmer to the Christian Workers church, founded in the 1890s by Rev. Peter Wiley Philpott. He was a former blacksmith and Salvation Army preacher who attracted working people with "the simple gospel over the social gospel." (The Christian Workers grew into the Associated Gospel, a small but influential fundamentalist denomination.)[42]

The Dominion Alliance was the Canadian branch of the Christian Alliance, an American denomination founded by an expatriate Canadian, Albert Benjamin Simpson (1843-1919). Simpson, who had been converted under Grattan Guinness in 1859, was one of the great Protestant mystics of the nineteenth century. Born in Prince Edward Island and raised in the "desolate wilderness" near Chatham, Ontario, he graduated from Knox College, Toronto, and held pastorates of churches in Hamilton, Louisville, Kentucky, and New York City. In 1883 he left the Presbyterian fold to found an independent faith

---

40. In 1994 Toronto became famous throughout the evangelical world for a spirit-filled revival known as "the Toronto Blessing," whose manifestations include being slain in the Spirit and "holy laughter." The Christian Institute must have been the Toronto Blessing of its day.

41. Frost, "Memoirs," p. 307. For Sandham, see biographical entry in Henry James Morgan, ed., *The Canadian Men and Women of the Time: A Handbook of Canadian Biography* (Toronto, 1898).

42. Kenneth L. Draper, "P. W. Philpott and the Christian Workers' Church: Conservative Premillennialism in the Social History of Hamilton" (unpublished paper, Canadian Baptist Archives at McMaster University).

mission in New York, the Home for Faith and Physical Healing. Four years later he created two "alliances," the Christian Alliance to reach the "lower classes, by highway missions and other practical methods," and an overseas wing, the Missionary Alliance; these merged into the Christian & Missionary Alliance in 1897. (The C&MA is still a prominent fundamentalist denomination in Canada and the United States, and supports many overseas missions.)[43]

Not only did Simpson found a denomination, he formulated a new theology that he called the "four-fold gospel": Christ the Savior, Christ the Sanctifier, Christ the Healer, and Christ the Coming King. The most controversial tenet was the "third blessing" of "divine health" — Christ the Healer. He taught that believers could "expect the Holy Spirit to strengthen their bodies and to keep them physically well. He described this as a higher reality than divine healing, something that one should comprehend while physically well." Simpson tried to keep away from "sensationalism, fanaticism, and the 'wonder-seeking spirit,'" but sometimes the power spilled out of control.[44] "We were a hilarious company in those early days," he recalled, "when with whole-souled enthusiasm, we were certified we should never have to adopt glasses, lose our teeth, behold falling or grey hair, nor suffer any impairment of physical faculties. . . . The cherished hope of passing from [ordinary] sleep into the presence of the Lord, should we be called ere his descent from heaven, was the ideal of expectation."[45]

Henry Frost remained at Attica, New York, until 1889, when Hudson Taylor returned for a second visit to North America and asked him to take up residence in Toronto as North American Director. Frost was a patrician Yankee, a Presbyterian, descended from post-*Mayflower* pilgrims, who counted Benjamin Franklin among his ancestors. His wife, Abbie Folger Ellinwood, had a better pedigree, descended from John and Priscilla Alden of the *Mayflower;* moreover, she was well connected in church work, for her father and

---

43. I am indebted to Lindsay Reynolds for his two-volume history of the C&MA in Canada: *Footprints: The Beginnings of the Christian and Missionary Alliance in Canada,* and *Rebirth: The Redevelopment of the Christian and Missionary Alliance in Canada* (Willowdale, Ont.: Christian and Missionary Alliance in Canada, 1982); and also to Darrell Reid for his doctoral dissertation, "'Jesus Only': The Early Life and Presbyterian Ministry of Albert Benjamin Simpson, 1843-1881" (Kingston: Queen's University, 1994).

44. Edith L. Blumhofer, *The Assemblies of God: A Chapter in the Story of American Pentecostalism,* vol. 1, *To 1941* (Springfield, Mo.: Gospel Publishing House, 1989), pp. 29-30. In the twentieth century the Alliance was often a stepping-stone to Pentecostalism.

45. Virginia Lieson Brereton, *Training God's Army: The American Bible School, 1880-1940* (Bloomington: University of Indiana Press, 1990), p. 11.

uncle were both on the American Presbyterian Foreign Mission Board.[46] Frost was born in New York City in 1858 (making him thirty) and had graduated in engineering from Princeton College. He moved to Attica, where he became a well-to-do industrialist who owned water and gas utilities. He was converted to premillennialism at the Niagara conference of 1885 by Jonathan Goforth, and like Goforth, applied to the CIM's London council. Taylor and Broomhall turned him down, too, on the grounds that as an American, the diplomatic problems between the British and American consuls would have been insurmountable. Frost confided that his trip to England was "a veritable bog of blasted hopes." Nevertheless, he remained hopeful, and acted as Taylor's host during the 1888 visit.

Frost must have been appalled when he moved to the Christian Institute, where the attic rang with holy laughter, while downstairs, in the street chapel, the poor threw away their canes and glasses. One thing was plain, he wrote, "that we were in a strange land and facing strange experiences."[47] (Toronto the Good, a strange land?) His first duty was to extricate the CIM from the Christian Institute. Sandham was "not as much in sympathy with our Mission service," and wanted to turn the Christian Institute into a training home to "thoroughly equip our would-be-missionaries both in the word of God and in practical service." Its teachings would include divine healing. Frost felt the CIM home should not be for "training" in Bible exposition and missionary methods, but for "testing," that is, how to live on faith.[48] Sandham resigned and the mission moved to a rented house on Shuter Street. A few years later, with the aid of wealthy members of the Toronto council, it rented a twelve-bedroom mansion at 632 Church Street, "in the best residential portion of the city." Henry Frost, his wife and seven children moved next door.[49]

The North American Council

With the zeal of a convert Frost accepted the CIM's faith principles without reservation. He resolved as an individual and a mission not to go into debt, even to the fraction of a penny; his engineering background ensured punctilious bookkeeping. The mission would not sign a lease, for example, since "the

---

46. Taylor and Taylor, "*By Faith*," p. 1. Frost, "Memoirs," p. 767.
47. Frost, "Memoirs," p. 273.
48. Ibid., pp. 310-11. Several applications in CIM Application Records (Toronto) were recorded from young men who gave their home address as the Institute, seemingly parentless Irish in their late teens.
49. Ibid., p. 390.

Lord might not enable us to fulfill" the rent, so the Toronto council members signed as individuals on its behalf.⁵⁰ Frost kept separate books for contributions designated "for China" and "Home." This meant he was remitting thousands of dollars to Shanghai, while there were thirty people — candidates and their families — living in the home with no food on the table. Then, miraculously someone would appear at the door with a brace of partridge, a ton of coal (councilor Elias Rogers owned a coal company), or a cheque in exactly the amount prayed for. "We lived from hand to mouth in those days," Frost recalled. "But we found before we were through that it was not our hand and our mouth, but God's hand and our mouth; and this is a distinction which makes a great difference. We gradually gathered, therefore, that our episodes of scarcity were intended to be new revealings of God's love and power, if only we could be attent to the inner meaning of things."⁵¹

In his choice of council members, Frost was certainly attentive to the inner meaning of Toronto evangelicalism. Toronto was a "city of churches," with the largest Protestant churches and the best preachers in the country. It also was the headquarters of the five national denominations, and had five theological seminaries. Since it was dominated by the churches, it was difficult for an interdenominational agency like the CIM (or the YMCA, the Salvation Army, or the Dominion Alliance) to gain a foothold. Frost made a tacit arrangement to seek broad approval among individual congregations while building an informal relationship with the national bodies. The CIM maintained cordial relations with three seminaries — Knox Presbyterian, Wycliffe low-church Anglican, and McMaster Baptist, but not with Victoria Methodist or Trinity high-church Anglican — which is surprising since the CIM did not accept ordained ministers.

The Toronto council was a narrow slice of Toronto evangelicals: all were men who could be called "proto-fundamentalists" on the basis of their Niagara connections, who believed in biblical inerrancy and premillennial dispensationalism.⁵² Yet if "fundamentalism" is a temperament as well as a theology — militant antimodernism — as some scholars argue, the CIM in Toronto was not "fundamentalist" in the twentieth-century sense. In 1889, modernism was not yet a cloud on the evangelical horizon among orthodox evangelicals. The historian of Knox church, which became a leading fundamentalist congregation within the Presbyterian denomination, put it suc-

50. Frost to Toronto council, 28 April 1891, and Frost to JHT, 29 May 1891, in ibid., pp. 389-91. Originals in CIM/ABGC, file 5/11.

51. Ibid., p. 397.

52. Ronald Sawatsky, "'Looking for That Blessed Hope': The Roots of Fundamentalism in Canada, 1878-1920" (Ph.D. diss., University of Toronto, 1985).

cinctly: "rather than get involved in sterile controversy, many evangelicals gave themselves to missionary work, to the preaching of the gospel, and in many cases to pietistic separatism."[53]

Whereas the London council was top-heavy with Brethren, Toronto was predominantly Presbyterian: seven of the eleven who can be identified (of fourteen) on the 1889 Toronto council were Presbyterian. In addition to Wallace they included Rev. Henry M. Parsons of Knox church, one of the "war-horses of premillennialism" and contributor to the Scofield Bible,[54] and Rev. William J. Erdman of Lockport, New York, a founder of the Niagara conference and Frost's spiritual mentor. Erdman, pastor of the Moody Church in Chicago and a founder of Moody Bible Institute, was reputed to possess "the best knowledge of theology and the Bible among all the ministers who taught at Niagara."[55] The appointment of Rev. Thomas Wardrope, secretary of the Foreign Missions Committee of the Presbyterian Church in Canada, cemented a semiofficial relationship that continued into the twentieth century under Wardrope's successor on both committees, Rev. R. Peter MacKay.[56]

The other semiofficial relationship was with the evangelical wing of the Church of England. In Canada as in England, no interdenominational association, liberal or conservative, could exist without Anglicans, who conferred an aura of legitimacy, dignity, and broad churchmanship. The ubiquitous layman Samuel Hoyles Blake, the brother of a former premier of Ontario, who sat on the CIM council from 1888 until his death in 1912, was a linchpin of interlocking boards and councils, including the Christian Institute, the Dominion Alliance, Toronto Bible Training School, Wycliffe College, and the Missionary Society of the Church in Canada.[57] T. C. DesBarres, the leading Anglican premillennialist, was the minister at St. Paul's, Yorkville, which happened to be two blocks from the CIM home. Among the applicants of 1888 were two of his parishioners, spinster sisters aged forty-five and fifty, who had to be politely declined on the grounds of age.

53. William Fitch, *Knox Church, Toronto: Avant-Garde, Evangelical, Advancing* (Toronto: Knox Presbyterian Church, 1971), p. 99.

54. Ronald Sawatsky, "Henry Martyn Parsons of Knox Church, Toronto (1818-1913)," *Canadian Society of Presbyterian History Papers*, 1982.

55. Sandeen, *Roots of Fundamentalism*, p. 142. Bradley J. Longfield, *The Presbyterian Controversy: Fundamentalists, Modernists, and Moderates* (New York: Oxford University Press, 1991), p. 135. Erdman's son Charles helped establish the CIM in Philadelphia after 1901 and ordained Frost as a Presbyterian in 1904.

56. For R. P. MacKay (a relative of George Leslie Mackay of Taiwan), see Austin, *Saving China*, and Brouwer, *New Women for God*.

57. Grant, *Profusion of Spires*, p. 180. For Blake and the Alliance, see Reynolds, *Footprints*.

Relations with Wycliffe College were cemented in 1910 when the principal, T. R. O'Meara, joined the CIM council. O'Meara provided a peculiarly Anglican service for the CIM: identifying high-church applicants. One man, he warned, attended a church "of an advanced ritualistic type. . . . I myself cannot see how any thoroughgoing Protestant who knows experientially the gladness and liberty of the Gospel of Christ would be comfortable and at home in such surroundings."[58] O'Meara was more comfortable with non-Anglicans in the CIM than with his own high-churchmen, though he could not share communion with the former for fear of launching the college into "public controversy."[59]

The careers of two other faculty indicate the continuing relations between Wycliffe College and the CIM. Howard K. Mowll, educated at Cambridge and ordained in Manchester, was teaching at Wycliffe in 1923 when he was appointed Assistant Bishop of the CIM/CMS diocese of East Sichuan, and later the successor of Bishop W. W. Cassels. In 1936 he became Bishop of Sydney, Australia, where he was prominent in evangelical causes. W. H. Griffith Thomas, another distinguished English scholar, came to Canada with a Keswick delegation and remained as professor of Old Testament at Wycliffe. He became a fundamentalist who helped found the Anglican seminary in Vancouver and Dallas Theological Seminary (which opened after his death in 1924).

Nevertheless, the CIM came into conflict with each of the Canadian missions that had representatives in China, both in the competition for recruits and money at home and overseas, and in the division of the fields. When Jonathan Goforth arrived in China, he claimed "North Henan" as a Canadian Presbyterian field. However, Taylor claimed the whole province of Henan because CIM missionaries had been making extended explorations for twelve years, although they had not yet opened a station in North Henan. Goforth's "unwise impetuosity," Taylor warned, and "the proposed incoming of a large body of inexperienced missionaries has alarmed the officials and greatly increased the difficulties." If Goforth wanted to advance into inland China, he concluded, "you must go forward on your knees." The problems evaporated when Taylor met Goforth in Shanghai and discovered a kindred spirit — and devolved the North Henan field to the Presbyterians.[60]

---

58. T. R. O'Meara to Frost, 4 April 1910, O'Meara papers, Wycliffe College Archives, Principal's Correspondence letterbooks. This is the only extant correspondence of a member of the Toronto council.

59. O'Meara to Frost, 1 June 1915, ibid.

60. Margaret Brown, "History of the Honan (North China) Mission of the United Church of Canada, Originally a Mission of the Presbyterian Church in Canada, 1887-1951" (typescript, Toronto: United Church of Canada Archives, 1970), chapter IX, p. 5. The Anglican mission in Kaifeng, Henan, ran against the CIM's territorial ambitions when the

A more immediate controversy was the CIM's faith principles of no solicitation, of never asking for money. The Presbyterians and Methodists paid missionary salaries of $750 a year, so the CIM's claim to support a missionary for $250 put pressure on the boards. "Mr. Frost tells me," wrote R. P. MacKay, the Presbyterian secretary and councilor of the CIM, "the 600 C.I.M. missionaries are satisfied — many of them — on $250, returning annually thank offerings of as much as 20%." When Donald MacGillivray, a North Henan pioneer, tried to live on $500, his experiment proved a failure. The CIM could live so cheaply, he charged, because they "number few educated men. Their missionaries are mostly from the bench and forge in Sweden and Germany and the U.K. . . . Their single men are constantly flying about and the equipment they use, not to say need, is very meagre." They did not have libraries, he said.[61]

The Toronto council had only one Methodist, William Gooderham, the philanthropist who founded the Christian Institute, but he died in 1889 and was not replaced. The Methodists, wary of any movement that diverted persons and money from connectional channels, was suspicious of the CIM because of its friends among the "pretended non-sectarian teachers" (i.e. Plymouth Brethren revivalists) scouring the Ontario countryside.[62] Relations were strained further when a former CIM missionary, Isabella Crossthwaite, started "operating" among the churches of southwestern Ontario. Miss Crossthwaite had gone to China in 1889, where she lasted a year before she was fired for instability, then went back two years later as an independent. By 1897 she was collecting money and spreading unorthodox teachings at home, so that the Methodist church warned its congregations to be "on their guard" against her.[63]

The Divine Healers

The CIM in Toronto, as in Britain, had to maintain a delicate balance with the churches, while letting enthusiasts in the back door. In Britain the sectarian

---

newly consecrated Bishop W. C. White built a hospital near the CIM "dispensary": Austin, *Saving China*, pp. 134-35. The Methodists in West China had a minor confrontation when they expanded into Chongqing in 1907: Methodist Church of Canada, West China correspondence in UCA.

61. Brown, "History of the Honan Mission," chapter XXIV, pp. 20-22.
62. Airhart, *Serving the Present Age*, p. 42.
63. See Miss Crossthwaite's application #43 in CIM Application Records, Toronto. See also correspondence of Alexander Sutherland, secretary of Methodist Foreign Mission Board, to Virgil Hart, Chengdu, 30 January 1897, in West China Mission correspondence, box 8, UCA.

influence came from the Brethren and the Salvation Army; in Canada it was the Christian & Missionary Alliance, with its controversial doctrine of faith healing. In England belief in healing was a minor undercurrent of evangelicalism because of its age-old association with witchcraft and "sedition." That was why many healing sects — Mother Anna Lee and the Shakers, for example — fled to the United States, where they could live in utopian communities.[64] By the 1880s healing was prominent among Christian Scientists, Seventh Day Adventists, and in the C&MA. Canadians tended to British skepticism, for as one Baptist preacher wrote, "Christianity has won most of its triumphs without the aid of miracles. The men and women who have best exemplified the power of Christianity have never experienced nor expected miraculous interference."[65] Nevertheless, by the turn of the century there was an interest in many forms of alternative medicine including folk remedies, patent medicines, and divine healing.

When Sandham was elected secretary of the Dominion Alliance in 1889, former mayor Howland was president and a young woman named Maggie Scott was elected women's vice-president. Born in a Presbyterian manse in Maxville, Eastern Ontario, Maggie had been paralyzed and blind until she was cured by Dr. Cullis of Boston — long-distance, over the telephone — who ordered her to "arise and walk." Within a few months, convinced of her own healing powers, the nineteen-year-old Maggie "stepped out on her own, travelling from town to town, holding evangelistic meetings and telling the story of her physical healing." Soon after founding the Dominion Alliance, she and her sister Christina joined the CIM and went to China. She contracted consumption and her journey back to Maxville caused a "solemn hush" wherever she went. Sister Tina lived a year longer and died in China. After their death, their brother volunteered to take their place, but was turned down on the grounds of health.[66]

One of the continuing controversies within the CIM was vaccination, which some objected to because the disease bacillus was given to healthy people. A few British expressed such views, but most of those who refused to be vaccinated were Scandinavians and Americans. After years of debate, the Toronto council made vaccination compulsory in 1893, followed by the China council in 1904.[67]

64. Butler, *Awash in a Sea of Faith*.
65. Reynolds, *Footprints*, p. 71.
66. Reynolds recounts the story of Maggie Scott at pp. 71-73, and her testimony at pp. 488-90. Her Alliance connection was not mentioned in the CIM records: her application listed her as "Presbyterian." Henry Frost discussed her in his "Memoirs," pp. 411-13.
67. Marcus Wood, London council, to Frost, 3 May 1904, in CIM/ABGC, file 3/48. Compulsory vaccination applied only to CIM and not to associate missions.

This did not end the debate though. In 1905 an American doctor, Arthur Shapleigh, who had served in China with another mission, was accepted by Toronto on condition that he and his wife and two sons were vaccinated. Within weeks of their arrival in Shanghai, Shapleigh and both boys died of smallpox, the very disease they had been inoculated against.[68]

Henry Frost's own attitude to healing was equally vexed. He made several trips to China, where he had witnessed, and experienced, divine healing. In later years he turned to a "somewhat peculiar mission which was quite apart from my work for the Mission, the cure of souls."[69] In his book *Miraculous Healing*, Frost concluded that Satan used the allure of supernatural healing to lead Christians "into unbalanced and extravagant positions . . . it is to be remembered that the occupying of any super-scriptural position will eventually lead one, if he is honest, into discouragement and . . . the darkness of despondency, amounting in some cases to despair."[70]

Frost's pilgrimage away from faith healing reflects a similar pilgrimage by Rowland V. Bingham, founder of the Sudan Interior Mission (SIM), a Canadian faith mission modeled on the CIM. Bingham was an English Salvation Army captain in Toronto who converted to the Alliance and set out in 1893 for "the Soudan" (not to be confused with the modern country of Sudan), the broad swath of Equatorial Africa known as the "White Man's Grave." Bingham vowed not to use medicines, not even quinine for malaria, relying on God's promise that the sun would not smite them by day, nor the moon by night. When his companions died, he returned to Toronto, his faith "shaken to the very foundation. First, I had gone out trusting in promises of healing that seemed plain, clear and explicit in the Bible, and yet I had buried in the Sudan two of the most faithful Christians whom I had ever met. Had the promises failed?"[71] The SIM had an appallingly high death rate and eventually Bingham, like the Alliance itself, repudiated divine healing: "To teach that healing is a part of the atonement and that all Christians have therefore the right to expect and experience it, is to cause heartbreak and disappointment."[72]

In the twentieth century the China Inland Mission and the Sudan Interior

---

68. Toronto council minutes, May 1904 and March 1905, in CIM/ABGC, file 3/48. Mrs. Shapleigh remained in the CIM until 1920.

69. Frost, "Memoirs," pp. 757-58. For his views on divine healing, see pp. 744-52.

70. Henry W. Frost, *Miraculous Healing: A Personal Testimony and Biblical Study* (London: Evangelical Press, 1951; reprint, 1972), pp. 11-14.

71. J. H. Hunter, *A Flame of Fire: The Life and Work of R. V. Bingham, D.D.* (Toronto: Sudan Interior Mission, 1961), p. 65.

72. Reynolds, *Rebirth*, p. 64.

Mission became intertwined in Toronto, different voices of the same call. Bingham and Rev. E. A. Brownlee, Frost's successor as Canadian director, sat on each other's boards, shared the same platforms, attended the same missionary conferences. Both were charter members of the Interdenominational Foreign Missions Association, the separatist organization that was established to rival the liberal Associated Boards of Foreign Mission Societies in 1917.

A New Beginning

From the beginning the Toronto CIM spoke in a babel of accents. Its deputation speakers were mostly British missionaries who "tarried" for a few weeks or months on their way home. Grace Stott, the Glasgow slum-evangelist who had been the matriarch of Wenzhou, was "a most impressive" speaker who "made many friends for herself and the Mission" from Los Angeles to Mississippi.[73] The candidates came from all parts of Canada and the United States, including some Swedish and Russian immigrants from the American Midwest who spoke "quaint, broken English."[74] The most unexpected accent was Japanese: Tozo Ohno, who taught Chinese language, was a former samurai who had been disinherited when he became a Christian and somehow ended up as butler to Frost's mother in New York City. He taught written Chinese, the radicals and simple characters, "in order to give us proof of the learners' prayerfulness." One wonders what sort of language he instilled, since he would have read Chinese characters with their Japanese pronunciation.[75]

Hudson Taylor visited North America six times after 1888: in 1889, to speak at Northfield and the Niagara conference again, and to establish a permanent North American council; in 1892; in 1894, for the SVM conference in Detroit; in 1897; in 1900, for the Ecumenical Missionary Conference, on the eve of the Boxer uprising; and finally as "an aged and broken-down old man" in 1905 on his way to China to die.

Considering the cool relations with London, Frost reported directly to Taylor, and did not consider it necessary to go to London until 1893. This was another crisis, when Taylor was refusing to meet with Broomhall and the council after they had rejected the *Book of Arrangements*. "Being an American," Frost

---

73. After many years in Canada, Mrs. Stott came to a sad senile end: Frost, "Memoirs," pp. 527-28. Minutes of Toronto council, 28 October 1919 and 2 February 1922, in CIM/ABGC.

74. Frost, "Memoirs," p. 415.

75. Ibid., pp. 299-305. Taylor and Taylor, *"By Faith,"* p. 139. Tozo Ohno died in Pottstown, New York, in 1896 while attending school; his last words were typically Japanese, and typically Christian, "It is victory to die!"

The New World

hoped that the "autocratic constitution" of the CIM could be "Americanized, that is, democratized,"[76] even if this meant opposing Taylor himself. Frost resolved the impasse by drawing up a constitution for the mission which confirmed the independence of the national councils, "mutually related and mutually helpful," and curtailed the autocracy of the general director.[77]

Frost also formulated the first credal statement of the CIM. Hitherto the CIM had not needed a creed — indeed no missions had such a statement — but with the spread of modernism, faith healing, and conditionalist views both within the mission and without, Frost felt the CIM needed to itemize its orthodox faith in black and white.[78] The CIM's statement had seven simple clauses with biblical references that did not mention controversial issues like adult baptism or premillennialism. The statement, which was reprinted in every issue of *China's Millions* from 1893 to 1950, reads:

1. The divine inspiration and consequent authority of the whole canonical Scriptures.
2. The doctrine of the Trinity.
3. The fall of man, his consequent moral depravity and his need of regeneration.
4. The atonement through the substitutionary death of Christ.
5. The doctrine of justification by faith.
6. The resurrection of the body, both in the case of the just and of the unjust.
7. The eternal life of the saved and the eternal punishment of the lost.

Once it was written down, the CIM's "doctrinal basis" took on a life of its own. Adopted by other organizations, such as Toronto Bible College and Moody Bible Institute, it became a shorthand creed for fundamentalism. Within the CIM itself it defined membership in an association, which was quite different from a family; the first person Frost attacked under the new provisions was Stanley Smith of the Cambridge Seven, "an old and esteemed member" who was preaching the heretical doctrine of the Larger Hope.

Frost returned from London determined to launch the CIM onto a "new beginning" in North America. He established a prayer union, groups in cities from New York to Los Angeles, from Toronto to Tennessee, which would

---

76. Frost, "Memoirs," p. 894.
77. Ibid., pp. 423-30, *HTCOC* 7, pp. 179-86, "Unanimity of Decision."
78. This itemization in black and white seems to have been an American pattern. For example, Brereton, *Training God's Army*, pp. 5, 22, noted that A. T. Pierson, a prominent mission theorist and ex officio CIM council member, formulated "The Six Successive Steps" of the Keswick Plan, having "a definite Beginning, Course and Culmination."

gather every week to pray for each station and each individual of the CIM (who numbered six hundred by this time). More significantly, he started a North American edition of *China's Millions* that would be "more representative of our part of the work."[79] The North American *Millions* was a different magazine, larger and better laid out, with photographs rather than the chinoiserie engravings that typified the British *Millions*. Canadian and American news was featured, less about England and Australia. Even Broomhall's cause, the anti-opium crusade, was seldom mentioned, although, of course, tragic stories of opium addicts remained a common trope. Frost described the *Millions* as "the chief deputation worker of the Mission in North America, being able to go to parts of the continent which missionaries cannot reach."[80] Just how far is shown with the story of Mary Brayton, who found a page blowing in the wind in Pueblo, Colorado; she came to Toronto, and stayed for thirty years, the "faithful, loving and devoted" bookkeeper.[81]

In 1919 the North American edition of *China's Millions* (edited in Toronto) had 4,100 subscribers.[82] One-quarter (1,120) were in Canada, and about 40% of those (447) were in Toronto. Vancouver, where the CIM had an office and receiving home, had 133 subscriptions, followed by London (72), Montreal (58), Hamilton (55), Ottawa (47), Winnipeg (36), Victoria, BC (30), Halifax (21), Belleville, ON (18), Calgary (16), and Galt, ON (14). In addition, Ontario had 119 subscribers in "scattered" centers, and Saskatchewan had 33 (making a total outside Toronto of 773).

In the United States, the 3,000 subscribers lived in 13 states. Illinois led with 363 subscriptions, of which 324 were in Chicago. New York State had 347 subscriptions, with 143 in New York City, 135 in Buffalo, 14 in Albany, and 55 in the rest of the state. Philadelphia, the CIM's North American headquarters, had 270 subscribers, with 70 in the rest of Pennsylvania. Other states included Michigan (Detroit, Grand Rapids, total of 112), Ohio (73) New Jersey (Atlantic City, total of 64), Missouri (St. Louis, 42), Massachusetts (31), Minnesota (Minneapolis, 30), and Maryland (Baltimore, 24). There seem to have been no subscribers in New England or the Midwest beyond Chicago. Los Angeles, where the CIM had an office connected to BIOLA, had 86 subscribers and 33 in the rest of California. Seattle, a branch plant of the Vancouver office, had 22 subscribers. Berea College, Kentucky, which had been founded as the first integrated college in the South, had 26 subscriptions.

79. Frost, "Memoirs," p. 431.
80. Ibid., p. 512.
81. Ibid., pp. 559-61.
82. Minutes of Fifth Annual Meeting of combined Toronto and Philadelphia councils, 26 June 1919, in CIM/ABGC, file 3/49.

The Great Design

As part of the new beginning, Frost decided to ally the CIM with the emerging Bible school movement. The CIM, he announced, "could not do better than take the equipment provided by a Canadian or American Bible Institute as a standard of preparation. We recognized, at the same time, that some men and women without such an equipment would be found acceptable; and we were convinced that Seminary-bred men were much to be desired." This was a return to the CIM's working-class roots, for, Frost continued,

> We were convinced that we should seek for the friendship, not of doctrinally and spiritually loose Christians, but of those who were sound in the faith, prayerful in spirit, devoted in service, evangelistic in purpose and, generally but not exclusively premillennial in attitude. We felt that one person of this quality would be worth to the Mission and China a hundred persons of another sort, and we were ready, as far as needed, to throw in our lot with the socially humble and financially poor, if only we could maintain scriptural and spiritual integrity in our friend-ships.[83]

The effect was immediate and phenomenal. When Hudson Taylor visited Moody Bible Institute in 1894, he received thirty-four applications, thirty men and four women — a most unusual proportion — of whom five men and two women went to China. That turned out to be the peak year, with seventy-one male applicants and forty-six females, of whom twelve men and thirteen women were accepted.

In 1895 the CIM printed a list of "approved Bible schools," which shows the fundamentalist movement in its infancy: Moody Bible Institute (Reuben A. Torrey); Boston Missionary Training School (Adoniram Judson Gordon, succeeded by Arthur Tappan Pierson); the Union Missionary Training School in Brooklyn (Mrs. Lucy Osborne); Pennsylvania Bible College (Cyrus Ingersoll Scofield);[84] Gospel Union Missionary Institute in Kansas City; and Toronto Bible Training School. The following year four more were added: the International Missionary Training School in New York City (later Nyack), of the Christian & Missionary Alliance, and schools in Philadelphia, Detroit, and Minneapolis. The CIM was becoming an arbiter of fundamentalist orthodoxy.

---

83. Frost, "Memoirs," pp. 431-32.
84. Dana Robert, *American Women in Mission: A Social History of Their Thought and Practice* (Macon, Ga.: Mercer University Press, 1996), chapter on "Women and Independent Evangelical Missions," pp. 189-254, particularly pp. 205-30, discussed the Africa Inland Mission, founded on CIM faith principles in Philadelphia in 1895.

After the CIM left the Christian Institute, Alfred Sandham started the Toronto Missionary Training Institute, which hobbled along for a few years as a precarious, faith-healing school.[85] But Toronto evangelicals felt they needed something better, a "real" Bible school which could guarantee orthodox teachings. In May 1894 twelve men gathered in the house of Elmore Harris — practically the entire CIM council — to found the Toronto Bible Training School. (Little TBTS grew into Toronto Bible College in 1912, Ontario Bible College in 1968, Ontario Theological Seminary in 1975, and in 1998 was renamed Tyndale University College and Seminary. It is a major evangelical institution in Canada.)

Elmore Harris spoke first. He had joined the CIM council the year before as its first Baptist representative.[86] He was a religious dynamo in a city filled with them. Independently wealthy, a director of the Massey-Harris farm implement company, he had already built, financed, and pastored two churches, Bloor Street and Walmer Road, the largest Baptist edifice in Canada. Located halfway between Harris's two churches was McMaster University, the Baptist seminary over which he cast a proprietorial eye and sat on the senate. He offered the Sunday school rooms of Walmer Road church to the new TBTS.

Henry Frost spoke next, and stated that "out of 500 applications for service with the C.I.M., many had to be refused because of want of proper training."[87] (The mission records indicate 400 formal applications by 1894, considerably more than any denominational mission.) The meeting agreed unanimously to establish Toronto Bible Training School, and formulated "The Great Design," its prospectus. It was to be for "the training of consecrated men and women as Sunday school workers, as Pastor's Assistants, and as City, Home, and Foreign Missionaries. It is intended for those who believe they have been called of God to Christian service, and who, from age or other reasons, cannot pursue a full collegiate and theological course of study."[88] In other words, the students were too old, too young, or did not have enough education ("other reasons") to pursue a six-year university course leading to ordination. Women, who formed the majority of the students, were of course precluded from ordination. The function of

---

85. Reynolds, *Footprints*, pp. 193-95.

86. As soon as Harris joined the council, the CIM applications began to have notations whether the applicant had been or intended to be immersed; on at least one occasion he rebaptized a candidate (Presbyterian) just before her departure. See also Ronald Sawatsky, "Elmore Harris: Canadian Baptist Extraordinaire" (Graduate paper, University of Toronto, 1980), copy in TBC Archives, Tyndale Seminary Archives).

87. Minutes of TBTS Board, 18 May 1894, in ibid. Interestingly, Frost's "Memoirs" do not mention this meeting or TBTS, which indicates how tightly he constructed his life (or at least his memoirs) around the CIM.

88. "The Great Design," Minutes of TBTS Board, September 1894.

the Toronto school, like those springing up throughout the United States, was to produce what Moody called the "gap men" — and women — Spirit-filled lay workers who could bridge the gap between the people and the clergy.

Henry Frost made an arrangement that all CIM candidates had to live in the mission home and attend Bible classes at the school. Often this was the only training they had in theology. By the end of its first year, TBTS reported five students had gone "to the Mission Field in China and six others have been accepted as missionaries for the foreign field."[89] By 1904 the Toronto newspaper could describe TBTS as a "hotbed of missions." "This is not a name we would ourselves have chosen," the school responded; "we should prefer to call it 'a Handmaid and Helper of Missions.' But understanding by the word 'Hotbed,' a place which promotes rapid growth or heated activity, we can desire nothing better for the Toronto Bible Training School than that it should continue to manifest this condition and spirit in relation to all missionary service, whether at home or abroad."[90]

On its fiftieth anniversary, E. A. Brownlee, Canadian director of the CIM, announced that five hundred graduates of TBTS/TBC had gone to foreign fields, with eighty to ninety in the CIM and a similar number in the SIM. This did not include the hundreds who attended for a few weeks or months but did not graduate.[91] The CIM was a major employer of TBTS graduates, who in turn infused the mission with scriptural knowledge and "common Canadian Christianity."

The Associates

Although Henry Frost tried to distance the CIM from the Christian & Missionary Alliance, its twin in the Christian Institute, Hudson Taylor went out of his way to court A. B. Simpson and Frederik Franson. He toured the Alliance congregations in Nebraska, Kansas, and Iowa, where some were proclaiming a spontaneous spiritual "fourth blessing" that already called itself pentecostal, or "the Latter Rain," or the "Evening Light." Its manifestations were extreme, with trances, jerks, holy laughter, and prostrations called being "slain in the Spirit." Some went beyond the "second blessing" of holiness, beyond the "third blessing" of divine health: one preacher said the believer

---

89. Ibid., March 1895, p. 1.
90. *TBTS Recorder*, December 1904.
91. *TBC Recorder*, December 1946, p. 5. Of these, 150 went out under various denominational boards, while 350 went out with interdenominational societies.

should expect an endless explosion of spiritual "blessings" that he called "dynamite," "lyddite," and "oxydite."[92]

Although such enthusiasts would have been at home with some members of the China Inland Mission, they were too radical for the mission hierarchy. Rather than accepting them as "full members," the CIM created a category of "associate missions," independent organizations run by boards in the homelands (a departure from the CIM headquarters in Shanghai), whose missionaries were "all but members of the CIM" — a significant phrase — in the field.[93] The connection between the revivals in the American Midwest and the associate missions in Europe indicates another transatlantic evangelical cable that linked the United States to Sweden and Norway. (They were the same country until 1906.)

In the mid-nineteenth century Sweden experienced a "second Reformation," as radical and profound as that of the sixteenth century, which denounced the "magnificent ice palace" of the Lutheran state church.[94] The movement was characterized by "preaching sickness," led by pious lay men and women called *lasare* ("readers") whose primary influences were sparked by American frontier revivals. The movement was marked in certain parishes in Norrland in the far north, a land of interminable forests where "superstition crept into every home," and in Smaland further south, which contained "the poorest soil and most versatile and energetic people." The historian George M. Stephenson described Smaland as "a fit habitat for goblins, elves, witches, and demons, whose pranks and deviltry have amused or tormented people since time immemorial." It was also the center of "America fever," the large-scale emigration from the poorer parts of Europe seeking religious freedom on the American frontier.[95] This cross-fertilization resounded back and forth across the Atlantic, where it produced such anomalies as a Swedish Mormon church and a quasi-state Lutheran Church in America.

A leading figure was Frederik Franson (1852-1908), "one of the most remarkable Swedish religious leaders who ever lived and [who] is said to have had

---

92. Vinson Synan, *The Holiness-Pentecostal Movement in the United States* (Grand Rapids: William B. Eerdmans, 1971), p. 82.

93. *HTCOC 7*, p. 57. "Associate Missions" were a new status. Previously denominations such as the Bible Christians and Quakers had joined as individual associate members, but an entire society independent at home and responsible to the CIM in the field was a new venture.

94. George M. Stephenson, *The Religious Aspects of Swedish Immigration* (Minneapolis: University of Minnesota Press, 1932; reprint, New York: Arno Press and New York Times, 1969), p. 2.

95. Ibid., pp. 27-29.

a more far-reaching influence than most of them."[96] Born in Vastmanland, Franson immigrated to Nebraska as a teenager where he was baptized and studied evangelism under Moody in Chicago. At twenty-nine he left for Europe carrying "neither purse nor script. His property consisted of a worn Bible, a plain costume, a satchel, and an umbrella." Possessions were "only an encumbrance that would slacken his mad pace to bring the gospel to the people of every land before the imminent crack of doom."[97] Franson remained in Europe for nine years, where he preached before the Queen of Sweden and was imprisoned in Denmark for sedition, before making his way to Turkey. He came in touch with Hudson Taylor as early as 1884, when he sent two Norwegian women to the CIM, Sophie Reuter (later Mrs. Stanley Smith) and Anna Jakobsen (later Mrs. Cheng Hsiu-chi). They were the governess and housemaid of a family in Kristians, southern Norway, which sent three of its own daughters to China.[98]

When Hudson Taylor issued his appeal for one thousand missionaries at the Shanghai conference in 1890, Franson took the challenge personally and dispatched so many missionaries they were known as "Franson's floods." Like Gutzlaff before him, he established national "Alliances" throughout Europe, in Germany, Sweden, Norway, and Finland, that became associate missions of the CIM: the German Alliance, the Swedish Alliance, Swedish Holiness mission, and so forth. Returning to the United States, Franson met A. B. Simpson, who deputized him to recruit two hundred missionaries for Simpson's newly established International Missionary Alliance (the foreign wing of the Christian Alliance). In addition Franson established his own Chicago-based organization, the Scandinavian China Alliance, which dispatched its first party in 1891 and had sixty members within three years.[99] (It *is* hard to keep all the Alliances straight. Suffice to say, some were European founded by Franson, while others were based in the United States among European immigrants, either founded by Franson or recruited by Franson for Simpson's C&MA. They eventually amalgamated to form The Evangelical Alliance Mission (TEAM), which now has 900 missionaries in twenty-two countries.)

Franson was so convinced of The End that the only training he gave was an eleven-day crash course called the Samaritan Aid Course. When he sent his first party of the Scandinavian Alliance from Chicago in 1891, the thirty-five men and women arrived in Shanghai, unannounced, with a letter "as cheerful as it was unbusinesslike," asking to be admitted to the CIM as associ-

---

96. Ibid., p. 127. *HTCOC 7*, pp. 122-25, 153-55. The Franson papers (in English and Swedish) are in ABGC, collection 87, with an excellent finding aid.
97. Stephenson, *Religious Aspects of Swedish Immigration*, p. 126.
98. *HTCOC 7*, p. 123.
99. Franson Papers finding aid (ABGC).

ate missionaries.[100] Their only encumbrance was a guitar. In China they became musical troubadours who epitomized sacrificial devotion; their theme was, "It's best to go singing, singing all the way."[101] They were sent to Shanxi, where they proved to be loose cannons, trying to replicate the preaching sickness among the Chinese peasants. Some "made trouble over many things" (rules concerning Chinese dress, marriage, furloughs, etc.) and had difficulty accepting the *Principles & Practice*. After two years the Scandinavian Alliance severed its association with the CIM and moved en masse to the neighboring province of Shaanxi.

One pilgrim can stand for the rest. Alfred Ogren was born on a farm in Smaland and moved to Jonkoping, a center of preaching fever, where he worked in a factory making safety matches. At fourteen he was "roundly converted" by Franson and went to China in one of the first Scandinavian Alliance Missionary (SAM) parties. Ogren was "young, of humble circumstances, not highly educated, full of zeal, meek in spirit, abounding in joy, and ready for service." He died during the Boxer uprising in 1900, at the age of twenty-six. "Singing, singing, all the way. . . ."[102]

The Candidates

One day in 1894, one month after Toronto Bible Training School opened, three young women arrived at the CIM home, unannounced, with empty purses, having come all the way from Avoca, Iowa. Anna Wood and two cousins, Emma and Effie Randall, were all trained schoolteachers and were welcomed at the CIM's meagre table. "It is the custom of the Mission to deal with missionary applications without reference to financial supplies," Henry Frost wrote. The three women "greatly commended themselves" and were accepted as candidates; they remained in Toronto for five months, offering a "special petition for funds," and enrolled as students at TBTS. One day a letter arrived from a women's college in Iowa, which was "so significant it was startling," announcing that they "wished to become financially interested in three young lady missionaries, [and] preferred ladies from the State of Iowa." Within a few weeks, the three friends sailed for China.[103] The most poignant part was never made public. Mattie, the younger sister of Emma Randall, also applied to the CIM, but there is a note on her application: "She is a good

---

100. *HTCOC 7*, p. 254.
101. Taylor and Taylor, *"By Faith,"* p. 223.
102. Forsyth, *The China Martyrs of 1900*.
103. Frost, "Memoirs," pp. 460-62.

house-keeper and after much prayer, it is clearly the Lord's will that she should give her life to China by becoming house-keeper for Effie's mother [her aunt] and releasing her [Effie] for a service on the field. It is to my mind a noble step." Greater love hath no woman.

The CIM in England was fairly homogenous both in class and theology: mostly Londoners with a scattering from the West Country, the industrial North, Scotland, and Ireland. In North America, the CIM was as heterogeneous as the continent. Nothing shows this better than the record of applications to the Toronto office between 1887 and 1915: a thick tome of 950 applications from 909 individuals. From 1887 to 1901 everyone had to apply to Toronto. During that time there were 751 applications, of whom 168 were accepted and went to China. Between 1901 and 1915, when most Americans applied to Philadelphia, there were only 108. The application forms contain considerably more information than the London records, including: name, address, next of kin, denomination, dates of residence in the CIM home, and dates of departure for China and arrival in Shanghai. A few list occupation, vaccination, adult baptism, deceased parents, and referees; some have only a surname and "application withdrawn," an indication how evanescent were some people's motives.

The number of applications seems to have had little correlation with the financial contributions, which increased steadily from 1888 to 1900, when it fell as a result of the Boxers:

1888	$ 3,400
1890	16,400
1895	33,300
1899	45,900
1900	40,700
1901	49,800[104]

The contrast with Canadian denominational missions is astounding: in 1899-1900 the Methodist church spent $10,000 on its West China mission out of a total overseas budget of $30,700; the Presbyterians spent $18,900 on North Henan out of $167,700 for its far-flung missions in Canada and overseas.[105] In other words, through hundreds of small donations, the CIM was

---

104. The annual income from 1888 to 1936 was tabulated in Taylor and Taylor, "*By Faith,*" p. 292.

105. John W. Foster, "The Imperialism of Righteousness: Canadian Protestant Missions and the Chinese Revolution, 1925-28" (Ph.D. diss., York University, 1977), pp. 555, 557.

raising one and half times as much for China missions as the Canadian Methodist and Presbyterian churches combined.[106] (The Anglicans did not yet have a formal mission in China.)

Chart 1
Applicants: Residence
1888-1901

	88	89	90	91	92	93	94	95	96	97	98	99	00	01	Total
CANADA															
Toronto	19	10	18	3	5	5	8	5	13	9	8	3	1	1	108
Rest of Ontario	28	20	20	4	5	6	7	5	8	2	1	4	7	2	119
Quebec	8	2	–	–	1	3	5	1	1	1	–	–	–	–	22
Manitoba	–	–	1	1	1	3	3	1	–	2	–	1	1	–	14
Nova Scotia	–	–	–	–	–	–	–	–	–	–	–	5	–		5
Br. Columbia	1	–	1	–	–	–	2	–	–	–	–	–	–	–	4
P.E. Island	–	–	–	–	–	–	1	–	–	–	–	–	–	–	1
Total Canada	56	32	40	8	12	17	26	12	22	14	9	8	14	3	273
UNITED STATES															
Illinois	–	8	2	5	5	1	36	16	13	5	6	6	8	2	113
New York	1	16	3	2	–	2	5	7	6	3	4	4	5	2	60
Nebraska	–	5	1	22	1	1	3	5	3	1	–	–	–	–	42
Pennsylvania	–	5	–	1	–	–	3	7	3	2	4	10	1	–	36
Minnesota	–	1	6	1	–	1	7	4	7	–	1	–	–	–	28
Massachusetts	3	2	3	1	–	–	3	5	3	3	1	2	1	–	27
Kansas	1	1	3	–	2	5	5	4	1	1	–	2	1	–	26
Michigan	3	2	1	3	1	–	5	4	1	–	2	–	2	–	24
Iowa	–	1	–	–	1	–	6	1	1	–	2	–	–	2	14
California	–	1	–	1	1	–	3	1	2	–	4	–	–	–	13
Missouri	–	1	1	–	–	–	–	1	2	–	3	2	1	–	11
Ohio	–	–	–	–	1	1	4	1	–	–	–	1	1	–	9
Virginia	–	–	–	–	–	2	2	–	–	–	2	–	–	–	6

106. Alvyn Austin, "No Solicitation: The China Inland Mission and Money," in Larry Eskridge and Mark A. Noll, eds., *More Money, More Ministry: Money and Evangelicals in Recent North American History* (Grand Rapids: William B. Eerdmans, 2000), pp. 207-34. In 1907 the North American edition of *China's Millions* began to list contributions according to the English formula, issuing numbered receipts which were acknowledged anonymously each month. In November 1932, an ordinary depression month, the Philadelphia office received 209 donations ranging from 50 cents to $3,000; two thirds (135) were for $10 or less. This proportion was more pronounced in Toronto, which received 99 small gifts and only 24 larger than $10.

The New World

	88	89	90	91	92	93	94	95	96	97	98	99	00	01	Total
Wisconsin	–	–	–	–	–	–	1	3	2	–	–	–	–	–	6
Maryland	–	–	–	–	1	–	1	–	–	1	–	–	1	1	5
New Jersey	–	2	–	–	1	–	1	–	–	–	1	–	–	–	5
Indiana	–	–	–	–	–	–	–	–	–	–	–	2	2	1	5
Texas	–	1	–	–	–	–	–	1	2	–	–	–	–	–	4
N. Carolina	–	–	–	–	–	–	–	–	2	–	1	–	–	–	3
Washington	–	–	–	–	–	–	–	–	–	1	–	2	–	–	3
Colorado	–	–	–	1	–	–	–	–	1	–	1	–	–	–	3
Connecticut	–	–	1	–	–	–	–	1	1	–	–	–	–	–	3
D.C.	–	–	–	2	–	1	–	–	–	–	–	–	–	–	3
S. Carolina	–	–	1	–	–	–	–	–	–	–	–	–	1	–	2
New Mexico	–	–	1	–	–	–	1	–	–	–	–	–	–	–	2
Georgia	–	–	–	–	–	–	2	–	–	–	–	–	–	–	2
Kentucky	–	–	–	–	–	–	–	2	–	–	–	–	–	–	2
West Virginia	–	–	–	–	–	–	–	1	–	–	–	–	1	–	2
Rhode Island	–	–	1	–	–	–	–	–	–	–	–	–	–	–	1
Wyoming	–	–	–	–	–	–	1	–	–	–	–	–	–	–	1
Mississippi	–	–	–	–	–	–	1	–	–	–	–	–	–	–	1
Vermont	–	–	–	–	–	–	1	–	–	–	–	–	–	–	1
South Dakota	–	–	–	–	–	–	–	–	1	–	–	–	–	–	1
Arizona	–	–	–	–	–	–	–	–	–	1	–	–	–	–	1
Louisiana	–	–	–	–	–	–	–	–	–	–	1	–	–	–	1
Total U.S.	8	46	24	39	14	15	91	64	51	18	33	31	25	8	467
Total U.S. & Canada	64	78	64	47	26	32	117	76	73	32	42	39	39	11	740
Residence Unknown	–	1	–	–	–	1	–	1	4	2	–	8	1	–	18
Totals	64	79	64	47	26	33	117	77	77	34	42	47	40	11	758

Chart 1 gives the residence of the 740 applicants to the Toronto office between 1888 and 1901 whose application form includes an address. It shows a wide fluctuation in applications from year to year. (Note: this list contains the applicant's place of residence at the time of application, not the birthplace or hometown, which would have shown an even broader diversity.) The chart can be read in two ways. First, chronologically, one can track the waves of applications, which seem to have come in three-year cycles. There was a great surge, 207 applications, at the beginning, from 1888 to 1890, when Hudson

Taylor was on his recruiting tours. This was followed by a slump from 1891 to 1893, years of financial depression, with only 106 applications. Henry Frost launched a "new beginning" in 1893, allying the CIM with the Bible college movement; coupled with Taylor's visit to Moody Bible Institute and Wheaton College, this led to an astounding 31 applications in the first three months of 1894 from MBI alone, with 8 more in the rest of the year. (Of these, only 8 were accepted and went to China, where most seem to have lasted only a few years before resigning. Interestingly almost half of these applicants — 17 — came from people born in Britain or Canada, with one lone New Zealander. The MBI applications leveled off to more realistic numbers, with 15 in 1895, and 11 in 1896.) The number of applicants dropped from 77 in 1896 to 34 in 1897, although the stream of applicants remained steady through the Boxer turmoil. In 1901, eleven brave souls applied to take the place of the martyrs. Hudson Taylor made extensive tours of North America in 1888, 1889, 1892, 1894, 1897, and 1900, and his personal charisma inspired hundreds of applications, yet applications were not entirely dependent on him.

Secondly, this chart can be read geographically. The applicants represent 6 provinces of Canada (Saskatchewan, Alberta, and Newfoundland were not yet provinces) and 36 states of the United States. Of the 740 applications, 273 were from Canada (plus another 20 Canadians living in the U.S.), who made up 40 percent of the total. Toronto, the CIM's hometown, provided 108 applications (40 percent of the Canadian total), with another 119 from the rest of Ontario. In other words, Toronto accounted for more applications than any state in the United States, except Illinois, and more than any two other states combined. The YMCA in Hamilton, which Hudson Taylor had inspired in 1888, provided 28 applications, the largest individual center. Montreal, where the Presbyterians were active in missions, provided most of the 22 applicants from Quebec.

In the United States, the pattern is so complicated as to defy description: 467 individuals from every corner of the country. For example, in May 1895, an ordinary month, the CIM in Toronto received applications from four men and three women: an Australian medical student in Philadelphia; a Methodist clergyman from Echo Bay, Ontario; a Syrian at the Presbyterian seminary in Omaha; a Toronto Bible Training School student from Minesing, Ontario; a 55-year-old widow from Melrose, Massachusetts; a nurse from Toronto; and an Irishman studying at MBI. (Two were accepted.) In the early years the CIM recruited directly from churches and from sympathetic ministers, such as William Erdman and R. A. Torrey of MBI, and T. C. Horton of Minneapolis. After the new beginning, most applicants were funneled through the Bible schools in Chicago, New York City, Minneapolis, and Boston. Despite its appeal to Americans, the CIM always retained a certain Britishness: 46 American applicants (10 percent) were born in the British Isles; other nationalities included Australia, New Zealand, Sweden, Norway, Iceland, Germany, Holland, and Syria.

The geographical distribution can also be correlated to the spidery deputation tours of people like Grace Stott who moved from place to place having a "serious talk" with one person here, selling a copy of Mrs. Howard Taylor's latest book to another person there.

- One-quarter (27 percent) of American applicants (128) were living in four northeastern states: New York (63), Pennsylvania (39), Massachusetts (26), and Ohio. (Only six came from the rest of New England.) This was the Moody Bible belt that stretched from New York and Boston to Northfield.
- Fully 60 percent (278) came from ten Midwestern states: Illinois (113), Nebraska, Minnesota, Kansas, Michigan (24), Iowa, Missouri, Ohio (9).... This was Moody's and Franson's territory that radiated from Chicago, where Moody Bible Institute and later Wheaton College supplied a steady stream of trained graduates.

Although Americans made up almost two-thirds of the applicants between 1888 and 1901, among those who were accepted and went to China (known as candidates) the ratio of Canadians (80) to Americans (88) was about equal. (The 168 candidates represented 22 percent of all applicants.) All the Canadian candidates (76), except for four from Montreal, came from the CIM's own backyard, from Toronto and small-town Ontario, the heartland that was fertile recruiting ground for Presbyterian and Methodist missionaries as well.[107] The American candidates correlate with the geographical distribution of applicants, representing 18 states: Illinois (30), New York (14), Nebraska (10), Pennsylvania (6), Minnesota and Kansas (5 each); Iowa and Ohio (3 each), Massachusetts and Maryland (2 each); and Missouri, New Jersey, Indiana, Virginia, D.C., West Virginia, Vermont, and Rhode Island (1 each).

In terms of age and gender, the CIM attracted extremes from seventeen to sixty, though most of the applicants were between twenty and thirty, the usual age for most mission societies. The men tended to be slightly younger, with 10 percent younger than twenty-one, the age of majority, compared with 5 percent of the women; 75 percent of the men and 65 percent of the women

---

107. Austin, *Saving China*, pp. 90-92. Gagan, *Sensitive Independence*, pp. 29-30.

were between twenty-one and thirty. Although the CIM had an upper limit of thirty, women continued to apply in their forties and fifties, many of them widows who had been released from family obligations. With its large institutional work, the CIM had places for motherly older women who did not need to speak Chinese, such as the Chefoo schools or the Shanghai office. In fact, Toronto sent thirty-six women over the age of thirty to China. Surprisingly, compared to ordinary mission societies, the CIM received equal numbers of men and women applicants. Of the 758 applications before 1901, there were 381 men and 377 women. Most mission societies around the world at the time reported that half, and sometimes as much as two-thirds of the missionary force were women: one-third single women and one-third wives.[108]

Chart 2
Denominational Affiliation
1887-1915

Summary of all applications to Toronto between 1887 and 1915. Numbers in parenthesis are included in the bold figures for the broader denomination.

	Canada		United States	
	Applicants	Candidates	Applicants	Candidates
Presbyterian	88 (34%)	31 (33%)	86 (21%)	35 (28%)
Cumberland			(2)	
United			(4)	(2)
Southern			(3)	(2)
Reform			(1)	
Baptist	67 (30%)	32 (34%)	64 (16%)	19 (15%)
Closed		(3)	(5)	
Swedish			(2)	
Free			(3)	
Methodist	41 (16%)	12 (13%)	60 (15%)	15 (12%)
Methodist Episcopal	(4)	(1)	(34)	(7)
Southern			(2)	
Norwegian			(2)	
Free			(1)	(1)

108. This paragraph is based on an analysis of 700 applications which give the person's age, 342 men and 358 women, between 1888 and 1915 (a somewhat broader scope, and the last date in the book). Of the men, 39 (11 percent) were twenty or younger; 252 (74 percent) in their twenties; 38 in their thirties, with only 6 older than that. By contrast, only 18 (5 percent) of the women applicants were twenty or younger; 236 were in their twenties; 87 (23 percent) in their thirties; and 14 women were older than forty. Altogether 36 women older than thirty were accepted and went to China.

The New World

	Canada		United States	
	Applicants	Candidates	Applicants	Candidates
Congregational	14 (5%)	4 (4%)	55 (14%)	18 (14%)
Swedish			(2)	
Anglican	25 (10%)	7 (7%)	16 (4%)	7 (6%)
Reformed Episcopal	(2)	(4)	(3)	
United Anglican	(1)	(1)		
Lutheran	—	5	(1%)	1
Evangelical	(2)	(1)		
Reformed Church USA			4 (1%)	3 (2%)
Dutch Reformed			(2)	(1)
Brethren	5 (2%)	3 (3%)	13 (3%)	7 (6%)
Plymouth	(2)	(2)		
United	(2)	(2)		
C&M Alliance	2		7	(2%)
Disciples of Christ	1	1	4	
Christian Workers	2			
Salvation Army	3	1	1	1
Quakers			5	
Mennonite			2	1
Amish			1	
Swedish Evangelical			1	
United Evangelical	1			
Evangelical Association	1	1		
Pentecostal		1	1	
Independent	1	1	3	1
Moody Church (only)	3		70	18
YMCA (only)	4	4		
Subtotal	258	95	401	127
Unknown	82	2	149	6
Total	340	97	550	133

In terms of denominational affiliation (Chart 2), distinct patterns emerge on either side of the border. Among Canadians, the vast majority, 90 percent (about the same proportion as the Protestant population of Ontario) belonged to the five national denominations, though not in the same ratio as the population: Presbyterians, then Baptists, Methodists, Anglicans, and Congregationalists. The American pattern is much more fragmented: 70 percent belonged to the traditional denominations, some in separatist branches like the Reformed Episcopal or Cumberland Presbyterian. This meant that whereas Baptists and Presbyterians made up two-thirds of Canadian applicants, they comprised barely one-third of Americans. This is explained by the presence of small denominations such as the Plymouth Brethren and Mennonites (from Lancaster, Pennsylvania, which provided a small but continuing stream from the 1890s on). Of American applicants, 17 percent, seventy individuals, listed membership in one church — the Moody Church in Chicago.

Henry Frost was not exaggerating when he said the majority of applicants were turned down for "lack of training," for the CIM accepted roughly one in seven applicants. Some were "not fitted in every way,"[109] such as a fifteen-year-old orphan living at Ontario Ladies College, or a widow in her sixties with three daughters asking to be considered as a group. There were retired ministers, divorced women, single parents, and two ex-Roman Catholic priests. The reasons for rejecting an applicant tended to be standardized: poor health, family objections, too young, too old, in debt. Few were rejected on theological grounds, although the terms "scripturally unsound" and "needs training" covered a multitude of cases. The sad story of a Methodist minister, Gilbert Robinson, illustrates exactly the sort of person the CIM was guarding against. He appeared at the Toronto office on Christmas Day 1895 and said his father was in the Hamilton asylum. He was "not accepted" but went to China independently; he came back to Canada "suffering from a delusion that his soul is damned eternally."[110]

The overwhelming cause for rejection was the CIM's peculiar policy on marriage. In Canada as in England, the CIM normally sent only unmarried men and women to China: of the fifty married couples who applied only seven were accepted. Rev. Edgar A. Brownlee, later Canadian director, was a rarity, an educated Baptist minister (B.A. and B.D. from McMaster University), married with a child. Even those who were engaged were questioned whether marriage or career had priority. Occasional remarks indicate broken engagements when one partner was accepted and the other turned down. The pattern seems to have been, if the man was accepted but not his fiancée, he tended to stay home and get married; if she were accepted but not he, more than likely she went to China as a single woman.

Few applications list previous occupations, except soul-saving among the "poor neglected ones" in Indian reserves and inner-city slums. The CIM did attract the "socially humble and financially poor"; in addition to home mission work, the occupations for men included harness maker, farm hand, me-

---

109. Application #626.
110. Newspaper clipping attached to his application.

chanic, upholsterer, shop employee, grocer, bookkeeper, and factory worker. Many women had cared for their parents, or worked as a teacher, dressmaker, tailor, housekeeper, servant, bookkeeper, stenographer, or nurse.

If two people can show the diversity of the CIM, one could not pick less similar candidates than Petrus Rijnhart and Kathleen Stayner. Rijnhart was (possibly) one of the great rogues of the China missions. Born in Rotterdam he came to Toronto in 1886 at the age of twenty, where he worked in a factory to learn English. He applied to the CIM in 1890 but before his case came up, he decided to walk to China — and he did walk as far as Chicago before someone gave him the money to take a train. In Shanghai, he applied directly to the China council and was sent to remote Gansu, where he created a "hornet's nest" of animosity. When rumors surfaced of Rijnhart's "dissolute life in Canada," he was "summarily dismissed," and returned to Toronto, vowing to wreck the CIM. Yet, somehow, he managed to marry the sweetest, most intelligent of women, Dr. Susie Carson, one of Canada's first female doctors, and took her to Tibet. After four years in northern Tibet — several stages beyond Annie Taylor, the lone wolf of Gansu — they set off across the roof of the world to Lhasa, a nightmare journey in which Petrus disappeared behind a rock and was never seen again.[111]

Kathleen Stayner represented the respectable side. She lived next door to the CIM, a twenty-year-old "orphan, very well educated, an heiress, free from hindrances which would keep her from China and deeply devoted to the Lord." She went to China, where her health was soon "shattered," and was invalided to a European spa; she went back to China three times, for a year or two each time until she was sent to Bath, England, where she died in 1907, aged thirty-five.[112]

When Hudson Taylor established the North American CIM, Benjamin Broomhall had commented that the British could never work with Americans. Americans — and Canadians — with no experience of an established

---

111. While recuperating in Toronto, Dr. Susie Rijnhart wrote *With the Tibetans in Tent and Temple: Narrative of Four Years' Residence on the Tibetan Border, and of a Journey into the Far Interior* (Chicago: Foreign Christian Missionary Society, 1901; reprint, New York: Fleming H. Revell, 1911), a classic of nineteenth-century Tibetan exploration. She subsequently returned to Tibet at the head of the Disciples of Christ mission, where she married another CIM missionary, James Moyes of Sichuan, who had to resign his connection to marry her. She was mentioned in histories of Tibet, such as Peter Hopkirk, *Trespassers on the Roof of the World: The Race for Lhassa* (London: J. Murray, 1982). Biographical entry by Alvyn Austin in *Dictionary of Canadian Biography*, vol. 13, pp. 175-76. *HTCOC 7*, pp. 194-96. Correspondence JHT to Frost, 15 July 1893 and 30 November 1893, in CIM/ABGC, file 5/11.

112. Frost, "Memoirs," pp. 421-22. Application record #264.

church could not comprehend the delicate balance Broomhall had created in Britain of Anglicans and Brethren, of working class yeomen and aristocrats, of tightly chaperoned unmarried men and women. He would have shared the common prejudice that Andrew Walls noted (quoting a Japanese Christian, Kanzo Uchimura): "the word *American* conveys, first of all, immense energy, resourcefulness, and inventiveness — a habit of identifying problems and solving them — and, as a result, first-rate technology. . . . Americans have a tendency to translate those very [religious] dimensions into technological terms, problems to be solved, something that can be all worked out — big boots in the Temple, as one might say."[113] That was certainly Broomhall's reaction when Frost came to London demanding that the CIM become "Americanized and democratized."

Mrs. Radcliffe's comment that there were big hearts and heavy purses in America proved to be prescient. The North American branch always contributed more than its share. By the 1930s, it was raising some $500,000 annually, one-half the operating budget of the entire CIM. Yet it supplied only one-third the missionaries.[114] By then British and Americans had learned to work together, but during Hudson Taylor's lifetime, the two branches of the CIM functioned as independent entities, communicating directly with Shanghai, each raising money to finance its own nationals rather than contributing to a common pot.

Just as the transplanting of the CIM to North America led to the rapid internationalization of the CIM, with branches and associates in Australia and Europe, this was reflected in the increasing American presence in China, as we shall see in the next chapter. In this process, it was not a coincidence that Canada was the pivot, the "hyphen in the Anglo American missionary alliance."[115] According to Harry Hussey, a witty observer of the China scene (he was a Canadian architect employed by the YMCA), the typical British expatriate was a younger son who expected to make his home there for forty years. He brought his club and his magazines — and his potted meat and marmalade — with him. "His children usually attended an English school somewhere in China until they were about twelve years old, when they were sent to England to complete their education. . . . This often meant that the parents

---

113. Andrew F. Walls, "The American Dimension in the History of the Missionary Movement," in Carpenter and Shenk, eds., *Earthen Vessels: American Evangelicals and Foreign Missions, 1880-1980*.

114. Austin, "Blessed Adversity."

115. Quoted in Peter M. Mitchell, "The Missionary Connection," in B. Michael Frolic and Paul A. Evans, eds., *Reluctant Adversaries: Canada and the People's Republic of China, 1949-1970* (Toronto: University of Toronto Press, 1990).

The New World

saw their children only a few times during the remainder of their lives. While this did little to strengthen the family ties it did make the children into loyal little Englishmen and Englishwomen." Americans on the other hand stayed in China until they made their "stake" and then returned to "God's country." They were "much friendlier with the Chinese, mixed with them more freely, ate their food, gave candy to their children and danced with their wives."[116] Except for the dancing wives, this was an apt description of the British and Americans in the CIM, with Canadians and Australians somewhere in the middle.

---

116. Harry Hussey, *My Pleasures and Palaces: An Informal Memoir of Forty Years in Modern China* (Garden City, N.Y.: Doubleday, 1968), pp. 81-82. One who epitomized the Yankee temperament was Edgar Knickerbocker of Lockport, New York, whom Frost initially turned down because of his inveterate habit of story-telling; the Chinese love stories and Knickerbocker made a successful missionary: Frost, "Memoirs," p. 479.

CHAPTER 10

God's Ambassadors
1888-1899

> At Kwei-k'i Hien [Guiqi Xian, Zhejiang], the native teacher, our excellent brother Ts'ai, has lost his wife by death. . . . Not an hour before she died, she professed her faith in Christ, and said she was not afraid to die; and a little while later said she felt she was going. Mr. Ts'ai said, "Are you trusting in the lord?" She replied, "Yes, I have seen him;" and lifting up her eyes and hands, added, "All clothed in white." Her mouth still continued to move, but the words soon became inaudible.
>
> J. E. Cardwell, annual report for Po-yang Lake District, Kiang-si, 1883[1]

The Third Generation

Now, another Pilgrim is at sea. It is January 1891, and Henry Frost, the North American home director of the China Inland Mission, is escorting four candidates, two men and two women, to China. Frost visited China four times between 1891 and 1904, for a total of over two years, to see the missionaries in their "habitat . . . the true home of the Mission."[2] He thus was the only CIM home director with field experience, since neither Benjamin Broomhall nor Theodore Howard ever visited China.[3] However, between 1904 and 1932, when he retired, he did not visit again, so his impressions of China were conditioned by what he saw before and soon after the Boxer uprising.

1. *China's Millions* (GB), August 1883, pp. 103-4.
2. Frost, "Memoirs," pp. 338-39. Taylor and Taylor, "*By Faith*," p. 184.
3. A. B. Simpson and Frederik Franson also visited China in the 1890s.

Hudson Taylor and the China council, 10 April 1905. On his return to China in 1905, Hudson Taylor (front center) met with the China council. Eleven members were present, but eleven more were scattered throughout inland China. The meeting included three of Taylor's relatives: D. E. Hoste, his successor, stands behind him next to Dr. Howard Taylor (fourth), and J. J. Coulthard, his son-in-law, is at the front left. Alexander R. Saunders, the first Canadian in the CIM and superintendent of Shanxi, is standing at the extreme right. Taylor died a few days later at Changsha, capital of the "bitterly anti-foreign" province of Hunan.
Source: *China's Millions* (NA), August 1905.

There was a dark side to Frost's character, which Mrs. Howard Taylor tried to whitewash in the official biography. He was subject to depression, amounting almost to nervous breakdowns, brought on by overwork, unfamiliar surroundings, or theological conundrums. "I have always been a great dreamer," he admitted, "my visions generally being vivid and filled with details."[4] China brought out the worst in him. Like many missionaries, he had a visceral reaction to heathenism, a physical nausea, and on each trip he had a vision of Satan. They were dark hallucinatory journeys, "a long and fearsome tunnel, in which there were a few rays of light and where the darkness grew deeper and deeper as I passed along. There were indeed rays of light, those missionaries, native pastors, evangelists, Bible women and church members shining radiantly with the very glory of God. But all of the rest was darkness, a darkness

4. Frost, "Memoirs," p. 383.

with no relief and indescribably profound."[5] If a rational, educated (Princeton, no less) man like Frost, with an engineer's mind and Presbyterian "common sense," was susceptible to panic, what could be expected of the rank and file?

In 1890, a year after Frost and his family settled in Toronto, the CIM in North America was still "largely and almost exclusively myself." Officially the secretary-treasurer, he was "also the Home Director, the deputation speaker, the head of the Mission Home, the teacher of candidates resident in the Home, the bookkeeper, the buyer of tickets for outgoing parties, the checker of missionary luggage, the packer of book-boxes, the shipper of freight-boxes, etc., etc."[6] That summer the CIM's benefactor, Archibald Orr Ewing, and his wife Mary (the daughter of the publisher Robert Scott) passed through Toronto and offered to pay the expenses for Frost to visit China. Orr Ewing had already donated, anonymously, the funds to erect the head office in Shanghai and the home in Newington Green, and by the time Frost returned from China, he had contributed to a new home in Toronto.

Frost and his party sailed from Vancouver, singing a new hymn, "Jesus, Savior, pilot me, Over life's tempestuous sea," and arrived at Shanghai one month later. The brand new home on Woosung Road was so grandiose that some called it "Taylor's Folly." It had accommodations for a hundred or more missionaries, but it was quickly filled when thirty-five men and women of the Scandinavian Alliance arrived unannounced, and asked to be admitted as associates. They were the first of "Franson's floods," the Swedish Americans who had been recruited by Frederik Franson from Michigan to Kansas and beyond (see Chapter 9). They were still there when Frost's party arrived, followed by three men from Australia and fifteen more Scandinavian Americans. Frost — used to living in penury in Toronto — was "impressed that our 'poor, faith Mission' had received some pretty generous treatment on the part of our Father in heaven; for first, there was an extensive compound which was beautifully bedecked with grass, palms and flowers, and then, there were large and splendidly equipped buildings reaching around three sides of the compound, one side being left open for sunlight and ventilation."[7]

To welcome Frost, Hudson Taylor invited the North American workers, who numbered thirty-one by this time, to come to Shanghai for a spiritual conference. Since most were in the adjacent province of Jiangxi, twenty-nine

---

5. Ibid., p. 374.
6. For Frost's first trip, see ibid., pp. 327-87; quote at p. 325. Taylor and Taylor, *"By Faith,"* pp. 183-99.
7. Frost, "Memoirs," pp. 339-40. Taylor and Taylor, *"By Faith,"* pp. 184-85.

did come. Frost could hardly recognize the probationers he had sent out a year or two earlier, since they were all wearing Chinese clothes, the men with moustaches and pigtails and the women in blue cotton trousers. The gathering was "radiant" in Swedish and English, and when it ended, they declared, "We have seen Jesus." But as soon as Frost left the tiny island of white man's civilization, he came face to face with Satan.

The summer of 1891 was not the safest of times for a white man to be wandering through Central China. A round of antiforeign, antimissionary violence had been sparked by a Roman Catholic agent's attempt to "purchase" a group of orphans in Hankou. The excited mob fell on the first foreigners they saw; within days, stations for hundreds of miles had been pillaged and the missionaries forced to flee to the treaty ports. The Catholic orphanages in Yangzhou and Anqing were burned to the ground, though the CIM language schools were unharmed. After an American missionary and a British official were killed at Hankou, Protestants and Catholics were attacked indiscriminately. The CIM was rioted out of the women's stations along Guangxin River, and the tremors were felt as far inland as Sichuan.[8]

Within the CIM, some debated whether they had the moral right to protect themselves with guns. At the height of the agitation, Hudson Taylor affirmed the CIM policy of neither demanding nor accepting remuneration from the Chinese government for property damage or personal injury. In an open letter he admonished his people to follow Christ's example: "We are in our stations at God's command, and as His ambassadors, and therefore have both promise of, and claim to, His protection. . . . A holy joy in God is a far better protector than a revolver."[9] Once again his pacific attitude put the CIM at the outer fringes of the foreign community, as businessmen and missionaries alike armed themselves with more than "holy joy" against the restless natives.

Although Frost passed through the district during the riot season, he does not mention it in his "Memoirs," except for a few outbursts of "foreign devil." His lack of political commentary indicates how insulated he was inside the CIM bubble. He did not attempt to use chopsticks or learn Chinese, beyond asking for hot water. His missionary guide took him through Shanghai, "showing me what I was justified in seeing, and leading me away from the sights which we did not wish to look upon." His nights were made "largely sleepless and often hideous" by the sound of wailing, gongs, and firecrackers,

---

8. Edmund S. Wehrle, *Britain, China, and the Anti-missionary Riots, 1891-1900* (Minneapolis: University of Minnesota Press, 1966).

9. *China's Millions* (GB), August 1891, pp. 113-14.

and during the day, "heathenism seemed always in sight and sound, its temples and shrines obtruding themselves upon one on every hand and its discordant cries and chants permeating the air one breathed."[10]

After the conference Taylor suggested that Frost escort a party of single women (including Maggie Scott, the healer, and her sister Tina, see Chapter 9) who were returning to their stations in Jiangxi. His companion was Stanley Smith, the "sunny" member of the Cambridge Seven. Smith, who was recovering from the death of his wife, Sophie Reuter, after two years of marriage, proved to be "a well informed missionary, a fluent speaker of the Chinese language, a godly man and, in every way, a most agreeable and likeable fellow."[11] They avoided the Yangtze and made their way up the small rivers that branch out from Hangzhou, over the hills and down the Guangxin River, the women's river.

Frost's fear and depression were intensified when Katie McIntosh, a gentle Scotswoman who held the Yushan "church and its adherents in the hollow of her hand," pointed out one convert, a "white-haired dame, with a heavenly face, who had had twenty-one children and had drowned with her own hand twenty of them. She told me tales of woe such as I had never before heard, of opium sots, gambling fiends, tyrannical and murderous women, and wives and children being sold into slavery and harlotry. In short, she revealed heathenism to me, till I could stand no more and wondered with a great wonderment how she could live, year in and year out, in such surroundings."[12]

One "ebony black" night, when their boat was moored outside the looming city walls, Satan appeared at the foot of Frost's bed. He was "attractive beyond all expectation. He was beautifully attired, his figure was perfectly formed and his face was strikingly handsome and benign. One feature of his face, however, was startling; his eyes, while lustrous, had in their depths the fire and venom of hell." "How long do you intend to go on?" Satan sneered, and, "I'll hound you to the day of your death." Frost understood instinctively that Satan knew Frost was trying to dispossess him of his kingdom, and he answered "calmly as if I had been speaking to Christ instead of his archenemy: 'Satan,' I said, 'whatever the result to me or mine may be, I intend to go on just as I am doing to the end of my life.'" With a murderous look, the apparition vanished.[13]

Frost fled to Shanghai, where a telegram urged him to return home im-

10. Frost, "Memoirs," p. 348.
11. Ibid., p. 350.
12. Ibid., p. 363.
13. Ibid., pp. 370-71. Taylor and Taylor, *"By Faith,"* does not mention this incident.

mediately. His companion across the Pacific was, again, Stanley Smith, who was returning to England on furlough. Smith was troubled by four conundrums that baffled Frost. Although they seem on the surface to represent Smith's "deep morass of spiritual legalism," they were extreme versions of views widely held within the mission. The first was sartorial: what should he wear when he reached England? Smith intended to dress in a business suit, but when he spent the weekends in the country homes of the gentry, should he dress for dinner? Why do you wear Chinese dress in China, Frost pointed out, if not to get close to the people? By analogy, in England Smith should dress like the gentry to "conform to the customs of the people." The second betrayed the anticlerical bias of the CIM. He could not use the word "Reverend," even when addressing bishops and high dignitaries, because it was one of the titles of God. Again from analogy, Frost noted that "Mister" was derived from Master, which was also one of God's titles, and that a man could be called Reverend because of his character and office.[14]

As he wandered the ancient mountains of Shanxi reading his Greek New Testament, Smith had developed an obsession with the Greek word *aiōn*. If an "eon" was infinite (eternity), then God stated the unregenerate would be punished forever in hell. Like W. T. Berger, Smith had come to conditionalist views concerning the existence of hell and the future life, which he called "the Larger Hope" — the name comes from Tennyson's *In Memoriam*, a Victorian panegyric that offered hope for a future life despite scientific doubt[15] — which "signified that all men will come to believe in Christ and so be saved, some in this life, and the others, as a result of adequate punishment and suffering, in the life to come."[16] In a sense Smith was fighting a rearguard action, for conditionalism may have been a living issue in the 1860s, but by 1890 it no longer troubled the consciences of orthodox evangelicals. In 1872 Berger had to resign immediately and secretly; but Smith published "almost tomes" on the larger hope, and the controversy dragged on for a decade.

Smith also came to "extreme views on the nonuse of medicines." He translated the Greek word *pharmakaeia* — translated in the Bible as "sorcery" — into a blanket condemnation of "the use of any kind of drugs, potions, or spells." Perhaps Smith came to these views because of his own use of morphine in treating opium addicts. He later repudiated his belief that medicine was sorcery, although he maintained a conscientious objection to vaccina-

---

14. Ibid., pp. 379-82.
15. Rowell, *Hell and the Victorians*, pp. 5-6, stated that "trust in 'the larger hope' became a keynote of much that was written on the subject" of conditionalism.
16. Frost, "Memoirs," p. 668.

tion. In 1900 he wrote "a heartfelt apology . . . for those misguided and offensive sentiments" to Hudson Taylor, published in the *Chinese Recorder*.[17]

Frost made his second visit to China for eleven months in 1895-96, when he was sent there to recover from a nervous breakdown brought on by overwork in Toronto. On board ship, his condition deteriorated physically and emotionally, until he was "more nearly dead than alive" and the ship's physician had to administer a "very strong heart stimulant." By the time he reached Shanghai, he was hallucinating that the tendrils of a vine outside his window were "serpents, with protruding and hissing tongues." He had a heart attack, and came to consciousness with the words "Blood, blood, blood!" ringing in his ears. During his convalescence, Hudson Taylor also fell critically ill: "First, we were up, and then, down; first, we were well, and then, sick."[18] During their life-or-death crisis, Frost experienced healing after being anointed with oil, and Taylor similarly responded "like one who had been raised from the dead."[19]

Here was another conundrum. Since faith healing was occurring regularly within the CIM, Taylor and Frost studied the scriptures together concerning the gifts of the Spirit. Frost came to the conclusion that the saints will not be "raptured up" before the Tribulation, i.e., *pre*-tribulationist premillennial dispensationalism. Rather, he came to the *post*-tribulationist belief that only the dead will be raptured up: the saints would live through the seven years of tribulation as a witness in the midst of furnace fires, after which they will rise to meet Christ in the air. The "trend of present events, religious, ecclesiastical, social, educational, economic and political, is making positively and rapidly in this direction." Thus, Frost's personal dark night of the soul was transmuted into a dark theology: "the giving up of old and happy prospects for new and less happy ones nearly broke my heart."[20]

Frost's pilgrimages parallel the chronology of this chapter, which starts with the missionary conference of 1890 and ends before the Boxer uprising. This was "the high tides of imperialism," when the Western powers redrew the map of China with railways and telegraph lines: the common expression

---

17. Stanley P. Smith, from Saffron Walden, England, 17 April 1900, "A Retraction," *Chinese Recorder*, July 1900, pp. 364-65.

18. For Frost's second trip, see "Memoirs," pp. 462-510; quotes at pp. 464-65, 471, 473, 476.

19. Ibid., p. 471. Frost, *Miraculous Healing*, p. 18.

20. Frost, "Memoirs," pp. 498-99. The shift from pre-tribulationist to post-tribulationist views was an important "revision of millennialism" adopted by other Toronto Bible teachers, such as Parsons and Harris. Marsden, *Fundamentalism and American Culture*, p. 241 note 17, stated that the controversy between pre-tribulationist and post-tribulationist groups shattered the American prophetic movement and led to the demise of the Niagara Bible Conference in 1901.

God's Ambassadors

was "carving the melon" into spheres of influence. After the Sino-Japanese War of 1894, Japan annexed Taiwan and loosed a "scramble for concessions." Germany occupied Jiaozhou Bay in Shandong, France invaded Yunnan, and Britain claimed the Yangtze valley from Shanghai to Tibet. China was "open": open for business, open for exploitation, open for opium, open for the gospel.

Wherever foreigners went, the CIM had been there first. The appeal for the Hundred in 1886-88 was the last of the CIM's great recruitment campaigns, simply because such drives were no longer needed. In 1888, when Hudson Taylor brought the North American party, the CIM had 296 missionaries (133 male, 163 female), three-quarters of whom (222) had less than five years' experience. Within seven years the CIM and its associates had doubled, and exceeded 800 by 1900. "There was scarcely a grey head in the Mission in those days," Mrs. Howard Taylor recalled, and "everything seemed possible."[21] In practical terms this meant the implementation of the CIM "system" in a hundred ways, as widespread itineration gave way to methodical visitation of smaller and smaller districts around established centers.

It would be too strong to say that Henry Frost, the passerby who "glimpsed into the heathen world," foresaw the Boxer terror, but he was not the only one to realize that China was a volcano about to explode. Timothy Richard and W. A. P. Martin thought the explosion could be channeled by education and modernization. They became advisors to the reformers gathered around the young Guangxu emperor. Under their influence, in 1898 the emperor enacted a sweeping series of edicts known as the Hundred Days of Reform. But then the Empress Dowager Cixi gained power, canceled the edicts, and put the emperor under house arrest until he died (in 1908, supposedly poisoned, one day before Cixi herself died). Thus ended any hope of reforming the Qing dynasty, at least as long as the "Old Buddha" was alive. The last years of the century witnessed increasingly violent confrontations between China and the West, and it was to the credit of the crumbling Chinese state that no CIM missionary died by violence until 1898.[22]

The High Tides

The trumpet call of the 1890s was sounded by the General Missionary Conference held in Shanghai from 7 to 20 May 1890. It was an august, self-

---

21. *Growth of a Work of God*, p. 458.
22. Two Swedish men, who were not formal associates, were killed in 1893 in Hubei: *HTCOC 7*, p. 171.

confident gathering, with 445 delegates comprising one-third of the missionary force. It was marked by the increasing presence of women (233 males and 212 females) and Americans: 213 British delegates, 206 Americans, 3 Canadians, 4 Europeans — and, distressingly, only two Chinese. Of the thirty-six societies represented, the CIM had by far the largest contingent: 84 delegates (47 men and 37 women), and had representatives on fifteen of the nineteen committees. The next largest, the American Presbyterians, had 49 delegates, and the Methodist Episcopal 35; among British societies the LMS had 20, and the CMS 19 (plus 6 women of the CMS Zenana Mission).[23]

They included learned sinologues and upcountry workers, who presented papers and discussed all aspects of the work, including "social, Biblical, evangelistic, educational, medical, and related political and social topics." They tried to steer away from the controversy that was beginning to widen between liberals and conservatives, and resolved long-standing divisions like the "term question," adopting the name *Shangdi* as the Protestant name for God, and promoting a standard translation of the Bible. Hudson Taylor gave the opening address on Jesus' feeding of the five thousand. He presented his vision that he had enunciated in *To Every Creature*, that China could be evangelized by one thousand foreign evangelists within three years (see Chapter 9). The conference did not consider Taylor's vision to be "chimerical," and issued a united appeal to Protestant churches worldwide to send "one thousand consecrated men" to China in the next five years, including evangelists, teachers, doctors, and nurses — the beginnings of the social gospel.

Unfortunately, when the delegates assembled for the commemorative group photograph, the scaffolding collapsed, injuring several. The collapse was symbolic of the discordant note when Gilbert Reid read a paper by W. A. P. Martin, a respected elder statesman who had resigned from the American Presbyterian mission to become president of a government college and edit a gazette that was influential among Chinese reformers. The title summed up Martin's paper: "The Worship of Ancestors — A Plea for Tolerance." Echoing Timothy Richard, Martin suggested that Christianity could be presented as "the successor of Buddhism" or "'Confucius plus Christ' and never 'Christ or Confucius.'" Although many delegates might have agreed in the abstract, they raised their eyebrows when Martin said he "accepted both the form and function of kneeling and bowing, affirming that while these actions were idolatrous in certain contexts, they definitely were not in others," such as making "salutations and announce-

---

23. *Records of the General Conference of the Protestant Missionaries of China, Held at Shanghai, May 7-20, 1890* (Shanghai: American Presbyterian Mission Press, 1890), p. xxiii. See also *HTCOC 7*, pp. 138-43, "The Third General Missionary Conference, Shanghai."

ments to the dead."[24] Reid added his own plea for the "mighty task" of reaching "the princes, ministers and censors in the central government."[25]

Hudson Taylor led the conservative attack. In the heated debate, he demanded that "a rising vote of dissent" be put to the conference. As the official report stated: "Without a motion to that effect he asked those who dissented from the conclusion of Dr Martin's paper to rise. Most of the audience then rose, upon which one of the preceding speakers [Reid or Richard] protested that this was not a fair way to treat such a subject."[26] Nevertheless, Martin asserted, "many missionaries have assured me that they concur in the general sentiment of the paper."[27]

The conference brought the CIM to unusual prominence, since treaty port residents would seldom see a foreigner in "the costume of the country." They found the presence of a hundred men and women in gowns and pigtails to be "incongruous, not to say bizarre." As one American from Canton sniffed, "Chinese dress too often means a Chinese house, pure and simple, and native furniture, native utensils, native food." He repeated the rumors that "one half of those who enter China under its [the CIM's] auspices, return within two years, either to their homeland on earth or the home above, and that the average term of service for the whole body is only three and a half years."[28]

Taylor wrote a carefully worded response, pointing out that the CIM had had sent 539 persons to China over the previous twenty-six years. Only 44 had left China during their two-year probationary period, of whom 21 were "removed by death," 5 were invalided home, 4 resigned, 5 were "requested to withdraw," and 9 left "on account of marriage or family claims." Of the 373 full members (those who completed their probation), 22 had died, 12 were invalided home, 4 were transferred to the home department, 21 had "retired," 9 were requested to resign, and 18 left on account of marriage or family. (This by his own admission amounted to one-quarter of the personnel.) Since one-half of the missionaries were recent arrivals, this explained the short length of service; some veterans had twenty-five years' service. He concluded somewhat ingenuously that "the Mis-

---

24. Covell, *W. A. P. Martin: Pioneer of Progress in China*, pp. 250-52.
25. Tsou Mingteh, "Christian Missionary as Confucian Intellectual: Gilbert Reid (1857-1927) and the Reform Movement in Late Qing," in Daniel H. Bays, ed., *Christianity in China*, p. 80.
26. *Records of the General Conference*, p. 659.
27. Covell, *W. A. P. Martin*, p. 252.
28. Rev. B. C. Henry, "Chinese Dress in the Shanghai Conference," *Chinese Recorder*, December 1890, pp. 550-52, noted that "fully one fourth" of the participants wore Chinese dress. To wear Chinese clothes for traveling was one thing, he said, but it was wrong to wear them in Shanghai or advocate them as a "duty." *HTCOC* 7, pp. 159-61.

sion is, by God's blessing, one of the healthiest in China, and that its policy has not led to any 'alarming sacrifice' of life, but rather the reverse."[29]

This was one of the "controversies within and attacks from without" that plagued the CIM in the 1890s.[30] Dr. Happer, an American Presbyterian in Canton, relayed "rumours prejudicial to the Mission," the old charge that the CIM prevailed upon its members to be rebaptized as Baptists. "The statements you have heard of proselytism are entirely false," Taylor replied. "Though a Baptist myself," the CIM had set aside certain districts for Baptists, Presbyterians, Anglicans, Methodists, and Plymouth Brethren.[31]

In 1891 a correspondent to the *North China Daily News* reported from Yichang, gateway to the Yangtze gorges, that CIM men and women were "promiscuously travelling in company overland" and were "huddled together" without chaperones, "aping Chinese dress and manners." "*Untrue*," Taylor responded. "Their man-servant was a quiet disciple, and the boat-woman who acted as their servant, there is some hope was converted and helped them to preach." By this time the CIM had considerable support among the missionary community and the rumours subsided. Besides, Chinese dress was now an expedient if eccentric mode of traveling.[32]

Nothing shows the respectability of the CIM so well as the near-hysterical reaction to A. B. Simpson's announcement in 1893 that he was sending two hundred Swedish Americans to China. These were "Franson's floods" going under the International Missionary Alliance, the overseas wing of the Christian and Missionary Alliance (C&MA, which was not a formal associate mis-

---

29. JHT, letter from Shanghai, 26 December 1890, in *China's Millions* (GB), January 1891, p. 35. JHT's statistics did not include those whose health was poor but not life threatening and thus were not "invalided" home. Such rumors circulated for years, and the annual reports took pains to refute them. *China's Millions* (NA), July 1896, p. 92, noted that deaths numbered nine out of 641, or "$17\frac{1}{6}$ per thousand — a very low rate for a semitropical climate." Yet, A. J. Broomhall commented, "still the deaths followed one upon another." *HTCOC 7*, p. 160.

By comparison, P. D. Coates, *The China Consuls*, p. 96, stated: "The health of the [consular] service was deplorable, due primarily . . . to malaria and intestinal diseases, and certainly made worse by the infrequency of home leaves. . . . Of the thirteen young assistants appointed in 1843, eight were dead by the age of 45 and three others had retired in broken health before reaching that age. Far too much food and alcohol cannot have helped." (See also Chapter 4, quotation from Dr. James Henderson.)

30. The CMS was similarly affected, for Eugene V. Stock, *The History of the Church Missionary Society*, vol. 3, used this phrase as the title of chapter 87.

31. China council minutes, 4 June 1890, in CIM/SOAS. See also *HTCOC 7*, p. 156.

32. *North China Daily News*, July 1891. This was an English business newspaper in Tianjin with an anti-missionary bias. A correspondent in Chongqing said that in eight years he had "never known anything improper" in the CIM's traveling arrangements. *HTCOC 7*, p. 159.

sion of the CIM, but cooperated closely). They were to arrive, the *Chinese Recorder* stated, in "batches of twenty, with only one month between the installments. Their pay, which is to cover all expenses, will be $200 (gold) a year." This was less even than the CIM, which also provided travel expenses and evangelists' salaries, and only one-quarter of most societies' salaries. The IMA was expected like "an invasion rather than a re-enforcement," since some could barely "intelligently correspond with the Directorate in America" because their education was so poor.[33]

By this time the *Chinese Recorder* tended to be circumspect regarding the CIM, if only because so many of its correspondents were CIM, including Stanley Smith and G. W. Clarke of Shanxi. When Hudson Taylor had started "his now great Mission," the editor commented, he was an experienced worker who "proceeded with due caution, and did not venture to bring large numbers into the service until from tested conditions he could discern success in the wider sphere." Nevertheless when the Alliance recruits did arrive, the veteran missionary W. S. Ament was charmed by their vitality and simplicity: "They have warm hearts, willing hands and strong bodies and are going to the rough country beyond and near the Great Wall. . . . They are as markedly called of God, and perhaps more so than many who have more extensive acquirements."[34] He wished them God-speed, and they were off, "singing, singing all the way" to the wilds of Inner Mongolia.

The consular authorities tried to control the flood of missionaries. Unfortunately they were still laboring under the old ruling, never rescinded, that missionaries had no right to reside outside the treaty ports and that consuls should not sanction their doing so. One consul in Chongqing, on hearing that a dozen CIM women were expected, asked for instructions: "if missionaries had no right of residence they had in theory only themselves to blame if they got into trouble; on the other hand, it was in practice hard to pass over in silence the public thrashing of a lady, and if a life were lost redress surely had to be sought."[35]

The consuls were overtaken by events, for a "game with such indeterminate rules could be played with success only when British and Chinese officials were sensible and firm and when missionaries [were] tactful and ready

---

33. *Chinese Recorder*, February 1893, pp. 94-95. The IMA was covered extensively over the next few months.

34. Ibid., July 1893, pp. 343-44.

35. Coates, *China Consuls*, pp. 180-81. Missionary cases took an inordinate amount of the consuls' time: in southwest China administered from Chongqing, for example, of the 240 British subjects, 232 were Protestant missionaries and their families. In 1881 there was one station in Sichuan; by 1900 there were nine, belonging to five societies (p. 310).

to co-operate with officials." The rules were changed "with vigorous insensitivity" in 1896 when the British Foreign Office appointed Sir C. M. MacDonald as minister plenipotentiary. He was "a curious intruder into diplomacy," P. D. Coates wrote in the official history of the China consular service, who had learned the rules of Empire in the British army in Africa. He declared that missionaries had a right to purchase property and travel anywhere in China, with a military escort if necessary.[36]

Anti-Christian disturbances were a fact of life throughout the 1890s, culminating in a grisly massacre in Gucheng (old spelling Ku-ch'eng, now Gutian), Fujian province, in 1895, in which nine CMS and Zenana missionaries and two children were killed by a secret society that called themselves the "Vegetarians."[37] The consul blamed the "want of discipline" among the women of the Zenana Mission, the women's branch of the CMS: their actions were "a danger and an obstacle to the spread of Christianity." Sixty-six unmarried missionary ladies of the Church Missionary and Zenana Societies were "rather a responsibility for an unfortunate consul. I cannot but think that more advance would be made by a smaller number, and that such an army is more calculated to excite opposition than to win converts." The diplomatic resolution of the Gucheng massacre was grisly, exactly what the CIM was trying to avoid. The provincial governor asked the consul how many heads he demanded; to avoid being hoodwinked, the consul reluctantly was present at the torture of the accused men (the only recorded occasion in the China service). Eventually twenty men were executed in installments.[38]

Historians have noted the collusion between disgruntled literati and unwise magistrates, but this was supplemented by new anti-Christian elements among the students and secret societies. Protestant missionaries had targeted the civil service examinations since Timothy Richard distributed tracts after the Shanxi famine. This was a volatile time when thousands of scholars would emerge from their ordeal, and a confrontation could escalate from stone throwing to a full-fledged riot, forcing the missionary to fold his table and beat a hasty retreat. The secret societies were more subtle, as the Gutian riot showed: it was carried out by a local religious sect who had been losing its

---

36. Ibid., p. 166. Esherick, *Origins of the Boxer Uprising*, p. 92, quoted Robert Hart, Inspector-General of the Chinese Customs, concerning MacDonald: "those of us who have succeeded so badly by treating Chinese as educated and civilized ought now to be ready to yield the ground to a man versed in negro methods and ignorant of the East."

37. *Church Missionary Intelligencer*, September 1895, pp. 656ff. Stock, *History of the CMS*, vol. 3, pp. 582-87.

38. Coates, *China Consuls*, pp. 214-15.

God's Ambassadors

members to the rival Christians; but, the missionaries emphasized, the sect was not anti-Christian, it was a revolutionary, anti-Qing society that attacked the Christians as a foil to get the Qing state into trouble with the Western powers.

The following charts give an overview of the explosion of the CIM between 1885 and 1899.[39] In Chart 3 the provinces are listed chronologically according to the date of the first station, so it provides a geographical synopsis of three generations of CIM stations. The first were the coastal provinces of Jiangsu, Zhejiang, and Anhui opened in 1867-70. The next group shows the bombshell scattering the missionaries inland in 1875-77, as they explored north from the Yangtze valley to Hubei and Henan; northwest to Shanxi, Shaanxi, and Gansu; and southwest to Sichuan, Yunnan, and Guizhou. Shandong and Zhili, the last provinces, were institutional — the Chefoo schools and a business office in Baoding that kept a line of communication to the inland provinces. Hunan, always the exception, was so "bitterly anti-Christian" that it was not "occupied" until 1897, when an outstation was established just inside the border.

The CIM expanded exponentially in all directions, but each province grew according to local persecution or enthusiasm. Certain points are worth noting. There were large institutions in Jiangsu, Shandong, Anhui, and Hubei. Organized "forward movements" led to dramatic spurts in Jiangxi and Shanxi in 1888-91, and in Shaanxi, Sichuan, Yunnan, and Guizhou in 1891-96. At the peripheries the CIM was thinly spread, in ones and twos, while in the established provinces new mission stations had to be shoehorned in, as missionaries took over chapels that had been established by native pastors, often displacing the local leaders in the process.

Chart 3
Growth of the CIM by Provinces

Number of missionaries, date founded, and (number of stations):

	1885	1888	1891	1896	1899
Jiangsu	18	22	57	55	57
1854	(2)	(5)	(6)	(6)	(6)
Zhejiang	21	24	36	65	91
1857	(9)	(12)	(11)	(20)	(25)

39. One could use other statistics to make the same point: In 1888 the CIM had 14 schools; by 1898 it had 114, with 1600 students, and employing 600 Chinese teachers, evangelists, and Biblewomen.

Anhui	13	21	28	54	56
1869	(4)	(5)	(9)	(12)	(14)
Jiangxi	5	15	48	51	89
1869	(2)	(6)	(13)	(15)	(24)
Hubei	10	17	8	16	13
1874	(3)	(5)	(2)	(3)	(3)
Hunan	2	—	—	—	7
1875	(1)	—	—	—	(3)
Henan	2	14	20	28	33
1875	(1)	(2)	(3)	(8)	(11)
Shanxi	23	41	64	77	103
1876	(6)	(12)	(15)	(22)	(25)
Shaanxi	12	17	29	74	78
1876	(2)	(4)	(5)	(16)	(21)
Gansu	13	20	26	35	42
1876	(4)	(5)	(6)	(9)	(10)
Sichuan	12	33	48	74	96
1877	(2)	(8)	(12)	(13)	(17)
Yunnan	10	16	23	35	20
1877	(3)	(4)	(6)	(6)	(4)
Guizhou	6	8	10	30	22
1877	(1)	(2)	(3)	(4)	(5)
Shandong	15	22	28	38	42
1879	(2)	(3)	(3)	(2)	(3)
Zhili	—	7	7	12	14
1887	—	(3)	(4)	(4)	(4)

Language Students, "missionaries absent," or "location undetermined"

—	43	32	50	29

Total Missionaries

1885	1888	1891	1896	1899
177	332	434	720	811

Total Stations

42	75	105	146	166

When Chart 3, the list of stations, is laid over Chart 4, the baptisms, a curious pattern emerges: generally speaking, the larger and more "foreign" the work, the fewer the baptisms; the more indigenous, the more converts. Zhejiang, which had been turned over to the Chinese church under bishop

God's Ambassadors

Wang Lae-djün, recorded an astronomical number of baptisms: 800 in 1896, more than fifteen per missionary, with a cumulative total of 5,700 by 1899. Another indigenous success was the Guangxin women's river in Jiangxi, where the work was largely conducted by native pastors and Biblewomen. By contrast, most provinces recorded fewer than one baptism per missionary; in fact one half of the stations recorded no baptisms at all.

Chart 4
Growth of the Chinese Church by Provinces

Baptisms per year (and cumulative):

	1885	1888	1891	1896	1899
Jiangsu	1	33	6	13	6
	(127)	(189)	(216)	(160)	(183)
Zhejiang	80	110	194	800	389
	(1297)	(1696)	(2167)	(4153)	(5709)
Anhui	43	49	23	7	62
	(180)	(274)	(376)	(470)	(673)
Jiangxi	10	40	14	53	262
	(43)	(142)	(303)	(627)	(1082)
Hubei	9	1	—	5	2
	(47)	(81)	(81)	(47)	(62)
Hunan	1	—	—	—	9
	(1)	—	—	—	(28)
Henan	—	24	3	58	117
	(3)	(33)	(57)	(254)	(649)
Shanxi	23	116	81	137	206
	(81)	(831)	(1055)	(1630)	(2205)
Shaanxi	20	13	39	61	41
	(131)	(159)	(277)	(492)	(638)
Gansu	—	9	3	13	22
	(5)	(38)	(64)	(109)	(135)
Sichuan	12	45	28	72	65
	(48)	(94)	(222)	(551)	(907)
Yunnan	6	7	5	8	—
	(9)	(19)	(34)	(71)	(43)
Guizhou	9	4	9	1	10
	(27)	(35)	(69)	(100)	(137)

Shandong	5	21	12	4	11
	(28)	(71)	(124)	(187)	(203)
Zhili	—	—	—	—	—
				(16)	(29)
Total Baptisms per year	1885	1888	1891	1896	1899
	219	472	417	1,262	1,202
Cumulative Total					
	2,206	3,587	5,045	9,276	12,964

At first, Taylor planned to designate Jiangxi as an "American" district, treating nationality the way he did denominational affiliation, grouping like-minded people together. The whole first party and most of the second were assigned to the women's stations along the Guangxin River, and the men further south along the Gan River.[40] But personnel needs changed quickly, and North Americans were dispersed throughout the CIM. Nonetheless Jiangxi retained a special place among Canadians: as late as 1898 half the CIM people in the province (35 of 77) were from Toronto. North Americans, one generation removed from the farm, made good pioneers. They were scattered throughout the northwest, in Shanxi (11 of 91) and Shaanxi (7 of 72), and the southwest, in Sichuan (5 of 84) and Guizhou (6 of 25).[41] Some of the first to take the gospel to the despised tribespeople of Guizhou were Canadians, for example, and the man who spent years trying to open Hunan was an American, Dr. Frank Keller.

Canadians were the chameleons of China missions. They could "pass" as British in Shanghai, as Americans in the interior, as fellow colonials among Australians; they could even present themselves (like Donald MacGillivray of the Christian Literature Society) as citizens of the world. And since Canada was the only nation to send both English-speaking Protestants and French-speaking Roman Catholics, French Canadians traveled on French passports and flew the *tricolore* over their chapels. Within the CIM, Canadians were the facilitators, those who explained the arcane British "mission-home etiquette" to enthusiastic Americans.

---

40. Austin, *Saving China*, pp. 15-20. The Gan River district was so inaccessible that thirty years later Mao Zedong established his first soviet there.
41. *China's Millions* (NA), February 1899, pp. 19-20.

God's Ambassadors

The Book of Arrangements

Satan's attacks from the outside were mirrored by "discord at the top." This discord, A. J. Broomhall stated, was continuous from 1886 to 1894. In fact, discord permeated the mission at all levels: the relations between junior and senior missionaries, between the rank and file and the superintendents, between Shanghai and London, but primarily between Hudson Taylor and his brother-in-law Benjamin Broomhall, the London secretary, over the issue of the mission's "final headship." "The rumble of distant thunder reverberates through letters of this period — references to the Book of Arrangements as 'a law of the Medes and Persians'; to another 'crisis' of Hudson Taylor's making; to some fearing a 'smash up' with 'deplorable injury to the work and sad humiliation' for him if he did not retract his new regulations — 'too much management — too much policy.'"[42]

The problems of Taylor's leadership went back to the beginning when he appealed for "helpers" — not colleagues, advisors or agents, not self-motivated missionaries — who would give him prompt and loyal obedience in fulfilling his vision of evangelizing China. In the early years, Taylor had been father figure, physician, pastor, language teacher, and superintendent for his far-flung flock. He had an intuitive understanding of each person's strengths and weaknesses and a big heart, adept at pastoral visits, gentle encouragement, patience and prayer. Those who could not take his autocratic leadership or the inadequate, uncertain stipends quietly resigned, joined another mission, or returned home. By the time the CIM reached three hundred people, Taylor had never met many of them personally, except when he attended the scattering of language students to their stations. The problem with the expansion and internationalization of the CIM was how to reconstruct his "family of helpers" into a "thoroughly efficient machine."[43]

Broomhall and the London council resented their advisory status as they watched the China council take an active role. The referees, dignitaries such as Charles Haddon Spurgeon, Dr. Barnardo, Theodore Howard, and Robert Scott, felt (in Taylor's words) "they are really nonentities and just carry out my or our plans and are not allowed to use their own discretion. . . . We must be careful that this contention is not a true one."[44] As complaints started coming from China that the superintendents were a layer of bureaucracy between the director and the ordinary missionaries, some evinced "a deplorable

---

42. *HTCOC 7*, pp. 191-200, "Discord at the top"; quote at p. 132.
43. Ibid., p. 145.
44. Ibid., p. 180.

new spirit" over the removal of their right to appeal to London or to Taylor himself. When educated, middle-class missionaries were placed over senior, working-class ones, more than one stalwart "refused to recognize the China Council unless he himself had a place on it."[45]

Was London to have the final headship? Taylor demanded. Why, he noted with desperation, London could not fulfill its own financial obligations. In January 1892 it had remitted only £497, of which 97 percent was earmarked for "special purposes," i.e., the salary of self-supporting missionaries who had regular stipends, and only £15 for "general purposes," for every one else, 400 adults plus children. "You have not funds to support 500 missionaries; you cannot protect them against an insurrection or in a riot," he wrote, listening to guns along the Yangtze, "you cannot come out here and administer the affairs of the Mission; we must walk before God. I am sure you will agree with me in this."[46]

The chief troublemaker in China was a man we met in Shanxi, Thomas Wellesley Piggott, the Anglo-Irish aristocrat of Taiyuan. He had fanned the "Shanxi spirit" into flames of "anti-CIM feelings" that threatened to disrupt the Shanghai conference. Since he was a wealthy benefactor — he paid for the Schofield Memorial Hospital and the land for the Woosung Road headquarters — he felt he deserved special treatment. He led the movement for "democracy" within the mission, demanding that the superintendents be "elective" rather than appointed. "Were self-opinionated men to stand like politicians for election by colleagues who barely knew them?" A. J. Broomhall asked rhetorically. "In fact, no missionary society chose its leaders that way."[47]

Piggott's next issue was the governess, cook, and schoolteacher he had brought from England. Although he was responsible for their passages and salaries, when the governess fell sick he demanded the CIM pay her return fare. This resulted in yet another coda to the *Book of Arrangements:* missionaries who brought a "friend, or sister, or servant, or governess to reside with them in the interior" needed the director's written approval because the "difficulties and responsibilities [were] so great."[48] The issue that broke the camel's back, though, was the ownership of the land on which the Schofield Hospital was standing. The *Principles & Practice* stated that missionaries must not "purchase or own as private properties, lands or houses in China, away from the Treaty Ports," referring to summer houses and shops that the

---

45. Ibid., p. 131.
46. China council minutes, 8 January 1892, in CIM/SOAS, file 73.
47. *HTCOC 7*, p. 131.
48. China council minutes, 24 November 1886, in CIM/SOAS.

missionaries would rent to converts to raise money. Since this rule had been introduced later, "as an old missionary he [Piggott] thought that a special exception should be made in his case. He stated that he was prepared to promise that the properties purchased by him should only be used for Mission purposes, and that plans of any proposed buildings, or the alterations of the outside of buildings should be first submitted to the Directors for approval."[49]

Chafing under Hudson Taylor's treatment, Piggott resigned from the CIM in 1893 and started recruiting a "band of independent labourers" for his own mission at Shouyang, Shanxi, fifty miles east of Taiyuan on the Big Road to Baoding, almost at the mountain pass known as the Gates of Heaven. "It is in my heart to establish a well-mannered station, having medical, evangelical, perhaps educational and it may be other branches," he wrote, with a backhanded slap against the less mannered stations. Piggott briefly joined the Baptist Missionary Society, which was staffed primarily with ex-CIM, and allowed his brother-in-law, Dr. Ebenezer Henry Edwards, to operate the hospital for the CIM.

Piggott's barbs and the "Shanxi spirit" were not confined to Shanxi, but were repeated on a larger or smaller scale throughout the CIM. In a New Year's editorial for 1892, Taylor wrote that after the Shanghai conference, "the opposition of the powers of darkness [has] been manifested; almost every little church and almost every station has had its trials; in some sickness or death of native Christians or foreign workers; in some through breaches of harmony; in some through distresses from flood or drought; in some through violent opposition and persecution; and in others through alienation of the minds of the heathen by the circulation of vile and blasphemous handbills and literature."[50]

The Breakdown

By the mid-1890s, the China council minutes take on a bureaucratic tone. There were few doctrinal or policy discussions, although they rumble below the surface. Rather, the minutes become lists: two or three pages document the arrival and departures from Shanghai; those receiving Junior and Senior Missionary Certificates; and the recent deaths. These are followed by twenty to forty pages of discussion concerning each case of furlough.

49. Ibid., 4 April 1889 and 2 June 1890.
50. New Year's editorial, *China's Millions* (GB), January 1892, p. 1.

Although most missions granted sabbaticals every five to eight years, the CIM did not standardize the process until the twentieth century. Except for medical and emotional crises, the *Book of Arrangements* granted a furlough every nine or ten years for a single person, or a total of eighteen years for a husband and wife. This meant that if one spouse came out later, the other would have to make up the difference by extending his or her own term. Consequently some missionaries stayed for fifteen years before their first furlough. F. W. Baller, for example, head of the language school, went twenty-one years between furloughs. Another missionary woman, who had no "home ties," was ordered to take a furlough after twenty years even though she was in good health and had no wish to take one.

Nevertheless, even after nine years, furlough was not automatic, and depended on the exigencies of the work — and the ability of the missionary to pay for the passage to Britain or North America. Since the council decided each case on its own merits, including reports from the physician and superintendent, each applicant had to prove why *he and his wife* needed a furlough, and why a short recuperation at Chefoo or one of the mountain resorts would not satisfy for an extra year or two. When the parents went on furlough, their children usually remained behind at the Chefoo School. Self-supporting missionaries were given more lenient treatment, which caused considerable resentment, when someone like Archibald Orr Ewing or Montague Beauchamp was granted a "special furlough" after two years.

The China council minutes make melancholy reading, sad litanies of the walking wounded asking for "immediate furlough." The minutes from January 1897 are typical: Mrs. Giffen's health was such that a milder climate was "the only hope of prolonging her life"; Miss Box's health was "very unsatisfactory" and she was sent to England; Mrs. Strong arrived in Shanghai "too weak to travel alone" and in the absence of a suitable escort Mr. Strong was allowed to accompany her home, which the council "regretted" because "he is in good health." Mrs. Joyce died at Hsiang Hsian. And so on, year after sad year.[51]

So many people had breakdowns that the doctors became adept in diagnosing nervous breakdowns. At the July 1892 meeting of the China council, for example, they considered the case of a Mr. Hutton, who suffered from "mental aberration characterized by undue restlessness and an excessive excitability of manner, alternating with depression and remorse." His attack seems to have been brought on by meetings "for seeking the fuller baptism of the Holy Spirit." Miss Bradbury "feigned" being unconscious: "She cannot

---

51. China council minutes, 6 January 1897, in CIM/ABGC, file 2/36.

tell how, but the devil tempted her so to act. She has undergone a *terrible* time of conflict, poor girl."[52]

Beyond the question of the patient's recovery, one can see the mission doctors groping toward a pre-Freudian psychology of mental illness, while explaining it in theological terms. Why was God allowing this to happen to his holy ones? Was it a sign of the times? Or a character flaw?

In "common sense" terms, they learned to distinguish between "mental" and "moral" conditions.[53] If a woman started tossing tables and chairs, or tore off her clothes, or if a man stormed at his Chinese co-workers, was this a "mental" collapse, something beyond the victim's control, when the mind shuts down? Or was it a "moral" failure, a collapse of the soul, a willful giving in to Satan? There were a few — very few — cases of overt "immorality" in the mission: one man "took liberties" with his fiancée, and another made "immoral suggestions" to the Chinese pastor's wife. Another said "things" to a male missionary. Immorality had to be rooted out branch and stem, and the offender was on the next boat home.

With their lively sense of the supernatural, how did they distinguish between a vision — like Henry Frost's vision of Satan — or a hallucination?

---

52. Ibid., 5 July 1892, CIM/SOAS, file 73.
53. See cases of Anna Munson, China council minutes, 17 April 1911, p. 16, in CIM/ABGC, file 2/37; and Miss R. M. Harris, July 1923, p. 6, file 2/39.

CHAPTER 11

The Middle Eden

1888-1899

> When Thou wouldst pour the living stream,
> Then I would be the earthen cup,
> Filled to the brim and sparkling clear.
> The fountain Thou and living spring,
> Flow Thou through me, the vessel weak,
> That thirsty souls may taste Thy grace.
>
> Pastor Hsi, "A Song of Sacrifice"[1]

The Venerable Chief Pastor

The Venerable Chief Pastor has brought his family to the Middle Eden. It is high summer of 1894, 110° (Fahrenheit) in the shade, the beginning of a yearlong drought — shades of the Great Famine of 1877-79 — the worst time for an old man to be traveling through the cauldron of central China.[2] Eight years earlier, in 1886, Hudson Taylor had made his first trip to Shanxi to calm an outbreak of the "Shanxi spirit" and to straighten out the Cambridge Seven, who were hoping to acquire the language supernaturally. He was charmed by Pastor Hsi Shengmo, the "Overcomer of Demons," and ordained him as "the watcher over and feeder of the sheep of God" in South Shanxi. More, he of-

---

1. Francesca French, trans., *The Songs of Pastor Hsi*, p. 11.
2. The trip is described in *HTCOC 7*, pp. 198-211. Mrs. Howard Taylor's diary was published in *China's Millions* (NA), September 1894 to May 1895. She also described the journey in *Pastor Hsi* (single volume, 1903). Pat Barr, *To China with Love*, pp. 139-40, presents an acerbic view of Pastor Hsi and the Middle Eden.

The Middle Eden

fered to finance his opium refuges — the "Heavenly Invitation Offices" — as "an auxiliary agency in opening up new districts and gaining the confidence of the people."[3] Those were days of heaven on earth, when anything seemed possible. Now, if only Hudson Taylor could get back to the garden.

The historian — like Hudson Taylor's contemporaries — is astounded at Taylor's stamina. He was sixty-two, an old man; he had been at death's door more times than he could count, his poor body had been wracked by malaria, fevers, concussion of the spine, paralysis, all the diseases that flesh was heir to in China. Yet he was planning to walk from Hankou to Xian to Taiyuan to Baoding — alone, with his wife Jennie if necessary. The "long overland journey to Shanxi invited the dangers of heat stroke, dysentery, typhoid, malaria, and quick tempers in places where the populace were unfriendly." Taylor himself wrote: "If the Lord has further work for us to do He will bring us safely through, and I think He will do so, but should it prove otherwise 'we ought to lay down our lives for the brethren.'"[4]

"Then let us come, too," his son Dr. Howard Taylor said with alarm, so they made a party of five. J. J. (Joe) Coulthard, Hudson Taylor's son-in-law and personal secretary, was a seasoned traveler, the superintendent of Henan province and a member of the China council. (He was married to Maria Hudson Taylor, Taylor's daughter by Maria Dyer, who was born in Hangzhou in 1867 and died in 1897.) Frederick Howard Taylor (1862-1946), Maria Dyer's second son, brought his bride, Geraldine Guinness (1862-1949), the daughter of Grattan Guinness, the silver-tongued Irish evangelist, whom he had married one month earlier, and they continued their honeymoon with the senior Taylors. The party left Hankou by houseboat on 22 May, changing to wheelbarrows and carts, and reached Xian on 26 June, and Pingyang on 17 July, where they remained for eight days.

There were two reasons why Taylor had to go to Shanxi at that moment, no matter how dangerous. One was the influx of Franson's floods, which was threatening not just the Scandinavians but the future of the CIM itself. Meanwhile there had been another outbreak of the "Shanxi spirit" of "dangerous individualism" and derelict morale, centered around Stanley Smith and Charlie Studd, the volatile members of the Cambridge Seven.

Hudson Taylor had recently returned from two years in England, and in New York City he had met with A. B. Simpson and a group of his International Missionary Alliance students about to sail for Hong Kong. He warned of the "[m]any grave difficulties in the way of superintending and aiding As-

---

3. *Pastor Hsi*, p. 214.
4. 11 May 1894, in *HTCOC* 7, p. 201.

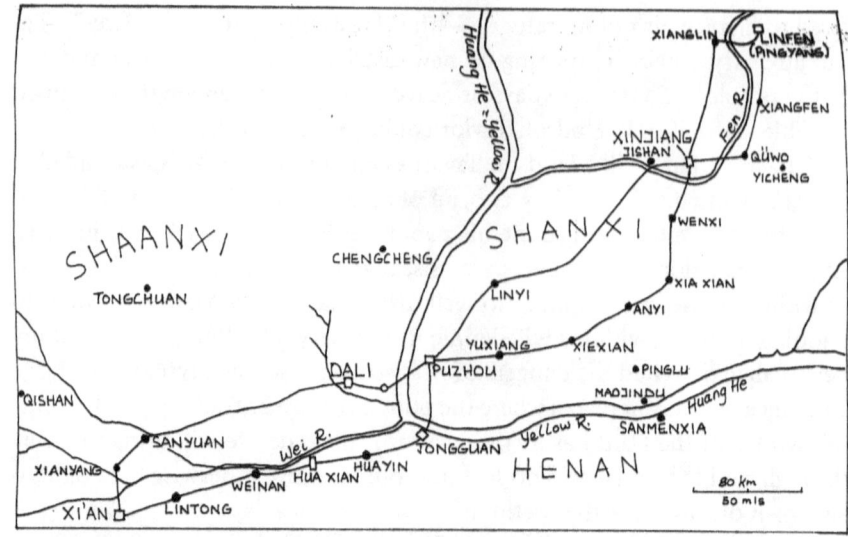

Map of South Shanxi with pinyin names. This map shows some of Pastor Hsi's opium refuges between Linfen (then called Pingyang) and Xian, capital of Shaanxi province. This map also illustrates the escape routes from the Boxers.
Source: A. J. Broomhall, *Hudson Taylor and China's Open Century,* book 6, *Assault on the Nine.*

sociate Missions."[5] In Shanghai the Swedish and Norwegian consul sent a friendly letter asking for Taylor's advice. The Swedish Foreign Office, he wrote, had had their attention called to a potential problem by a German newspaper in Shanghai, that "twenty unmarried unprotected females" were in danger in the far north of Shanxi without male missionaries to help them. "Can the Chinese fathom their good intentions — without the current of suspicion running in another direction?" the consul asked. "Do you consider a female more protected in China generally than a man?" Taylor had his own misgivings, as A. J. Broomhall commented: "A women's language school near Shanghai was a very different matter from congregating young women together at Guihuacheng near the Mongolian border."[6]

The British minister plenipotentiary — who happened to be an Irish Catholic, Sir N. R. O'Conor, and thus suspicious of Protestant enthusiasm — was also "making very minute inquiries and watching our proceedings very jealously."[7] An English traveler named George Littledale, who came upon

---

5. China council minutes, 11 April 1892, in CIM/SOAS, file 73.
6. *HTCOC 7,* p. 201.
7. Ibid., p. 203. Coates, *The China Consuls,* p. 181, stated that O'Conor stressed "the

twenty-five CIM women in a Shanxi market town, confirmed these reports in a letter to the Foreign Office. "It is hard to speak temperately of the individual or society that sends girls wholesale into the interior of such a country as China unprotected, practically uncared for and with the most inadequate means.... These poor, unfortunate women, with the merest smattering of the language, are being sent about, sometimes in pairs and sometimes alone, to pray, play the guitar and sing hymns in the street, a life that none but an improper woman in China would lead, and which fosters the idea in the native mind that these girls were too bad to be allowed to remain in their own country; and they openly express the opinion that one girl must have been very bad indeed to have been sent from her own country so young. . . ."[8]

Twenty-one members of the Scandinavian Alliance (Franson's Chicago-based mission) had delivered an ultimatum: unless Hudson Taylor rescinded the *Principles & Practice*, they would sever their connection and form an independent mission. Since they were associates, not full members, they did not feel bound by the *P&P*, particularly the restrictions concerning Chinese dress. "All too many of the CIM and Scandinavians in Shanxi," A. J. Broomhall commented, were wearing "a Chinese gown, but leather boots, pith helmet and no queue, a clownish hotch-potch scorned by the Chinese."[9] The most difficult hardship was the two-year probationary period before marriage. Since the men were constantly itinerating, they had no permanent home and their health was suffering as a consequence, and the single women were forced to live with a married couple. If they did not have to wait for two years, a couple could marry immediately on arrival and resolve the problem of housing.[10]

Geraldine Taylor, the future author of thirty books, kept a diary of the journey — a writer practicing her craft — which was published in installments in *China's Millions*. She had joined the CIM in 1886 and thus was a veteran of eight years as a single woman working in several provinces, which gave her a wide knowledge of the field. She and Howard Taylor, who joined the CIM in 1890, had been friends since childhood, but they postponed their marriage so she could write *The Story of the China Inland Mission*, the first official history, published in two volumes in 1893. She had an eye for dramatic snapshots, and her diary bubbles over with divine providence. "Excellent,

---

duty of Chinese authorities to enable missionaries to settle peaceably in the interior and was at the same time authorizing him [the consul] to withhold passports for dangerous areas where the situation was genuinely beyond the control of the Chinese authorities."

8. Barr, *To China with Love*, p. 132.
9. *HTCOC* 7, p. 207.
10. Ibid., pp. 201-3. P. E. Holman to J. W. Stevenson, China council minutes, 23 April 1894, in CIM/SOAS, file 73.

hard-working, ingenious people!" she enthused. "Now we are getting up amongst the mountains. Oh marvelous land! What roads — what means of progression! Over these sheer steeps of rock . . . persistently, relentlessly we travel from four o'clock in the morning until the sun goes down, our springless barrows, creaking and squeaking like perpetual bagpipes."[11]

Her tone changed as they went inland: "June 13. 6 am. This is indeed a moment of misery. We are sitting waiting in our carts in this filthy inn-yard, all ready to start — as we have been for over an hour — while the rain pours steadily down. . . . There being only one room, Mother and I occupied it; Father, Howard and Joe slept in the carts outside."[12] The next day, a swollen river barred their path and her journal was reduced to notes: "Dreadful-looking people — no inn — place dangerous. Had to return." Then, it stops altogether. ("An absence of records," A. J. Broomhall noted parenthetically, "suggests 'the less said the better.'")[13]

At every stop they tried to engage the people with tea-shop evangelism and tract distribution. At one congregation Hudson Taylor used "Mr. Hsi's little parable of the candle." A recent convert had asked Pastor Hsi if he needed to study the Word before he could witness for Jesus. "Ah!" Hsi responded. "Do you use candles in your part of the world? . . . Do you expect to remain in darkness for an hour or two after you have lighted the candle, or do you look for some illumination a little earlier?" Why, answered the young man thoughtfully, "I expected it to shine, of course, immediately it is lighted."[14]

Their first stop was Xian, the capital of Shaanxi province, an ancient city that had been the capital of China for fifteen hundred years. "[A]ll around Sian stretched the vast plain, fertile, populous, unreached: twelve thousand square miles of country; with twenty-one walled cities, sixty market towns, and almost countless villages."[15] The CIM pioneers had itinerated throughout the plain for fifteen years — "fleeing in circles," they called it — because they could not gain a foothold within the city itself. The arrival of the Scandinavians in the plain set off an expansion of stations that alarmed the cautious CIM, though it was symptomatic of what was happening throughout all China missions in the 1890s.

To put it bluntly, the "forward movements" had moved too far, too fast:

11. Mrs. Howard Taylor (née Geraldine Guinness), "Through the Heart of China," *China's Millions* (NA), February 1895, pp. 16-17.
12. Ibid., September 1894, pp. 104-5.
13. *HTCOC 7*, p. 206.
14. Taylor, "Through the Heart of China," *China's Millions* (NA), May 1895, p. 58.
15. *Pastor Hsi*, pp. 218-20.

The Middle Eden

there were too many missionaries and not enough places. Taylor wrote that "anything like a rush into a large number of unoccupied cities (in Shaanxi) might be attended not only with riot and danger (murder) to the missionaries concerned, but also to those who are now safely and usefully settled in centres already open." Thomas Botham, the man who invented the term "one man and a mule," warned, "We hope never to see a very large staff of foreign workers on the (Xian) plain. I think there can be too many missionaries in a place. I should not like to see foreign pastors of all the Chinese churches any more than I should like to see Russian pastors of all English churches."[16]

At Xian, Taylor met with a conference of eleven Scandinavians and four CIM men. He was impressed by the way they had adapted: "Very few of our men after three years in China are as competent as they have become, or as careful. . . . Their plans for independent work seem so matured . . . they are looked on with much favour and get on well and wisely with the officials." Taylor appointed a system of superintendents, with a "Senior Missionary Associate" over each Alliance mission who reported to the CIM provincial superintendents of Shanxi, Shaanxi, and Gansu. Recognizing that the two-year marriage rule was unrealistic, he simply waived it. "This capacity for being master of the rules he made," A. J. Broomhall praised, "instead of being mastered by them, stands out as one of Hudson Taylor's strong characteristics."[17]

Leaving Xian and crossing the Yellow River into Shanxi, Hudson Taylor succumbed to "cerebral congestion" and heat stroke, and arrived as frail as paper. Everything was in disorder. He met the "restless Swedes" at Yuncheng and Quwu, and held an eight-day conference at Pingyang of thirty-five CIM and eleven Scandinavians, with special sessions for church members. Even these meetings could not resolve the difficulties. Taylor appointed Dixon E. Hoste of the Cambridge Seven, the former artillery officer who "sort of steered Pastor Hsi" as his companion and colleague, to be superintendent of South Shanxi. To general rejoicing, Hoste announced his engagement to Gertrude Broomhall, Hudson Taylor's niece (the third of Amelia and Benjamin Broomhall's children to join the CIM), thus joining Taylor's extended clan. Above all, Taylor realized he had to placate Pastor Hsi; everything — the CIM's publicity in England, the anti-opium crusade, the blitz-conversion of China, the creation of an indigenous Christianity — depended on the publicity about him.

After the conference, Pastor Hsi invited "the Venerable Chief Pastor" to the Middle Eden, which he had expanded into a utopian community. He

16. *HTCOC* 7, pp. 203.
17. Ibid., pp. 205-6.

would invite enquirers to live there free for three months, paying their food and expenses, while he cured their addiction and instructed them in the Word. Afterwards, they could remain and live under his rules, or return to their homes, if any. Sometimes, there were a hundred people living in the compound, addicts in various stages of rehabilitation, staffed by Hsi's family and his in-laws.

Geraldine Taylor picked up her diary in the Middle Eden. It was half a day's journey across the plain, and the travelers arrived at the lantern-lit courtyard at dusk. Pastor Hsi had constructed a "roomy summer guest-hall" on the threshing floor, where tea was set out on a "clean white tablecloth" illuminated by a foreign kerosene lamp. When he and Mrs. Hsi escorted their guests to their sleeping quarters, Geraldine's enthusiasm knew no bounds: "it was almost a royal pavilion: a whole suite of apartments, beautifully arranged . . . with clean white towels and new cakes of the best Pears' soap. The whole place, in a word, was so clean and attractive, so polished and radiant."[18]

The next morning, with a dramatic gesture, Pastor Hsi astonished his guests with a piece of nonconformist thaumaturgy that Taylor would have appreciated. He had been praying for Dixon Hoste's father, General Hoste, who was ill in England, and the Holy Spirit had revealed the cure, just as he had revealed the recipe for the anti-opium pills many years earlier. Hsi produced two bottles of pills for General Hoste, along with an eight-page letter on "ornamental notepaper." One kind of pills, the red ones, were called "Ho-lo-shu" [*huoleshu*, literally "releasing the living chords," i.e. blood vessels, or "Promoting Circulation"], which Hsi described as "a supplementary pill, good for curing all kinds of weakness in hands or feet. Take eight pills in the evening with boiling water." The black pills, twenty every morning, were called "Huan-sha-tan" [*huanshadan*, literally "Restoring Youth Pill"], which "helps to strengthen aged people, either man or woman may use it."[19]

Far, far away, that very same day — 25 July 1894 — the Japanese sank a Chinese troopship off Korea and declared war on China.

The Venerable Chief Pastor spent a few days in the Middle Eden, and with the black and red pills in his packsack, he resumed his pilgrimage. His family now numbered seven, for Gertrude Broomhall and Dixon Hoste were going to Tianjin to get married. The CIM had fifteen stations in South Shanxi, some Swedish, some English, some female, some male, and Pingyang, the flagship

---

18. *Pastor Hsi*, vol. 2 (1903), pp. 325-29 (omitted from single volume).
19. Ibid., pp. 330-32, has the photograph of the original letter, which was also reproduced in *China's Millions* (NA), January 1895, p. 10. (The 1962 single volume has no illustrations.)

The Middle Eden

which had two married couples plus four unmarried men and four women. "Travelling from city to city for meetings with Chinese Christians and missionaries who could not get to the conferences, Hudson Taylor found a disgraceful state of affairs. Two factions, for and against Hsi Shengmo, lived in a permanent state of friction which their unbiased colleagues could not overcome. At Taiyuan this 'dread of Hsi' was compounded by a recurrence of the 'Shanxi spirit,' the 'Christianized Confucianism.'"[20]

The disorder was too much to clear up, but Taylor did make two decisions. "'Chinese dress' meant correct Chinese dress and deportment, unreluctant adaptation winning Chinese approval. That included the conventional hair style. . . . He advocated courtesy to the Chinese by ceasing the charade of neither one proper dress nor the other." He won the compliance of most missionaries, including Stanley Smith and Dr. Ebenezer Henry Edwards, the doyen of Taiyuan, who were both "loose on the dress question." Dr. Edwards, who "would be pleased to have no more dealings with Hsi," was threatening to resign and join his brother-in-law T. W. Piggott in the Shouyang mission, taking the Schofield hospital with him. To rally him, Taylor appointed him superintendent of North Shanxi with a seat on the China council.[21]

By the time Taylor's party reached Tianjin, he was suffering from enteritis and dysentery. Japanese gunboats blockaded the harbor. The city was preparing for war. They caught the last boat to Shanghai. After meeting with the China council, Taylor set out again — alone — to return to Shanxi, retracing his steps from Tianjin. Going by mule cart across "a sea of mountains — solid waves," taxed his endurance. With no wife or daughter-in-law to see to his needs, no son to arrange carts and inns, he appeared "very aged and tired." The war was going poorly. The Japanese had driven the Chinese out of Korea and were about to annex Taiwan. "All seem to think," Taylor wrote, that "the dynasty [was] unlikely to survive the shock."[22]

Taylor was returning to Shanxi to "reinforce discipline among the still recalcitrant," lest they dash against the rocks and shipwreck the mission. He met Stanley Smith, "vacillating again but as charming as ever," at his isolated station at Luan, where he was preaching his views on healing and the larger hope. At Taiyuan, Dr. Edwards "agrees, thank God," to live according to the *P&P*, and was growing his hair. Finally, at a great celebration at Hongdong, the mud-brick cathedral where Pastor Hsi held sway, the people welcomed

20. *HTCOC 7*, p. 207.
21. Ibid., pp. 207-8.
22. Ibid., pp. 209-11.

Dixon and Gertrude Hoste with a blue silk banner with gold characters, which read "With one heart serving the Lord." At a gathering attended by four hundred converts, sixty-nine men and women were baptized and several deacons appointed. "This was the true Shanxi," A. J. Broomhall commented, not the nasty Shanxi spirit of Taiyuan.

Taylor wrote pointedly, "Had I not been able to visit Shan-si [Shanxi] and Shen-si [Shaanxi] we should have lost a good many workers."[23] By the time he arrived back in Tianjin, having been on the road for seven months, snow was falling. Mukden had fallen to the Japanese.

In May 1895, a year after Taylor's epic journey, Frederik Franson, the Swedish firebrand, also journeyed to try and resolve the Shanxi spirit among the Scandinavians. He held a prayer meeting in Pingyang, which lasted from morning to afternoon, followed by a Bible reading until supper, with an evangelistic service in the evening. He "got hold of two of the schoolboys, Miss Jacobsen [sic] interpreting," and within a few minutes they were sobbing "on their knees . . . confessing their sins and asking forgiveness from God." Gertrude Hoste commented, "It is impossible to say how many of those who came forward for prayer were really seeking salvation," for most were already church members. Nevertheless, she concluded, she "could not but feel they were face to face with God, and with their own sins." Frederick Franson was not invited to the Middle Eden. For one who had tried to convert the Queen of Sweden, two schoolboys must have seemed a paltry harvest.[24]

North Shanxi

Shanxi was the success story of the CIM. From 1886 to 1900 it was the largest province in the numbers of missionaries, stations, schools, hospitals, and opium refuges. Except for Zhejiang, which was under Pastor Wang Lae-djün, Shanxi had the most converts. In 1885 the CIM had two stations, Taiyuan and Pingyang; by 1900 it had twenty-five stations with one hundred missionaries (including associates). Taiyuan was the largest inland station in the CIM (eleven missionaries), but in 1891 it recorded only one baptism, the first in three years. Meanwhile in Pingyang, Pastor Hsi baptized 214 men and women on one day in 1887, and by 1900 his church counted 400 "communi-

23. Ibid., p. 211.
24. Mrs. D. E. Hoste, "Mr. Fransen [sic] at Hung-t'ung," *China's Millions* (NA), October 1895, pp. 134-35. China council minutes, 19 March 1895, in CIM/SOAS, file 73, noted that Franson had just opened North Shanxi for the Scandinavian Alliance Mission, and that all SAM missionaries in Zhejiang and Jiangxi were to go north without unnecessary delay.

The Middle Eden

cants in fellowship." (One indigenous church in Zhejiang had 1,000 communicants and two had 400 each; no other CIM congregation approached that number.)[25]

Taiyuan was an unrewarding station ("dead" was a common description), despite hundreds of patients at the hospital and opium refuge, and flourishing schools and women's work. In 1881, when Hudson Taylor ordered the CIM to separate themselves from Timothy Richard and his "heretical" teachings, most of the CIM people resigned to join the Baptist Missionary Society. Even after the departure of Timothy Richard in 1884, the BMS remained fractious; in 1893 one-half of the twelve missionaries packed up and moved west of the Yellow River to the neighboring province of Shaanxi.[26] The BMS also had a small station north of Taiyuan.

When Thomas Wellesley Piggott, the Irish autocrat, resigned from the CIM the same year, 1893, he joined the BMS briefly before he returned to Britain to recruit a "band of independent labourers" to establish a mission at Shouyang. Shouyang was a major commercial center fifty miles east of Taiyuan, the first city on the Big Road west of the mountain passes. As mentioned in Chapter 10, Piggott kept the deed for the Schofield hospital, although he allowed his brother-in-law, Dr. Ebenezer Henry Edwards, to operate it within the CIM. After years of equivocating, Dr. Edwards also resigned from the CIM, claiming the Schofield hospital as his personal property.[27] With three missions in one city, the CIM "handed over its commitments in Taiyuan to Dr Edwards and the 'Shouyang Mission,'" and reestablished its provincial headquarters at Pingyao, seventy-five miles south, on the other side of the Oberlin mission.

The superintendent at Pingyao was the respected Canadian, Alexander Saunders, Goforth's friend. Born in Scotland, he had grown up in Toronto, where he graduated from Knox College. When he first arrived at Taiyuan, he had been shocked by the "luxury" of Piggott's home and was convinced that the missionaries were "living too much above the ordinary people."[28] After six years, he concluded that "the one-man preaching from a given text system was not the best for China," since people would wander in and out of the chapel. He devised a "new order of services for the Lord's Day," similar to Chinese sectarian worship, which "will make each worshipper take part in the

---

25. Statistics from *China's Millions* (NA), July 1900.
26. H. R. Williamson, *British Baptists in China 1845-1952* (London: Carey Kingsgate Press, 1957), p. 49.
27. *HTCOC 7*, p. 245. China council minutes, 1 January and 6 April 1896, in CIM/SOAS, file 73.
28. *China's Millions* (GB), February 1890, p. 25.

work of the Lord's Day. We meet at, say 10 a.m. for prayer, when intercession is made for our fellow-worshippers throughout the world, and for our own meetings." This was followed by a period of private Bible study, including literacy classes, memorization, and catechism, then an "open meeting" in the afternoon, "when they rehearse, in their own words, the Bible story read in the morning, with a few words from the leader. This makes a full and interesting day, and the brightest of our Christians take up the plan heartily."[29]

Pingyao was once a rich and prosperous city, but had fallen on bad times, an entrepôt for goods from the Silk Road and the headquarters of the empire-wide system of "native banks." Their branches from Canton to Manchuria to Japan were staffed entirely with Pingyao men, Saunders reported proudly, "not merely the branch managers, but all the clerks, and even the cooks go from our city."[30] In our time, more than a hundred years later, Pingyao has recently (1997) been declared a World Heritage Site by UNESCO, because it is the last walled city left in China, and it is being restored as a museum city of Ming-Qing architecture. Its city walls, built 2,700 years ago, loom above the plain like a fortress, four miles in diameter, with seventy massive watchtowers, encircling the city in the shape of a turtle: the main gate on the south side with its twin towers is the head and eyes, the north gate is the tail, while gates on the east and west represent the legs.[31]

The CIM had several stations in North Shanxi. At Datong, the Buddhist shrine town, the seven missionaries operated a school, a clinic and opium refuge, and counted twenty communicants in 1899. Beyond, at Guihuacheng and Inner Mongolia, the Scandinavian associates were still doing pioneer itinerations. If Taiyuan was unrewarding because city people were too sophisticated, in Mongolia the problem was to catch desert nomads before they moved on. Neither Muslim merchants nor Tibetan lamas, the travelers in these parts, were easy converts; Guihuacheng, where at least the people were "civil," recorded one baptism in ten years.

The senior missionary at Datong was George W. Clarke, whom we met as

---

29. "Diary of Mr. Alex Saunders," 1 October 1894, in *China's Millions* (NA), April 1895, p. 45.

30. A. R. Saunders, "Important Business Centre in North China," ibid., May 1898, p. 68.

31. Liu Yuan, "Life in a Museum: Pingyao represents the struggle between history and modernity," *Asiaweek*, 15 December 2000, rated Pingyao as one of the best cities in Asia. Poverty saved Pingyao from destruction in the twentieth century, but as the people are moved outside the city to create private museums, the question arises: What is the purpose of restoration? See also Elisabeth Rosenthal, "Where Walls Saved History: Pingyao, the last fortress city in China, offers a detailed look at life in the late Ming China," *New York Times*, 4 October 1998, travel section 1.

one of the orphans Annie Macpherson sent to Canada (see Chapter 9). His stint working on the railways stood him in good stead, for he would enter the encampments of Manchu soldiers, timidly, to distribute tracts and perform simple medicine such as lancing boils and abscesses. He made a banner for outdoor preaching consisting of the colors of the wordless book, black, red, white, and yellow, which he used to explain the gospel to the soldiers. This is only the second mention of the wordless book in the CIM literature, after its invention as a silk purse in Taiyuan. He described it as "a large calico scroll, in black and white, to represent the broad and narrow ways, the kingdoms of darkness and light. The gate of the City of Darkness is very large; on each side are the words, 'Broad is the way.' The gate of the City of Light is very narrow, with the words, 'Narrow is the way,' etc. The streets are selections of suitable texts. The goal of each street is a city in colours — a red city for hell, and a gold city for heaven, with texts describing each. I carry a nail fastened to a string, so that I can always fix it up. . . . The unlettered soon learn the meaning, and I trust may be led thereby to a knowledge of the truth as it is in Jesus."[32] Obviously, Clarke's banner was a variation on the Two Roads, an illustration used by both Protestant and Roman Catholic missionaries, based ultimately on *Pilgrim's Progress*.

This unproductive desert was the training ground for "Franson's floods," and the CIM devolved its northern work to Franson's Scandinavian Alliance and Simpson's International Missionary Alliance. The pioneers of the Chicago Mission Among the Mongols, a branch of the Scandinavian Alliance founded in 1896, "lived in tents in the broad plains of Mongolia, living on native food, and without a settled home." With money from America, they bought "a large tract of land in Mongolia, and were founding a farm colony. . . . It was hoped that some of the Mongols would be induced to settle at least for a time, and place themselves under Christian instruction."[33]

The Opium Dream

Compared to the dry reports from Taiyuan and Datong, the reports from South Shanxi were like drugged epistles. In one of the most startling letters ever published in *China's Millions*, Priscilla Livingstone Stewart (later Mrs.

---

32. G. W. Clark [sic], "News from Shan-si," *Chinese Recorder*, February 1887, p. 84.

33. Ebenezer Henry Edwards, *Fire and Sword in Shanxi: The Story of the Martyrdom of Foreigners and Chinese Christians* (Edinburgh: Oliphant, Anderson & Ferrier, 1900), pp. 100-109; Forsyth, *The China Martyrs of 1900*, pp. 80-82.

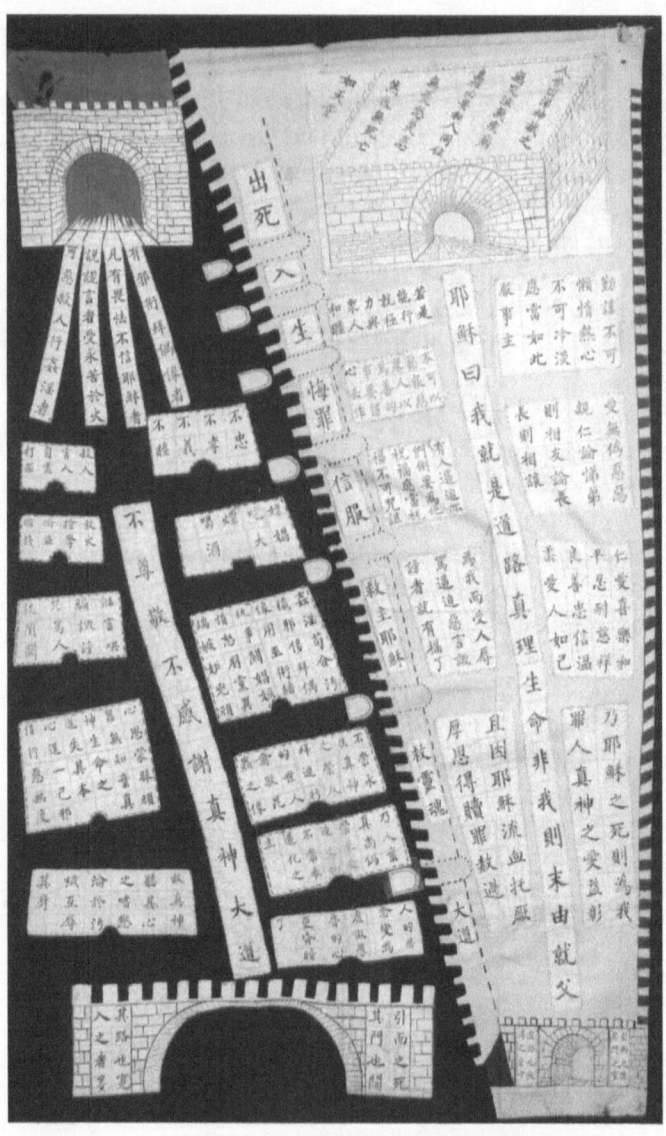

"The Two Roads" evangelistic banner. It is made of cotton, with black and white fields joined obliquely with a toothed edge, appliquéd with white panels and Bible verses. Broad is the way that leads from the black city of sin to the red city of Hell; narrow is the path that leads from the white city of holiness to the golden gates of Heaven. The main inscription on the right reads, "Jesus said, I am the Way, the Truth and the Life; no man cometh unto the Father except through me." This banner was used by George Leslie Mackay, who established a successful indigenous church in Taiwan. Source: Royal Ontario Museum.

The Middle Eden

Charlie Studd) poured out her despair in visions that show the graphic violence of her interior landscape. The air was "thick with devils," she wrote, "and the people seem literally possessed by the devil — held in bondage, spellbound, deafened, blinded, hardened by the devil — DEAD in trespasses and sin. But GOD's own voice . . . has come to us as a mighty, rushing torrent, sweeping AWAY the EVIL heart of unbelief. . . . He is letting us hear THE VOICE which breaketh the cedars, which can divide the flames of fire, which is able to shake the wilderness. . . . He has indeed made the devil real to us, sin real to us, hell real to us, eternity real to us; and very real that these people are DEAD, and that nothing but the voice of the GOD OF GLORY thundering forth can awake them."[34]

Back in 1886, when Hudson Taylor committed the CIM to using Pastor Hsi's opium refuges as an auxiliary agency in opening up new districts, he set in motion a train of events that produced Miss Stewart's vision and culminated in the Boxer massacre. Within six years, Hsi had opened forty refuges in four provinces, employing two hundred men and women and treating two to three thousand addicts a year. So, during the 1890s, the high tides of imperialism, two Christian institutions were growing in South Shanxi, the missionaries in the cities and Pastor Hsi in the rural villages — and both were based on the treatment of opium addicts.

In Chapter 7, I discussed the use of morphine (morphia) for the treatment of opium addiction, weaning the addict through the humane "withdrawal" method rather than the heroic "cold turkey" method. By 1890 the use of hypodermic morphine and the black market smuggling of morphine pills was so pervasive that the Shanghai Missionary Conference expressed "unflinching opposition to the opium-traffic." Further, they expressed "alarm" at "the rapid increase in the consumption of morphia . . . largely owing to the indiscriminate sale and consequent abuse of the so-called anti-opium medicines." On the advice of the Medical Missionary Association, the conference resolved that "all missionaries discourage, and, as far as possible prevent, the sale of such anti-opium medicines as contain opium or any of its alkaloids." In a footnote, the committee stated this did not refer to "carefully managed opium refuges."[35]

The CIM felt singled out by this resolution, as the minutes of the China council make clear. The council's reaction was puzzling, considering that not one member was a medical doctor. They did acknowledge that morphine was

---

34. *China's Millions* (GB), June 1888, pp. 66-67; capitalization in the original.
35. *Records of the General Conference of the Protestant Missionaries of China, Held in Shanghai, May 7-20, 1890*, p. li.

used by inexperienced missionaries and converts — with a reference to Pastor Hsi's business — who were dependent on it and had no alternative treatment. The minutes are revealing:

> Mr. Taylor mentioned that some young missionaries had felt puzzled how to act with regard to the medical missionary conference's decision to discourage the sale by church members of opium curing pills or powders which contain morphia. Some church members were occupied in this business, who had been encouraged to enter upon it, by missionaries with a view to help people to give up opium smoking. After a long conversation it was decided to recommend such younger missionaries to go on as they are now doing being careful in the use of the medicine and to wait till their hands are strengthened by the receipt of an official letter from their superintendent discouraging the use of such medicine and suggesting or providing a substitute. Dr Douthwaite was asked to prepare a suitable tract on the subject and take steps to see that a suitable substitute for the morphia pills should be available.[36]

The subject of morphia was never mentioned again in the China council minutes. It is impossible to track the use of morphine during the 1890s since it is seldom mentioned by name: "tincture . . . pills . . . medicine," the reports say elliptically.[37] Nevertheless, a conference of Shanxi missionaries admitted they were still using morphine in 1892. W. G. Peat of the CIM presented a paper which "protested against the indiscriminate opening of refuges by men whose Christianity had not been previously tested. As far as possible he would have such a work under foreign supervision" — which implies the use of hypodermic morphine rather than in pill or powder form. At the missionary-run refuge at Pingyao, Peat "had withdrawn all narcotics at once and simply encouraged the patients to hold out" — which explained why only two in a hundred patients had "stood" — "but this method he would not now employ." He stated that the refuges should be "as bright and comfortable as could be, and [he] would use morphia and tonics in the breaking off." Nevertheless, the conference passed a motion that "views with alarm the indis-

---

36. China council minutes, 29 May 1890, in CIM/SOAS, file 73.
37. R. H. Newman, "Opium Smoking in Late Imperial China: A Reconsideration," *Modern Asian Studies* 29, no. 4 (1995), p. 774, agrees that morphine use "cannot be quantified." In 1903 when imports of morphia reached 146,000 ounces, the Chinese government imposed a heavy tax which drove the trade into the hands of smugglers. "Morphia smuggling became a serious matter in the 1930s, but in 1906 the problem was still in its infancy."

criminate sale, in Opium Refuges and otherwise, of medicines containing opium and its alkaloids."[38]

With the CIM's financial and moral support, Hsi turned his Heavenly Invitation Offices into a flourishing business, but there were always questions about the propriety — and the profits — of such a venture. Between 1886 and 1890, he established refuges along the Big Road from Pingyang as far north as Pingyao; Hongdong had enough addicts to support eleven refuges. A chain went to Daning, west of the Fen River, where Pastor Ch'ü, the former Buddhist sect leader, led his own indigenous work, and southeast to Stanley Smith's mountain station at Luan. In the early 1890s Hsi extended his system into the adjoining provinces, east to Zhili, southeast to North Henan, and southwest across the Yellow River to Xian and then northwest into Shaanxi and Gansu.[39]

Hsi's "keepers" were reformed addicts who came through his system as patients, enquirers, converts, assistant refuge keepers, apprentices and preachers, whom he personally trained in his drug-preparation rooms. He would send them somewhere to open a refuge where addiction was rampant, and supply his famous red pills at a certain price. Some refuges were decent "clean" surroundings run by semi-honest keepers; most were in abject poverty, comparable to Samuel Drake's experimental refuge in a cave (see Chapter 8). In a remote mountain village named Fensi, the keeper Wang "entirely lost his reason" when he was left alone. He went into debt, saying that the Jesus Religion had lots of silver. The refuge was "a wretched place, tumbledown, filthy, and in the most hopeless disorder." Eventually Hsi made good the debts, amounting to 8,000 cash, and closed the refuge. This, D. E. Hoste reported, was the only time Hsi closed a refuge.[40]

The opium work brought a tougher, younger class of men into the church, who changed Pastor Hsi's little Bible-reading and exorcism sect. Normally the only paid employment at a mission was as evangelist, colporteur, cook, servant, or coolie, or for women, amah or Biblewoman. All were demanding jobs

---

38. A. R. Saunders, "Shansi Conference of Foreign Missionaries," *Chinese Recorder*, April 1893, pp. 178-86; quotes at p. 184, p. 186. In the issue of July 1893, p. 350, an American Baptist, George L. Mason, reported that "native Christians still sell the [morphine] pills as opium remedies, while admitting the cures are exceedingly rare. The native shops have dozens of preparations, liquids, powders, pills, lozenges, put up in attractive shape and flamingly advertized as sure cures of the opium habit. Some are prepared by foreign druggists. But most of them are native mixtures, in which morphia or opium is the chief ingredient."

39. Partial list in *Pastor Hsi*, p. 214.

40. Ibid., pp. 227-30.

operating under the missionaries' noses. Hsi offered something better: to set up rehabilitated addicts in business. Most of the keepers were upright and kindly if one is to trust the stories, but with confiscated opium coming in and anti-opium pills going out, operating a refuge could corrupt the best men. Beyond the orthodox refuges was a shadowy underworld of "spurious" and "renegade" refuges set up by non-Christians and former Christians — like Mr. Fan of Chapter 8 — who thought they would get onto a good thing.

Despite Taylor's hopes, Pastor Hsi's system never caught on outside Shanxi, even though every mission in China experimented with some sort of opium work. W. W. Cassels, the Anglican clergyman of the Cambridge Seven, took some of Hsi's helpers to East Sichuan where they set up a replica of Hsi's system, which folded within a year, as did those in Zhejiang and elsewhere.[41] As late as 1899 the CIM had forty missionary-run refuges in Shanxi and uncounted native ones, but only five in Shaanxi, and one each in Gansu, Jiangxi, and Zhejiang. There was not one other opium refuge in the entire China Inland Mission.

The opening of Xian shows how Pastor Hsi's opium refuges paved the way for the expanding missionary presence. Since the missionaries could not rent a house there, Pastor Hsi decided to go personally — his first trip outside his home province — and open a refuge. Traveling alone, he joined up with a Muslim military mandarin, a general who, finding "that Hsi was a doctor, prepared to undertake the cure of opium smokers," confessed he was a "slave" to the habit. The general introduced Hsi to his opium-smoking friends and "materially helped him in securing suitable premises." The refuge prospered under two "reliable keepers" who helped a Swedish missionary named Holman to become the first Western resident. Holman was an innocent, who slept in the back room and refused to be evicted when the magistrate and his assistants called on him. He welcomed the magistrate as an honored guest and "asked if they were fond of music, and would like to hear his guitar. . . . Inwardly crying to God for protection, Holman sang hymn after hymn to simple Swedish melodies, until somehow prejudice was disarmed. . . . Half-interested and half-amused, his would-be opponents went away, won to neutrality if not friendship."[42]

North Henan, the cut-off corner north of the Yellow River, was also opened by Pastor Hsi's refuges. Despite extensive itinerations, the CIM had been forced out of every city in the province, except for two stations in the south. Pastor Hsi sent a trusted agent named Ch'eng to open a refuge in

---

41. Ibid., pp. 221-24.
42. Ibid., pp. 218-21. Annual report in *China's Millions* (NA), September 1893, p. 117.

Huaiqing, east of Luan. Ch'eng was rebuffed at every turn until he came upon a "forlorn" stranger who had been robbed by bandits; like the Good Samaritan, Ch'eng befriended the man, who turned out to be a "gentleman." This act of charity impressed the people who allowed Ch'eng to open a refuge.[43]

When the Canadian Presbyterians arrived five or six years later, they did not have a high opinion of the so-called Christian opium refuge. "Taylor claims to have begun actual work at Changte [Zhangde, now Anyang]," Jonathan Goforth wrote. "This amounts to Pastor Hsi, a Chinaman connected with CIM, who has discovered the art of making opium pills. He sells these at a good profit and has sent men in all directions to start opium refuges."[44] Nevertheless, Goforth's first convert was a man named Wang Fu-lin, who had tried to break his addiction unsuccessfully using Hsi's medicine and was working as a "sort of assistant" at the refuge. He stayed with the Goforths for three weeks, where their "treatment" was to feed him tea and cakes and show him photographs of the West. By the fifth day Wang seemed demented, his "mind, body, soul hung in the balance." He had a dream in which a "horrible being" urged him to jump over the wall. On the fifteenth day, the craving ceased, and he never again touched the stuff. "The Lord raised up a wonderful instrument for our work in the person of Wang Fu-lin," Jonathan and Rosalind Goforth wrote in *Miracle Lives of China*. Before his conversion, Wang had been a professional storyteller, and afterwards, he kept his profession but changed the stories and was known as "the Spirit filled preacher."[45]

A Wealthy Place

When Hsi Shengmo was a young Christian, he would storm about exorcising devils and terrorizing magistrates, even demanding an audience with the provincial officials to protect his flock. God had given him a position like Moses, Stanley Smith commented, and "in expecting the subjugation of others to his authority, he thought he was carrying out the Divine Will."[46] Neverthe-

---

43. *Pastor Hsi*, pp. 222-23.

44. Jonathan Goforth, North Henan Mission, to Thomas Wardrope, Convenor of Foreign Mission Committee, Presbyterian Church in Canada, 24 May 1890, in North Henan Mission files, UCA.

45. The biography of Wang Fu-lin is in Jonathan and Rosalind Goforth, *Miracle Lives of China* (London: Marshall, Morgan & Scott, 1931, and Grand Rapids: Zondervan, 1931), chapter 1, "Earliest Trophies of Grace," part 3; "A Broken but Filled Vessel (Wang Fu-Lin)," pp. 14-20.

46. *Pastor Hsi*, p. 191.

less, Pastor Hsi continued to assert the treaty rights not to pay the idol taxes. It was not until 1891, the year of the Yangtze riots, that the churches of South Shanxi resolved "unanimously" not to appeal for legal protection but to rely on "God alone for succour and defence." This policy was "clearly explained to every candidate before baptism; lest afterwards, when tested and tried by persecution, he should repent."[47] As Pastor Hsi grew older — he was fifty-eight in 1894 when Taylor visited — he "mellowed," and thanks to the missionaries, God had brought him into "a wealthy place," as one chapter in his biography was entitled.

When missionaries started arriving in South Shanxi in numbers, they followed the example of the Cambridge Seven and put themselves under Pastor Hsi's protection and guidance. His mellowness made his relations with some missionaries easier, those who came with no experience or settled theories of their own and were willing to accept his authority. But others would tell him to his face that his opium work was dangerous and his hold over the people misguided. On occasions like that, Hsi would retreat politely and murmur, "As far as I know, I was led of God to open that Refuge. I am simply His servant. He is responsible. How dare I venture, without orders, to close my Master's business?"[48]

Nothing shows the dichotomy between the missionaries and Pastor Hsi as clearly as the mission stations at Pingyang and Hongdong, and his own home at the Middle Eden. Pingyang, the prefectural *(fu)* city that had been the epicenter of the famine, became the CIM's largest inland station after Taiyuan was closed, with eleven missionaries. In this city of grandiose temples, the CIM had built a model station with schools, opium refuges, and two hospitals, one for men and one for women. Dr. Millar Wilson, a Scottish physician who went out under a special dispensation, financed the entire medical and opium work. At Hongdong, the county *(xian)* town twenty miles north, was Pastor Hsi's chapel, where he presided as "bishop" and Dixon Hoste, the only foreign resident, lived in a room behind. Mrs. Hoste described her first view of Hongdong: "A large door on the 'Grain Market Street,' surmounted with heavy handsome carved wood-work, leads first into the opium refuge court. . . . There are nearly always men standing and sitting around this yard, and very often someone singing in a strong unmusical voice a very monotonous hymn tune. . . . The chapel is a long, rather imposing building, with a high-pointed roof. . . . It has evidently been a fine ancestral hall in some by-

---

47. Roger Thompson, "Twilight of the Gods," pp. 66-68, discussed Pastor Hsi and persecution.
48. *Pastor Hsi*, p. 227.

The Middle Eden

gone day." Gertrude Hoste also provided one of the few eyewitness descriptions of Pastor Hsi, a small man "with sharp eyes. One eye is particularly piercing; there is a slight cast in the other. His manner is quick and imperious."[49]

The credulous people would flock around him, calling him "Our Shepherd" and "Living Jesus," as if he was an avatar, a Living Buddha. Feeling this was "the devil's scheme" to puff him with pride, Hsi stopped the people and humbled himself, "taking on the heart of a bond-slave." (There is a self-serving tone in his statement, "I could not stop them," but his attitude of holy servitude is common among religious leaders.) Every spring and autumn, four or five hundred Christians would converge on Hongdong for four days of worship, singing, and testimony — and free food — culminating in a mass baptism. The missionary would catechize and baptize some of the men, while Hsi baptized the rest of the men and all the women.

As the fourth son of a wealthy peasant family, Hsi had inherited a corner of the ancestral home, which he expanded by purchasing derelict property. He had intended to call his home simply "Eden," the story goes, but this name was stolen by Mr. Fan for his spurious refuges. "So Hsi added the one word *Chong* [pinyin *Zhong*], so full of meaning to every Chinaman [i.e. *Zhong-guo*, the Middle Kingdom], and after that it was always known as 'The Middle Eden.' It was there one really had to see him, really to know him at his best."[50]

Pastor Hsi's own family is seldom mentioned: one of his brothers was baptized and had something to do with the refuges; his only child, a daughter, died in infancy; and his adopted son became an opium addict, "a prodigal, and almost broke his [father's] heart."[51] The Middle Eden, like many Chinese sects — indeed, like the CIM in a curious way — was run by the distaff side, by Mrs. Hsi (who was fourteen years younger than her husband), her mother, aunts, and her sister, Mrs. Sï. Before her conversion Mrs. Hsi had been an ordinary Chinese wife, illiterate and sharp-tongued; when her husband became a Christian, she became apoplectic, possessed of an evil spirit which her husband cast out of her, his first experiment in exorcism. On at least one occasion Mrs. Hsi herself cast out devils: once when Pastor Hsi was away, a possessed man came to the gate and she exclaimed, "We save men through faith in God! Are we dependent on the Pastor?"[52]

49. Mrs. D. E. Hoste, "Hung-t'ung and its Autumn Conference," *China's Millions* (NA), March 1895, pp. 33-34.
50. *Pastor Hsi*, p. 258.
51. Ibid., pp. 26-61.
52. Hsi's autobiographical account in ibid., p. 262.

Mrs. Hsi, the second, younger wife of Pastor Hsi. As a bride Mrs. Hsi sold her jewelry to open a station at Huozhou, and she remained her husband's helpmeet in his ministry. Since he was often absent, she ran the Middle Eden, the utopian community at his family's home. After she was widowed and dispossessed of her inheritance in 1896, she took on her own ministry, working with women addicts in Huozhou. Source: OMF/Toronto.

The Middle Eden

After her husband taught her to read, she became his partner in the full sense of the word. He was often away for weeks and months opening refuges, visiting the flock — traveling in a cart emblazoned with a scarlet banner that read "Holy Religion of Jesus" — and she was in charge of the Middle Eden, including the worship services and the pill-making operation. Moreover, she also often took to the road, supervising the women missionaries and the women's refuges under her care. Other women also held prominent positions in the sect: when three "substantial farmers" were vying for the position of deacon, rather than elevate one and factionalize the church, Pastor Hsi appointed a "dear old lady" who had "quite a power." "Why not recognize the position the Lord has evidently given this woman, and let her be set apart as a deaconess?" he asked.[53]

"For many years past," Pastor Hsi wrote in his autobiographical sketch, "there have been both a Refuge and a Gospel Hall in my own house, where through the power of God I have healed diseases, cured opium-smokers, and preached the Gospel." (The order is significant: healing, opium addicts, then preaching.) He continued, "There are several others, both men and women, who had diseases that no man could cure; but by regularly attending the services in our home, they gradually recovered, and were led to trust in the Lord."[54] Among his disciples was a "young fellow who was a priest, and is now in a tailor's shop; . . . he is a man of prayer and faith, and was the means of healing one or two in a village near P'ing-yang, where he used to live; his plan is to keep on praying about a person until the disease is removed."[55] Pastor Hsi's ultimate miracle occurred at the Middle Eden during the drought of 1894 when he announced that the One True God, who "understood farming much better than he did," had appeared in a vision and told him, "Harrow the land at once, but sow late." He persisted despite his neighbors' ridicule and when the rains came too late for them to plant, he was ready. "The moral needed no pointing" when their fields were barren and his were fertile.[56]

Every day at the Middle Eden began and ended with public worship, Bible reading, hymn-singing and prayer "to keep the Refuges from calamity." Charles Wesley's genius was to set the people singing, to take religious music out of the churches and into the marketplace, and to bring secular tunes into the churches, putting new words to popular songs. "Pastor Hsi was himself

---

53. Ibid., pp. 234, 275-76.
54. Ibid., p. 262.
55. D. E. Hoste, letter from P'ing-yang Fu, 18 April 1886, in *China's Millions* (GB), October 1886, p. 138.
56. *Pastor Hsi*, pp. 263-64.

always singing," said Geraldine Taylor, and "the life of the Hung-tung Christians was set to song. The outcome was not always musical, but it was full of blessing."[57]

Although Chinese religious music consisted of congregational chanting, bells, and instruments — or the disreputable "singing people," a hereditary outcaste group in Shanxi who provided dirges for funerals[58] — Pastor Hsi realized the power of singing in Christian worship. He became a prolific hymn writer, and "a nice little volume" of his hymns was published in Chinese, with additions by Stanley Smith. Several were copied in the CIM hymn books of the 1920s, and are still used in Chinese churches. The English translation, *The Songs of Pastor Hsi*, by Francesca French, made him well known in the West. "Many of the airs he adopted were of native origin; and others, European by extraction, 'had their heads shaved like the missionaries and were put in Chinese dress.' These naturalised melodies took wonderfully with the people. Hsi also had his own way of leading. He loved to pitch the tunes as high as possible, and keep them up to a good, swinging pace. There was nothing dull or drowsy about the Hung-tung services when he was present."[59]

It is worth pausing to consider Pastor Hsi's hymns. Except for a few autobiographical excerpts in *Pastor Hsi* (his conversion, heavenly visions, and the revelation of the pills), his letter to General Hoste, and the rules for the Middle Eden, the hymns are the only texts from Pastor Hsi's own hand. What message was he telling the people? What do these hymns reveal about the people who sang them? I have quoted his best known composition, "A Song of Sacrifice," as the epigraph at the beginning of each of the Shanxi chapters (5, 8, 11, 12, and 13). The opening lines of each stanza are as follows:

> When Thou wouldst light the darkness, Lord,
>   Then I would be the silver lamp . . .
> When Thou wouldst slay the wolves, O Lord,
>   Then I would be the keen-edged sword . . .
> When Thou wouldst pour the living stream,
>   Then I would be the earthen cup . . .
> When Thou wouldst warn the people, Lord,
>   Then I would be the golden bell . . .
> When Thou wouldst write the records, Lord,
>   Then I would be the ready pen . . .

---

57. Ibid., pp. 186-87.
58. Spence, *The Search for Modern China*, p. 88.
59. *Pastor Hsi*, p. 187.

The titles of other hymns suggest their mood: "A Song of Consolation," "A Song of Compensations" ("For the faith's sake, my home is poor . . ."), and "Song for Aged Men":

> The evening shades of life have crept across your sunset sky,
> My fathers, I would plead with you, for your immortal soul. . . .

"A Song of Opium Woes" starts:

> Of opium's woe you should certainly know,
> Its evils are many, they blight your whole life . . .
> When you light up the flame of the opium lamp,
> The devil enfolds you in sepulchral gloom. . . .[60]

Some hymns commemorate an occasion, such as the departure of "two native brethren" from Hongdong to open a refuge in North Henan:

> Despising Earthly pleasure,
> Esteeming Heavenly treasure,
> To preach the Truth in Ancient Wei, ye go;
> Exhorting and beseeching
> The churches ye are leaving
> That mutual love should ever fostered be.
>
> CHORUS
> May travelling mercies be vouchsafed by God to thee,
> May cities you pass through hear Jesus preached by you.
>   Then — Satan defeated,
>   Your mission completed —
> Chanting songs of Victory, Return.[61]

It has been said that Chinese Christian hymns, betraying their Buddhist roots, portray the sadness and transience of this world. Sacrifice, transience, and impermanence have always been minor chords of Christian hymnody, too: "Only one life, 'twill soon be past, Only what's done for God will last . . ." as one popular hymn said. Keswick Holiness, with its emphasis on the "Higher Life," intensified this longing for heaven and transcending of earthly

---

60. French, *Songs of Pastor Hsi*, p. 39.
61. "Tell Abroad God's Truth," *Pastor Hsi*, vol. 2 (1903), p. 270.

cares. So, Pastor Hsi's songs of consolation drew on a dual heritage, Christian and Chinese, glorying in the value of being poor and persecuted and small because "Jesus loves me."

There are hints, too, of Hsi's sectarian roots in the Religion of the Golden Pill, the black-and-white Manichean fatalism that recalls the yin-yang dichotomy of good and evil, word and flesh, spirit and soul. These are expressed as themes of transformation and redemption, of good triumphing over evil, another congruence with nineteenth-century evangelicalism. The "Church militant" of the next verse of the Hongdong farewell could compare with "Hold the fort, for I am coming":

> With Jesus for our Leader,
> Our Captain and Preceder
> We follow trump and standard to Lu-an:
> To-day we meet together,
> By grace we'll meet hereafter,
> Enjoying even more the love of God.

Behind the King James phraseology, there is something else behind Pastor Hsi's hymns: the wordless book. Reading *China's Millions* and *Pastor Hsi* through the prism of the wordless book, one can make sense of the converts' testimonies and the growth of Pastor Hsi's church among illiterates and opium addicts. So far, we know that the wordless book was introduced in 1880 by the CIM ladies after the Great Famine as a four-colored silk purse, a simple mnemonic device for "gossiping the gospel" among widows and orphans in the shelter. Seven years later, G. W. Clarke created his calico banner at Datong. The next occasion the wordless book appeared, it was in the hands of Mrs. Howard Taylor, immediately after her visit to the Middle Eden. (It is significant that she does not mention it before, on her trip into Shanxi.) After accompanying the senior Taylors to Tianjin, Howard and Geraldine returned to Henan, where she used it to teach a congregation of Buddhist nuns, "religious women . . . [who] belonged to an organized order of religious worshippers." She also introduced the gospel glove at that meeting. (See Introduction.)

I am suggesting a certain line of transmission: it was introduced by missionaries but it quickly slipped out of their hands. Pastor Hsi incorporated it into his indigenous sect because of its congruence with the ancient *wuxing* color cosmology, and then returned it back to the missionaries. What evidence do we have for the wordless book at the Middle Eden? Through his study of the Religion of the Golden Pill, Pastor Hsi had a keen sense of the ceremonial application of colors. He dressed for dramatic effect, with a white

The Middle Eden

gown and scarlet sash, that would have singled him out as a religious practitioner, such as an exorcist or priest who officiated at funerals. Embedded in the converts' testimonies are suggestions that they learned their simple catechism through the four-stage progression of the wordless book. When William Key catechized the candidates, who included illiterate peasants and old grannies, he was "much pleased with the answers most of them gave; two or three were rather dull, and knew little more than that they were sinners, and that Christ died for them, which, I believe, is sufficient to admit them into the Kingdom."[62] Black sin, red salvation, white baptism, the golden Kingdom: there in the grannies' testimony are the four colors of the wordless book. (Compare this with Pastor Hsi's own testimony in Chapter 5: "I know my sins are great; I ought to go to hell. I know, too, that Jesus is able to forgive my sins, able to save me from sin, able to save me from hell, and to give me to live in heaven forever.")[63]

Many of Pastor Hsi's hymns utilize color references to symbolize a Pilgrim's Progress in song: lighting the darkness, sounding the golden bell, inscribing the names in the Book of Life. These tantalizing clues suggest that the wordless book was used among indigenous Chinese churches, until its origins were forgotten and it became part of the background of missionary Christianity.

The Rules for the Middle Eden

The final text from Pastor Hsi's hand consists of the "Rules for The Middle Eden," which he "mounted on a board . . . like an official proclamation" inside the gate of the compound. These were so detailed they took four pages to summarize in *Pastor Hsi*, the book. "There were no unimportant matters with him," Geraldine Taylor explained. "'Everything has a great truth underlying it,' was one of his characteristic sayings. He believed that the highest principles should be applied to the smallest details of everyday affairs, and that the true state of the heart shows itself in just these little things. It is a deeply earnest view of life."[64]

"By the grace of God," the rules began, "these Regulations are appointed for learning the Heavenly Doctrine." Rule One stated: "On the Lord's Day all

---

62. William Key, "Baptisms at P'ing-yang," *China's Millions* (GB), October 1886, pp. 132-33.
63. Ibid., January 1887, p. 6.
64. *Pastor Hsi* (single vol.), p. 261.

must attend public worship three times," and that persons "who have fallen into sin and not repented, may not be entertained." During the week, "each one shall arise at daybreak. All are to watch and pray; and having combed hair and washed faces, must diligently sweep out the rooms and courtyards, set the children to work, and go to their own occupation, not daring to be lazy." Rule Four set out the order of the services every evening, which were held outdoors in summer and in the chapel in the winter. Monday was Exposition of the Scriptures; Tuesday was a Prayer Meeting; Wednesday, "Singing of Hymns: ten hymns shall be practised, new and old"; Thursday was "Gospel Preaching . . . that they may more easily understand and remember: from shallow going on to deep, from less to greater, making daily progress"; Friday was "Prayer for All Men"; and Saturday night, more hymn singing and prayer. Finally, the rules stated, "no one is permitted to attend fairs, or theatricals; no one may smoke either the dry pipe or the water pipe; and on no account is wine to be used. . . . Gossiping is not allowed from door to door."[65]

Beyond the religious observances, the rules for the Middle Eden regulated everyone's life like clockwork, down to the smallest children. Elders Sï, Cheo, and Yüen were to "make up the various pills, not omitting united prayer that by the help of the Holy Spirit the medicine may be properly prepared, may be able to rescue people from opium-smoking, and lead them to believe in the Gospel; also that the pills may be well-made, smooth, and attractive looking." "Brother Yü is to look after matters of husbandry, feeding the animals, the use of mules and carts, drawing water, collecting manure. . . . He will employ some of the children to help him. . . . If they are disobedient, upon return from the fields Elder Sï is to see that those under ten years of age receive twenty blows on the hand, those over ten, thirty. . . . If they disobey the heavenly laws of God, they are to be beaten with sticks according to the above regulations." Gentle Princess, one of Pastor Hsi's many nieces, "is to sweep out the three rooms on the south of the courtyard; after breakfast she will spin thread; after dinner study, and feed the chickens." If she was naughty, "her old Aunt with a small stick is to beat her five times on the hand." Little Silver Bells, another niece, "is not to let the baby rest on other people's beds."

If Pastor Hsi's hymns show his spiritual, suffering side, these regulations depict him as a stiff-necked Confucian patriarch. Since the One True God had chosen him, Pastor Hsi reasoned, he needed to reinforce God's heavenly discipline as revealed in the Bible. Lack of discipline was the cause for the addicts' opium habit in the first place, and only through discipline could they be brought back to their filial duty and the correct path. The "Rules for The

65. Ibid., pp. 258-61.

Middle Eden" concluded with a Confucian exhortation: "Any unwilling to follow these regulations will be earnestly exhorted to repent. If they choose rather to leave The Middle Eden, they are at liberty to do so. Regulations in force A.D. 1894. Trusting the Lord, Hsi, Overcomer of Demons."

The Converts

"I should like you to know these men," Duncan Kay wrote of his "encouraging" congregation at Quwu, South Shanxi: twenty-eight of forty-one baptized converts were reformed opium addicts. In Pingyang the proportion was one-half; and "nine out of ten in the large church at Ta-ning [Daning], the best church that we have in Shan-si, have been delivered from opium. . . . Many people say that opium-smokers cannot be brought under the power of the Gospel. They have been," Kay concluded. "Some of our best men in the church have been opium-smokers."[66]

The CIM reports stressed the new life of the convert, of "lives quieted by the Spirit." Doubtless many were simple peasants wanting to be good and have some protection in a world gone crazy, but even Stanley Smith admitted that the opium refuges brought in "scamps and vagabonds in every sense of the term, but God loves them; that is enough."[67] Charlie Studd reported on one inquirer who stated, "I am a murderer, an adulterer, I have broken all the laws of God and man again and again. I am also a confirmed opium smoker. He cannot save me." This man was "soundly converted" and returned to his town to preach where he "had done all this evil and sin." Even when brought before the magistrate and beaten severely, he would not desist, preaching through the window of his prison cell. "Such men are worth saving," Studd commented.[68] In Shandong, another missionary said, "If I had gone through the city in order to select THE VILEST AND MOST DISGRACEFUL MAN that could be found, and the greatest ruffian, I should certainly have picked out that man. And now he adorns the doctrines of GOD our SAVIOUR."[69]

Those who came were the poorest of the poor: why else would they let themselves be "bewitched" by the Christians? Many were old and sick, looking for a happier land in the next life: "The LORD seems to save so many just

---

66. Duncan Kay, "Encouraging Progress in South Shan-si," *China's Millions* (GB), August 1893, pp. 110-11.
67. Ibid., July-August 1887, p. 101.
68. Grubb, *C. T. Studd: Athlete and Pioneer*, pp. 84-85.
69. Charles H. Judd, "Turned to God from Idols," *China's Millions* (NA), July 1895, p. 91, capitalization in the original.

to take them home," one missionary wrote.[70] In other words, the Christians provided good funerals. There are no accounts of life inside the refuges, but one list of fifty-four men in Ningxia indicates a cross-section of the rural population:

> 4 carpenters, 3 tailors, 6 curriers, 5 labourers, 4 bakers, 9 small tradesmen, 1 innkeeper, 1 opium dealer, 2 shoemakers, 1 cabman, 1 paperhanger, 1 blacksmith, 1 Buddhist priest, 1 stonemason, 2 teachers, 1 painter, 1 felt maker, 1 tax gatherer, 3 soldiers, 2 brasiers, 1 butcher, 1 horn maker, 1 dyer. Average age began to smoke, 23 years, youngest began at 11; oldest began at 41; the youngest entered the Refuge at 21; the oldest and the first at 51. On average a man smokes 2 drs. 2 scr. 20 grs per day.[71]

(Except for the Buddhist priest and the opium dealer, this could be the roll of a dissenting chapel in Yorkshire.)

There seem to have been many religious seekers among the converts: members of the White Lotus and Golden Pill sects and other, more secretive societies, Buddhist priests and nuns, Daoist exorcists. The star convert in Studd's station at Lucheng was a former "sorceress" and opium addict. "She is evidently determined to press on the heavenly way, and has been here several times, during the winter, to attend service. She has a cart and a donkey of her own, and so she can come better than some others, although she lives fifteen miles away."[72]

Outsiders were suspicious of the inflated statistics; one Bible Society agent doubted that "one in 15" of the six hundred converts claimed by the CIM "was really interested in the truth." The Oberlin Mission, wary of "make-believe work," quoted one "Baptist missionary operating in South Shansi" — probably Dixon Hoste — who baptized two hundred people solely because they came to him and "it was not his place to reject them." The Oberlin Mission developed a "stiff examination" — far more rigorous than the wordless book — to weed out inquirers with questions like: "What is it to be a Christian? What is sin? What is the meaning of baptism?" and finally, "Why do you love the Lord?"[73]

Normally the CIM demanded two years' probation before baptism, but this was honored more in the breach than the observance. Pastor Hsi's para-

70. *China's Millions* (NA), November 1895, p. 153.
71. *China's Millions* (GB), September 1888, p. 113.
72. Hattie Rice, letter from Lu-ch'eng, 6 April, in *China's Millions* (NA), June 1895, p. 82.
73. Francis Price, "Description of Mission Work in Shansi, 1877-1889," in Nat Brandt, *Massacre in Shansi*, pp. 116-17.

ble of the candle shining as soon as it was lit produced an expansionist church but it garbled the message. It pushed some converts beyond their capabilities when they were dispatched to some far-off place to cure addicts and preach the gospel. And there remains the unanswerable question: what happened to the backsliders, those who got a little religion and gave up when God did not bring good luck?

The Cambridge Seven

If the articles in *China's Millions* are any indication, Pastor Hsi had the official support of the CIM and probably of most of its people. Three groups — the Cambridge Seven, the single women, and the Scandinavians — made the virtually unprecedented decision to work *under* Hsi's direction, and not *over* him. Going native, living in a courtyard with a constant stream of guests and only one or two foreign companions brought out the worst aspects of their character: love of power, priggishness, anger, class and racial condescension, difficult marriages, and Western clothing. These were "the onslaughts of Satan" that plagued relations between foreigners and Chinese everywhere. It also brought out their best: their sweetness, spirit of adventure, adaptability, optimism, self-sacrifice and their love of the Chinese.

The "sporting hearties" of the Cambridge Seven arrived in Pingyang in 1885 and each reacted in his own way. W. W. Cassels, "Will the Silent," the Anglican clergyman, was shocked by the ecclesiastical laxity he saw and moved as quickly as possible to East Sichuan where he established a proper Church of England enclave. Arthur Polhill Turner joined him and remained his right-hand man until Cassels's death in 1925. Cecil Polhill Turner went pentecostal and joined Annie Royale Taylor, the lone wolf at the borders of Tibet. Montague (later Sir Montague) Beauchamp, the benefactor, remained in the CIM in various provinces, until he returned to war-torn Sichuan to die in 1939. Dixon Edward Hoste, the artillery officer who loved order, swallowed his pride and remained balanced and orthodox, though distant and unemotional. Stanley Peregrine Smith, "the percussion cap," and Charlie Studd, "the roman candle," were loose cannons who careened from enthusiasm to enthusiasm, progressively unbalanced and unorthodox.

Hoste, like Hudson Taylor, was a visionary a generation ahead of his time, who believed missionaries were building the "scaffolding" of a Chinese church under Chinese leadership, self-governing, self-supporting, and self-propagating. Living as a single man in a corner of the Hongdong chapel, Hoste had to walk a delicate line between recognizing Hsi in his "God-given position" and becoming "one of his lieutenants; that you cannot be." Content to remain in the background, the coxswain, the "little man to sort of steer" the boat, while Hsi provided the energy, Hoste remained Hsi's closest associate for ten years. Pastor Hsi gave his own tribute: "In all matters connected with Church or Refuges, Mr. Hoste and I have united in prayer and consultation. . . . We mutually help one another, without any distinction of native or foreigner, because the Lord has made us one."[74]

One incident reveals the indirect, high-minded nature of their relationship. During the drought of 1894, when Pastor Hsi received his divine vision to sow his wheat late, Hoste knew he was in "great privation" and felt the urge to give him some money. While walking to the Middle Eden, he came to the "unwelcome conviction" that he should not give the money, rather that he could do more through "loving sympathy." Later, when Hoste revealed what he had thought, Pastor Hsi thanked him for not giving the money; the One True God had sent the drought as a "blessing," and a gift from the missionary, at a time when many Christians were hungry, would have been a "hindrance in the work."[75]

Hoste never had "much opportunity to develop household skills," as Hudson Taylor delicately put it, and took to eating at street food stalls, with the health problems that that entailed. Taylor was worried and sent a companion, an enterprising young American named Edwin M. McBrier. "I understand you Americans are very adaptable," Taylor wrote, asking him confidentially to make sure Hoste had certain "home comforts." McBrier was a born salesman, for he had given up a promising business career: a few years earlier, he and his cousins, C. S. and F. W. Woolworth, had opened the first "5-and-10 cent" store, in their hometown of Lockport, New York. (Lockport was an important CIM center, through the ministry of William J. Erdman and his son Charles.) Unfortunately McBrier remained only two years at Pingyang, before he resigned to return to America and marry his fiancée, who had been rejected by the CIM. He went back into the family business, which was now the Woolworths' empire, and became vice-president. But he never lost his interest in China missions. For many years, until the 1950s when he was in his eighties, he sat on the New York–based United Board for Christian Higher Education in Asia, and contributed funds for a building at Cheeloo University in Shandong. He also established the McBrier Foundation for Biblical Instruction and Christian Work, an institution which lasted from 1929 to 1945.[76]

---

74. *HTCOC 7*, p. 245.
75. *Pastor Hsi*, pp. 232-33. Phyllis Thompson, *D. E. Hoste: "A Prince with God*," pp. 6-67.
76. Thompson, *D. E. Hoste*, pp. 73-76. McBrier's application # 66 in CIM Application

The Middle Eden

Meanwhile, after two more years of the bachelor life, Hoste married Gertrude Broomhall, and brought her to Hongdong.

Stanley Smith and Charlie Studd had offended Pastor Hsi during the episode with Elder Fan and the spurious opium refuges, and had to be reassigned to Luan, an isolated station 130 miles southeast of Pingyang in the Taihang mountains. Before they departed, though, Pastor Hsi married the two men and their fiancées in a "sham marriage," which had to be repeated in front of the British consul at Shanghai. Smith married Sophie Reuter, the Norwegian governess who had been recruited by Frederik Franson (see Chapter 9), and "whose grace of manner and goodness of heart speedily endeared her to all." Studd married Priscilla Livingstone Stewart, author of the startling passage quoted above, a "real Salvation Army lassie" from Belfast. With both couples deeply in love, Luan, Studd said, was like a "honeymoon with Jesus!"[77]

Abandoning the unobtrusive "tea-shop evangelism," they started preaching on "Salvation Army lines, with a good deal of banners and processing on the streets and beating of gongs and drums; we did not place any faith in them," Smith concluded, "but we thought that the Lord would bless our efforts. I am not aware that the Lord did bless them particularly, but the Lord blessed us in our souls very much."[78] Hudson Taylor was alarmed, warning that a "reckless S.A. band might easily drive us all out of any province in China." Smith would not "bear too much stimulus with safety," and as for Studd, "we must do all we can to knit him more closely to us *for his own sake*. We can do better without him than he can without us."[79]

Enthusiasm cannot be sustained indefinitely. Luan was an unrewarding station — twenty-four baptisms in seven years, mostly immigrants from Henan and Shandong — and after a year, the Studds moved to the next town of Lucheng. One year later, after only two years of marriage, Sophie Smith died suddenly of typhus, plunging Stanley into a maelstrom of grief. He drifted around the mission for a while until he volunteered to act as Henry Frost's traveling companion through the riot-torn Yangtze valley in 1891 and on their long voyage across the Pacific (see Chapter 10). When Frost persuaded the CIM to adopt its statement of faith, which specifically included the eternal punishment of the unregenerate, Frost then demanded that the *P&P* be revised. It had stated that a member "must be prepared to resign" if

---

Records (Toronto). His papers are in Archives of the United Board for Christian Higher Education in Asia, Yale University Divinity Library, Special Collections # 11.

77. *China's Millions* (GB), October 1886, p. 138.
78. Stanley Smith, "Six Years in China," *China's Millions*, July 1892, pp. 88-92.
79. *HTCOC* 7, pp. 58-60.

he held unorthodox views, leaving the decision up to the general director; now this was changed to read the member "*must* resign."

Frost's first target was Stanley Smith: he must resign. The "Smith controversy" dragged on for years, and became the flash point for the power struggle between Hudson Taylor and the councils. One of the reasons for Hudson Taylor's trip to Shanxi in 1894 was to bring Smith and Studd back into the fold and reinforce discipline concerning Chinese dress. Taylor believed that "tolerance for an old and esteemed member" — family — was more important than theological conformity. Against the opposition of the London council, Henry Frost, future fundamentalist, was determined to rid the CIM of liberals and modernists. Although Frost managed to convince the China council to censure Smith, Smith was reinstated after he repented, until finally in 1900 the China council allowed him to remain at Luan but prohibited him from preaching his views to the Chinese.[80]

Four years later the matter came up again. Dixon Hoste had been appointed general director, successor to Hudson Taylor, and at his inaugural meeting in 1904, at the first joint gathering of the China, London, North America, and Australia councils, the primary business was Stanley Smith. Hudson Taylor, an invalid in Davos, Switzerland, as well as the majority of the London, Australian, and China councils, wanted to show tolerance, but Frost convinced them that Smith must resign to maintain evangelical purity. Using arguments that were repeated a decade later by many American fundamentalists in the wars against modernism, Frost launched one of the opening salvoes of militant orthodoxy, that preserving "the faith once delivered to the saints" was more important than family, friends, or denominational loyalty. Frost wrote at length about the Stanley Smith affair in his "Memoirs" with such strong feeling that he was obviously reliving it thirty years later.

Stanley Smith, with his son Algernon and his second wife Anna M. Lang, remained at their old station of Luan as independents, even though there was also a CIM station there. He became a correspondent for the *Chinese Recorder*, where he promoted his views, and wrote two books: *China from Within: Or the Story of the Chinese Crisis*, a history of the Boxer Rebellion published in 1901, and *"The Spiritual Condition of the Heathen": A Reply to Mr. Henry W. Frost, Director of the China Inland Mission in North America*.[81] After his wife died in 1926, Smith applied to join the Canadian Presbyterian

---

80. Ibid.
81. Stanley Smith, *"The Spiritual Condition of the Heathen": A Reply to Mr. Henry W. Frost, Director of the China Inland Mission in North America* (Shanghai: Commercial Press, n.d.).

mission in North Henan, but was turned down because of his eccentric style. He died in China in 1933. Stanley Smith founded a missionary dynasty that is now in its fifth generation. His son Algernon (Algie) Stanley Smith went to South Africa as a missionary. All four of his children served in Africa, and the eldest married a CMS bishop. The next generation all served in various parts of the world, and their children have done service abroad.[82]

Charlie and Priscilla Studd resigned their formal membership in the CIM in 1890 — leaving only three of the Cambridge Seven in full communion — but they too remained at Lucheng until 1894, when they retired to England in poor health. He itinerated throughout the United States and Britain for six years before moving to India as pastor of an English-speaking congregation. Again in poor health, he returned to Britain in 1906 to resume his preaching ministry. In 1910, at the age of fifty, Studd went to the Belgian Congo alone, against the wishes of his ailing wife. He founded the Heart of Africa Mission, later the Worldwide Evangelization Crusade, and remained there until his death in 1931. Priscilla, who remained in England except for a single visit to Africa in 1928, died in 1929.[83]

The Pastor's Wife's Dream

Mrs. Hudson Taylor brought the first unmarried women into Shanxi in 1878, Anna Crickmay and Celia Horne, but both defected to the Baptist mission, and the experiment was abandoned. When Taylor visited the Middle Eden in 1886, Pastor Hsi said he had been impressed with the "young unmarried ladies, free to devote all their time to schools and evangelistic work" in Taiyuan. When Taylor proposed a forward movement, Hsi asked for single women to open women's opium refuges and work under Mrs. Hsi. The CIM had never stationed single women alone, but always with a married couple or a brother, so these women were the first to live alone in the interior without a white male escort.

At first, they were two, Sophie Reuter (later, Mrs. Stanley Smith) and Anna Jakobsen, in Huozhou (now Huo Xian), a county town three stages north of Hongdong on the Big Road. Then there were women at three stations, at Xiaoyi, near Taiyuan, and at Daning, to the west, a triangle. By 1899 there were

---

82. I am grateful to Sue Anderson, Stanley Smith's great-granddaughter, who works at the Henry Martyn Trust, University of Cambridge, for this information.
83. Biographical entry in Gerald H. Anderson, ed., *Biographical Dictionary of Christian Missions*, p. 649.

The women's Bible school at Huozhou, about 1904. Evangeline French was one of the pioneer women in Shanxi, a high-spirited and educated woman who had to learn how to be dowdy. At Huozhou, she worked under Mrs. Hsi's supervision, and they are shown at the far left sharing a book. Eva was later joined by Mildred Cable, standing center, and her sister Francesca. In the 1920s, when Eva was 53, they set out to walk to Central Asia, where they became nomads at the oases along the Silk Road. The sign seems to read: "Women's Bible School — Erected in the [?] — of — Westminster Chapel London [?] — 1904." Source: A. Mildred Cable, *The Fulfilment of a Dream of Pastor Hsi's: The Story of the Work in Hwochow* (London: Morgan & Scott, and CIM, 1917).

forty-four unmarried women in Shanxi, ten at women-only stations. Of the eleven who pioneered these stations in 1886-87, two died young, one committed suicide, two were sent home to die, and two died at the hands of the Boxers. Only four survived past 1900.

Huozhou started with a dream of Mrs. Hsi — one of the touching legends — in which the One True God promised to provide 30,000 cash to open a refuge there. Mrs. Hsi sold her jewelry, the rings and hairpins that marked her as a prosperous woman, saying, "Let Hwochow have the Gospel."[84] (If one uses

---

84. *Pastor Hsi*, pp. 143-44. A. Mildred Cable, *The Fulfilment of a Dream of Pastor Hsi's: The Story of the Work in Hwochow* (London: Morgan & Scott and CIM, 1908; reprinted 1917, 1920), pp. 6-8.

The Middle Eden

the usual calculation of 1,000 cash to one tael [one ounce] of silver, 30,000 cash would be the equivalent of 30 taels, or one-third of the annual salary of a poor teacher.)[85]

Hsi sent an evangelist named Ch'eng Hsiu-chi, probably the same Ch'eng who opened the refuge in Huaiqing, North Henan. He was a native of Huozhou, and had been a wild youth who "had wandered far in the paths of sin" and had a "fire of passion, hatred, and ignorance always burning in his heart." When he joined the Christians, he refused to pay the idol taxes and was disinherited by his family. Pastor Hsi took him in and gave him a job in the Hongdong refuge, before sending him to Huozhou to start a refuge and chapel.[86]

Sophie Reuter and Anna Jakobsen, enthusiastic Norwegians consumed with preaching sickness, living in one small room of a women's opium refuge in a hostile city, were prey to anyone who wanted to take advantage of them. Since they did not have the mobility of the male missionaries, they could not venture outside the compound for a walk through the countryside. Frustrated at the drugged stupor of the women, they were willing to do anything to "blow the trumpet in the ears of the people," even if it meant the "loss of reputation" and to have "evil spoken" of them.

The first scandal was wearing wadded trousers like a peasant woman, rather than the gown of a mandarin lady. "As pioneer workers, enthusiasm sometimes overstepped discretion, and ... the public playing of stringed instruments and open-air preaching to mixed congregations, led to misunderstanding, and even to the gathering around them of some whose presence was far from helpful." No wonder the people craned to see the spectacle, "their hungry eyes rivetted: the whole crowd seemed spellbound."[87] Following Pastor Hsi's example the women started providing "a simple mid-day meal" for the hungry people who had walked a considerable distance to attend Sunday worship. This gesture was misinterpreted, and they were besieged by "beggars

---

85. Henrietta Harrison, *The Man Awakened from Dreams*, pp. 43-44, states that Liu Dapeng was paid an annual salary of 100 taels as a live-in schoolteacher for a wealthy family; another teacher in a village school earned only 20 taels a year. Thirty taels was the same amount that David Hill offered as the first prize in the literary competition in 1879, which was calculated at the time as the equivalent of £7 10 shillings (or about $40 U.S.). See "The Hung-t'ung Conference, Aug. 1st and 2nd. Deeply Interesting Native Testimony," *China's Millions* (GB), January 1887, p. 5.

86. Cable, *Fulfilment of a Dream*, p. 22. *HTCOC* 7, p. 252, gives his pinyin name, Chéng Xiaoyu.

87. *China's Millions* (GB), June 1888, pp. 66-68. This description is of the first women's service in Huozhou.

and impostors." Pastor Hsi warned that the people "believe in Jesus for the food," and suggested that instead of serving a noon meal, the women themselves should fast for the whole Sunday, for their own good.[88]

Anna Jakobsen, a former housekeeper, came to the fore. She was an "idealist, strong, capable, and critical, . . . independent in thought and action." She mastered the local dialect "to a remarkable degree, and with a praiseworthy tenacity she studied the classical works of the Chinese."[89] The worst suspicions concerning single women were confirmed when she became secretly engaged to Pastor Ch'eng Hsiu-chi, the evangelist. Ch'eng felt a "strong admiration" for her, and she felt a "mysterious something" for the "one man who loved the pilgrim soul" in her. Moreover, she believed, marrying a Chinese would bring a "wider sphere of usefulness." Pastor Hsi did not condemn their marriage on racial grounds, but he did warn that "the time had not yet come for such unions to be desirable."[90]

Their engagement provoked a major crisis in the CIM. George Parker had married a Chinese woman some years earlier, but they had been sent to Gansu, far inland. Miss Jakobsen's case was different. Parker's marriage, Henry Frost indelicately put it, was "unnatural but not serious," but Miss Jakobsen's engagement was both "unnatural and serious."[91] Diplomatically, in the precarious world of international diplomacy, a white woman marrying a Chinese man would have to renounce her own citizenship and become a Chinese citizen, subject to Chinese law. The Swedish ambassador, fed up with the problems of single women, again threatened to recall all his nationals and revoke everyone's passport. Hudson Taylor refused to sanction the marriage, "good woman as she is," warning it would expose all women to "unwanted attentions from unsuitable men." He sent Miss Jakobsen with another Chinese evangelist to attempt the impossible, to open a beachhead in Hunan, where the men had failed. After five years living on the Jiangxi-Hunan border she established a small opium refuge five miles inside Hunan, the first foreigner to live in the province.[92]

Miss Jakobsen obeyed Taylor's orders until 1896, when Pastor Hsi, her only advisor, died. She and Pastor Ch'eng found an American missionary in Tianjin who would consent to marry them. Ostracized by foreigners and Chinese alike, the couple disappeared from the record, except for one cryptic no-

---

88. Cable, *Fulfilment of a Dream*, p. 21; *Pastor Hsi*, p. 241.
89. Cable, *Fulfilment of a Dream*, p. 20.
90. The Ch'eng-Jakobsen marriage is in ibid., pp. 22-24; *HTCOC* 7, pp. 252-53. It is not mentioned in *Pastor Hsi*.
91. Frost, "Memoirs," pp. 548-49.
92. *HTCOC* 7, p. 52. Marshall Broomhall, *The Jubilee Story of the CIM*, pp. 231-32.

tice that the CIM women in Jiangxi asked Mrs. Ch'eng not to complicate her sisters' lives by going there. Pastor Ch'eng "proved himself worthy in all ways of the confidence she had placed in him," and after she died he "faithfully served the Lord" until he "passed to his reward" in 1915.[93]

After Miss Reuter and Miss Jakobsen left Huozhou, they were replaced by women of a different sort. Jane Stevens, a Mildmay deaconess nurse, and Mildred Clarke, a YWCA worker, were determined that the Chinese "all should early understand the impossibility of intercourse outside the most rigid observance of etiquette, Chinese and Western." They were formal and "aloof," and since they would not eat Chinese food, "a simple, but foreign menage, took the place of the hitherto free-and-easy conditions." Neither woman spoke Chinese well — the language was "a real obstacle" to Miss Stevens — and to keep the people at a distance the work became institutional: Miss Clarke ran a girls' school and Miss Stevens did visitations in the city. The converts were baffled by this abrupt change of attitude and many drifted away. The women persevered, and must have been successful for Huozhou was the largest congregation in South Shanxi outside of Hongdong.[94]

The Pastor's Death

In 1895, one year after Hudson Taylor's visit to Shanxi, Pastor Hsi called a conference of all the refuge keepers and church leaders, two hundred guests, at the Middle Eden. He was filled with energy and preached with "solemnity and power" on the "great gulf" of the next life. This was his last public appearance. A few days later he fainted and "seemed strangely weak." Slowly he faded away, while he settled his affairs. He put the refuges on a self-supporting basis, closing some and amalgamating others so that the system would remain stable after he was gone.[95] Somehow, through extraordinary faith and charisma Pastor Hsi had held his disparate flock — the people of this book, Chinese and foreign — in a spiritual family that transcended nationality, class, religious beliefs, temperament, and drug addiction.

On 19 February 1896, at the age of sixty he was "translated to higher service." It was an omen-filled day. A Muslim rebellion was threatening northern

93. Cable, *Fulfilment of a Dream*, p. 24.
94. Forsyth, *China Martyrs of 1900*, pp. 437-39. Except for these conventional obituaries, the only record of Miss Stevens and Miss Clarke is in Cable, *Fulfilment of a Dream*, pp. 27-28. The only mention in *China's Millions* during their four years at Huozhou was one four-line report.
95. *Pastor Hsi*, pp. 289-92.

Shanxi, and the Big Road was thronged with troops marching north and refugees fleeing south.

One month after Pastor Hsi's death, Dixon Hoste bade his friends farewell and left Hongdong on furlough, his first in eleven years. Since his wife Gertrude had not yet fulfilled ten years of service, she remained there, where she was joined by her brother Marshall Broomhall, the future London director and CIM historian. After her husband returned, she was granted a few months' holiday in Australia. Afterwards, instead of reassigning Hoste to Shanxi, Hudson Taylor appointed him assistant China director, the youngest member of the China council, and assigned him to Shanghai. In 1900, after Taylor was invalided, Hoste became acting general director, and then general director in 1904. Thus, Hudson Taylor's generation, the generation of pilgrims, gave way to Dixon Hoste's generation of soldiers.

At its first meeting after Pastor Hsi's death, with D. E. Hoste in attendance, the China council approved future arrangements for "the Opium Refuges and work of the late Mr. Hsi," without specifying what those arrangements were. Expressing "thankfulness to God for Mr. Hsi's devoted life and unceasing toil, which have produced such wide-spread results in blessing to his fellow countrymen," the council extended heartfelt sympathy to his widow.[96] After that, the usual sources fall silent. *Pastor Hsi*, the biography, ends in 1896, and Dixon Hoste, the most incisive correspondent, moved away. Hoste's replacement, his brother-in-law Marshall Broomhall, wrote a few articles for *China's Millions,* such as "Discipline and Progress at Hung-tung, Shan-si," and a pamphlet about Hongdong called "A Mission Station in China" (1899).

As soon as Pastor Hsi was gone, the wolves descended. In villages where petty persecution had rumbled below the surface, there was "constant persecution." Invariably the trouble stemmed from the Christian's refusal to pay for "idolatrous theatricals," which were an important part of village life. Broomhall blamed the trouble on the village elders who refused to make a distinction between "public and idolatrous expenses" or "profitable and unprofitable" expenses. (This is the famous 40 percent off deal discussed in Chapter 5.)

> [At one village, An-loh] several men made profession of Christianity and applied to the village Council for exemption from the idolatrous portion of the taxes. This the council refused to allow, and as four villages were dependent on the same water channel for irrigation, the several village Councils unitedly determined to oppose any attempt to

---

96. China council minutes, 14 April 1896, in CIM/SOAS, file 73.

The Middle Eden

break the ancient custom of their villages as to taxes. The Christians conscientiously refused to pay, whereupon the water supply was cut off. For three years they persisted in their decision, only obtaining poor crops where irrigation would have produced profitable returns. At length, weary with the contest, they yielded to the pressure and paid as before. Although they still profess faith in Christ, they have ceased to give any public acknowledgement and have fallen from public worship.

At another village, the council refused "to accept even the lawful taxes from them, and thereby free themselves from all responsibility for them as to their property and persons." To withdraw legal protection, Broomhall declared, "was tantamount to a public declaration that any evil-disposed person might steal their property and otherwise molest them without fear of being arrested."[97]

The people elected Elder Sï Ch'ing-lan — Pastor Hsi's brother-in-law, his widow's younger sister's husband (see page 162) — as their leader and protector. Elder Sï was a simple man who had been one of Gatekeeper Sung's first converts and came from the same village, Fancun ("Fan Village"), as Gatekeeper Sung, Elder Fan, and Mrs. Hsi. His father, a member of a secret society, had formerly been rich but was reduced to poverty through opium. At the age of twenty-seven, he came in contact with the gospel and was cured in the refuge. Hsi sent Sï to open a refuge at Zhaocheng, and later appointed him the "chief helper in the management and oversight of the many refuges." Although the missionaries felt he "displayed in a beautiful manner the humility and gentleness of Jesus Christ," some Chinese accused him of using the foreigners, of "personal ambition, and unfaithfulness in the discharge of his office."[98] Baptisms in South Shanxi, which had numbered one hundred fifty annually, dropped to eleven the year following Hsi's death. Twenty or thirty had to be suspended for "cases of discipline," mostly growing and smoking opium. Since no one, Chinese or foreign, could supervise the district, many drifted away, in Hongdong and elsewhere, and went back to growing opium.[99]

As a childless widow Mrs. Hsi's position was precarious. According to

97. Marshall Broomhall, "A Mission Station in China" (CIM, 1899). This pamphlet was discussed by Thompson, "Twilight of the Gods," pp. 66-68.
98. Marshall Broomhall, "The Late Elder Si, of Hung-t'ung, Shan-si," *China's Millions* (NA), November 1902, p. 137.
99. Statistics for 1897 in *China's Millions* (NA), June 1898, p. 80. Opium cultivation had been expanding for several years: Marshall Broomhall, "Discipline and Progress at Hung-tung, Shan-si," *China's Millions* (NA), April 1899, p. 58.

Chinese custom, she was placed under the protection of her husband's nearest male relative, a nephew — were his elder brothers dead? — who turned out to be an "opium smoker, gambler, and unregenerate heathen." He confiscated the "anti-opium medicine" and stole her grain.[100] Evicted from the Middle Eden, Widow Hsi did the most extraordinary thing: she unbound her feet and set out on a new life, her "second gift" to Jesus. She became the keeper of a women's refuge in Zhaocheng, a small town north of Hongdong. "The women's Refuge is quite separate from the men's and they have their own chapel," wrote Miss E. Gauntlett. "As a rule, Mrs. Hsi has about fifty or sixty women to service on Sunday and she leads them herself... and the early comers sit around in the chapel in groups, some reading, some learning to repeat texts, and some singing hymns."[101] Eva French remembered that Mrs. Hsi would sleep with the "dirty, coarse, and repulsive" women addicts "to comfort them and pray for them during the night watches."[102]

The year is 1899, the stage is set. The sound of thunder is heard far, far away. On the last day of the year, a missionary in Shandong, walking alone late at night, was beset by a gang of Spirit Boxers and killed. In her fitful nightmares, did Mrs. Hsi dream, as Timothy Richard had predicted so many years before, that Shanxi was a volcano about to explode? That the Middle Eden would go up in flames, and she, the widow of the Overcomer of Demons, would become the epicenter of Boxer terror?

100. Cable, *Fulfilment of a Dream*, pp. 77-82.
101. Miss E. Gauntlett, letter from Hung-t'ung, dated 2 May, *China's Millions* (NA), September 1900, p. 146.
102. Cable, *Fulfilment of a Dream*, p. 82.

CHAPTER 12

The End of the Middle Eden

1900

*When Thou wouldst warn the people, Lord,
Then I would be the golden bell,
Swung high athwart the lofty tower,
Morning and evening sounding loud;
That young and old may wake from sleep,
Yea, e'en the deaf hear that strong sound.*

Pastor Hsi, "A Song of Sacrifice"[1]

The Spirit Boxers

The Spirit Boxers arrived in Shanxi in the spring of 1900. By the end of April they were "secretly drilling" at Hongdong. By early May, the Boxers United in Righteousness — *Yihe Quan* (old spelling I Ho Ch'üan), or the old translation, "Righteous and Harmonious Fists" — had plastered posters throughout the province calling for the extermination of Christians. By June they had shrines in "every street and alley" of Taiyuan, and a Dragon King "boxing ground" in front of the main gate of the provincial government building. Thus, says a Chinese historian, "Taiyuan came under Yi Ho Tuan [*Yihetuan*, or Boxer] control. And so, soon after, did every sub-prefecture, county and many villages of Shan-si."[2]

---

1. Francesca French, trans., *The Songs of Pastor Hsi*, p. 11. This poem with the phrase, "the golden bell," was written about the same time as the Armor of the Golden Bell, the progenitor of the Boxers, was arising in Shandong (1895). This suggests how common the term was in Chinese sectarian thought.

2. Compilation Group for the "History of Modern China" Series, *The Yi Ho Tuan Movement of 1900* (1976), quoted in Esherick, *Origins of the Boxer Uprising*, pp. 304-5.

THE THIRD GENERATION

No one knew where they came from, young men with wild hair and red turbans. They appeared in the villages one day, offering to teach the local boys their invulnerability rituals, how to become spirit soldiers. Some said they had arrived with the entourage of the newly appointed governor, Yuxian (or Yu Xian, old spelling Yü Hsien), as he journeyed along the imperial highway from Beijing to Taiyuan, thus giving official approval.[3] Others said that eight million spirit soldiers had flown down from heaven to exterminate the foreigners from China. For a second year, the rains had failed, and famine stalked the land. Memories of '77 fanned the fear and social unrest. One Chinese scholar in Taiyuan described a terrified population inclined to violence and ready to believe almost anything.[4]

How few they were at the beginning — and how young! At Fenzhou, the Oberlin station, two Boxers tried unsuccessfully to organize young men and had to recruit ten-year-old boys.[5] At Daning, west of the Fen River, May Nathan reported that a placard called on "schoolboys" to form a "Children's Witchcraft Band." Her sister Edith wrote: "Truly these 'Child Boxers' are devilish, and a device of the devil. We in England know little of what the power of Satan can do over the mind of a child."[6] Olivia Ogren at Yongning (now Zhongyang) explained that a "large proportion of the Boxers were boys, as they were more susceptible to the spirits than mature men. Many children were won from among the poorer people, by the promise of perpetual safety from all calamity if they would give their sons to this righteous crusade."[7]

Yet once the Boxer movement was imported into Shanxi, it "swept over the country like a flood carrying all before it."[8] The summer of 1900 was the hottest on record, and the famine in Shanxi was, "if anything, even worse than in Zhili." The missionaries blamed the drought for the movement's success. Rowena Bird of the Oberlin Band wrote: "These are most trying times — famine threatens the people with starvation — the dry, hot weather makes all ill, and the Boxers are threatening the destruction of the country by robbing and killing missionaries and Christians. . . . The country is full of the wildest rumors and threats. The people have nothing to do but talk and they talk of killing the foreigners and Christians and we feel that the end may not

---

3. Brandt, *Massacre in Shansi*, p. 18.
4. Paul A. Cohen, *History in Three Keys: The Boxers as Event, Experience, and Myth* (New York: Columbia University Press, 1997), p. 149.
5. Brandt, *Massacre in Shansi*, pp. 155, 187.
6. Cohen, *History in Three Keys*, pp. 116-17, 329-30 note 72.
7. Cohen has an excellent discussion (pp. 114-17) of children and witchcraft, including the Salem witch trials.
8. Louise Partridge of the Oberlin Mission, in ibid., p. 327 note 60.

be far off for any of us . . . things grow worse and worse and if the rains hold off it is hard to say what violence may not ensue. We know God could send relief thru rain if He thot best, and we know all our interests are in His hands."[9]

As the Boxers infiltrated the cities and towns of Shanxi, they treated the people well, "paying good prices in cash for all they bought," and ingratiated themselves with the local officials.[10] They inquired who were the "doctrine lovers," who had eaten the Jesus doctrine? They would set up an altar at the town boxing grounds or in front of the main temple, with placards to the various deities who were said to possess their bodies. As a crowd gathered, they would put on a show; as Paul Cohen says, "spirit possession makes good theater."[11] It was easy to learn the simple rituals. A local gazetteer from Anze County, Shanxi, stated: "They write an incantation on a piece of paper. After rinsing their mouths [for ritual purification] and chanting the incantation they suddenly fall to the ground. After a short while they get up and begin to dance in a frenzied manner and talk as if in their sleep. Then they either state that Guandi has descended [*xiajiang*] or that Kongming has attached himself to their bodies [*fushen*]."[12]

The Boxers were spirit mediums who were possessed by familiar characters from the popular operas, particularly *The Romance of the Three Kingdoms*: Guandi, the God of War (also known as Guangong, born Guan Yu), and his blood-brothers, Liu Bei (Zhang Fei), Zhao Zilong (Zhao Yun), and Kongming (Zhuge Liang). Another powerful deity was the trickster Monkey (Sun Wukong) with his distinctive red and yellow face from *The Journey to the West*. (In the spirit world, the Boxer uprising could be considered as a replay of the Taiping Rebellion, a heavenly battle between Guandi and Shangdi, the God of War with his sidekick Monkey versus Jehovah God Almighty.) These gods, Guandi and Kongming, had a particular resonance in Shanxi, since Guandi's birthplace and cult center was located near Pingyang. One might expect his spiritual power to be more warlike there than elsewhere.

Within days, a town would become full of entranced men and boys practicing their Boxing Drills. An unfriendly scholar-official in Tianjin at the time described their bizarre behavior:

> There are those who move slowly with their eyes closed and those who stare straight ahead and walk forward with erect bearing. There are

---

9. Ibid., pp. 79-80.
10. Marshall Broomhall, *Martyred Missionaries of the China Inland Mission*, pp. 104-5.
11. Cohen, *History in Three Keys*, p. 105.
12. *Anze xianzhi* (Anze county gazetteer), in ibid., p. 97.

cases in which a few people hold one person up and cases in which a person supported by two other persons staggers like one who has had too much to drink. In some instances, holding a sword, they dance about wildly, and pedestrians don't have time to get out of the way. In other instances several of them, clutching weapons, walk in single file. Sometimes, mounted on horses, they provide people with protection and guidance. Sometimes they place those who have been wounded or are already dead on their shoulders and take them home. There are even cases in which a bandit [i.e., a Boxer] will hold a stick embellished on the top with a bloody object which he claims is the heart and liver of a foreigner. Coming or going, they are unaware of what they are doing. Confused, disoriented, they don't seem like normal people.[13]

After performing their ritual, the senior brother-disciple would go up to village elders and say, "Our drill is finished. We are turned into Boxers. Now whom shall we kill?"[14]

The late Pastor Hsi's sect was so prominent in South Shanxi that it was singled out as the symbolic first target of the Boxer violence: destroy the powerful demon's nest, then the lesser demons will disperse. On 14 May, in Hongdong, the gang of Boxers stopped in the middle of their drilling and announced they would go immediately to Fancun, Fan Village, the site of Elder Fan's first opium refuge, and kill Elder Sï, Pastor Hsi's successor. They looted his home and stabbed him with a sword, which left him bedridden. The gang moved across the plain to the Middle Eden, which they plundered on 23 May. Widow Hsi and her aged mother were badly beaten and had to hide in the fields.[15]

These incidents highlight the ambiguities at the beginning. Few neighbors

---

13. Ibid., p. 99.
14. Rowena Bird to her brother, 11 July 1900, in Harrison, "Village Politics and National Politics: The Boxer Movement in Central Shanxi." I am grateful to Professor Harrison for providing me with this paper which gave me an understanding of Catholics in Shanxi who, of course, are entirely absent from Protestant accounts. Her book, *The Man Awakened from Dreams: One Man's Life in a North China Village, 1857-1942* (Stanford: Stanford University Press, 2005), is a biography of Liu Dapeng, a poor scholar who lived near Taiyuan and never held public office. "Through the story of his family, the author illustrates the decline of the countryside in relation to the cities as a result of modernization and the transformation of Confucian ideology as a result of these changes. Based on nearly 400 volumes of Liu's diary and other writings, the book illustrates what it was like to study in an academy and to be a schoolteacher, the pressures of changing family relationships, the daily grind of work in industry and agriculture, people's experience with government, and life under the Japanese occupation" (from publicity copy).
15. Broomhall, *Martyred Missionaries*, pp. 103-6, 261; HTCOC 7, p. 321.

The End of the Middle Eden

Boxers setting fire to a church. The Boxers were brought into Shanxi with the collusion of the governor Yuxian, but they spread like wildfire in the parched land. About 80 Protestant missionaries were killed in Shanxi, most in the CIM, and 80 more in the adjacent areas of Inner Mongolia. Source: *Quanfei jilüe* (A brief chronicle of the Boxer bandits) (Shanghai: Shangyang Shuju, 1903). The picture also appears in Paul A. Cohen, *History in Three Keys: The Boxers as Event, Experience, and Myth.*

participated in the looting. Some stood by, while others bought loot and grain at low prices, returning them surreptitiously later. The magistrate sent soldiers, who took no "energetic action beyond giving the village elders a beating," thus blaming the elders. The friendly *daotai*, the prefectural official, gave a "very satisfactory" response that the offenders must "be brought to justice at once, and that Christians be protected." As a result one group of Boxers caught trying to pawn stolen goods was thrown into jail; the Boxers retaliated, attacking the yamen, and in the skirmish two were killed and five sent to Pingyang as criminals. As a result the rumors subsided, for the moment.

At first the Boxers seemed almost conciliatory, trying to make the "path to denial as easy as possible." Pay a fine, sign a certificate, spit on a cross, bow to an idol, burn some incense: anything to show that a Christian had forsaken the foreign religion. "No matter whether you mean it or not!" they said.[16]

16. Forsyth, *The China Martyrs of 1900*, p. 347.

Many Christians recanted for outward conformity while remaining secret believers. Some resisted even this simple denial, so the Zhaocheng magistrate devised a blanket declaration using "the very words they use to enter the Church": "I promise to repent."[17] In some places the pastor or elder was allowed to recant on behalf of the whole congregation. After considerable soul-searching some yielded, becoming the scapegoat to protect the flock.

Once the missionaries fled, the Boxers returned to kill and torture. Eighteen Christians had crosses carved into their foreheads because they would not recant, and were made to stand in the sun until the scars were permanent. Elder Sï, confined to his bed, weeping for the sufferings of his people, recanted, as did Pastor Hsi's widow, and her aunts and cousins. Elder Sï managed to preserve the church by stationing guards at the Hongdong chapel, and was instrumental in saving escaping missionaries, providing them with news and money. "Cringing with shame," he told the people he was unworthy to be called elder; the Christians insisted, and he remained titular head of the one Protestant congregation in Shanxi that kept worshiping throughout the conflagration.

By the middle of May, communications within Shanxi had collapsed and the telegraph lines had been cut. When the postal service was closed a week later, Shanxi was entirely cut off from the rest of the world.

Making Sense

Joseph Esherick has stated that "there is no major incident in China's modern history on which the range of professional interpretation is as great" as the Boxer Uprising.[18] My contribution is modest, to document one lacuna in the historical record: the Boxer movement in Shanxi from the viewpoint of the victims, Pastor Hsi's sect of Protestant god worshipers.

Most scholars have concentrated on Shandong, where it all began, or on the siege of the legations in Beijing, the thrilling second act. From that perspective, they argue that there was a disjunction between the spontaneous events in Shandong, where the Boxers sprang from the soil like a many-headed hydra (in Esherick's apt term), and the "officially inspired Boxer 'militia'" in Shanxi, which were promoted at the highest state level.[19] In Shanxi,

---

17. Cable, *Fulfilment of a Dream*, pp. 30-33, noted that many Christians regarded this declaration as "the overruling of Providence" and accepted it without any "verbal recantation of their faith."

18. Esherick, *Origins of the Boxer Uprising*, p. xiv.

19. Esherick discussed Shanxi in about two pages, pp. 90-91, 304-5.

The End of the Middle Eden

strangely enough, even in the old missionary records, identifiable Boxers were few and far between. After 1901 it was easy to blame the governor, Yuxian — "the butcher of Shanxi" — as though he were single-handedly responsible for the murders. Even now, traditional historians such as A. J. Broomhall see the Shanxi Boxer movement as a vast conspiracy between the "evil" Empress Dowager and her "henchman" Yuxian on one hand and the Boxers on the other. But other questions need to be asked. Was Shanxi merely the third act, where events were played out that had their origin elsewhere? Why was Shanxi the place where it all ended?

The most eminent study of the Boxers in Shandong is Joseph Esherick's *The Origins of the Boxer Uprising*. This is Big History writ local, as he examines the village-by-village spread of the Boxers in Shandong from the mid-1890s as a village self-protection militia, a secret society known as the "Armor of the Golden Bell," in the southeast. This was a restless border area where endemic famine and banditry was compounded by the "mailed fist" of German imperialism. Suppressed in one area, they sprang up in another place, and by 1899 they had spread to northwestern Shandong and Zhili. By then they had gained their distinctive invulnerability rituals and anti-Christian focus, and started attacking churches in isolated communities.

The governor of Shandong in 1899 was the same Yuxian who became governor of Shanxi in 1900. He could not — or would not, charged the foreigners — control the Boxers in Shandong, so he was recalled to Beijing under foreign pressure a few days before Christmas. On 31 December, S. P. Brooks, a Society for the Propagation of the Gospel missionary, was murdered, and the new governor, Yuan Shikai, an enlightened reformer who was friendly with the West, moved quickly to "decapitate and disperse" the Boxer movement and protect the missionaries. Tensions increased as anti-Christian incidents multiplied in the early months of 1900. The Boxers, an inchoate mass of bored, restless young men, started streaming towards Beijing. By January the xenophobic, reactionary faction at the Qing court had become ascendant, and the Empress Dowager Cixi — known as the Old Buddha — issued an edict that encouraged legitimate self-defense societies (i.e., the Boxers) and vowed to exterminate secret societies *(hui)*, which included both Protestant and Roman Catholic Christianity.

Rather than being degraded or cashiered for his failure in Shandong, Yuxian was rewarded by the Empress Dowager "with special marks of favour, and in recognition of his services, was appointed to the governorship of Shan-si."[20] He arrived in Taiyuan on 20 April. It was said that he brought

---

20. Forsyth, *China Martyrs*, p. 32.

three companies of Boxers, "mounted and armed," with him from Shandong.[21] Modern scholars think that is inconceivable, just one of many false rumors swirling around during 1900. In Shandong, he had legitimately tried to suppress the Boxer movement, and had executed the top leaders. In Shanxi, one can say that he was zealous, perhaps over-zealous, in obeying the Empress Dowager's orders. He was a loyal Confucian official — and a Manchu — and he certainly owed her fealty after she sent him to Shanxi with honor rather than handing him the silken cord as the Germans demanded. Finally, one can say with some assurance, he was extremely anti-foreign — perhaps with good reason.[22]

If history cannot blame Yuxian entirely, then we must look elsewhere for the spontaneous volcano of violence at the grass-roots level. The eminent Chinese historian of the Boxers in Shanxi and the editor of several volumes of historical documents is Qiao Zhiqiang, who even-handedly made a distinction "between the reactionary violence against missionaries ordered by Yuxian in Taiyuan on 9 July 1900 and the anti-imperialist struggle carried out by the Boxers in other localities" elsewhere in the province. He argued that the violence was directly related to Yuxian's presence from April 1900, when he arrived in Taiyuan, until mid-summer, when he began to distance himself from the anti-Christian violence. Qiao argued against a connection between the Boxers and the secret societies or White Lotus, as was common in Shandong, and noted that there was in Shanxi no martial-arts tradition that could help explain the rapid development of the movement.[23]

Right up to the end — while Beijing was in flames — the Shanxi missionaries had an overwhelming sense of danger, but they went about their usual business, holding conferences, itinerating through the countryside, working with women and children, and running the opium refuges. Shanxi was not Shandong, they reasoned. In twenty years of Christian missions, there had *never* been a major riot, although there had been plenty of petty persecutions and "missionary cases." As one missionary wrote: "In disposition the people are more mild and amiable than those of any other portion of the empire. They are patient and uncomplaining to a high degree. The common people are tolerant in their attitude toward Christianity and foreign missionaries except when instigated by the monstrous misrepresentation of the literati and

---

21. Brandt, *Massacre in Shansi*, p. 18.
22. I am indebted to Andrew T. Kaiser for providing me with his unpublished manuscript, "A History of Protestant Missions in Shanxi"; chapter 2, "The Boxer Turmoil," especially, helped me formulate the structure and conclusions for much of this chapter.
23. Summarized in Roger Thompson, "Twilight of the Gods," p. 68.

The End of the Middle Eden

officials. Almost invariably their first judgement of us is 'they are just like us, they do good to accumulate merit.'"[24]

The most outspoken critic of the missionary version is Roger R. Thompson, who has stirred a scholarly debate by dismissing the martyrologies concerning the execution of the missionaries. Thompson defended Yuxian, arguing that "the evidence, while it does not exonerate Yuxian, certainly does not lend itself to scapegoating the governor."[25] Essentially, he noted the lack of substantiation in contemporary Chinese and foreign conciliar records as well as similarities between the supposed "eyewitness" accounts and *Foxe's Book of Martyrs*. For example, Thompson claims that a memorial from Yuxian to the Emperor describing the execution of the missionaries, which is often used as evidence in favor of the traditional narrative, may be a forgery. Rather than a deceitful play on Yuxian's part followed by a summary execution, Thompson argues for either a more general riot which left many dead, or an execution of foreigners and local Christian leaders motivated by Yuxian's need to quell local fears of a foreign invasion.[26]

In order to understand the violence of 1900, Thompson argues, one must go back to the compromise of 1861, when the Franciscans reclaimed the mission property seized from their predecessors a century and a half earlier (see Chapter 5). This was the policy of the Zongli Yamen and the French government that Catholic converts did not have to pay the idol taxes, the "wasteful" portion used to support temple festivals and opera performances, while they were still responsible for "useful" 60 percent taxes such as road building, crop watching, and water rights. This was *the* most contentious issue between Christians and their neighbors, Thompson argues, because their refusal to pay idol taxes upset the economic and moral order of the villages. As evidence, he cites the meeting between returning Protestant missionaries and Chinese officials in Taiyuan on 13 July 1901, one year after the uprising, to resolve the indemnity question. Typically, the officials blamed banditry, famine, drought, and administrative incompetence, but the new governor issued a proclamation which stated that

> the greatest number of murders of Christians during last year's Boxer disturbance took place in Shanxi. In every local community *(xiangshe)* there has been a vibrant tradition of opera. The intense violence that

---

24. Brandt, *Massacre in Shansi*, pp. 148-49, argued that the missionaries' ignorance of the Boxer threat was a sign of their "insularity.... They never did understand why the animosity was directed against them, or the reason for its intensity."
25. Thompson, "Twilight of the Gods," p. 54.
26. Kaiser, "Protestant Missions in Shanxi."

broke out so suddenly was a result of grudges that had been building up for a long time because Christians had been refusing to pay opera subscriptions. For the time being opera performances are forbidden. Later, should Christians wish to attend opera performances they must contribute money like everyone else. As for useful public projects in rural areas *(xiangcun)* it is appropriate for everyone to donate money. This should put an end to the conflicts."[27]

The most perceptive historian of the Boxers in Shanxi is Henrietta Harrison, who has combined Roman Catholic narratives and Chinese historical records to examine the power relationships between Catholic and non-Catholic villages. She disputes the common view that the violence arose from preexisting tensions between Christians and their neighbors *within* the villages. "Christianity was certainly problematic in Chinese villages, but in central Shanxi most deaths occurred when one village fought against another, rather than within villages." The Roman Catholic Church in Shanxi had a trajectory distinct from the Protestants, because the Catholic villages had roots that went back to the 1700s. With their complexes of churches, schools, and seminaries, they became important regional centers. It was not accidental that some were located higher up the hills, and thus controlled the water supplies for several (non-Christian) villages below. Harrison's insight about intervillage fights is applicable to the Protestants, as the attacks on Fancun and the Middle Eden show. One surprising difference, though, is that "most Catholics in the villages of the central Shanxi plain had been born and brought up in the faith: of the 533 people killed during the uprising in this area and later recorded by the church as martyrs only 11 were converts." In other words, she suggests that "Chinese Protestants were few in relative numbers and that Protestantism was far less integrated into local communities."[28]

As the Boxers spread through Shanxi in May 1900, there were sporadic killings, but the victims were not Christians; rather there were suspicious

---

27. Qiao Zhiqiang, ed., *Yihetuan zai Shanxi diqu shilao* (Historical documents of the Boxers in Shanxi), in Thompson, "Twilight of the Gods," p. 52. See also Edwards, *Fire and Sword in Shansi*, p. 53.

28. Harrison, "Village Politics," p. 4. See also her biography of Liu Dapeng, *The Man Awakened from Dreams*, whose diary is an important record of the Boxer movement in Shanxi, pp. 84-86. Liu commented: "The uprisings are all caused by foreigners and Christians tyrannizing the common people, and the fact that the officials cannot protect them. If the common people oppose the priests of the foreign religion, they are accused of being rebels and soldiers are used to put them down. The people cannot accept this so I suspect that incidents of murders of officials, and killing of soldiers, will occur in more than one place."

The End of the Middle Eden

strangers, such as vagrants and a Buddhist monk, who were accused of poisoning wells. The senior brother-disciple of the Boxers at Shitie, southeast of Taiyuan, was a fifteen-year-old peasant boy, Jiang Jinhua, whose group grew rapidly after the first murder, and who received permission from the magistrate to train in a temple in the county town. "Shortly afterwards Jiang Jinhua led a group of Boxers into Taiyuan city, wearing a red head cloth and riding a horse through streets packed with wildly excited crowds. Yuxian was said to have come out to welcome him to the provincial government compound."

About 6 June, three weeks after the attack on Fancun, three hundred Yuci county Boxers attacked the Catholic stronghold of Wangdu and burned the church. This was the first of a series of Boxer assaults on Catholic communities in Central Shanxi. "In Sanxian, where there had been a Catholic community since 1760, a large group of Boxers from the town of Beige marched to attack the Catholics who had taken refuge in the church. The resistance was fierce; the men fired guns from the church roof while the women sprinkled holy water on the Boxers (to drive out the spirits that possessed them)." The account in the *Historical Records* states that the leader of the Catholic women, who was called "Green-Fisted Lantern," had a full-blown battle with her nemesis, the senior brother-disciple Jiang Jinhua, which involved fire, rain, and thunder — and even levitation.[29] "These attacks set the pattern for the violence, with large, well-armed groups of Boxers fighting pitched battles against Catholics, also armed and usually besieged in the village church. By the end of the fighting whole lineages had been entirely wiped out."[30]

"Village financial disputes, drought and the acceptance of violence all played a part in the rapidly escalating tensions between Christians and their neighbours," Harrison concluded. "Together with the political decisions of the court in Beijing reflected in Yuxian's shifting and ambiguous policies, they created the conditions for the violence." Yuxian had been eager to use the Boxers in the spring of 1900, so they could claim to be a legitimate self-defense militia protecting the good people from the powerful Christian criminals. "At the local level, Boxer ideals were also morally acceptable to many members of the elite, who hoped, like Yuxian, that foreign invasion could be resisted by calling the people to arms. The belief that the government should take a firmer line against Christian heterodoxy was also widespread among this group." A local scholar in Jinci county, south of Taiyuan, named Liu Dapeng, whose diary is an important primary document, argued that the Boxer movement began because the officials had failed to deal with the Chris-

---

29. In Kaiser, "Protestant Missions in Shanxi."
30. Harrison, "Village Politics."

tians: "The court could not execute them and the officials did not dare, so the Boxers executed them. Even those who were not Boxers all also wanted to catch the Christians and kill them. Surely it was their cruelty and selfishness that caused Heaven's awe-inspiring anger of which the Boxers were the tool."[31]

All global events are ultimately local, and Andrew T. Kaiser, who lives in Taiyuan and works for Shanxi Evergreen Service, a Christian development and aid organization, brings Big History down to earth by placing the Boxers on the ground. Unofficially, Taiyuan was recently described by Zhu Rongji, the architect of China's modernization, as the most *luan* (chaotic) of *shengcheng* (provincial capitals). During the 1999 war in Kosovo, Kaiser witnessed first-hand how rumors can spread at a time of national humiliation.

> I spent most of my adult years saying China could never have another Cultural Revolution [he wrote], until I witnessed first-hand the reaction of Shanxi's people (especially rural) to the bombing of their embassy in Belgrade. In an almost literal 100 year time-warp, fantastic rumors began circulating (my coworkers had supposedly written letters to Bill Clinton asking him to do such a thing; we had supposedly held a celebratory dinner the night before the bombing; etc. . . .), [and] these rumors were believed by many who did not know us personally, and otherwise intelligent people grasped at the opportunity to blame someone else for the problems Shanxi was facing (then as now, corruption and inequality, heat and drought, and — particularly in modern Taiyuan — tremendous actual unemployment).[32]

As to the missionary records, all martyrologies are framed in the same rhetoric, going back to *Foxe's Book of Martyrs*, just as all pilgrim allegories ultimately descend from *Pilgrim's Progress*. As Kaiser says, "While it is certainly true that primary sources relevant to the events of June and July are spartan often relying on 'eye-witness' accounts with little hope of verification, the general course of events as portrayed by foreign and local Christians is by no means implausible. On the contrary, the simple fact that they have stood for so long — giving ample opportunities for contradiction — suggests that while details may be questioned, the general narrative stands as most likely."[33]

If the "inside story" of Pastor Hsi's indigenous sect has any larger mean-

31. Ibid.
32. Andrew T. Kaiser, letter to author, 13 September 2003.
33. Kaiser, "Protestant Missions in Shanxi."

The End of the Middle Eden

ing, it suggests an alternate line of descent for certain Boxer manifestations, such as magic, mass shamanism, and invulnerability rituals. At one level South Shanxi was representative of Christian churches in late Qing China. They may have been attached to a foreign mission, but each took on the character of the individual leaders, pastors, Biblewomen, and converts, many of whom had been members of organized religious sects. At least from the Taiping rebellion onwards, demon possession and its good twin, exorcism, had been prominent in rural Christian congregations. As John Livingston Nevius said, exorcisms were common among rural Chinese Christians, though seldom mentioned in missionary publicity. "No Protestant missionary, so far as I know, has ever given native converts instructions as to casting out spirits; and few, if any, have dreamed that their converts would have the disposition, the ability, or the opportunity to do so."[34] From the Boxers' point of view, their losses in battle were not due to Western fire power but rather superior magic. That was what their shamanism and magic were all about: spirit boxing to counteract Christian exorcism. Their rituals, as simple as the wordless book, took on certain characteristics, in negative (or intaglio) form, of the Christian enemy.

Let us look at some rumors that spread like wildfire during that parched summer of 1900 to see how Boxer magic reflected Christian claims through a glass, darkly. The first and most persistent rumors were that Christians were poisoning wells. This had been a frightening prospect since the beginning of time, that sinister forces would poison the drinking water; but in poor, parched Shanxi, control of water — whether as wells, irrigation canals, holy water, clouds or rain — seems to have been an underlying foundation for subsequent rumors. "Sometimes the poison was said to be shaken from a sleeve, sometimes a great green bottle was said to be inverted over the well."[35] (This is reminiscent of the charges back in the 1850s against Mary Anne Aldersey, Hudson Taylor's nemesis in Ningbo, mentioned in Chapter 2. The Chinese called her a "witch" because she would walk along the city wall at night and open a bottle of smelling salts, which released demonic powers.)

Dr. E. H. Edwards of the Shouyang Mission reported:

> So great was the terror spread by these reports that numberless persons were killed who had no connection with Christianity whatsoever, for, in consequence of the long-existing drought, many people were wandering

---

34. Nevius, *Demon Possession*, p. 14; see also Chapter 8 note 20.
35. Oberlin Mission, "Report of women's work for T'ai-ku [Taigu] for 1899," in Harrison, "Village Politics."

about picking up a precarious living; and not a few of them were accused of being in the pay of foreigners, and killed at sight. It was extremely dangerous even for respectable foot-travellers to go about singly, especially if they happened to stop at a village well to drink. Immediately they might be seized and their belongings searched, to see if they had anything in the shape of medicine with which they could poison the water. For months many of the village wells were guarded day and night; and even in T'ai Yuan Fu the well-to-do people for three months would not drink any water drawn from the city wells, or employ the usual water carriers, but made their own servants fetch a supply from special wells outside.[36]

Charles Price of the Oberlin mission at Fenzhou recorded one of the most entertaining rumors, that the Christians were holding back the rain clouds.

Various stories were set afloat as to the power of the missionaries to prevent rain, ascribing almost superhuman strength in the way of controlling the elements. Clouds were continuously being driven away by fierce winds, which led to the story — thoroughly believed by all the people — that we went into our upper rooms and drove the clouds back by fanning with all our might. The story was changed as regards the T'ai Yuan Fu missionaries, that they were naked when doing the fanning.[37]

As we have seen, Pastor Hsi and the missionaries prayed for rain like the biblical Elijah and the prophets of Baal — supernatural control of the elements — and took credit when God sent rain clouds. So there was a certain truth to this rumor.

Finally, at a microcosmic level, the end of the Middle Eden sect raises the troubling question of opium, which has figured prominently throughout this book. Did the opiated condition of the people create a predisposition for hallucinations? What was the role of opium among Shanxi Christians? By 1900, the Heavenly Invitation Offices, somewhat diminished in numbers, still operated a network of opium refuges throughout four provinces, treating thousands of patients a year. Did anyone catch on that these might have been

---

36. Edwards, *Fire and Sword*, pp. 54-55. A Boxer poster translated in A. Henry Savage-Landor, *China and the Allies* (New York: Scribner, 1901), pp. 22-24, included a "divine prescription" for a powerful antidote to be swallowed after drinking water from a poisoned well: "Dried black plums — half an ounce. Solanum dulcamara — half an ounce. Liquorice root — half an ounce."

37. Edwards, *Fire and Sword*, p. 269.

thinly disguised fronts for the morphine black market, an easy place to acquire some "Jesus opium"?

The Killing Time

The Boxer tragedy went through three distinct stages in Shanxi: the "Fining Time" from Yuxian's arrival in April 1900 to 26 June, when he received the declaration of war from Beijing; the "Killing Time" until September; and the "Torturing Time," which lasted spasmodically until the end of the year.[38]

By the end of May, tens of thousands of Boxers were streaming into Beijing from all over North China ready to defend the dynasty and exterminate the foreigners. Beijing went up like a tinderbox when the mobs torched the Roman Catholic East and South cathedrals. The carnage was horrible, wrote the journalist George Morrison: "Attack of Boxers. Cries of Boxer incantations. Passing the French Legation I found all on guard. 'The Boxers are coming.' . . . Awful cries in the west part of the city all through the night. The roar of the murdered. Rapine and massacre."[39] Watching the small-footed women, panic-stricken and distraught, running down the streets was "like watching a herd of terrified deer fleeing before a predator."[40]

The first victim of the siege of the legations was Francis Huberty James, the pioneer of the Shanxi Famine, who was killed while on an act of mercy that earned him a niche in the Boxer annals. After resigning from the CIM, Huberty James and his wife had joined the Baptist Missionary Society in Shandong, where he was known for his "good communication" with the native church and officials. He continued his interest in occult religion, and wrote learned papers on the "Secret Sects of China." He resigned from the Baptists "owing to fundamental changes in his religious beliefs," and after doing "lecturing, preaching and literary work" in England and America, he returned to China in 1897 as a professor at the Imperial University, where he was known as a "kindly and trusting" gentleman.[41]

At the beginning of the siege, Huberty James and Morrison rescued hundreds of Chinese Christians stranded at the Catholic cathedral and brought them to the legations. Since there was no room for a refugee camp, they requisitioned the palace next door by persuading the prince "it would not only be

38. Forsyth, *China Martyrs*, pp. 351-52.
39. Cyril Pearl, *Morrison of Peking*, pp. 112-13.
40. Diana Preston, *Besieged in Peking: The Story of the 1900 Boxer Rising* (London: Constable, 1999), p. 63.
41. Obituary in Broomhall, *Martyred Missionaries*.

kind, but wise" for him to depart, leaving "all of his treasure and half his harem." By rescuing those Christians, Morrison and James set a precedent for thousands of other Chinese to seek asylum in the legation district, providing much needed coolie labor. The siege of the legations began at four o'clock on 20 June, and a few minutes later Huberty James was crossing a little bridge to the refugee camp when he was set upon by Chinese soldiers and hacked to death.[42]

The next day, 21 June, the Empress Dowager issued a formal declaration of war against the Powers: Great Britain, the United States, France, Germany, Holland, Austria-Hungary, Russia, and Japan. This was followed by a flurry of edicts, including the most horrifying: "The foreigners must be killed, even if they try to escape, they must be killed." The declaration of war was sent to the governors of every province, and it arrived at Taiyuan post-haste, on 26 June. Governor Yuxian posted a proclamation "withdrawing protection" from foreigners and ordering them to leave by the next day. After that, it is difficult to keep track, everything happened at once. "From the human standpoint," one wrote, "all places are equally unsafe."[43]

The next day, the Schofield Memorial Hospital in Taiyuan, the foreigners' showplace, went up in flames.[44] The day started quite typically. At the girls' school, located in a far corner of the compound, Miss Edith Coombs was dismissing the students for the summer, as this was the first day of the sixth moon of the lunar calendar. Eleven girls had not left yet, due to various circumstances. Dr. Lovitt saw around thirty outpatients at the dispensary. A few missionaries read the Imperial Decree which had been posted in the nonfunctioning Taiyuan Telegraph office, but since it did not bear the official seal they treated it as simply another rumor.

That evening a crowd collected outside of the front gate. Efforts to parlay with the crowd were met by stones, and then the crowd began to set fire to the buildings of the compound one by one. As midnight approached the situation became desperate with few buildings remaining and most of the Chinese helpers gone. The staff decided to force a passage through the mob. Shielding their young charges as best they could, the group of teachers, students, doctors, and patients dashed through the fire set at the entrance to impede their escape. They used their arms to ward off the stones and bricks hurled by the crowd as they raced for Rev. Farthing's compound.

Miss Coombs, upon exiting the gauntlet, noticed that two girls whose feet

---

42. Pearl, *Morrison of Peking*, pp. 113-14.
43. Broomhall, *Martyred Missionaries*, p. 29.
44. This account is summarized from Kaiser, "Protestant Missions in Shanxi." See Edwards, *Fire and Sword*, pp. 60-67, especially pp. 60 and 67 for lists of who was where on the night of 27 June. See also Williamson, *British Baptists in China 1845-1952*, p. 64.

The End of the Middle Eden

were slowly being unbound had been left behind. She raced back into the maelstrom and carried the first child free of the flames. She returned again to the burning compound and as she was dashing out through the fire at the gate with the second child in her arms, she stumbled and fell. Immediately they were assaulted with bricks and stones. The girl was yanked from beneath Miss Coombs's body and whisked away to safety as Miss Coombs herself was forced back into the fire. Fuel was heaped onto the fire as she knelt in prayer; and though she twice rose from the flames the crowd would not allow her to escape. (One official Chinese history of religion in Shanxi, published in the 1980s, described Miss Coombs raving in front of the school brandishing a flaming torch and a pistol.) The next morning her ashes were recovered and buried by Chinese friends in the mission garden.

For the next week or so the missionaries in Taiyuan were held in separate compounds. The Protestants — twenty-six in all, eight men, ten women, and eight children — were at three places in the south of the city: the two stations of the BMS, Farthing's and Silvester Whitehouse's nearby (Whitehouse had been Hudson Taylor's personal secretary during his 1888 visit to North America, see Chapter 9); or Mr. Beynon's of the British and Foreign Bible Society. The Roman Catholics — two aged Franciscan bishops, one Belgian and one Dutch, three priests, and seven Sisters of Mary who had only arrived in 1899 — were at the cathedral in the north. These premises were all "guarded" by soldiers, as were the now closed gates and walls of the city proper. Since these homes were in residential areas they were deemed safe from fire (since their immolation would necessarily imply the torching of all neighboring buildings).

Dr. Millar Wilson managed to smuggle a letter out to F. C. Dreyer at Pingyang: "It's all fog, but I think, old chap, that we are on the edge of a volcano, and I fear Taiyuan is the inner edge. I'd rather be where you are." On 5 July, their names were recorded and they were informed by an official that they must all move to the abandoned railway bureau where their safety might be better guaranteed.[45] They eventually arrived under escort late on the night of the 6th to find that they were to share a residence with the twelve Catholics. They were in fact under arrest.

The next day the party was brought from Shouyang, Thomas Wellesley Piggott; his wife and thirteen-year-old son Wellesley; Wellesley's tutor, John Robinson, a graduate of London University; a governess, Mary Duval; and two Atwater girls from the Oberlin mission.[46] Living on the imperial highway

---

45. *HTCOC 7,* pp. 377, 379.
46. Edwards, *Fire and Sword,* pp. 72-82. Forsyth, *China Martyrs,* pp. 34-38, 424-29. Brandt, *Massacre in Shansi,* pp. 214-22.

to Zhili, Piggott was always sensitive to the movement of troops. At the beginning of June, he had reported that "this place is full of [rumors], the people being fully assured that we shall all very soon be killed. . . . I am told that all shopkeepers have received notice in the form of a 'circular' or tract, and that this states that wherever idols have been put away, there all will be killed." On 23 June, he listed more rumors: "The ocean has receded 9 *li* from the shore — no foreign troops can land. A great iron trident has erected itself in the sea. Boxers' food multiplies itself in their hands, so that they may never suffer from want. The foreign legations in Peking are all destroyed."[47]

The Shouyang missionaries did not decide to flee until 29 June — ironically a day of heavy rain — and hid in caves in the hills for a week, where they were protected by local Christians. As the Boxers cut a swath through the neighborhood, they were quickly discovered, and brought to the magistrate. He was a new man, one of Yuxian's appointees, and bewildered, he kept them in his yamen for three days before sending them to Taiyuan. For "protection," he "suggested" the men should wear "loose handcuffs," to convince the Boxers they were state prisoners. Like St. Paul-in-chains, Tom Piggott could not stop preaching, standing in the cart in shackles, much to the amazement of the onlookers.[48]

On Monday morning, 9 July, Yuxian ordered another census of the foreigners in Taiyuan. He then pretended to leave Taiyuan on a journey to the north, but suddenly turned around and arrested everyone, including some hapless Chinese who were present on business. They were all marched to the courtyard between the governor's yamen and the street outside where a large group of soldiers awaited them.[49] The governor then asked each missionary where he or she was from, and as each answered with the name of a foreign country, he gave the order to the soldiers: "Kill!" According to the declaration of war, Yuxian was justified in killing them upon proof (or confession) of their status as foreigners. Hence, his line of questioning. They were killed in order of seniority, Protestants first, starting with Rev. Farthing and ending with the women and children, then the Catholics. Later that afternoon the Shouyang seven were beaten and then killed in the same spot — again, on the governor's orders.

47. Edwards, *Fire and Sword*, pp. 73 and 75.
48. Ibid., pp. 80-82, provides a gripping account of the transportation and execution of the Shouyang group. Edwards and his wife, who happened to be on furlough, were the sole survivors of the Shouyang Mission; Piggott was his brother-in-law. *HTCOC* 7, pp. 341-42.
49. A photograph taken from the central tower, printed in *Fire and Sword*, p. 29, shows the governor's compound in 1902: the gate is still visible on Fudong Jie, but a large screening wall or *zhaobi* has created a small square in front.

That fateful day, forty-five foreign men, women, and children were killed in front of the governor. Their heads were hung on the city gates as a warning, while their bodies were given a temporary burial outside the South Gate. It is not known how many Chinese Christians died, although Yuxian's "petition" to the Emperor claimed seventeen Chinese "helpers" were executed.[50] After the foreigners were dispensed with, local Chinese Christians were rounded up for execution as well. One missionary who managed to escape reported that Christians were forced "to kneel down and drink their [the foreign missionaries'] blood, and as they knelt, were killed — not one denied Christ."[51] Elder Liu Dingxuan, steward of the Taiyuan church, who escaped, remarked years later that: "God had not counted him worthy to die for Him in 1900."[52]

There is still disagreement over the total number of foreigners who were killed in Shanxi, ranging from an official figure of 78 Protestants (56 adults and 22 children) before September 1900, to A. J. Broomhall's estimate of 159, including adjacent areas of Inner Mongolia. In Inner Mongolia, 40 Scandinavians, 9 Catholics, and 3,000 Christians were killed, the highest toll of converts in any province. Shanxi and Inner Mongolia sustained the killing of one-half the foreign martyrs in China.[53]

North of Taiyuan, all was in ruins. At Xinzhou, the Baptist station, three men and three women survived for a month by moving every night from one cave to another. They were captured by soldiers and thrown into the common jail, and on 9 August the magistrate put them into four carts to escort them "to the coast." They were murdered by a "mob" outside the city gates.[54] At Datong, the "friendly Prefect" put a guard around the CIM station until the storm broke, when the guards melted away. Under these circumstances, Mrs. McKee gave birth to a baby. On 12 July "the house was surrounded by three hundred horse and foot soldiers, and sword and fire soon did their deadly

---

50. Kaiser, "Protestant Missions in Shanxi." The BMS claimed that nine Christians died in Taiyuan: Williamson, *British Baptists*, p. 66.

51. Uncited letter from May Nathan, in *HTCOC 7*, pp. 383-84.

52. Williamson, *British Baptists*, p. 66.

53. Kenneth Scott Latourette, *A History of Christian Missions in China* (New York: Macmillan, 1929; reprint ed., New York: Russell & Russell, 1967), pp. 514-17, gave the official figure of 78 Protestants but listed 94 individuals plus uncounted others. Esherick, *Origins of the Boxer Uprising*, pp. 305 and 406, note 101, adjusted several estimates to come up with a total of 130 foreigners in Shanxi. *HTCOC 7*, p. 624, gives a total of 159 Protestants killed in Shanxi and Inner Mongolia, 113 adults and 46 children; they comprised 85 percent of the 188 Protestant martyrs. One missionary was killed in Shandong, 17 in Zhili, and 11 in Zhejiang.

54. Edwards, *Fire and Sword*, pp. 96-98. Forsyth, *China Martyrs*, pp. 43-64, including three diaries; biographies on pp. 443-51.

work." Six adults and five children died, as well as a hundred Christians in the city.⁵⁵

At Shuoping, two stages west of Datong, the Swedish Holiness Union was "entirely blotted out" when its ten members gathered to commemorate the mother-church in Sweden. With them were two couples from the Christian & Missionary Alliance. On 27 June, they were taken outside the city, where "the crowd was waiting for them."⁵⁶ Further north in Mongolia, where the various Scandinavian Alliances were located, the carnage was worse. The six members of the Chicago Mission Among the Mongols, which had tried to establish an agricultural commune, died on 1 September.⁵⁷ The Christian & Missionary Alliance had thirty-eight missionaries at Guihuacheng and other towns: twenty-one adults and fifteen children — "all in flight" — perished.⁵⁸

South of Taiyuan was the same. At Xiaoyi, two women were beheaded while they were kneeling in prayer, and buried where they fell, in the baptistery, "where no man had been baptized." Their Chinese followers were tracked down after their names were noted on a silk banner that they had presented to the missionaries and hung on the chapel wall.⁵⁹ The two deaconesses who had taken over Huozhou after Anna Jakobsen married the Chinese evangelist, Jane Stevens and Mildred Clarke, were caught at Taiyuan. May Nathan and her sister from Daning "wandered about among the hills . . . [and] took refuge in a cave, but were discovered, brought back to Ta-ning, and murdered outside the west gate." One party from Ho-tsin, west of the Fen River, made it as far as the Yellow River, where they were killed at the ferry dock.⁶⁰

The Oberlin Band survived almost to the end. At Taigu, forty miles south of Taiyuan, they held a "council of war" on 1 July amidst conflicting rumors and supposedly "reliable" reports, to discuss the moral dilemma whether to use revolvers in "strenuous self defense." They hesitated. One day. Two days, too late. "We talk of fleeing can't decide," one wrote. "Terror everywhere." The Chinese begged them to leave, especially one young Christian man named K'ung Hsiang-hsi (H. H. Kung), then aged nineteen, who remained their faithful companion, following their execution carts and then taking the sad news to the coast.⁶¹

Two years later, in May 1902, Eva Jane Price's parents received a package of

---

55. Edwards, *Fire and Sword*, pp. 98-99. Forsyth, *China Martyrs*, pp. 77-78, 459-61.
56. Edwards, *Fire and Sword*, pp. 99-100. Forsyth, *China Martyrs*, pp. 79-80, 461-64.
57. Edwards, *Fire and Sword*, pp. 100-109. Forsyth, *China Martyrs*, pp. 80-82.
58. Forsyth, *China Martyrs*, pp. 82-84.
59. Thompson, "Twilight of the Gods," p. 60. (See Chapter 8.)
60. Edwards, *Fire and Sword*, pp. 88-96. Forsyth, *China Martyrs*, pp. 73-77.
61. Brandt, *Massacre in Shanxi*, pp. 243-45.

letters from the mission board, with an accompanying letter that said: "These letters of our friends in Shansi were found by the workmen excavating the cellar of Dr. Nobli's house, and I sent them to you at once. They were evidently hidden by Mr. Pitkin in the ashes in the basement. The letters seem like voices from the dead. How intensely interesting and pathetic it is to receive these letters almost two years after they were written."[62]

The Exodus

After reading the harrowing details of suffering . . . it is a relief to read of the escape of a party of missionaries.[63]

Even before the Empress Dowager issued the declaration of war on 21 June, the evacuation began. Almost three thousand frightened Protestant missionaries and their children, plus Roman Catholics and other foreigners made their way from inland China to the coast. The edict had stated bluntly, "the foreigners must be killed," but the governor of Shandong, Yuan Shikai, courageously changed the words to read: "the foreigners must be protected." Consequently, the provinces south of the Yellow River were safe. One of the safest was Shaanxi, across the Yellow River, where the "humane" governor Duanfang was "so distressed that he wept in the presence of other high officials" and issued "stringent orders that at any cost and all hazards order was to be maintained." He was personally responsible for saving ninety missionaries from Shanxi, Shaanxi, and Gansu, by giving them a military escort to Hankou.[64]

By August, the survivors started to trickle out of Shanxi. One of the most harrowing journeys was that of Alexander Saunders, who wrote an account called *A God of Deliverances*. They were rioted out of Pingyao on 26 June, when a rain procession destroyed the compound, and headed for the supposed safety of Taiyuan, but they met a group of Christians on the road who warned that the Schofield hospital had been destroyed and the missionaries imprisoned. They turned back, and headed through the mountains to Lucheng, 130 miles southeast, where they were joined by another couple and

---

62. Judson Smith, secretary of American Board of Commissioners for Foreign Missions, quoted in Price, *China Journal*, p. 243.
63. Forsyth, *China Martyrs*, p. 85.
64. *HTCOC* 7, p. 331.

two single women, making a group of fourteen including six children. "We trudged on as best we could, carrying the smaller children, the others walking, and all of us exposed to the full blaze of a semi-tropical sun. All that day and the two following days, through village after village, we were subjected to the cruelest treatment. . . . Although we were now almost naked, without shoes or stockings, the people would not believe that we had no silver secreted about us. . . . The people of one village would follow us to the boundary of the next, stoning us and throwing hard lumps of clay, beating us on the back and head with sticks and bricks."[65]

Two women, too exhausted to go on, stopped in a deserted hut: Miss Rice was beaten to death, while Miss Huston died of her injuries on the road a month later. When the group reached the Yellow River, the magistrate was so enraged that he stamped his feet, saying an edict had arrived that very day ordering all foreigners had to be protected and escorted to Hankou. "Had you come here yesterday, I would have had you all killed." Instead he sent them onward in carts that normally carried criminals to the execution grounds. During this part of the journey, Mrs. Cooper and her baby, and two of the Saunders's children died of "fatigue."

We all had visions in those days, J. W. Stevenson said of the 1880s: how much more so in 1900 when every stone seemed charged with supernatural significance, when a peasant offering a "cup of water" was a signifier of "the restraining Hand of God." One poignant vision can stand for the rest. Archibald E. Glover, a young Oxford graduate and Church of England clergyman, who described his journey as *A Thousand Miles of Miracle in China*, escaped from Luan (Stanley Smith's station, though Smith was on furlough) a few days before the Saunders party passed through. His family included his pregnant wife Flora, two infants, and Caroline Gates, a single woman. One shadeless afternoon, the children too weak to cry, Flora collapsed, crying, "God has forsaken us!" Instantly Miss Gates was at her side and in "music of heavenly utterance . . . she poured forth passage after passage, promise after promise, from the Scriptures, exalting His name, declaring His faithfulness." Flora, filled with glory, exclaimed, "Oh, I will never, never doubt Him again." Four days after their arrival in Hankou, she gave birth to a baby girl they named Faith. Faith lived eleven days. Flora died in October.[66]

---

65. Alexander R. Saunders, *A God of Deliverances: The Story of the Marvellous Deliverances Through the Sovereign Power of God of a Party of Missionaries, When Compelled by the Boxer Rising to Flee from Shan-si, North China* (London: CIM, 1901). Saunders's letter to *The Times*, 29 September 1900. Marshall Broomhall, *Martyred Missionaries*, pp. 68-76. Forsyth, *China Martyrs*, pp. 116-33.

66. Archibald Edward Glover, *A Thousand Miles of Miracle in China: A Personal Record*

Archibald E. Glover and his family, Flora and children Hedley and Hope, six months before they had to flee from the Boxers, March 1900. The Glovers had a harrowing journey from Luan to Hankow, where Flora gave birth to a baby named Faith. Mother and baby both died.   Source: Archibald E. Glover, *A Thousand Miles of Miracle in China: A Personal Record of God's Delivering Power from the Hands of the Imperial Boxers of Shan-si* (London: CIM, 1904).

The Last Pilgrim

In the early hours of 15 August 1900, the Empress Dowager set out for Shanxi. The day before, the Allied armies had fought their way into Beijing after a desperate, bloody campaign, and had lifted the siege of the legations. "And Beijing, like Tianjin before it, was left for the armies and missionaries of the 'civilized nations' to wreak their terrible revenge."[67]

That night was a scene of "chaos in the moonlit courtyards of the Forbidden City." The Empress Dowager, like a madwoman, "ransacked her closets, overturning boxes of blue and yellow silk handkerchiefs as she snatched up handfuls." She had her fingernails clipped, and taking off her elaborate court head-

---

of God's Delivering Power from the Hands of the Imperial Boxers of Shan-si in China (London: CIM, 1904), pp. 101-2. Glover's "plain unvarnished tale" of ordinary people caught up in extraordinary events went through twenty-one printings during the author's lifetime (he died in 1954 at 95), and was reprinted in an abridged edition to celebrate the OMF's 125th anniversary in 1991.

67. Esherick, *Origins of the Boxer Uprising*, p. 310.

dress, she cut her hair. Fearing to leave the Emperor where he might become a hostage, she ordered him and his wife into rickety peasant carts, with a few officials. They looked, a local magistrate noticed, like "dejected jackals," and even the palace guards could not recognize the wrinkled peasant woman.[68]

The party made slow progress, as the roads were clogged with refugees and the countryside had been devastated by the Boxers and disaffected troops. "Even the wells were said to be polluted with piles of floating heads." Since they had brought no food, her troops "pillaged, murdered and raped along the whole route," and stole the food from her table. Rather than fleeing south, towards the Allied armies, the party proceeded to Kalgan, 140 miles northwest, then on to Datong, which had been cleared of foreigners one month earlier.

The royal progress became grander and less pathetic the further the distance from Peking and the greater the certainty that the allies were not pursuing them. It was easier now for the Emperor and Empress Dowager to sustain the myth that they were making an official "tour of inspection," as the decrees grandly called it, rather than a panic-stricken dash from the clutches of a vengeful enemy.[69]

The imperial family reached Taiyuan in mid-September. Labor was conscripted from the countryside to build small villages outside the city for their entourage. Despite the famine and hardships, the people were ordered to pay 170,000 *jin* (85,000 kilos) of grain, 100,000 *jin* of coal, over 10,000 *jin* of red meat, hundreds of fowl and other goods. "September of 1900 must have been a difficult time for the people of Shanxi," Andrew Kaiser comments.[70] Fearing a foreign invasion would sack Taiyuan, the Empress Dowager and her retinue, several thousand people in full regalia, left the city in early October and set out down the Big Road to Xi'an, safe beyond the passes. The road had been paved as far as the bend in the Yellow River. A couple of years later, Francis Nichols, traveling *Through Hidden Shensi* (Shanxi, the title of his 1902 book), was amazed at the quality of the roads and guest-houses south of Taiyuan. He was told that one bad stretch had taken five thousand soldiers two weeks just to make it passable.[71]

68. Preston, *Besieged in Peking*, pp. 191-97.
69. Ibid.
70. Kaiser, "Protestant Missions in Shanxi." He based this on Liu Dapeng's account in Qiao Zhiqiang, ed., *Yihetuan zai Shanxi diqu shiliao* (Historical materials concerning the Boxer Movement in Shanxi).
71. Francis Nichols, *Through Hidden Shensi* (1902), pp. 88, 90.

The End of the Middle Eden

Little did the Empress Dowager know as she passed Pingyang — the epicenter — that within the sound of her procession, three isolated pockets of foreigners had survived: a widowed man and two women at Quwu, four Catholic priests at Hongdong, and a Swedish couple, Alfred and Olivia Ogren and their infant Samuel in the Pingyang prison.

The Last Exodus

Four months later, on 16 February 1901, long after the madness had passed, a pitiful procession appeared in Hankou, "three mule litters containing the last of the poor salvage saved from the deplorable wreck of foreign life in Shansi."[72] Somehow ten foreigners had survived for eight months while everything burned around them.

Alfred Ogren was introduced in Chapter 9, briefly, as a Swedish Everyman, a carpenter from Jonkoping who fell under the spell of Frederik Franson. He and his wife Olivia were "young, of humble circumstances, and not highly educated, yet, full of zeal, meek in spirit, abounding in joy in the Lord, always ready for service." In 1899, as members of the CIM, they opened a new station in Yongning, five stages southwest of Taiyuan, near Fenzhou. When the Boxers came, the "kindly disposed" magistrate gave them money and soldiers to escort them to the Yellow River. They reached the river where they hired a boat that sailed down-river between menacing gangs on either side. After two hundred miles, they were forced to disembark near Daning, the same dock where the Ho-tsin party had been killed a few days earlier. Captured by bandits, they were sold to a group of Boxers who inflicted "misery and untellable sufferings." (This was their only encounter with Boxers.) Alfred escaped when the Boxers fell on him with their swords but he crawled out from underneath; Olivia and the infant were released and told to go away. Separated, each thinking the other dead, they hid in caves near Daning until they were rescued by the magistrate's secretary who locked them in the common jail, the safest place in the world.

The deprivation proved too much and Alfred died of starvation, "a mere living skeleton." Olivia and the baby survived and they were joined in the jail by the other foreigners. By this time, the Empress Dowager's edict had been rescinded, and the foreigners were given intensive security. Nevertheless, they refused to leave until Olivia Ogren's confinement, when she was delivered of a baby daughter, "sound in mind and body" in early December.

72. Forsyth, *China Martyrs*, p. 135.

In the vast literature on the Boxers, Olivia's story is a quiet testament to simple faith: "God only knows the horror of those hours," she wrote. "No human words are full enough of sadness to tell my awful loneliness. No tears were bitter enough." She and the babies returned to Sweden and never came back.[73]

---

73. Olivia Ogren's account is quoted at length in ibid. This famous narrative is notable for the small role played by the Boxers themselves. See also Olivia C. Ogren, *The Last Refugees from Shansi: In the Hands of the Chinese Boxers (An Eyewitness Account)*, trans. Samuel Ogren Sr. (Victoria, B.C.: Trafford Publishing, 2004).

CHAPTER 13

The Aftermath

When Thou wouldst write the records, Lord,
Then I would be the ready pen,
A medium subtle for Thy thought,
Desirous to write it true.
That when the Book of Life is read,
Therein those names be found inscribed,
Which hell nor death can e'er blot out.

Pastor Hsi, "A Song of Sacrifice"[1]

The Blood of the Martyrs

Nothing was ever the same after 1900.
Although much perished, yet something of that pre-Boxer world did survive. Call it the Shanxi spirit. This was not just the derelict spiritual malaise that A. J. Broomhall talked about, the gossiping and factionalism; it was also the birth pangs of an independent, indigenous church. In this chapter, I will summarize the aftermath within Shanxi, as the province and the mission moved from the Boxer catastrophe to become the "model province" after 1911 under the warlord Yan Xishan. In the conclusion, I will consider the broader, international ramifications of the story of Pastor Hsi and the missionaries.
As Shanxi emerged from its hermetic isolation, rumors were many and news scarce. Well into the spring of 1901, there were pitched battles which involved en-

---

1. Francesca French, trans., *The Songs of Pastor Hsi*, p. 11.

tire villages. These seem to have been motivated by fear, revenge, and hunger, as powerful Catholic villages took revenge on their non-Catholic neighbors, and non-Christians took the law into their own hands.[2] When the priests returned, they acted with a heavy hand. They demanded, through the French minister, that reparations should include either the governor's compound, the Confucian school, or the military officers' school; that the people of two villages be expelled and the land reserved for Chinese Catholics; plus 10,000,000 taels of silver (£1,300,000 or $6.6 million U.S.) indemnity. When the Chinese officials reacted with incredulous stares — Shanxi was too poor for such a vast expense — the priests called upon the French government to invade the province. The Catholics seized the Confucian school, and forced the other villages to pay for elaborate funeral masses. Eventually, the governor reminded the priests that they had no foreign protection and therefore their passports were invalid. They settled for one-fifth indemnity, 2,250,000 taels, which was extracted from the non-Christian villages, what they had formerly paid for opera performances.[3]

In February 1901 a Christian photographer in Taiyuan smuggled out a letter which vividly described the suffering of the Protestant Christians. "With houses burned, their friends killed, their property looted, their grain stolen, and made again to pay the temple taxes, no one inquires into their case. They will soon be either frozen or starved to death. The officials still expect them to pay the taxes. Pray, quickly have a telegram sent to the Governor to say that the Christians need not this year pay the taxes, as they have passed through such heavy troubles. The Christians of Fen Chou Fu [Fenzhou], T'ai Yuan Fu, Hsin Chou [Xinzhou], and Tai Chou [Daizhou], — altogether fifteen districts, — amounting to more than four thousand people, have had eight-tenths or nine-tenths of their property destroyed. We have also had a very bad year (famine), and if we do not obtain relief by next spring all the Christians will starve. We trust that at an early date our pastors may be able to return to Shansi, by the grace of God, to help His church."[4]

On 25 April, the German troops were ordered to remove the Chinese troops guarding the Guguan Pass, the Gates of Heaven where the Big Road enters the province. The pass was taken with little resistance, and this, everyone presumed, was the prelude to a full-scale invasion and the sacking of Taiyuan, the site of the massacre. The frightened peasants fled from the bor-

---

2. For the information that follows, I am indebted to Andrew T. Kaiser, "A History of Protestant Missions in Shanxi," and to Henrietta Harrison, "Village Politics and National Politics: The Boxer Movement in Central Shanxi." The diarist Liu Dapeng gave examples of these conflicts: two are translated in Cohen, *History in Three Keys*, p. 158.

3. Edwards, *Fire and Sword in Shansi*, pp. 165-72.

4. Translation in ibid., p. 116.

The Aftermath

der regions, causing havoc throughout Central Shanxi. In desperation, the new governor named Zhou Erxun — Yuxian had been exiled by this time, and would soon be executed — sent a telegram to Timothy Richard, the great conciliator, imploring him to help settle the "missionary affairs" before the military occupation could be accomplished.[5]

Richard immediately left Shanghai for Beijing, where he was joined by Dr. Iranaeus Atwood, the sole surviving member of the Oberlin mission, and Dr. Ebenezer Henry Edwards, likewise of the Shouyang mission. (Dr. Edwards's book, *Through Fire and Sword in Shan-si*, is regarded as the most authoritative account of the post-Boxer settlement.) They met with the venerable statesman, China's foreign minister Li Hongzhang, and presented a list of seven demands which they hoped would resolve the problems to everyone's satisfaction. They argued for leniency for the rank-and-file Boxers, but the leaders must be punished — eventually 107 Boxer leaders were executed[6] — and the local people had to pay a fine to support the widows and orphans. Monuments were to be erected in each area where Christians were murdered, stating clearly that the deaths were without cause. Finally, a total of 500,000 taels of silver over a ten-year period was to be extracted from the entire province for the establishment of a Western institution of learning. (Edwards estimated that 500,000 taels were about £66,000, or $330,000 U.S. He also noted that the annual penalty, £7,000, was what the city of Pingyao spent every year for opera festivals.)[7] This indemnity was to establish Shanxi University — Richard's dream since he had come out of the Great Famine — which would become China's second Western-style university. Li Hongzhang was sympathetic and supported the recommendations.

On 22 June, representatives of the four missions working in Shanxi set out for the province, and arrived in Taiyuan — entirely by accident — on 9 July 1901, one year to the day after the massacre. The CIM was represented by Dixon E. Hoste, Hudson Taylor's designated heir, Archibald Orr Ewing, the benefactor (who among other things financed Pastor Hsi's opium refuges — see Chapter 8), and Ernest Taylor (no relation of Hudson Taylor), along with C. H. Tjader of the Swedish Mission. The others were Rev. Moir Duncan and Dr. Creasy Smith of the Baptist Missionary Society, Dr. Atwood of Oberlin, Dr. Edwards of the Shouyang mission, and, in an unofficial capacity, Major Pereira of the Grenadier Guards.[8]

---

5. Ibid., Chapter 3, "After the Massacres," pp. 111-72; the full telegram is at p. 120.
6. Ibid., p. 135.
7. Ibid., pp. 122-24.
8. *HTCOC 7*, pp. 470-78, describes this visit.

On the road outside Taiyuan, they were met by the governor himself, who kowtowed in the dust at their feet. Every gesture was calculated to humiliate: the governor had to provide a banquet "in semi-foreign style . . . most tastefully decorated," and conduct a state funeral for the Boxer martyrs, which was repeated in every city. The Martyr Memorial Cemetery outside the city was the first of many monuments erected throughout the province. The railway bureau where they had been imprisoned and an ancient pagoda overlooking the yamen were blown up with explosives, and a public garden erected with yet another monument.

Hoste conducted the state funeral, following speeches by various Chinese officials. "It was a beautiful day," Dr. Edwards recalled, "and as from the pavilion one looked over the thirty-four new graves to the city and plain beyond and the high mountains to the west, all so peaceful, it was hard, nay almost impossible, to realise what actually happened only a year and ten days before. Outwardly a great difference between now and then, and yet one instinctively felt the difference to be only superficial. It is true that representatives of the gentry were at the cemetery, but neither they nor any of the merchants' guilds gave any tangible token even of respect . . . although six of these guilds combined to erect a memorial tablet extolling the monster Yu Hsien [Yuxian]. The people appeared to be sullen rather than repentant."[9]

When the missionaries met with the Chinese officials, publicly everyone agreed that Yuxian must be the scapegoat, that he must take full responsibility for allowing the violence to occur. As to underlying, more disturbing causes, the missionaries tended to blame the drought while the evasive officials blamed the opera taxes. This was the compromise discussed in Chapter 5, that Christians had to pay the 60 percent of taxes that were considered "useful" but not the 40 percent for "useless" temple ceremonies and opera performances. Behind the scenes, though, as Roger Thompson has noted, the Chinese officials secretly accepted the 60/40 formula. If Western missionaries could use local tax money to build their chapels, schools, and hospitals, they argued, the Chinese government could too. The following year, December 1902, in order to pay the 50,000 taels of annual indemnity, the governor directed that all local opera taxes should be diverted towards building new-style schools. "Rural communities had always had resources extracted by the state; this was not new," Thompson noted. But the message of this directive was something else: "Combining Confucian distaste for popular practices with the Western effort to split rural society into secular and sa-

---

9. Edwards, *Fire and Sword*, pp. 138-39.

The Aftermath

cred spheres, Zhang Zhidong [governor of Shanxi in 1882-84 and now the leading reformer at court] was laying claim to local resources with the voice of a secular, modernizing state. This message was just as unfathomable to rural Chinese as the missionaries' arguments that opera was frivolous and idolatrous."[10]

This settlement was over and above the reparations for the whole country. "The [Boxer] indemnity imposed on the Chinese was huge: 450 million taels (U.S. $333 million), to be paid in thirty-nine annual installments along with a 4 percent interest on unpaid principal."[11] When the Japanese war broke out in 1937, China had not yet finished paying the Boxer indemnity. The dilemma of whether to ask for reparations was to bedevil relations between missionaries and converts for the next generation. The extreme view, expressed by the united American mission boards, asked the United States government to include "indemnities for societies, individuals and Chinese who had suffered 'in person or in property in consequence of their being in the service of foreigners.'" Being in the service of foreigners implied a mercenary relationship, not membership in a religious society, which was to trouble the Chinese church and its struggle for independence.[12]

As usual, the CIM bucked the imperialist rhetoric of the time, affirming Hudson Taylor's dictum that faith in God was better than a revolver. According to the *Principles & Practice*, the CIM refused to ask for reparations or to accept them if they were offered for damage to property or for suffering of foreign missionaries: "no appeal and no demands." As a result, it gained respect in the eyes of both the foreign and Chinese officials, and a selling point at home, since the CIM was known for its policy of "no solicitation."[13]

Although the CIM was praised for rejecting "blood money," they were eager to press for compensation for Chinese believers who lost their lives during the turmoil. This was "a separate matter between the Chinese government and its own subjects. They were not 'in the service of foreigners' or under the 'protection' of the Mission, although everything possible would be done to help them." Dr. Edwards recorded the official settlement as granted by the governor:

---

10. Roger Thompson, "Twilight of the Gods in the Chinese Countryside," pp. 69-71.
11. Cohen, *History in Three Keys*, p. 56.
12. Kaiser, "History of Protestant Missions in Shanxi."
13. *HTCOC 7*, pp. 462-70, discussed the CIM's dilemma concerning the indemnity.

	Number of adherents killed	Compensation granted
China Inland Mission	156	73,156 taels [£10,700]
Baptist Mission	112	35,776 taels
American Board (Oberlin)	79	25,000 taels
Shouyang Mission	27	5,600 taels[14]

Not only were the demands made by the Protestant societies relatively light, but they also brought with them 26,000 taels of silver to be distributed for famine relief. They were officially and publicly praised by the governor for their leniency and generosity. In fact, on 11 October 1901, he posted a proclamation in every location where the CIM and its associate missions had worked:

> The Mission, in rebuilding these churches with its own funds, aims in so doing to fulfill the command of the SAVIOUR OF THE WORLD, that all men should love their neighbours as themselves, and is unwilling to lay any heavy pecuniary burden on the traders or the poor. I, the governor, find . . . that the chief work of the Christian religion is in all places to exhort men to live virtuously. From the time of their entrance into China, Christian missionaries have given medicine gratuitously to the sick and distributed money in times of famine. . . . They regard other men as they do themselves, and make no difference between this country and that. Yet we Chinese . . . have treated them not with generous kindness, but with injustice and contempt, for which we ought to feel ashamed . . . contrasting the way in which we have been treated by the missionaries with our treatment of them, how can anyone who has the least regard for right and reason not feel ashamed of this behaviour.[15]

Returning to the Ruins

Of the twenty-three CIM missionaries who escaped from Shanxi during the Boxer time, an astounding twenty-one returned as the core of the new work, along with others among the Scandinavian associates. They were joined by a new generation who did not know what had happened. Before 1900, the "free and irresponsible life of the itinerant missionary" was already being reined in;

---

14. Edwards, *Fire and Sword*, pp. 157-58.
15. *HTCOC 7*, p. 481.

The Aftermath

by 1905 most missionaries had "accepted the calling of teachers, and allowed ourselves to be tied to the numberless claims and responsibilities of institutional life."[16]

One of the first to return, in September 1901, was Evangeline (Eva) French (see Chapter 6), who had matured under Mrs. Hsi's guidance from a high-spirited tomboy into an experienced veteran of seven years. During the Boxer terror, she had guided the women to Jiexiu, "a quiet country town less likely to see disturbances." When they joined Alex Saunders's party, she told one official "plainly that unless everything was satisfactory we would not move." That saved their lives, for the magistrate gave them — ten women, two men, and two children — an escort to Hankou. What Eva remembered was not the horror, but the kindness of strangers "who would have helped us if they had dared," such as one mandarin who sent seventy eggs and a basket of apples.[17]

Miss French brought a new missionary to Shanxi, Mildred Cable, a "supersensitive, over-controlled, too intense girl," who was to become an articulate author and platform speaker. They were joined in 1909 by Eva's sister Francesca, who had been released from obligations by her mother's death. The three women became so inseparable that they referred to themselves in the third person plural, "the Trio." The Trio were stationed at Huozhou, a turbulent market town north of Hongdong which had been opened as a result of Mrs. Hsi's dream when the Holy Spirit had commanded her to sell her jewelry so Huozhou could have the gospel (see Chapter 11). When Anna Jakobsen married the Chinese evangelist and Sophie Reuter married Stanley Smith, their successors had been the aloof deaconesses Miss Stevens and Miss Clarke; since they had perished, the Trio had to rebuild Huozhou for the third time. Mildred Cable's account, *The Fulfilment of a Dream of Pastor Hsi's: The Story of the Work in Hwochow* (1917), provides a candid snapshot of the problems of establishing a "proper" women's institution from the blood of the martyrs.

Miss Cable learned to speak Chinese through tears, for she spent her first years weeping with the women, some of whom had crosses branded onto their foreheads. "It was necessary for the missionaries to stay in every village, visit every Christian home, and spend long hours in listening to heart-rending stories, before it was possible to begin with encouragement."[18] Suspi-

---

16. Cable, *Fulfilment of a Dream*, p. 71.
17. *HTCOC 7*, pp. 338-40, 389-92.
18. Mildred Cable and Francesca French, *Something Happened* (London: Hodder & Stoughton, 1935; CIM, 1934), p. 106.

cious of those who had recanted — the majority, it seems — the missionaries were appalled by their greed for indemnity money.[19]

By 1905, when a "mass movement" towards Christianity spread throughout China, hundreds of inquirers came into the Shanxi churches who were of a higher, educated class, mainly young men who wanted to learn English. It was easy to lose sight of the old Christians who needed pastors. "It is a case of sheer neglect," one complained. "I have been a church member for fifteen years, and all the notice they have taken of me is to spend one paltry day in my home, whereas they were three whole days in the village of Peace and Harmony, where there are only heathen and not a Christian to receive them." Eva recounted the poignant story of an aged "military mandarin," who had been a church elder for twelve years. When she did not pay sufficient respect to him, he stormed into their courtyard with "blood-curdling yells . . . throwing himself in the classical position of the Chinese brave." He told her to go somewhere else and "and leave us alone; *our* missionaries must shepherd *our* Church." The "old members have stood in the way long enough," she declared, and if they did not welcome new converts, "the old ones must go."[20] With no ties to the older generation, the women "viewed the nurturing of a small band of discontents as of very secondary importance to the opportunity of spreading the news of the Gospel far and wide amongst the heathen."[21]

Elder Sï, Pastor Hsi's successor, died of his injuries in 1901, and Widow Hsi died in 1906. After their deaths the Shanxi sect was a new church in a new world. Elder Sï was replaced by Elder Hsü (Hsü-pu-üin in one letter,[22] or pinyan probably Xu Buyuan), "a man of advanced ideas" who "aimed to make his church renowned throughout the province. There were to be no poor among its members." He told the people to stop growing wheat and plant opium instead: "Of course, being Christians, you won't smoke opium. But . . . if you grow opium, you will have all the money to make our church flourish." As a result, many Christians went back to smoking opium. Under Hsü's direction "the church established a large cash shop in the city [Hongdong]. . . . Then the leaders became more covetous and issued bogus money. The bank went smash, and the reputation of the church or what was left of it went down with it."[23]

---

19. *HTCOC 7*, "The Most Painful Experience," pp. 474-78, discussed degrees of recanting among believers.

20. Cable, *Fulfilment of a Dream*, pp. 49-53.

21. Ibid., p. 50.

22. D. E. Hoste, Shanghai, to Geraldine Taylor, 26 October 1901, in CIM/SOAS, file # 9322.

23. Jonathan Goforth, *"By My Spirit"* (London: Marshall, Morgan & Scott, 1929), pp. 71-73. For a different view of Hsü, see *HTCOC 7*, p. 474, quoting D. E. Hoste.

The Aftermath

Elder Hsü [Hsü-pu-üin], third leader of the Christians in South Shanxi, in 1900. After the Boxer catastrophe, Hsü went to Beijing to confer with the government concerning reparations for the destitute Chinese Christians. After Elder Sï died of his injuries, Elder Hsü was elected as his successor. He inherited "not a few of the special gifts" of Pastor Hsi. There were to be no poor Christians, he said, and they should start growing opium, but not smoking it, to become rich. Jonathan Goforth felt that the "very devil" took control of him.
Source: Mrs. Howard Taylor, *Pastor Hsi*, vol. 2, *One of China's Christians*.

After the Boxer famine — just as after the Great Famine — the people took to opium smoking on a mass level. The Shanxi Christians were merely following social trends, as vast tracts of South Shanxi were planted with poppy fields. By the early twentieth century Shanxi produced much of the domestic opium for the entire empire. Efforts by the officials to suppress it produced riots from the peasants: they needed the extra revenue to pay their escalating taxes.[24] When Francis Nichols entered Shanxi in 1902, he encountered entire "opium villages" which had slipped over the edge into drug addiction:

Even from a distance the difference between the sad village and the rest is very marked. The walls at the entrance to it are crumbling as though

---

24. Williamson, *British Baptists in China 1845-1952*, p. 73.

the inhabitants had ceased to take any interest in spirits, good or evil. The roofs of the houses are dilapidated and full of holes. A nearer approach reveals windows from which the paper panes are missing and doors supported by only one hinge. No one is selling vegetables in the road, and the one or two shops which the village possessed are closed. In the shadow of the houses a few men and women are lying or squatting — apparently in a stupor. Their faces are drawn and leathery, their eyes glazed and dull. Their clothes are masses of rags, and, what is most hopeless of all, the men have neglected to braid their queues; their hair is disheveled and matted. Even some of the babies the women carry in their arms have the same parched skins and wan haggard faces. And the cause of this is *opium.*

Such a village, whose wretchedness and degradation I have inadequately described, is known throughout the surrounding country as an "opium village." No matter how cheerful and gay my escort of Shansi police might be, they always became silent, and their faces grave and serious, whenever we passed a place of this kind.[25]

Another thing that did not change, Miss Cable revealed, was the number of "demoniacal manifestations," which was such an important subject that she devoted a chapter to it. Noting that exorcism among Chinese Christians was "too numerous" to mention, she described one young woman "chanting the weird minor chant of the possessed, the voice, as every case I have seen, clearly distinguishes it [spirit possession] from madness." Miss French commanded the devil to leave her, whereupon she sneezed fifty or sixty times and came to herself, seated, clothed and in her right mind. Like Pastor Hsi, the "Overcomer of Demons," who "understood the conflict in the Heavenly Places," Eva learned to distinguish between greater and lesser devils, and warned "young believers" they were "in serious danger" tampering with the Chinese spirit world.[26]

In 1908 Jonathan Goforth came to Shanxi. He was the Canadian firebrand who became the leading proponent of militant fundamentalism in China. The year before, he had "got up" a "Holy Ghost" revival in Manchuria and Korea, which, like the Welsh revival a few years earlier, swept through the meetings like a mighty rushing wind. He did not aim his message at the unconverted but at reviving the churches, and the meetings climaxed in confession of sin and, a new phenomenon, public weeping. Shanxi was his attempt to take his revival

---

25. Francis H. Nichols, *Through Hidden Shensi* (London: Newnes, 1902), pp. 57-58.
26. Cable, *Fulfilment of a Dream,* pp. 109-23.

on the road. When he arrived in Taiyuan, he visited the sacred ground and preached with such power that people outside the church remarked that a "new Jesus" had arrived. As he proceeded southward, he sensed sin and hypocrisy. At Xizhou, a Mr. Kuo, a Boxer hero, was expelled for getting drunk with the local mandarin while "consulting" over indemnities, and almost killing his wife. Kuo confessed his sins and was reinstated. At Hongdong, "the Spirit of Burning was very much in evidence." When Elder Hsü came into the room, the "very devil appeared to take control of the meeting"; when he left, the "conviction of sin, and the sense of God's nearness returned."[27]

Why did Goforth feel the devil at Hongdong? The blood of the martyrs had been spilled there too. Was it the crosses branded into their foreheads? Was it the greedy Christians? Was it the opium? The sources do not say. But it was far from the last gasp of the Shanxi spirit.

Beyond the Jade Gate

Although the CIM became less wild and wooly after 1900, it still appealed to adventurers who sought to escape from the compound — what Pearl Buck described as "the small white clean Presbyterian American world of my parents and the big loving merry not-too-clean Chinese world"[28] — and go native. There were always individuals who felt called to "the regions beyond," to the unevangelized areas on China's frontiers. When Raymond Joyce walked across the Gobi Desert in the 1930s, he was following a tradition of apostolic wandering that went back a century to Karl Gutzlaff.

The most famous of the semi-independent missionaries were the Trio — Eva (Evangeline) French (1869-1960), Mildred Cable (1877-1952), and Francesca French (1872-1960) — who took the Shanxi spirit to Central Asia, living among the nomads along the Silk Road. But they had to wait until Eva and Francesca were in their fifties before the mission authorities would sanction their traveling without a male escort. Until then, the Trio remained at Huozhou, and had to satisfy their craving for adventure by taking the Trans-Siberian railway to England, stopping at Munich and Paris to view the art galleries. After the First World War, the CIM inaugurated a "forward movement" to China's minorities: to the Muslims in Chinese Turkestan (Qinghai) in the northwest, to Tibet on the west, and among the tribespeople of Guizhou and

---

27. Goforth, "*By My Spirit*," pp. 64-65 (Taiyuan), pp. 66-68 (Xizhou), pp. 71-73 (Hongdong).

28. Theodore F. Harris, *Pearl Buck: A Biography* (New York: John Day Co., 1969), p. 81.

The Trio and Topsy in England: Francesca French, Topsy, Mildred Cable, Evangeline French. The Trio were nomads along the Silk Road from 1923 to 1940, living with the people and "gossiping the gospel." On Christmas Eve 1928, they bought an unwanted girl (for 17 shillings, sixpence), a deaf-mute of mixed race, Mongol father and Tibetan peasant mother, whom they formally adopted and named Topsy. Topsy was "a true Mongol, fearless and proud, and completely at home with a horse." In England her "hugely pleasant and extroverted personality" won her many friends. Source: OMF/Toronto. See also Hugh P. Kemp, *Steppe by Step* (London: Monarch Books, and OMF, 2000).

Yunnan in the southwest. Since these were non-Han Chinese, this necessitated learning another language, such as Uighar or Miao. The Trio tentatively asked the China council: "Are the conditions in the North-West such that experienced, middle-aged missionaries, with a working knowledge of the Chinese language, would be useful, or do they more definitely demand young people who lack experience, but have greater physical vigor?" Although some council members felt "Experience, in this case, is more valuable than youth," the opposition was so "distressing to all concerned that they were not permitted to leave Huozhou until 1923."[29]

29. Cable and French, *Something Happened,* pp. 120, 122-23. This opposition is dis-

The Aftermath

The Trio set out to walk from Huozhou to the Jade Gate, the armed border post at the entrance to Central Asia, normally a fifty-day journey, or about one thousand miles. It took them a full year because they stopped to teach the scriptures to groups of Buddhist monks. Settling at a border post, they rented a supposedly haunted house, "an airy summer house, standing in a flower garden," where they lived during the winter, while spending the other eight months following the trade routes. "On trek," traveling in a dilapidated cart called "the Flying Turki," they wrote that "all personal belongings were reduced to a minimum, as space must be left for the Christian literature without which the journey would be useless. A frying-pan, a kettle and one big pot made up the cooking outfit, along with a little iron tripod for the camp fire. Each of the three had an officer's sleeping bag with blanket and pillow, and they carried a small tent, just large enough to hold them. Everything superfluous was simply abandoned." After a decade of the "homeless" life, they put it delicately, the Trio "preferred to travel without a mirror."[30]

About 1925, the women befriended a beggar girl "with rags tied round her anyhow" who came knocking at their door. She was about seven years old, and her legs were badly bitten by roaming dogs. She was a deaf-mute, and in her silent world, she did not hear the dogs barking and could not run away. Her name was Gwa-Gwa ("Little Lonely"), and she would come around every day begging for food. When they went on trek, she would forlornly follow their cart as long as she could keep up, and would visit their courtyard daily while they were away, where the cook would provide her with a cup of soup and some bread. Hearing her story from Christian friends, the women decided to adopt her.

"Thus on Christmas Eve 1928, she joined their household for seventeen shillings and sixpence and from that day on they became her 'three mamas.'" They changed her name to Ai-Lien ("Love Bond"), but as this was difficult for her to lip-read, they called her "Topsy." In due course, she acquired a British passport and UK citizenship under the name of Eileen Guy, which combined the sound of her Chinese name Ai-Lien with Mildred Cable's Chinese surname Gai. The women wrote an affectionate book, *The Story of Topsy: Little Lonely of Central Asia*, in which they described her early years: "She really was very happy, and life would have been perfect, she thought, if only she could always have her own way about everything. But that could not be, for now she

---

cussed by Linda Benson, "French, Cable and French: Women Evangelists of the China Inland Mission" (paper presented at the annual meeting of the Association of Asian Studies, March 2000).

30. Cable and French, *Something Happened*, pp. 143-44, 157, 244.

had to find her place in a picture where there was a background of home, and while the solitary Topsy had looked quite all right as an isolated beggar-maid, the great big TOPSY in the pretty picture looked very ugly." Under their love and guidance, "she developed a hugely pleasant if extroverted personality."[31]

Virtually the only Western residents between the Great Wall and Urumchi, the Trio's books — they wrote twenty books individually or collectively — thrilled generations of readers with their exploits in an unknown corner of the globe. *The Gobi Desert* (1942) is a scholarly work of Central Asian history, from the time of the Buddhist monk Xuanzang in the 600s C.E., including an art critic's description of the fantastic Buddhist sculptures of Dunhuang, up to the art of hiring a carter during the Mongolian rebellion.[32] The eminent authority, Sven Hedin, the Swedish explorer who traveled the Silk Road from Samarkand, regarded their books as the only reliable information about "events in these hermetically sealed regions" during the Republican period of the 1920s and '30s.[33] Now, at the beginning of the twenty-first century, with conflicts and *jihads* looming in these same hermetically sealed regions, their books have attracted scholars with more urgency as they seek to understand the history of the holy wars of Central Asia.[34]

The Trio toured the northwest Gansu oases six times, a round trip of thirty days, and made four visits to Urumchi, thirty-six days' travel beyond Kansu. Like generations of pilgrims, they went to Dunhuang, the ancient "lost city" of the Caves of the Thousand Buddhas. Although they were awed by the "Elysian gardens of the Chinese paradise," their mission was to climb the mountainsides, over rickety ladders and rope bridges, and deposit a tract at the entrance of each cave. "Their fervent hope was that some weary pilgrim, sitting down to rest on his toilsome penance, might find there the end of his quest, in the story of the Lamb of God."[35]

When the Trio returned to England on furlough in 1935, they brought

---

31. Mildred Cable and Francesca French, *The Story of Topsy: Little Lonely of Central Asia* (London: Hodder & Stoughton, 1937). Hugh P. Kemp, *Steppe by Step: Mongolia's Christians — From Ancient Roots to Vibrant Young Church* (London: Monarch Books and OMF Publishing, 2000), pp. 458-71, quote at pp. 465-66. See also article by Julia Cameron, "The Trio and Topsy," at website of OMF Australia: http://www.au.omf.org/content.asp?id=12669.

32. Mildred Cable and Francesca French, *The Gobi Desert* (London: Hodder & Stoughton, 1942, and New York: Macmillan, 1944). This was reprinted with a new introduction by Marina Warner in 1984 by Virago Press, the feminist publisher in London.

33. Sven Hedin, *The Silk Road*, p. 295.

34. Linda Benson, an historian of the Uighars of Central Asia, is working on a scholarly study of the Trio.

35. Cable and French, *Something Happened*, p. 241.

Topsy with them. Topsy immediately caught the public's imagination. An article in *China's Millions* described the last meeting of their furlough, before they returned to Qinghai. When Eva French, the eldest, aged sixty-seven, was asked, "Are you not thrilled to be going back?" she responded. "Picturing conditions of the Gobi, its stony floor, the filth of its inns, the hard bread and unappetizing food, the uncertainties of life, the rumours, the brigands, etc," these things, she said, made poor thrills. But contacts with needy souls, the evidences that kind deeds did bear fruit, were thrills worthwhile. But the only true thrill was to be able to say, as the Master did, "I delight to do thy will."

"People had asked if Topsy was thrilled at going back to her native land, but Topsy's bitter experiences in the land of her birth were poor preparations for being thrilled at the prospect of return. But there were a few things that Topsy wanted to say, and though she had been born deaf and was consequently dumb, she had been taught to know about 500 words. At Miss French's invitation, Topsy then rose and said 'Good bye' and 'Forget-me-not,' waving her hand as she did so. Topsy will not be forgotten, and the memory of her will speak for her people."[36]

Their final trip lasted only one year before it was cut short by another civil war, and all four retired to England. Mildred Cable died in 1952, and the French sisters within a month of each other in 1960 — Eva reached the fine old age of ninety-one. When Topsy died in 1998, she too received a respectful obituary in the newspapers.

The Model Province

Two years after the Boxers, in June 1902, Timothy Richard, the visionary of modernism, returned to Shanxi for the official opening of the Western Studies Department of Shanxi University. This was the first time he had visited since he was ordered not to return twenty years earlier. At the Beijing discussions, he had urged the government to set aside 500,000 taels (£66,000 or $330,000 U.S.) of the indemnity funds, "not for foreigners or for the Christians, but for the opening of schools throughout the province, where the sons of the officials and gentry could obtain useful knowledge." This would be capped by Shanxi University, built by the government and run by missionaries. The conservative Chinese officials felt this school would not actually *teach* anything, but merely be a tool for propaganda. The compromise — a noble compromise — was reached that a single institution would teach both West-

---

36. *China's Millions* (NA), August 1935. Kemp, *Steppe by Step*, pp. 466-67.

ern subjects and the Chinese classics, run by the state and outside of mission control.

Here was Richard's New Jerusalem in bricks and tiled roofs. Shanxi University became a famous center for traditional learning in northwest China. It had compulsory "worship" of Confucius, but did not permit Christian teaching even outside school hours, even though most of the staff were missionaries. After the abolition of the old examination system in 1905 and the Revolution of 1911, it became an agent of modernization in this ancient heartland.[37]

After 1911, with the collapse of the central government and the beginning of the warlord period, Shanxi was taken over by a warlord named Yan Xishan (old spelling Yen Hsi-shan), who withdrew from the turmoil in the rest of China and made Shanxi into "the model province." He paved the Big Road from Baoding to Taiyuan, and south along the Fen River to the bend in the Yellow River. This was paralleled by a railway, the major route from Beijing to Xian. Moreover, Yan exploited the resources of coal and iron, and established heavy industries such as cement factories.

One component of Yan's model province was his prohibition of opium. After 1906, when opium growing was outlawed throughout China, the law was so strictly enforced in Shanxi that Sir Alexander Hosie, veteran of the British consular service, saw no opium fields there during his visit in 1913.[38] Opium was not entirely stamped out, for into the 1920s "at least 10 per cent of Shansi's 11 million people were habitual consumers." Yan set up a Society for the Suppression of Opium Smoking, which instituted severe laws to jail addicts, and built "sanitariums" that "dispensed medicinal compounds designed to assuage and gradually destroy their craving." By the 1920s the "curse of opium" was one of the planks of Chinese nationalism and anti-imperialism. The students of Shanxi University took to the streets chanting "How pitiful are the drug addicts! Save them! Save them! Save them!"[39]

---

37. Donald G. Gillin, *Warlord: Yen Hsi-shan in Shansi Province 1911-1949* (Princeton: Princeton University Press, 1967), p. 75. One of Shanxi University's sponsors was H. H. Kung, the Oberlin convert who had tried to rescue the missionaries during the Boxer Uprising (Chapter 12) and was now influential in Shanxi politics. He would later be finance minister of the Republic of China after his marriage to Ailing Soong.

38. Hosie, *On the Trail of the Opium Poppy*. Newman, "Opium Smoking in Late Imperial China: A Reconsideration," p. 773, said that in 1906 Shanxi produced 30,000 piculs of opium (four million pounds), the sixth largest producer after Sichuan (238,000 piculs), Yunnan (78,000), Shaanxi, Guizhou, and Gansu.

39. Gillin, *Warlord in Shansi*, pp. 38-40. The "medicinal compounds" of the weaning treatment sound like morphine.

The Aftermath

Although Yan was an orthodox Confucian, he was on exceptionally good terms with the missionaries, for he employed them as economic, medical, rural, and educational advisors. They proved indispensable during the famine of 1919-22 — the second Great North China Famine — when they distributed relief and set up cooperatives for weaving and road building. Eventually roads were constructed to villages so remote that "the inhabitants had never seen a cart, much less a bicycle or bus."[40] He also contributed to an indigenous (i.e. nonmissionary) Protestant church in Taiyuan.

Yan incorporated Christian ideas into a moral reform movement he "deliberately patterned" on the Christian church that he called the "Heart-Washing Society" (a name both Buddhists and Christians would approve). He established a branch in every town for the gentry and students, and a "Good People's Movement" in every village among the peasants. Meetings of the Heart-Washing Society culminated in confessions of sin, self-criticism, and "hymns in praise of Confucius."[41] Also, according to Donald Gillin's biography, Governor Yan urged "his subjects to place their faith in a supreme being which he called *shang-ti* [pinyin *Shangdi*] and for whom he professed to find a sanction in the Confucian classics." Yan described the deity in terms of regeneration, salvation, and retribution. Shangdi, of course, was the name of the ancient deity who was killed in Shanxi by the new god named *Tian*, Heaven, many thousands of years ago. It was also the Protestant name for Jehovah God, "the One True God" of the Taipings and Pastor Hsi. Was this the culmination of Gutzlaff's dream of the blitz-conversion of China? Was Yan trying to convert the people of Shanxi into god worshipers?

Yan boasted that his ideology embodied the best features of "militarism, nationalism, anarchism, democracy, capitalism, communism, individualism, imperialism, universalism, paternalism, and utopianism." Gillin concluded: "No combination of ideas was incongruous for him."[42]

The same, I think, can be said of some in the China Inland Mission. As George Eliot said, "Religious ideas have the fate of melodies, which once set afloat in the world, are taken up by all sorts of instruments."

---

40. Ibid., pp. 75-77 (education), pp. 36-38 (medical and famine), pp. 90-91 (roads).

41. Mao Zedong would certainly have known about Yan's society, since Shanxi was a communist base camp during the Yanan period (1935-45). It is interesting the way different ideas get picked up, and Mao may have adapted the public confession of sin in Yan's program for his reeducation campaigns.

42. Gillin, *Warlord in Shansi*, pp. 60-63.

Postscript

This is not the end. In 1988, almost forty years after "the reluctant exodus" following the Communist liberation of 1949, some children of the CIM returned to Shanxi. Hakon Torjesen and Kari Torjesen Malcolm, the son and daughter of Norwegian associates Peter and Valborg Torjesen, were allowed to visit their childhood home in Hequ (old spelling Ho-ch'ü), northwestern Shanxi, where their parents had lived for almost twenty years. During the anti-Japanese war, they opened their home and church premises to shelter thousands of refugees. Tragically, Peter, whose Chinese name meant "Leaf Evergreen," was killed in a Japanese bombing raid.

During the Torjesens' 1988 visit, the Hequ county officials informed the family that Peter Torjesen's name was on the county roll of the people's martyrs, and that they wanted to erect a monument on the fiftieth anniversary of his death. Three generations of the family attended the unveiling of a marble monument in 1990, upon which the story of Peter's life and work was engraved in gold characters. On that occasion, a request was made to Peter's grandson Finn Torjesen, who spoke Chinese and had extensive international experience, to return with his family to work in Shanxi "in the same spirit as Peter Torjesen served." This invitation came from the highest government level, the Executive Vice Governor's office.

In 1993 Finn Torjesen founded Shanxi Evergreen Service, a Christian development and aid organization, which operates three centers in Taiyuan City, Jinzhong Prefecture, and Yangqu County, where its teams offer medical services, classes in English, and consulting and economic development. Evergreeners are proud of their historical roots, as can be seen in their mission statement: "To assist Shanxi and other Chinese provinces by developing public benefit services for the common people, continuing the good works of Ye Yongqing ("Leaf Evergreen," i.e., Peter Torjesen), acknowledging God's gracious calling in our lives and reflecting the credibility of Christ."

The statement continues:

> Since we are an openly Christian organization, excellence in our work provides the opportunities to reflect Christ; our ministry comes through our work.... Both Joseph in Egypt and Daniel in Babylon contributed greatly to the countries in which they lived, even in servitude. They were known and respected for their wisdom and God-given skills and brought glory to God through their lives and their work. Evergreeners seek to live out similar lives of work and faith in China to-

The Aftermath

day. To the degree that we invest ourselves in the lives of those around us, we hope to reach people at all levels of society for the spiritual and physical benefit of Shanxi.[43]

Those too were the ideals of their spiritual forebears in the China Inland Mission.

---

43. The story of the Torjesen family in China and the birth of the Evergreen organization is in Kari Torjesen Malcolm, *We Signed Away Our Lives: How One Family Gave Everything for the Gospel* (Downers Grove, Ill.: InterVarsity Press, 1990; reprint ed., Pasadena: William Carey Library, 2004). See also Shanxi Evergreen Service website, www.evergreenchina.org/index.htm.

CONCLUSION

Something Happened

I have begun teaching them in this way. On a piece of yellow paper these words are written in large Chinese characters: "In heaven there is a true spirit called God; He is lord of Heaven and Earth." The children repeat it over and over again until it is known. As soon as they get one idea into their heads (and I trust their hearts) then they will learn another.

China's Millions, February 1896.[1]

The Shanxi Spirits

Thirty years after the Boxers, when the Trio came to write their joint autobiography, they called it simply, *Something Happened.*

We have come a long way from Barnsley. But exactly what did happen?

In the preface, I said I intended to use the China Inland Mission as a prism to shed light on two large questions. I would like to return to those questions in this conclusion. First I want to review certain events in this book to examine how Hudson Taylor's (and before him, Karl Gutzlaff's) vision of the blitz-conversion of China's millions played out on the ground. I will then enlarge the perspective to the larger evangelical movements of the twentieth century to show how the "Shanxi spirits" — the experimental spirituality loosed by the encounter of evangelical Christianity and indigenous religious sects — continued to reverberate far beyond the borders of Shanxi.

In fact, so many key leaders of the CIM had worked in Shanxi before 1900, and had learned the lessons of Pastor Hsi, that the religious controversies of

---

1. *China's Millions* (NA), February 1896, p. 26.

the twentieth century — fundamentalism versus modernism versus pentecostalism — sound like a family squabble within the CIM. The leaders with Shanxi experience included Dixon E. Hoste, Hudson Taylor's nephew and the general director from 1901 until his death in a Japanese internment camp; Frank W. Baller, the linguist and superintendent of the language school; W. W. Cassels, the CIM/CMS Bishop of East Sichuan; Marshall Broomhall (another of Taylor's nephews), the London secretary; his sister Gertrude (Mrs. Hoste), and three other siblings; and important superintendents such as Alex Saunders and F. C. Dreyer. Thus, through the fanciful pens of the mission's authors — Mrs. Howard Taylor, Marshall Broomhall, and the Trio — the strange story of Pastor Hsi Shengmo, the formidable "Overcomer of Demons," became a model for mass evangelism in twentieth-century China.

I would like to consider the second question first, which I posed in a deceptively simple fashion: how did evangelical Christianity become Chinese? One might as well try to define the Shanxi spirits.

Pastor Hsi was, of course, unique. He arose from an unusual set of circumstances — Shanxi after the Great Famine — and came out of a particular sectarian background, the Golden Pill. He was important, not just in his own time as the founder and leader of the largest indigenous Protestant sect between the Taipings and the Boxers. He was also the forerunner and prototype of many other charismatic Chinese church leaders of the twentieth century, such as Jonathan Sung and Watchman Nee. Indeed, compared with manifestations among Chinese Christians today, Pastor Hsi seems almost tame. Nowadays exorcisms, dreams, visions, and healing are common, and many Christians read their Bibles literally — "in quaint and surprising ways," as Geraldine Taylor put it — which would not have seemed out of place a century ago. The major difference between then and now is opium.

The pattern of Pastor Hsi and the missionaries was, in microcosm, the birth of evangelical Christianity as Chinese folk religion and the subsequent reassertion of missionary control. If I had to select one incident that marks that moment, it would be the decision made by the Cambridge Seven to put themselves under Pastor Hsi's guidance and protection. Many missionaries went native, but seldom did they deliberately become disciples of the native convert; fewer still decided to put themselves in the background, as Dixon Hoste did, content to be the exotic white disciple who lived in the backroom. Stanley Smith, more susceptible, started to cast out devils and administer morphine; he got lost, preoccupied with notions that medicine was sorcery and that all humankind will be saved, if not in this life, then the next. Charlie Studd and Cecil Polhill Turner went pentecostal. Each made a unique decision, but what larger patterns can be detected?

CONCLUSION

In order to succeed at the grassroots level, evangelical Christianity had to be born again. It had to become simple. When Hudson Taylor was young, he believed in the widespread dissemination of tracts and gospels, which were printed without "denominational" commentaries or explanatory notes — just the pure unvarnished Word of God. But these appealed to only one segment of society, literate elite males who could understand the obscurantist god-talk of the awkward translations. Christianity had to have intellectual appeal for the scholar gentry at the imperial court, yet also be simple enough to be understood by a bound-foot peasant granny. The conflict between those who sought to inculcate Christianity at the elite level and those who believed in the blitz-conversion of the peasants was the first outbreak of the Shanxi spirit.

As the Great Famine abated in 1879, the missionaries in Taiyuan were quite experimental in their methods of evangelism, releasing the spirits. On one hand, Timothy Richard was creating his Christianized Confucianism aimed at the "worthies" in Chinese society, the scholars and leaders of reformed religious sects. While the male missionaries were targeting the civil service examinations, distributing tens of thousands of printed tracts, the CIM women were turning the wordless book into a little silk purse. The wordless book is what both Daniel Bays and Murray Rubinstein call a congruance, one medium through which simple Christianity could enter Chinese society (see Introduction). Thus the evangelical message was reduced to four colors, black, red, white, and yellow, which happened to coincide with the ancient color cosmology called the *wuxing*, the five colors. I have sinned; Jesus saves me; Jesus loves me; I am going to heaven.

The second stage was to attract seekers, those who were already on a spiritual pilgrimage. As Pastor Hsi shows in vivid detail, most of the CIM's early converts were former members of the collapsing religious sects: "vegetarian friends," the Golden Pill, the Secret Religion, and White Lotus. New religions in China were (and still are) deliberately syncretic; that is, they claimed to be better than existing religions because they incorporated the best elements of each. Christianity, both Catholic and Protestant, can thus be seen as part of a continuum of sects which promised to save suffering humanity from the coming cataclysm. And the Middle Eden was one of many utopian, patriarchal communes scattered through the deep countryside of China.

Opium was the downfall of Gutzlaff's Chinese Union in 1850, when opium addiction was just becoming a national problem; fifty years later, at the high tides of imperialism, opium dragged Pastor Hsi's sect into the twilight zone of narcotic Christianity. One of the primary attractions of any new religion was a promise of healing, either by medicines, breathing exercises (such as *taiqi*), divine intervention, or exorcism — or better yet, some combination of all four. (These are still the primary attractions to Christianity in China today, as the health care infrastructure collapses.) Exorcism was Pastor Hsi's specialty, as his name proclaimed, but when the missionaries started supplying his rival, Elder Fan, with foreign "anti-opium pills" — morphine — he saw the chance to make a lot of money. A few years later, when Taylor decided to finance the spread of his Heavenly Invitation Offices, things spun out of control. After years of publicity, the CIM had to support him, even if it meant relocating or firing missionaries and censoring their reports. The "cocoon of silence" descended, and Hudson Taylor's policy of "only sell success" meant that only positive news emanated from Shanxi.

The Cambridge Seven's decision to work in one of Pastor Hsi's refuges set off a chain reaction. They started casting out demons and curing the sick, entering the Chinese spirit world to battle the gods. They were followed by the single women, who placed themselves under Mrs. Hsi's personal protection. But when Anna Jakobsen married the Chinese evangelist, the CIM tried to rein in the free spirits. Stanley Smith's and Miss Jakobsen's generation was replaced by women of a sterner sort, who demanded "the most rigid observance of etiquette, Chinese and Western." They alienated the Chinese with their formal, condescending attitude. This, too, was a common pattern throughout China, as foreign missionaries took control of indigenous congregations and displaced the native elders and Biblewomen.

After 1900, with the slate wiped clean, this process of missionary control was completed as the CIM became more like conventional institutions. Hudson Taylor's generation of pilgrims — the people of this book — gave way to the generation of soldiers, Dixon Hoste and Henry Frost.

The City of Brotherly Love

To return to the first question I posed, how did nineteenth-century British evangelicalism feed into twentieth-century American fundamentalism, and eventually into worldwide Protestant patterns of the twenty-first century? When Jonathan Goforth brought his Holy Ghost revival to Shanxi in 1908 (see Chapter 13), this was one indication that Shanxi was increasingly a battleground for theological conflicts that originated elsewhere. These were primarily connected with the CIM's shift to militant fundamentalism and its attempts to separate itself, first from the modernists, then from the pentecostals.

Henry Frost, who moved the North American headquarters from Toronto to Philadelphia in 1901, became a charter member of the emerging American fundamentalist movement, a key member of an interlocking directorship of missions, Bible schools, and conservative associations. He contributed a manifesto on "What Missionary Motives Should Prevail?" (1915) to *The Fundamentals,* the series of booklets which gave the movement its name. It is well known that the oil millionaires Lyman and Milton Stewart (Union Oil of California) financed the distribution of three million copies of *The Fundamentals* to every minister and YMCA secretary in the United States and Canada. Less known is that they also exported *The Fundamentals* to China, financing the same number in Chinese. This was funneled through the Bible Union of China, a cooperative agency of Goforth and the CIM which sponsored Keswick conferences and provided Bibles and antimodernist booklets in Chinese.[2]

Frost made his third trip to China in 1900, at the height of the Boxer tragedy. Hoste, the acting director, invited the national directors to come to Shanghai to console the victims. Walter B. Sloan, the successor to Benjamin Broomhall, went from London, and Frost from Toronto. Like Frost's other trips, this was a morbid, hallucinatory journey. While he was at sea, he prepared a sermon entitled "the privilege and joy of suffering." He wrote, "I am going to tell them that it is fitting that we should suffer and if need be die for Christ, for He is worthy." How dare *he* speak of the "joy of suffering"? one survivor asked. What did *he* know? Frost felt "unworthy" as a post-traumatic grief counselor (to use today's jargon), and came to realize "the missionaries needed sympathy more than exhortation." He remained in China for three months, and sailed for home via England. He was shipwrecked four times and lost everything except a grimy tropical suit. He arrived back in Toronto in July 1901 "as one raised from the dead."[3]

The next day he set off on a pilgrimage of a different sort. While he had been in China, Howard and Geraldine Taylor had been touring American universities on behalf of the Student Volunteer Movement. They traveled in the *haute monde* of transatlantic evangelicalism — the first volume of *Pastor Hsi* was just off the press — and mingled with the rich and powerful. A "new friend," Horace Coleman of Norristown, Pennsylvania, introduced himself with a check for $5,000, "the largest donation which we had ever received." He was a "bachelor business man" who had previously shown no interest in missions, but now he offered to donate a house if Frost would move to Philadelphia. Coleman took Frost and the Taylors for a walk up De Kalb Street. He

---

2. Marsden, *Fundamentalism and American Culture,* pp. 168-69. Goforth's papers in UCA and ABGC are important sources for fundamentalism in China.

3. For Frost's third trip, see his "Memoirs," pp. 601-30; quotes at pp. 612-15, 627.

Something Happened

pointed to a large house, and said, "You can have it if you want." At a second house: "You can have it if you want." And a third, on the crest of a hill "where the houses and grounds were more inviting," he asked Frost to look out of the corner of his eye. Frost was "deeply moved . . . too grateful to speak." The next day Coleman donated the house as the North American headquarters of the China Inland Mission.[4]

Without putting too fine a point on it, Coleman, who became a member of the North American council and generous donor for thirty years, bought his way into the CIM. He showered it with money, donating two houses in succession and contributing several hundred thousand dollars. "We were finding out that divine leadings were sometimes very strange, but that they always went from good to better and from better to best. Mr. Coleman had his way."[5]

Like many expatriate Americans, during his twelve years in Toronto (1889-1901), Frost "never gave up looking for a new movement of the cloud, this time toward the States."[6] By 1901, the CIM was in an anomalous situation. Although its headquarters were in Canada, one-half of its missionaries and three-quarters of its constituency were south of the border. As Frost put it, "Mr. [Joshua S.] Helmer [treasurer in Toronto] and I were Americans, but we were living on British soil. *China's Millions,* our monthly paper, was printed in Toronto, but its chief circulation was in the States. Our Prayer Union was centralized in our Canadian center, but the larger part of its membership in America. And, most interestingly, our greatest opportunity for witnessing to the needs of China was in the States, but almost all our speakers were from Great Britain."[7]

Coleman's offer was the movement of the cloud, Frost believed, and he moved his family to Philadelphia so precipitously he did not have time to notify the Toronto council. They felt deserted by a key leader in Canada's evangelical coalition. Elmore Harris, president of Toronto Bible Training School,

---

4. Ibid., pp. 593, 634-36. The official history by Dr. and Mrs. Howard Taylor, *"By Faith": Henry W. Frost and the China Inland Mission,* pp. 259-62, toned down Coleman's questions and wrote the Taylors (the authors) out of the story. They mention Coleman only once by name, even though they stayed at his "summer camp" many times, and thereafter refer to him as "the giver."

5. For the financial history of the American CIM, see my chapter, "No Solicitation: The China Inland Mission and Money," in Noll and Eskridge, eds., *More Money, More Ministry: Money and Evangelicals in Recent American History.* Miss Charlesanna Huston, a wealthy heiress in Germantown, bequeathed $700,000 to the CIM; she was not mentioned in *"By Faith,"* except for one brief citation (p. 331). William Borden, the milk company heir, bequeathed $250,000 and rated a martyrology by Mrs. Howard Taylor, *Borden of Yale* (London: CIM, 1926).

6. Frost, "Memoirs," p. 570.

7. Ibid., p. 523.

realized that without the CIM students, TBTS would be reduced from a continental institution to a local one. They felt, Frost wrote, that "I had no right to abandon a work to which I had given my life." Yet, thirty years later, Frost regretted, "I lost in the hour of my departure from Toronto something in the way of spiritual fellowship which — except in certain individuals — has never been restored to me."[8]

Frost's first years in Philadelphia were a "dismal failure" because of his "utter isolation and loneliness." He went from Toronto, where he was in demand as a speaker, to a city where he was unknown. The few who dropped in tended to be "cranks and had vagaries of faith and prophecy which they desired to set forth in detail." During Frost's sojourn in Canada from 1889 to 1901, the religious climate in the United States had sharpened. Now he was convinced that the "standard of doctrine and life in the States is much lower than that which prevails in Canada, and apostasy has increased so rapidly in these eastern parts that it is impossible to tell what one is going to meet with, even in the most apparently spiritual persons." This was a sign of "the great apostasy which the Scripture connects with the last days."[9] Thus the dark night of the soul Frost experienced in his trips to China was transmuted into a universal principle.

Frost's move to Philadelphia proved to be a decisive event in the history of American fundamentalism. By then the giants of the first generation were gone, D. L. Moody, A. T. Pierson, and A. J. Gordon. The Niagara prophetic Conference had collapsed. The YMCA and YWCA had gone liberal. One of the most important figures of the second generation was Cyrus Ingersoll Scofield, editor of the *Scofield Bible*, a pre-millennialist annotated King James Bible, who moved to Philadelphia in 1914 to found Philadelphia School of the Bible. Another ally was Charles Erdman, son of Frost's mentor William J. Erdman, who arranged for Frost to be ordained as a Presbyterian minister. Once again, the CIM found itself at the center of a very large circle, a continental octopus, until by the 1920s, it had become the favorite foreign mission of American fundamentalists.

In order to remake the CIM into a fundamentalist institution, Frost led a campaign within the mission to expel those who held liberal or conditionalist views. This had been simmering since 1893, when Frost went to England determined to "Americanize, that is, democratize," the autocratic constitution of the CIM, even if that meant opposing Hudson Taylor and the London council. He forced the CIM to adopt a credal statement that stated in black and white the conditions of "membership" in an association, not a family. The first per-

8. Ibid., pp. 638-39.
9. Ibid., pp. 698-99.

son Frost attacked under the new provisions was Stanley Smith, despite Taylor's pleading for "tolerance" for "an old and esteemed member" of the family.

In 1904, when Hoste was officially appointed general director, he convened the first ever joint meeting of the combined councils in Shanghai. This was Frost's fourth and final trip to China, so everything he knew about the field was conditioned by what he had seen before and after the Boxers. The main issue on the agenda was Stanley Smith, who had been reinstated at Hudson Taylor's personal pleading, but was prohibited from preaching to the Chinese. But Smith could never hold his tongue for long, and soon he was attacking Frost in a pamphlet entitled *"The Spiritual Condition of the Heathen": A Reply to Mr. Henry W. Frost, Director of the China Inland Mission in North America,*[10] and articles in the *Chinese Recorder.* Every member of the China council and both the British and Australian home directors opposed Frost's hard-line approach, except Dr. Howard Taylor, who had lived so long in America that he too had become a leading fundamentalist speaker. Using terms common a decade later, Frost and Howard Taylor convinced them that Smith must resign according to the *Principles & Practice.* Allowing him to remain would "imperil the spiritual interests of the other members" and would change "the character of the Mission and [result in] the losing of its evangelical testimony." The councils agreed, and Smith was forced to resign, although he remained at the same station, Luan, Shanxi, for the next thirty years.[11]

A few years later, the British CIM supported the Edinburgh Missionary Conference of 1910, which marked a watershed of ecumenical cooperation in missions. Walter Sloan was its official representative on the Continuation Committee, which worked on the final recommendations. In 1915 Frost forced the CIM to withdraw from the committee. "We could not approve of this relationship," he wrote, because of "the unscripturalness of co-ordinating evangelical and nonevangelical missionary agencies." This — reminiscent of the Plymouth Brethren idea of second-degree separation — "gave us in North America a new sense of spiritual freedom."[12] In 1917 Frost withdrew the CIM from the Associated Boards of Foreign Mission Societies of North America to establish the Interdenominational Foreign Mission Association, which is still a fundamentalist bastion. Finally, in 1922 the CIM in China

---

10. Stanley P. Smith, *"The Spiritual Condition of the Heathen": A Reply to Mr. Henry W. Frost, Director of the China Inland Mission in North America* (Shanghai: Commercial Press, n.d.)

11. Ibid., pp. 653-63. Alvyn Austin, "Blessed Adversity: Henry W. Frost and the China Inland Mission," in Carpenter and Shenk, eds., *Earthen Vessels: American Evangelicals and Foreign Missions 1880-1980*, pp. 64-65.

12. Frost, "Memoirs," pp. 791-94.

joined the National Christian Council, but withdrew in 1926, at the height of the civil war raging in China, because, as the China council stated, "Separation is forced upon us."[13]

Thus did Henry Frost, descendant of Puritans, bring the CIM into the tent of the hardest of hard-liners.

Yet, because of its British and Canadian roots, the CIM as an international institution did not entirely "go fundamentalist." Michael Griffiths, the general director of the Overseas Missionary Fellowship (the renamed CIM after 1950) in the 1960s, remarked that

> the US section was more 'fundamentalist' than the rest of us even as late as the fifties, sixties and seventies: Americans were premill [pre-millennial], creationist, anti-ecumenical, anti-socialist and later anti-charismatic. The mainland Europeans were at the opposite pole, with the Brits somewhat intermediate as usual — mainly amill [a-millennial, that is, not professing a stand on pre- or post-millennial eschatology], not indisposed to the Creator using evolution, sympathetic to evangelicals within the WCC [World Council of Churches] (many were Anglicans after all); delighted with the post-war social reforms that gave us a welfare state and unpolarised over the charismatic movement, always trying to see both sides. An amusing example was the American candidates questionnaire which enquired 'Do you have any experience of charismatic gifts?' The politically correct anticipated reply was 'No!' to which I, writing from the Singapore International Headquarters as General Director, wrote, 'Who wants a missionary with no experience of charismatic gifts? (in their Biblical sense, that is!).' It seems common sense that mission groups are bound to be influenced and shaped by their own environment and church history — and thus the differences. The danger always is that people (Americans particularly) want the rest of the world to fall into line with them: some kind of evangelical Monroe Doctrine would seem overdue.[14]

Testing the Spirits

If the CIM's militant antimodernism was predictable, its opposition to pentecostal manifestations was neither predictable nor straightforward. The CIM had always tolerated, and sometimes encouraged, prayer and anointing with

13. China council minutes, 12 March 1926, in CIM/ABGC, file 2/39.
14. Michael Griffiths, communication to the author, 16 June 1998.

oil when a patient was beyond human aid. Hudson Taylor, Henry Frost, and a host of other worthies had experienced some sort of divine healing. But the compulsory vaccination policy tended to weed out the extremists who refused medicine of any sort, or at least it forced them to conform to standard medical practice. Confined to a few individuals in remote stations — the more remote the better — these manifestations were quite different from the "tongues movement" which arrived like a mighty rushing wind in 1906.

The first sign was the Welsh revival of 1905, which some called the Third Great Awakening, the evangelical revival of the early 1800s. being the Second. "The Welsh revival defied description," wrote Edith Blumhofer. "It ignored the methods with which Christians typically approached revival. Spontaneity and seeming disorder replaced promotion, scheduling, regular preaching, financial planning, and even systematic evangelistic outreach." G. Campbell Morgan, a British evangelist, noted, "It is Pentecost continued, without a single moment's doubt." With reference to Acts 2, he concluded: "If you put a man into these meetings who knows nothing of the language of the Spirit, and nothing of the life of the Spirit, one of two things will happen to him. He will either pass out saying, 'These men are drunk,' or he himself will be swept up by the fire into the Kingdom of God."[15]

This revival in the coal towns of South Wales was only the beginning, the prelude to a worldwide "outpouring of the Holy Spirit." News spread rapidly, particularly through the Keswick circles and the CIM. Goforth replicated it in Manchuria. The next outpouring occurred in April 1906 in an abandoned shop-front church on Azusa Street, in a poor, black area of Los Angeles. This was the first modern instance of speaking in tongues on a mass level, and it is credited as the birth of the pentecostal movement. One woman claimed to be able to speak Chinese and Tibetan and set out immediately for China. Pastor M. L. Ryan of Salem, Oregon, and "a large part of his congregation sent themselves off around the world as faith missionaries." Within the year pentecostal missionaries had crossed the Pacific to China, India, and other fields. By 1914, when the Assemblies of God, the largest pentecostal denomination in the United States, organized its own mission board, there were over 150 British and North American pentecostal missionaries at thirty places in China.[16]

Invariably, as Daniel Bays notes, "most of the first Pentecostals who felt called to foreign lands fully believed they had been or would be given instant

---

15. Blumhofer, *The Assemblies of God*, vol. 1, *To 1941*, pp. 100-102.
16. Daniel H. Bays, "The Protestant Missionary Establishment and the Pentecostal Movement," in Blumhofer, Spittler, and Wacker, eds., *Pentecostal Currents in American Protestantism*, p. 56.

fluency of speech.... This claim or expectation of language was a typical and general one among early Pentecostals, as far as I can tell. That the disappointment which inevitably ensued did not totally discourage them all is a tribute to their adaptability and stubbornness, as well as to their strength of conviction in the new creed."[17]

Many CIM missionaries, with their lively sense of the supernatural, were attracted to these "waiting meetings," which seemed similar to Keswick conferences for the deeper spiritual life. There was a distinct progression, as those who had experienced the "second blessing" of holiness sought the "third blessing" of divine health, and then the "fourth blessing" of divine utterance. Among the most susceptible were the CIM associate missions, Frederik Franson's Swedish Holiness Mission and Scandinavian Alliance, as well as A. B. Simpson's Christian and Missionary Alliance (which was not an associate). These were the Swedish and Norwegian troubadours who had suffered so severely from the Boxer violence. Thus the pentecostal currents reached the CIM from many directions, from Wales via Keswick, from Sweden and continental Europe, and directly from Los Angeles.

Among those who made the pilgrimage to Azusa Street was Cecil Polhill Turner, the most adventurous of the Cambridge Seven. (Another was Charlie Studd's brother George, who remained in Los Angeles as a pentecostal preacher.)[18] Polhill Turner had come full circle: in 1885 he had tried to gain the Chinese language supernaturally, but had given up when it proved a failure. During the 1890s, he and his wife had joined Annie Royale Taylor, the lone wolf of Tibet, first in Gansu and Qinghai, then at Darjeeling in northern India. They had differed over strategy: her goal was to reach Lhasa herself by small incremental stages, while he wanted to convert Tibetans to take the gospel themselves to Lhasa.[19] After Polhill Turner received the baptism of the Holy Spirit at Azusa, he returned to England, where he founded the Pentecostal Missionary Union for Great Britain and Ireland, the first organized pentecostal foreign mission. In 1909, at the age of fifty — the same year Charlie Studd was escorting the Heart of Africa Mission to the Belgian Congo — Polhill Turner announced he was bringing a party of twelve PMU workers, mostly Scandinavians, and intended to "plant them on the Tibetan border."[20] He made an arrangement for the members of his group to work as individual CIM associates, not as a formal associate mission.

17. Ibid., pp. 53, 60.
18. Blumhofer, *The Assemblies of God*, vol. 1, *To 1941*, p. 222.
19. *HTCOC 7*, pp. 162-65.
20. China council minutes, 14 April 1909, in CIM/ABGC, file 3/37.

Something Happened

Another CIM missionary at Azusa Street was Hector McLean, a rarity among the seekers, an experienced China missionary who spoke the language. An Irish Canadian, he had joined the CIM in 1901 and was stationed in Yunnan, where he married Sigrid Bengtson from Sweden. In 1907, they were granted an emergency furlough because of her precarious heath and also for their infant daughter Karin, who had been born partially blind. They sought healing in Sweden and Toronto, then went to Los Angeles, where, according to Henry Frost, they "joined the so-called Pentecostals." Frost had "no choice" but to demand their resignation, but they returned to Yunnan as independent missionaries, where they joined Polhill Turner's PMU.[21]

The pentecostal movement was troubling in two ways. The first was theological. According to pentecostal theology, the gifts of the Spirit that had been withdrawn in apostolic times — "the cessation of charisms" — were being restored in these end times as a witness to the Second Coming. Thus instances of healing, tongues, or exorcism in remote Shanxi were interconnected, as part of God's unfolding plan, with the revivals in Wales and America. They were manifestations of "the latter rain" or "the evening light." This was quite different from the traditional CIM explanation that demons still existed in China just as in the Holy Land at the time of Jesus, so apostolic methods of healing and exorcism were appropriate. Spiritual gifts were cultural, not to be distributed generally among the Christian public at home.

The second problem was that pentecostal missionaries, once they discovered their tongues could not be understood by the Chinese, turned their attention to other missionaries and native Christians. More troubling was their exclusivity, their insistence that tongues were a necessary "evidence" of Spirit baptism. By 1909, the CIM — again led by Henry Frost and D. E. Hoste — decided to expel the pentecostals from its ranks. The China council stated that there had "already been meetings carried on in one part of China by persons professing to have the gift of tongues, which meetings have been characterized by undesirable proceedings." However, they would not reject candidates "simply on the ground that they professed to speak in a tongue," but they certainly would need to be "assured as to their soundness of judgement, and their willingness to associate and work with all who love the Lord and not merely with such as see eye to eye with them in this one manner."[22]

The CIM's suspicion of the charismatic movement was paralleled by

---

21. I am grateful to the late Karin McLean for information concerning her family. Bays, "Protestant Missionary Establishment," p. 56. Minutes of Toronto council, September 1909, in CIM/ABGC.

22. Minutes of China council, Special Meeting, 3 Feb. 1909.

other fundamentalists, such as Roland V. Bingham of the Sudan Interior Mission and A. B. Simpson of the Christian and Missionary Alliance. Some felt that Alliance teachings were congenial to pentecostal manifestations, and Simpson was receptive at first. But he himself never experienced the gift of tongues despite years of seeking. The official C&MA policy concerning tongues was expressed succinctly: "seek not, forbid not."[23] "Eventually the lines were drawn fairly sharply," noted Daniel Bays.

The more the fundamentalists in the CIM tried to suppress the charismatic movements, the more they would erupt at some other place. Since the associates were concentrated in the northwest, in Shanxi, Shaanxi, and Gansu, naturally these were the most fertile ground for supernatural manifestations and indigenous movements. In 1914 the Norwegian Mission in Shanxi — which had been "entirely blotted out" during the Boxer Uprising — reported that ten of its eleven members had received the Spirit baptism under the guidance of a C&MA veteran, W. W. Simpson (no relation to A. B. Simpson), and that "a few of the Christians, including the Linhsien Evangelist, had had a similar experience."[24] This time the CIM took a harder stand: it severed its associate relationship with the Norwegians and forbade the practice of tongues. This was repeated with other associates, such as Franson's Scandinavian Alliance and the German Liebenzell Mission.

In 1914-15 the CIM's China council debated the issue at length, soliciting correspondence from the home directors, provincial superintendents, and senior missionaries. They proceeded with "the utmost care and circumspection." The final policy — which stood until the 1970s — was that pentecostalism contained manifold doctrinal errors. Furthermore, the meetings were "characterized by disorder and manifestations which in some cases has led to mental derangement and maniacal ravings. . . . For one thing, the strain upon the brain occasionally is such that in some cases insanity has ensued, etc."[25] Besides, with one eye on the home constituencies, it concluded that the "highly controversial character" of pentecostalism would be inconsistent with keeping faith with "supporters at home who have entered into fellowship with us on the basis of an understanding, alike as to doctrine and methods, which do not include such new departure."[26]

23. Blumhofer, *Assemblies of God*, vol. 1, *To 1941*, p. 123.
24. China council minutes, 3 December 1914, pp. 16-17. There was one loophole: although "waiting meetings" could not be held on CIM premises and missionaries could not attend Chinese pentecostal services, individuals could continue to attend foreigner-only services: Minutes, 3 December 1915, p. 16.
25. Ibid., 14 April 1915.
26. Ibid., 9 Sept. 1914.

Something Happened

Did the CIM miss the boat? As it pulled back from that twilight zone represented by Pastor Hsi in the 1880s and 1890s, did it also cut itself off from indigenous grassroots Christianity? That was what Bob Whyte meant (see Introduction) when he wrote that the CIM functioned as "a separate denomination with its own congregations," and in this sense was more of an obstacle to the development of a Chinese church than denominational societies.[27] To put the question another way, were the Shanxi spirits precursors to the worldwide pentecostal movements of the twentieth century, an irruption of the divine into history as a warning to the nations? Or did they grow out of the yellow earth, rooted in the history of that sad, sad land?

After 1900, Protestant Christianity in China became more diverse than Pastor Hsi's exorcism and opium sect. (One difference was that opium disappeared from the missionary radar.) Missions offered a wide variety of social, medical, educational and religious services, each attracting a different segment of society. Some converts came to Christianity *because* it was modern and foreign: they wanted to learn English and wear smart Western clothes, and they thought that the Christian church could save China through social service and regeneration. During the religious wars between the modernists and anti-modernists in the 1910s and 1920s, the CIM staked out its own ground, rejecting both the liberals and the enthusiasts. Henry Frost put it best, in his usual florid tone.

> The CIM were a peculiar people. We are evangelicals, and hence, liberalists are not attracted to us. We are evangelistic, and hence, educationalists prefer other organizations. We are, in personnel, largely premillennial, and hence, those who hold this view of truth are specially sympathetic to us. And what has been, in these particulars, is likely to be.... It is my earnest prayer, whatever separation from others our position may require, that we shall never allow to rise up amongst us the critical and censorious spirit.... It has been the glory of the China Inland Mission, that, remaining pre-eminently true to God, it has sought to be to men, the poor as well as the rich, the false as well as the true, the bad as well as the good, their servants for Jesus' sake.[28]

That was the view from Philadelphia. From the perspective of grassroots Shanxi, as the CIM separated itself from pentecostal manifestations, it also

---

27. Bob Whyte, *Unfinished Encounter: China and Christianity* (London: Fount Paperbacks, 1988), pp. 119-23.
28. Frost, "Memoirs," pp. 347, 900.

abdicated its responsibility for or fellowship with an important sector of indigenous Christianity. This was picked up by the pentecostals and the independent churches. Pentecostalism, says Daniel Bays, was historically a "revolt against hierarchy in the church." By the 1920s it facilitated the emergence of indigenous churches, such as the Jesus Family and the True Jesus Church, which offered all believers egalitarian "access to spiritual enlightenment and knowledge of God's will through the indwelling Holy Spirit, and also provided for self-interpretation of this revelation via the gifts of prophecy, tongues and their interpretation. Any Chinese believer could have access to all this, and capable ones could easily claim equality with, or superiority to, any foreign missionary."[29] That was what Pastor Hsi was saying forty years earlier.

The Delectable Mountains

The Venerable Chief Pastor has been brought to the end of the road. He stands amid the Delectable Mountains and can see across the river to the Heavenly City. He can almost hear the angels.

Hudson Taylor made his last public appearance on 23 April 1900 — ironically less than a week after governor Yuxian arrived in Shanxi — when he gave the opening address at the Ecumenical Conference of Foreign Missions in New York City. Six months earlier, in September 1899, after two strenuous years in China — "the hammer blows," A. J. Broomhall called them — he had left Shanghai with his wife Jennie for a two-month tour of Australia and two months in New Zealand. The Ecumenical Conference proved to be a great flag-waving union of church and state, attended by President Theodore Roosevelt and the governor of New York State. Of the two thousand delegates, 779, including 13 from the CIM, were missionaries representing 108 societies. When Taylor spoke on "The Source of Power in Foreign Missions," Henry Frost recalled, "there was almost an audible sigh of spiritual relief, so many of his hearers realising that they understood as never before the will and way of God."[30]

A few days later he "lost his train of thought," the result of a minor stroke. After recuperating in Philadelphia, Hudson and Jennie returned to London just as vague reports were coming out of China. They went on to Davos, Switzerland, a health spa, where they were joined by Howard and Geraldine Taylor. She was in the middle of writing the first volume of *Pastor Hsi*, the biog-

29. Bays, "Protestant Missionary Establishment," p. 63.
30. Frost, "Memoirs," pp. 313-16.

raphy. As the news of the Boxer tragedy arrived, Hudson Taylor wept. "I can not read, I can not pray, I can scarcely think — but I can trust!"[31] All his life he had felt that the CIM — his vast pigtailed tribe, now 800 strong — had a spiritual passport that allowed them to pass in safety. Now he felt as though God had withdrawn "His restraining hand."

It must have been a tragic scene as the great man slipped into senility, and understandingly the sources become vague. Jennie died in 1904, and he had "the awful temptation," an unpublished note in the Taylor papers states, "even to end his own life."[32] The only uncensored account is chilling. Hudson Taylor was putting his affairs in order and had written his last will and testament (quoted in Chapter 3) to the CIM and his successor, D. E. Hoste, which concluded ominously: "If the Directors and Members of our Councils are godly and wise men, walking in the spirit of unity and love, they will not lack Divine guidance in important matters, and at critical times; but should another spirit ever prevail, no rules could save the Mission nor would it be worth saving."[33]

Henry Frost, the militant, was deputed to report the decision of the united councils that Stanley Smith must resign directly to Hudson Taylor in Switzerland. "For the first time in my life, I shrank from meeting Mr. Taylor," he wrote. Like many British evangelicals, Taylor had become "less dogmatic" in his interpretation of eternal damnation.[34] In fact, he told Frost, if the CIM were organized in 1901 instead of 1865, the clause on "the eternal punishment of the lost" would have been worded differently. When Frost delivered his ultimatum, Taylor's face was like granite. Then he crept into a corner "as if he were in China, expecting a riot and felt it best to have the protection of a wall behind him," and waved his cane in Frost's face. He called Frost's position "a temptation of the evil one.... Have faith in God, dear brother, and hands off, and He will do well and wisely." Nevertheless Frost felt compelled to write "frankly" and "sever" the intimate relationship with Taylor.[35]

Meanwhile, Geraldine Taylor had completed the first volume of *Pastor Hsi*, subtitled *One of China's Scholars*, which was published in the fall of 1900, and had begun writing the second, *One of China's Christians*, published in 1903. How to explain this antediluvian world? How could she make sense of a peasant sect in "the regions beyond" for an English audience? *Pastor Hsi* is more than a curious, sentimental story. Read against the background of the Boxer

---

31. *HTCOC* 7, p. 604.
32. *Christian History*, vol. XV, no. 4 (1996), p. 2.
33. See Chapter 3 note 94.
34. For the decline of dogmatism, see Rowell, *Hell and the Victorians*, pp. 3-4, 16-17, and 190-92.
35. Frost, "Memoirs," p. 691.

uprising, which engendered widespread anti-Chinese attitudes, it was a brave statement against the virulent imperialism of the times. Its purpose was to evince "a larger sympathy for and appreciation of the Chinese" and "to awaken an intelligent interest in the Chinese Christians as fellow members of the body of Christ, and not simply as the objects of the missionaries' labours."[36]

There is a file in the CIM Archives at SOAS, labeled "Pastor Hsi," which contains three letters from D. E. Hoste to Geraldine Taylor concerning the draft of volume one of *Pastor Hsi*, which he had read. Hoste, who had been Pastor Hsi's colleague for ten years, was Mrs. Taylor's main informant, and in that sense, the book was *his* manifesto, the spiritual secrets *he* had learned during his own hidden years. First, he replied that Mrs. Taylor's draft had given "undue prominence to the peace, gentleness and love which undoubtedly did characterize [Hsi] in no small degree." But his chief characteristic was "strenuous warfare against evil in himself and others . . . [which] made him . . . over-severe in his rebuking and exhorting."[37]

Hoste's second point was Pastor Hsi's touchy "relationships with foreign missionaries." He said that "in view of past controversies," he as general director did not wish to be "drawn into, possibly, heated discussions with sundry members." In the Introduction to volume two, he explained that just as "the Western Church in her primitive days grew along the lines of existing institutions," the transitional Chinese leaders would show signs of "despotism," the "typical faults of his race." Nevertheless, often the fault lay with the Western missionaries, for those faults were also "characteristic to some extent to the races from which they were drawn."[38]

Privately, Hoste then raised *the* troubling question, "whether the frequent mention of demoniacal possession and casting out of devils, is not rather strong meat for a Home public? What would you think of a paragraph in the preface, or introduction alluding to the topic, saying that it has been thought best to let the accounts stand much as they come from the actors in them, as serving to illustrate their actual point of view, rather than indicating the author's adherence in a dogmatic way of explanation?"[39] In other words, he and the mission would condone manifestations of Chinese folk religion such as exorcism as long as they did not tie the CIM to any theological position.

As soon as it was published, *Pastor Hsi* took on a life of its own, and has not been out of print for a century. Its first life coincided with the fundamen-

---

36. JHT, Preface to *Pastor Hsi*, vol. 1 (1901).

37. D. E. Hoste to Geraldine Taylor, 26 October 1901, CIM/SOAS, file 9322.

38. *Pastor Hsi*, vol. 2 (1903), pp. xvii-xviii. Hoste's statements were collected into a manifesto entitled *If I am to Lead* (London: OMF, 1968).

39. Hoste, Philadelphia, to Geraldine Taylor, no date, CIM/SOAS, file 9322.

Something Happened

Three veterans: W. A. P. Martin, Griffith John, and Hudson Taylor, Shanghai, April 1905. After Jennie Taylor died in Switzerland, Hudson Taylor returned to China, where he died. In Shanghai, he met with the China council for the last time and formally passed the directorship to Dixon E. Hoste. He posed for a photograph with W. A. P. Martin and Griffith John, who had all gone to China in the 1850s, and who had each spent more than fifty years in China's service. Source: Dr. and Mrs. Howard Taylor, *Hudson Taylor and the China Inland Mission*, vol. 2, *The Growth of a Work of God* (London: CIM, 1918).

talist and pentecostal movements that coalesced after 1906. *Pastor Hsi* could be read either way, as a model of "apostolic Christianity" in demon-possessed China or as a precursor of the baptism of the Holy Spirit. Sixty years later, in the heyday of the sex-and-drugs revolution, *Pastor Hsi* gained a new life among the "Jesus People" as "God's freedom fighter" in the battle against

457

drug addiction and satanism.[40] As evangelists like David Wilkerson (*The Cross and the Switchblade*) entered the inner cities to work with drug addicts, gang members, and street kids, they found a resonance between modern urban addicts and the Middle Eden.[41]

In 1905 Hudson Taylor, by now a tiny aged elf with wild white hair and a long white beard, accompanied by Howard and Geraldine, slowly made his way home, to China. In London, he made his peace with Benjamin and Amelia Broomhall, and their son Marshall, recently recalled from Shanxi to be home secretary. In Philadelphia, relations with Henry Frost remained strained. At Shanghai he was welcomed as founder and father, and sat for a historic photograph with W. A. P. Martin and Griffith John, who between them had served 156 years in China. From Shanghai Taylor pushed on to Hunan, symbolically the last province to be opened by Christian missions, formerly the most bitterly anti-Christian province.

Hudson Taylor arrived at Changsha, the capital, on 2 June, where Dr. Frank Keller was hoping to build a modern hospital. That afternoon, despite the oppressive heat, Taylor visited the site of several acres that the provincial governor had offered them for the hospital. The next morning he addressed a group of Hunan Christians in the mission chapel, which Howard thought was another high point of his father's missionary career. In the afternoon he came down from his room for a reception for the Changsha missionaries, thirty guests from six societies. After, he retired to his room where he told Dr. Barrie, "There is nothing small and there is nothing great; only God is great, and we should trust him fully." Geraldine brought a tray of "good things" for him to eat, and while she was "in mid-sentence" Hudson Taylor "turned his head on the pillow and took a quick breath. . . . No cry, no word, no choking or distress."

The Changsha Christians bought the best coffin they could, and his body was escorted downriver to Zhenjian, where he was buried in the Protestant cemetery next to his first wife, Maria, and three of their children.

After the funeral, Geraldine wrote to Theodore Howard, "Surely this is not death. He is gone from us. We know it. . . . But *life* it is that has come suddenly into our midst, not death. He was caught away from us, he did not seem to die. . . . We look up rather than into the grave, and cry instinctively — 'My father, my father! — the chariots of Israel and the horsemen thereof.'"[42]

---

40. D. M. Lloyd-Jones, "Foreword" to abridged single volume (1972) of *Pastor Hsi*, pp. vii-x.

41. David R. Wilkerson, *The Cross and the Switchblade* (1963).

42. *HTCOC 7*, pp. 503-11.

Bibliography

Archives

CIM London Archives, at School of Oriental and African Studies, University of London (cited as CIM/SOAS).
CIM Toronto Archives, at OMF, Toronto (cited as OMF/Toronto).
CIM Philadelphia Archives, at Archives of the Billy Graham Center, Wheaton College, Collection #215 (cited as CIM/ABGC).
    Frederik Franson Collection #87.
Toronto Bible College Archives, at Tyndale College and Seminary, Toronto.
Royal Ontario Museum, Toronto (cited as ROM), Church of Canada Archives, Toronto.

Periodicals

China Medical Missionary Journal.
China's Millions, published in British, North American, and Australian editions [Note: British edition consulted from 1875 to 1888, and North American after 1888]. Retitled since 1950 as *East Asia's Millions.*
The Chinese Recorder, 1867-1941. See also Kathleen L. Lodwick, *"The Chinese Recorder" Index: A Guide to Christian Missions in Asia, 1867-1941*, in 2 volumes (Wilmington, Del.: Scholarly Resources Inc., 1986).
The Christian Advocate. The Christian Advocate was published by the Methodist Book Concern in New York City under various names from 1826-1956.
Church Missionary Intelligencer.
Hamilton (Ontario) Spectator, 1886-1990.

North China Daily News, 1865-1910. This was an English business newspaper in Tianjin with an anti-missionary bias.
North China Herald.
Times (London), 1865-1901.
Toronto Bible Training School Recorder, 1894-1912; *Toronto Bible College Recorder*, 1912-1967.

Books and Unpublished Manuscripts

Adeney, David. *China: The Church's Long March*. Singapore: OMF, 1985.

Airhart, Phyllis D. *Serving the Present Age: Revivalism, Progressivism, and the Methodist Tradition in Canada*. Kingston and Montreal: McGill-Queen's University Press, 1992.

Anderson, Gerald H., ed. *Biographical Dictionary of Christian Missions*. New York: Macmillan Reference USA, 1998.

Austin, Alvyn J. "Blessed Adversity: Henry W. Frost and the China Inland Mission." In Joel A. Carpenter and Wilbert R. Shenk, eds., *Earthen Vessels: American Evangelicals and Foreign Missions 1880-1980*. Grand Rapids: William B. Eerdmans, 1990.

———. "Carson, Susanna (Rijnhart; Moyes)" and "Mackay, George Leslie." In *Dictionary of Canadian Biography*, vol. 13. Toronto: University of Toronto Press, 1994.

———. "Hotbed of Missions: The China Inland Mission, Toronto Bible College, and the Bible School Movement." In Grant Wacker and Daniel Bays, eds., *The Foreign Missionary Enterprise at Home: Explorations in North American Cultural History*. Mobile: University of Alabama Press, 2003.

———. "No Solicitation: The China Inland Mission and Money." In Mark Noll and Larry Eskridge, eds., *More Money, More Ministry: Money and Evangelicals in Recent American History*. Grand Rapids: Eerdmans, 2000.

———. "Only Connect: The China Inland Mission and Transatlantic Evangelicalism." In Wilbert R. Shenk, ed., *North American Foreign Missions, 1810-1914: Theology, Theory, and Policy*. In the Studies in the History of Christian Missions series. London: Curzon and Grand Rapids: Eerdmans, 2003.

———. *Saving China: Canadian Missionaries in the Middle Kingdom 1888-1959*. Toronto: University of Toronto Press, 1986.

———. "Scholars, Archaeologists and Diplomats: China Missions and Canadian Public Life." In Marguerite Van Die, ed., *Religion and Public Life in Canada: Historical and Comparative Perspectives*. Toronto: University of Toronto Press, 2001.

———. "The Transplanted Mission: The China Inland Mission in Toronto 1888-1901." In George A. Rawlyk, ed., *Aspects of the Canadian Evangelical Experience*. Kingston and Montreal: McGill-Queen's, 1997.

Bibliography

Austin, Alvyn, Peter M. Mitchell, and Margo S. Gewurtz. *Guide to Archival Sources on Canadian Missionaries in East Asia.* Toronto: University of Toronto–York University Joint Centre for Asia Pacific Studies, 1989.

Bacon, Daniel W. *From Faith to Faith: The Influence of Hudson Taylor on the Faith Missions Movement.* Philadelphia: OMF, 1984.

Bagnell, Kenneth. *The Little Immigrants: The Orphans Who Came to Canada.* Toronto: Macmillan of Canada, 1980.

Baller, Frederick W. *An Analytical Anglo-Chinese Dictionary.* London: CIM, 1900.

——. *Letters from an Old Missionary to his Nephew.* Originally in *Chinese Recorder,* 1907. Shanghai: American Presbyterian Mission Press, 1907.

——. *Mandarin Primer.* Shanghai: CIM, 1887. Twelve editions by 1911.

Barnett, Suzanne Wilson, and John King Fairbank, eds. *Christianity in China: Early Protestant Missionary Writings.* Cambridge: Harvard University Press, 1985.

Barr, Pat. *To China with Love: The Lives and Times of Protestant Missionaries in China 1860-1900.* London: Secker & Warburg, 1972.

Bays, Daniel H. "Christian Tracts: The Two Friends" and "Christianity and Chinese Sects: Religious Tracts in the Late Nineteenth Century." In Suzanne Wilson Barnett and John King Fairbank, eds., *Christianity in China: Early Protestant Missionary Writings.* Cambridge: Harvard University Press, 1985.

——. "The Protestant Missionary Establishment and the Pentecostal Movement." In Edith Blumhofer, Russell Spittler, and Grant Wacker, eds., *Pentecostal Currents in American Protestantism.* Urbana and Chicago: University of Illinois Press, 1999.

Bays, Daniel H., ed. *Christianity in China: From the Eighteenth Century to the Present.* Stanford: Stanford University Press, 1996.

Beard, A. E. *South of the Great Wall.* Whangarei, Australia: private, 1976.

Beauchamp, Montague. *Days of Blessing in Inland China: Being an Account of Meetings held in the Province of Shansi.* London: Morgan & Scott, 1887.

Beaver, R. Pierce. *American Protestant Women in World Mission: A History of the First Feminist Movement in North America.* (Original title, *All Loves Excelling,* 1968.) Reprint, Grand Rapids: William B. Eerdmans, 1980.

Bebbington, David. *Evangelicalism in Modern Britain: A History from the 1730s to the 1980s.* London: Unwin Hyman/Routledge, 1989. Reprint, Grand Rapids: Baker Book House, 1992.

Benson, Linda. "French, Cable and French: Women Evangelists of the China Inland Mission." Paper presented at the annual meeting of the Association of Asian Studies. March 2000.

Berridge, Virginia, and Griffith Edwards. *Opium and the People: Opiate Use in Nineteenth-Century England.* London: St. Martin's Press, 1981.

Binfield, Clyde. *George Williams and the Y.M.C.A.: A Study in Victorian Social Attitudes.* London: Heinemann, 1973.

"The Bishop White Gallery: Wall Paintings and Wood Sculptures from Shanxi Province, China." Toronto: Royal Ontario Museum, 1990.

Blumhofer, Edith L. *The Assemblies of God: A Chapter in the Story of American Pentecostalism.* Vol. 1, *To 1941*. Springfield, Mo.: Gospel Publishing House, 1989.

Blumhofer, Edith L., Russell Spittler, and Grant Wacker, eds. *Pentecostal Currents in American Protestantism.* Urbana and Chicago: University of Illinois Press, 1999.

Bohr, Paul Richard. *Famine in China and the Missionary: Timothy Richard as Relief Administrator and Advocate of National Reform, 1876-1884.* Cambridge: East Asian Research Center, Harvard University, 1972.

Boyd, Robert. *The Lives and Labours of Moody and Sankey.* Toronto: A. H. Hovey, 1876.

Brandt, Nat. *Massacre in Shansi.* Syracuse: Syracuse University Press, 1994.

Brereton, Virginia Lieson. *Training God's Army: The American Bible School, 1880-1940.* Bloomington: University of Indiana Press, 1990.

British Foreign Office. *British Parliamentary Papers.* Vol. 29, *China: Correspondence, Dispatches, Circulars and other Papers Respecting Missionaries in China 1868-72.* Shannon: Irish University Press, 1971.

Broomhall, A. J. *Hudson Taylor and China's Open Century.* 7 vols. Sevenoaks, UK: Hodder & Stoughton and OMF, 1981-1989.
  Book 1: *Barbarians at the Gates* (1832-50). 1981.
  Book 2: *Over the Treaty Wall* (1850-56). 1982.
  Book 3: *If I Had a Thousand Lives* (1856-65). 1982.
  Book 4: *Survivors' Pact* (1865-67). 1984.
  Book 5: *Refiner's Fire* (1867-75). 1985.
  Book 6: *Assault on the Nine* (1875-86). 1988.
  Book 7: *It Is Not Death to Die!* 1989.

Broomhall, Benjamin. *The Truth About Opium Smoking.* London: Hodder & Stoughton, 1882.

———. *The Opium Question from a New Point of View.* London: Morgan & Scott, 1906.

Broomhall, Marshall. *The Chinese Empire: A General and Missionary Survey.* London: Morgan & Scott and CIM; New York: Fleming H. Revell, 1907.

———. *F. W. Baller: A Master of the Pencil.* London: CIM, 1923.

———. *Heirs Together of the Grace of Life.* London: Morgan & Scott and CIM, 1918.

———. *John W. Stevenson: One of Christ's Stalwarts.* London: CIM, 1919.

———. *The Jubilee Story of the China Inland Mission.* London: CIM, 1915, reprinted 1929.

———. *Martyred Missionaries of the China Inland Mission, With a Record of the Perils and Sufferings of Some who Escaped.* London: CIM, 1901.

Bibliography

———. "A Mission Station in China." Toronto: CIM, 1899. [Pamphlet about Hongtong, Shanxi.]

———. *W. W. Cassels: First Bishop in Western China*. London: CIM, 1926.

Brouwer, Ruth Compton. *New Women for God: Canadian Presbyterian Women and India Missions, 1876-1914*. Toronto: University of Toronto, 1990.

Brown, Margaret H. "History of the Honan (North China) Mission of the United Church of Canada, Originally a Mission of the Presbyterian Church in Canada, 1887-1951." 4 vols. Typescript. 1970. In United Church Archives, Toronto.

Bunyan, John. *The Pilgrim's Progress from this World to that which is to Come*. London: 1678; republished London: Thomas Nelson & Sons, no date.

Burgess, Alan. *The Small Woman*. London: Evans Brothers, 1957. A biography of Gladys Aylward.

Burkinshaw, Robert K. *Pilgrims in Lotus Land: Conservative Protestants in British Columbia 1917-1981*. Montreal and Kingston: McGill-Queen's University Press, 1995.

Burns, Islay. *Memoir of the Reverend William C Burns, M.A.; Missionary to China from the English Presbyterian Church*. London: James Nisbet & Co., 1870.

Butchart, Reuben. *The Disciples of Christ in Canada Since 1830*. Toronto: Disciples of Christ Publications, 1949.

Butler, Jon. *Awash in a Sea of Faith: Christianizing the American People*. Cambridge: Harvard University Press, 1990.

Cable, A. Mildred. *The Fulfilment of a Dream of Pastor Hsi's: The Story of the Work in Hwochow*. London: Morgan & Scott and CIM, 1908; reprints, 1917, 1920.

Cable, Mildred, and Francesca French. *Ambassadors for Christ*. London: Hodder & Stoughton, 1935.

———. *The Gobi Desert*. London: Hodder & Stoughton, 1942. New York: Macmillan, 1944. Reprint, with an introduction by Marina Warner, London: Virago Press, 1984.

———. *Something Happened*. London: Hodder & Stoughton, 1934.

———. *The Story of Topsy: Little Lonely of Central Asia*. London: Hodder & Stoughton, 1937.

———. *A Woman Who Laughed: Henrietta Soltau Who Laughed at Impossibilities and Cried: "It Shall he Done."* London: CIM, 1934.

Cameron, Julia. "The Trio and Topsy." OMF Australia website: http://www.au.omf.org/content.asp?id=12669

Carpenter, Joel A. "Propagating the Faith Once Delivered: The Fundamentalist Missionary Enterprise 1920-1945." In Joel A. Carpenter and Wilbert R. Shenk, eds., *Earthen Vessels: American Evangelicals and Foreign Missions 1880-1980*. Grand Rapids: William B. Eerdmans, 1990.

———. *Revive Us Again: The Reawakening of American Fundamentalism*. New York: Oxford University Press, 1997.

Carpenter, Joel A., and Wilbert R. Shenk, eds. *Earthen Vessels: American Evangeli-*

cals and Foreign Missions 1880-1980. Grand Rapids: William B. Eerdmans, 1990.

Carter, Betty Smartt. *I Read It in the Wordless Book: A Novel.* Grand Rapids: Baker Book House, 1996.

Carwardine, Richard. *Trans-atlantic Revivalism: Popular Evangelicalism in Britain and America, 1790-1865.* Westport, Conn.: Greenwood Press, 1978.

Chang, Irene, James Hudson Taylor III, James Hudson Taylor IV, Joyce Wu, Janey Yiu, Lisa Yu, eds. *Christ Alone: A Pictorial Presentation of Hudson Taylor's Life and Legacy.* Hong Kong: OMF Hong Kong, 2005.

Chesney, Kellow. *The Anti-Society: An Account of the Victorian Underworld.* Boston: Gambit Incorporated, 1970.

Cleveland, Marion Elinor. "Lay Leadership Training for Rural Women of the China Inland Mission in West Szechwan." Master's thesis, Biblical Seminary, New York, 1938.

Cliff, Norman. *A Flame of Sacred Love: The Life of Benjamin Broomhall, Friend of China, the Man Behind Hudson Taylor, 1829-1911.* Carlisle, UK: OM Publishing, 1998.

———. "A History of the Protestant Movement in Shandong Province, China, 1859-1951." Ph.D. diss., University of Buckingham, 1995.

Clifford, Nicholas R. *Spoilt Children of Empire: Westerners in Shanghai and the Chinese Revolution of the 1920s.* Hanover, N.H.: University Press of New England, 1991.

Coad, F. Roy. *A History of the Brethren Movement: Its Origins, its Worldwide Development and its Significance for the Present Day.* London: Paternoster Press, 1968.

Coates, P. D. *The China Consuls: British Consular Officers, 1843-1943.* Hong Kong: Oxford University Press, 1988.

Cohen, Paul A. *China and Christianity: The Missionary Movement and the Growth of Chinese Antiforeignism 1860-1870.* Cambridge: Harvard University Press, 1963.

———. *History in Three Keys: The Boxers as Event, Experience, and Myth.* New York: Columbia University Press, 1997.

Collier, Richard. *The General Next to God: The Story of William Booth and the Salvation Army.* New York: E. P. Dutton, 1965.

Collis, Maurice. "Morality and the Opium Trade." In Molly Joel Coye and Jon Livingston, eds., *China Yesterday and Today.* Toronto: Bantam Books, 1975.

Compilation Group for the History of Modern China Series. *The Yi Ho Tuan Movement of 1900.* Beijing: Foreign Languages Press, 1976.

Covell, Ralph R. *W. A. P. Martin: Pioneer of Progress in China.* Washington: Christian University Press, 1978.

———. *Confucius, the Buddha, and Christ: A History of the Gospel in Chinese.* Maryknoll, N.Y.: Orbis Books, 1986.

Bibliography

Coye, Molly Joel, and Jon Livingston, eds. *China Yesterday and Today.* Toronto: Bantam Books, 1975.

Cross, Whitney R. *The Burned-over District: The Social and Intellectual History of Enthusiastic Religion in Western New York, 1800-1850.* Cornell: Cornell University Press, 1950. Reprint, New York: Harper & Row, 1965.

Davies, Rupert, and E. Gordon Rupp, eds. *A History of the Methodist Church in Great Britain.* 4 vols. London: Epworth Press, 1965-88.

Day, Clarence Burton. *Chinese Peasant Cults: Being a Study of Chinese Paper Gods.* Shanghai: Kelly & Walsh, 1940.

de Groot, J. J. M. *The Religion of the Chinese.* New York: Macmillan, 1910.

———. *The Religious System of China: Its Ancient Forms, Evolution, History and Present Aspect, Customs and Social Institutions Connected Therewith.* Leyden: E. J. Brill, 1892.

———. *Sectarianism and Religious Persecution in China: A Page in the History of Religion.* 2 vols. Amsterdam: Johannes Muller, 1903.

Dikotter, Frank. *The Discourse of Race in Modern China.* Stanford: Stanford University Press, 1992.

Dingle, Edwin J. *Across China on Foot; Life in the Interior and the Reform Movement.* Bristol: J. W. Arrowsmith, 1911.

Draper, Kenneth L. "P. W. Philpott and the Christian Workers' Church: Conservative Premillennialism in the Social History of Hamilton." Manuscript. McMaster University. Canadian Baptist Archives.

Drummond, Lewis A. *Spurgeon: Prince of Preachers.* Grand Rapids, Mich.: Kregel Publications, 1992.

Duncan, Sara Jeannette. *The Imperialist.* Toronto, 1904. Reprint, Toronto: McClelland & Stewart, 1984.

Eames, James Bromley. *The English in China: Being an Account of the Intercourse and Relations between England and China from the Year 1600 to the Year 1843 and a Summary of Later Developments.* London: Curzon Press, 1909. Reprint, New York: Barnes and Noble, 1974.

Edkins, Joseph. *Religion in China: Containing a Brief Account of the Three Religions of the Chinese: With Observations on the Prospects of Christian Conversion Amongst that People.* 3rd edition. London: Trubner & Co., 1884.

Edwards, Ebenezer Henry. *Fire and Sword in Shansi: The Story of the Martyrdom of Foreigners and Chinese Christians.* Edinburgh: Oliphant, Anderson & Ferrier, 1900.

Ekvall, Robert B., H. M. Shuman, et al. *After Fifty Years: A Record of God's Working through the Christian and Missionary Alliance.* Harrisburg, Pa.: Christian Publications, 1939.

Eliot, George. *Scenes of Clerical Life.* 1857. Republished London: Penguin, 1973.

Elliott, Brian. *The Making of Barnsley.* Barnsley: Wharncliffe Publishing, 1988.

———, ed. *Aspects of Barnsley: Discovering Local History.* 5 vols. Barnsley: Wharncliffe Publishing, 1993.

Embley, P. L. "The Early Development of the Plymouth Brethren." In Bryan R. Wilson, ed., *Patterns of Sectarianism: Organisation and Ideology in Social and Religious Movements*. London: Heinemann, 1967.

Esherick, Joseph W. *The Origins of the Boxer Uprising*. Berkeley: University of California Press, 1987.

Eskridge, Larry, and Mark Noll, eds. *More Money, More Ministry: Money and Evangelicals in Recent American History*. Grand Rapids: Eerdmans, 2000.

Fairbank, John King. *Chinabound: A Fifty Year Memoir*. New York: Harper & Row, 1982.

Findlay, James F. Jr. *Dwight L. Moody: American Evangelist 1837-1899*. Chicago: University of Chicago Press, 1969.

Forsyth, Robert Coventry. *The China Martyrs of 1900: A Complete Roll of the Christian Heroes Martyred in China in 1900, With Narratives of Survivors*. London: Religious Tract Society, 1904.

Foster, John W. "The Imperialism of Righteousness: Canadian Protestant Missions and the Chinese Revolution, 1925-1928." Ph.D. diss., York University, 1977.

French, Francesca, trans. *The Songs of Pastor Hsi*. London: Morgan & Scott and CIM, 1920.

Frolic, B. Michael, and Paul M. Evans. *Reluctant Adversaries: Canada and the People's Republic of China, 1949-1970*. Toronto: University of Toronto Press, 1991.

Frost, Henry W. "The Days that are Past." In CIM/Toronto and CIM/ABGC. Typescript memoirs, 932 pages.

———. "What Missionary Motives Should Prevail?" In *The Fundamentals*, vol. 12. Chicago: Testimony Publishing, 1915.

———. *The Great Commission*. Philadelphia: CIM, 1934.

———. *The Heathen*. Findlay, Ohio: Fundamental Truth Publishers, 1938.

———. *Miraculous Healing: A Personal Testimony and Biblical Study*. London: Evangelical Press, 1951. Reprint, 1972.

Gagan, Rosemary. *A Sensitive Intelligence: Canadian Methodist Women Missionaries in Canada and the Orient, 1881-1925*. Montreal and Kingston: McGill-Queen's University Press, 1992.

Garfield, Simon. *Mauve: How One Man Invented a Colour that Changed the World*. London: Faber and Faber, 2001.

Gelber, Harry. *Opium, Soldiers and Evangelicals: Britain's 1840-42 War with China and Its Aftermath*. New York: Palgrave Macmillan, 2004.

Germani Ian, and Robin Swales, eds. *Symbols, Myths and Images of the French Revolution: Essays in Honour of James Leith*. Regina: Canadian Plains Research Centre, 1998.

Gernet, Jacques. *China and the Christian Impact: A Conflict of Cultures*. Translated by Janet Lloyd. Cambridge: Cambridge University Press, 1985.

———. *Daily Life in China on the Eve of the Mongol Invasion, 1250-1276*. Ori-

ginally published as *La vie quotidienne en chine, à la veille de l'invasion mongole, 1250-1276*. Translated by H. M. Wright (Stanford: Stanford University Press; London: Allen & Unwin, 1962.
Gilbert, Alan D. *Religion and Society in Industrial England: Church, Chapel and Social Change, 1740-1914*. London: Longmans, 1976.
Gillin, Donald G. *Warlord: Yen Hsi-shan in Shansi Province 1911-1949*. Princeton: Princeton University Press, 1967.
Glover, Archibald E. *A Thousand Miles of Miracle: A Personal Record of God's Delivering Power in China from the Hands of the Imperial Boxers of Shan-si in China*. London: CIM, 1904. 22nd printing 1957. Abridged ed. Singapore: OMF, 1991.
Goertz, Donald. *A Century for the City: Walmer Road Baptist Church 1889-1989*. Toronto: Walmer Road Baptist Church, 1989.
Goforth, Jonathan. *"By My Spirit."* London: Marshall, Morgan & Scott, 1929.
Goforth, Jonathan, and Rosalind Goforth. *Miracle Lives of China*. London: Marshall, Morgan & Scott; Grand Rapids: Zondervan, 1931.
Goforth, Rosalind. *Goforth of China*. Grand Rapids: Zondervan, 1937.
Gosse, Edmund. *Father and Son: A Study of Two Temperaments*. London: Heinemann, 1907. Reprint, 1958.
Grant, John Webster. *A Profusion of Spires: Religion in Nineteenth Century Ontario*. Toronto: University of Toronto Press, 1988.
Greenhalf, Jim. *Salt and Silver: A Story of Hope*. Bradford, Yorkshire: Bradford Libraries, 1998.
Grubb, Norman P. *C. T. Studd: Athlete and Pioneer*. London: Religious Tract Society, 1933. Reprint, Grand Rapids: Zondervan, 1937.
Guinness, Geraldine. See Mrs. Howard Taylor.
Guinness, Joy. *Mrs. Howard Taylor: Her Web of Time*. London: CIM, 1949.
Guinness, Michelle. *The Guinness Legend*. London: Hodder & Stoughton, 1989.
Hamilton, Michael S. "Wheaton College and the Fundamentalist Network of Voluntary Associations, 1919-1965." Paper presented at Conference on Evangelicals, Voluntary Associations and American Public Life, Wheaton College, June 1991.
Hamilton, Pauline G. *To a Different Drum: An Autobiography*. Singapore: OMF, 1984.
Harris, Theodore F. *Pearl Buck: A Biography*. New York: John Day Co., 1969.
Harrison, Henrietta. *The Man Awakened from Dreams: One Man's Life in a North China Village, 1857-1942*. Stanford: Stanford University Press, 2005.
———. "Village Politics and National Politics: The Boxer Movement in Central Shanxi." Unpublished paper, courtesy of the author.
Harrison, J. F. C. *The Second Coming: Popular Millenarianism 1780 1850*. New Brunswick, N.J.: Rutgers University Press, 1979.
Hedin, Sven A. *The Silk Road*. Translated by F. H. Lyon. London: Routledge, 1938.
Hill, Justin. *A Bend in the Yellow River*. London: Phoenix House, 1997.

Hilliard, David Lockhard. *God's Gentlemen: A History of the Melanesian Mission, 1849-1942*. St. Lucia, Queensland, Australia: University of Queensland Press, 1978.
Hopkirk, Peter. *Trespassers on the Roof of the World: The Race for Lhasa*. London: J. Murray, 1982.
Hosie, Sir Alexander. *Three Years in Western China: A Narrative of Three Journeys in Ssu-ch'uan, Kwei-chow, and Yun-nan*. London: George Philip & Son, 1890.
———. *On the Trail of the Opium Poppy: A Narrative of Travel in the Chief Opium-Producing Provinces of China*. Boston: Small Maynard & Company, 1914.
Hoste, D. E. *If I am to Lead . . .* London: OMF, 1968.
Houghton, Frank. *George King: Medical Evangelist*. London: CIM, 1930.
Hunter, Alan, and Kim-Kwong Chan. *Protestantism in Contemporary China*. Cambridge: Cambridge University Press, 1993.
Hunter, Jane. *The Gospel of Gentility: American Women Missionaries in Turn-of-the-century China*. New Haven: Yale University Press, 1984.
Hunter, J. H. *A Flame of Fire: The Life and Work of R. V. Bingham, D.D.* Toronto: Sudan Interior Mission, 1961.
Hussey, Harry. *My Pleasures and Palaces: An Informal Memoir of Forty Years in Modern China*. Garden City, N.Y.: Doubleday, 1968.
Hyatt, Irwin T. *Our Ordered Lives Confess: Three Nineteenth-Century American Missionaries in East Shantung*. Cambridge: Harvard University Press, 1976.
Isichei, Elizabeth. *Victorian Quakers*. London: Oxford University Press, 1970.
James, Francis Huberty. "The Secret Sects of Shantung, with Appendix." *Records of the General Conference of the Protestant Missionaries of China, Held at Shanghai, May 7-20, 1890* (Shanghai, American Presbyterian Mission Press, 1890), pp. 196-202.
Jen Yu-wen. *The Taiping Revolutionary Movement*. New Haven: Yale University Press, 1973.
Johnson, David, Andrew J. Nathan, and Evelyn S. Rawski, eds. *Popular Culture in Late Imperial China*. Berkeley: University of California Press, 1985.
Jordan, David K. *Gods, Ghosts and Ancestors: Folk Religion in a Taiwanese Village*. Berkeley: University of California Press, 1972.
Jordan, David K., and Daniel L. Overmyer. *The Flying Phoenix: Aspects of Chinese Sectarianism in Taiwan*. Princeton: Princeton University Press, 1986.
Kaijage, F. J. "Working-Class Radicals in Barnsley, 1816-20." In Sidney Pollard, ed., *Essays in the Economic and Social History of South Yorkshire*. Barnsley: South Yorkshire County Council, 1976.
Kane, H. H. *The Hypodermic Injection of Morphia: Its History, Advantages and Dangers. Based on the Experience of 360 Physicians*. New York: Chas. Bermingham, 1880.

Bibliography

Kemp, Hugh P. *Steppe by Step: Mongolia's Christians — From Ancient Roots to Vibrant Young Church.* London: Monarch Books and OMF Publishing, 2000.

Kent, John. *Holding the Fort: Studies in Victorian Revivalism.* London: Epworth Press, 1978.

———. "The Wesleyan Methodists to 1849." In *A History of the Methodist Church in Great Britain,* vol. 2, edited by Rupert Davies et al. London: Epworth Press, 1978.

Kruppa, Patricia Stallings. *Charles Haddon Spurgeon: A Preacher's Progress.* New York: Garland Publishing, 1982.

Kuhn, Hans, and Julia Ching. *Christianity and Chinese Religions.* New York: Doubleday, 1989.

Lary, Diana. "Chinese Reds." In Ian Germani and Robin Swales, eds., *Symbols, Myths and Images of the French Revolution: Essays in Honour of James Leith.* Regina: Canadian Plains Research Centre, 1998.

Latimer, Dean, and Jeff Goldberg. *Flowers in the Blood: The Story of Opium.* New York: Franklin Watts, 1981.

Latourette, Kenneth Scott. *A History of Christian Missions in China.* New York: Macmillan, 1929. Reprinted New York: Russell & Russell, 1967.

Lears, T. J. Jackson. *No Place of Grace: Antimodernism and the Transformation of American Culture 1880-1920.* New York: Pantheon Books, 1981.

Lindesmith, Alfred R. *Opiate Addiction.* Bloomington, Ind.: Principia Press, 1947.

Lindsell, Harold. "Faith Missions since 1938," in Wilber Christian Hart, ed., *Frontiers of the Christian World Mission since 1938: Essays in Honor of Kenneth Scott Latourette.* New York: Harper, 1962.

Lodwick, Kathleen L. *"The Chinese Recorder" Index: A Guide to Christian Missions in Asia, 1867-1941.* Wilmington, Del.: Scholarly Resources, 1986.

———. *Crusaders Against Opium: Protestant Missionaries in China, 1874-1917.* Lexington: University Press of Kentucky, 1996.

Long, Kathryn Teresa. *The Revival of 1857-58: Interpreting an American Religious Awakening.* New York: Oxford University Press, 1998.

Longfield, Bradley J. *The Presbyterian Controversy: Fundamentalists, Modernists, and Moderates.* New York: Oxford University Press, 1991.

Lutz, Jessie G. "Karl F. A. Gützlaff: Missionary Entrepreneur." In Suzanne Wilson Barnett and John King Fairbank, eds., *Christianity in China: Early Protestant Missionary Writings.* Cambridge: Harvard University Press, 1985.

Lutz, Jessie G., and R. Ray Lutz, "Karl Gützlaff's Approach to Indigenization: The Chinese Union." In Daniel H. Bays, ed., *Christianity in China: From the Eighteenth Century to the Present.* Stanford: Stanford University Press, 1996.

Malcolm, Kari Torjesen. *We Signed Away Our Lives: How One Family Gave Every thing for the Gospel.* Downers Grove, Ill.: InterVarsity Press, 1990. Reprint, Pasadena: William Carey Library, 2004.

Marsden, George M. *Fundamentalism and American Culture: The Shaping of*

Twentieth-Century Evangelicalism 1870-1925. Oxford: Oxford University Press, 1980.

Martin, W. A. P. *A Cycle of Cathay: Or China South and China North with Personal Reminiscences*. New York: Fleming H. Revell, 1896.

Mathews, R. H. *Kwoyu Primer: Progressive Studies in the Chinese National Language*. Shanghai: CIM, 1938.

McKay, Moira Jane. "Faith and Facts in the History of the China Inland Mission 1832-1905." Master's thesis, University of Aberdeen, 1981.

McKenzie, Brian. "History of Toronto Bible College." Manuscript. 1970. In TBC Archives.

Michell, David J. *In God's Way: The Impressive Centennial Story of the China Inland Mission/Overseas Missionary Fellowship in North America*. Toronto: OMF, 1988.

Michie, Alexander. *Missionaries in China*. London: Edward Stanford, 1891.

Miller, Sheila. *My Book about Hudson*. Singapore: OMF, 1975. Reprint 1988.

———. *Pigtails, Petticoats and the Old School Tie*. Sevenoaks, UK: OMF, 1981.

Mitchell, Peter M. "The Missionary Connection." In Michael B. Frolic and Paul A. Evans, eds., *Reluctant Adversaries: Canada and the People's Republic of China, 1949-1970*. Toronto: University of Toronto Press, 1990.

Moody, William R. *The Life of Dwight L. Moody, By his Son*. New York: Fleming H. Revell, 1900.

Morgan, Henry James, ed. *The Canadian Men and Women of the Time: A Handbook of Canadian Biography*. Toronto: 1898.

Morse, Hosea Ballou. *The International Relations of the Chinese Empire*. 2 vols. London: Longmans, Green, & Co., 1918.

Moser, Leo J. *The Chinese Mosaic: The Peoples and Provinces of China*. Boulder, Colo.: Westview Press, 1985.

Moyles, R. G. *The Blood and Fire in Canada: A History of the Salvation Army in the Dominion, 1882-1976*. Toronto: Peter Martin, 1977.

Müller, George. *A Narrative of Some of the Lord's Dealings with George Muller. Written by Himself*. N.p. 1850.

Mungello, David E. *Curious Land: Jesuit Accommodation and the Origins of Sinology*. Honolulu: University of Hawaii Press, 1989.

Najarian, Nishan J. "Religious Conversion in Nineteenth-Century China: Face-to-face Interaction Between Western Missionaries and the Chinese." In Sidney L. Greenblatt, Richard W. Wilson, and Amy Auerbacher Wilson, eds., *Social Interaction in Chinese Society*. New York: Praeger, 1982.

Naquin, Susan. *Millenarian Rebellion in China: The Eight Trigrams Uprising of 1813*. New Haven: Yale University Press, 1976.

———. "The Transmission of White Lotus Sectarianism in Late Imperial China." In David Johnson et al., eds., *Popular Culture in Late Imperial China*. Berkeley: University of California Press, 1985.

Naquin, Susan, and Evelyn S. Rawski. *Chinese Society in the Eighteenth Century.* New Haven: Yale University Press, 1987.
Needham, George C. *The Life and Labours of Charles H. Spurgeon: The Faithful Preacher, The Devoted Pastor, The Noble Philanthropist, The Beloved College President, and the Voluminous Writer, Author, Etc., Etc.* Boston: D. L. Guernsey, 1883.
Nevius, John Livingston. *Demon Possession.* 1898. 8th edition, Grand Rapids: Kregel Publications, 1968.
Nichols, Francis H. *Through Hidden Shensi.* London: Newnes, 1902.
Niklaus, Robert L., John S. Sawin, and Samuel J. Stoesz. *All for Jesus: God at Work in The Christian and Missionary Alliance Over One Hundred Years.* Camp Hill, Pa.: Christian Publications, Inc., 1986.
Nock, David A. *A Victorian Missionary and Canadian Indian Policy: Cultural Synthesis vs Cultural Replacement.* Waterloo: Wilfrid Laurier University, 1988.
Noll, Mark A. *A History of Christianity in the United States and Canada.* Grand Rapids: William B. Eerdmans, 1992.
Ogren, Olivia C. *The Last Refugees from Shansi: In the Hands of the Chinese Boxers (An Eyewitness Account).* Translated by Samuel Ogren Sr. Victoria, B.C.: Trafford Publishing, 2004.
Orr, J. Edwin. *The Second Evangelical Awakening in Britain.* London: Marshall, Morgan & Scott, 1949.
———. *The Fervent Prayer: The Worldwide Impact of the Great Awakening of 1858.* Chicago: Moody Press, 1974.
Overholtzer, Ruth. "That Little Book." The Child Evangelism Fellowship website http://www.gospelcom.net/cef/wordless.
Overmyer, Daniel L. *Folk Buddhist Religion: Dissenting Sects in Late Traditional China.* Cambridge: Harvard University Press, 1976.
———. *Precious Volumes: An Introduction to Chinese Sectarian Scriptures from the Sixteenth and Seventeenth Centuries.* Cambridge: Harvard University Asia Center, 1999.
Owen, David Edward. *British Opium Policy in China and India.* New Haven: Yale University Press, 1934.
Page, I. E., ed. *John Brash: Memorials and Correspondence.* London: C. H. Kelly, 1912.
Palmer, Alan, ed. *The Age of Optimism.* "Milestones of History," vol. 8. London: Weidenfeld and Nicholson, 1974.
Parker, Michael. *The Kingdom of Character: The Student Volunteer Movement for Foreign Missions (1886-1926).* Lanham, Md.: American Society of Missiology, University Press of America, 1998.
Pearl, Cyril. *Morrison of Peking.* Sydney: Angus & Robertson, 1967.
Peel, J. D. Y. *Religious Encounter and the Making of the Yoruba.* Bloomington: Indiana University Press, 2000.
Pettifer, Julian, and Richard Bradley. *Missionaries.* London: BBC Books, 1990.

Piggin, Stuart. "Assessing Missionary Motivation." In D. Baker, ed., *Religious Motivation: Biographical and Sociological Problems for the Church Historian.* Oxford: Oxford University Press, 1978.

Pill, David H. "Barnsley." In *Yorkshire: The West Riding.* London: Batsford, 1977.

Platt, W. J. *Three Women: Mildred Cable, Francesca French, Evangeline French: The Authorized Biography.* London: Hodder & Stoughton, 1964.

Pollock, John C. *A Cambridge Movement.* London: Marshall, Morgan & Scott, 1953.

———. *The Cambridge Seven.* Basingstoke, UK: Marshall, Morgan & Scott, 1955. Reprint 1985.

———. *Hudson Taylor and Maria: Pioneers in China.* New York: McGraw-Hill and OMF, 1962.

Preston, Diana. *Besieged in Peking: The Story of the 1900 Boxer Rising.* London: Constable, 1999.

Price, Eva Jane. *China Journal 1889-1900: An American Missionary Family During the Boxer Rebellion.* New York: Scribner's, 1989.

Quanfei jilüe (A brief chronicle of the Boxer bandits). Shanghai: Shangyang Shuju, 1903.

Qiao Zhiqiang, ed. *Yihetuanzi Shanxi Diqu shiliou* (Historical materials concerning the Boxer movement in Shanxi). Taiyuan: Shanxi renmin chubanshe, 1982.

Rabe, Valentin H. *The Home Base of American China Missions, 1880-1920.* Cambridge: Harvard University Press, 1978.

Rawlyk, George A., ed. *Aspects of the Canadian Evangelical Experience.* Kingston and Montreal: McGill-Queen's, 1997.

Rawlyk, George A., and Mark A. Noll, eds. *Amazing Grace: Evangelicalism in Australia, Britain, Canada, and the United States.* Grand Rapids: Baker Books, 1993.

Records of the General Conference of the Protestant Missionaries of China, Held at Shanghai, May 7-20, 1890. Shanghai: American Presbyterian Mission Press, 1890.

Reid, Darrel Robert. "'Jesus Only': The Early Life and Presbyterian Ministry of Albert Benjamin Simpson, 1843-1881." Ph.D. diss., Queen's University, Kingston, 1994.

Ren Ch'eng-yuan. *A Tamarisk Garden Blessed with Rain: Or the Autobiography of Pastor Ren.* Translated by Herbert Hudson Taylor and Marshall Broomhall. London: CIM, 1930.

Reynolds, Lindsay. *Footprints: The Beginnings of the Christian and Missionary Alliance in Canada.* Willowdale, Ont.: Christian and Missionary Alliance in Canada, 1982.

———. *Rebirth: The Redevelopment of the Christian and Missionary Alliance in Canada.* Willowdale, Ont.: C&MA in Canada, 1992.

Bibliography

Richard, Timothy. *Forty-Five Years in China: Reminiscences by Timothy Richard.* New York: Frederick A. Stokes Company, 1916.
Rijnhart, Dr. Susie C. *With the Tibetans in Tent and Temple: Narrative of Four Years' Residence on the Tibetan Border, and of a Journey into the Far Interior.* Chicago: Foreign Christian Missionary Society, 1901. Reprint, New York: Fleming H. Revell, 1911.
Robert, Dana L. "'The Crisis of Missions': Premillennial Mission Theory and the Origins of Independent Evangelical Missions." In Joel A. Carpenter and Wilbert R. Shenk, eds., *Earthen Vessels: American Evangelicals and Foreign Missions, 1880-1980.* Grand Rapids: William B. Eerdmans, 1990.
———. *American Women in Mission: A Social History of Their Thought and Practice.* Macon, Ga.: Mercer University Press, 1996.
Rowdon, Harold H. *The Origins of the Brethren 1825-1850.* London: Pickering & Inglis, 1967.
Rowell, Geoffrey. *Hell and the Victorians: A Study of the Nineteenth-Century Theological Controversies Concerning Eternal Punishment and the Future Life.* Oxford: Clarendon Press, 1974.
Rubinstein, Murray A. *The Protestant Community on Modern Taiwan: Mission, Seminary, and Church.* Armonk, N.Y.: M. E. Sharpe, 1991.
Russell, C. Allyn. *Voices of American Fundamentalism: Seven Biographical Studies.* Philadelphia: Westminster Press, 1976.
Saeki, P. Yukio. *The Nestorian Monument in China.* London: Society for Promoting Christian Knowledge, 1916. Reprint 1928.
Sandall, Robert. *The History of the Salvation Army.* Vol. 1, 1865-1878. London: Nelson, 1947. Reprint 1964. Vol. 2, 1878-1886. 1950. Reprint 1966.
Sandeen, Ernest R. *The Roots of Fundamentalism: British and American Millenarianism 1800-1930.* Chicago: University of Chicago Press, 1970.
Sauer, Christof. "Reaching the Unreached Sudan Belt: Guinness, Kumm, and the Sudan-Pioneer-Mission." D.Th. diss., UNISA, South Africa, 2002.
Saunders, Alexander R. *A God of Deliverances: The Story of the Marvellous Deliverances Through the Sovereign Power of God of a Party of Missionaries, When Compelled by the Boxer Rising to Flee from Shan-si, North China.* London: CIM, 1900.
Savage-Landor, A. Henry. *China and the Allies.* New York: Scribner, 1901.
Sawatsky, Ronald. "Elmore Harris: Canadian Baptist Extraordinaire." Graduate paper, University of Toronto, 1980. Copy in TBC Archives.
———. "Henry Martyn Parsons of Knox Church, Toronto (1818-1913)." In *Canadian Society for Presbyterian History Papers,* 1982.
———. "'Looking for That Blessed Hope': The Roots of Fundamentalism in Canada, 1878-1920." Ph.D. diss., University of Toronto, 1985.
Scott, J. M. *The White Poppy: A History of Opium.* London: Heinemann, 1969.
Scott, Paul H. *The Jewel in the Crown.* London: Heinemann, 1966.

Scovel, Myra, and Nelle Keys Bell. *The Chinese Ginger Jars*. New York: Harper & Row, 1962.
Seagrave, Sterling. *The Soong Dynasty*. New York: Harper & Row, 1985.
Shen Fu. *Six Records of a Floating Life*. 1809. Translated by Leonard Pratt and Chiang Su-hui. Markham, Ont.: Penguin, 1983.
Showalter, Nathan D. *The End of a Crusade: The Student Volunteer Movement for Foreign Missions and the Great War*. Lanham, Md.: Scarecrow Press, 1998.
Skinner, G. William, ed. *The City in Late Imperial China*. Stanford: Stanford University Press, 1977.
Smith, Arthur H. *The Uplift of China*. New York: Young People's Missionary Movement, 1909.
Smith, Stanley Peregrine. *China from Within: Or the Story of the Chinese Crisis*. London: Marshall Brothers, 1901.
———. *"The Spiritual Condition of the Heathen": A Reply to Mr. Henry W. Frost, Director of the China Inland Mission in North America*. Shanghai: Commercial Press, n.d.
Soothill, William E. *Timothy Richard of China: Seer, Statesman, Missionary & the Most Disinterested Adviser the Chinese Ever Had*. London: Seeley, Service & Co., 1924.
Sorrell, Mark. *The Peculiar People*. Exeter: Paternoster Press 1979.
Spence, Jonathan D. *Chinese Roundabout: Essays in History and Culture*. New York: W. W. Norton & Company, 1992.
———. *God's Chinese Son: The Taiping Heavenly Kingdom of Hong Xiuquan*. New York: W. W. Norton, 1996.
———. *The Memory Palace of Matteo Ricci*. New York: Viking Penguin, 1984.
———. *The Search for Modern China*. New York: W. W. Norton, 1990.
———. *To Change China: Western Advisors in China 1620-1960*. New York: Little, Brown & Co., 1969.
Spurgeon, Charles Haddon. *C. H. Spurgeon's Autobiography*. Compiled from his diary, letters, and records, by his wife [Susannah T. Spurgeon] and his private secretary [Rev. W. J. Harrald]. 4 vols. London: Passmore and Alabaster, 1897-1900.
———. *Sermons*. 63 vols. London: Passmore & Alabaster. Republished as *Metropolitan Tabernacle Pulpit*. Pasadena, Tex.: Pilgrim Publications.
Stackhouse, John G., Jr. *Canadian Evangelicalism in the Twentieth Century: An Introduction to Its Character*. Toronto: University of Toronto Press, 1993.
Stanley, Brian. *The History of the Baptist Missionary Society 1792-1992*. Edinburgh: T&T Clark, 1992.
Stauffer, Milton T., ed. *The Christian Occupation of China: A General Survey of the Numerical Strength and Geographical Distribution of the Christian Forces in China Made by the Special Committee on Survey and Occupation, China Continuation Committee 1918-1921*. Shanghai: China Continuation Committee, 1922.

Steer, Roger. *George Müller: Delighted in God*. London: Hodder & Stoughton, 1975.
Stephenson, George M. *The Religious Aspects of Swedish Immigration*. Minneapolis: University of Minnesota Press, 1932. Reprint, New York: Arno Press and New York Times, 1969.
Stevens, Keith. *Chinese Gods: Fo Hsiang Shen Hsiang*. London: Collins & Brown, 1997.
Stock, Eugene V. *The History of the Church Missionary Society: Its Environment, Its Men and Its Work*. 4 vols. London: CMS. Vol. 3, 1899. Vol. 4, 1916.
Stott, Grace. *Twenty-Six Years of Missionary Work in China*. London: Hodder & Stoughton, 1897.
Styles, John. *Titus Salt and Saltaire: Industry and Virtue*. Shipley, Yorkshire: Salts Estates, 1994.
Sultzberger, Hartmann Henry. *All About Opium*. London: Wertheimer, Lea and Company, 1884.
Sunzi. *The Art of War*. Translated by John Minford. New York: Viking, 2002.
Synan, Vinson. *The Holiness-Pentecostal Movement in the United States*. Grand Rapids: William B. Eerdmans, 1971.
Taylor, Harold. "Bleachworks of Barnsley & their Industrial Archaeology." In Brian Elliott, ed., *Aspects of Barnsley: Discovering Local History*. 1993.
———. "Taylor Row and the Handloom Weavers of Barnsley." In Brian Elliott, ed., *Aspects of Barnsley*, vol. 5. Barnsley: Wharncliffe Publishing, 1993.
Taylor, Geraldine. *Pastor Hsi: A Struggle for Chinese Christianity*. Inverness, Scotland: Christian Focus Publications, 1997.
Taylor, Mrs. Howard, under her maiden name Geraldine Guinness. *The Story of the China Inland Mission*. 2 vols. London: Morgan & Scott and CIM, 1892.
Taylor, Mrs. Howard. *Borden of Yale*. London: CIM, 1926.
———. *Pastor Hsi*. London: CIM. Vol. 1, *One of China's Scholars: The Culture and Conversion of a Confucianist*. 1901. Vol. 2, *One of China's Christians*. 1903.
———. *Pastor Hsi: Confucian Scholar and Christian*. Abridged edition. London: CIM, 1903. 28th printing 1991.
———. *Guinness of Honan*. London: CIM, 1930.
Taylor, Mrs. Howard, and Dr. Howard Taylor. *Hudson Taylor and the China Inland Mission*. London: CIM. Vol. 1, *Hudson Taylor in Early Years: The Growth of a Soul*. 1911. Vol. 2, *The Growth of a Work of God*. 1918.
———. *Faith's Venture*. London: CIM, 1932. U.S. edition: *Hudson Taylor's Spiritual Secret*.
———. *"By Faith": Henry W. Frost and the China Inland Mission*. Philadelphia: CIM, 1938.
Taylor, James. *The Age We Live in: A History of the Nineteenth Century, from the Peace of 1815 to the Present Time*. London: William Mackenzie, 1900.
Taylor, James Hudson. *China: Its Spiritual Need and Claims*. London: CIM, 1865. Republished in several editions as *China's Spiritual Need and Claims*.

———. *A Retrospect*. London: CIM, 1875. Reprint. *Hudson Taylor*. Minneapolis: Bethany House Publishers, 1986.
Thompson, E. P. *The Making of the English Working Class*. London: Victor Gollancz, 1963.
Thompson, Phyllis. *D. E. Hoste: "A Prince with God": Hudson Taylor's Successor as General Director of the China Inland Mission 1900-1935*. London: CIM, 1947.
———. *Each to Her Post: Six Women of the China Inland Mission*. Sevenoaks: Hodder & Stoughton and OMF, 1982.
Thompson, Roger R. "Twilight of the Gods in the Chinese Countryside: Christians, Confucians, and the Modernizing State, 1861-1911," in Daniel H. Bays, ed., *Christianity in China: From the Eighteenth Century to the Present*. Stanford: Stanford University Press, 1996.
Trevor-Roper, Hugh R. *The Hermit of Peking: The Hidden Life of Sir Edmund Backhouse*. London: Macmillan, 1976.
Tsou Mingteh, "Christian Missionary as Confucian Intellectual: Gilbert Reid (1857-1927) and the Reform Movement in Late Qing." In Daniel H. Bays, ed., *Christianity in China: From the Eighteenth Century to the Present*. Stanford: Stanford University Press, 1996.
Van Die, Marguerite, ed. *Religion and Public Life in Canada: Historical and Comparative Perspectives*. Toronto: University of Toronto Press, 2001.
Varg, Paul A. *Missionaries, Chinese and Diplomats: The American Protestant Movement in China, 1890-1952*. Princeton: Princeton University Press, 1958.
Wacker, Grant, and Daniel H. Bays, eds. *The Foreign Missionary Enterprise at Home: Explorations in North American Cultural History*. Mobile: University of Alabama Press, 2003.
Wagner, Gillian. *Barnardo*. London: Eyre & Spottiswoode, 1979.
Wagner, Rudolf G. *Re-enacting the Heavenly Vision: The Role of Religion in the Taiping Rebellion*. Berkeley: Institute of East Asian Studies, University of California Press, 1982.
Wakeman, Frederic W. Jr. *Strangers at the Gate: Social Disorder in South China 1839-1861*. Berkeley: University of California Press, 1966.
Walker, William O., III. *Opium and Foreign Policy: The Anglo-American Search for Order in Asia, 1912-1954*. Chapel Hill: University of North Carolina Press, 1991.
Walls, Andrew F. "The American Dimension in the History of the Missionary Movement." In Joel A. Carpenter and Wilbert R. Shenk, eds., *Earthen Vessels: American Evangelicals and Foreign Missions, 1880-1980*. Grand Rapids: William B. Eerdmans, 1990.
Watson, Mary E. *Robert and Louisa Stewart: In Life and in Death*. London: Marshall Brothers, 1895. Available at http://anglicanhistory.org/asia/china/stewart/05.html.
Wehrle, Edmund S. *Britain, China, and the Anti-Missionary Riots, 1891-1900*. Minneapolis: University of Minnesota Press, 1966.

Bibliography

Westermeyer, Joseph. *Poppies, Pipes, and People: Opium and Its Use in Laos.* Berkeley: University of California Press, 1982.

White, William Charles. *Chinese Temple Frescos: A Study of Three Wall Paintings of the Thirteenth Century.* Toronto: University of Toronto Press, 1940.

———. *Chinese Jews: A Compilation of Matters Relating to the Jews of K'aifeng Fu.* 3 vols. Toronto: University of Toronto Press, 1942. Reprint. 1 vol. 1966.

Whyte, Bob. *Unfinished Encounter: China and Christianity.* London: Fount Paperbacks, 1988.

Williams, Samuel Wells. *The Middle Kingdom: A Survey of the Geography, Government, Literature, Social Life, Arts, and History of the Chinese Empire and its Inhabitants.* New York: Charles Scribner's Sons, 1895. Reprint, New York: Paragon Book Reprint, 1966.

Williamson, H. R. *British Baptists in China 1845-1952.* London: Carey Kingsgate Press, 1957.

Wilson, Bryan R. *Patterns of Sectarianism: Organisation and Ideology in Social and Religious Movements.* London: Heinemann, 1967.

Wood, Frances. *No Dogs and Not Many Chinese: Treaty Port Life in China 1843-1943.* London: John Murray, 1998.

Wu Jingzi [Wu Ching-tzu]. *The Scholars.* Translated by Yang Hsien-yi and Gladys Yang. New York: Columbia University Press, 1992.

Articles

Baller, Frederick W. "A Visit to Mr. Hsi." *China's Millions* (GB), April 1886.

Bays, Daniel H. "Chinese Popular Religion and Christianity Before and After the 1949 Revolution: A Retrospective View." *Fides et Historia: Journal of the Conference on Faith and History,* Winter/Spring 1991.

———. "Christianity and the Chinese Sectarian Tradition." *Ch'ing Shih Wen-t'i* 4, no. 7 (June 1982): 33-50.

Cardwell, J. E. "Annual Report for Po-yang Lake District, Kiang-si, 1883." *China's Millions* (GB), August 1883, 103-4.

Carpenter, Joel A. "Fundamentalist Institutions and the Rise of Evangelical Protestantism, 1929-1942." *Church History,* March 1980.

Drake, Samuel B. "The Story of Mr. Fan, of P'ing Yang Fu, Shan-si." *China's Millions* (GB), September 1883, 127-29.

———. "Shan-si Province: Eighteen Persons Baptised." *China's Millions* (GB), September 1884.

Dudgeon, John. "Is Morphia Volatilizable?" *Chinese Recorder,* January-February 1883, 56-63.

———. "Notes of a Bible Tour in South Eastern Shansi." *Chinese Recorder,* January 1871.

———. (Unnamed author, probably Dudgeon.) "Report of the Opium Refuge at Peking for 1878-79," *Chinese Recorder*, May-June 1880, 196-207.
Elliston, W. L. "The Work of God in P'ing-yang, Shan-si Province." *China's Millions* (GB), April 1881.
"F." "Colour-Names in Mencius." *Chinese Recorder*, January-February 1880, 59-64.
Gewurtz, Margo S. "Do Numbers Count? A Report on a Preliminary Study of the Christian Converts of the North Henan Mission, 1890-1925." *Republican China* 10, no. 3 (June 1985): 18-26
Hervey, G. N. "Spurgeon as a Preacher." *Christian Review* 22 (1857): 296-316.
Hill, David. "The Kü Jän Examination." *Chinese Recorder*, March-April 1880, 143-46.
———. Speech to CIM annual meeting. *China's Millions* (GB), July-August 1881, 89-93.
———. "The Triennial Examinations for the Kü Jän Degree." *Chinese Recorder*, November-December 1979, 463-64.
Hoste, D. E. "Tidings from Kuh-wu Hien" [Quwu Xian]. *China's Millions* (GB), January 1886, 8.
"The Hung-t'ung Conference, Aug. 1st and 2nd: Deeply Interesting Native Testimony; Testimony of Mr. Hsi." *China's Millions* (GB), January 1887, 7.
Liu Yuan. "Life in a Museum: Pingyao represents the struggle between history and modernity." *Asiaweek*, 15 December 2000.
Moule, G. E. "The Opium Refuge and General Hospital at Hangchow." *Chinese Recorder*, September-October 1874, 256-62.
Newman, R. K. "Opium Smoking in Late Imperial China: A Reconsideration." *Modern Asian Studies* 29, no. 4 (1995).
Overmyer, Daniel L. "Alternatives: Popular Religious Sects in Chinese Society." *Modern China* 7, no. 2 (April 1981): 156-57.
Piggott, Thomas W. "Shan-si Province: The Work in P'ing-yang Fu and the Surrounding Towns and Villages." *China's Millions* (GB), September 1884.
Richard, Timothy. "Christian Persecutions in China — Their Nature, Causes, Remedies." *Chinese Recorder*, July-August 1884.
———. "The Political Status of Missionaries and Native Christians in China." *Chinese Recorder*, March 1885.
Schofield, R. H. A. "Medical Mission, T'ai-yüen Fu, 1882." *Chinese Recorder*, p. 136.
"Sermons and Sermonizers." *Fraser's Magazine* 55 (1857): 84-94.
Shek, Richard. "The Revolt of the Zaili, Jindan Sects in Rehe (Jehol), 1891." *Modern China* (April 1980): 162-86.
Smith, Stanley Peregrine. "A Retraction." *Chinese Recorder*, July 1900, 364-65.
———. "Six Years in China." *China's Millions* (GB), July 1892.
Taylor, Mrs. Howard (née Geraldine Guinness). "Through the Heart of China." *China's Millions* (NA), September 1894-May 1985.
Taylor, James Hudson. "Itineration Far and Near as an Evangelizing Agency"

(speech to the Shanghai Missionary Conference, 12 May 1877). *China's Millions* (GB), October 1877, 122-25.

———. "Special Notice." *China's Millions* (GB), October 1875, 44.

———. "To Every Creature." *China's Millions* (GB), December 1889, 171-73; February 1890, 14-17.

"The Testimony of Mr. Hsi." *China's Millions* (GB), January 1887, 5-6.

Tiedemann, R. Gary. "Christianity and Chinese 'Heterodox Sects': Mass Conversion and Syncretism in Shandong Province in the Early Eighteenth Century." *Monumenta Serica* 44 (1996): 339-82.

Wong Læ-djun. Annual report for "Cheh-kiang, North." *China's Millions* (GB), August 1883, 105-6.

Websites

"Armchair Traveller: Shanxi Province." http://essl.ps.uci.edu/~oliver/shanxi.html.

Book reviews: www.acloserlook.com/.

OMF Australia website: http://www.au.omf.org/content.asp?id=12669.

Carter, Betty Smartt. bettycart@juno.com.

Child Evangelism Fellowship. http://www.gospelcom.net/cef/wordless.

"The Christian Hall Of Fame." Canton, Ohio: Canton Baptist Temple. http://www.cantonbaptist.org/halloffame/spurgeon.htm.

Etler, Dennis A. "The Fossil Evidence for Human Evolution in China." http://www.cruzio.com/~cscp/index.htm.

Shanxi Evergreen Service website: www.evergreenchina.org/index.htm.

Wally the Gospel Walnut, "a Creative Object Lesson made from a Jumbo Sized Real Walnut with wordless book Ribbons Inside that scroll in and out of the mouth." See website www.kedhelper.com/CCM/walnut.htm.

Watson, Mary E. *Robert and Louisa Stewart: In Life and in Death.* http://anglicanhistory.org/asia/china/stewart/05.html.

Index

Aldersley, Mary Ann, 75-76
Alliance, Christian and Missionary. *See* Christian and Missionary Alliance (C&MA); *and see also* CIM and Associate Missions
Alliance missions. *See* CIM, Associate Missions of; Christian and Missionary Alliance; German Alliance Mission; Scandinavian Alliance Mission; Swedish Alliance Mission; The Evangelical Alliance Mission
American evangelicalism, 293-95, 298-99, 304, 317-18; and denominations, 326-27; and faith healing, 304, 310-11; and Franson's floods, 319-20, 334; and fundamentalism, 306-7, 386; and American temperament, 9, 306, 312-13, 330. *See also individual evangelists by name:* Finney; Franson; Moody; Palmer; *and see also* fundamentalism; pentecostalism
American evangelicals and transatlantic revivalism, 298-99; American influence on British evangelicalism, 46; and on Canadian evangelicalism, 295, 301, 303-5; and on Swedish evangelicalism, 317-20; and Moody network, 9-10, 167, 188, 301; and Niagara Conference, 294, 299;
and Revival of 1857-59, 83-85. *See also* British evangelicals and transatlantic revivalism; Canadian evangelicals and transatlantic revivalism; Sweden, revivals in
American government (United States) in China, 71, 305, and Boxer Indemnity, 425
American missions in China, 340, 425; and Chicago Mission Among the Mongols, 343, 364-65, 414; and Christian and Missionary Alliance (International Missionary Alliance Mission), 304, 319, 342-43, 355, 365, 414; and Franson's floods, 319-20, 334, 365, 414; and Oberlin Band, 274-77, 396, 408, 414-15, 426; and Scandinavian Alliance Mission, 268, 319-20, 334, 357, 365, 414
American missionaries in CIM. *See* CIM organization in United States
Anglican churches: Church of England, 84, 98-99; and Brethren movement, 55, 57, 86, 98, 210; and Anglicans in CIM: as applicants, 100, 109-10, 114, 192-93, 207-8, 281, 330, 416; and as referees, 211-15; C. of E. and conditional immortality, 189; and interdenominational cooperation, 19, 98; and Mildmay Insti-

Index

tute, 99. *See also* Church of England Zenana Mission; Church Missionary Society; Holiness teachings; Keswick movement; Mildmay Institute

Anglican churches: Anglican Church of Canada, 299; and Anglicans in CIM: as applicants, 307, 327; and on Toronto Council, 306-8; and Anglican missions, 302; and Wycliffe College, 306-8

Anglican churches: Episcopalian Church of United States, 327

Anglo-Chinese Society for the Suppression of the Opium Traffic/Trade (SSOT). *See* Society for the Suppression of the Opium Trade

Anhui. *See* China, provinces of CIM work: Anhui

anti-Christian (anti-foreign) reaction in China, 115-17, 134, 344-45, 351, 385; anti-Christian pamphlets, 115-16; persecution of converts, 256, 284, 372, 378, 381, 392-93; riots, 26, 129-31, 335, 359, 372; Chinese suspicion of women missionaries, 122-23, 240, 356-57, 389. *See also* Boxer Uprising; Chinese government and missionary cases; Hsi

anti-opium lobby. *See* CIM and anti-opium lobby; opium: and anti-opium lobby; opium refuges

anti-slavery lobby, 89, 92, 190

Assemblies of God, 449. *See also* pentecostal currents in CIM; revivals, and pentecostal revivals

Associate Missions of CIM. *See* CIM, Associate Missions of

Associated Gospel Churches of Canada, 303

Australia. *See* CIM organization in Australia

Baller, Frederick William, 352; and *Baller's Primer*, 228; and CIM language school, 29-30, 228, 231-32; scholar, 25; in Shanxi, 231, 281, 441

Baller, Mrs. Frederick William (Mary Bowyer), Lammermuir party, 100, 106 (photo), 107, 110; rebaptized, 114

Baptist church in Australia, 301

Baptist churches in Britain, 84, 88, 189; and Baptists in CIM: as applicants, 101, 102, 109-10, 205, 234; and as referees, 194, 210-12, 214, 216; Baptists and other denominations, 19, 57, 114, 342; and JHT, 47, 94; Pastors' College, 88, 298. *See also* Spurgeon

Baptist churches in Canada, 310; and Baptists in CIM: as applicants, 326-28; and on Toronto Council, 316; and Baptist missions, 302

Baptist churches in China: Baptist enclave of CIM, 268, 342. *See also* Baptist Missionary Society

Baptist churches of United States, 342; and Baptist applicants to CIM, 326, 328

Baptist Missionary Society (BMS), 92; and Boxer Uprising, 410-12, 423, 426; and CIM, 149, 167, 268; and CIM missionaries join BMS, 267, 268-69, 272-73, 351, 363, 387, 409; and Richard, 102-3, 143, 149, 268-74; in Shandong, 103, 167, 270; in Shanxi, 143 (map), 149, 167, 268-69, 284, 363. *See also* Baptist churches in China

Barnardo, Thomas, 21, 89-90, 207; rejected by CIM, 102, 302; as CIM referee, 193, 211, 215, 349

Barnardo Homes, 88, 218, 237; in Canada, 88, 298; and CIM, 20, 90, 97, 102

Barnsley, Yorkshire, 38 (photo), 53, 440; JHT's childhood in, 36-38, 41-43; later visits to, 64; Wesley in, 38 40; and Miss Rose, 100, 110, 114

Beauchamp, Sir Montague, 86; and Cambridge Seven, 208, 219 (photo), 220 (photo), 221, 383; in Shanxi, 222, 281, 284; and pentecostal tongues, 222; and philanthropy, 208, 221, 352

Berger, William Thomas, 94, 107, 187, 296; and CIM: co-founder of, 62-63, 93-94; financial contributions to, 93, 96, 190;

481

INDEX

home director of, 103, 105, 131; resignation from, 182, 188-90; and Chinese Evangelisation Society, 62, 93; and conditional immortality, 188-89, 337; advice to JHT, 188, 190. *See also* CIM organization in Britain; CIM organization in Britain: London Council
Berger, Mrs. William Thomas (Mary), 63, 94, 122
Bible college movement in Britain, 97, 188, 298. *See also* East London Missionary Training Institute; Mildmay Institute; Pastors' College; Spurgeon
Bible college movement in Canada, 298, 315-17. *See also* Toronto Bible College; Vancouver Bible Training School
Bible college movement in United States, 188, 207, 298, 314, 315, 324. *See also* Bible Institute of Los Angeles; Christian and Missionary Alliance: Nyack Institute; Moody Bible Institute; Philadelphia College of the Bible
Bible Institute of Los Angeles (BIOLA), 298, 312, 314
Bible Union of China, 444
Billy Graham Center Archives, 19
Bingham, Roland Victor, 311-12, 452. *See also* Sudan Interior Mission
Blatchley, Emily, 194; Lammermuir party, 101, 106 (photo), 107, 110; JHT's mouthpiece, 182-83, 190. *See also* CIM organization in Britain, under Miss Blatchley
blitz-conversion: Gutzlaff's goal of mass conversion, 119-20, 437; adopted by JHT, 3-4, 75, 359, 297, 340, 440-43; thunder and lightning conversion, 39, 52, 69, 176. *See also* evangelistic methods; Gutzlaff
Booth, General William, 61, 63, 90, 207, 239. *See also* Salvation Army
Botham, Thomas, 239, 359
Bourne, Consul F. S., 18, 29

Boxer Indemnity, 425, 431, 435; Boxer settlement in Shanxi, 422-24
Boxers: Boxers United in Righteousness, 395; and children join Boxers, 396; invulnerability rituals of, 396-98, 401, 407, 412; and origins in Shandong, 394, 400-402; and Boxers in Shanxi, 394-402, 405, 419
Boxer Uprising in China: Allied armies, 417-18, 422; and siege of the Beijing legations, 400-402, 409-10, 417; and fight of Empress Dowager, 417-18; and Frost's visit to China, 444; in Gansu, 415; in Inner Mongolia, 413-14, 418; and killing edict, 410, 415; in Shaanxi, 415
Boxer Uprising in Shanxi, causes of: as anti-Christian movement, 401, 406; as anti-foreign (anti-imperialist) movement, 402, 412; and chaos, 403, 406; and CIM's train of events, 367, 394; and drought, 405, 408, 424; and idol taxes, 158, 403-4, 423, 424; and government support, 396, 399-400, 405-6; and village tensions, 404-5; and opium, 408-9; and Roman Catholics, 404-6; and rumors, 406-8, 412, 414, 421; and sorcery by Christians, 405-8; and Yuxian (governor), 396, 401, 409, 410, 412-13, 424
Boxer Uprising in Shanxi, events of, *in chronological order:*
Fining Time (April to 26 June 1900): 409; and Boxers and burning churches, 399 (illustration), 404; and looting, 398-99; missionary reaction to, 396, 402-3, 407-8, 410, 414; and recanting Christians, 399-400, 404, 428
Killing Time (26 June to September 1901): 400, 409, 410-15, 419; and deaths of Chinese, 162 (photo), 398, 400, 403, 404-6, 407-8, 413, 414, 422-23, 425-26; and deaths of missionaries: execution by governor, 403, 411-13, 415; and elsewhere in Shanxi, 413-

482

Index

15, 419; and flight of Empress Dowager, 142, 418-19; and flight of missionaries, 415-16, 417 (photo), 419-20
Torturing Time (September to December 1900), 400, 409, 421-22, 427, 431
aftermath (after 1901), 421-26; and Boxer settlement, 422-26; and demoniacal manifestation, 430; and Goforth's revival, 430-31; and opium, 428-30; and *Pastor Hsi*, 455-56
and rebuilding the missions, 426-27; and Shanxi spirits, 421, 431, 441; and Shanxi University, 423, 435-36. *See also* China, government of, and Boxer Uprising; CIM, and Boxer Uprising. *For individual places, see* Shanxi: cities

Brethren movement: in Britain, 55-57, 85, 89, 188, 301; in Canada, 310, 327; and influence on CIM, 193, 210, 237, 310, 330; and as CIM referees, 210-15; Brethren and Church of England, 55, 57, 86, 98-99; and conditional immortality, 189; and Open Brethren, 57, 62, 94, 188, 193; and prophecy, 55-57, 89, 97; and influence on JHT, 54, 57-58, 62, 92-94, 96-97; and in United States, 327. *See also* Berger; Groves; Guinness; Howard; Müller

Brethren, Plymouth (PB), 21, 86; and in Canada, 295, 298, 309, 327-28; and influence on CIM, 94, 102, 193, 197, 295, 301; and as CIM referees, 210, 213; and PB exclusiveness, 19, 57, 447; and prophecy, 55-57; and influence on JHT, 47, 54-55, 60, 76, 94, 188; PBs in United States, 328. *See also* Darby

British evangelicals and transatlantic revivalism: American influence on British evangelicalism, 46, 413; British influence on American evangelicalism, 9, 188, 209, 293, 298-99, 308, 319, 324; and on Canadian evangelicalism, 295-96, 298-99; and Moody network, 9-10, 167, 188, 301; and Niagara Conference, 293-94, 299; and Revival of 1857-59, 83-85. *See also* American evangelicals and transatlantic revivalism; Canadian evangelicals and transatlantic revivalism

British government, 49-50, 130-31, 200-201; and anti-opium lobby, 199-201; and British Empire, 49, 209, 218, 292, 301; and CIM, 20, 131, 201; and Foreign Office, 20, 117-18, 130-31, 357; and Opium Wars, 48-50, 77; and British treaties with China, 50, 51, 53, 115, 118-19, 158-60, 163, 201.

British government in China: ambassadors of, 116-17, 129-30, 344, 356; and Boxer Indemnity, 423-25; and Boxers, 403; and CIM, 118-19, 123, 129-32; consuls of, 15, 18, 26, 29, 51, 115-18, 130, 137, 184, 284, 343-44; and consuls threaten to revoke passports, 17-18, 132, 221; and high tides of imperialism, 297, 338-39, 367; and opium / morphine trade, 15, 48-50; and threats of violence against Chinese (gunboat diplomacy), 116-17, 130-32, 187, 234, 236; and treaty rights, 18, 50, 118-19, 129-31, 160, 163, 284, 343-44. *See also* Chinese government; Opium Wars

Broomhall, Anthony James, CIM historian, 19, 22-24, 65-66, 125, 227, 233, 401; and CIM/OMF Archives, 19. *See also citations in text and footnotes*

Broomhall, Benjamin, 21, 92-93, 190-92, 201; and anti-opium lobby, 14, 191, 199, 201-2; and anti-slavery lobby, 190, 199; as CIM home secretary, 191-92, 194, 196, 225, 227, 237, 332; and CIM North American branch, 300, 329-30; *The Evangelisation of the World*, 209, 292; and Methodist church, 190, 192, 194, 214; retirement from CIM, 202; relations with JHT, 22, 26, 93, 191, 300, 312, 458; and YMCA, 92, 190, 199, 237

Broomhall, Mrs. Benjamin (Amelia Hudson Taylor): JHT's sister, 21, 43, 47, 53,

483

INDEX

92, 114; home mother of CIM, 21, 93, 107, 190-91, 196-97, 458
Broomhall, Edith. *See* Wallace, Mrs. Robert (Edith Broomhall)
Broomhall family, 21, 187, 191, 227n.30, 234, 236
Broomhall, Gertrude. *See* Hoste, Mrs. Dixon Edward (Gertrude Broomhall)
Broomhall, Marshall, London Home Director, 191, 458; as CIM historian, 208; and China Council, 227n.30; in Shanxi, 392, 441
Brownlee, Edgar A., Canadian Home Director, 312, 317, 328
Buck, Pearl, 431
Burma, CIM in, 137, 193, 226
Burns, William Chalmers, 68-69, 119; translates *Pilgrim's Progress*, 71, 157, 252; opposes Shangdi (as name of God), 157

Cable, A. Mildred, 388 (photo), 432 (photo); author, 197, 427, 440; in Central Asia, 25, 431-35; in Shanxi, 427, 429-30; and Topsy, 432-35; and the Trio, 25, 197, 431-35, 440
Cambridge Seven, 206-9, 219 (photo), 220 (photo), 291-92; and their arrival in China, 221-22; in Shanxi, 222-23, 280-81, 383, 387; work under Pastor Hsi, 280-81, 283, 288, 372, 383, 441, 443. *See also individual members by name:* Beauchamp, Cassels, Hoste, A. Polhill Turner, C. Polhill Turner, Smith, Studd.
Canada: Hamilton, 83, 295; Toronto the Good, 299, 301-9, 322, 324; Vancouver, 298, 308, 314
Canadian evangelicalism, and CIM Toronto Council, 296, 306-9; and denominations, 295, 299, 301-2, 306-10, 326-27; and fundamentalism, 292, 299, 306-7; overseas missions of, 301-2; and orphanage movement, 88, 295-96, 298; and Revival of 1857, 83, 295; and Student Volunteer Movement, 301; and Canadian evangelical temperament, 299, 317. *See also* CIM organization in Canada; Sudan Interior Mission; Toronto Bible College; Vancouver Bible Training School
Canadian evangelicals and transatlantic revivalism: British associations in Canada, 298-99; and Canada as hyphen in Anglo-American missionary alliance, 294-95, 298-99; and Canadian influence on American evangelicals, 293-94, 298-99; and CIM as linchpin of evangelical alliance in Toronto, 299, 302, 306-7, 311-12, 445; and in Vancouver, 298n.26; and CIM expands from Canada to U.S., 315, 317, 320-29, 445; and JHT's visits to North America, 293-97, 301-2, 304, 312, 315, 317, 324
Cassels, Bishop William Wharton, and Cambridge Seven, 207-8; and Church of England, 205, 207-8; bishop of East Sichuan, 208, 281, 308, 370; in Shanxi, 222-23, 281, 383, 441. *See also* Cambridge Seven
Catholics, Roman, 68, 328; and Boxer settlement, 421-22; and Boxer Uprising in Shanxi, 403-5, 411-13, 415, 419; and Catholic missions in China, 14, 115-16, 184, 335; and in Shanxi, 146, 148, 153, 158-60, 274, 283; and contextualization of Christianity, 6, 121, 136, 169, 156-58; and idol taxes, 158-59, 403, 421
Chefoo Schools, 186, 326, 330, 345, 352. *See also* CIM organization in China
Ch'eng Hsiu-chi. *See* Jakobsen, Anna
Chicago, 10, 188, 329. *See also* Franson; Moody; Moody Bible Institute; Scandinavian Alliance Mission; Wheaton College
Chicago Mission Among the Mongols, 343, 364-65, 414. *See also* China, provinces of CIM work: Inner Mongolia; CIM, Associate Missions of
Child Evangelism Fellowship, 5n.6, 10

484

Index

children, evangelism of, 5, 9, 88-89, 241. See also orphanages

children, treating Chinese like, 5, 19, 119-20, 240-41, 443

China, Qing government of, in Beijing, 49-50, 116-17; and Boxer Indemnity, 425; and Boxer Uprising, 401-2, 405, 410, 413, 415; and Empress Dowager, 339, 401-2, 415, 417-19; and Hundred Days of Reform, 272, 339; and missionary cases, 116, 158-60, 344; and morphine trade, 15; and opium trade, 15, 49, 199, 202, 243-44, 247; and Opium Wars: First, 43, 48-50, 53, 129; Second, 48, 77, 115, 116; and Sino-Japanese War (1894), 360-61; and unequal treaties, 50-51, 115-17, 158-60, 163; and Zongli Yamen (Foreign Office), 15, 116-17, 158, 403

China, government of, at local level: magistrates, 14, 27, 117, 158, 236, 259, 370; provincial governors, 129, 236, 284, 344, 401, 415

China, government of, in Shanxi: and Boxer settlement, 422-26; and Boxer Uprising, 395-96, 399-400, 401-3, 405-6, 411-13, 419, 427; and civil service exams, 170; and Governor Zhou Erxun, 423-24; and Governor Yuxian, 396, 401-3, 409-10, 412-13, 423; and Pastor Hsi, 256, 259, 264, 371; and Shanxi as model province, 421, 435-37. See also Boxer Uprising in Shanxi; Hsi; opium refuges in Shanxi; Shanxi

China, government of, and control of religion: Chinese government and CIM, 17, 117, 129-30, 132; and Chinese church today, 29; and Falun Gong, 29, 165; and Sacred Edict, 158, 229, 250-51; and secret societies, 12, 133, 165, 229, 265; and Taiping rebellion, 53, 67, 114-16, 158

China, missions in: missionary cases, 116, 130-32; and Roman Catholic missions, 14, 115-16, 184, 335; statistics of missionaries, 66, 79, 80-81, 118, 125, 297, 453

China, provinces of CIM work:

Anhui, 129, 136, 345-47; and men's language school in Anqing, 186, 231-33, 335

Gansu: CIM in, 137, 239, 415, 434, 450; opium refuges in, 369, 370; Scandinavian Alliance in, 268

Guizhou, 52, 136, 236

Henan: Canadian Anglican Mission in, 302, 308n.60; Canadian Presbyterian Mission in, 302, 308, 371; CIM in, 144, 308, 345-47; opium refuges in, 161, 369-71. See also Anglican Church of Canada; Presbyterian Church in Canada; Goforth

Hubei, 346-47

Hunan: anti-foreign character of, 115-16, 236, 345; CIM in, 137, 220, 345-48, 390, 458; and Taiping Rebellion, 64, 115

Inner Mongolia, 343, 356, 364-65; and Boxer Uprising, 399, 413-14, 418

Jiangsu, 128, 136, 345, 347; and Jiangsu cities: Nanjing, 64, 71-73, 77, 115, 142; and Yangzhou, 22, 113, 221, 229, 236, 233, 335

Jiangxi, 334, 346-48, 370; indigenous work in, 236-37; and women's river, 237, 240, 335-36

Qinghai, 431-35, 450

Shaanxi: Baptist Missionary Society in, 363; and Boxer safety, 415, 418; CIM in, 13, 52, 142, 345-48, 356 (map); opium in, 202, 369, 370; and Shaanxi cities: Hanzhong, 236, 238; Xi'an, 15, 164, 236, 355, 358-59, 362

Shandong, 11, 52; and Baptist Missionary Society, 103, 167, 270; Boxer Uprising in, 395, 401-2; 330, 345, 352; CIM in, 345-46, 348; and CIM's Chefoo Schools, 186, 326

Shanxi. See Shanxi

Sichuan, 52, 345-47; and CIM/CMS diocese of East Sichuan, 208, 281, 308

Tibet, 136, 208, 238, 329, 431, 450

485

INDEX

Yunnan, 115, 248; CIM in, 25, 137-38, 202, 236, 273, 296, 345-47, 432, 451

Zhejiang, 13, 52; CIM in, 226, 233-36, 239, 332, 345-46, 369-70; and native agency, 129, 233-34, 362-63; and Zhejiang cities: Hangzhou, 123, 125-27; Ningbo, 50, 68-70, 75-77, 79, 120-21, 134; Taizhou, 234-35; Wenzhou, 108, 118, 123-25, 128-29, 133-34, 235. See also CIM organization in China; native agency; Shanghai

Zhili province, 280, 345-46, 348; and Boxer Uprising, 396, 401

China Inland Mission (CIM), and anti-opium lobby, 14-15, 62, 89, 191, 199-202, 298, 314, 359; and archives of CIM/OMF, 16-17, 19-20, 204; and Boxer Indemnity, 425-26; and Boxer Uprising, 410-20, 443; conspiracy of silence surrounding, 16-19, 26-27, 131-32; named Constantly in Motion, 128; critics of, 24, 26, 28, 185, 240, 351, 356-57; as separate denomination, 28, 453; as God's ambassadors, 2, 335; as octopus, 185-86, 196, 217, 227, 233; pioneer explorations by, 136-38, 139-40, 142, 144, 239, 339, 331-35, 388; as special agency, 91; and treaty rights, 18, 118-19, 129-31, 160, 163, 284, 343-44, 350-51. See also individual denominations by name; and also British government in China, and CIM; China, Qing government of, and CIM; evangelistic methods

CIM and Associate Missions, 2, 273, 318-20, 330, 342-43, 355-57, 359; and Boxer Uprising, 414, 427; and Franson's floods, 319-20, 334; and CIM's marriage policy, 320, 357, 359; and pentecostal currents, 317-18, 450, 452. See also Christian and Missionary Alliance; Franson; Simpson; Swedish American missions; Swedish missions

CIM, Associate missions of: Chicago Mission Among the Mongols, 343, 364-65, 414; Finnish Alliance Mission, 319; German Alliance Mission (Germany), 319; Liebenzell Mission, 452; Norwegian Alliance Mission, 450, 452; Pentecostal Missionary Union, 450-51; Scandinavian Alliance Mission (Chicago), 268, 319-20, 334, 414, 450, 452; Swedish Alliance Mission (Sweden), 319; Swedish Holiness Mission (Sweden), 319, 414

CIM and Chinese dress, policy of, 121-22, 206, 233, 235, 248, 235, 337, 357, 361. See also Chinese dress

CIM forward movements: in China, 345, 358-59, 431-32; recruitment campaigns, in chronological order:

Lammermuir party (1865-66), 100-102, 106-10; in China, 120-29, 136, 195, 204, 233-35, 248; and Lammermuir pact, 103-4, 121, 128, 235

the Eighteen (1875-76), 136-37, 139-40, 184-86, 204, 205, 230, 238

the Thirty (1878-79), 186, 204, 230

the Seventy (1882-85), 186, 204, 226

the Cambridge Seven (1885), 206-9, 219 (photo), 292; in China, 220 (photo), 221-23, 280-81, 283, 288, 291, 372, 383, 387;

the Hundred (1886-88), 204, 230 (photo), 339

the Thousand (1890-95), 340

CIM and other mission societies, 273; and Baptist Missionary Society, 149, 267-69, 272-73; and Canadian Presbyterian Mission, 273, 308, 371; and Church Missionary Society, 76, 126, 182, 185, 206, 208, 281; and Oberlin Band, 274, 277, 287

CIM missionaries, applicants in Britain: class background of, 91, 112, 136, 139, 184, 203-5, 206, 248, 321, 330; health of, 203; as JHT's helpers, 104-5, 118, 121, 349; medical education of, 92, 204-5, 246, 278; and ordination, 204-5; qualifications of, 91-92, 181, 203-5, 231; statistics of, 100, 109-10, 186, 192, 195, 197,

486

Index

204-5. *See also* women missionaries in CIM

CIM missionaries, applicants in Canada: class background of, 312, 315, 328-29; denominational background of, 305, 310, 326-28; qualifications of, 302, 307, 316; recruitment of, 295-96, 300, 305, 310, 312, 315-18, 320; statistics of, 316-17, 321-29, 339; and vaccination, 310-11

CIM missionaries and candidates in China: appeals to London, 191, 227, 235, 239, 350; deaths of, 128, 136, 198, 351-52; democracy movement among, 105, 226, 269, 279-80, 330, 350; and experiences in China, 186, 227-29, 231-36, 248-49; and family relationship with CIM, 103, 195, 226, 232, 239, 248, 349, 386, 446-477; as explorers and pioneers, 136-38, 220, 226, 231, 233-40, 389, 431-35; and furloughs, 351-52; health of, 136, 185, 198, 329, 341-42, 351-52, 384; and language study, 125, 221-22, 227-29, 231-33, 250-54; and madness, 352-53; and marriage, 109-10, 120, 198, 204-6, 226-27, 232-33; and interracial marriage, 22, 238-39, 390-91, 427; resignations of, 136, 272, 341; and resignations for theological reasons, 189, 385-86, 447; and the scattering, 140, 192, 227, 233; and settled work, 76, 125-26, 233, 240; and the Shanxi spirits, 268-69, 283-84, 350-51, 354-55, 361-62, 421, 431, 440; and statistics of CIM missionaries, 131, 136, 185-86, 192, 204, 339, 341-42, 345-46, 349, 426; and suicide, 277, 388; and JHT, 126-28, 226-27, 232-33, 235, 239, 273; as a voluntary association, 105, 226, 313, 330, 446-47. *See also* CIM and Chinese dress; CIM principles and practice; Chinese dress; evangelistic methods; women missionaries in CIM

CIM and money, 16, 19, 35-36, 96, 248; and Boxer Indemnity, 425-26; and Chinese employees, 65, 133, 162, 177, 183, 276, 285; and famine relief, 147, 149; and financial contributions in Canada, 305-6, 321-22, 330; and in Britain, 65, 93, 95-96, 131; and in China, 133, 234; and in United States, 294, 330; and CIM's financial principles, 18, 184, 195, 305-6; and Pastor Hsi's refuges, 285, 288, 367-69, 423; money in the bank, 107, 183-84; no solicitation, 18, 21, 44, 46, 63, 66, 81-82, 107, 133, 185, 309, 425; remittances to China, 65, 68, 100, 104, 183-84, 309, 349-50. *See also* CIM principles and practices: policies; Hsi and opium refuges

CIM organization, Councils: relations among Councils, 103-5, 190, 300, 304, 312-13, 446-48, 452; and discord at the top, 16, 195, 227, 349-50, 386; and joint Council meetings, 312-13, 334-35, 386, 444, 447; and JHT's family, 16-17, 19, 22, 90, 193, 227, 296, 333 (photo), 392, 441. *For national Councils and home directors, see* CIM organization *by country*

CIM organization: directors: Deputy China Director, 225; General Directors: 22, 103-5, 225, 283, 447-48. *See also* Griffiths; Hoste; JHT. *For national home directors, see* CIM organization *in each country; and also individuals by name:* Broomhall, Benjamin; Broomhall, Marshall; Brownlee; Frost; Sloan

CIM organization in Australia, 16, 85, 193, 308, 324, 331, 392, 454; founding of Australian branch, 301, 330, 334; Australian Council, 383, 386, 447

CIM organization in Britain, 9, 192-98, 218; and anti-opium lobby, 14, 20, 191, 199-202; and archives of British CIM/OMF, 16-17, 19, 22; evangelical constituency of, 92, 182, 193, 205, 210-16, 237; and financial contributions, 65, 93, 95-96, 131; and organization under Berger, 93-94, 105, 182-84; and under Miss Blatchley, 182, 190; and under

487

INDEX

Broomhall, 190-96, 225, 237, 300; secrecy surrounding CIM, 16, 18, 19, 131, 226; and women's training home, 196-98, 218. *See also* Anglican churches: Church of England, and CIM; Brethren movement, influence on CIM; Brethren, Plymouth, influence on CIM; Milday Institute; Spurgeon; women missionaries in CIM

CIM organization in Britain: London Council, 93, 182; and selecting applicants, 191, 194-98, 218; and China Council, 16, 183-84, 191, 195, 226-27, 239, 248, 349-50, 386, 444; and Council of Management, 190, 192-94, 210-11; and Edinburgh Missionary Conference, 447; function of, 104-5, 194-95, 349-50; members of, 21, 190, 192-95, 196, 210-11; and North American Council, 300-301, 312-13, 329-30, 447; referees of, 190, 192-94, 211-16; and Scottish Council, 205, 194, 214, 258; and JHT, 26, 191, 195, 227, 312-13, 349-50, 386; and JHT's family, 19, 90, 193, 227, 441; and women's training home, 196-98. *See also* Berger; Broomhall; CIM missionaries in China, appeals to London; Henrietta Soltau

CIM organization in Canada, North American branch: applicants to, 294-96, 297, 305, 307, 310-11, 320; and their class background, 309, 315, 321, 324, 328-29; and their denominational background, 298-99, 326-28; and their qualifications, 296, 315, 321, 328-29; and archives of Canadian CIM/OMF, 19; and beginning of North American branch, 295-301, 313-14, 324; and Bible college movement, 298, 315-17, 324; and Canadians in CIM, 220, 292 (photo), 294-96, 321-29; *China's Millions*, North American edition, 314, 445; and CIM's evangelical constituency: local (Toronto), 295, 299, 302-3, 306-9, 316-17, 322, 324-25, 329; and national (Canada), 295-96, 302, 306, 322, 324-29, 445; and continental (United States), 291, 295, 298-99, 308, 315, 317-19, 321-28, 445; CIM and faith healing, 304-5, 310-11; faith principles of, 315; financial contributions to, 294, 305-6, 321-22, 330; financial principles of, 16, 300, 309, 320-21, 328; and fundamentalism, 292, 306-7, 313; and statistics, 294, 322-29, 339, 348. *See also individual denominations; and also* Canadian evangelicalism; Canadian evangelicals and transatlantic revivalism

CIM organization in Canada: Toronto Council, 297, 304, 305, 445-46; and Brownlee, 312, 317, 328; and London Council, 300-301, 312-13, 329-31, 386; members of, 306-9, 313n.78; and North American headquarters (Toronto home), 291-99, 305-6, 312, 320-21; and Sudan Interior Mission, 311-12; and JHT's visits to Canada, 293-97, 300-302, 304, 312; and Toronto Bible College, 316-17; and Vancouver Bible Training School, 298, 308. *See also* Frost

CIM organization in China, 185-86, 225-29, 248-49; and Chefoo Schools, 186, 326, 330, 345, 352; and archives of China CIM/OMF, 19-20; and CIM system, 248, 339, 345-48, 356-57; and concentration and diffusion, 85, 233, 343, 345; and denominational enclaves in CIM: Baptist, 268, 342; and Church of England (East Sichuan), 208, 281, 308, 370; and Head Office in Shanghai, 129, 186, 221-22, 300, 318, 326, 334; and language schools, 186, 228-29, 231-33, 239, 248, 250-54, 280, 335, 346; and medical work, 76, 204-5, 241-42, 245, 278, 365; and statistics of CIM missionaries in China, 131, 136, 186, 192, 204, 339, 340, 345-48; and superintendents, 226, 281, 349-50, 359. *For CIM work in individual provinces, see* China, provinces of

488

Index

CIM work. *See also* British government in China, and CIM; China, Qing government of, and CIM; Christianity as a Chinese religion; evangelistic methods

CIM organization in China: China Council, 190, 193, 225-29, 280, 284, 310, 333 (photo), 349-53; and accepts candidates, 301, 329; and Ladies Council, 229; and health of missionaries, 352-53; and London Council, 16, 183-84, 191, 195, 226-27, 239, 248, 349; and morphine, 367-68; and National Christian Council, 227n.30, 448; and North American Council, 300, 330, 451-52; and pentecostal movement, 451-52; and JHT, 16, 105, 361, 386, 457; and JHT's family, 193, 227, 333 (photo), 392, 441

CIM organization in United States, 205, 292 (photo), 294-95, 310-12, 320-31, 348, 444; Americanization (democratization) of CIM, 313, 330, 446-48; and archives of American CIM/OMF, 19-20, 22; and beginning of North American branch, 295-301, 313-14, 324; and evangelical constituency (US), 314-15, 322-28, 326-28, 446, 448; and faith healing, 317; and fundamentalism, 292, 298, 313, 443-48; and JHT's visits to US, 293-95, 312

CIM organization in United States: Philadelphia Council, 298, 321, 443-48; members of, 296, 313n.78, 445; and office in Los Angeles, 298, 312-14; and Interdenominational Foreign Missions Association, 312. *See also* Frost

CIM, *Principles & Practice of the C.I.M.*, 227, 248, 279, 300, 350; and Boxer reparations, 425 and Chinese dress, 235; devotional study of, 229; and marriage policy, 198; theology of, 385-86, 447

CIM principles and practice: policies (practice) of: and Boxer Indemnity, 425-26; and comity, 273; and denominational enclaves: Baptist, 268, 342; and Church of England (East Sichuan), 208, 281, 308, 370; and interdenominational principles, 18-19, 98, 104, 107, 131; and lay organization, 194; and marriage policy, 198, 204-5, 226-27, 232-33; and interracial marriage, 238-39, 390-91; and self-protection (guns), 335, 372, 425; and women as equals, 91, 198, 231, 237-38, 240. *See also* CIM and Chinese dress; CIM missionaries in China; Chinese dress; evangelistic methods; opium refuges; women missionaries in CIM

CIM principles and practice: theology (principles), 453; and conditional immortality, 198-90, 206, 272, 385-86, 446-47; and doctrinal (credal) statement, 313, 385-86, 446-47; and ecumenical movement, 447-48; and faith healing, 241, 310-11; and faith principles, 18, 44, 63, 315; and financial principles of, 18, 184, 195, 305-6; and fundamentalism, 2, 22, 292, 386, 441, 443-48, 453; mottos of, 96, 183-84; and ordination, 48, 92, 194, 234, 316, 328; and pentecostal tongues, 222, 228, 288, 354-55, 449-52. *See also* CIM and money; conditional immortality; fundamentalism; pentecostal currents in CIM; prophecy and prophetic movement; JHT, theology of

CIM publications: histories, 16-17, 19, 20-22, 24-27, 209, 357; devotional study of, 229, 252-53; publications: *Book of Arrangements of the C.I.M.* (1886), 103, 195, 206, 227, 229, 300, 312, 349-50, 352; *Candidates' Schedule*, 203; *China: It's Spiritual Need and Claims* (1865), 25, 80, 93, 99, 212, 229, 251; *Christ Alone*, 22n.51; *Evangelisation of the World* (1885), 209, 292; *Occasional Papers*, 25, 131, 182-83, 234; *To Every Creature* (1889), 297, 340. *See also individual authors by name:* Broomhall, A. J.; Broomhall, Benjamin; Broomhall, Marshall; Taylor, Mrs. Howard; JHT.

489

INDEX

See also CIM, *Principles & Practice;*
China's Millions; Hsi: *Pastor Hsi*
China's Millions, 19, 25-27, 45, 140, 193, 234, 261; and anti-opium information, 14, 191, 199, 202-3; and doctrinal statement, 313; and famine information, 149; first issues of, 140-41, 185; and publicity about Pastor Hsi, 176-77, 258, 287, 359, 383; and inner dialogue of CIM, 26; North American edition of, 314, 445; and propaganda, 25-27, 189, 287
China's millions (image), 3-4, 53, 79-80, 181, 189, 293-94, 297. *See also* JHT, theology of: imagery (storytelling)
Chinese church. *See* Christian churches in China
Chinese dress, 1-3, 90, 113, 118, 121-27, 186, 337; Chinese dress outside CIM, 51, 67-69, 121, 127, 271; and critics of, 123, 127, 236, 240, 341-42, 356-57; female missionaries in, 24, 122-23, 124, 126, 240, 335, 342, 356-57, 389; and going native, 121, 123, 383; male missionaries in, 2, 4, 23-24, 121, 220, 335; and CIM policy, 121-22, 206, 233, 235, 248, 235, 337, 357, 361; and its rationale (spiritual passport), 2, 24, 28, 67, 119, 121-22, 127, 455; and refusal to wear, 18, 123, 126-28, 136, 279-80, 357, 361, 383; and pigtail mission, 2, 76, 120, 455; and Western clothes inspire respect, 2, 122, 127, 233-35, 453. *See also* CIM and Chinese dress, policy of; JHT, in Chinese dress
Chinese Evangelisation Society (CES), directors of, 62-63, 79, 92, 103; and Gutzlaff, 53-54, 61; and JHT, 47, 54, 61, 68
Chinese (Qing) government. *See* China, Qing government of; China, government of, at local level; China, government of, and control of religion
Chinese Union, 51-53, 119, 133. *See also* blitz-conversion; Gutzlaff
Christian and Missionary Alliance

(C&MA), 303-5, 317, 319; and Boxer Uprising, 414; in Canada, 303-5, 306; and CIM, 303-5, 310, 315-16, 317, 319, 327; and faith healing (divine health), 304, 310-11, 316, 317; and International Missionary Alliance Mission, 342-43, 355; and Nyack Institute (International Missionary Training Institute), 315; and pentecostal movement, 450, 452; and Sudan Interior Mission, 311. *See also* Bingham; CIM and Associate Missions; Franson; Simpson
Christian churches in China, and Boxer Uprising, 398-400, 403-6, 410-14, 422, 425-26, 427-29; and Chinese church today, 11, 28-29, 235, 441, 443
Christianity as a Chinese religion, 135, 157-58, 256, 281, 369-70, 440-43; and Christianized Confucianism, 189, 269-72, 274, 276, 361; and congruences of Christianity and Chinese religions, 11, 241, 249, 378-79, 407-8, 442; and contextualization, 6, 121, 136, 169, 156-57; and Gutzlaff's vision, 119-20; and Heart Washing Society, 437; and indigenous churches, 2, 236-37, 260-63, 265, 359, 421, 437, 440-43, 452-54; and as a heterodox secret society *(hui),* 133, 158, 229; and National Christian Council, 227n.30; and native control, 129, 233-34, 362-63; and Nestorians, 135, 154, 164-65; and sectarian conversion, 11-14, 69, 77, 237, 262-63, 270, 281, 344, 382, 441-42; and Shanxi sect, 161, 164, 166, 171, 265-66; and Three-Self Protestant Church, 2, 28, 270; and worship services, 363-64. *See also* blitz-conversion; Hsi; native agency; religious sects in China
Church Missionary Society (CMS), 79, 90, 98, 119, 340, 387; and CIM, 20, 76, 92, 125-26, 182, 185, 192, 206; and CIM diocese of East Sichuan, 208, 281, 308, 441; and Fujian massacre, 6, 295, 344; and wordless book, 6-9. *See also* Anglican churches: Church of England

490

Church of England. *See* Anglican churches: Church of England
Church of England Zenana Mission, 217, 340, 344
Clarke, George W., 296, 343, 364-65
Clarke, Mildred, 391, 414, 427
Cliff, Norman, 21, 25, 192, 196
Coleman, Horace, 444-45
conditional immortality, 89, 188-90, 206, 272; Larger Hope, 188, 197, 224-25, 313. *See also* Berger; CIM principles and practice: theology; Smith
contextualization of Christianity in China. *See* Christianity as a Chinese religion
Coulthard, Joseph J., 227n.30, 333 (photo), 355; and Mrs. Coulthard (Maria Hudson Taylor), 355
Crimean War, 86, 200
Crombie, George, 121; and Mrs. Annie Crombie, 136

Dallas Theological Seminary, 308
Darby, John Nelson, 55-57, 62, 94, 295
demoniacal manifestations (spirit possession), 28-29, 172, 260-63, 276, 367, 430, 451, 456; and Boxers, 397-98; in Chinese church today, 28-29; and exorcism, 70, 241, 260-63, 283; and Pastor Hsi, 10, 171-72, 175-77, 255, 262; among missionaries, 328, 352-53; and spirit mediums, 148, 156, 165. *See also* exorcism, Christian
divine healing. *See* healing, faith
Douthwaite, Arthur, 205, 231, 368
Drake, Samuel, 167, 265, 269, 272; and anti-opium pills, 266-67, 369; and Pastor Hsi, 258; and Mrs. Drake (née Sowerby), 269
Dudgeon, John, 245-46
Duncan, George, 101, 106 (photo), 107-9, 136; and Mrs. Duncan, 196

Eason, Arthur, 202, 248

East London Missionary Training Institute, 17, 97, 296, 298. *See also* Guinness
Edkins, Joseph, 250, 254; and Chinese sects, 12, 67, 189; and JHT, 67-68
Edwards, Ebenezer Edward, 206, 279-80; and Boxer settlement, 407-8, 423-24; and opium treatment, 247; and Mrs. Edwards (Florence Kemp), 205-6, 279; and Shouyang mission, 268, 351, 363
England. *See* British evangelicalism; British government
Erdman, William J., 307, 324, 384, 446
Evangelisation of the World, The, 209, 292. *See also* CIM publications
Evangelization of the World in This Generation: watchword of Student Volunteer Movement, 209
evangelistic methods in Britain, 39-40, 46, 51, 82-86, 92. *See also* children, evangelism of; Revival of 1859
evangelistic methods in China, 3-4, 6-8, 10, 15, 124, 128, 138, 236; and agricultural commune, 365, 414; and blitz-conversion, 3, 39, 50-52, 69, 75, 119, 133, 176, 297, 340, 440; and faith healing, 11, 24, 28-29, 177, 241, 262, 375; and feeding the poor, 150, 259, 264, 373, 384, 389-90; and gossiping the gospel, 4-6, 24, 167, 169, 237, 240; and itineration, 24, 124, 144; and itineration by pioneers, 27, 50-51, 68, 119, 136-37, 140, 236, 238, 297, 339, 357, 426, 431; and "Itineration Far and Near as an Evangelizing Agency," 4, 132-33; and evangelization among literati (worthies), 169-71, 271-72, 341-42, 344-45; and famine relief, 148-50, 426; and funerals, 381-82; and miracles, 24, 82, 217, 225, 375, 384, 408; and native agency, 51-53, 119, 129, 133, 236, 359; and native evangelists, 69, 119, 140; and opium refuges, 10, 241, 244, 285, 368, 370; and preaching, 7, 133-34, 167, 236, 371, 389; and preaching with guile, 144; and printed word, 3-4, 232, 236, 247-48, 340, 358, 363, 433; and processions, 385;

INDEX

and sectarian conversion, 11-14, 69, 77, 237, 262-63, 270, 281, 344, 382, 442; and settled work, 76, 119, 125-26, 233, 240, 339, 431; and singing, 241, 320, 343, 357, 370, 375-79, 389, 394; and teashop evangelism, 4, 236, 358, 385; and wordless book, 4-10, 167-69, 236, 240, 365, 378-79, 382, 407, 440. *See also* blitz-conversion; Christianity as a Chinese religion; demon possession; exorcism; Hsi; native agency; opium refuges; wordless book

exorcism, 28-29, 70, 241, 260-63, 283, 441, 443, 456. *See also* CIM principles and practice: theology; demoniacal manifestations; evangelistic methods; pentecostal currents in CIM

extraterritoriality. *See* British government in China: treaty rights

Fairbank, John King, 23, 160
faith healing. *See* healing, faith
faith missions, 21, 94-95, 97, 211, 298, 387, 449; in Canada, 302, 303, 311. *See also individual missions by name; and also* CIM and Associate Missions
faith principles. *See* CIM principles and practice: theology; Müller; JHT, faith principles of
Falun Gong, 29, 165
famines: Great North China Famine (1877-79), 138, 144-50, 160, 396, 441; and its aftermath, 167-70, 223; and famine relief, 147-50, 160, 167, 169, 426; and famine of 1921-22, 437. *See also* Shanxi
Fan, Elder, 265, 280, 285-86, 393; and spurious refuges, 266-67, 286, 370, 443
Faulding, Jennie. *See* Mrs. JHT #2
Faulding, Nellie. *See* Fishe, Mrs. Charles
Finnish Alliance Mission, 319
Finney, Charles Grandison, 46, 84, 275
Fishe, Charles Thomas, 194, 213, 215; and Mrs. Fishe (Nellie Faulding), 213
Franson, Frederik, 295, 317-20, 357; in China, 332n.3, 362; Franson's floods, 319-20, 334; and Scandinavian Alliance Mission (Chicago), 319-20, 334, 450. *See also* Christian and Missionary Alliance; Simpson

French, Evangeline, 197, 388 (photo), 432 (photo); in Central Asia, 25, 431-34; and exorcism, 430; in Shanxi, 394, 427-28, 430; and Topsy, 432-35; and the Trio, 25, 197, 431-35, 440

French, Francesca, 388 (photo), 432 (photo); as author, 197, 218, 376, 434, 440; in Central Asia, 25, 431-34; in Shanxi, 394, 427-28, 430; and Topsy, 432-35; and the Trio, 25, 197, 431-35, 440

Frost, Henry Weston, North American director in Philadelphia, 443-48; and in Toronto, 19, 297-98, 300, 304-7, 312-13, 332, 334, 445-46; and applicants, 292, 328; in China, 311, 332-39, 444, 447; and Christian and Missionary Alliance, 305, 317; and doctrinal statement, 385; and faith healing, 305, 311, 338; and financial principles, 305-6, 309, 444-45; and fundamentalism, 292, 305-6, 313, 315, 444-48; and *The Fundamentals*, 444; memoirs of, 19, 291n.1, 386; ordination of, 446; and pentecostal movement, 451; and Smith, 225, 336-38, 385-86, 446-47, 455; and JHT, 297, 305, 312, 454-55, 458; visions, 333, 336-38, 446. *See also* CIM organization in Canada; CIM organization in United States

Fujian province: massacre at Gutian, 2, 295, 344. *See also* Church Missionary Society

fundamentalism, 2; in China, 302, 430; in CIM, 292, 306-7, 313, 315, 440-41, 443-48; and fundamentalist temperament, 306-7, 386, 446-48; and *The Fundamentals*, 444; in United States, 298-99, 299n.30, 300, 306-8, 386, 444, 446. *See also* CIM principles and practice: theology of

Gansu province. *See* China, provinces of CIM work: Gansu

492

Index

German Alliance Mission, 319
Germany, 52, 94-95, 339, 400, 422. *See also* Gutzlaff; Müller
Goforth, Jonathan, 302, 305, 308, 371; and fundamentalism, 302, 444; and Holy Ghost revivals, 429, 430-31, 443, 449. *See also* fundamentalism, in China; Presbyterian Church in Canada, missions of
going native. *See* Chinese dress
Golden Pill, Religion of. *See* religious sects in China: Golden Pill
Gordon, Adoniram, 315, 446
Griffiths, Michael, 448
Groves, Anthony Norton, 55, 57, 95
Guinness, Geraldine. *See* Taylor, Mrs. Howard
Guinness family, 97, 301; Guinness, Lucy (Mrs. Karl Kumm), 97
Guinness, Grattan, 17, 78, 107, 182, 213, 218, 355; applies to CIM, 96-97; and Brethren, 94, 96-97; referee of CIM, 194, 212, 215; East London Missionary Training Institute, 17, 97, 296, 298
Guizhou province. *See* China, provinces of CIM work: Guizhou
Gutzlaff (or Gützlaff), Karl Friedrich August, 43, 50-53, 431; and blitz-conversion, 39, 52, 69, 119, 133, 440; and Chinese Union, 51-53, 119, 133, 442; in Europe, 52-53; *Gutzlaff's Bible*, 64, 157; and Taiping rebellion, 53, 61, 64, 75; and JHT, 51, 61. *See also* blitz-conversion; Chinese Evangelisation Society

Hangzhou. *See* China, provinces of CIM work: Zhejiang: cities
Harris, Elmore, 316, 446-47
healing, faith (divine healing): in CIM, 24, 198, 241, 338; in Chinese church today 11, 28-29, 443; and Christian and Missionary Alliance, 304-5, 310, 316; in England, 86, 197n.58, 198, 310; and Frost, 311, 338; and Pastor Hsi, 177, 262; and Jesuits, 70; and medicine as sorcery, 337-38; and skepticism, 24, 310-11; and in Sudan Interior Mission, 311; and JHT, 241, 338; in United States, 310, 313; and vaccination, 310-11, 337-38. *See also* CIM organization in China: medical work; CIM principles and practice: theology; evangelistic methods; exorcism; pentecostal currents in CIM
Heavenly Invitation Offices, 255, 267, 369, 443. *See* Hsi and opium refuges; opium refuges
Hedin, Sven, 23, 434
hell and eternal punishment. *See* conditional immortality
Henan. *See* China, provinces of CIM work: Henan
Hill, David, and essay contest, 169-71; and Pastor Hsi, 171-72, 176; and Shanxi Famine, 146, 149, 160-62, 168; and wordless book, 168-69
Hill, Richard, 94, 190, 193, 196; as CIM referee, 210, 215; and Mrs. Hill (Agnes Soltau), 193, 196, 210
Holiness teachings, 83, 182, 186-88, 237, 377-78; exchanged life, 187, 203; second blessing (holiness), 186, 197, 317, 450; third blessing (divine health), 197, 450; fourth blessing (tongues), 317, 450. *See also* CIM principles and practice: theology; healing, faith; Keswick movement; Oberlin College; tongues, speaking in
homeopathy, 242
Hong Xiuquan, 50, 53, 61, 64, 70-75, 114; visions of, 70-71, 74. *See also* Taiping Rebellion
Horne, Celia, 150, 167, 268, 272, 387
Horton, T. C., 324
Hosie, Sir Alexander, 25, 436
Hoste, Dixon Edward, 191, 219 (photo), 220 (photo), 282 (photo); and Boxer settlement, 423-24; and Cambridge Seven, 208-9, 383; as General Director of CIM, 104, 227n.30, 333, 386, 392, 423, 447, 451; and Pastor Hsi, 172, 258, 280-

493

83, 287, 359-62, 372, 383-84, 441; and *Pastor Hsi* (book), 172-73, 456; and penetcostal movement, 451; in Shanxi, 222-23, 280-83, 287, 359, 392, 441; and Smith, 222-23, 281, 283, 383, 386

Hoste, Mrs. Dixon Edward (Gertrude Broomhall), marriage of, 359, 362, 372-73, 385, 392; and JHT's extended family, 227n.30, 191, 441

Howard & Sons, quinine manufacturers, 62, 190, 200, 242

Howard family, 68, 94, 107, 190, 200, 211

Howard, John Eliot, 62; as CIM referee, 194, 211, 215

Howard, Luke, 62, 80, 114, 190

Howard, Robert, 62, 190

Howard, Theodore, London Home Director, 62, 190, 193, 211, 215, 239, 458

Hsi, Pastor (Hsi Liao-chih, and name in religion Hsi Shengmo, pinyin Xi Shengmo), preface (photo), 257, 441-43; autobiography (testimony) of, 171-72, 176, 189, 375, 376, 379; character of, 171, 173-77, 255-58, 371-73, 375; and Chinese officials, 173, 176, 256, 259, 264, 371; death of, 391-92; family of, 171, 173-74, 177, 263-64, 373, 380; and Famine, 173-74; and Golden Pill, 165-66, 171, 174, 176, 256, 265, 269, 378, 441-42; and idol taxes, 163, 257-58, 372, 392-93; Hsi as model for mass evangelism, 441-43, 456-58; and money, 171, 177, 285, 288, 367-70, 373, 384, 388, 391, 423; and name in religion: Shengmo (Overcomer of Demons), 171, 175-76, 255, 441; and Nestorian Christianity, 165; and publicity, 232, 359, 383; and Taiping movement, 173; Hsi's visions, 172, 174-75, 255, 267

Hsi, Pastor, and the Middle Eden, 284-85, 354, 359-60, 362, 373, 391, 442; run by Mrs. Hsi, 374-75; Rules for the Middle Eden, 375-76, 379-81; and JHT's visits, 284-85, 359-60, 378

Hsi, Pastor, ministry of, 176-77, 249, 256-59, 268, 362, 375-81; at his chapel, 177, 264, 375; and divine will, 371-72, 380-81; and exorcism, 175-77, 255, 262-64, 369, 371, 441, 443, 456; and feeder of the sheep, 281, 283, 285, 354; and feeding the poor, 259, 264, 373, 384, 390; and healing, 177, 360, 375; hymns of, 139, 255, 354, 372, 375-79, 380, 395, 421; and mass baptisms, 284, 287, 362, 382, 393; and parable of candle, 358, 383; and wearing scarlet banner, 375; and under-shepherds, 256, 375, 391: Elder Chü, 281, 285; and Elder Fan, 265-67, 280, 285-86, 443; and Elder Sï, 262, 285, 393; and Gatekeeper Sung, 162, 171, 173, 176, 393; Hsi and wordless book, 10, 378-79; and worship services, 380

Hsi, Pastor, and missionaries, 176, 255-26, 264, 267, 443, 456; Hsi's anti-foreign attitude, 171, 173, 177, 258; and anti-Hsi factions (dread of Hsi), 265, 280, 287, 361; and Cambridge Seven, 280-83, 383, 441, 443; and CIM, 258-59, 265, 280-83, 372-73; and Hsi's conversion, 175-77; and cured of opium addiction, 171, 174-76, 243, 255-56; and essay contest, 171-72, 255; and Hoste, 172-73, 258, 280-83, 287, 359-62, 369, 376, 383-84, 441, 446; and interracial marriage, 390; and missionaries work under Hsi, 280-83, 285, 288, 372, 383, 443; and Hsi performs marriage of, 385; and Shanxi spirits, 268-69, 283; and JHT, 281, 284-86, 358, 359, 367, 378; and treaty rights, 256. *See also* Hsi: *Pastor Hsi*

Hsi, Pastor, and opium, 442; and anti-opium medicines, 370, 367-68, 394; and Gospel Hall, 265; and Hsi's red pills, 264, 267, 285-86, 360, 376; and missionary medicines, 175, 255, 266-67, 368; and morphine, 15, 257, 266-67, 368. *See also* opium

Hsi, Pastor, and opium refuges, 14-15, 266-67, 356 (map), 372, 391-92; and CIM financial support, 285, 288, 367-

Index

69, 423, 443; as evangelistic agency, 10, 283, 367, 369-70, 380; as Heavenly Invitation Offices, 255, 267, 369; at Middle Eden, 360, 375; as philanthropic business, 257, 285-86, 367-70, 443; and refuge keepers, 257 (photo), 369-70, 383, 389, 391, 393; and spurious refuges, 266-67, 286, 370. *See also* opium refuges in Shanxi

Hsi, Mrs., 173, 177, 240, 374 (photo); and CIM women work under her, 240, 285, 387, 388 (photo), 443; and exorcism, 373; Mrs. Hsi's dream, 265, 374, 388-89, 427; and mother of Hsi's sect, 173, 263, 265, 285, 374-75; relatives of, 264, 360, 373; as widow, 374, 393-94, 398, 400, 427-28; and women's refuges, 263, 374, 394

Hsi: *Pastor Hsi* (book), 172-73, 232, 243, 262, 444; and its significance, 455-58. *See also* Hoste and *Pastor Hsi*; Taylor, Mrs. Howard, and *Pastor Hsi* and its influence

Hsi, Pastor, and Shanxi sect after his death, 162 (photo), 392-94; and Boxer Uprising, 162, 398-400, 407-8, 413; and after Boxers, 427-31; and Hsi's successors: Elder Sï, 162, 285, 393, 428; and Elder Hsü, 428, 429 (photo), 431

Hubei. *See* China, provinces of CIM work: Hubei

Huberty James, Francis. *See* James, Francis Huberty

Hunan. *See* China, provinces of CIM work: Hunan

idol taxes, 69; exemption from paying, 13, 158-60, 163, 163, 257, 372, 389, 392-93; as cause for Boxer Uprising, 403-4, 421, 423-25

idols, idolatry, 30, 120, 332, 340; Chinese iconoclastic attitudes to images, 170, 237; destruction of idols, 14, 160, 161, 240-41, 281; as museum objects, 14, 61, 81-82, 155, 160; and missionaries' idols (possessions), 225, 233, 319, 363; and in Shanxi, 154-57, 163, 176, 263

imperialism. *See* British government in China

indigenous Christianity. *See* Christian churches in China; Christianity as a Chinese religion; Hsi

Inner Mongolia. *See* China, provinces of CIM work: Inner Mongolia

International Missionary Alliance Mission, 342-43, 355. *See* Christian and Missionary Alliance

Interdenominational Foreign Mission Association, 312, 447. *See also* CIM organization in United States; fundamentalism

Ireland, 81; Brethren movement in, 55; and Irish in CIM, as missionaries, 96, 100, 109, 218, 279, 305n.48, 321, 385; and as referees, 211, 213-14; and Revival of 1857-59, 83, 85, 96. *See also* Guinness

Irving, Edward, 46, 51

Jakobsen, Anna, 238, 319, 362, 387; marries Ch'eng Hsiu-chi, 370-71, 389-91, 414, 427, 443

James (Huberty James), Francis, and CIM, 139, 144, 238, 273; and Chinese sects, 11, 139, 409; and Mrs. Huberty James (Marie Huberty), 273; and Shanxi Famine, 145-46, 149, 167, 170

Jesus family, 454

Jesus opium. *See* morphine

Jiangsu. *See* China, provinces of CIM work: Jiangsu

Jiangxi. *See* China, provinces of CIM work: Jiangxi

John, Griffith, 67, 248, 457 (photo), 458; and his tracts, 250-53

Joyce, Raymond, 431

Kaiser, Andrew, 151, 153, 406, 418
Kansas, 295, 315-17, 334
Keller, Frank, 348, 458

495

Kemp, Florence. *See* Edwards, Mrs. Ebenzer Henry
Kemp, Jessie. *See* Piggott, Mrs. Thomas Wellesley
Keswick movement, 20, 98, 182, 185, 279, 298, 444; in Canada, 299, 308; and Keswick teachings, 9, 126, 187-88, 197, 237, 249, 377-78, 450
King, George, 238
Kung, H. H., 414

Lammermuir party. *See* CIM, forward movements of: Lammermuir party
Landale, Robert J., 220, 258, 268; and Pastor Hsi, 265
liberal churches, 47; and liberal missionaries in China, 1-2, 189, 268-69, 272, 340-41, 453; and modernism, 187, 306-7, 313, 443, 446. *See also* CIM, critics of; CIM principles and practice, theology; conditional immortality; Martin; Richard
Liebenzell Mission, 452
London, CIM in East London, 78, 90, 94, 97; East London Missionary Training Institute, 17, 97, 296, 298; CIM in Islington, 182, 191-92; CIM missionaries from London, 100, 109-10, 205; and CIM referees, 193, 210-15
London Missionary Society (LMS), 46, 75, 90-92, 119, 340

McBrier, Edwin M., 384
Mackay, George Leslie, 238, 366 (banner)
McKay, Moira Jane, 21, 192, 195, 254. *See also references in text and footnotes*
Mackee, Maggie, 30
McLean, Hector, 451
Macpherson, Annie, and House of Industry, 88, 102, 218, 295; in Canada, 88, 295-96, 365; and CIM, 101, 218
Malcolm, Kari Torjesen, 438
Margary, Consul Augustus, 115, 137, 184
Martin, W. A. P., 65, 252-53, 339, 457 (photo), 458

Mathews, R. H., 25
Meadows, James, 81, 128, 226, 233-35; and Mrs. Meadows (Elizabeth Rose), 110, 114, 120, 235
Medhurst, W. H., 130
Mennonites, 327-28
Methodist churches in Britain, 84; in Barnsley, 38-40, 110; and Broomhall, 190, 192, 194, 214; and Methodists in CIM: as missionaries, 110, 114, 194; and as referees, 193-94, 213-14, 216; and Methodist missions, 43, 149; and Reform Secession, 47-48; and JHT, 38, 43, 47-48
Methodist churches in Canada, and CIM, 306, 309, 326-27, 328; missions of, 302, 321-22
Methodist churches in United States, 340
Middle Eden, the. *See* Hsi and the Middle Eden
Mildmay Institute, 92, 99-100, 182, 218; and CIM, 100, 109-10, 114, 126, 192, 391; and Holiness movement, 182, 187-88. *See also* Anglican churches: Church of England; Holiness movement; Pennefather
missionary conferences: in Edinburgh (1910), 447; in New York (1900), 312, 454; in Shanghai (1877), 4, 132; in Shanghai (1890), 1-2, 297, 338-42, 351, 367-68
Mitchie, Alexander, 24, 26, 28
modernism. *See* liberal churches. *For anti-modernism, see* fundamentalism
Mongolia. *See* China, provinces of CIM work: Inner Mongolia
Moody, Dwight Lyman, 295, 446; in Britain, 185, 188, 298; and Cambridge Seven, 207, 209, 293; in Canada, 301; institutions of, 10, 188, 312; international networks of, 9, 298, 317; and Moody Church, 10, 327-28; and JHT, 185, 291, 293, 298; and wordless book, 9, 167

Index

Moody Bible Institute (MBI), 188, 207, 294, 298, 307, 313, 315, 324
Morgan, Richard Cope, 85, 194, 334; as CIM referee, 214, 215
Morley, John, 21, 212, 215
morphine, 7-8, 200, 337, 441, 443; and black market, 245-46, 409; and British government, 15; and Pastor Hsi, 257, 266-67; and Jesus opium, 15, 409; and medical (hypodermic) treatment of opium addicts, 15, 200, 245-49, 276, 278; and Shanghai conference, 367-68; spread of, 368-69; tinctures of, 242, 368
Morrison, George, 23, 409-10
Morse, Hosea Ballou, 119
Moule, George E., 125-27, 208n.99
Mowll, Howard K., 308
Müller, George, 94-96, 119, 207, 232; and contributions to CIM, 96, 131, 190; and CIM referee, 193, 212; faith principles of, 95; mottoes of, 96; and orphanages, 85, 95
Murray, Mariamne, 229

Nanjing. See China, provinces of CIM work: Jiangsu: cities
National Christian Council (of China), 227n.30, 448. See also Christian churches in China
native agency, 51-53, 119, 129, 133, 346-47, 359, 407, 443; and Biblewomen, 119, 347, 369, 443; and native evangelists, 69, 119, 140, 276, 281; and Wang Laedjün, 129, 233-34, 347, 362-63. See also blitz-conversion; Chinese Union; evangelistic methods in China; Hsi; Wang
native, going. See China dress
Nee, Watchman, 441
Nestorians, 135, 154, 164-65. See also religious sects in China: Nestorians
Nevius, J. L., 270, 261, 407
Niagara Believers' Conference, 293, 299, 305-7, 312, 446
Nicol, Lewis and Eliza, in Lammermuir party, 100-101, 106 (photo), 107, 109, 112; in China, 124, 126-27
Ningbo. See China, provinces of CIM work: Zhejiang: cities
Norway, 318; Norwegians in CIM, 319, 389, 450, 452
Norwegian Alliance Mission, 450, 452. See also CIM, Associate Missions of

Oberlin Band, 143, 269, 274-77; and Boxer Uprising, 396, 408, 414-15, 423, 426; and CIM, 274, 276, 281; and Oberlin College, 274-75
Ogren, Alfred and Olivia, 320, 396, 419-20
O'Meara, T. R., 308
opium, medical properties of, 199; and smoking opium, 174, 248, 270; and opium suicides, 30, 76, 174, 242-43
opium refuges, and anti-opium medicines, 175, 242-48, 266-67, 285-86, 367-68, 370; in CIM, 247-48, 368-71, 408; and conversion of opium smokers, 4, 257, 270, 276, 287, 336, 458; as an evangelistic agency, 10, 241, 244, 285, 368, 370; and medical treatment, 15, 76, 200, 242-49, 278, 368; and morphine, 15, 245-49, 276, 278, 367-68; as Salvation Hall, 247-48
opium refuges in Shanxi, 15, 169, 266, 408; and Boxer Uprising, 402; as Gospel Hall, 265; as Heavenly Invitation Offices, 255, 267, 369, 408; and Pastor Hsi's refuges, 10, 14-15, 257, 267, 367-71; and missionary refuges, 245-49, 266-67, 278, 363-64, 368, 372; and refuge keepers, 257 (photo), 368-70, 383, 389, 391, 393; and spurious refuges, 266-67, 286, 370; and women's refuges, 169, 263. See also Fan, Elder; Hsi and opium refuges
opium trade, and anti-opium lobby, 14-15, 20, 49, 89, 191, 199-202, 298; and Chinese anti-opium societies, 244, 436; and Chinese government, 199, 202, 243-44, 247; missionary attitude to (perfidious Albion), 7-8, 30, 202-3; and

497

opium in Shanxi, 144, 161, 169-70, 174, 248, 269-70, 408, 428-31; and opium villages, 174, 257, 429-30; and Society for the Suppression of the Opium Traffic/Trade (SSOT), 14, 199-201; Taiping suppression of, 73. *See also* Broomhall; CIM and anti-opium lobby

Opium Wars: First, 43, 48-50, 129; and Treaty of Nanjing, 51, 53; and Second, 48, 77, 115, 116; and subsequent treaties, 115, 158. *See also* British government, and treaties with China; China, Qing government of.

orphanages, in Britain, 9, 88-89, 99, 102; in China, 76, 150, 167, 335; in U.S., 188

Orr Ewing, Archibald, 285, 288, 334, 352, 423; and Mrs. Orr Ewing (Mary Scott), 334

Overholzer, Ruth, 5n.6, 10

Overseas Missionary Fellowship (OMF), 19-22, 28, 444. *See* China Inland Mission (CIM)

Palmer, Phoebe, 83-84

Parker, George, 238-39, 390; and Mrs. Parker (Minnie Mianzi Shao), 238-39

Pastor Hsi. See Hsi: *Pastor Hsi*

Pastors' College, 88, 298. *See also* Baptist churches in Britain; Spurgeon

Pearse, George, 54, 61-62, 68

Pennefather, Canon William, 99-100, 187, 193-94; as CIM referee, 212-13, 215. *See also* Mildmay Institute

pentecostal currents in CIM, 228, 440-41, 443, 448-54; and exorcism, 28-29, 70, 241, 260-63, 283, 443; and faith healing, 24, 177, 198, 241, 262, 305, 310-11, 337-38, 443; and Holy Ghost revivals, 430-31, 443; and Pentecostals in CIM, 317-18, 327, 441, 451-52; and speaking in tongues, 222, 228, 288, 355, 449-52. *See also* CIM principles and practice: theology: faith healing; *and also* tongues; Christian and Missionary Alliance; healing, faith; tongues, speaking in

Pentecostal Missionary Union for Great Britain and Ireland, 450-51

pentecostal movement, 448-52

Philadelphia. *See* CIM organization in United States

Philadelphia School of the Bible, 298

Pierson, Arthur Tappan, 313n.78, 315, 446

Piggott, Sophia, 187, 279

Piggott, Thomas Wellesley, as Boxer martyr, 411-12; and CIM, 167, 279-80, 284, 350-51, 361; and Pastor Hsi, 280; and Mrs. Piggott (Jessie Kemp), 206; and Shouyang Mission, 137, 143, 268, 351, 360

pigtail mission, 2, 76, 120, 455. *See* CIM and Chinese dress policy; Chinese dress

Pilgrim's Progress, 27, 36, 59, 61, 65, 71-72; and Chinese translation, 71-72, 252; as metaphor, 29-30, 61, 116, 365, 406

Plymouth Brethren. *See* Brethren movement: Plymouth Brethren

Polhill Turner, Arthur, 219 (photo), 220 (photo); and Cambridge Seven, 208, 222. *See also* Cambridge Seven

Polhill Turner, Cecil, 219 (photo), 220 (photo); and Cambridge Seven, 208, 222; in India, 238; and pentecostalism, 222, 238, 450-51. *See also* Cambridge Seven; Pentecostal Missionary Union

possession by spirits. *See* demon possession; sorcery

premillennial dispensationalism. *See* prophecy and prophetic movement; *and also* Brethren Movement; CIM, principles and practice: theology; Darby; Frost; Guinness

Presbyterian churches in Britain, 46, 57; and CIM, 234, 302; as CIM referees, 194; and Great Disruption, 47; and missions, 112

Presbyterian Church in Canada, missions of, 302, 308, 371; and Presbyterians in CIM: as applicants, 326-28; and on Toronto Council, 306-8

Index

Presbyterian church in United States, and CIM, 326-28
Price, Charles and Eva Jane, 275, 277, 287, 408, 414-15
prophecy and prophetic movement, 446, 448, and Blessed Hope, 54, 97, 294, 319; and Brethren movement, 54-58, 89, 97; and Christian and Missionary Alliance, 304, 319; and Franson, 317-19; and Niagara Believers' Conference, 293-94, 299, 304, 306, 446; and premillennial dispensationalism, 56-58, 89, 249, 294, 299, 304, 306, 338, 448, 453; and JHT, 54, 57-58, 97, 294, 299, 319. *See also* Brethren movement; CIM principles and practice: theology; Christian and Missionary Alliance; Darby; Franson; Guinness; Simpson

Qinghai. *See* China, provinces of CIM work: Qinghai
Quakers, 31, 63, 83, 188; and Beaconite schism, 47, 62; among the Brethren, 57, 62; and CIM, 194, 327
quinine, 62, 190, 200, 242. *See also* Howard & Sons quinine manufacturers; opium, and anti-opium medicines

Radcliffe, Reginald, 293-94, 330
Radstock, Lord, 85-86, 208; as CIM referee, 215
Regions Beyond Missionary Union, 97, 211. *See also* faith missions
religious sects in China, 133, 154-58, 229, 260, 409; Buddhist sects, 27, 29, 69, 134-35, 155, 237, 244, 265-66, 281; Daoist sects, 29, 69, 135, 155, 157, 161-66, 237, 244, 265-66, 382. *See also* Falun Gong
religious sects in China, and healing, 262, 442-43; and opium, 244, 266; and Sacred Edict, 158, 229, 250-51; and secret societies (*hui*), 12, 133, 164-65, 229, 265, 344-45; and spirit mediums, 148, 156, 165; and sutra reading sects (*jiao*), 133, 281; syncretic character of, 135, 155, 442; teachings of, 11-13, 133-34, 161-66; and vegetarian sects, 12-13, 27, 29, 30, 77, 237, 265, 344. *See also* Christianity as a Chinese religion; evangelistic methods: sectarian conversion

religious sects, Chinese: Boxers United in Righteousness, 395-98; and Former Heaven (Xiantian), 13; and Golden Pill (or Golden Elixir), 163-66, 171, 173, 256, 265-66, 269, 283, 378, 382, 441-42; and Muslims, 154, 164; and Nestorians, 135, 154, 164-65; and Pure Land Buddhism, 154; and Secret Religion, 157, 265-66, 442; and Taiping god-worshippers, 70-71, 74, 157; and White Lotus, 135, 154, 165, 283, 442; and Zaili (vegetarians), 165. *See also* Christianity as a Chinese religion

Reuter, Sophie. *See* Smith, Mrs. Stanley Peregrine
revivals: evangelical revival of early 1800s, 46; and Holy Ghost revivals, 430-31, 443, 449; and Methodist revivals, 38-40; and pentecostal revivals, 317-18, 449-52; and revival of 1857-59, 82-86, 167, 185; and Welsh revival (1905), 449
Richard, Timothy, 121, 270-74, 271 (photo), 394; and Baptist Missionary Society, 103, 167, 270; and Boxer settlement, 423, and CIM, 102-3, 143, 268-74, 278, 284; and Christianized Confucianism, 189, 269-72, 274, 276; and Reform movement in Beijing, 274; and religious sects, 164, 170, 270-72; in Shanxi, 146, 149-50, 167, 205, 273-74; and conversion of worthies, 169-70, 271-72, 442; and scriptural colportage, 258, 272, 276; and Shanxi University, 423, 435-36. *See also* Baptist Missionary Society
Richard, Mrs. Timothy (Mary), 150, 268, 271 (photo), 272
Rijnhart, Petrus, 329
Roberts, Issachar, 61, 65
Roman Catholics. *See* Catholics

INDEX

Royal Ontario Museum, 155, 366 (banner)
Rudland, Will, 101-2, 106 (photo), 107-9, 234-35

Salt, Sir Titus, 35
Salvation Army, in Canada, 306, 327; and CIM, 90, 194, 237, 310, 385; and equality of women, 91, 237. *See also* Booth
Sandham, Alfred, 297, 303, 305, 310
Saunders, Alexander, 302, 333 (photo), 363-64, 441; and Boxer Uprising, 415-16, 427
Scandinavian Alliance Mission (Chicago), 268, 319-20, 334, 414. See also CIM, Associate Missions of
Schofield, Robert Harold Ainsworth, 205-6, 241, 275; death of, 247, 278-79; and opium treatments, 205, 242-43, 246-47; and Richard, 205, 268, 278; and Mrs. Schofield, 205, 278-79; in Shanxi, 159-60, 205-6
Schofield Memorial Hospital, 206, 247, 278-79, 351, 361
Scofield, Cyrus Ingersoll, 315, 446
School of Oriental and African Studies, 19, 458
Scotland, 81, 83-85; and Scottish branch of CIM, 205; Scottish missionaries in CIM, 100-101, 108-9, 137, 205, 218, 220, 226, 229; and as CIM referees, 194, 214, 258
Scott, Maggie, 310, 336
sects, Chinese. *See* Christianity as a Chinese religion; religious sects in China
sectarian conversion. *See* Christianity as a Chinese religion
Seed, Sarah, 277
Shaanxi. *See* China, provinces of CIM work: Shaanxi
Shaftsbury, Lord, 20, 201, 218
Shandong. *See* China, provinces of CIM work: Shandong
Shangdi (Lord on High): enfiefment of the gods (*Shangdi* versus *Tian*

[Heaven]), 155-56; and Good People's Movement, 437; and Roman Catholic name for God, 156-57; and Protestant name for God, 157, 257, 340; and Taiping name for God, 157, 259, 397
Shanghai, 50, 66-67; and CIM Head Office, 129, 186, 221-22, 300, 318, 326, 334. *See also* CIM organization in China
Shanxi province of China, 141-77, 143 (map), 222-25, 246-47, 255-87, 345-47, 354-94, 356 (map), 395-420, 421-32, 435-39, 440-43; and Boxer Uprising, 395-420, 421-26; geography of, 142, 144-45, 150-54, 358; and geography of the Big Road, 137 (photo), 142, 157, 351, 387, 392, 423, 436; history of, 23, 151-56; as model province, 421, 435-37; and native banking system, 152, 364; and Shanxi art in world museums, 155, 160; and Shanxi today, 151-53, 406, 438-39; and *Shanxiren* (Shanxi native), character of, 152, 376, 402-3, 406; and Wutaishan (Five Peaks Mountain), 154-55
Shanxi, Christian missions in, 81, 142, 144, 152, 160, 402; and Baptist Missionary Society, 102-3, 143, 149, 167, 268-74, 284; and Boxer Uprising, 396, 402-3, 406-8, 410-17, 419-20, 422-26; and CIM, 21, 143-46, 148-150, 278, 283-86, 345-46, 426-31, 440-43; and CIM Associate Missions, 320, 452; and Chinese church today, 153; and Pastor Hsi's sect after his death, 162 (photo), 392-94, 398-400, 407-8, 413, 427-31; and Oberlin Band, 143, 269, 274-77, 363, 396, 414-15, 423; and Roman Catholics, 146, 148, 153, 158-60, 274, 283, 404-5, 411-12; and Scandinavian Alliance Mission, 268, 414; and JHT's visits, 345-48, 354-62; Swedish missions, 277, 356, 383, 419-20. *See also* CIM and Associate Missions; Hsi
Shanxi famines: Great North China Famine (1877-79), 138, 140-45, 160, 441; and its aftermath, 167-70, 223, 378, 442; and

500

Index

famine of 1900, 405, 408, 424; and famine of 1921-22, 437
Shanxi, opium in. *See* Hsi and opium refuges; opium refuges in Shanxi; opium trade, in Shanxi
Shanxi, religious sects in, 148, 154-58, 161, 164, 166, 171, 260. *See also* religious sects in China
Shanxi, cities of CIM work:
Daning, and Boxer Uprising, 396, 414, 419; indigenous sect in, 281, 369, 387
Datong, 151, 154; and Boxer Uprising, 414, 418; CIM in, 273, 296, 364-65, 378, 381
Fenzhou, and Boxer Uprising, 396, 414-15, 422; Oberlin Band in, 275
Hongdong, 162 (photo), 284, 286-87, 392, 393-94, 428; and Boxer Uprising, 400; and Pastor Hsi's cathedral, 372, 383; and opium refuges, 283, 369, 394, 389, 428; and religious sects, 154; and Taiping Northern Expedition, 157-58
Huozhou, 387-91; and Boxer Uprising, 414, 427-28, 431-33
Luan, 286, 361, 369, 377-78, 385-87; and Boxer Uprising, 416
Pingyang (now Linfen), 143 (map), 151, 153, 160, 259, 273, 285, 287, 359; and Cambridge Seven, 223, 280-83; and Boxer Uprising, 411, 419; and Great Famine, 145, 160; and Pastor Hsi, 258; and opium refuges, 369, 372; and religious sects, 155-56, 157, 160, 164; and Taiping Northern Expedition, 157-58
Pingyao, 143 (map), 363-64, 369; and Boxer Uprising, 415, 423; and native banking system, 152, 363-64
Shouyang, and Boxer Uprising, 411-12; Shouyang Mission in, 137, 143, 268, 351
Taigu, and Boxer Uprising, 414; Oberlin Band in, 275-76
Taiyuan, 143 (map), 151-54, 406, 436,
438; Baptist Missionary Society in, 273-74, 363; and Boxer settlement, 422-24, 431; and Boxer Uprising, 395-96, 401-2, 405, 408, 410-12, 415, 418; CIM in, 167, 222, 224, 259, 264, 268-69, 273-74, 278-80, 284; and Great Famine, 145, 167; opium refuges in, 15, 246-47, 363; Roman Catholics in, 153, 158, 405; and Schofield Memorial Hospital, 206, 247, 278-79, 351, 363; and Shanxi University, 435-36
Xiaoyi, 284, 387, 414
Xizhou (Xi Xian), 281, 285
Xinzhou, Baptist Missionary Society in, 413, 422
Shanxi Evergreen Service, 151, 153, 406, 438-39
Shanxi spirits, as derelict morale, 268-70, 354-55, 361-62, 421, 431; and democracy movements in CIM, 269, 283-84, 350-51; and Pastor Hsi, 269; and indigenous Christianity, 283-84, 421, 440, 453; and Richard, 268-69
Shanxi University, 423, 435-36
Shouyang Mission, 137, 143, 268, 361; and Boxer Uprising, 411-13, 423. *See also* Edwards; Piggott; Shanxi, cities of CIM work: Shouyang
Sï Ch'ing-lan, Elder, 162 (photo), 285, 373, 380; as Pastor Hsi's successor, 393, 428-29
Sichuan. *See* China, provinces of CIM work: Sichuan
Simpson, Albert Benjamin, 96, 298; in China, 332n.3; and Christian and Missionary Alliance, 303 4, 317; and faith healing, 304, 311, 317; and Franson, 319, 342; and International Missionary Alliance, 342-43, 355-56; and pentcostal movement, 452; and JHT, 317, 355. *See also* CIM and Associate Missions; Christian and Missionary Alliance; healing, faith
Sloan, Walter B., London home director, 444, 447

501

INDEX

Smith, Stanley Peregrine, 219 (photo), 220 (photo), 224 (photo), 343; and Cambridge Seven, 206-7, 383; converts of, 380; and Frost, 225, 313, 336-38, 385-86, 446-47; works under Pastor Hsi, 281, 283, 286, 369, 376, 385, 441; and Larger Hope, 187, 224-25, 313, 337; and morphine, 248, 441; resigns from CIM, 385-86, 447; in Shanxi, 222-23, 237, 281, 283, 287-88, 385-87; and Shanxi spirits, 355, 361, 443

Smith, Mrs. Stanley Pergrine, #1 (Sophie Reuter), 319, 385, 389, 391, 427; #2 (Anna Lang), 386

Society for the Suppression of the Opium Traffic/Trade (SSOT), 14, 199-201. *See also* CIM, and anti-opium lobby; opium, and anti-opium lobby

Soltau, Agnes. *See* Hill, Mrs. Richard (Agnes Soltau)

Soltau, George, 193, 196, as CIM referee, 211, 215

Soltau, Henrietta, 190, 196-98, 218, 229; and CIM's Ladies Council, 196

Soltau, Henry W., 193, 196, 210, 215, 301

sorcery, and Boxer Uprising, 396-98, 407-8; and converted sorceress, 382; and medicine *(pharmakaeia)*, 337-38; missionaries accused of, 75-76, 116, 122-23, 144, 381

Spurgeon, Charles Haddon, 86-89; and CIM, 192, 218; as CIM referee, 194, 215-16, 349; and Metropolitan Tabernacle, 81, 86-87, 192; and orphanages, 9, 88-89; and Pastors' College, 88, 298; and JHT, 9, 87, 107, 185; and wordless book, 9, 87-88, 167

Stevens, Jane, 391, 414, 427

Stevenson, John W., 185, 233, 284; Deputy China Director, 226

Stewart, Lyman and Milton, 444

Stewart, Robert, 6, 344

Stock, Eugene V., 98, 126, 182, 206

Stott, George, 108, 118, 121, 133-34, 138, 234; refuses to wear Chinese dress, 121, 128, 235

Stott, Mrs. George (Grace Ciggie), 108, 118, 235; and exorcism, 265; in North America, 312, 325

Studd, Charlie, 219 (photo), 220 (photo); and Cambridge Seven, 206-7; as cricketer extraordinaire, 206; and Pastor Hsi, 385; and pentecostalism, 441, 450; philanthropy of, 207; in Shanxi, 222, 232, 288, 385, 387

Studd, George, 293, 450

Student Volunteer Movement, 209; in North America, 293, 303, 312, 444

Sudan Interior Mission, 303, 311-12, 317. *See also* Bingham; faith missions

Sudan United Mission, 97. *See also* faith missions

Sung (Song-Ch'ang-Keng), Gatekeeper, 162 (photo), 285, 393; autobiography (testimony) of, 140, 161-62; conversion of, 161; as gatekeeper, 160-64, 167, 265; and Golden Pill, 162-63; and Pastor Hsi, 163, 173

Sung, Jonathan, 441

Sweden, revivals in, 317-20; Swedish consuls in China, 356, 390

Swedish Alliance Mission, 319

Swedish Americans, and CIM Associate Missions, 21, 312, 318-19, 325-27; and Franson's floods, 295, 319-20, 365; in China, 309, 334-35, 342-43. *See also* Chicago Mission Among the Mongols; CIM and Associate Missions; Christian and Missionary Alliance; Franson; Scandinavian Alliance Mission

Swedish Holiness Mission, 319, 414, 423, 450

Swedish missionaries in China, 21, 277, 309, 318-20, 356, 359-60; and Boxer Uprising, 414, 419-20, 450; and penetcostal movement, 450, 452. *See also* CIM and Associate Missions

Taiping rebellion, 64, 67-68, 70-75, 76-77;

and its aftermath, 4, 114-17, 119, 124-25, 236; and color symbolism *(wuxing)*, 64, 71, 74; and Northern Expedition in Shanxi, 64, 157-58, 162, 173, 259; as godworshippers, 53, 61, 64, 116, 133, 236; JHT's reaction to, 74-75

Taiyuan. *See* Shanxi: cities of CIM work: Taiyuan

Taylor, Amelia Hudson (JHT's sister). *See* Broomhall, Mrs. Benjamin

Taylor, Annie Royale, 238, 383, 450

Taylor (JHT) family: ancestors, 38-41; and his father, James Taylor, 41, 43-45; and mother, Amelia Hudson, 41, 44, 107; and JHT's children: Grace, 34, 77, 100, 107-9, 128; and Herbert Hudson, 22, 100, 109; and Maria (Mrs J. J. Coulthard), 333, 355; and JHT's descendants, 21-22; and grandson, JHT II, 189

Taylor, Henry, 144

Taylor, Howard (Frederick Howard, JHT's third child), 17 (photo), 97, 100, 109, 293, 444, 454, 458; as member of China Council, 227n.30, 333 (photo); in Shanxi, 355-57

Taylor, Mrs. Howard (Geraldine Guinness), 17 (photo); and Brethren, 94; and *By Faith*, 291n.1; and CIM archives, 16-17, 19; as CIM historian, 16, 19, 44, 47, 75, 97, 112; and *Pastor Hsi*, 172, 176, 258n.9, 262, 285, 360, 441, 444, 454-58; and Philadelphia office, 444; in Shanxi, 355, 358, 360, 376, 378; and wordless book, 6. *See also* Brethren movement; Guinness; Hoste; Hsi: *Pastor Hsi*

Taylor, James Hudson (JHT), photos of, 3, 60, 106, 333, 457; biographies of, 16, 19-22, 25, 65, 75; and British government, 17-18, 26, 130-32; critics of, 24, 26, 28, 340-43; including Oberlin Band, 274, 276, 281; and Martin, 65, 340-41; and Moule, 125-27; and *North China Herald*, 127, 128, 130; JHT's oratorical skills, 81, 340, 454; and physical description, 35, 76, 81, 355, 458

JHT, biography of, *in chronological order:* childhood (1832-48), 36-37, 43-46; and Methodist Reform Secession (1848), 47-48; and Chinese Evangelisation Society (1850-60), 47, 54, 61-64; and medical education, 54, 63-64, 79, 205; and first term in China (1853-60), 64-77; and marriage to Maria Dyer (1858), 20, 75-77; and return to England (1860), 33-35, 70, 77; and hidden years (1860-65), 78-80; and ordination, 47-48, 79, 205; and vision at Brighton (1865), 3, 78-80, 87, 99, 106, 129, 293; and founding of CIM (1865), 80, 87, 92, 99, 189; and recruiting Lammermuir party, 80-82, 83, 91, 100-105; and voyage of Lammermuir (1866), 100, 106, 109, 111-12; in China (1866-71), 118, 120-32, 136, 182; and marriage to Jennie Faulding (1871), 182; in England (1871-72), 72, 182, 188; in England (1874-77), 136, 182-86, 190, 194; and second vision (1875) at Brighton, 181; at Shanghai Missionary Conference (1877), 4; and Cambridge Seven (1885), 206, 291; in Shanxi (1886), 283-86; in North America (1888), 291-97; in England (1889), 300; in North America (1889-1900), 304, 312, 315, 317, 324; Shanghai Missionary Conference (1890), 2, 297, 319; in Australia (1890), 300; in Shanxi (1894-95), 351-62; at New York Missionary Conference (1900), 454; in Switzerland (1901-5), 454-55; returns to China (1905), 333 (photo), 457 (photo), 458; and death (1905), 312, 333, 458

JHT as author and editor, 16; and *Book of Arrangements of the C.I.M.* (1886), 103, 195, 206, 227, 229, 300, 312, 349-50, 352; and *China: Its Spiritual Need and Claims* (1865), 25, 80, 93, 99, 212, 229, 251; and *China's Millions*, 25-26, 45, 140, 149, 185, 189; and *Occasional Papers*, 25,

INDEX

182-83, 234; and *Principles & Practice of the C.I.M.*, 227, 229, 279, 300, 350, 385-86; and *To Every Creature* (1889), 297, 340. *See also* CIM publications

JHT and CIM, General Director of, 103-5, 182-84, 225, 455; and authoritarian rule, 90, 103-5, 190, 248-49, 269, 300, 302, 313, 349, 359, 390; in Chinese dress, 34, 65-69, 74, 76, 81, 121; and democracy movements in CIM, 105, 226, 269, 279-80, 313; and family relationship with missionaries, 103-5, 126-28, 195, 232-33, 349-50; and with women missionaries, 100, 114, 126-27, 196, 239. *See also individuals by name; and also* CIM missionaries, personal relationship with JHT; CIM organization in Britain; CIM organization in China

JHT and CIM Councils, 16, 103-5, 190, 313, 386, 455; and Broomhall, 26, 190-92, 194-95, 225, 300, 312, 349, 458; and China Council, 26, 195, 225-27, 239; and London Council, 26, 93, 103-5, 182-84, 188, 193-95, 225-27, 300, 312; and London Council of Management, 190, 192-94, 210-11; and London Ladies Council, 196; and North American Council, 296, 297, 300-301, 304, 312-13; and JHT's family, 16-17, 19, 22, 90, 193, 227, 296, 333 (photo), 392, 441

JHT, theology of (personal), and Baptists, 47, 94, 342; and Brethren, 54, 57-58, 60, 62, 92-94, 96-97; JHT repudiates Plymouth Brethren, 94, 188, 342; and conditional immortality, 89, 188-90, 206, 272, 455; and doctrine, do not confuse people with, 4; and faith healing, 241, 338; and faith principles (personal), 54, 63, 65, 96; financial principles (personal), 44, 54, 64, 81-82, 96, 104; and Holiness teachings (exchanged life), 182, 186-88, 203, 237; and imagery (storytelling), 2-3, 53, 79-82, 140-41, 181, 189, 293-94, 297; and interdenominational principles, 47-48, 114; and last will and testament, 104-5; and mottoes, 96, 183; and liberal missionaries, 1-2, 47, 189, 268-69, 272, 340-43; and suspicion of priest-craft, 48, 123, 194; and prophecy, 54, 57-58, 97, 294, 299, 319; and wordless book, 9. *See also* Brethren movement; Brethren, Plymouth; CIM principles and practice: theology; healing, faith; Methodist churches in Britain; prophecy and prophetic movement

Taylor, Mrs. JHT: Maria Dyer (#1), 20, 22, 36, 70, 75-77, 355, 458; in Chinese dress, 34, 76, 122; death of, 108, 136, 182; in England, 34-36, 70, 78-79, 87; and Lammermuir party, 100, 103, 106 (photo), 107-9, 114, 126, 129; and LMS, 75, 92; and love story, 20, 75-77, 120

Taylor, Mrs. JHT: Jennie Faulding (#2), 3 (photo), 194; in China, 120, 124, 150, 167, 195, 355, 358; death of, 103, 455; and Lammermuir party, 101, 106 (photo), 107, 109; and marriage to JHT, 110, 136, 182-84, 454; as JHT's mouthpiece, 196; and wordless book, 167. *See also* Faulding, Nellie

The Evangelical Alliance Mission (TEAM), 319. *See also* CIM and Associate Missions; Christian and Missionary Alliance; Scandinavian Alliance Mission; Swedish Alliance Mission

Thompson, E. P., 38-39, 71-72

Three-Self Protestant Church, 2, 28, 270. *See also* Christian church in China

Tibet. *See* China, provinces of CIM work: Tibet

tongues, speaking in, 317; and Cambridge Seven and, 222, 228, 288, 355; and Irving, 46; and JHT, 222; *See also* CIM principles and practice: theology; pentecostal currents in CIM; Pentecostal movement

Toronto. *See* Canada; CIM organization and structure in Canada

Toronto Bible College, 298, 307, 313, 316-

Index

16; TBC graduates in CIM, 317, 320-21, 324, 445-46
Torrey, Reuben A., 315, 324
treaty rights. *See* British government in China; China, government of
Trio, the. *See individuals by name* Cable, A. Mildred; French, Evangeline; and French, Francesca
True Jesus Church, 454
Turner, Joshua J., and CIM, 139, 161, 272, 274; and Pastor Hsi, 176, 258; and Mrs. Turner (Anna Crickmay), 150, 167, 242; and Shanxi Famine, 139, 144-46, 149, 238

Unequal Treaties. *See* British government in China; China, government of
United States. *See* American evangelicalism; American evangelicals and transatlantic revivalism; American government (United States) in China; American missions in China; CIM, organization in United States; Oberlin band; Scandinavian Alliance Mission; Swedish Americans

Vancouver Bible Training School, 298, 308
visions: Frost's visions, 333-34, 336, 441; and Hong Xiuquan's visions, 70-71, 74; and Pastor Hsi's visions, 172, 174-75, 255, 267, 293-94, 297; interpretation of, 70; and JHT's visions, 3, 78-80, 87, 99, 106, 129, 181; and we all had visions, 185-86, 416. *See also* Taiping Rebellion

Wales, 83; Welsh missionaries in CIM, 218, 270; Welsh revival, 449
Wallace, Robert W., and Mrs. Wallace (Edith Broomhall), 296
Wang Lae-djün, as bishop of Zhejiang, 35, 129, 233-34, 347, 362; and conversion, 68-70; in England, 33-34, 36, 77, 78-79, 87, 95. *See also* China, provinces of CIM work: Zhejiang; native agency

Wenzhou. *See* China, provinces of CIM work: Zhejiang: cities
Wesley, John, 38-40, 82, 111
Wheaton College, 324
White Lotus sect. *See* religious sects in China; religious sects, Chinese: White Lotus
Whitehouse, Silvester, 293, 411
Whyte, Bob, 28, 453
Wilkerson, David, 458
Williams, Sir George, 190, 218; as CIM referee, 194, 215
women, Chinese, and Boxer Uprising, 405; and Pastor Hsi, 259, 263-64, 284, 286, 373-75, 399; and Chinese women in religion, 6, 28-29; and converted sorceress, 382
women missionaries in CIM, 100-101, 106-8, 186, 195-98, 230-31; and avoidance between sexes, 198, 232; in Chinese dress, 2-3, 24, 122-24, 127, 240, 335, 342; Chinese suspicion of, 75-76, 122-23, 240, 356-57, 427-28; class background of, 204-5, 315-16, 325-26, 328-29; and Pastor Hsi, 285, 383, 387-91, 427-28; and language school, 228-29; and settled work, 76, 136, 167-69, 240-41, 387-91; and single women in CIM, 27, 119, 122-23; and in Shanxi, 150, 195, 198, 231, 240, 285, 357, 387-91; and women's river, 240, 335; and women unsuitable as missionaries, 196, 231. *See also* CIM principles and practice; Church of England Zenana Mission
women missionaries and CIM's marriage policy, 100, 108, 195-98, 204-5, 231-33, 238-39, 328, 357, 359, 390-91; and equality of women, 91, 198, 231, 237-38, 240; and interracial marriage, 238-39, 390-91
wordless book, 4-10, 366 (banner); and gospel glove, 4, 6, 240, 379; in China, 5-8, 167-68, 236, 240, 365, 378-79, 382, 407, 440, 441; and used by CMS in Africa, 8-9; in England, 9-10, 87-88; pure symbolism of, 5, 8-9, 88-90, 167-68; and

505

wuxing (Chinese color cosmology), 5-6, 11, 70-71, 168-69, 378-79, 441

wuxing (Chinese color cosmology), 121, 154-55; and congruences with wordless book, 5-6, 168-69, 378-79, 441; and Golden Pill, 166, 168, 378; and Taiping Rebellion, 64, 71, 74

Yan Xishan (warlord), 436-37

Yangzhou. *See* China, provinces of CIM work: Jiangsu: cities

Young Men's Christian Association (YMCA), 21; and Broomhall, 92, 190, 199, 237; in Canada, 295, 298, 306; in China, 330; and CIM, 192, 209, 212, 218, 220; and Holiness teachings, 187-88; in United States, 275, 444, 446

Yuan Shikai (governor), 401

Yuxian (governor of Shanxi) 396, 401, 409, 410, 412-13, 424, 454

Yunnan. *See* China provinces of CIM work

Zeng Guofan, 114-15, 129, 149n.26, 236, 270

Zhejiang. *See* China provinces of CIM work: Zhejiang; CIM organization in China; Shanghai

Zhili. *See* China provinces of CIM work: Zhili

www.ingramcontent.com/pod-product-compliance
Lightning Source LLC
Chambersburg PA
CBHW031539300426
44111CB00006BA/114